The Films of Stan Brakhage in the American Tradition
of Ezra Pound, Gertrude Stein, and Charles Olson

R. Bruce Elder

Wilfrid Laurier University Press

This book has been published with the help of a grant from the Humanities and Social Sciences Federation of Canada, using funds provided by the Social Sciences and Humanities Research Council of Canada. We acknowledge the support of the Canada Council for the Arts for our publishing program. We acknowledge the financial support of the Government of Canada through the Book Publishing Industry Development Program for our publishing activities.

Canadian Cataloguing in Publication Data

Elder, Bruce (R. Bruce)
 The films of Stan Brakhage in the American tradition of Ezra Pound, Gertrude Stein, and Charles Olson

Includes bibliographical references and index.
ISBN 0-88920-275-3

1. Brakhage, Stan – Criticism and interpretation.   I. Title.

PN1998.3.B74E42 1998   791.43′0233′092   C98-930429-9

© 1998
WILFRID LAURIER UNIVERSITY PRESS
Waterloo, Ontario, Canada   N2L 3C5

Cover design by Leslie Macredie, using a still from the film *Dog Star Man* by Stan Brakhage

Printed in Canada

Contents

With Gratitude

This book began many years ago. I was an aspiring poet who, not too long before, had just published his first chapbook, and was about to begin studies for a Ph.D. when I suddenly had a change in heart. I had done my utmost to drill my attention down on the more technical, logico-mathematical areas of philosophy, so as to keep my artistic and my intellectual lives as widely separated as possible (primarily to give my artistic urges a safe harbour from the tumult of the academies); but I was suddenly beset by doubts about whether I could sustain over many decades the degree of interest in such technical areas as would allow me to make genuine contributions. I needed an alternative, and set upon the possibility that industrial filmmaking might be a means for obtaining the necessities of living, and allow me to go on writing poetry. So I enrolled in film school to learn a trade. Owing to the paucity, at the time, of academic film programs, my interest in aesthetics, and the happy coincidences that film studies was then a burgeoning discipline and the school where I studied was embarking on a drive that would transform it from a trade-training institution to a university, I was asked to teach there. Having no better opportunities at hand, I accepted, and immediately set out to find how film history, film analysis, and film theory were taught elsewhere. My wife and I headed to a summer graduate school in New England, where she enrolled in a course taught by Prof. Gerald O'Grady; from her notes, which she discussed with me nightly, I learned a great deal, and it would be no exaggeration to say that what I learned changed my life, by allowing me to see films more deeply. Throughout the years, I have remained in touch with Prof. O'Grady, and his unstinting drive to discover ever more about the art of the cinema has remained a model for me.

At that same summer session I met another person who was to profoundly change my life: Stan Brakhage, who taught a course on the *Songs*. I was not enrolled in his course, but each instructor at the summer institute presented to the entire student body an evening that dealt with the topic they were teaching. On one of the first evenings, Stan Brakhage presented a number of his films; what I saw struck me with the force of revelation. My plans were in ruins, for I sensed I had to become a maker of such "poetic" films. I knew that Stan Brakhage had accomplished in film everything I dreamt of doing as a poet; so, straightaway, I began sitting in on his classes. My wife somehow persuaded the school's administration to loan us money, and I purchased a Bolex camera from a schoolteacher who, the previous year, had been inspired by Brakhage's example to take up filmmaking, but had come to the conclusion that he and the medium were not congenial.

I also set out to see as many avant-garde films as I could. Innumerable times my wife and I made the trip between Toronto and Buffalo, where Prof. O'Grady had established a centre that screened avant-garde films and presented many distinguished lecturers on avant-garde films. I hunkered down to a life of teaching, to support my "unorthodox" filmmaking, and resolved to do the best I could at it. It has been a blessing: my students have long been a source of great delight (and in the past few years all the more so), and have annually renewed my commitment to the subjects I teach. Year after year, they have responded with enormous enthusiasm to avant-garde cinema; and several of them now devote themselves, either part-time or full-time, to making and exhibiting it. They have done much to shelter me from the criticism of parties who do not share their, or my, enthusiasm for the practice. Indeed, circumstances have occasionally called upon them to take direct action to fend off such attacks, and they have risen most effectively to the task. And recently, when I was in distress, and in doubt about going on with my work on this book, a group of them let me know that they simply would not countenance my reneging on my responsibilities. Earlier, one of that group, Izabella Pruska, had taken on the responsibilities of tracking down, photocopying, and checking every quotation in this book (even though I had hired her as a filmmaking assistant), and she did so with a very touching sense of being fortunate to be required to read the writings of Brakhage et al. with such fine care; at that juncture she went to pains to convey her desire to reread the book under different conditions, and the disappointment she would feel if she could not.

I am grateful to the Humanities and Social Sciences Federation of Canada for providing funds for the publication of this book. The Office of Research Services at Ryerson Polytechnic University provided funds that helped defray the costs of indexing. I am also grateful to their anonymous reviewers who made many valuable suggestions (the inclusion of a glossary was one), and who drew to my attention several errors in detail. Barbara Schon did a splendid job on this brutally difficult-to-index manuscript (the most difficult she has ever had to do, she tells me). I have also received support that goes far past the call of duty from the entire staff of Wilfrid Laurier University Press. Leslie Macredie has handled many design, production, and marketing details in exemplary fashion (and with notable good cheer). Doreen Armbruster agreed to take her work on the manuscript with her into retirement (and the manuscript benefited greatly from her, experienced eye for detail). Carroll Klein had to go to enormous pains to work a sprawling manuscript, produced by one who does not write easily, into a more seemly shape; the book has benefited greatly from her scrupulous care. Sandra Woolfrey, WLU Press's director, took personal interest in the project, and at every turn and in a thousand practical ways conveyed her deep commitment to it. She also provided immensely wise counsel that salvaged the project at one crucial moment.

While I was reviewing the page proofs for this book, on an airplane bound for New York City, where I was to present a film that concerns the mystery of the resurrection, and at a juncture when reflection was appropriate, I came across a beautiful passage quoted in German, and tears of thankfulness for all that my father taught me welled up in my eyes. He gave me a very good example that some of our ideals cost us dearly and demand appalling sacrifice, but are worth holding out for, even in the teeth of barbarous criticism; his example makes it possible for me to continue. Even though he was barely acquainted with Brakhage's films, he took a real interest in this book, partly because he knew I believed Brakhage to be a "poetic" filmmaker and he held the spirit of poetry in reverence, but mostly because he understood that Brakhage's films have given my soul the ballast necessary for that spiritual gravity which is requisite for real thinking. When it seemed the funding for the book was unlikely, he was most distressed. I wish he were here now, so that he could have seen the happy resolution of that trial.

My wife, Kathryn, has listened to more complaints from me (and many of them about my labours on this book) than anyone should have to, and she has listened very sympathetically. She also did many of the endless chores that confront one in making a book such as this when I became too busy, too blue, too distracted by my filmmaking, or too swamped by the demands of teaching to carry on. She has stood by me through the successive assaults that came our way during the time we worked on this book, and really made me believe that somehow, come what may, we would survive. She has accepted our many financial misfortunes over this period with impressive dignity and grace, and let me know in ten thousand ways that she believes maintaining one's ideals is more valuable than seeking the remuneration that another discipline might have provided us. She has, against all reason, encouraged my filmmaking. She brightens my every moment.

Stan Brakhage's films have enriched my life immeasurably. But he means as much to me personally as his films do. I have had him as a friend for thirteen years, and during this entire time, he has taken a great interest in my doings, been concerned when I have become ill or fallen under attack, and been a wonderful companion with whom to talk about painting, music, literature, and film. Over the years, he has been a bulwark of support. He has cheered me when (and it is not infrequent) I became terribly blue; he has watched my films, and written illuminatingly on them. Our exchanges on the many topics on which we differ has enlivened my thinking. The breadth of his knowledge in the arts astonishes me. I consider myself very fortunate to have him to talk with. His friendship has remained steadfast through many trials to which the making of this book, and the horrid politics of experimental filmmaking, has subjected us. I dedicate this book to him, with love.

Acknowledgments

The author and publisher wish to thank the following for permission to use copyright materials by other authors:

Carcanet Press/New Directions Publishing Corporation for material from William Carlos Williams, *Spring and All*, "Young Sycamore," "Della Primavera Transportata Al Morale" from *The Collected Poems of William Carlos Williams*, Vol. 1: *1909-1939*, edited by A. Walton Litz and Christopher McGowan (Paladin Grafton Books, 1991); and for material from William Carlos Williams, "Writer's Prologue to a Play in Verse" from *The Collected Poems of William Carlos Williams*, Vol. 2: *1939-1962*, edited by A. Walton Litz and Christopher MacGowan (Paladin Grafton Books, 1991).

Dover Press for material from Gertrude Stein, "Sentences and Paragraphs" from Gertrude Stein, *How to Write*, with a new Preface and Introduction by Patricia Meyerowitz (Dover, 1975); and for material from Arthur Schopenhauer, *The World as Will and Representation*, Vol. 1, translated by E.F.J. Payne (Dover, 1960).

Faber and Faber Ltd./Georges Borchardt Inc. for material from George Steiner, "Language and Silence" from *George Steiner: A Reader* (Oxford University, 1984). Copyright © 1967 by George Steiner. Reprinted with the permission of Faber and Faber Ltd. and Georges Borchardt Inc. for the author.

Faber and Faber Ltd./Harcourt Brace and Company for material from T.S. Eliot, "The Love Song of J. Alfred Prufrock" and "Preludes, II" from T.S. Eliot, *Collected Poems 1909-1962* (Faber and Faber, 1963).

Film Culture for material from Stan Brakhage, *Metaphors on Vision*, edited with an Introduction by P. Adams Sitney (Film Culture, 1963).

Allen Ginsberg for material from Allen Ginsberg, *Improvised Poetics*, edited by Mark Robison (Anonym, 1971); and for material from Allen Ginsberg, "When the Mode of the Music Changes the Walls of the City Shake" from *Esthetics Contemporary*, edited by Richard Kostelanetz (Prometheus Books, 1978).

Grove/Atlantic Press for excerpts from Michael McClure, *Star* (Grove, 1970).

Harcourt Brace and Company for excerpts from "Litany in Time of Plague" and "Edward" from *The College Survey of English Literature*, shorter revised edition, edited by Alexander Witherspoon (Harcourt Brace and Company, 1951).

Calman A. Levin and the estate of Gertrude Stein for material from Gertrude Stein, *Four in America* and "Bee Time Vine" from *Gertrude Stein and the Making of Literature*, edited by Shirley Neuman and Ira B. Nadel (Northeastern University, 1988); for material from Gertrude Stein, "An Elucidation," "If I Told Him, A Completed Portrait of Picasso," "Composition as Explanation," and "Doctor Faustus Lights the Lights" from *A Stein Reader*, edited and with an Introduction by Ulla E. Dydo (Northwestern University, 1993); for material from Gertrude Stein, "Stanzas in Meditation" from *The Yale Gertrude Stein Selections*, with an Introduction by Richard Kostelanetz (Yale University, 1980); for material from Gertrude Stein, *How Writing Is Written*, Vol. 2 of the *Previously Uncollected Writings of Gertrude Stein*, edited by Robert Bartlett Haas (Black Sparrow, 1974).

Michael McClure for excerpts from Michael McClure, *Scratching the Beat Surface* (North Point, 1982).

McPherson and Company for excerpts from Stan Brakhage, *Brakhage Scrapbook: Collected Writings 1964-1980*, edited by Robert A. Haller (Documentext, 1982).

New Directions Publishing Corporation for material from Robert Duncan, "Often I Am Permitted to Return to a Meadow" from Robert Duncan, *The Opening of the Field* (New Directions, 1960). Copyright © 1960 by Robert Duncan. Reprinted with the permission of New Directions Publishing Corporation; for material from Charles Olson, "The Human Universe," "Apollonius of Tyana," "Equal, That Is to the Real Itself," "Projective Verse," "The Resistance," "Letter to Elaine Feinstein" from Charles Olson, *Selected Writings of Charles Olson*, edited by Robert Creely (New Directions). Copyright © 1949 by New Directions Publishing Corporation. Copyright © 1966 by Charles Olson. Reprinted with the permission of New Directions Publishing Corporation; for material from Kenneth Rexroth, "Snow Storm" from Kenneth Rexroth, *One Hundred Poems from the Chinese* (New Directions, 1965). Copyright © 1971 by Kenneth Rexroth. Reprinted with the permission of New Directions Publishing Corporation; for material from Kenneth Rexroth, "Introduction" from D.H. Lawrence, *Selected Poems* (Viking Press, 1959). Reprinted with the permission of New Directions Publishing Corporation; for material from Ezra Pound, "In a Station of the Metro" from Ezra Pound, *Selected Poems*, edited with an Introduction by T.S. Eliot (Faber and

Faber, 1948). Copyright © 1935 by Ezra Pound. Reprinted with the permission of New Directions Publishing Corporation; for material from Ezra Pound, "Fratres Minores" from Ezra Pound, *Collected Shorter Poems* (Faber and Faber, 1948). Copyright © 1937 by Ezra Pound. Reprinted with the permission of New Directions Publishing Corporation; for material from Ezra Pound, "Introduction to Calvacanti Poems" from Ezra Pound, *Translations*, with an Introduction by Hugh Kenner (New Directions, 1963). Copyright © 1963 by Ezra Pound. Reprinted with the permission of New Directions Publishing Corporation; for material from Ezra Pound, "Psychology and Troubadours" and "Dante" from Ezra Pound, *The Spirit of Romance* (New Directions, 1968). Copyright © 1968 by Ezra Pound. Reprinted with the permission of New Directions Publishing Corporation; for material from Ezra Pound, "LXXXI," "XLVII," "LXXVII," "LXXXVI," "LXXIV," "CV," "LXXXIII," "XVI," "LII," "XIII," "XXVI," "XLIV," "XLV," and "LXXXVII" from Ezra Pound, *The Cantos of Ezra Pound* (New Directions, 1950). Copyright © 1966 by Ezra Pound. Reprinted with the permission of New Directions Publishing Corporation; for material from William Carlos Williams, "The Delineaments of the Giants" in William Carlos Williams, *Paterson* (New Directions, 1963). Copyright © 1958 by William Carlos Williams. Reprinted with the permission of New Directions Publishing Corporation.

Penguin UK/HarperCollins Publishers Inc. for material from Allen Ginsberg, "THE CHANGE: Kyoto-Tokyo Express" from *Allen Ginsberg: Collected Poems 1947-1980* (Viking 1985). Copyright © 1968, 1984, by Allen Ginsberg; and for material from Allen Ginsberg, "Howl" from *Allen Ginsberg: Collected Poems 1947-1980* (Viking, 1985). Copyright © 1956, 1984, by Allen Ginsberg.

Random House Inc. for material from W.H. Auden, "The Composer" from *W.H. Auden: Collected Poems*, edited by Edward Mendelson. Copyright © 1976 by William Meredith and Monroe K. Spears, Executors of the Estate of W.H. Auden. Reprinted with the permission of Random House Inc.; for material from Gertrude Stein, "Objects" and "Tender Buttons" from *Selected Writings of Gertrude Stein*, edited by Carl Van Vechten and F.W. Dupee (Random House, 1972); and for material from Gertrude Stein, *Lectures in America* (Random House, 1935). Copyright © 1935 and renewed 1963 by Alice B. Toklas. Reprinted with the permission of Random House Inc.

University of California Press for material from Charles Olson, *The Maximus Poems*, edited by George Butterick (University of California, 1983); and for material from Hugh Kenner, *The Pound Era* (University of California, 1971).

Visual Studies Workshop Press for material from Hollis Frampton, "A Pentagram for Conjuring the Narrative" from Hollis Frampton, *Circles of Confusion: Film, Photography, Video: Texts 1968-1980*, with a Foreword by Annette Michelson (Visual Studies Workshop, 1983).

Preface

The agencies of modernity collude to reduce experience to a single mode. Among the agencies of this reduction are the narrative's linguistic effects. Syntagmatic structures (see glossary) that are essentially homologous with linguistic structures organize the narrative, and the effect of their insistent repetition is to enfold all experience within a system of language—to submit all experience to the shaping force of language and its handmaiden, narrative. More deleteriously, a *post hoc ergo propter hoc* principle constitutes the majority of narrative relations which we rely upon to order experience; so all experience, through the agencies of language and narrative, is brought under the causal principle.

We use narratives to impose order on our circumstance, and that will to impose order on reality (instead of discovering order in experience and attempting to conform oneself to that order) is characteristic of modernity. Some narratives operate in secret, without our being aware of them, and shape our understanding of the world in ways we are not conscious of. These patterns of unconsciousness impose familiarity on new experiences, and so render less intense our experience of novelty (which experience opens us to the Creator).

There are three damaging implications to the role that the *post hoc ergo propter hoc* principle has in founding modernity's explanatory narratives. First, it elevates the principle of temporal succession to a privileged position. The status of the elements that belong to temporally successive sequences was long a contentious issue among philosophers and theologians, just as the contrast between two orders of time concerned artists from Homer to Pound. The elevation of the *post hoc ergo propter hoc* principle to the supreme position it now occupies has rendered all these concerns

---

Notes to the Preface are on pp. 473-74.

1

between orders of existence irrelevant, through the same dynamic that it has rendered obsolete all modes of experience that are not implicated in the regime of technique. Second, this *post hoc ergo propter hoc* principle has come to serve as a principle of explanation in all domains not amenable to quantitative analyses, and the causal sequences it serves to construct have the same role in these fields that deductive patterns of calculative reason have in the various areas that science and technology comprise, that of bolstering the sense that humans, because they possess reason, are lawgivers to reality. Third, as modernity extends the scope of narrative, to that same degree the spiritual practice of memory diminishes; those who have observed children's memory weakening as they become more involved with books are aware of how external, public, material forms can substitute for inward, private, spiritual forms.

Diminishing the experiential faculties in favour of an outward form is a Faustian gambit, for the cost moderns pay for this exchange is the price of the soul. The gambit involves sacrificing our intimate acquaintance with the power of prayer, with the sublimity of *participation mystique*, with the ecstasies of contemplation, with the transports of identification with other spirits—generally, with a variety of forms of experience that cannot be translated into the language of positivist reason. In political theory, it has led to our inability to understand the function of community and to challenge contemporary political thinkers' emphasis on the rights of the individual. For the ties that bind us into a community are matters of affective relatedness that reach across time, and thus are relations that modern, positivistic reason cannot apprehend, for modern reason recognizes only concrete, localized existents. This form of reason has become the sole arbiter of truth recognized by the cultural apparatus.

Examine any feature of the postmodern practice—from the concern with theory and with popular culture, the adherence to a contextual aesthetics which has had the effect of reducing art to commentary, or, what is most telling, to the treatment of poems as "texts"—and one discovers that they all give evidence of the process of reducing experience to a common mode, making it less varied, less disruptive, less complex. Let's note, as just one example, that it is not a theory grounded in modernity's *paideuma* (see glossary) that could appreciate the manner in which James Herbert's films call forth the experience of nakedness. A complete debasement of spiritual forms of experience is evident in the currently fashionable theorization of "the body" which has managed to convert the last site of resistance to the hegemony of the word into yet another empty, metanarrative signifier.

Few have understood the dynamic by which linguistic consciousness has enfolded us. The occasional great artist like Stan Brakhage has. Between

1990 and 1997 he made films almost exclusively by applying paint to clear strips of film, creating works that look a tiny bit like a Jackson Pollock painting from 1952 that has "come to life" and begun to move. Recently, he has foresworn creating films that use "moving photographs," for he wants not to incorporate what he refers to as "nameable things" in his films (i.e., objects we can identify such as "a cat," "a car," "a little boy," or "a sofa"). He recognizes that when nameable things are included in a film, then a linguistic form of consciousness begins to operate—and among its effects is to close us off from the glory and beauty of that which has no name.

Postmodern practice, at least in its better-known (if not more significant) examples, is not at all radical—it is simply the form that modernity's most recent efforts to become an all-comprehending regime have taken. That the historical role of postmodernity is one of consolidating modernity explains the discursive, even balefully academic, character of the writings of so many postmodern theorists: the sort of meaning that the postmodern theorists actually employ, despite their theoretical denials, is the theory of meaning embedded in modernity's *paideuma*, for it is a discursive/representational conception of meaning. Postmodern theorists, after all, frequently note that an artwork reflects the conditions of its production, and how else could it reflect the conditions of its production but through discursive/representational meanings?

The major shift between modernist and postmodernist literary theory is that modernism carved out a special domain of "literary meaning," while postmodernism has rejected the distinction between "everyday meaning" and "literary or artistic meaning": postmodernist theory has collapsed all meaning into a single type (just as the regime of modernity has collapsed all experience into a single type). The postmodernist theorists' motivation for rejecting the idea of "literary language" and "artistic meaning" is to discredit the claim that alternative types of meaning make available alternative types of experience. Admittedly, their dismissal of the distinctiveness of literary meaning was meant to suggest that all uses of language (or, at least, all uses of written language) have the same qualities that literary works do; that is, they use language that, because it is not definite, and not unambiguous, cannot be reduced to definite meaning—cannot, in fact, be reduced to propositional meaning. And, because propositional meaning is the only type of meaning that modernity acknowledges, this meant that statements of any type (or, at least, written statements of any type) cannot be experienced as offering propositions, but only as invitations to free play (to, at the extreme, *jouissance*). The postmodernist theorists collapsed all meaning into literary meaning; it is this that has allowed them to treat culture, and even everyday life, as texts. In practice, however, the consolidation of all types of meaning into the monolithic model of non-propositional meaning has had exactly the opposite effect: it has collapsed all meaning into the discursive practices of modernity—practices that are based on a propositional conception of meaning. Postmodern theorists treat literary texts as though they were the declarations of self-aware individuals concerning cultural practices (and do so even while, as theorists, they write about unconscious motivations and unconscious meanings).

Their acceptance of a discursive/representational conception of meaning that has shaped postmodernist practices explains why those who celebrate such practices prefer theory to art (for, if the truth be told, the meaning of a work of art is never discursive) and why they prefer writing commentary on theory to writing commentary on real works of art. Postmodernists often write as though artworks illustrated concepts. It strikes me that this is a very serious confusion, and one purpose of this book is to argue that point. I believe the postmodern theorists' conception of the activity of a poet or painter relies on a notion of "meaning" in poetry and painting that allies it with propositional truth, and that this conception has little or no relevance to the arts. I believe that artworks elicit sensations of a particularly raw, primordial, and intense sort, but they do not illustrate doctrine. New art irks many—a proposition that can be confirmed by considering the history of the abuse it has been accorded, in the form of riots, denunciations, invective, censorship, boycotts, and negative reviews from journalists and aficionados of theory, to list just a few—because it turns us over to modes of experience that lie outside the approved modality. Our tradition extols as evidence of God's goodness His taking the form of human *logos* and so looks askance at ideas that have a non-textual experiential basis. Our preference for textually authorized experience privileges the same mode of experience that modernity wishes to make a hegemonic regime.

The conception of *logos* that grounds much of the postmodernists' practice (even though, in their theory, the exponents of postmodern practices deny this) is the very notion that modernity transmuted into its notion of reason. The consequence is a logomachy that results from identifying the ideals of a political theology of language with the positive languages of humanity—an identification that is really part of modernity's *paideuma*.

Evidently, some find it unpalatable that we cannot reduce such experiences to the apprehension of propositional truths. Some are troubled that much poetry develops from silly notions and that its statements are announced with embarrassing intimacy. Art has a strange, primitive appeal. The notions that inspire artists to make their work are sometimes silly, but they represent, in however distorted a form, a connection with a tradition far older—and, we might hope, stronger—than modernity, and their art draws strength from such ideas. Many commentators yearn to tame art's unruly power by turning it into a form of assertoric discourse. They want to convert the unruly, raw, and strange aesthetic experience into a cognitive experience, to flatten it into a form that modernity might validate. They do this by writing criticism that dismisses not only those vague but powerful intimations of the Divine that drive artists to make art, but also those non-categorical apprehensions that artworks elicit. Modernity's power enfolds us more surely and completely every year. If art is to endure (and I am not sure it will), we require critical practices that are open to unauthorized modes of experience. It is to this enterprise that this book is dedicated. I attempt here to develop a theory of poetic meaning that, I hope, transcends the limitations of fashionable (but, I believe, internally inconsistent) literary theories that we have come to call "postmodernist."

But before any further perpension on the topic, one must consider the issues of sexually explicit depictions of the body and the appalling proliferation of unseemly representations of the body that recent times have known, which have brought such deliberation on images of the body into disrepute. It is true that no era has been without its pornography, but it is also true that, as we approach the present, the rate of increase in production of such material seems to rise exponentially—and this, so it seems, has been true since about the time of Gustave Flaubert (1821-80). Hence two questions impose themselves on us: Why, the body, now? and Are explicit, non-pornographic, life-enhancing images of the body possible, in this era when matters of the spirit are scanted to an unprecedented degree?

Conjectures readily suggest themselves as possible responses: The rise of technology is turning us from creatures of flesh into objects of metal. We have broken with nature as a whole and, most destructively, with our own embodied nature. Hysteria has resulted, and this hysteria is the cause of the incessant, repetitive production of these compulsive deformations of the lost pleasure of the body. Or again: The rise in the inhuman profligacy of the pornographic imagination parallels the rise of capitalism. Pornography, like prostitution, represents the conversion of the human body into just one more commodity among others and the reduction of orgasm to just another entertainment that one can purchase (at an ever-lower price).

Both conjectures are certainly persuasive and, likely, a part of the complete explanation. That the seminal realist work, Daniel Dafoe's *The Fortunes and Misfortunes of the Famous Moll Flanders* (1722), thematizes the relation between capital and pleasure, and indicates just how plausible the second conjecture is. But another possible account, related to the second, has been put forward by no less a commentator than George Steiner. It concerns a possible relation between sexually explicit images and tyranny.[1] The concern Steiner expresses about the proliferation of sexually explicit material raises another worrying point, one that relates to the conjoint effect of the use of realistic, photographically produced images of sexual behaviour and narrative structures in film.

As much as pictures usually depend upon vanishing points around which to order their linear-spatial systems, narratives depend upon focal centres to unify all the various actions that they contain into all-embracing, well-ordered systems. One common device of narrative artworks is to parallel two or more plot structures; such parallelism gives the impression that order which subsumes these various elements does not depend primarily upon the causal relation, but upon similarities, analogies, repetitions, and mirroring functions (though, to be sure, these relations do sometimes disguise themselves as causal, through a Gnostic doctrine of correspondence, according to which similarity implies influence). The creation of work that depends upon similarities, analogies, repetitions, and mirror structures reflects a Gnostic faith in a lost but recoverable world not ordered by logic but by analogy. Thus such forms arrogate to narrative, the claim to have the powers that attend rediscovering this lost origin—to have the means to return humans to this primal source where they may be refreshed by their experience at the wellspring of creative order. And so they bolster modernity's universal principle of explanation, the causal principle.

Furthermore, narratives provide explanations for the actions that lead to their focal event, though these explanations are based partly on identification, regression, and primary process thinking as well as on logic and reality testing. Narratives make use of devices such as analogical parallels that help us make sense of the succession of events they recount. They embody attitudes toward the characters who create or react to the events the narratives depict.

Thus, narratives offer an interpretation on the incidents and characters they represent—or, at least, they guide their readers toward a specific attitude and interpretation. They instruct us on the attitudes we should take towards their characters, the morality of their behaviour and the explanations we are to give about why the characters behave as they do. What is more, narratives, and especially realistic narratives, rely on devices, most of which derive from analogical thinking, that encourage their readers to respond unwittingly to these instructions.

Readers are unwitting of the effect of these devices for two reasons: First, because they engage primary process thinking, the operation of which is usually preconscious or unconscious; and second, because the realistic effect of the narrative structure conceals these devices and their mode of operation. Sexually explicit narratives almost always encourage negative attitudes toward their personages—it seems that such narratives must submit to the moral law that uncommon forms of sexual pleasure come only at the cost of ultimate unpleasure. With sexually explicit narratives, moreover, the reader is even less free than with other sorts of narrative, precisely because his or her libidinal investment in them is so much greater.

The mechanism that locks the spectator into a film narrative demands more specific commentary. Film images have photographic origins, and one of photography's principal characteristics is its profligate, promiscuous intimacy with the body of the real world. Traditional forms of visual representation encourage us to engage in what Wittgenstein called "seeing-as."[2] Van Dyke's *Bust-Length Figure of an Apostle with Folded Hands* (1620) encourages us to see the representation not as a depiction of the real person who modelled for it (who happens to have been the messenger of the Antwerp painters' guild) but as a portrait of an Apostle gazing upwards during the miracle of the Pentecost. Photography is different in this respect; its ability to get us to see "X" as "Y" is vastly more restricted than that of other representational media. When we see a woman and infant in a photograph, we do not see the picture as portraying Madonna and Child—we see, simply, a particular, real child. Similarly, when we see a photograph of a human body, we don't see the represented figure as a Nude (that is, as an instance of one of the ideal subjects of classical art); we see a particular person without clothes. This difference explains why a photograph of a naked person prompts more embarrassment than a Nude painting. We see what is there in the photograph, and we do not see it as something other than what it really is. That what we see in a sexually explicit photograph is a real man or, far more usually, a real woman, only increases our feelings of aversion to any ill-treatment the subject received in being so depicted. Our recognition of their reality adds weight to the historically based fears to which Steiner gave such forceful expression, concerning a relationship between the prevalence of pictures of naked bodies and the occurrence in our civilization's recent past of incidents in which lines of real men and women were forced, under threats of whipping (which often came anyway), to strip and fornicate for the amusement of the "master race."

Because we take what a photograph presents to be real, photographs elicit strong identificatory responses. Indeed, it elicits nothing less than a modified form of magical thinking—modified by the recognition that what we take as real we simultaneously know to be unreal, to be merely phantasmal. Thus, narratives recounted in photographic representations, to a degree unmatched by narratives recounted in other media, induce us to surrender to their effect and to allow them to shape our responses. Our strong identifications with the subjects of photographic images lead us to adopt the attitudes implicit in a film narrative as our own. Our responses exacerbate the lack of freedom that Steiner decried. And when the attitude toward sexuality implicit in the narrative structure is a negative one, as it usually is, the identificatory mechanism encourages us to adopt negative attitudes towards our own bodies and desires. At the same time, the realism of the photographic image, a realism that depends upon seeing what is there in the photograph for what it actually is, inflects the moral regime under which sexually explicit narratives generally operate; it makes it appear that the moral law of exchange that ensures that uncommon sexual pleasure comes only at the cost of overwhelming unpleasure obtains in the order of the real—makes it appear that, as much as Newton's laws of motion are, this moral law is a law of nature.

But perhaps there are film forms that can restore freedom to the viewer. I suggest that there are, and that forms that do so dispense with narrative and its latent protocols for interpretation. Such a form might, for example, offer spectators an array of elements that they can freely combine and recombine. Most commentators it seems, including Steiner, seem to feel that sexually explicit images and texts invariably deny the viewers/readers freedom, since they always provide interpretations of and attitudes toward what they represent, rather than allowing the viewers/readers to construct these interpretations and attitudes for themselves. He offers no hope that sexually explicit images or texts can be incorporated into forms that afford an adequate measure of freedom to those who look at them or read them. But our sexuality is basic to our experience and, if we cannot deal with our sexuality honestly and fully in words and pictures, then art is closed off from a key domain of human awareness and sensitivity. One purpose of this meditation is to explain why I believe Steiner's pessimism on this matter is unwarranted.

To do so we must return to the topic of why our time is so concerned with the body, for only this will allow us to understand what demands we, citizens of modernity, place upon Eros. To carry out this task we must engage in historical considerations.

From the Givenness of Nature to the Encumbered Modern Body

The account of nature that was generally accepted in the West before the early modern period (that is to say, roughly, 1600 CE) took as its first principle that nature was created by God. Because God created nature, all objects possessed value. This account implied that what is good, either as a means or in itself, is given in the order of the world and that humans could apprehend nature's value as an objective fact.

Moderns repudiated the proposition that nature was created by a Being who belonged to an order other-than-nature, from Whom the goodness of nature derived. The modern dogma is that an account of beings and processes must petition only to facts about material beings and physical processes. What followed from this, in a historical line that is too intricate to trace here, was that material beings and phenomena appear increasingly as having no ground for their existence. Having lost their status as beings that God created, they seemed merely accidental—to be, in the end, nothing. Nature fell from being a created order ruled by and revelatory of the Good to a raging chaos of ungrounded and ultimately worthless beings. Thus humans lost their grounding in nature.

A twentieth-century American poet, Charles Olson (1910-70), states the fear this sense of the ungroundedness of nature arouses:

> Void is what's left when the kosmos breaks down as the interesting evidence of order, Man falls when that purpose falls, and so Void is the only assumption left; that is, Kosmos infers [sic] Chaos as precedent to itself and Man as succeeding, and when it goes as a controlling factor, only Void becomes a premise of measure. Man is simply filling an empty space. Which turns quickly by collapse into man is skin and flesh surrounding a void as well. Void in, void out. It is the counsel of despair.[3]

The prodigious interest contemporary culture takes in the body is partly a reaction to the terror of nihilism that Olson expresses here. We have made the body the instrument of our last-ditch efforts to re-establish a salutary connection with nature. This is nowhere more evident than in the "New French Feminism." Motivating their efforts is the desire to establish a salutary relation between language (thought) and the body—and especially the female body, which they consider as socially repudiated or, at least, as set apart from male discourse and marginalized. These writers resort to a celebration of the body—in their cases, specifically the *woman's* body—that derives from feelings of grandiosity (since it results from primary identification). This regressive grandiosity is a reaction to the devaluation of the body that occurred when thinkers separated nature from the Divine and, ultimately, left it valueless.

Olson attempts to establish contact with the field of the being beyond the limits of the limited (lyrical or egotistical) self. He is enough of a modern (or "postmodern") as he called himself, long before the vogue for the term, that he accepts that reality is flux. He proposes a poetics that construes the creative process as one that begins beyond the self of the individual poet, and is affected by—in tune with—all the fluctations in the circumambient field. Because representational language puts the outside world at a distance, Olson proposed to reconstruct poetic language, so that the poetic image would have its basis in rhythm (which seems to be Olson's term for the pri-mordiality that is a principle subject of this book). Thus the image is a vec-tor, Olson states. The New Critics, and modernist poets they celebrated, conceived of the image as a transcendent entity, with a higher reality than the world of ordinary objects: the image is apprehended through a pure (i.e., bodiless) act of intuition; it does not address itself to reason, as befits an entity of another order of reality; it is insubstantial and non-material, and, most crucial of all, unchanging (here we see the legacy of the Symbolists). All this is implied in Wallace Stevens's poem "Anecdote of a Jar." The great advance of Pound, Williams, Stein, and Open Form poets (see glossary) was to have tilted against the conception that the image is a transcendent entity. To guarantee its meaningfulness, they ensured that the image is connected with—indeed embedded in—the world (for, after all, they all believe that the world is the meaning of the image); one of the great advances in Pound's writing, and that of W.C. Williams and Gertrude Stein, is the development of the means of embedding the image in the world. The real world is energy, they said, so let the image be an active thing—"a vector," as Olson says.

Brakhage argues similarly for a conception of *poesis* that takes place out-side the limited (egotistical) self, and is in touch with the field of being. Like Olson, he argues that it is rhythm, that is, a somatic pulse, that establishes contact with the larger field of being. Through the primordiality of the body, evident in dynamic activity of all sorts (but of which rhythm is the exem-plar), we are attuned to all the flux in the field of being.

We can trace similar moves played out in the latter years of the nineteenth century, in the writings of Friedrich Nietzsche (1844-1900). It was Nie-tzsche's sad fate to be the first thinker to clearly envision, and thematize, the appalling, abysmal absence of permanence and truth. That defect, which he believed characterized all previous philosophers—a "lack of historical sense"—utterly scandalized Nietzsche. Nietzsche was the first to realize that in the modern age becoming is the rule, even in spiritual matters. Everything that exists, spiritual or material, human or non-human, we con-sider as having a history. But, as Nietzsche argued, "only that which has no history can be defined"—so, when nothing is permanent, nothing can be defined. There are, therefore, no true assertions we can make, no truths and no knowledge. The language of permanence, truth, and being had developed only to mask the primal chaos.

Previously, humans believed they possessed a distinctively human virtue—love or reason, in consequence of their place within a divinely ordained order. Nietzsche recognized that, when we lost our sense of belong-ing to a permanent order, we gave up our claim that a cosmic order sustains our system of values. We no longer believe that our purposes and ends have their foundations in the nature of things. This realization opened up an abyss, and Nietzsche's way of confronting and responding to this abyss has proved typical. Nietzsche's Zarathustra informed his listeners: "But the awakened and knowing say: body am I entirely, and nothing else; and soul is only a word for something about the body. . . . Behind your thoughts and feelings, my brother, there stands a mighty ruler, an unknown sage—whose name is self. In your body he dwells; he is your body."[4]

No logical necessities required Nietzsche to exempt the body from his allegation that there is no truth, that our understanding of things is always an interpretation, perspectively informed and shaped by our desires and our will. Given the total context of Nietzsche's philosophy, the exemption seems disingenuous and implausible. Hence the inevitable historical development has occurred; thinkers applied Nietzsche's own instrumentalist and perspectivalist theories of knowledge to the body itself. The first who did this was Michel Foucault (1926-84). In *Discipline and Punish* (1975), Foucault applied Nietzsche's methods to elucidate the contributions that language and learning make to our understanding of our bodies and our sexualities. In fact, Foucault's first reference to the body occurs in "Nietzsche, Genealogy, History" (1971) where he refers to the body as "the inscribed surface of events (traced by language and dissolved by ideas), the locus of a dissociated Self (adopting the illusion of a substantial unity), and a volume in perpetual disintegration."[5]

Foucault goes the full distance in separating sexuality from any presumed "natural given," for Foucault's writing depicts sexuality as a product of discourse. Foucault points out insistently that sexuality is a product of culture, not nature. Foucault does not even recognize such a thing as completely natural desire. We cannot get back to some natural, lyric sexuality by dispensing with the sick-making social order, Foucault argues, for there is no natural order we can return to—there are only different formations of power. There is not even a natural human body-self to which we can revert.

Panic over loss of reality is undoubtedly one of the forces that motivated Nietzsche's Dionysian affirmation of the body. It is also one of the factors that has contributed to the prodigious production of imagery of the body engaging in pleasurable activities: for we use the naturalizing power of the photographic image in our efforts to convince ourselves that such pleasure is entirely natural.

Our bodily selves seem to be the only certainty we possess. Yet we recognize, at the same time, that the body is no more real than nature, which we, moderns, view as an abysmal, raging chaos. So we prodigiously produce imagery of the body to prevent ourselves from being disabused of this one last idea which, nonetheless, we recognize subconsciously to be mere delusion.

The Signifying Body

Artistic theory and practice in this century display a similarly conflicted response to nature's slide into chaos and to the body. Still, we must admit that, in the first part of the century, most thinkers conceived the body in the way that Western thinkers traditionally have, that is, as the prime matter, as the yet-unformed hylic factor that makes up the material content of signifiers and to which only meaning can bring form. On this conception, meaning is not self-given or self-present within the body; the body becomes a signifier only through the shapes or forms that humans impose on it.

This view traditionally associated with the belief that the body is, or can be if properly trained, the instrument by which interior desires and passions become manifest; at its best, it is a special voice that speaks to us of the most valuable parts of ourselves, our most fundamental and exemplary human feelings. The polemics issued by the exponents of early American concert dance in the first decades of this century most forcefully promulgated these beliefs. The makers of this dance, Ruth St. Denis (1880-1968), Isadora Duncan (1878-1927), Loie Fuller (1869-1928), Mary Wigman (1886-1973), Doris Humphrey (1895-1958), Charles Weidman (1900/01-75), and, most prominently, Martha Graham (1895-1991), demanded that dance be reformulated so that it would become the medium most expressive of primal human feeling. They believed they could make dances that would convey profound intuitions and deep, almost unconscious, feelings that otherwise have no means of expression. They associated these primal feelings with the body, and so they searched for a natural way of moving and an organic choreography whose gestures were motivated by the sensations and impulses of the natural body. They endeavoured to discover, for example, rhythms that arose from the natural cycle of breathing. They used the body's centre of gravity in falls and recoveries, to perform choreographic gestures whose motivations arose within the body's natural "centre of movement"; so they put a greater emphasis than had traditional ballet on the torso (as the centre out of which human movement emanates) and on continuous movement that extends across adjacent parts of the anatomy (to suggest the flow of the movement out of the centre and to reinforce the spectator's sense of the unitary, well-integrated character of the ideally trained body). Dance, these pioneers averred, has the potential of returning an overly civilized humanity, which has lost touch with the vital energies of its physical being, to a sense of wholeness.

These dance pioneers thought of the body as a physical instrument that can give expression to the interior realm, an instrument that, when trained to be sufficiently compliant with the ebb and flow of energies of the inner soul, can furnish us with dynamic image of ineffable human truths. Once she has established contact with the proprioceptive sensation—a feat that, in our too-rational culture, is no mean achievement, and indeed is one that often occurs only after years of specialized training—the dancer discovers both a source of truths more primal than those available through any other means and the wherewithal for converting proprioceptive sensations into dynamic images. Thus in *My Life* (1927) Isadora Duncan speaks of "long days and nights in the studio seeking that dance which might be the divine expression of the human spirit through the medium of the body's movement.... I ... sought the source of the spiritual expression to flow into the channels of the body filling it with vibrating light—the centrifugal force reflecting the spirit's vision."[6]

By repeatedly doing basic exercises, the dancer undoes the effects of upbringing (of "nurture") on posture, bearing, and locomotion—effects that separate us from the natural, corporeal self—and recovers a natural, essentially human, way of moving. The study that takes place in the dancer's studio serves to return the dancer to the primal, energetic sources of movement and it ends only when she has formed an Adamic language of the sort sought by the Emersonian tradition.

Among the theorists who propounded such ideas was François Delsarte (1811-71). He believed that the human physique and human movement directly manifested the human spirit. He based his teachings on the physical culture movement that had proclaimed the possibility of inspiring self-expression by exercises that promoted relaxation, mental and physical balance, and flexibility. From the insights of the physical culture movement, Delsarte developed a system that aspired to make the body a perfect, transparent instrument of the soul—a condition Delsarte conceived to be ideal and, more significantly, natural. Thus, according to the system he taught, to express a certain emotion the choreographer/dancer must sense the particular qualities of the dynamics of the energy exchanges associated with that emotion—to express sadness, for example, the choreographer/dancer first must become aware of the flow of energies experienced in sadness, with the particular agitation of the soul, vigour of emotions, and mental judgments that are part and parcel of the experience of sadness. Then she must channel that energy into the body, using it to project a dynamic image that makes those energies and feelings manifest. Delsarte and his followers argued that a thorough and intimate understanding of the inner world of our emotions and ideas coupled with adequate physical training allows the choreographer/dancer to replicate thoughts and feelings within the domain of the body.

The founding idea of the Delsarte system, and the idea that drove Delsarte and the early American pioneers in the modern dance movement to examine the body's dynamics, was the belief that corporeal nature's gift is that by it we are attuned to Being, for our embodied nature grants us a form of understanding more primordial and more radical than that which emerges through reason or in our involvement with mass society. By the grace of our embodiment, we bear within ourselves a felt sense of the meaning of Being more primordial than that which is conveyed within the socially constituted misrepresentations of the "everyone-and-anyone." To overcome the deleterious effects of mass society, mass language, and mass thinking, we must learn to live in accord with the primordial ground of our individual being, with the felt understanding of the way that, through our corporeality, we are in-and-with-the-world and always already related to Being. Thus, flesh grants us a primordial enjoyment of the field within which we have our being. Our bodies relate us, feelingly, to the situations in which we find ourselves and found a context for meanings. What is more important, our embodied nature makes possible the disclosure of Being. This is our fleshy nature's most precious endowment to us, for the disclosure of Being constitutes our guardian awareness.

Primordial awareness is preverbal. It is the awareness of the child—it is formed as a cross between the awareness that we come closest to tapping in our dreams and proprioceptive experience. It constantly undergoes change and, more than that, it is synaesthetic. As we grow up and assume our roles within the social economy, we become increasingly distanced from that form of awareness. With the acquisition of language, percepts that had previously been subject to continual change become fixed, and primordial synaesthetic perception differentiates into the various sensory modalities; sight, hearing, taste, touch, and smell become quasi-distinct.

A central proposition of Brakhage's film aesthetics is that film can revivify this primordial, corporeal awareness. His film style relies on intense camera movement—to the extent that detractors often identify him as the exemplar of the shaky camera school of filmmaking. Besides its philistinism, what makes the remark especially galling is that Brakhage's style, far from being merely a way of surrendering to accident, or even of overcoming the arbitrary, actually rests on profound psychological insight. Brakhage somehow learned from his own experience that before a child acquires language, his or her visual percepts are unstable and undergo continual transformation (an insight psychoanalytic studies have confirmed). Corporeal changes register in perception, altering its form. Saccadic eye movements, emotional changes, changes in light, all alter what we see. The acquisition of language transforms perception, by stabilizing the percept.

Great effort is required to get ourselves back in touch with primordial, corporeal awareness, as the extreme rigour of modern dance training testifies. For this form of awareness is not definite, bounded, fixed, and framed as is the instrumental thinking of technique and the representational thinking of scientific reason. It is an awareness reliant on mood, attuned to a sense of wholeness, global, synthetic, and all-encompassing. It reveals the matrix of Being from which it emerges. It dissolves the ego's boundaries. It is, as the titles of so many of Martha Graham's dance compositions imply, night-thought, not day-thought. It resides in darkness, not sunlight. It is feminine rather than masculine.

So the dance theorists argued. But this conception of the body is riddled with paradoxes. For these beliefs accord the body value only insofar as the body vanishes into transparency to reveal the inner workings of the soul. They require that the body not enunciate itself, for its ideal is to convert the body into a pure medium for revealing what is other-than-itself, namely, the soul. This conception of the body depends on a hierarchically structured opposition between body and soul that accords greater value to the soul and less to the body. After the dancer has absorbed the preliminary discipline of dance classes, "[t]he body itself must then be forgotten, "Duncan says.[7] The goal of dancing is spiritual transcendence and spiritual transcendence involves overcoming the body's natural weight, the pull that brings us down to earth. While she knew the body's glory, Duncan nonetheless accepted the traditional normative distinction between body and soul, which accords greater value to the soul than to the body. For this reason she believed that the only power that can satisfactorily guide the body is the inspiration of the soul.

The contradiction at the heart of the expressionist dancer's conception of the body is that it views the body both as a manifestation of the integrity and indivisibility of the human being and as merely a part of what makes up a human being (the other part being the soul)—and, what is more to the point, as the lesser part, the earthbound and less sacred part. The first of these contradictory beliefs was the basis for the expressionist dancer's assertion that getting in touch with the body's proprioceptive sensations is tantamount to getting in touch with our deepest feelings and emotions, with our true self. On this side of the contradiction, the expressionist dancer conceives body and soul as an identity. Because she conceives the body in this way, the expressionist dancer believes that training the body is a spiritual discipline and that expanding our awareness of emotion is the best facilitator of physical movement. She views the body as the site of our deepest wishes, a reservoir of the passionate, libidinal, and unconscious aspects of human existence, and the source of human liberty and truth. She avers that getting in touch with the body will elevate our emotional and spiritual awareness and strengthen the true self.

On the other side of the contradiction, the expressionist dancer sees the body as simply an instrument for the soul's self-expression. And from this it follows (as the quotations from Isadora Duncan make abundantly clear) that the body should efface itself to afford the soul complete self-expression. This conception does not consider the body to be identical with the soul, but as subject to it. This conception is a product of the Western metaphysical tradition that divides body from soul and accords the spiritual dimension a higher value. Proposing that the two separated terms have an apophantic (see glossary, apophansis) relation is a common mark of the tendency to dichotomize and to formulate distinctions that are merely conceptual, not distinctions between actual properties of actually existing entities. Apophantic relations (as I use the term) are relations between two terms that exhibit the feature that as one term appears, the other is hidden. Apophantic relations, because they are relations in which one of the relata eclipses the other, suggest opposition; yet their co-ordinated operation (in which one term disappears whenever the other appears) hints that there is an ontological link between the two, that between the two there is a link strong enough to suggest their identity—to suggest that the two terms apply to different aspects of the same being. In proposing that the body is only an instrument for the soul's self-expression and that it should efface itself so as to make the soul apparent, the expressionist dancer proposes an apophantic relation between body and soul; she proposes that whenever the body presents itself, it eclipses the soul and, conversely, whenever the soul makes itself evident, the body effaces itself. We would be wise to suspect that the expressionist dancer's contradictory conception of the body, and the apophantic relation she proposes, indicate that the body and soul are really identical—that they are simply different aspects of the same underlying reality (or, to express the notion in Spinozistic terms, different modes of the same substance).

The relation between the earthbound body and the body as spiritual is a principal theme of Duncan's autobiography (*My Life*), that both sees body and soul as one and, at the same time, privileges the soul above the body. For her, narrative insists on the importance of carnal love and decries the restrictions that Puritanism has placed on love, which is so important for inspiration and creation; however, it also indicates a conflict between carnality (which she alternately defends and decries) and artistic commitment. Not the least intriguing feature of that extraordinary text is its manner of not acknowledging any possible resolution or sublation of these two desires, even while she insists on the key role that physical love plays in inspiration and creativity; so, as *My Life* shows, Duncan alternates between committing herself wholeheartedly to the one and then to the other, but never to both at once, and the tension between the two commitments wracked her. An apophantic conception of the body is evident in Duncan's oscillating between life choices, too. The problems that arise from the expressionists' apophantic conception of the body motivated a later generation of American choreographers, among whom Merce Cunningham (1919-) was the paradigmatic figure, to sever choreography's relation with both music and human feeling. By dissociating feeling, music, and movement, Cunningham gave unprecedented independence, and hence a degree of emphasis, to the tangible human machinery which is the true material of dance. He helped to bring the body into full self-presence.

Or so the argument ran. But how ever could the body be fully given? What would the experience of the body in full givenness be? And how would one go about rendering the body fully present? Philosophers since Kant have offered a variety of arguments to prove that "the actual" or "the given" is not given in direct, full presence (see glossary); rather it is the result of that which is not *given as such* but is *represented* within the given. Expressionist, and more generally, modernist dance theory conceived of the body as that which is outside representation—as being natural in Jacques Derrida's sense of the term, as that which is constituted as the effacement of the necessity of the (supposedly supplementary) level of representation. To put the point otherwise, the notion of natural body such as we find in expressionist and modernist dance theory is constituted only by the effacement of the sign, mimesis, culture, history, time, and space. Modern dance theory conceived the body to be the origin of all that of which experience is both the sign and the result. Thus, modernist dance theorists (and, as we shall soon see, theorists of poetry who worked on the cusp of the transition between modernism and postmodernism) conceived the moment of contact with the body itself to be the moment of evidence that founds knowledge and truth. This way of formulating the conceptual basis of modernist dance theory exposes the constitutive desire behind those aesthetic formulations to be the desire for a truth that does not need the support of a signifying system in order to be formulated—a truth that is pure, undivided, transparent, and totally exposed in its presence-to-itself. Thus, modernist dance theory, like modernist art theory generally, presumed the equivalence of presence, evidence, and truth.

Mid-twentieth-century American poetic theory assumed a similar equivalence. To better understand the significance of these ideas, we must consider their provenance; we must also consider some ideas that Schopenhauer and Nietzsche offered.

The Two Bodies in the Philosophy of Arthur Schopenhauer: The Body Observed Externally and the Body Experienced from Within

Between 1814 and 1818 Arthur Schopenhauer (1788-1860) who was then, judging from the single portrait we have of him from the period, a good-looking young man (he was actually between the ages of twenty-six and forty) with full, sensuous lips, a pellucid complexion, a high forehead surrounded by delicate curls of auburn and black hair and given to expensive and fashionable dress (he was, after all, from a rich merchant family) and, according to the best reports available, irascible, sharp-tongued, neurotically anxious and prone to depression, arrogant, brooding, truculent, and possessed of a powerful sexual drive—wrote a book that waged a ferocious attack on the way his arch-rationalist rival, Georg Wilhelm Friedrich Hegel (1770-1831), had developed the philosophy of Immanuel Kant (1724-1804).[8] Enormously self-assured in all matters, he was convinced (not without reason) that he, of all post-Kantians, provided the most penetratingly understanding extension of Kant's philosophy, and even conceived the belief that "subject to the limitations of human knowledge, my philosophy is the real solution to the enigma of the world." The certitude of this conviction he maintained from his early manhood (he formulated the essential principles of his philosophy at the age of eighteen) throughout the remaining years of his life.

The conviction that the clue to the riddle of life had been vouchsafed to him was not the only belief Schopenhauer maintained from early manhood until the time of death. Schopenhauer, in fact, was one of the rare individuals who, by reason of a remarkable confluence of complementary ideas, formulate the essentials of the system while still young and prone to influence, and spend the remainder of their lives clarifying its exposition or elaborating upon fine details. Schopenhauer himself acknowledged that his philosophy could only have been conceived by one into whose mind the rays of the Upanishads, Plato, and Kant shone simultaneously. While living in Dresden, the orientalist Friedrich Majer (who in 1819 published *Brahma, or The Religion of the Hindus*) introduced Schopenhauer to the Upanishads, in Anquetil Duperron's Latin translation from the Persian rendering of their original Sanskrit, which went under the title *Oupnekhat*. From the Upanishads, Schopenhauer took the idea that the world we perceive is a *mâyâ*, a veil of illusion. They impressed upon him too that underlying this veil of illusion there is something that is truly real, but which cannot be seen or understood by reason, something that can only be grasped by a higher form of awareness (the nature of this form of awareness is a principal topic of the rest of this work, but to anticipate a little, what Schopenhauer contributed to understanding its nature was the insight that this form of awareness is linked to inner awareness of our bodies). The Upanishads also confirmed Schopenhauer in his belief that the realm of illusions engenders suffering, and that to overcome suffering one must find release from this realm.

Vedanta philosophy was the third ingredient to be added to the mix from which Schopenhauer forged his philosophy. Schopenhauer initially attended university at Göttingen, where his first teacher of philosophy was the sceptical Kantian Gottlob Ernst Schulze. Schulze had introduced Schopenhauer to the philosophies of Plato and Kant, and Schopenhauer was to spend much of the rest of his life attempting to effect a synthesis between their works.

Kant was the first to highlight the role the subject plays in constructing the world of which he is aware—in staging the shadow show that proceeds in consciousness. In this regard, as in so many others, Kant is the exemplary philospher of modernity. I suggested several pages ago that the modern paradigm takes hold when the belief that material beings are grounded in the divine is rejected; the modern belief in the ungroundedness of matter is a key reason for the recrudescence of Gnosticism in the last century and a half. As matter comes to seem ungrounded, the order of beings presents itself less and less as an order ordained by a Higher Being; and as the order of beings loses that authority, it seems less and less something to command our respect and our love—less and less a source of instruction about the nature of the Good. Values lose their being, and humans must search within—or, rather, as Nietzsche pointed out, must bring out of themselves, by a creative act—the values that will guide their lives, since no values are given in the order of being.

Kant did not take the notion of subjectivity so far, of course (he wrote too early in the modern era for that to be possible), but he was among the first to point out that the mind does not conform to the outer world in apprehending objects (as the Scholastics had asserted), but rather that appearances must submit themselves to the activity of the mind—must subject themselves to being structured by the imposition of basic forms or categories that the mind imposes on raw sensation—before we can become aware of them. When an object affects our senses, and we perceive it, the object's actions on our nerves produce the raw material of sensation. But the manifold of sensation so produced has to be organized, i.e., brought under the categories, in order for us to become aware of it. The categories are not derived from experience; father, they belong to the mind, and are the means by which the mind organizes experience. We are aware only of the appearances that the mind has structured (see glossary, phenomena) and not objects as they are in themselves. Nevertheless, the "thing-in-itself" (see glossary, noumenon) is required to explain the fluctuations in the content of the manifold of sensation.

Many philosophers found Kant's manner of treating the thing-in-itself—it ends up as a peculiar X, about which we know only that it must exist (if we accept Kant's argument)—and several subsequently jettisoned the idea of the thing-in-itself altogether. Kant in fact had an ulterior motive for maintaining the existence of a noumenal reality. The capstone of Kant's philosophy was really his ethical theory, and his epistemology, which is the part of Kant's system most read today, was really a means to establish arguments on the topics of ethics and, to lesser extent, aesthetics; thus Kant's First Critique, the *Critique of Pure Reason* (*Kritik der reinen Vernunft*, 1871) which presents Kant's arguments on the topics of epistemology, was to provide the groundwork for the Second and Third Critiques, the *Critique of Practical Reason* (*Kritik der praktischen Vernunft*, 1788) and the *Critique of Judgement* (*Kritik der Urteilskraft*, 1790), which respectively present his arguments on the topics of ethics and aesthetics and the topics of aesthetics. In the matter of ethics, Kant attempted to show that even though our knowledge is limited to the determined entities of the phenomenal realm, we cannot believe that our being is limited in the same, for we must believe that we, in ourselves, are free and capable of exercising pure reason. To act morally, one must able to exercise choice, that is, to escape the determinism to which all phenomena are subject; therefore (that "therefore" depends on the legitimacy of his transcendental method of inquiry) the transphenomenal thing-in-itself must be within. Ethical behaviour (and Kant argued somewhat similarly in regards to aesthetic experience) carries us beyond the realm of appearances and puts us in touch with the thing-in-itself.

The philosophers who were most immediately affected by Kant's philosophy generally took up the later two Critiques, which purported to show how the sense of duty and aesthetic experience afford us some knowledge of the noumenal realm, as the summit of his work.[9] They wanted to develop that aspect of Kant's philosophy. They demanded greater clarity on the question of what the world in itself is like, what the self—the 'I'—that structures the world of appearance is like. Kant's epistemology had done so well in divorcing the phenomenal and the noumenal realms that his theories on ethics and aesthetics could not stick them back together again. The task of doing so philosophers took up immediately. They wanted to penetrate to the heart of things, to know what the thing-in-itself was like, what the self is like, and what the relation between the thing-in-itself and self is. Fichte developed his ideas on the matter around the concept of the 'ego,' Schelling developed his ideas around the concept of 'natural subject,' Hegel around the concept of 'objective spirit' (see glossary, spirit), Feuerbach around the concept of 'body,' and Marx around the concept of 'the proletariat.' Schopenhauer's proposal was that both the self and the *Ding an sich* (the thing-in-itself) are Will.

Whatever the troubles subsequent philosophers had with Kant's positing of the thing-in-itself, his assertion that the subject plays a role in constituting experience, that experience does not conform itself to the world, but the world conforms to its conditions of experience, was a key development in the history of thought. The idea that 'ego' plays a formative role in creating the world provided the basis for a new way of thinking of the relation between subject and object, self and world—it led to the claim that the object belongs to the subject, that the world belongs to the self, not the other way around. Foucault points out that in the pre-modern *épistème* (see glossary) the subject of all mental acts vanished into the object: thinking disappeared into what was thought, perception into what was perceived, willing into what was willed, believing into what was believed. Kant's philosophy exemplifies the modern paradigm in making evident that the subject plays a constitutive role in all experience. Claims for the constitutive role of the subject would become central to the philosophy of Romanticism, including the paradigmatic Romantic philosophers, Johann Gottlieb Fichte (1762-1814), G.W.F. Hegel, F.W.J. Schelling (1775-1854), and Arthur Schopenhauer. Indeed, it became the basis for the Romantic celebration of the imagination (which Brakhage has taken up, and adapted for his own purposes).

The Romantics considered the imagination just as Brakhage has, as the human faculty for producing images. An image has powers that words lack, for language is used to make assertions about the world, but without making contact with it. Language is complicitous with reason, and both language and reason have the effect of putting the world at a distance. However, an image is apprehended through an intuitive act, which fuses the subject that knows and the object known. Moreover, the most fundamental structure of language is the subject-predicate form used to make assertions, and the subject-predicate structure of assertions tends towards suggesting that reality is made up of timeless substances forever qualified by certain attributes. Thus, language presents reality as though it is static, but an image can convey the dynamism of reality. Furthermore, language presents us with abstractions, while the image presents us with concrete reality. Finally, while language presents the world as something pre-existent, that can be commented upon, the image presents the world as a product of created human activity. This opposition between abstract thinking and a more primordial form of apprehension puts us in touch with something concrete, central to Schopenhauer's philosophy. It is also central to Brakhage's commentary on the image and imagination, which, for the most part, adopts these Romantic claims (though he, like Pound and Olson, has a more radical conception of the image as activity).

Schopenhauer agreed with Kant that, for the most part, our knowledge is structured by categories that the mind imposes on that with which it is acquainted; this is true of our understanding of material things, for example. He accepted Kant's distinction between appearance and the thing-in-itself. He agreed, too, that the phenomenal world did not exist in itself, but was given its form by the activity of mind, which imposes space, time, and causal relations on phenomena. In fact, Schopenhauer interpreted these Kantian ideas in a fashion that made Kant's system resemble somewhat that of the great Advaita Vedantic philosopher, Shankara. For Schopenhauer wrote as though the empirical world were simply a world of appearances (*Vorstellungen*, he called them, which means "representations," but also "mental representations"; thus when Schopenhauer says that the empirical world is an organization of *Vorstellungen*, he can be seen to be saying that the world is made of ideas in the mind—ideas structured by the mind and, as we shall see, by the interests of Will—almost like the realm of illusion from which, according to Vedantic philosophy, we can be released only by *moksha*, an experience of enlightenment). But, while agreeing with Kant that our concepts of space, time, causality, relation, et al. organize the familiar world of objects into the form in which we know it, Schopenhauer asked whether there is anything behind these appearances that we can know. Schopenhauer's claim against Immanuel Kant was that we have knowledge not just of representations or phenomena (appearances presented to the mind, which Schopenhauer identifies with being-for-another) but also of noumena (objects as they are in themselves, apart from our awareness of them, which Schopenhauer identifies with being-in-itself). What we know, immediately and without concepts—what appears not as a representation but as it is in itself—is will. Or rather, as we shall call it, Will, since Schopenhauer showed that our experience of particular acts of willing provides a window onto the fundamental reality. The world in its existence for another is representation, but in itself it is Will. 'To-exist-for-another' is 'to-be-represented,' Schopenhauer says, but to be 'being-in-itself' is to will.[10]

Plato remained for Schopenhauer the philosopher who taught that the objects we know through the senses belong to a low grade of reality; but above the transient entities of the world disclosed by the senses, there is a higher realm that can be apprehended by an elevated form of awareness beyond sense experience, beyond even reason, and *grasped* through an experience very much like mystical intuition. Schopenhauer noticed that the same sort of distinction between illusion (sense experience) and reality that one finds in the Vedanta is also the basis of Plato's philosophy. That the world of objects which come into being and pass away is illusory, of the nature of shadow-play, is an insight that Plato developed in the allegory of the cave presented in *The Republic*. Plato further represented to Schopenhauer the ideal of the philosopher who maintained that the beatific vision (the Vision of the Good referred to *The Republic*'s allegory of the divided line) was possible to achieve. Kant was the philosopher who revealed more clearly than any other the limitations of our understanding, but Plato was the philosopher who held out the possibility of transcendence, and surcease from sorrowing.

The first synthesis of Platonic and Kantian philosophy Schopenhauer arrived at was all too simple: he crudely identified the Platonic Forms with the thing-in-itself—the Forms represented what reality is like in itself, not as appears to the sense, but reality it itself. Since Kant has shown that space and time are a priori representations that underlie outer appearances, it could be taken that Kant believed that the noumenal realm was atemporal and aspatial; and Plato's eternal Forms are certainly beyond time, and, as immaterial, beyond space as well.

Schopenhauer soon realized that the domain of Platonic Ideas could not be identified with Kant's noumenal realm; the Platonic Ideas are static entities, and Schopenhauer, as we shall see, conceived of the thing-in-itself in more dynamic terms. Nonetheless Schopenhauer, to the end, continued to construe Kant's philosophy in Platonic terms. The pressure of interests in the Vedantic philosophy and in the philosophy of Plato, read through the Vedanta, led Schopenhauer to interpret Kant's philosophy as presenting an idealism closer to Berkeleian idealism than the transcendental idealism—as arguing that what we know through sense experience is merely an appearance in the mind, akin to illusions. Kant's phenomena he construed as almost phantasmal, not as structured appearances, so intricately co-ordinated with one another as to constitute a world.

The historical importance of Schopenhauer's philosophy rests partly on his having grounded our understanding of ultimate metaphysical concepts on corporeal experience (experience I frequently refer to in this book as "primordial experience"). The Will itself, in its very essence, is disclosed in such primordiality—"primordiality" because, indeed, this noetic-noematic structure has not yet separated into a subject and an object; there is awareness, and this awareness is not ontologically distinguished from what is disclosed in this awareness (just as in my inner awareness of my body, my body is indistinguishably the agent and object of awareness, for I am not outside my body, and my understanding does not conform itself to its object as to an other). Schopenhauer recognizes that his theory of the Will expands the concept beyond its usual range—he refers to the "requisite extension of the concept" that is necessary if one is to understand his system, and explains that the requirement arises because we use nouns to refer to "objects"—entities "thrown over against us"—while the primordiality of Will knows no distinction between known and known. In the end, what Schopenhauer means by the Will is simply a form of striving. Striving is the essence of our inner lives, and that of World; striving is the essence of the noumenal realm, of the thing-in-itself. This is a knowledge that each person possesses concretely, as feeling.

> This is the knowledge that the inner nature of his own phenomenon, which manifests itself to him as representation both through his actions and through the permanent substratum of these his body, is his *will*. This will constitutes what is most immediate in his consciousness, but as such it has not wholly entered into the form of representation, in which object and subject stand over against each other; on the contrary, it makes itself known in an immediate way in which subject and object are not quite clearly distinguished, yet it becomes known to the individual himself not as a whole but only in its particular acts. The reader who with me has gained this conviction . . . will recognize that same will not only in those phenomena that are quite similar to his own, in men and animals, as their innermost nature, but continued reflection will lead him to recognize the force that shoots and vegetates in the plant, indeed the force by which the crystal is formed, the force that turns the magnet to the North Pole, the force whose shock he encounters from the contact of metals of different kinds, the force that appears in the elective affinities of matter as repulsion and attraction, separation and union, and finally even gravitation, which acts so powerfully in all matter, pulling the stone to the earth and the earth to the sun; all these he will recognize as different only in the phenomenon, but the same according to their inner nature. He will recognize them all as that which is immediately known to him so intimately and better than everything else, and where it appears most distinctly, is called *will*. It is only this application of reflection which no longer lets us stop at the phenomenon, but leads us on to the *thing-in-itself*. All representation, be it of whatever kind it may, all *object*, is *phenomenon*. But only the *will* is *thing-in-itself*; as such it is not representation at all, but *toto genere* different therefrom. It is that of which all representation, all object, is the phenomenon, the visibility, the *objectivity*. It is the innermost essence, the kernel, of every particular thing and also of the whole. It appears in every blindly acting force of nature, and also in the deliberate conduct of man.[11]

Schopenhauer's proposal that the highest form of knowledge is the knowledge our body grants us of the Will—that is to say, of striving—marks a decisive repudiation of the traditional conception of knowledge. Classical philosophy, as the example of Aristotle's philosophy shows well, had claimed that the highest form of knowledge was the abstract knowledge acquired by reason; to attain such knowledge one had to put bodily sensations at a distance, detach the mind from body's energetics (from the dynamic exchanges within the body that constitute a permanent substratum underlying all awareness), and apprehend general truths through the abstracting power of reason. The idea that the highest form of knowledge is granted through the body, that expanding awareness of the stirrings of the body is required if one is to attain knowledge of the ultimate, is a claim that classical philosophers (and, for that matter, almost all philosophers prior to Schopenhauer, who, to a greater or lesser extent, were still under the spell of the *mathesis univer-salis*) would have found preposterous. Yet it is exactly this claim that Schopenhauer asserted, and that he did so is one of the reasons his philosophy is so important to our inquiry. Schopenhauer understood himself not as the subject of cognition, as most traditional philosophers had understood human beings (consider Aristotle's notions that humans are rational animals), but as the subject of volition. Cognition depends upon representation, Schopenhauer understood, and so give us purchase only on *Vorstellungen*, not on the thing-in-itself.

Furthermore, both classical philosophy and the religious tradition considered the body as the part of us that condemns us to die. Plato and Saint Paul both taught that the body, and the senses, must be controlled if the soul is to find the peace that is its rightful element. Prior to Schopenhauer, no philosopher had taught that body, the *feeling* body, was the source of knowledge of what is ultimate. Certainly, the Cynics had taught that it is important that one feel at ease with one's fleshy being, but this really was a counsel on how to adjust to misfortune; and admittedly, a few philosophers through the ages celebrated the body. But that position was adopted largely by way of thumbing their noses at respectability, a gesture that depends upon the idea that the body is a degraded thing. Schopenhauer, however, wrote of the body, the *feeling* body, as though it vouchsafed secrets about the inner nature of reality. If one only sets aside that thinking in representations has been the method that philosophers have used in the past, and attunes oneself to the throbs and surges and strives of the body, one will discover the answer to the riddle of existence. Such was the radical cast of Schopenhauer's philosophical temper.

Many other thinkers were to follow Schopenhauer's lead in formulating a radical conception of the body's role in our understanding of ultimate things; indeed, as we shall see, it is an important feature of twentieth-century thinking that the body has been required to sustain the burden of grounding our our relation with reality—a burden that, in the absence of help from above (in the form of a warrant for belief that existents have a ground), it cannot possibly sustain. It is for this reason that so many twentieth-century thinkers have argued that theoretical reason is a vain and fruitless activity, and that is through practical understanding that we acquire knowledge of the ultimate, if only we look inwards. Schopenhauer's historical importance also helps explain why so many twentieth-century thinkers have cast the will in the role of rational agent that, if it knows enough about its circumstances, will act in accord with the principles of self-interest.

In fact, Schopenhauer's claim that we have knowledge of something behind appearances depends upon the realization that we possess two distinct types of bodily self-awareness:

In fact, the meaning that I am looking for of the world that stands before me simply as my representation, or the transition from it as mere representation of the knowing subject to whatever it may be besides this, could never be found if the investigator himself were nothing more than the purely knowing subject (a winged cherub without a body). But he himself is rooted in that world; and thus he finds himself in it as an *individual*, in other words, his knowledge, which is the conditional supporter of the whole world as representation, is nevertheless given entirely through the medium of a body, and the affections of this body are, as we have shown, the starting-point for the understanding in its perception of this world. For the purely knowing subject as such, this body is a representation like any other, an object among objects. Its movements and actions are so far known to him in just the same way as the changes of all other objects of perception; and they would be equally strange and incomprehensible to him, if their meaning were not unravelled for him in an entirely different way. Otherwise, he would see his conduct follow on presented motives with the constancy of a law of nature, just as the changes of other objects follow upon causes, stimuli, and motives. But he would be no nearer to understanding the influence of the motives than he is to understanding the connexion with its cause of any other effect that appears before him. He would then also call the inner, to him incomprehensible, nature of those manifestations and actions of his body a force, a quality, or a character, just as he pleased, but he would have no further insight into it. All this, however, is not the case; on the contrary, the answer to the riddle is given to the subject of knowledge appearing as individual, and this answer is given in the word *Will*. This and this alone gives him the key to his own phenomenon, reveals to him the significance and shows him the inner mechanism of his being, his actions, his movements. To the subject of knowing, who appears as an individual only through his identity with the body, this body is given in two entirely different ways. It is given in intelligent perception as representation, as an object among objects, liable to the laws of these objects. But it is also given in quite a different way, namely as what is known immediately to everyone, and is denoted by the word *will*. Every true act of his will is also at once and inevitably a movement of his body; he cannot actually will the act without at the same time being aware that it appears as a movement of the body. The act of will and the action of the body are not two different states objectively known, connected by the bond of causality; they do not stand in the relation of cause and effect, but are one and the same thing, though given in two entirely different ways, first quite directly, and then in perception for the understanding. The action of the body is nothing but the act of will objectified, i.e., translated into perception.[12]

The cardinal distinction that Schopenhauer makes here, between two aspects of the body—the body as it appears phenomenally and as it presents itself as it is in itself, noumenally, as an objectification of will—he believed was the key that unlocks the riddle of the world, the entire solution to which he presented to the world in his magnum opus, *The World as Will and Representation* (1819). The world was not immediately taken by his discovery, however. Seventeen years after its publication, he inquired of its publisher concerning its sales and was informed that there had been none. An incident that had occurred some twenty years earlier must have made that disclosure all the more painful for Schopenhauer: Schopenhauer's mother, Johanna, had become, after the death of Arthur's father, something of a literary lioness, who conducted *the* salon in Weimar, which was attended by such luminaries as Johann Wolfgang Goethe (1749-1832), the Grimm brothers, Jakob (1785-1863) and Wilhelm (1786-1859), and Friedrich von Schlegel (1772-1829). When Schopenhauer had finished his thesis, he had it printed and bound at his own expense and took a copy to Weimar to present to his mother. Looking at the title, *The Fourfold Root* (1813), she remarked offhandedly that it must be something for druggists. Schopenhauer was so upset that he replied hotly that his first book would remain available long after the trash she produced had been forgotten. His mother sweetly agreed with him, remarking that, indeed, the entire press run would still be available.

But, as Schopenhauer predicted in the preface to the vastly expanded second edition of *The World as Will and Representation* (1844), his ideas did at last rise up out of the turmoil and clash of philosophical disputation. Others came to recognize the importance of our privileged awareness of our own bodies known not externally, as part of the furniture of the world, but known first hand, intimately, from within, and as related to our feelings and desires. Instead, this recognition became central to American poetry, painting, and filmmaking at the middle of this century and has remained so.

Schopenhauer's way of characterizing our awareness of the body tells us much about crucial phenomenological differences concerning our awareness of our own bodies and our awareness of other bodies. One way to indicate the difference is to state its nature extravagantly: while our bodies structure each and every act of perceptual awareness, they are only rarely, and never in their entirety, a thematized object of our own experience. When I watch a film, read a book, type at my word processor, or allow myself to wander off in my thoughts, or when I work with my body, doing carpentry or household repairs, or even when I take my film camera in hand and photograph in a manner that involves a great number of bodily movements (both large and small), I pay attention to the task at hand, not to my bodily states. For the most part, our own bodies are absent from our experiences at least as thematized objects, though their nature and condition affect every experience that we have.

Schopenhauer's distinction between our two forms of bodily awareness and bodily knowledge is one that must inform any deliberation on the topic of how the body figures in the advanced arts of our time, including avant-garde cinema. One feature of avant-garde film, much celebrated in the 1960s when its transgressive aspirations seemed to strike a resonant chord, was its assertion of its right to incorporate sexually explicit imagery. But its engagement with the body took other forms as well—forms that, arguably, had greater importance. Like the poets and painters who were his contemporaries, the American avant-garde filmmaker Stan Brakhage attempted to ground his aesthetics in the internal awareness we have of the body. For Brakhage, a film is ideally a construction that conveys its maker's visionary experiences, and vision—or at least vision in its primal condition—he conceives as a somatic activity. Though living in society and being trained in its modes of experiencing makes each individual's unique way of seeing more like that of other people, at its origin and in its essence each person's vision is unique precisely because each person's body is unique, and seeing is a bodily act. The film artist, Brakhage insists, must attempt to recover, so far as possible, the forms of visionary experience proper to his or her own body.

Brakhage maintains, too, that every change in one's bodily state affects one's faculty of sight; indeed, he believes that the organ of vision is ultimately the entire body. He consequently maintains that all emotional events register in sight. He advocates that the film artist should become aware of this interplay between emotion and seeing for, he points out, the interplay actually can be disclosed by a meticulous examination of our internal awareness of ourselves, though most of us do not take the trouble to conduct such a close study of our perceptual faculties. Brakhage has even argued our bodily nature shapes artistic forms; this is especially evident of rhythmic forms.

But there is an even deeper similarity between Brakhage's ideas and Schopenhauer's system, for both of them expound, almost paradoxically, idealist notions about reality even while they maintain a view of consciousness that identifies consciousness with the physiological processes that are associated with activities of consciousness.[13] Schopenhauer's Spinozistic claim (quoted above) that "The act of will and the action of the body ... do not stand in the relation of cause and effect, but are one and the same thing, though given in two entirely different ways, first quite directly, and then in perception for the understanding" provides some clue as to his views on the matter of the relation of consciousness to matter, but he is quite expansive on the topic, and more in in the second volume that he appended to the second edition of his magnum opus. All that he says, though, comes down to the radical proposition that the body is simply the Will objectified. He states baldly that, if we consider self-consciousness objectively, we understand that all the mental processes are "nothing more than the physiological function of an internal organ, the brain."[14] According to this position, our mental representation of a world of objects in space and time, is not a product of our brain function: it is our brain. But this rather odd position, that allows no ontological (or even modal) distinction between the physiological processes that underlie a conscious experience and the conscious experience itself, is one that Brakhage argues. In lectures and in the column "TIME . . . on dit" in *Musicworks*, the Canadian publication on experimental music, Brakhage insists that "the firings of the synapses" are actually experienced, and the project of much of his film work is to construct forms that will convey equivalents of that experience to the view.

There are more telling similarities between Brakhage's belief in the material nature of consciousness and Schopenhauer's systematic analysis of the topic. The purpose of Schopenhauer's philosophizing was to demonstrate the implicit unity of the self and the cosmos (to demonstrate, in Vedantist terms, the unity of *atman* and *Brahman*, to show as the Sanskrit saying has it, "That thou art" (*Tat tvam asi*). Thus Schopenhauer argues that all manifestations of the Will belong to a One, and that our individual belongs to the Will. Thus Schopenhauer integrates the individual back into the field of being from which modernity had separated him (consider in this regard Cartesian consciousness). But Stan Brakhage's methods of artmaking, too, are directed towards making contact with, and finally integrating the maker into, the field of being, just exactly as Charles Olson advocates in his writings on poetics.

Perhaps more telling is that both Schopenhauer and Brakhage justify these efforts towards integration in functional terms. This aspect of Schopenhauer's thought is most evident in the discussion he offers in the second edition of *The World as Will and Representation*, the objective view of the intellect. If we adopt an objective standpoint (that is, if we consider consciousness not from within, but from the outside, as we might any other phenomenon) then, Schopenhauer asserts, we can discern that the configuration of our bodily parts, and the assignation of their functions, expresses the Will—or, more, are manifestations of the Will, or, in other orders, aspects of the Will.

> Just as the intellect presents itself physiologically as the function of an organ of the body, so is it to be regarded metaphysically as a work of the will, the objectification or visibility of which is the whole body. Therefore the *will-to-know*, objectively perceived, is the brain, just as the *will-to-walk*, objectively perceived, is the foot; the *will-to-grasp*, the hand; the *will-to-digest*, the stomach; the *will-to-procreate*, the genitals, and so on.[15]

Stan Brakhage uses similar functional terms—in his case, specifically adaptational terms—to integrate the body into the field of being when he formulates evolutionary arguments.

Schopenhauer's philosophy gives us two senses in which to interpret "the body in film": the body as viewed from the outside, as it becomes an aspect of the content of films, and the proprioceptive body (the body experienced internally) as it affects the form of films. But besides these two senses of the phrase, we could give to the phrase another, admittedly a more extended, but nonetheless important, meaning: as the body that figures in film we could take the film's own body—its own material nature. I have treated the topic of the representation of the first body, the body as viewed from the outside, in another volume, *A Body of Vision*. In this volume, I offer a series of ruminations on the proprioceptive body, the body that experienced in inner sensation: and especially I deliberate on how that body came to be conceived in dynamic terms. The interrelations among the three bodies—the human body viewed as an object like other objects in the world, the personal body given in our internal awareness and the film's own body—will also be a major subject of our concern.

The Modern Body's Unbearable Burden of Being

Arthur Schopenhauer regarded himself as having furnished the most lucid development and trenchant critique of Kant's philosophy. The primary relationship between Schopenhauer's philosophy and Kant's is their shared conviction that there exist divisions between the phenomenal and noumenal realms and between phenomenal and noumenal aspects of the self—i.e., between the self as it appears as an object of awareness and the self as it is in itself. Unlike Kant's, however, Schopenhauer's philosophy provided a unified conception of human being; for Schopenhauer showed that human being is essentially a single reality, though one that we can view under two aspects, viz., body and will.

Schopenhauer emphasized (and in this, too, his philosophy accords with Kant's), the hidden, yet distorting, operations of will in the self's quest for knowledge. He believed that only in art are human beings able to escape from the distorting influence of Will; in free aesthetic experience, humans contemplate the noumenal realm with an attention undistorted by the corrupting and misrepresenting operations of the Will—and because the apprehending faculty is undistorted by Will, what is revealed through that attention is veridical.

To attain a more complete understanding of the primordiality that is Will, it is necessary to consider Schopenhauer's ideas on art in general, and on music in particular. Schopenhauer's ideas on aesthetic experience constitute one area of his philosophy where the Platonic concept of the Ideas have a key role. Schopenhauer accepts the arguments that universals have an objective existence (that is, that the world is populated not only by particular horses, but also by an entity that represents what all horses have in common; and the same is true for all general terms such as "horse"). In fact, not only do universals have objective existence, the representations of universals are, Schopenhauer asserts (using rather tormented arguments), closer to the thing-in-itself than the representations of particular objects. The Platonic Idea "is the most *adequate objectivity* possible of the will or of the thing-in-itself; indeed it is even the whole thing-in-itself, only under the form of the representation. Here lies the ground of the great agreement between Plato and Kant, although in strict accuracy that of which they both speak is not the same."[16]

The Idea, as a general form and not a particular existent, does not come into being or pass out of existence. Schopenhauer uses these characteristics of the object Ideas to explain the nature of aesthetic experience. Aesthetic experience opens us to the realm of the Ideas; in aesthetic experience, we apprehend pure Ideas. The nature of the aesthetic experience, like all experience, is determined by the nature of objects that experience apprehends, that is to say the Ideas. Because the Ideas are eternal, aesthetic experience has a contemplative character. Because Ideas do not come into and go out of existence, aesthetic experience brings an end to the suffering of watching things come into and go out of existence. And what is perhaps most important, because the Idea is a universal, the apprehending subject is divested of his or her individuality and becomes the pure subject of knowing. Finally, because in aesthetic experience the pure subject of knowing apprehends the pure Idea—the Idea that possesses nothing of particularity—this experience is an immediate experience, one in which differences are overcome, and in which there is no distinction between subject and object.

All of this resembles suspiciously that form of thinking that Jacques Derrida has criticized as "logocentrism" (thinking in abstract terms, terms derive from language), and logocentrism is the very form of thinking we have claimed that Schopenhauer struggled to overcome. The uneasiness the reader might feel in considering this prospect is allayed by taking Schopenhauer's remarks on music into account.

Schopenhauer, unlike most philosophers, accorded music the place of greatest privilege. That he was unique in this regard is related to the fact that Schopenhauer was the first thinker to conceive a critique of what we would now call "logocentrism," and to strive to overcome thinking in the general categories of language (that he was the first to assert that the form of knowledge arising from the feeling body grants us the highest form of knowledge, knowledge of the Will to Live). Schopenhauer's analysis of the effects of music anticipated the founding ideas of the musicological system of Heinrich Schenker, which so long dominated the study of music. Schopenhauer, like Schenker, argued that the pleasure we experience in listening to music depends upon our sense that music is movement that strives for resolution (harmonic resolution, rhythmic resolution, and melodic resolution, felt as melody to the tonic), and that the tension music arouses results from the digression away from immediate resolution. This alone would be reason to take an interest in Schopenhauer's commentary on music; but it what he does with this analysis—essentially, using it to show that music is, in the end, mimetic, for it imitates the striving, not of objectifications of the Will-to-Live, but of the Will-to-Live itself—that makes it especially important to our purposes.

> Thus . . . the nature of melody is a constant digression and deviation from the keynote in a thousand ways, not only to the harmonious intervals, the third and dominant, but to every tone, to the dissonant seventh, and to the extreme intervals; yet there always follows a final return to the keynote. In all these ways, melody expresses the many different forms of the will's efforts, but also its satisfaction by ultimately finding again a harmonious interval, and still more the keynote. The invention of melody, the disclosure in it of all the deepest secrets of human willing and feeling, is the work of genius, whose effect is more apparent here than anywhere else, is far removed from all reflection and conscious intention, and might be called an inspiration. Here, as everywhere in art, the concept is unproductive. The composer reveals the innermost nature of the world, and expresses the profoundest wisdom in a language that his reasoning faculty does not understand, just as a magnetic somnambulist gives information about things of which she has no conception when she awake. . . . Even in the explanation of this wonderful art, the concept shows its inadequacy and its limits.[17]

Schopenhauer recognized that the form of knowledge which music engenders is viewed askance by the reasoning faculty, and therefore has little currency in the world; but he did not flinch from asserting that this form of knowledge (which we may consider that of the *feeling*, and not the reasoning, body) is actually the higher form.

> All possible efforts, stirrings, and manifestations of the will, all the events that occur within man himself and are included by the reasoning faculty in the wide, negative concept of feeling, can be expressed by the infinite number of possible melodies, but always in the universality of mere form without the material, always only according to the in-itself, not to the phenomenon.[18]

He goes so far as to say that since in music we apprehend the pure nature of striving, the complete music would constitute the truest philosophy.[19]

'Will,' Schopenhauer's term for the inner world of sensations, desires, impulses, and energy forms the whole of that of which we have direct and immediate acquaintance. Schopenhauer encapsulated the key insight his philosophy offers in the assertion, "My body and my will are one."[20] Thus, whereas Kant had made an insuperable division between the phenomenal realm of appearance and the noumenal realm of the *Ding an sich* (thing-in-itself), Schopenhauer collapsed the distinction, for one existent, by asserting that body is the phenomenal form of the Will and the Will the noumenal form of the body. But though the phenomenal coincides with the noumenal only for one's inward sensation of the body, this single domain of identity suffices to establish our route of contact with noumena. We can discover the character of noumenal being, Schopenhauer averred, we are not shut away from the world in itself. The momentous, world-historical impact of this was to reveal that thought was more physical than people had previously assumed it to be. If Nietzsche found that reading Schopenhauer's *The World as Will and Representation* was a catalytic experience, it was partly because Schopenhauer's assertion that the highest form of knowledge is granted through the body, that expanding awareness of the body's stirrings is required if one is to attain knowledge of the ultimate, was key to his project of replacing the Apollonian mode in philosophy with the Dionysian mode.

In his remarkably wide-ranging "Prize Essay," Schopenhauer undertook to argue for the often-repeated slogan *quidquo fit necessario fit* ("whatever happens, happens necessarily") and for the proposition that it is ignorance alone that is responsible for the illusion of freedom. This slogan states a principle that philosophers often call the principle of sufficient reason. The principle of sufficient reason maintains that all things occur for a reason, that no event would occur if its reason for being did not exist, and that any event would be constituted differently if its reason for being were different. Schopenhauer interpreted the principle in a remarkably Kantian fashion, according it a status similar to the principle that Kant established through his (notoriously difficult) transcendental deduction of the categories (see glossary). For Schopenhauer showed that the way we represent the world to ourselves results from applying the principle of sufficient reason to four key areas: the interrelations among our sense impressions; our judgments; our spatial and temporal intuitions; and our motivations. To achieve a truer understanding of our representation of the world, we must learn to separate out what is primarily responsible for its form—which turns out to be Will, not reason or sensation. This acknowledged, it follows (according to Schopenhauer) that all else of which we are aware is formed by the Will and is an objectification of the Will. Even the body is an objectification of Will. Human existence is a manifestation of the Will, for the Will is a force that permeates all reality. Or, to express the idea in yet another way, if human thought and sensation are an objectification of one's Will and if, by a principle of parity, what is true of human beings is true of reality as a whole, then the world itself is a representation of the Cosmic Will. Human sensation and thought belong to the realm of phenomena, but human will belongs to the noumenal realm.

By conceiving the Will in this manner, Schopenhauer really had done what he claimed to have done—to have extended Kant's philosophy by exfoliating and, in some cases, extending, principles inherent in it. For Kant, too, had proclaimed that practical reason is the key to self's true nature, and that it is in the exercise of the will that the self actualizes its potentials. Who, having read the opening sentence of *Laying the Groundwork to a Metaphysics of Morals*—"Es is überall nichts in der Welt, ja überhaupt auch ausser derselben zu denken möglich was ohne Einschränkung für gut könnte gehalten werden, als allein ein guter Wille"—could ever forget the exalted place to which Kant elevated the will? Schopenhauer took this action with greatest seriousness, and deliberated on its consequences.

Nietzsche testified to the overwhelming impact that Schopenhauer's masterwork, *The World as Will and Representation*, had upon him. Late in October 1865, Nietzsche was prowling through a bookshop and discovered himself irresistibly drawn to a book:

> I took it in my hand as something totally unfamiliar and turned the pages. I do not know which demon was whispering to me: 'Take this book home.' In any case, it happened, contrary to my principle of never buying a book too hastily. Back at the house I threw myself into the corner of the sofa with my new treasure, and began to let that dynamic, dismal genius work on my mind. Each line cried out with renunciation, negation, resignation. I was looking into a mirror that reflected the world, life and my own mind with hideous magnificence.[21]

Nietzsche was swept away by the book's initial assertion that the world "is my idea (representation)," that the only objects in our direct ken are ourselves, and that we know our bodies as extended in space and time only indirectly.

Nietzsche accepted most features of Schopenhauer's philosophy heretofore described. One proposition that he did not accept—and this difference with Schopenhauer affected the entire cast of his philosophy—was the claim that we have immediate awareness of an aspect of noumenal reality. Nietzsche rejected any claim that what we call knowledge corresponds to the real, or that we can have any acquaintance with the real. Above all else, it is his assertion that what we call knowledge lacks any ground that gives his philosophy its world historical significance, for it encapsulates a fundamental truth about the condition of thinking in the era of modernity.

Nor did Nietzsche accept the next step in Schopenhauer's philosophy. Schopenhauer went on to argue that, though the world consists of representations (that is, of individual things that objectify a Will driven to create pain and suffering), release from this domain of misery is possible. For, above the spatial and temporal *principia individuonis* is a hierarchy of beings that have essentially the form of Platonic Ideas. The first step towards liberating oneself from domination by the Will is to contemplate these timeless realities. Another step is overcoming of the ego by developing compassion, since compassion produces insight into the unity of all beings.

Schopenhauer rejected the Christian doctrine that the rational plan of a benevolent deity establishes the design of the universe. Rather, he argued, the universe is the product of a blind Will. He even went so far as to pass moral judgments on the Will, describing it not just as amoral but as downright malevolent. Schopenhauer claimed, as did Nietzsche, that the appetite for each person's life drive conflicts with life drives of all others. Consequently, suffering is the common lot of all humans and, indeed, of all sentient beings.

Schopenhauer's pessimism had a major influence on the young Nietzsche. In 1866, a post-Kantian philosopher and natural scientist, F.A. Lange (1828-75), reinforced the anti-Platonic strain in Nietzsche's developing thought. Lange's *Geschichte des Materialismus und Kritik seiner Bedeutung für die Gegenwart* (*History of Materialism and Critique of Its Significance for the Present*), argued against Schopenhauer's Platonically inspired conception of the *Ding an sich* (thing-in-itself). He averred that it is impossible to draw a meaningful distinction between appearance and reality. Ultimate reality itself is unknowable, Lange argued, and any conception we can form of it belongs exclusively to the world of appearance, not reality. Anything that enters our minds belongs to the realm of appearances. We cannot attain accurate knowledge even of our own bodies, for our bodies are as much a manifestation of an unknowable reality as any other objects in the visible world. As George Berkeley (1685-1753) and Baruch Spinoza (1632-77) had argued before him, Lange proposed that everything that enters our minds results from the interaction of the perceiving organ and the external world. Thus, against Schopenhauer's claim that the body's interior knowledge of itself grounds our knowledge of ultimate, cosmic reality, Lange countered that our belief that we possess sure knowledge of the Cosmic Will is groundless.

Nietzsche concurred with the point Lange's arguments were intended to establish. Accepting it drove him into a thoroughgoing perspectivism that denies the possible existence of any authoritative, independent criterion for evaluating the relative validity of competing systems of thought. Nietzsche concluded that many alternative systems of concepts and beliefs can interpret reality equally well. In *Der Wille zur Macht* (*The Will to Power*), a major book that appeared only in 1901, Nietzsche wrote, "Against Positivism, which halts at phenomena—'There are only facts'—I would say: No! Facts are precisely what there are not, only interpretations."

In 1873, still a young man at twenty-eight, Nietzsche had already arrived at an insight that would become central to twentieth-century philosophy: that words do not deliver objective truths about external reality. His most often quoted passage asserts this, and more:

> What then is truth? A mobile army of metaphors, metonyms, and anthro-pomorphisms—in short, a sum of human relations, which have been enhanced, transposed and embellished poetically and rhetorically, and which after long use seem firm, canonical, and obligatory to a people: truths are illusions about which one has forgotten that this is what they are; metaphors which are worn out and without sensuous power; coins which have lost their pictures and now matter only as metal, no longer as coins.[22]

The essay in which this passage appears, "Über Wahrheit und Lüge im aussermoralischen Sinn" (On Truth and Lie in an Extra-Moral Sense), argues that we have no real, objective knowledge of the interior functioning of our body. It is only our nearly unlimited capacity for delusion and decep-tion that allows us to think that we do.

Language cannot designate the *Ding an sich* (thing-in-itself), but only our relations to things, Nietzsche proclaimed. Two intermediaries intervene between words and things: first, by the stimulus the thing produced, and, second, by the percept we form of it. Words refer to these percepts, not to things themselves. Every other form of animal perceives a different world than humans do, so their worlds and our world are utterly incommensurable. And so are the various competing systems of interpretation that different people form.

Nietzsche's most terrifying proposal concerns the morality of knowledge. Against the Positivists of the eighteenth and nineteenth centuries, who pre-sumed that objective, value-free knowledge exists, Nietzsche offered the view that knowledge is the product of the Will and so subject to being evalu-ated morally. Our knowledge takes on shapes that reflect the compelling urge to acquire knowledge; this urge is a creative force that moulds what we think of as knowledge. Facts do not exist in themselves—thus Nietzsche exposes the baselessness of the realists' or naturalists' assertions that their world-pictures meticulously represent the world just as it is. Against those who (like the expressionist dancers of later times) claim to be revealing the secrets of the soul, Nietzsche points out that they actually create these secrets in the processes of articulating them. "This is how I wish the soul to be" is all that they say in the end.

Thus, in a statement that could find a place in a refutation of Stan Brakhage's reflections on moving visual thinking, Nietzsche wrote:

> Language depends on the most naive prejudices.
> . . . [W]e read disharmonies and problems into things because we think *only* in the form of language. . . .
> *We cease to think when we refuse to do so under the constraint of language;* we barely reach the doubt that sees this limitation as a limitation.
> *Rational thought is interpretation according to a scheme that we cannot throw off.*[23]

Nietzsche was the first to articulate the beliefs that have undone modern civilization. Nietzsche uncovered the views that we, moderns, have accepted at the cost of our salutary relation to truth a hypertrophy of the power of Will: that nature itself is without value; that the strength of the Will derives from nature; and that those of strong will and great power do not disown the Will but acknowledge it is their innermost being and allow it to steer their action. Such individuals are not constrained by the false teachings of sickly humility or by the erroneous conviction they must submit to a non-existent objective good. Those who have such power of Will, the *Übermensch*, can disencumber themselves of that cargo of shame and guilt with which the belief in the real existence of good and evil (as actualities that exist outside the Will) burdens the self.

However, the view that we do not love things because they are good but that they are good because we choose to love them—and that frequently what we choose to love does not even exist but is only the projection of our desires—assigns to the self the awesome task of creating value. Things themselves are pitched into the abyss of valuelessness, and this abyss becomes a constant element in the self's experience—it is always on the horizon of the self's experience when it is not central. So the self, in its turn, is understood as the mysterious, free, creating (and value-creating) centre of our being that confronts an abyss of non-existence.

This picture, which really is the *imago hominis* of the modern era, depicts whatever belongs to the outer realm as cast into the darkness of nihilism, while what belongs to the inner realm—the realm of subjectivity, the realm disclosed through self-reflection, but above all else, the realm that Protestant Christianity depicted as the place where the human and Divine have intercourse—resides in the lighted clearing that is the emptiness within which creative making (creation *ex nihilio*) arises. The inner and outer worlds become detached from one another as the outer world dissolves in raging chaos and the inner world becomes the source of all value and the arbiter of all truths. But the burden placed on the self becomes too great. It is this of which the prolific production of pornographic pictures is the symptom. We have asked Eros, one of the body's most basic drives, to carry the entire burden of giving meaning to life, but even Eros cannot sustain such a burden.

The Harmony of Spirit and Body

The philosopher Hegel exhibited remarkable powers of prescience regarding this division; for he had predicted that artistic production would bifurcate into those art works that are concerned primarily with the inner world of Spirit (see glossary) and those that are concerned with the outer realm of matter. Hegel had traced the antithesis between these two realms back to the end of the Roman era, and had predicted that this antithesis would be the downfall of art. Hegel celebrated the time of the classical Greeks as the apogee of the history of art. He praised especially Greek sculpture, the sculpture of the naked human body. Hegel explained the special excellence of this sculpture by saying that it displayed the ideal unity of the matter (the stuff of the body) and Spirit. In the art of classical Greece, bodily matter and the Spirit were reconciled with each other, for the Soul provided the corporeal material its ideal form. The Spirit entered the body of the world and illuminated it. The Real became Ideal and the Ideal became Real.

Hegel took this balance as showing that in the classical world, the realms of inward and outward existence reached a perfect accord, as inner meaning and outer form found their perfect unity. But this perfect accord was short-lived. Owing to its nature, Spirit wants to be free of all sensuous encumbrances and to achieve absolute freedom. Consequently, the next stage in the history of art, Romantic art (for Hegel's lexicon designates all postclassical art "Romantic"), deals with the inwardness of the Spirit's existence, with human subjectivity in itself, with Spirit freed from the limitations imposed by its involvement in matter and come into its own.

But Romantic art had a falling out, not just with the content of Greek art but also with the various art media, especially language. Thus, such writers as Hugo von Hoffmannsthal (1874-1929), Stephane Mallarmé (1842-98), and Rainer Maria Rilke (1875-1926), among others, issued statements about the inadequacy of language, or any material form, for expressing the true inwardness of human subjectivity. In Romantic art, the Spirit sought to free itself from commerce with any sensuous medium and to dwell solely within itself. So in Romantic art, we witness the inner and the outer realms, Spirit and medium, separating from one another. We find there, for the first time in the history of art, works that highlight the purity of the medium (or, to use more contemporary terminology, foreground their material and language). We can also find there works that offer an unprecedentedly precise description of the phenomenal realm, that is, of consciousness. For when the marriage of the Spirit and the sensuously real dissolved, all that remained for art to do was to display either the inner operations of consciousness or its own material conditions.

Even works of "scientific realism," which might seem to offer objective descriptions of the external world, actually describe (usually in painstaking detail) how objects appear to consciousness. It is, though, for depicting the subjective realm rather than the landscape that Romantic art is renowned. Walter Pater asserted that all the arts aspire to the condition of music and Schopenhauer proclaimed music as the highest of all the arts—of all philosophers, it was Schopenhauer who possessed the most profound under-standing of the relation between the understanding of music and the understanding of the self. Many Romantics committed themselves to pre-senting the process of human subjectivity, or the inward movements of the Spirit, by using musical forms and musical orderings.

Romantic art has endeavoured to escape the solid, and stolid, encum-brances of the material world and to depict what appears to the mind's eye alone. It has attempted to dispense with words and patterns that are too heavy with the burden of material reality. Romantic art shows verbal thought and the thought that belongs to the deepest levels of human inward-ness moving farther and farther apart; and, as T.S. Eliot's "East Coker" shows, the struggle with the divorce between them became the subject of some Romantic artworks.

A later strain of Romantic art became concerned with displaying subjectiv-ity. This strain of Romanticism limited its interest in the external world to the extent to which the external world can serve as signs of the inner world. Romantic art increasingly adopted the principle that when the external world can be eliminated or, at least, its externality overcome (as the artist trans-mutes external objects into the internal visual forms that make up our "brain movies"), it should be eliminated; and so they did. Cinematic representa-tions possess the capacity to transmute external objects into visual forms that seem to belong to the internal world, for its material—light—seems so intangible and immaterial as to be unreal—or, rather, to have the status of phenomenal (phantasmagoric) appearances. Even when the artist or film-maker does not eliminate the external occasions that condition creative endeavour, he or she reduces these external events to momentary configu-rations of coincidences devoid of genuine substance or, as Romantic dis-course on artmaking often has it, the pretext for the work. But the momentary conjunctions that prove evocative for one individual's conscious-ness likely will not possess that power for another's: the memory of a swal-low against a certain curve of cloud or the taste of a particular tangerine usually proves to have entirely private significance. If language is to have a common significance, it must refer to a common reality. When that reality dissolves and all that remains is the internal realm of our own private aware-ness, language at the very least loosens (if it does not completely detach) itself from referential significance. All we can claim for a non-referential lan-guage is what the Black Mountain poets claimed for language in general, that language is a reality sui generis, whose significance belong to its sounds alone. Words cannot mirror reality, nor can works of art represent, refer to, or describe a world outside that of the poem itself; but a flow of sounds can form an autonomous reality.

Hegel predicted accurately when he suggested that the historical development of the Spirit would leave behind "picture thinking," and through that
overcoming, would lead to the final separation of Spirit from figurative, sensuous form. As he foresaw, the course of history brought art to the point of
attempting to present to absolute truth in its absolute form—as pure
thought. In this stage, as Hegel predicted, the Idea took itself as its object:

> art cannot work for sensuous intuition. Instead it must, on the one hand,
> work for the inwardness which coalesces with its object simply as if with
> itself, for subjective inner depth, for reflective emotion, for feeling which, as
> spiritual, strives for freedom in itself and seeks and finds its reconciliation
> only in the inner spirit. This *inner* world constitutes the content of the
> romantic sphere and must therefore be represented as this inwardness and in
> the pure appearance of this depth of feeling. Inwardness celebrates its tri-
> umph over the external and manifests its victory in and on the external itself,
> whereby what is apparent to the senses alone sinks into worthlessness.[24]

How apt Hegel's commentary on Romantic art is as a description of the
poems of Rainer Maria Rilke or the films of Jordan Belson! The Domain of
the Invisible of Rilke's *Duineser Elegien* is the domain that Hegel foresaw, in
which the Spirit has separated from matter—or more exactly, it is a domain
in which the Ideal strives for (even if does not attain) complete freedom from
material embodiment. Hegel foresaw the program of Romaticism:

> For at the stage of romantic art the spirit knows that its truth does not con-
> sist in its immersion in corporeality; on the contrary, it only becomes sure
> of its truth by withdrawing from the external into its own intimacy with
> itself and positing external reality as an existence inadequate to itself. . . .
> The true content of romantic art absolute inwardness. . . . In this Pantheon
> all the gods are dethroned, the flame of subjectivity has destroyed them.[25]

Imagination becomes the paramount force in Romantic art, as it becomes
understood as the force that brings forth reality. And since imagination creates reality, whatever represents the inner workings of imagination are the
truest documentaries. These documentaries, Brakhage tells us, are the real
works of art.

But Hegel failed to realize that the quest for absolute freedom is not the
Spirit's only goal—or, at least, it is not a goal for which the Spirit can strive
without pain attending the quest. The reason why the Spirit feels such pain
is easy to understand: the Spirit craves to have a home, a place where it can
truly be and can have intimate relations. As the Symbolists were later to
learn, the total self-enclosure of Hegel's Absolute is a parlous feature, as its
existence becomes unreciprocal when it lacks relation to matter. Its being
becomes too one-sided when it lacks embodiment in the flesh of the world—
finally, its existence becomes too undialectical for it to maintain itself in
existence. So thinkers have attempted to discover, or invent, a realm in

which the dynamics of consciousness might find material embodiment; and they frequently used the concept of energy to found such a world. Two thinkers who have been instrumental in formulating a worldview in which the dynamics of consciousness and the energetics of the world are at one are D.H. Lawrence (1885-1930), a woefully underestimated influence on recent art theory, and A.N. Whitehead (1861-1947), through his own writings and his influence on so-called "process philosophy" (see glossary). We shall see that proprioceptive experience plays a central part in both thinkers' works. Thus, the harmony that Greek art exemplified, between Spirit and the body experienced externally, was displaced in Romantic art only to be replaced, in due course, by a harmony of the Spirit with the body that we experience internally. The earliest place where we can see this new harmony emerging is Schopenhauer's philosophy and it is this that gives his philosophy its historical importance.

The Primacy of the Subject Body and the Recessiveness of the Subject Body

Western metaphysics is an onto-theology of presence. It accords value to that which comes forth, out of nothingness, into presence. Derrida has shown that the onto-theology of presence accords with the priority that Western culture grants to speech over writing and to the present over the past and the future. Schopenhauer's distinction between types of bodily experience makes it possible to understand why a culture founded in the metaphysics of presence must denigrate the importance of the body. This understanding will help us to assess a claim that poets and poetic theorists have consistently advanced this century, that the breaking point of traditional Western culture was the division between self and nature, and that they are developing a poetics that points the way towards overcoming that distinction.

My proposal is simple: it is that the signal importance of Schopenhauer's stress on inner bodily experience lays the foundation for a conception of being that challenges the grounding principles of Western metaphysics. The apprehension of the body from within constitutes a primordial form of awareness, and this form of awareness must be fundamental to any proper analysis of experience. For just as our moods affect everything that we experience— just as, for example, when I fear, objects are disclosed to me as sources of peril, to be avoided, and when I feel loving, objects are revealed as things to possess and hold near—so too does the state of our body condition all that it discloses. My feelings and emotions are conditions of my body, but they are also instruments through which the features of the world "out there" make themselves known to me. (These are the grounds on which we can refute the common belief of the transcendentality of higher forms of cognition—subjects participate moment by moment in making the world in which they dwell, and any form of cognition whatever furnishes information only about a world the subject has had a role in bringing to awareness.)

Thus, primordial experience is first in the order of experience, even if it is not first in the order of being. However, our internal experience of the body is not the experience of a being that comes into full presence as our experience of objects is; and because the body does not come into full self-presence as an object among other objects in the world, it is not experienced as being replete with being. Consequently the proprioceptive body always seems to be something phantasmal, ephemeral, without substance, somehow unreal.

Our experience of "the subject body," to adopt Merleau-Ponty's nomenclature, has a property that I characterize as "recessive." Ordinarily, our awareness of the body is tacit awareness—we register the impact that objects around us make on the body and direct our attention towards the objects that make the impact. We are hardly aware, if at all, of the condition of the body, for the subjective body is recessive. The internal body, because it is the medium of all experience, hides itself. It eschews disclosure. If we try to bring the body to awareness—that is, if we make the body the centre of our focused awareness, then the body that we experience is no longer the same body, for the subject body (the body experienced from within) recedes from focal awareness and, in an apophantic alternation, the object body (the body as experienced as just one object among others in the world) comes forth to take its place. In attempting to thematize the body, we change the object of awareness.

The French philosopher Mikel Dufrenne, possibly the philosopher who has extended Merleau-Ponty's aesthetics in the most interesting way, comments on the deepest implications of experiencing through the recessive body:

> For example, when I am all ears, I no longer have ears, for the sonorous completely inhabits me; I then live the primitive distinction between subject and object, just as I live it between self and other in the ecstatic moments of love. At this juncture I am in contact with the ground: the sensuous offers me a face of Nature that is, of course, for me, but for "a me" that has barely been born, still immersed in Nature, still situated in the vicinity of the originary. Here I am close to experiencing what I am in principle forbidden to experience: the ground.[26]

The comment goes quite a way towards explaining why so many poets and artists of the twentieth century have wanted to provide a splendid image not of the body (for the represented body is the object), but of the subject body. The recessive body can only be experienced, insofar as it can be experienced at all—and it is certainly true that we experience it only fleetingly, as we catch a glimpse of the texture it imposes upon the sensuous elements that it discloses to us—as the subject body; but nonetheless, I shall argue that it is the recessive body that brings us into relation with something grand that transcends our individual being.

The shift between experiencing the subject body and the object body is crucial to how we become aware of our bodies. The subject body eludes thematization and can never be the focal object of directed attention, for in making the body the object of focused awareness, its phenomenological status changes. The recessiveness of the subject body is already a challenge to the onto-theology of traditional metaphysics. Still more destructive to traditional metaphysics is the conceptual and experiential primitiveness of our awareness of the inward body's recessive character—our awareness of the inward body is not something that we could arrive at by scrutinizing our experience of the world (that is to say, by studying the impact that objects belonging to the external world have upon the body) and factoring out the contributions that the body makes to that experience. For the subject body is a precondition of experience and can no more be an object of immediate and direct awareness than the Kantian categories or the transcendental self can. The efficiency with which we act relates directly to this capacity of the body to recede from awareness. Recessiveness is the essence of bodily skill: when we play a musical instrument or perform an intricate feat of choreography, we must surrender any focalized awareness of the actions our bodies engage in; for when we attend to the movement of our fingers or our bodies, we falter. When we cannot carry out the steps in the choreography as one smooth, flowing, rhythmically marked gesture, we focus on the movements we make with our feet, legs, torsos, arms. Under these conditions, we direct our attention towards our muscles and how we use them to shape the required form—we attend to the manner in which a certain rotation of an extended leg enables the line from the hip through to the toes to project into space and to how that rotation must integrate into the movement of the leg into that position and out of it again. But our bodily operations become awkward when we allow this happen. Only when, by performing the gesture repeatedly, we incorporate the knowledge of how to perform into our musculature—and only when we arrive at the stage where we can allow the body to recede from focal awareness and use our body as an instrument for experiencing space, dynamics, and rhythm—can we perform the gesture effectively.

These examples show that the experience of the subject body is necessarily recessive because it comes forth only as the body fades from focal awareness. The subject body is fundamental to all our experience, for it mediates all our experience; yet, we cannot thematize that experience. The subject body is the body we experience when, in performing a piece of choreography, we experience space and movement *through* the body, rather than making the body itself the focus of awareness. As I master the movements of the choreography, the body recedes to allow space or movement to come forth as presence. The condition for experiencing movement—for becoming fully aware of the feelings of movement—is that the awareness of the body recedes to form a background for the experience of movement, or, more accurately, the condition for experiencing movement as an immediate presence is that the body become an instrument *through* which movement discloses itself to me.

This shows that one's awareness of one's body is bound in an apophantic relationship with one's experience of the world: as the world and the body have an apophantic relationship in experience, only the body's self-concealment allows experience to be world-disclosing rather than self-disclosing. The body must recede so as to allow the Other to emerge as presence. The Other cannot reveal itself unless my body conceals itself. The world reveals itself to me only through my body, yet my body as an object within the world must become absent itself in order for me to experience the world of beings as presences.

A central paradox of our existence, then, is that the subject body emerges only as it conceals itself. If we attempt to thematize the subject body it disappears, and the object body takes its place. Only when we allow it to recede from the focus of experience so that the Other might reveal itself does the lived body emerge. The subject body has a mysterious mode of being (not unlike Being itself) for the subject body becomes present exactly as it fades into absence, and it fades into absence just when it emerges in full presence. But a mode of being which so inextricably links presence and absence defies explanation through the categories of traditional metaphysics which, being founded on the law of the excluded middle, cannot abide any term's being involving non-being. The inexplicability, according to metaphysical categories, of the subject body explains the hostility Western metaphysics has harboured towards the body.

We experience the subject body more immediately than we do any object. It is a stream of sensations, of various types—visceral, kinesthetic, proprioceptive, auditory, visual, affective, etc. The subject body does not coincide with the object body, for its being is more that of energy than of mass. It is unstable, for inner experience undergoes rapid alteration both in the sensory modality that predominates the moment of experience and in the object that experience reveals. Inner experience is also temporally disjunctive, for it can shift instantly from the present to the future or the past. What is more, it has access to non-present things. Consequently, Western metaphysics deems that there is something unreal—or, at least, less than fully real—about the subject body.

Chapter 1

Four for America: Williams, Pound, Stein, Brakhage

Styles of English Metre

The various styles of discourse and the various representational forms that rose to dominance, one after the other, during the period that spans the years between the beginning of the Age of Reason (around the start of the seventeenth century) and the middle of the nineteenth century, exhibit a consistency so thoroughgoing that we can characterize that interval as a historical epoch. To acknowledge that this period was the epoch of the dominance of the bourgeoisie, we shall call it "the bourgeois epoch." Since the ideology of the bourgeoisie rests on the idea of the individual, the canonical poetic tradition of this epoch is the poetry of the individual voice. The various poetic forms and devices that we find in this epoch were means for creating the impression that an individual has the status that a monad does in Leibniz's philosophy, that he or she is an internally homogeneous and independent element—an atom that carries its nature within itself and that does not alter inwardly as it forms relations with other atoms. Its unified, internally homogeneous nature determines that the relations into which this monad enters are purely extrinsic.

In *Les Mots et les choses* (1966, trans. *The Order of Things*, 1973), the French philosopher of history, Michel Foucault, describes the transformation in the modes of representation that took place as the Age of Reason began. Foucault argues that each historical epoch has its own *épistème*, a preconceptual scheme that underlies its science, religion, philosophy, art, political theory, and methods of governance, and that provides the parameters and limits of the theories, beliefs, and practices that might appear in that epoch.

Notes to Chapter 1 are on pp. 474-512.

He further proposes that the different *épistèmes* of various societies vary more than people commonly realize. The people of the medieval epoch made themselves a world that differed greatly from the world the people of the Renaissance or the Age of Reason constructed for themselves, or that, in our time, people of Western European descent have created for themselves.

Foucault claims that analogical thinking was the cardinal feature of the *épistèmes* of both the Middle Ages and the Renaissance. The citizen of the Middle Ages or the Renaissance thought in terms of resemblances. There were four sorts of resemblance crucial to the *épistème* of the Renaissance: *convenientia*, by which things close to one another on some scale (e.g., earth and sea, animal and plant) were related; *aemulatio*, direct comparison, as the face and the sky are alike because a face has two eyes, while the sky has the sun and the moon; *analogy*, indirect comparison, a similarity in ratios; and *sympathy*, which brought every thing into likeness with all other things (so sympathy drew together human destiny and the movements of the planets and the stars, and the momentary condition of the cosmos and the relation between the various humours). Until the Age of Reason, the structure of ideas that Western societies used rested on the concept of resemblance. It was the concept of resemblance that shaped the exegesis and the interpretation of texts, that organized the use of symbols, that permitted acquaintance with things visible and invisible, and that guided the art of representing them. The world revolved around itself; the earth repeated the sky, stars reflected faces, painting imitated space. Representation, whether in art or in learning, took the form of repetition. Its resemblance to the world—its being a theatre of life or a mirror of the world—gave language its validity, its mode of proclaiming itself and of formulating its right to speak. Philosophers of this period generally assumed that language has purchase on the world because its structure reflects the structure of the world. Foucault proposes that citizen of the Renaissance lived within a web of resemblance, which knit words and things together into a undivided unity.

Consider the principle of the Divine Right of Kings. Foucault claims that people living during the Renaissance or the medieval epoch could think of God only by way of analogy to the king or to a father—and therefore as the King of kings or as the Father in heaven. Conversely, they conceived of the king's earthly power as a reflection of the Divine Majesty's glory and so believed that the king commands his subjects' loyalty in just the same way as God commands our faith and devotion. Considered as a product of analogical thinking, the principle of the Divine Right of Kings is hardly the preposterous piece of nonsense that it commonly is presented as (viz., nonsense that James I invented as justification for the Stuart regnum and, more particularly, as self-justification).

Or take Saint Thomas's theory of political authority as another example, this one to show how an understanding of analogical thinking makes what might seem an exotic piece of speculation seem reasonable and wholly understandable. According to Saint Thomas, the signal condition to which a king's government must conform to be a justified government is that it must imitate God's government of nature. As God created the world, the king must found cities; as God guides natural beings towards realizing their various purposes, the king must lead humans to their rightful end. Considered in the terms of contemporary reason—in the terms that the predicate calculus codifies—this reasoning seems to rest on an unwarranted and erroneous identification of the secular kingdom with God's Kingdom, of the earthly ruler with the Lord of the Heavens, of the power of secular authority with Divine Power. Considered as an example of analogical thinking, however, it seems defensible: it conceives of the earthly city as exemplifying the pattern that the Heavenly City establishes.

Foucault shows that from the time of the Stoics until the Renaissance, philosophers of language argued that resemblance, i.e., *convenientia*, emulation (*aemulatio*), analogy, and sympathy, formulate the links between the signs of language and the objects of the world that they intend. Because resemblance, emulation, analogy, and sympathy depend on properties that belong to signs themselves, these links are inherent in signs themselves. Philosophers of language maintained, accordingly, that words and things belong to the same logical category and, consequently, that we can count words as just one sort of thing among many others. Holding words and things together in an undivided integrity was a concept that the Symbolist poets did much to resurrect, the idea of correspondence through the signatures; indeed in Renaissance thought the term "signature" is the sign of similarity of every possible variety.

People of the Renaissance era believed that God had stamped every thing with an image (which they called a "signature") that is proper to things of its sort—all brains, for example, are stamped with a common signature proper to the class of brains, all walnuts with a common signature proper to the class of walnuts. These signatures are usually hidden, so it took special, often arcane, knowledge—an *eruditio* that, often, was tantamount to *divinitio*—to identify them. However, this knowledge afforded understanding of the secret potencies of things, according to the principle of like affecting like: thus, if the signature of two types of objects were similar, then one of these could affect the other. For example, the signatures of brains and walnuts are similar; therefore eating walnuts can improve the intelligence. Such was the thing that bound all existents together in a seamless web (even divination, of course, involves a participation of the knowing mind in the divined essence).

From the Renaissance on, however, "Things and words were to be separated from one another," as people began to consider words and things as belonging to distinct logical categories. In the seventeenth century, the concept of resemblance was decisively repudiated, and the concept of representation took the place that the concept of resemblance had occupied. The analysis of representation replaced divination of resemblance as the principal method of inquiry and as the key principle of right reason. No longer was thinking conceived in intuiting, through sufficient training to have acquired *eruditio*, the resemblance between things that allowed thinkers to draw them into a unity; rather, thinking came to be conceived as carving out fine distinctions.

To get an inkling of the importance of the concept of representation, just consider the political baggage that has burdened it in our own time. Out of representation, moreover, arises the idea of a *mathesis universalis* that we are only just recovering from. Knowledge sought to replace intuition of the whole with the ability to manage—i.e., to calculate finite differences. In its effort to apprehend and to manage difference, taxonomy became the regnant discipline of the era.

Foucault expresses this insight by saying that with the Renaissance, language retreated and discourse took its place. By "language" Foucault intends language insofar as it is self-referential and ontogenic (i.e., world-creating or, more literally, being-creating). The vector of language points inward, toward itself as language (in Foucault's sense of the word) and takes itself as the world. The vector of discourse, on the other hand, points outward, for its sole function is to act as a transparent representation of objects and ideas that exist outside language. Thus, when language retreats, as Foucault argues it did in the seventeenth century, what it leaves behind is its function as representation—representation that unfolds in the sign itself, and not by virtue of relation based on resemblance—and, hence, its nature and function become that of discourse.[27]

Foucault sometimes characterizes this change by saying that a ternary system of signs gave way to a dyadic system (such as that represented by Ferdinand de Saussure's bilateral sign, which he conceives of as a "two-sided psychological entity" binding together a *"concept"* and a *"sound-image"*).[28] From the time of the Stoics to the Renaissance, philosophers of language claimed that the signifier—represented in Saussure's semiology by the sound-image—and the signified—represented in Saussure's semiology by the concept—relate to one another through resemblance, which Foucault characterizes as a "conjuncture" of signifier and signified. We can understand the ternary nature of the function by comparing the function of analogy, the most general form of strict resemblance (sympathy being another matter entirely) to the mathematical idea of proportionality (A:B::B:C), i.e., A is to B as B is to C, with the "as" invoking a relation similar to that of resemblance. Thus, the concept of representation would be unpacked into the claim that the sign is to a concept as the concept is to a thing; where the relation between the sign and the concept (itself a form of resemblance) resembles the relation between the concept and the thing (again, a form of resemblance); or, similarly, the concept of Divine Right would be unpacked into the claim that God is to the king as the king is to the people, for the relation between God and the king (itself a form of resemblance) resembles the relation between king and people (again a form of resemblance). Or, to formulate the idea differently, we could consider the third element as stating the ground of the sign—as stating in what respect that representamen (see glossary) resembles the object signified. From the Renaissance until recent times, thinkers no longer considered this relation to be ternary but dyadic, without connection to any external reality. With the Port-Royal Logic of 1683, which helped make explicit some of the foundational principles of the post-Renaissance *épistème*, the sign is explicitly understood as involving a dyadic relation between the idea of one thing and the idea of another, between the idea of that which represents (the signifier) and the idea of that which is represented (the signified); what is more, in Port-Royal Logic, the relation between signifier and signified is understood as being arbitrary. The post-Renaissance *épistème* dispensed with the third term, resemblance, altogether. But in doing so, the sign and its object became separated, and words were no longer thought to afford direct access to things. Knowing became a matter of discourse, of representation, and of criticism. In due course, the mind, which possesses the representing sign, was divorced from the world objects that sign represents.

Foucault regards this semiotic change as the basis for a new way of thinking, or a new *épistème*. The Age of Reason inaugurates a way of thinking which deems only that which is measurable to be real. As the philosophy of René Descartes makes evident, the criterion of truth becomes the clarity and distinctness of ideas. Because mathematics deals with precisely definable quantities, it became central to the intellectual project of the era. The new *épistème* measures out reality, cuts it up, defines, and arranges it in taxonomic categories.

Francis Bacon, writing in 1605, stated the principle that drove this change when he condemned writing that concerned itself with style more than with subject matter:

> men began to hunt more after words than matter; more after the choiceness of the phrase, and the round and clean composition of the sentence, and the sweet falling of the clauses, and the varying and illustration of their works with tropes and figures, than after the weight of matter, worth of subject, soundness of argument, life of invention or depth of judgment.[29]

Foucault's thesis can serve us as our starting point for considering the importance of Ezra Pound's poetic theory and practice. In Canto LXXXI (*inter alia loci*), Pound stated, "[t]o break the pentameter, that was the first heave." Pound proclaimed that a more flexible metre should replace iambic pentameter, a metre that could adapt to the variability of human nature and yet, for all that, would be absolute, since it would have a basis in the structure of the poet's emotional life. In the Credo section of his essay "A Retrospect" (in which he presents a string of thoughts on the significance of *vers libre* [see glossary]), he wrote: "I believe in an 'absolute rhythm,' a rhythm, that is, in poetry which corresponds exactly to the emotion or shade of emotion to be expressed. A man's rhythm must be interpretative, it will be, therefore, in the end, his own, uncounterfeiting, uncounterfeitable."[30]

Pound did not set out his reasons for making iambic pentameter the focus of his first attack on poetic conventions; however, I conjecture that his reasons have to do with a belief that iambic pentameter did not afford the requisite flexibility. Iambic pentameter serves similar functions in poetry as linear perspective serves in painting. For example, both are what I term "thoroughly determining forms," i.e., forms that regulate all the elements that become part of a composition. We can gauge how thoroughly determining iambic pentameter is—how pervasive its influence on a poem's construction is—by contrasting the effect that metre has on a poem's architectonic with the effect that the common metre of earlier English verse (i.e., Old, Middle, and early Modern English verse) had.

The most common metre of earlier English poetry consisted of a recurrent pattern of four stressed syllables per line, with each line presenting a quasi-independent thought or fact. Northrop Frye has argued that this metre has roots in the nature of the English language. "A four-stress line seems to be inherent in the structure of the English language. It is the prevailing rhythm of the earlier poetry, though it changes its scheme from alliteration to rhyme in Middle English; it is the common rhythm of popular poetry in all periods, of ballads and of most nursery rhymes."[31]

The rules for accentual metre specify only that a line must contain a specific number of stressed syllables; they stipulate nothing about the use of unstressed syllables. The rules for iambic pentameter, on the other hand, decree that stressed and unstressed syllables must alternate and that the total number of syllables (both stressed and unstressed) must be ten. Iambic pentameter dictates both the stress and syllable count, while common metre required only that each line have four stressed syllables.

However, the additional form-generating power that iambic pentameter possesses, compared with common metre, cannot be entirely accounted for on the basis that iambic pentameter regulates a greater number of features in a line. The pattern of alternation of stressed and unstressed units established by that metre reverberates through the whole of the poem's architectonic, and effects all the other aural patterns that have to work in concert with it, whether by reinforcing the pattern of alternation or by acting in counterpoint (see glossary) with it. One effect of iambic pentameter is a tendency towards isochrony—a reader's tendency to eliminate variations in the length of vowels (or even, at times, to elide what a non-metric reading would pronounce as two syllables, with a pause between them, into a single syllable) so as to maintain an even and periodic recurrence of the beat. Another sort of example that shows how pentameter shapes the poem's entire aural effect results from the character of English metre's stress system. In English poetry stress is primarily a matter of aural intensity, and not of vowel quality, which correlates more closely with intonation. Because in English poetry loudness determines stress, a recurrent pattern of stresses invites the poet to use strongly marked, heavy syllables, or even to create a bass-drum-like "di-BOOM-di BOOM-di BOOM-di BOOM-di BOOM" effect. Much of Algernon Charles Swinburne's (1837-1909) poetry could illustrate this effect.

Most English verse, to be sure, avoids a coincidence between a pattern of stressed syllables with a second rhythmic pattern that is formed by marking syllables with variations in intonation, pauses, phrasal division, inversions of word order, or any other stressing factors. It is even common for the intonation or phrasal patterns of a line or a series of lines to establish a secondary rhythm. Thus, Gerard Manley Hopkins (1844-89) insisted on the importance of this secondary metre and on the tension between the primary (iambic) and secondary metre—a tension he referred to as "counterpointing," a term of tellingly musical provenance. Hopkins described the effect as:

> the superinducing or *mounting* of a new rhythm upon the old; and since the new or mounted rhythm is actually heard and at the same time the mind naturally supplies the natural or standard foregoing rhythm, for we do not forget what the rhythm is that by rights we should be hearing, two rhythms are in some manner running at once and we have something answerable to counterpoint in music, which is two or more strains of tune going on together, and this is Counterpoint Rhythm.[32]

These general comments are overly broad; however Hopkins's technical analysis limits the range of counterpoint more narrowly than our description suggests and, for that matter, more than his own choice of the term would suggest, to the results of the systematic reversal of iambic stress (for which effects use of the term "syncopation" might form a more precise analogy).

Wellek and Warren argue that counterpoint, in the sense that we have been using the term, is the norm of English poetry: "English verse is largely determined by the counterpoint between the imposed phrasing, the rhythmical impulse, and the actual speech rhythm conditioned by phrasal divisions."[33] We can scan many lines in iambic pentameter verse both as iambic and as dactylic or anapaestic—just think of almost any line from John Keats's (1795-1821) "Ode to a Nightingale" for an example:

> My heart aches, and a drowsy numbness pains
> My sense, as though of hemlock I had drunk,

I defy anyone to read those lines aloud and not want to make "pains/ My sense," into three consecutive stressed beats—that desire itself suggests that the lines involve an interplay of dactylic and anapaestic metres, or at least that some principle is at work that breaks the alternation of one stressed with one unstressed syllable. And it continues so:

> Thou wast not born for death, immortal Bird!

Note how one tends to read "born for death" as ambiguously stressed—either as three consecutive stressed syllables or as alternating heavy/light/heavy stresses; the word "for" in this phrase is therefore a variable syllable and has a hovering stress (see glossary).

> No hungry generations tread thee down;

The same comments apply to "tread thee down" as apply to "born for death," with "thee" being the variable syllable with a hovering stress.

> The voice I hear this passing night was heard
> In ancient days by emperor and clown:

The same analysis applies to "emperor and clown" as applies to "born for death" and "tread thee down," with "and" being the variable syllable with hovering stress.

The counterpoint Wellek and Warren speak of usually involves duple and triple metres, as it does in "Ode to a Nightingale"; that is, it is a pulse that arises when a pattern formed by stressing every other syllable interacts with a pattern formed by stressing every third syllable. Counterpointing duple and triple metre is so common as to be practically the norm in English.

There may be historical reasons for the interplay between duple and triple metre being as common in English verse as it is. The mensural rhythms of pre-polyphonic music had their grounds in the belief that units of three were the perfect measure and the various rhythmic modes that emerged around the tenth century all grouped notes in time measures of three beats. Whatever the reason, Western music composed since the beginning of the homophonic period, in which duple metres achieved their current predominance, has had a penchant for hemiola (the use of a two-against-three or a three-against-two cross-pulse [see glossary, cross-rhythm]), just as English verse, ever since iambic pentameter became the most prevalent metre, has leaned towards an analogous effect by using lines that are amenable to being read in either anapaestic or dactylic and in iambic scansion.

This interplay between two coexistent systems is an example of what Classical prosodists called "epiploce" (see glossary), a term that denotes the various possibilities of scansion. Epiploce generally, and more specifically the particular interplay we have been examining between a metrically determined and a phrasally determined scansion, creates and organizes variations in stress and intonation. Since intonational stresses are highly flexible, these variations often moderate what would otherwise be the thumping alternation of heavy and light beats characteristic of doggerel, for example. It is principally this moderation of the metrical schema by the actualized particular—this softening of a rigid abstract form by the complexities of the actual instance and the mitigation of the severity of normative metre by the subtleties of actual speech acts—that prevents iambic pentameter from falling into a steady hoofbeat measure.

Thus, in comparison with accentual metre, which admits of considerable variation in line lengths, iambic pentameter is a highly formalized, preconceived construct, a systemic whole that strictly regulates a variety of features (alternating stresses, line length, vowel length, etc.); the variety that it tolerates arises from the interaction between iambic metre and anapaestic or dactylic metre. Iambic pentameter closely resembles linear perspective in the way that it organizes nearly all a poem's features. Iambic pentameter has other similarities with linear perspective: a similar counterpoint between abstract schema and actualized instance, with a similar effect of concealing the highly formalized abstract system, obtains in painting based on linear perspective; thus, spatial anomalies, whether Mannerist anamorphosis, or Cézannesque *passage*, or any one of a number of other sorts, abound, even in perspectival painting, and these deviations from the universal, geometrical schema introduce considerable flexibility into what would be, if such deviations were not encouraged, a too-rigid system.

The softening of iambic pentameter's insistent stress pattern by a superinduced pattern in triple metre also bolsters the conceit that the poem records natural speech; what is more, it creates the sense that readers can put the stress where they want, and so it affords an illusion of spontaneity. Contrapuntal rhythms, because they more closely approximate the rhythms of speech, lend a quality of being natural to the artifices and contrivances of metrical construction.

Combining iambic pentameter with a rhythm that gives the semblance of being a close approximation to "natural (i.e., everyday) speech," creates the effect—and here I am using the term also in the sense in which filmmakers and stage people use it when they speak of "special effects," that is, in the sense of "an illusion"—of being delivered by a spontaneous voice, of being unstudied and uncontrived speech. At the same time, the precision and formal rigour of the undergirding structure produces a strong sense of univocity, of a single voice whose integrity and coherence the metrical uniformity guarantees. The regularity of the pulse encourages identification with the assumed speaker, for it allows the reader to predict the speaker's speech pattern and so to feel that he or she could take the speaker's place. This identification with a coherent, unified speaker produces the effect of a coherent, unified subject.

Furthermore, what is just as important, this identification eludes being thematized, for that identification (indeed all identification) has an apophantic relation with awareness. The fixity of the speaker/reader's position, and the reader's identification with the voice of a highly distinctive individual, foster our belief that the poem's coherent, unified subject has the character of a transcendental ego, for that fixity ensures that the speaker/reader occupies a position that shields her from change. Furthermore, just as counterpointing iambic pentameter with anapaestic or dactylic metres conceals the artificial nature of iambic pentameter and so contributes to creating a semblance of natural speech, so too the textual continuity of most iambic pentameter verse—its long, flowing lines and the regularity of its metre—conceals the role that language plays in creating a position for the subject. This fluent continuity, by creating an undisturbed, unfissured subject—a subject that doesn't really appear, that lies outside the realm of experience because of the apophantic masking of the subject by the continuity of the text, but which we can consider as the unifying principle that lies behind the various experiences of the ego—renders that subject as though transcendental, i.e., presents it simply as the agency that imposes on experience the conditions to which it must conform in order to be experienced. This convention reinforces the impression that the very same factors that produce the subject's coherence are also responsible for the coherence of the poem; indeed that impression does much to explain the reasons the convention favouring fluent writing arose in the first place.[34]

While the line closings in iambic pentameter verse more frequently than not do coincide with line boundaries, the formal pressures leading to such coincidence are more relaxed in comparison with four-stress accentual metre. Lines in four-stress metre often break into two units of two. The pentameter line exhibits no such proclivity toward internal division, since a line resists being divided internally into unequal or asymmetrical parts. The conventional coincidence, in iambic pentameter verse, of line boundaries and line closings (or line lengths and thought lengths) reinforces this effect, for this coincidence produces the impression that the very same factors produce the coherence of the subject as produce the coherence of the poem. The lack of textual pressure, in iambic verse, to create a closure at the end of a line to pair with an internal division point within a line, steers iambic verse towards using a more extended line-unit. At the same time the use of a more extended line-unit reduces the pressure for the line end to register the completion of one unit and the beginning of the next. Because the lines are not end-stopped, the poem has the texture of a long and intricately woven, but nonetheless unified, syntagma (see glossary) that holds all the elements in the poem in place. The integrity and coherence of these poetic elements often give the impression of a unified diegesis and this diegetic unity further encourages the reader to identify with the world the poem represents. The coherence of the subject produced by this identificatory process is a source of pleasure and the subject's own reflective unity in turn has the reflective effect of making the diegetic unity of the poem seem all the greater; that diegetic unity, in its turn, becomes the source of further satisfaction.

This subjective integrity and diegetic uniformity gives pentameter a flowing quality—these features explain why pentameter verse generally flows smoothly from line to line. Consider lines as abstract and philosophical as those of the well-known reflective section of William Wordsworth's (1770-1850) "Lines Composed a Few Miles Above Tintern Abbey":

> For I have learned
> To look on nature, not as in the hour
> Of thoughtless youth; but hearing oftentimes
> The still, sad music of humanity,
> Nor harsh nor grating, though of ample power
> To chasten and subdue. And I have felt
> A presence that disturbs me with the joy
> Of elevated thoughts; a sense sublime
> Of something far more deeply interfused,
> Whose dwelling is the light of setting suns,
> And the round ocean and the living air,
> And the blue sky, and in the mind of man:
> A motion and a spirit, that impels
> All thinking things, all objects of all thought,
> And rolls through all things. Therefore am I still
> A lover of the meadows and the woods,
> And mountains; and of all that we behold
> From this green earth; of all the mighty world
> Of eye, and ear,—both what they half create,
> And what perceive; well pleased to recognise
> In nature and the language of the sense
> The anchor of my purest thoughts, the nurse,

> The guide, the guardian of my heart, and soul
> Of all my mortal being.[35]

The sentence that starts with "And I have felt" runs across several line-breaks. The line-breaks themselves occur at places where the thought is incomplete. "I have felt" ends with a transitive verb, and so leads us on, towards the object "A presence that disturbs me." That line ends with an incomplete prepositional phrase "with the joy" and so leads us on, towards that phrase's completion, "Of elevated thoughts." This leads immediately to a second object for the verb "felt"—"a sense sublime." Starting with a noun phrase suggests an ellipsis—a lack of completeness that we resolve only when we come to recognize that the phrase's anaphoric reference leads back to the verb form "have felt." Furthermore, the parallelism between "I have felt/ A presence that disturbs me with the joy/ Of elevated thoughts;" and "a sense sublime/ Of something far more deeply interfused" links the two noun phrases and smooths the flow from line to line and from phrase to phrase. This linearity, this unfissured syntagma, has the effect of creating a single, coherent position for the subject in the text.

The poem continues in a similar manner. The use of a long, continuous line that flows over line-breaks is characteristic of Wordsworth's style—and not only Wordsworth's but also those of several of his contemporaries. This contrasts markedly with the form of ballads in which line-breaks coincide with the conclusion of thoughts and, consequently, each line represents a distinct thought (and sometimes even a separate sentence). The effect of this coincidence of syntactical and poetic forms is to impel the poem towards using paratactical constructions. The most famous of the early English ballads, "Edward," exemplifies this drive:

> "Why dois your brand sae drap wi bluid,
>   Edward, Edward,
> Why dois your brand sae drap wi bluid,
>   And why sae sad gang yee O?"
> "O I hae killed my hauke sae guid,
>   Mither, mither,
> O I hae killed my hauke sae guid,
>   And I had nae mair bot hee O."
>
> "Your haukis bluid was nevir sae reid,
>   Edward, Edward,
> Your haukis bluid was nevir sae reid,
>   My deir son I tell thee O."
> "O I hae killed my reid-roan steid,
>   Mither, mither,
> O I hae killed my reid-roan steid,
>   That erst was sae fair and frie O."

"Your steid was auld, and ye hae gat mair,
>> Edward, Edward,
Your steid was auld, and ye hea gat mair,
> Sum other dule ye drie O."[36]

The mother's repetitive and unrelenting questioning and Edward's evasive prevarication create suspense that continues to build even after the ballad has revealed that the "dule" (grief) that Edward "dries" (endures) is that he has killed his "fadir deir"—and this tension building continues despite the remainder of the ballad being mostly a list of penances he must undergo. This suspense leads towards the poem's famous "surprise" ending (which we can take to suggest that an illicit desire and an unspeakable hope motivate the mother's relentless questioning):

"And what wul ye leive to your ain mither deir,
>> Edward, Edward?
And what wul ye leive to your ain mither deir?
> My deir son, now tell me O."
"The curse of hell frae me sall ye beir,
>> Mither, mither,
The curse of hell frae me sall ye beir,
> Sic counseils ye gave to me O."[37]

The effect is clearer, perhaps, in Elizabethan lyrics. Here is Thomas Nashe's extraordinary poem, "Litany in Time of Plague" (from his play *Summer's Last Will and Testament*):

Adieu, farewell earth's bliss,
This world uncertain is;
Fond are life's lustful joys,
Death proves them all but toys,
None from his darts can fly.
I am sick, I must die.
> Lord, have mercy on us!

Rich men, trust not in wealth,
Gold cannot buy you health;
Physic himself must fade,
All things to end are made.
The plague full swift goes by;
I am sick, I must die.
> Lord, have mercy on us!

Beauty is but a flower
Which wrinkles will devour:
Brightness falls from the air,
Queens have died young and fair,
Dust hath closed Helen's eye.
I am sick, I must die.
> Lord, have mercy on us!

Strength stoops unto the grave,
Worms feed on Hector brave,
Swords may not fight with fate.
Earth still holds ope her gate;
Come! come! the bells do cry.
I am sick, I must die.
        Lord, have mercy on us!

Wit with his wantonness
Tasteth death's bitterness;
Hell's executioner
Hath no ears for to hear
What vain art can reply.
I am sick, I must die.
        Lord, have mercy on us!

Haste, therefore, each degree,
To welcome destiny.
Heaven is our heritage,
Earth but a player's stage;
Mount we unto the sky.
I am sick, I must die.
        Lord, have mercy on us![38]

Nearly every line presents a separate item in the list of what Death undoes: "Brightness falls from the air,/ Queens have died young and fair,/ Dust hath closed Helen's eye./ I am sick, I must die." Some items, like the splendour of youth and beauty, the poet refers to only metaphorically; others the poet mentions explicitly. However, the general form of the piece evens out the differences between these levels of reference. The poem has the character of a list, with each item separated from all the others.

The rhyming couplets emphasize the closure at the end of each line. Ending each line on a metrically accented syllable lends additional strength to the closure. Furthermore, the couplet has the effect of stopping every other line with a firm caesura (see glossary). Each pair of end-stopped lines forms a unit, the repetition of which integrates the poem's phonetic, syntactical, and semantic dimensions. The couplet form imposes an intonational pattern that bolsters the impression that each line and each rhyming couplet is distinct. We tend to read the second line of a rhyming couplet as answering the first. We read the first rhyming word with a higher intonation, to suggest a pause rather than a full stop, and the second with a lower intonation, to indicate that we will not continue the line or thought after a break. This manner of reading has the effect of dividing the poem into quasi-separate modules.

The gravitational pull exerted by the line's end provides the lines' phonetic pattern while the line-stop and line length shape the syntax. This pattern influences the poem's semantic structure as well, through the requirement that a thought be completed either at the end of every line (or, if not at the end of every line, at the end of every couplet). Parallelism further reinforces the effects of the metre and rhyme, giving the closure at the end of each line a strong sense of inevitability.

All these factors have the effect of separating each line, conceptually and syntactically. The separation of line from line leads the lyric form towards the list form and towards paratactical construction generally. The unity that joins these modules in a whole is different from the organic unity that pentametric verse favours. The relations that one element has to other elements in an organic whole affect that element internally and alter its intrinsic characteristics. Verse in rhyming couplets accords greater integrity and a higher degree of independence to a poem's formal elements than the organic unity of pentametric verse allows. The greater integrity of the units that make up a poem in rhyming couplets, and their quasi-autonomy, are among the reasons that poems in rhyming couplets tend towards using repeated formal elements. The systematic use of formal repetition elicits an expectation of continuation, not finality. Try rereading "Edward" and you will see that the effect of using similar modules of meaning is to mitigate the dispersal that the parataxis of the list form produces.

Among the reasons Pound was so deeply committed to non-pentametric verse, *vers libre*, and Chinese poetry and troubadour poetry, surely, is that all share the impulse towards parataxis that Pound's own verse manifests. Pound's verse foregrounds the distinctness of each image and each action to an uncommon, and perhaps unprecedented, degree. What is more, Pound's mental processes seemed to tend towards the epigrammatic, and towards speed. Iambic pentameter favours a different form of thought.

Parataxis, the contiguity relation among signifiers that four-beat metre favours, produces a loose and 'open' syntagmatic chain. Use of juxtaposition encourages us to think, even if only unconsciously, of paradigmatic substitutions for the elements that appear in the poem. Just think of how often, in reciting from memory poems that incorporate lists, we substitute items of our own for items that appear in the list, and of how often we reorder the list and shuffle modifiers around to qualify items other than those the actual poem has them modifying.

Poems in iambic pentameter are different in all these regards. Take Wordsworth's verse as an example, and consider his use of intricate sentence construction. He favours long sentences with several subordinate clauses and frequently employs digressive (and therefore apparently loose grammatical) constructions and parallelism to create relations between phrases that are far separated from one another. These constructions give the impression that his poems represent speech—elevated speech, admittedly, but speech nonetheless. We can find examples in almost any of his shorter poems and even in *The Prelude* and *The Excursion*. The following poem, dedicated to the poet's daughter who died at the age of three years, exemplifies the quality:

> Surprised by joy—impatient as the Wind
> I turned to share the transport—Oh! with whom
> But Thee, deep buried in the silent tomb,
> That spot which no vicissitude can find?
> Love, faithful love, recalled thee to my mind—
> But how could I forget thee? Through what power,
> Even for the least division of an hour,
> Have I been so beguiled as to be blind
> To my most grievous loss!—That thought's return
> Was the worst pang that sorrow ever bore,
> Save one, one only, when I stood forlorn,
> Knowing my heart's best treasure was no more;
> That neither present time, nor years unborn
> Could to my sight that heavenly face restore.[39]

Wordsworth frequently reinforces the effect that his poems represent a speaking voice by including deictic (see glossary) markers, or shifters, in his poems. Another excerpt from "Lines Composed a Few Miles Above Tintern Abbey" can illustrate the effect. The emphases are mine.

> Five years have past; five summers, with the length
> Of five long winters! and *again* I hear
> *These* waters, rolling from *their* mountain-springs
> With a soft inland murmur.—*Once again*
> Do I behold *these* steep and lofty cliffs,
> That on a wild secluded scene impress
> Thoughts of more deep seclusion; and connect
> The landscape with the quiet of the sky.
> *The day is come when I again* repose
> *Here*, under *this* dark sycamore, and view
> *These* plots of cottage-ground, *these* orchard-tufts,
> Which *at this season*, with *their* unripe fruits,
> Are clad in one green hue, and lose themselves
> 'Mid groves and copses. *Once again* I see
> *These* hedge-rows, hardly hedge-rows, little lines
> Of sportive wood run wild: *these* pastoral farms . . . [40]

Deictic signifiers mark the passage with signs of enunciation. They foreground the act of utterance and in doing so they turn the text into a representation of the speaking voice that is the subject of the enunciation. It is a fact that could easily be established with a selection of examples that the subjectivity that we so frequently ascribe to Romantic lyrics results from the use of devices that foreground the subject of the enunciation over the enounced subject. Privileging enunciation sutures the reader to the poem, for the voice that reads the poem is prone to identify with the voice represented in the poem. This privileging of enunciation over the enounced subject has a second effect that can best be explained using Benveniste's ideas about the grammatical notion of a person. Benveniste points out that, whereas Indo-European languages generally distinguish among three persons, Arabic grammarians distinguish between only two. Arabic grammar's first class, those who are present, comprises two subcategories, the one who speaks (i.e., the first person) and the one who is spoken to (i.e., the second person). But the essential distinction contrasts the class of those who are present with the class of those who are absent (the person spoken of, i.e., the third person).[41]

A poem's use of deictic signifiers contributes to the effect of giving the speaker a place within the virtual space of the poem—of making the subject seem to be present in the poem. These signs of presence promote an identification that collapses the first and second persons of Indo-European languages into the single category of the Arab grammarians, of those who are present. These deictic signifiers thus encourages the addressee of the message (the reader) to merge with the addressor (the poet).

The following remarks by Benveniste identify a related basis for the identificatory effect that Romantic lyrics mobilize: "very generally, person is inherent only in the positions 'I' and 'you.' The third person, by virtue of its very structure, is the non-personal form of verbal inflection. . . . They contrast as members of a correlation, the *correlation of personality*: 'I-you' possesses the sign of person; 'he' lacks it."[42]

Use of the first-person pronoun in Wordsworth's poem, and in Romantic lyrics generally, not only represents the presence of a speaker, but also personalizes the speaker. In short, the use of the first-person pronoun dramatizes the subject of the enunciation. Wordsworth's poem may represent an extreme of such dramatization, but the mechanism we have used to explain this example applies almost as well to the majority of Romantic lyrics, and to most pentameter verse generally.

Another device contributes to mobilizing these identificatory mechanisms. The implicit representation of a subject of the enunciation within a poem cooperates with the impression of linearity that the suppleness of iambic pentameter engenders and the impression of continuity and fluency that this linearity creates in its turn. The joint effect is to reinforce the feeling that the subject represented in the poem is the transcendental subject. The regularity of pentameter creates the impression that the subject is self-consistent while the contrapuntal rhythm embodied in the pattern of intonation fosters the feeling that the subject is free and the dramatization of that subject suggests that the subject has fundamental importance.

The general effect is unlike that of common metre verse. The coincidence of accentual and intonational stress in four-beat metre prompts us to stress the marked syllables heavily. This implied performance pattern made four-beat metre congenial to choral reading—that is likely why it is mainly in verse that is chanted in chorus (nursery rhymes, sports cheers, lines sung out at political demonstrations, and the like) that the four-beat metre survives.

The lack of coincidence between the two rhythmic patterns that coexist in most iambic pentameter verse, and the lack of any criterion that determines how much emphasis a reader should give either, along with its more fluent style, make pentameter verse's implied performance style more free and more open to individual variation. Consequently, when assessing a reading of a poem in iambic pentameter, we are likely to assume that the reading reflects the richness of the individual reader's interpretation, and so conveys his or her sensitivity and emotional depth. We assume that the quality of the reading reflects the performer's character, since the cross-pulse creates the illusion that no single rhythm constrains the reader's performance to a particular result, and that the reader, consequently, is free to choose—or rather, what is more important, to create—the rhythm of his or her reading. The long line further strengthens this effect of the triple-metre cross-pulse that iambic pentameter frequently employs, for it bolsters the impression of the reader's freedom. A long line allows the reader greater freedom of inflection and stress. How the reader handles this freedom, what he or she does with the latitude of interpretation that the cross-pulse and the long line afford, we take as evidence of the reader's character. We value characteristics that suggest that the reader possesses a highly developed sensitivity; our high regard for such sensitivity is the reason we prize recordings of poems by great interpreters. The picture of the free individual, set apart from the collective and valued for the richness of his or her sensibility, is one that appears commonly wherever and whenever bourgeois humanism holds sway.

The identification of the performer/reader with the voice represented in the poem renders the poem's linguistic material transparent. The accentual counterrhythms that enable us to slip easily between rhythms and that allow the movement from one to another to seem "natural" (i.e., so thoroughly habituated as to be effortless) make the poem's textual mechanisms still more transparent. Further, these counterrhythms enable the poem to accommodate idiomatic and idiolexical expressions; the presence of such expressions strengthens the impression that the poem embodies natural speech. The seeming naturalness of the represented voice makes the actual words withdraw from consciousness, leaving behind only pure, amaterial sound and meaning. This effect of "language," as Foucault terms it, contrasts with the effect of the heavy stresses that the coincidence of intonational and accentual patterns in the four-stress line lends itself to, for the degree and metronomic regularity of the stress characteristic of common metre are marks of what Foucault terms "discourse," since they throw the material of language into relief.

Mukařovský has pointed out that foregrounding the signifier indicates that language is "being used for its own sake."[43] His insight helps explain the widespread use of four-stress metre in nonsense verse. The pleasure that we take in nonsense verse results primarily from escaping the iron laws of meaning. Only when we are free of meaning can we enjoy language for its material, rather than its referential, properties. Uses of language that isolate the material of language from sense allow us to play with language without paying the cost of illogic or breaching the taboo of misstatement. Modernity is founded in a triangular relationship among discourse (in the sense Foucault used that term in *Les Mots et les choses*, of a seemingly transparent language), bourgeois humanism, and the idea that the cardinal attribute of the individual is the transcendentality of the ego (as this feature guarantees the individual's inviolability and the freedom and the consistency and coherence of his or her experience); this triangular relationship ensures that culture will privilege meaning.

The hostility that such Romantic poets as William Wordsworth showed towards rigid metres is evidence enough that the Romantic poets harboured the ideal of a transparent language. They prized this effect of transparency because it enabled the subject of enunciation to dominate the enounced subject. The privileging of the subject of enunciation over the enounced subject conforms with the individualistic and humanistic ideas that undergirded the Romantic movement. Wordsworth, for example, believed that poetic language should be free from artificial and inflated poetic diction and should avoid the mechanical adoption of figures of speech and other conspicuously poetic devices—in sum, that poetry should be transparent. Only this conviction could have allowed him to identify good poetry with the spontaneous overflow of powerful feelings. Wordsworth did not say that good poetry *represents* powerful feelings. He said, rather, that good poetry *is* feelings—that it is strong feelings actually come into language. Wordsworth's manner of expression is evidence of the role that the Imaginary (see glossary) played in the formulation of his beliefs about the creative process.

Meaning and Personal Being: Pound and Brakhage

Pound's wish to create a work that is true to the individual experience of the particular thing and to maintain the "amicable accentuation of difference" gave life to his notion of "absolute rhythm." As he described it, absolute rhythm "corresponds exactly to the emotion or shade of emotion to be expressed."[44] He spoke about the common use of ordinary language imposing a grid on experience. He railed against traditional poetic language and poetic form because, he suggested, traditional poetry imposes symmetry everywhere. The contours of true poetry should derive from the impulse that impels its making. A poem should be an exact "rendering of the impulse."

> As far as the "living art" goes, I should like to break up *cliché*, to disintegrate these magnetised groups that stand between the reader of poetry and the drive of it, to escape from lines composed of two very nearly equal sections, each containing a noun and each noun decorously attended by a carefully selected epithet gleaned, apparently, from Shakespeare, Pope, or Horace. For it is not until poetry lives again "close to the thing" that it will be a vital part of contemporary life.[45]

Here, his suspicion about imposing symmetry on experience finds expression, for he speaks of lines divided into two equal parts, with each bifurcated in itself, one part adjectival, the other nominal, but every line conforming to the same pattern. The influence of Hulme's ideas on clichéd language and conventional form are evident. The passage's most important point, however, is the stress it lays on "the drive" of poetry.

Pound was enamoured of the diversity of experience. We have seen him arguing that the form of a poem should not be something conventional—that it should not be wrought into stanzas composed of the inevitably bifurcated lines that English poets got from Horace by way of the Renaissance. The form of a poem should evolve out of the unique impetus that motivates the poet to make it. Pound also cherished the diversity of each person's experience, for he cited, approving the Emersonian attitude it expresses, a passage from the *Analects* in which Confucius (Kung) asked each of his disciples the same question and received a different answer from each. When asked which of them had answered correctly, Confucius replied, "They have all answered correctly,/ That is to say, each in his nature."[46] Openness to difference explains Pound's admiration for both Confucianism and paganism, his dislike for Christianity and, possibly, a small portion of his virulent antisemitism. For he probably believed that monotheistic religions, unlike Confucianism and paganism, impose too great a unity on experience, denying the individual his or her unique way of experiencing and denigrating those forms of experience that are inconsistent with the mode it makes dominant.[47]

Pound's poetry embodies in its construction the principles that Pound expounded in the quoted passage. Pound's work is renowned for its highly dissociated style. Lines in the *Cantos* are disrupted, broken off in mid-thought, as another thought is begun, apparently quite arbitrarily. He opens a sentence form and abandons it before bringing it to completion. Pound rarely uses symmetry to round off statement forms or to suggest the completion of a thought. Different metres sometimes abut one another, for the shifts from one metre to another do not always coincide with the caesurae in his verse. Readers often take Pound's poetry as registering the kinetics of consciousness and these fissures, dislocations, and lacunae as suggesting the movement of his thought as it leaps from one topic to another. These ideas are not so much incorrect as insufficient: they leave Pound's conception of the nature of the subject unanalyzed, and that conception is the basis of his formal innovations; what is more, that very idea (often derived from sources other than Pound) has had enormous influence in several arts, including film.

We have already seen that the poetic forms that the Romantics developed effaced the signifier and created an effect of presence whereby the reader feels he or she has immediate contact with the inner voice of the poet. They are strategies for evoking what the French psychoanalyst Jacques Lacan calls the Imaginary, a mental mechanism that makes the subject feel it is fully present to itself, even though what furnishes that feeling of wholeness and self-presence is fictitious. The feeling that the self is immediately present to itself—that it does not come to self-presence through any representing token but through its own nature—arises from an illusion, since an image of the integrated self mediates the self's awareness of itself. This fiction of an integrated self that is present to itself in the immediacy of self-presence is (as Descartes's use of the *cogito* shows) one of the ruling fictions of the modern paradigm—perhaps, even, the fundamentum of its master narrative. Romantic literary thinking, in proposing the conception of direct seeing, denied language a constitutive role in the formation of thought; its denial was double pronged (just as it conceived the problematic of thinking was the integration of the subject and object which had lost their identity) for it denied language a constitutive role in the formation of the self, just as it denied representational systems any role in constituting the object of representation. The idea of direct perception and immediate experience (probably familiar to readers from Wordsworth's "Preface") are undergirded by the conviction that experience is outside language and prior to signification. The conception of language associated with this belief maintains that the means of enunciation do not affect the enounced: reality and experience are simple data, and the order of language so conforms to the order of the things that language can refer directly to reality (including experience), without imposing upon it. Just as, according to the modern paradigm's master narrative, no representing token presents the self to the self, so no system of representation mediates our relation to reality—reality, our narrative implies, is given to us in a direct and immediate presence, for our experience is a self-presenting self-presence.

Sometimes, this notion of language expands into a nominal theory of language according to which the most important terms in language are nouns, and verbs are merely qualifiers of nouns.[48] The order of words and the order of things are similar, inasmuch as reality is made up of substances that are qualified by properties and discourse is a string of nouns qualified by so many predicates (verbs do the work of predication). Grammar decides that subjects and verbs, nouns and adjectives, etc., agree—i.e., they regulate word use so that a discourse ascribes properties of the right number and category to objects; it is at least plausible, then, that the attributions of discourse match the ways that properties and qualities belong to objects. Thus grammar ensures the isomorphism of speech and reality. The problem of meaning, then, is essentially that of correctly aligning the tokens that language uses to represent things (whether objects in the world or ideas in the mind) with the objects that they represent. The development of an *epistémè* based on such a view about the relation between the tokens of language and the furniture of the world is essentially what Foucault intended when he wrote that with the Renaissance, what he calls discourse took the place of what he calls language.

The empiricists were the first thinkers to promulgate this conception of language. We recognize too infrequently just how important this view of language was to the empiricists: time after time their writings claim that the broadening of language's scope and the amplification of linguistic style results in the conceptual mischief we know of as philosophy (especially speculative philosophy or metaphysics, but ethics, theology, and aesthetics as well), that our language should be brought back to the point when people delivered so many things in an equal number of words, to a natural way of speaking, to a plainness that clearly reflects the order of reality. This idea of language subtends Coleridge's *Biographia Literaria*, Shelley's *Defense*, and Wordsworth's "Preface" to the *Lyrical Ballads*.

The superior powers of poets, in this view, are that they can make their most inward thoughts and feelings show "sincerely" and truly—that they have special powers for making the inward outward, i.e., can make them show through language without being affected by the medium of representation so that they appear just as they are—that poetry is "the spontaneous overflow of powerful feelings." Romantic poetics condemned poetry whose language obtrudes upon a reader's consciousness. When we read good poetry we are gripped by the powerful feelings it expresses and are oblivious of the machinery that conveys those feelings to us; this is why we feel immediate contact with the poet's soul. Good poetry seems like natural speech and, as Jacques Derrida shows, the illusory power of speech makes language recede and its material content come to the fore, so that it appears as direct presentation of the speaker's thoughts.[49] The sound of speech echoes experience. Thus, speech minimizes the difference between experience and statements about experience. The enunciatory medium becomes transparent as the *énoncé* (see glossary) effaces the *énonciation*.

The correspondence theory of meaning implicit in these views is probably the semantic theory embedded in what we call the commonsense standpoint. Pound's poetic practice challenged this "commonsense" theory of meaning and the conception of the subject that goes along with it. Pound recognized that enunciation is a material process, with material effects, and that what enunciation makes present is a verbal artifact, not thoughts or feelings.

The means that poetry traditionally used to efface enunciation was to yoke sound and sense together structurally, to give to a poem's form the shape of a feeling—to create a poem that has, as the philosopher S. Langer has it, the virtual shape of a feeling. Thus Dryden counsels poets to contrive sense "into such words that the rhyme shall naturally follow them, and not they the rhyme." The rhyming couplets of Augustan poetry often strike the contemporary reader as the very height of artifice; yet to their contemporaries, they were the essence of plain speaking. Dryden recommends the "Plain and Natural Style," which offers instructions on how to present objects in the most natural way possible. Writers of the time preached the virtues of avoiding swelled-up verbiage and of striving to deliver so many things in an equal number of words. Thinkers of the period insisted that a taxonomic relation between thought and nature ensured there exists an isomorphism between the order of words and the order of things. The use of a natural manner in expression ensured that language would convey its signifier to the reader without the reader having to expend undue effort.

The homology between the order of words and the order of things guarantees the subject a stable place within the order of language, for the high degree of syntagmatic continuity that produces an effect of transparency ensures the subject an uninterrupted existence. The rhyme scheme in pentameter verse in rhyming couples has a similar effect. In rhyming couplets, the line ending is closed phonetically (by use of rhyme), syntactically (by the coincidence of phrase and sentence boundary with the line and couplet endings), and semantically (by the completion of a thought in each couplet). The high degree of isomorphism between the phonetic, syntactic, and semantic structures suggests a highly regulated, closed order in which the individual is ensured of his or her place. The "return of the same," the essence of the rhythm of rhyme, is always pleasurable. The reasons for the pleasure are interesting to speculate on: The poem's rhyme scheme encourages us to expect repetition, and the strictly defined phonetic, syntactic, and semantic order of the rhyming form evokes the mechanism of identification, for we feel that our expectations steer the course of the text and cause it to resolve according to our wishes. Thus, our very being is held in suspense awaiting its reappearance. The appearance of the rhymed element satisfies that expectation and returns us to the fullness of being from which the suspense had separated us. The rhythm of the self's vicissitudes, alternating between alienation and integration, itself is a stable order explicable only by the perseverance of the transcendental self.

Pound's rhythmic ideas overlap those of the French composer of sacred music, Olivier Messiaen (1908-92), though they are not nearly so formalized. Like Messiaen, Pound eschews the repetition of elements of equal measure—whether that measure be a quantity of stress or a metric duration. Like Messiaen's, Pound's rhythms take their inspiration from the movements of nature, movements that are free and unequal in length. Like Messiaen's, Pound's rhythms lack any feeling of a dominant tactus. All these are attributes of the rhythms of Brakhage's films as well. One can even find in Brakhage's *Songs* (especially the earlier among them), a type of rhythmic structure that we have come to associate with Olivier Messiaen, viz., palindromic (or, as Messiaen calls them, non-retrogradable) rhythms.

Pound's paratactical poetry dissolves the coherence of the syntagmatic chain. Ruptures, dismemberments, fissures, and lacunae appear where formerly there was metonymic continuity. The verse form breaks off, reassembles itself, only to break off again. The self who identifies with the broken unity dies and is replaced by a new self with every shift in direction. The sense that the self dies and is reborn continually is the deepest implication of Pound's paratactical forms—as it is of Stein's use of repetition with difference. It is also the deepest implication of what I term Brakhage's "perpetually regenerating structures" (see glossary). Such a self has neither a past nor a future, however. Hence, the time of the continually altering self is the continuous "now." The continuous "now" is also the time of the body, for the body knows only pulsations, movement, and energy, and nothing of the continuities of mental life. The push to provoke this sense of time is the deepest connection between paratactical forms of poetry and the concern with the body that is so evident in the works of Stein, Pound, and Brakhage.[50]

As Cubist paintings repudiated the simple correspondence between their visual forms and the form of the object, so too do Brakhage's films. The qualities of the visual forms that make up his films change from moment to moment. These changes foreground the *énonciation* over the *énoncé*, the signifier over the signified, and they make one aware that the order of images is separate from the order of the real. Brakhage has practised what he preached—using self-reflexive references and discontinuity to "kick spectator out of his illusionistic wrap-up," as he put it in *Metaphors on Vision*.[51] The lack of syntagmatic continuity creates a feeling of a continually altering "now," the time of ecstatic intensity, the time of the body of energy.

Near the end of his great essay on Dante in *Spirit of Romance*, Pound undertakes the daunting task of comparing the verse of Dante and Shakespeare. No person should be so foolish as to attempt the chore, of course; yet Pound manages to assemble some splendid insights into the topic. Among them are the following comments on rhythm in verse.

> Dante has the advantage [over Shakespeare] in points of pure sound; his onomatopoeia is not a mere trick of imitating natural noises, but is a mastery in fitting the inarticulate sound of a passage to the mood or to the quality of voice which expresses that mood or passion which the passage describes or expresses. Shakespear [*sic*] has a language less apt for this work in pure sound, but he understands the motion of words, or, if the term be permitted, the overtones and undertones of rhythm, and he uses them with a mastery which no one but Burns has come reasonably near to approaching. Other English poets master this part of the art occasionally, or as if by accident; there is a fine example in a passage of Sturge Moore's *Defeat of the Amazons*, where the spirit of his faun leaps and scurries, with the words beginning: "Ahi! ahi! ahi! Laomedon."
>
> This government of speed is a very different thing from the surge and sway of the epic music where the smoother rhythm is so merged with the sound quality as to be almost inextricable. The two things compare almost as the rhythm of a drum compares to the rhythm (not the sound) of the violin or organ. Thus, the "surge and sway" are wonderful in Swinburne's first chorus in the *Atalanta*; while the other quality of word motion is most easily distinguished in, though by no means confined to, such poems as Burns' *Birks o' Aberfeldy*, where the actual sound-quality of the words contributes little or nothing to the effect, which is dependent solely on the arrangement of quantities (*i.e.*, the lengths of syllables) and accent. It is not, as it might first seem, a question of vowel music as opposed to consonant music.[52]

The Seachange: Or, How Pound Came "To Break the Pentameter"

Romantic ideals held sway over poetry when Pound began writing. Vorticism (see glossary) changed that. Vorticism was a revolutionary art movement. *Blast*, the house organ of the Vorticist movement shrieked, "BLAST years 1837 to 1900," to demand the destruction of Victorianism so that staid, old England might enter twentieth-century life. The signatories of the first

Blast manifesto, Lawrence Atkinson, Jessica Dismore, Henri Gaudier-Brzeska, Cuthbert Hamilton, William Roberts, Helen Saunders, Edward Wadsworth, Wyndham Lewis, and that inveterate joiner of causes, Ezra Pound—a tremendously talented group of young people by any reasonable measure—claimed for themselves the cocky role and title of Primitive Mercenaries in the Modern World. They proclaimed with utter self-confidence derived from the assurance that science (in their case, the science of thermodynamics) provided that "a movement towards art and imagination could burst up here, from this lump of compressed life, with more force than anywhere else."[53] Augustus John's pseudo-Roman classicism, and any backwards-looking art, was anathema to them, as were the Camden Town Group's portrayals of London's quietly fading gentility. In language that echoed its precursor movement, Italian Futurism, the Vorticists declared that theirs was to be an art of the machine age:

> "Vorticism" accepted the machine-world: that is the point to stress. It sought out machine-forms. The pictures of the Vorticists were a sort of *machines*. . . . It was cheerfully and dogmatically external. . . . [It] was not an asylum from the brutality of mechanical life. On the contrary it identified itself with that brutality, in a stoical embrace, though of course without propagandist fuss.
>   It did not sentimentalize machines, . . . it took them as a matter of course: just as we take trees, hills, rivers, coal deposits, oil-wells, rubber-trees, as a matter of course. It was a stoic creed: it was not an *uplift*.[54]

The Vorticists heralded England as the country of the machine and proclaimed that England, therefore, should produce the art for the modern, machine age. They undertook the obligation enthusiastically.

> [T]he Modern World is due almost entirely to Anglo-Saxon genius—its appearance and its spirit. Machinery, trains, steam-ships, all that distinguishes externally our time, came far more from here than anywhere else. . . . But busy with this LIFE-EFFORT, [England] has been the last to become conscious of the Art that is an organism of this new Order and Will of Man.[55]

This statement valorizes will; this valorization of will relates to Pound's crucial distinction between receptive artists and constructive artists—the latter are those who can impose their will on materials.

The Vorticists astutely observed that the Machine Age had remade humankind in its image and, even more astutely, that the human faculty that the machine had primarily affected was the will. The Vorticist manifesto in *Blast* stated: "Our industries, and the Will that determined, face to face with its needs, the direction of the modern world, has reared up steel trees where the green ones were lacking: has exploded in useful growths, and found wilder intricacies than those of Nature."

English peoples' affinity with the machine should make them the enemy of Romanticism:

> [O]nce this consciousness towards the new possibilities of expression in present life has come . . . it will be more the legitimate property of Englishmen than of any other people in Europe. It should also, as it is by origin theirs, inspire them more forcibly and directly. They are the inventors of this bareness and hardness, and should be the great enemies of Romance.[56]

What, more than anything else, the new art should derive from the machine is dynamism of the mechanical kinetic: "The vortex is the point of maximum energy. It represents, in mechanics, the greatest efficiency. We use the words 'greatest efficiency' in the precise sense—as they would be used in a text book of MECHANICS." Pound and his co-factionalists in the Vortex movement admired the precision of the machine, its ability to accomplish the ends for which it had been designed without sentimentality, fuss, melodrama, or murky emotional gush. They spoke for an art that would capture the machine's essence, its dynamic energy. In an instance of exaggerating small differences, they chastised Futurism for being too rhapsodically Romantic in its celebration of the beauty of the machine and too picturesque in technique (the latter charge amounting partly to the accusation of being realistic/representational and partly to a condemnation of Futurism's Symbolist provenance). They lambasted Cubism for being too lifeless (i.e., static and lacking in energy). They conveyed their contempt for Cubism's favourite motifs—citing guitars, posed models, vases of flowers, and tables set with bottles of wine—by referring to the Cubists' favourite subjects (through a pun on *nature morte*) as "dead matter." These subjects were the same motifs of hoary old studio painting. Vorticists criticized the Cubists not only for the deadness of their art, but also for presenting a picture of the world that was all too domesticated for Vorticist taste.

Wyndham Lewis, the movement's principal theorist, summed up its program.

> By Vorticism we mean (a) *Activity* as opposed to the tasteful *Passivity* of Picasso; (b) SIGNIFICANCE as opposed to the dull or anecdotal character to which the Naturalist is condemned; (c) ESSENTIAL MOVEMENT and ACTIVITY (such as the energy of a mind) as opposed to the imitative cinematography, the fuss and hysterics of the Futurists.[57]

Activity, significance, and essential movement are what the Vorticists intended the image of the vortex to capture; they meant the vortex to convey the idea of a whirling force, sweeping up whatever comes into its field and holding it in place as the field itself turned around its own still centre. Pound described the vortex as "a fluid force" and "a radiant node or cluster . . . from which, and through which, and into which, ideas are constantly rushing."[58] But his definition of the vortex was more natural, more organic than Lewis's, who conceived of the vortex as a machine form. For Lewis, the vortex is a dynamo, for Pound, a whirlwind. Both stressed the dynamic properties of the art with the image of the vortex, and for a while that was enough to unite the two; but soon the difference would split Lewis and Pound and lead to the movement's early demise.

Before Vorticism, during the years 1912-14, Pound had preached the doctrine of Imagism (see glossary). A statement that Pound drew up with H.D. (Hilda Doolittle) and Richard Aldington set out the fundamental principles of Imagism.

1. Direct treatment of the 'thing' whether subjective or objective.
2. To use absolutely no word that does not contribute to the presentation.
3. As regarding rhythm: to compose in the sequence of the musical phrase, not in sequence of a metronome.[59]

For Pound, these tenets served as a valuable brake against effusive rhetoric and subjective blather. Though Pound would not like to admit it, his concept of an image as "an intellectual and emotional complex in an instant of time" had strong roots in the Romantic movement.[60] One recalls Wordsworth's "spots of time" and the widespread idea of epiphanic moments in Romantic poetry. Indeed the Romantic poets, Ezra Pound and Stan Brakhage, have all created great trouble for themselves by according a central role to the image. For Keats and Wordsworth, Pound and Brakhage, all celebrate the particular instant of epiphany—that is why all of them create works that belong to the temporal modality of immediacy. Yet all of them, and especially Wordsworth and Pound, hanker to create an epic work that will chronicle in its entirety "the growth of the poet's mind." But it is difficult to reconcile the desire to convey the unique intensity of a particular moment in time and the epic desire to present events that develop over a long span. If Pound abandoned Imagism almost as soon as he developed its principle, it is largely because of his desire to extend what he had learned about concision and condensation from Imagism (throughout his life he offered the slogan that Brakhage, too, has used, "dichten = condensare," i.e., to write poetry is to condense) to the large field of the long poem. Brakhage, for his part, resolved the tension by repudiating his epic ambitions after he had made Dog Star Man (which, of course, itself establishes him as a major artist of the epic form), and accepting his status as a lyric poet.[61]

Vorticism was also a revolt on behalf of individualism. Blast, and the Vorticist movement generally, depicted the artist as an autonomous individual who rejects the legacy of tradition and conventions handed down by the past and for whom humanism, society, and good taste have become out of date—

as an autonomous creator who cannot find any truths outside him- or herself, or discover there the standard of truth or the criterion of beauty. So complete was their devaluation of the external world that they asserted that the artistic will remakes a person thoroughly. As the *Blast* manifesto says, "The moment a man feels or realizes himself as an artist, he ceases to belong to any milieu or time."[62] The Vorticists insisted on the self-sufficiency of the artist. This conviction set them in opposition with both society and tradition, both of which they announced they intended at least to revolutionize, if not to destroy.

The Vorticists' extreme conception of the artist's self-sufficiency led them to a voluntaristic aesthetic. "Make it new!" was Pound's constant counsel.[63] Too many readers take the advice platitudinously, as admonishing artists to find fresh and vital means for making works of art, lest they find their audiences turn away in tedium. There is more to Pound's dictum. Pound declared Vorticism to be in favour of the "creative faculty as opposed to the mimetic": the artist must *make* something new, not imitate something that already exists.[64] In making something new, artists affirm their constructive or generative powers, while in imitating, they display only a greater or lesser receptivity to existing forms. Accordingly, Pound criticized Impressionism for having "set a fashion of passivity" and proclaimed that Impressionists "DENY the vortex. They are the CORPSES of VORTICES."[65]

T.E. Hulme (following Worringer) set up the conceptual categories the Vorticists used to condemn the Futurists by distinguishing between "vital" (i.e., Romantic) art and "geometrical" (i.e., Classical) art. For these terms, Hulme drew on Bergson (though, while Bergson celebrated the vital, Hulme, now distancing himself from his erstwhile mentor, celebrated the geometrical impulse).[66] The former develops out of a happy pantheistic relation with nature and follows the shapes and movements one finds in nature; hence, it prizes organic unity. The latter imposes forms that possess the shapely elegance of human thought on the messiness and confusion of the natural world; its preference for the shapeliness of thought over the messiness of nature gives this art a tendency towards abstraction.

In his essay expounding the principles of Vorticism, Pound reworked Hulme's distinction between vital and geometric art into one based on the direction in which the creative impulse moved, and so between active and passive intelligence.

> [F]irstly, you may think of him [the artist] as that toward which perception moves, as the toy of circumstance, as the plastic substance *receiving* impressions; secondly, you may think of him as directing a certain fluid force against circumstance, as *conceiving*. . . . In the [eighteen] eighties there were symbolists opposed to impressionists, now you have vorticism, which is, roughly

speaking, expressionism, neo-cubism, and imagism gathered together in one camp and futurism in the other. Futurism is descended from impressionism. It is, in so far as it is an art movement, a kind of accelerated impressionism. It is a spreading, or surface art, as opposed to vorticism, which is intensive.[67]

While Pound here lays stress on differing vectors of impulse in Futurism and Vorticism, it is his derogation of Futurism as "a spreading art" that is especially interesting, for that criticism turns back on the movement whose principles he had once expounded, for the Vorticists themselves proclaimed Vorticism as an art of surfaces, as an art without depths.

But every opposition arises from a limitation, and so it was the Vorticism. No more than the Imagist does Vorticist art give expression to the full scope of an image's possible dynamic. Perhaps this was due primarily to the powerful influence Wyndham Lewis exerted on the movement. In *Time and Western Man*, Lewis struck out against Western humanity's abiding concern with time; passages of the book attack Henri Bergson and Albert Einstein for their obsession with time, and even Pound for his interest in music and the musical qualities of poetry. Lewis wrote the book as a call for a spatial conception of relationships and praised painting over music as a model for poetry. Lewis's own paintings and drawings indicate something of the quality he sought: they confine movement within space by creating an intricate pattern of interlocking relationships. While the Futurists created forms that spiraled out across the canvas, ultimately shattering any boundary that would confine it, the Vorticists recomposed fragments of moments into an almost Cubistically conceived nexus of interacting relationships that, finally, gave the whole a static quality. As the quotation from Pound shows, the Vorticists refused any stance that might imply passivity, and so they insisted upon using forms that indicated the mind dictates to reality; to do so, they shattered natural forms and recomposed the resulting fragments into patterns that evidenced the mind's shaping role. Hence the Vorticists favoured geometrical over organic forms, and appealed to the intricacy of geometrical interrelations to reveal the power of the mind to recompose reality. But this very intricacy locked the forms that appeared in their works in tautly conceived patterns that forbade change.

A cruel, if culturally typical, dilemma respecting the body trapped the Vorticists. In speaking for energy, dynamism, thrust, and power, they advocated values connected with corporeality. The sentimentality and gentility they despised in traditional art had its basis in discorporate conceptions of mind and soul. Against that, they proposed an art that presented the movement and energy of a mind—but not a disembodied mind, rather a mind with the strength and physical force of the body. However, they conceived of the body as a machine. Their conception of the body was marked with features that derive from the fantasy that identifies the whole body with the phallus. It is from this fantasy that Vorticism derived its emphasis on hardness, thrust, power, and the machine. Vorticists despised the body of soft flesh. In poem entitled "Fratres Minores," lines of which the printers of the first issue of *Blast* blacked out because they so flagrantly violated contemporary standards of decorum, Pound accused certain English and French poets in the following terms:

> With minds still hovering above their testicles
> Certain poets here and in France
> Still sigh over established and natural fact
> Long since fully discussed by Ovid.
> They howl. They complain in delicate and exhausted metres
> That the twitching of three abdominal nerves
> Is incapable of producing a lasting Nirvana.[68]

To distinguish Vorticism from Futurism, Wyndham Lewis referred to Futurism's continuing concern with serving life. Lewis maintained that we should consider life only as "a good dinner, sleep, and copulation," and as nothing more, not even emotion. Because the Futurists maintained humanism's interest in emotions, Lewis described Futurism as "a hospital for the weak and incompetent." Lewis has his spokesperson, Tarr, proclaim in his eponymous novel, "*deadness* is the first condition of art.... The second is the absence of *soul*, in the sentimental human sense.... It has no inside. This is another condition of art; *to have no inside*, nothing you cannot *see*." Even Lewis's co-factionalists among the Vorticists had trouble with the extremity of his views; nonetheless, his antipathy for all that was soft, sentimental, and delicate—for all that was not hard like the phallus—typified the attitudes of the Vorticists. Thus, while the Vorticists strove to reunite art and mind with the body, the body they dreamt of was hardly one that could rescue us from the delirious fantasies of reason that Western metaphysics had produced. Only a more fluid conception of the body—a conception of the body as composed of labile forces and shifting energies—can possibly accomplish that.

Bergson, Hulme, Pound, and Brakhage on the Body and Energy

Among the sources of the Vorticists' ideas was the philosopher Henri Bergson (1859-1941). Bergson was the most renowned philosopher of his day and his ideas had nearly as great an impact on many important thinkers and artists of the first three decades of this century as Jean-Paul Sartre's (1905-80) thought had in the 1950s and 1960s or Jacques Lacan's (1901-81) had in the 1970s and most of the 1980s; among the English-speaking artists attracted to Bergsonianism (at least for a time) was T.S. Eliot (1888-1965), who attended Bergson's lectures and underwent a temporary conversion. Bergson's ideas garnered such wide enthusiasm that, while the Holy Office placed his books on proscription, the Swedish government awarded him the Nobel Prize for literature in 1927. Indeed Bergsonianism reached giddying heights of appeal: in the last years of the first decade of the century, intellectuals from a range of disciplines, artists, and philosophers were joined at Bergson's Friday evening lectures at the *Collège de France* by women of high society who had sent their servants, in the late afternoon, to reserve them seats. The excited reception that Bergson's philosophy attracted was due in part to Bergson's fortuitous situation in the Paris of *la belle époque*, a time and place of real intellectual fervour. It was also due in part to the occult revival taking place in France.

The occult revival began with the publication in 1884 of an extraordinary decadent novel, *A rebours*, by Joris-Karl Huysmans (1848-1907). Prior to *A rebours*, Huysmans had written stories in the style of the formalized naturalism of the Goncourt brothers; all that really marks these works as aesthetically progressive are some stylistic mannerisms derived from Flaubert. *A rebours* marks Huysmans's move to Symbolism.[69] Huysmans's ideal of beauty, like that of the great Symbolist poet Charles Baudelaire (1821-67), was of a beauty that was withdrawn, inward, intimate, vague, and utterly melancholy—a beauty that could comprise even what is unhealthy or evil. The completely odd hero of *A rebours*, Des Essenintes, withdraws from the material world into an aesthetic world, in an amoral quest for rare, exquisite, and decadent sensations; the novel's greatness, however, is that one cannot discern with certainty whether Huysmans's description of Des Essenintes is meant as parody or eulogy. Huysmans's next novel was *Là-bas* (1891), a spiritual adventure into black magic. Huysmans became disenchanted with the artificial realities of decadence and magic, wrote a transitional work on the monastic life entitled *En route* (1895), converted to Christianity, and wrote *La cathédrale* (1898) and *L'oblat* (1903), which collected essays on the aesthetic sensations that Christian rituals and Christian edifices provoke.

Religious emotion and a quest for that which reason cannot seize were central first to the occult and then to the Christian revival. A part of this emotion was contempt for the external world and for all efforts to reproduce the external world with exactitude. The hero of Huysmans's novel is a type for the person attracted to occultism—disgusted with the prevailing order, he, like the Great Beast of Kenneth Anger's film *Inauguration of the Pleasure Dome* (which displays remarkable resemblances to the Huysmans's novel), attempts to construct an artificial paradise closed to the loathsome squalor of everyday life, and where aesthetic sensation is everything. Artistic and bohemian circles in France witnessed the rise of many groups that turned away from material reality towards inner truth. Erik Satie (1866-1925), Charles Baudelaire, Paul Verlaine (1844-96), and Arthur Rimbaud (1854-91) took an interest in such goings-on. Rosicrucianism, Cabalism, Blavatskyism, astrology, alchemy, spiritism, Satanism, and neo-Buddhism were as common in Paris in the 1910s as they were in San Francisco in the late 1960s and early 1970s. Among the most prominent of the occult circles in Paris, as in London, was The Order of the Golden Dawn. This group first attracted widespread attention in London in the 1890s, under the leadership of Samuel MacGregor Mathers. Mathers's wife, Mina, who had initiated W.B. Yeats (1865-1939) into the Order, was Henri Bergson's sister. Mina caused a stir in Paris when she presented a theatre-piece, entitled *The Rite of Isis*, to great acclaim. And, as in the United States in the 1960s, a scholarly interest in mystical knowledge accompanied the popular vogue for the occult. The publication of *Varieties of Religious Experience* by William James (1842-1910) and *Mysticism* by Evelyn Underhill (a former member of The Order of the Golden Dawn) contributed considerably to the development of a more level-headed interest in religious experience. So responsible scholars became familiar with the central teachings of occult groups.

The same forces that revived interest in mysticism and the occult gave shape to Bergson's philosophy. The most important of these was the desire to transcend the data concerning external reality with which the senses present us, in order to discover the higher truths of the inner life. Bergson owed much to that line of French thinkers who opposed materialism and mechanism. Bergson said that in his lectures he strove "to develop a taste for the internal life." The taste for the internal life, for Bergson, was a counterweight to modernity, for Bergson shared his age's distaste for industry, for modern urban existence, and for mechanization. In books such as *Time and Free Will* and *Introduction to Metaphysics*, Bergson systematized the discoveries he made using an intuitive method of introspection that owes a not inconsiderable debt to Maine de Biran's thesis that a primary inner experience is the "flow" of life and to Felix Ravaisson's claim that philosophy should take directly intuited noematic objects as its proper subject. Bergson extolled the value of the truths one discovers by following the inner way.

Of all the ancient thinkers, it was Neo-Platonist mystic Plotinus in whom Bergson took the greatest interest. In this mystical bent to his thinking—a bent that increased with the passing of years (even though Bergson denied ever having had any mystical experiences himself)—and in several other respects, Bergson's taste for the inner life coincided with that of Symbolists. So the formidable Belgian Symbolist writer, Maurice Maeterlinck (1862-

1949) extolled Bergson as "a great writer and a great artist" and "the great-est thinker in the world."[70] Bergson reciprocated the interest, as he counted among his favourite writings Maeterlinck's plays and Pierre Loti's (1850-1923) exotic, vague, dreamy, and subjective fictional chronicles of a melan-choly, death-haunted soul coming across exotic civilizations in remote cor-ners of the world.

While Symbolism seems the antipodes to Pound's Vorticism, and while Pound had nothing but contempt for the Symbolists' vague, mystical yearn-ings, or for their often morbid, listless style, one can recognize, nonetheless, through the mediating ideas of Bergson, some similarities between them. Both Mallarmé and Pound (at least in his Imagist and Vorticist periods) cre-ated works that revolve about a central image or recurrent form. Both of them use elliptical phrasing. Furthermore, like Mallarmé and Baudelaire, Pound had a great concern for the music of language and, even though the music of Pound's poetry is not nearly so dreamy as Mallarmé's, some pas-sages in the *Cantos* figure among the most musical written in the English language.

Stan Brakhage has drawn ideas and inspiration from these areas where Symbolism and Vorticism overlap. Brakhage shares Maeterlinck's beliefs that the referential or denotational powers of language are incapable of describing the contents of the inner life and that only the rhythm and music of language can convey the make-up of the inner world. Brakhage admires as well Messiaen's ideas on chromo-harmony and, more generally, those Sym-bolist ideas with which Messiaen displayed an affinity. Brakhage often bases his film forms on properties of the film medium that most filmmakers neglect (either by overlooking or rejecting) and which he invests with psy-chological or spiritual significance; in this regard, too, his work resembles Messiaen's. Thus, just as Messiaen has created compositions that depend upon timbre or tonal colour, Brakhage has constructed compositions that depend on grain, or spots that appear on a film because of optical aberra-tions, or tiny movements at the edges of the frame.

Messiaen's example helps explain the peculiar convergence of self-reflexive forms and Symbolistic interests we find in Brakhage's work. For like Brakhage, Messiaen often uses self-reflexive forms to isolate each ele-ment in the work both from extrinsic referents and from seamless interac-tion with one another. Messiaen subscribes to the post-Webernian aspiration to bring all attributes of sound (intensity, duration, pitch, and attack) under complementary sets of rules. He has made use of scales of volumes, attacks, intensities, and pitch, as he did in his 1949 piano composition for Darstadt, *Modes de valeurs et intensités*, in which he manipulates a set of scales, one comprising thirty-six pitches, one comprising twenty-four durations, one comprising twelve types of attack, and another comprising seven volumes. Each note in the composition has a set of values, one drawn from each type of scale (one from the scale of pitches, one from the scale of durations, one from the scale of attacks, one from the scale of volumes). Few successive notes have the same duration, or attack, or volume, for Messiaen attempted to change the entire set of parametric values from note to note. Even more than Webern's music is, works based on such methods are very angular, elliptical, and fragmentary, as each note comes forth as a quasi-independent sonic event. By way of comparison, Brakhage characteristically varies the intensity, length, speed, and content of each shot, preserving almost none of the parametric values from shot to shot, though in his case parametric variations are not systematic but instead respond to what he feels from moment to moment as he shoots. The results of both cases have similarities, however, for each shot in a Brakhage film presents itself as quasi-independent unit, just as each note in an Olivier Messiaen composition does.

Furthermore, like Baudelaire, Messiaen, and Debussy (whose music Messiaen admired), Brakhage believes in correspondences between the different sensory modalities (synaesthesia) and between emotion and the mind's visual representations. Brakhage's affinities with Symbolism, however restricted they may be, are also evident in the preference he shows for ellipsis, for extreme condensation, for composing works that suggest an analogy between the material and spiritual realms, and for vivifying his forms by using repetition. Brakhage's devotion to the music of Claude Debussy, revealed in his radio series *The Test of Time*, indicates the Symbolist inclinations of his work; his films reveal a similar commitment to the inner life, as does Debussy's music which has so often been linked to Bergson's thought.

One form of the quest for the supernatural, so important in Symbolist art and Brakhage's films alike, is based on a sense of the body that identifies it with the cosmos. Proprioceptive sensations are especially important to us because they provide the grounds for our being-with-our-bodies. Because they are so important to us, we sometimes project our proprioceptive sensations (modified by what we identify them with) onto the structure of the cosmos—or, rather, what we imagine this structure to be. This mechanism explains how attentiveness to the subjective realm and to the qualities of the subjective world can so easily become the basis for a cosmological art (or for an art that concerns itself with myths of cosmogenesis). Such a conception of the body is evident in the films of Harry Smith and, especially, Kenneth Anger (both of whom, reportedly, have been chosen by the Aleister Crowley cult—a splinter group that separated from The Order of the Golden Dawn—as members of its circle of Seven Wise Men). This process is evident in the works of several poets and filmmakers who have taken an interest in Bergson's ideas. They have identified proprioceptive sensation with insight and have taken inner awareness as primary; for them, proprioception becomes the basis for a cosmology, for they maintain that propriception's intuitive capacities disclose the very structure of reality.[71]

Though Bergson had little philosophical concern with the body as such—indeed he argued that our minds survive the death of our bodies—the painstaking attention he devotes to apprehending the qualities of the flow of inner sensations make his remarks about our inner awareness of the body important for those concerned with how our culture has interpreted the body. Bergson describes as forms of the inner life what others have interpreted as the inward sensation of the body. Bergson takes as the primary data for his philosophical system the experience of consciousness as it entwines with the body, before the separation of matter and mind. He made the body experienced from within central to philosophy. The body is the ground of all our sensations, Bergson acknowledged. "As my body moves in space, all the other images vary, while that image, my body, remains invariable. I must therefore make it a centre, to which I refer all the other images. ... *My body* is that which stands out as the centre of these perceptions."[72] By this statement, Bergson expounded what has been affirmed in the Preface to the present volume, that it is the body's (unthematized) inward awareness of itself that makes perception possible in the first place, and so at least a component of that inward awareness is a constant element in sensation; but where his spiritual interests prompted him to take this insight is another matter (though it did mark out a trail that many of the artists discussed in this work were to follow).

Bergson pointed out that in most philosophers' understanding of perception, the body is accorded too small a role. The common understanding of perception holds that it resembles a photographic process and results in pictures of what is perceived being formed in the mind. Against this erroneous view Bergson argued that since images are spatially extended, they cannot belong to the mind (or, conversely, nothing mental can resemble pictures since pictures are spatially extended). Perception is a process of selection and is directed towards action, not knowledge; it does not need to result in the formation of visual representations in the mind. Acknowledging that selecting among actions does not require consciousness, Bergson explained why we are conscious of our perceptions by saying that perceptions are impregnated with memory.

Bergson conducted a painstaking analysis of our inner experience of the body; that care yielded many rich insights into our inner experience of the body. Bergson recognized, first, that the proprioceptively experienced body is an instrument for acting in the world, for he claimed that the body is turned towards actions, which do not necessarily produce intellectual representations. Second, Bergson acknowledged the phenomenon of body knowledge and body memory; in fact, his most succinct description of one type of memory represents it as a collection of habits that have accumulated in the body and are reactivated, often without any intervening image, when some stimulus provokes a body to repeat previous actions. (At the same time, he thought that a second type of memory, one that restores images to consciousness, belongs to a higher mnemic form and, as essentially spiritual, belongs exclusively to human beings, unlike the body's memory of habits, which animals also have.) What is more important, he recognized that raw experience of the inner body is a strictly indivisible flow of inward sensations—it is neither laid out before us under the form of an extensive homogeneity nor is it divisible according to sensory modality. Before our senses separated into their various modalities, our feeling of being in the world was synaesthetic; then all the senses were equiprimordial in a fused, inner sensation. Understanding of the relation between body and mind is granted not through intellectual perpension (for the mind does not belong to space, and besides, the intellect only considers matter external), but through action, as it is action that reveals that body and mind converge in time.

Time was the principal protagonist of Bergson's philosophy, just as it was in the thought of Bergson's European contemporary, Edmund Husserl (1859-1938). The Polish philosopher Leszek Kolakowski encapsulates the essence of Bergson's thinking: "[W]e may sum up his [Bergson's] philosophy in a single idea: time is real."[73] Kolakowski's claim is close to correct, but it just misses utter comprehensiveness, for what he should have said is that we can sum up Bergson's philosophy in a single idea: time is a fluid reality. Bergson repeatedly pointed out that time—time as it really is—cannot be conceived as a series of static instants analogous to frames on a strip of cinematographic film. Run the frozen moments by however you wish, and you still don't get genuine movement (just as there is no genuine movement in a motion picture) or real change. Time and again, he returned to draw further insights from what is really the axiomatic foundation of his philosophical system: there is no way to get from static being to becoming, so if time and change are fluid realities, then common notions, both of philosphy and so-called common sense, are mistaken.

One member of Pound's circle in London, T.E. Hulme (1883-1917), had translated Bergson's *Introduction à la metaphysique*. He took many of Bergson's ideas, mixed them with ideas from Georges Sorel (1847-1922, an engineer-turned-philosopher who rejected all conceptions of history as deterministic and adopted the Bergsonian idea of creative freedom as an instrument partly of historical analysis but primarily of political advocacy on behalf of anti-bourgeois violence), Friedrich Nietzsche, and others to produce not so much a philosophy as a collection of ideas whose appeal synergized each other. One can get an inkling of what Hulme took from Bergson by considering Bergson's own summary of his metaphysical position that he presented in his *Introduction to Metaphysics*.

> II. . . . [R]eality is mobility. . . . *All reality, therefore, is tendency, if we agree to mean by tendency an incipient change of direction. . . .*
>
> V. . . . But because we fail to reconstruct the living reality with stiff and ready-made concepts, it does not follow that we cannot grasp it in some other way. . . .
>
> VI. But the truth is that our intelligence can . . . place itself within the mobile reality, and adopt its ceaselessly changing direction; in short, can grasp it by means of that *intellectual sympathy* which we call intuition. . . . Only thus will a progressive philosophy be built up. . . .
>
> VII. . . . The most powerful of the methods of investigation at the disposal of the human mind, the infinitesimal calculus, originated from this very inversion. . . . *[T]he object of metaphysics is to perform* qualitative *differentiations and integrations.*
>
> VIII. . . . From the overlooking of this intuition proceeds all that has been said by philosophers and by men of science themselves about the "relativity" of scientific knowledge. *What is relative is the symbolic knowledge by pre-existing concepts, which proceeds from the fixed to the moving, and not the intuitive knowledge which installs itself in that which is moving and adopts the very life of things.* This intuition attains the absolute.
>
> IX. That there are not two different ways of knowing things fundamentally, that the various sciences have their root in metaphysics, is what the ancient philosophers generally thought. Their error did not lie there. It consisted in their being always dominated by the belief, so natural to the human mind, that a variation can only be the expression and development of what is invariable. . . . Now it is the contrary which is true. . . . [W]hile science needs symbols for its analytical development, the main object of metaphysics is to do away with symbols.[74]

Hulme's discovery of Bergson had a momentous effect, both on him and on other members of his circle. The shock of exhilaration it produced reverberated through the modernist movement; it was not, however, long-lasting, for as Michael H. Levenson shows in his crucial study *A Genealogy of Modernism*, Hulme's intellectual career is cleaved in the middle, with those works written before 1912 being exuberantly Bergsonian and those written after 1912 being anti-Bergson.[75] The first questions that had attracted Hulme's intellectual energies were those of the late Victorians—questions concerning the place of value in a world made up exclusively by matter and, more broadly, the reconcilability of science and religion. Hulme tells us that he found the claim that the world is made up exclusively of material atoms that move according to the gigantic mechanism of cause and effect intolerably unsettling, for "There cannot be any good or bad in such a turmoil of atoms."[76] Bergson provided Hulme with (at least temporary) relief from the mental turmoil that his encounter with scientific materialism had induced, releasing him from "a nightmare which had long troubled [his] mind"; later a reactionary anti-Romanticism was to serve the same role for him.[77] His first encounter with Bergson's ideas induced an excitement so expansive as to be "an almost physical sense of exhilaration, a sudden expansion, a kind of mental explosion."[78] Bergson persuaded him that it is confusion to conclude that the evident success of science's deterministic materialism made obsolete the belief that humans are free moral agents; rather, Bergson convinced him that humans are creatively unconstrained; he showed him that material determination obtains only in the realm of matter, not in the realm of mind. Those who apply categories taken from the external world and apply them to the subjective realm engage in spurious analogizing. Pointing out the error of thinking about inner life using categories derived from the external world was the primary lesson that Bergson taught Hulme.[79]

Bergson did not discount the scientific account of nature; rather he pointed out that it distorts or neglects aspects of conscious experience. Scientific materialism takes the categories that are appropriate to the analysis of the external world (such as quantity and causality) and extends them everywhere, and when it uses them to analyze experience, it uses them inappropriately.[80] By extending these categories to the realm of experience, scientific materialism makes the inner, "intensive" realm coextensive with the external, "extensive" realm. Bergson's efforts to counter the global claims of scientific materialism took the form of arguing that there are phenomena, or as he called them, "intensive manifolds" that are not amenable to analysis "in terms of space." That we do not adequately represent such phenomena by conceiving them as discrete entities occupying the "extensive manifold of space" was one of Bergson's central themes. Furthermore, a strain of antipathy towards logic, and rational methods of any sort, appears in Bergson's writings from time to time, giving his philosophy an irrationalist cast that has made it attractive to present-day philosophers such as Gilles Deleuze.

An acquaintance with Bergson's ideas about the method that humans use to uncover truth is essential to understanding what Hulme believed he had found in Bergson. Darwin's *On the Origin of Species* (1859) had greatly influenced Henri Bergson, as it had many other thinkers of the period. He had even for a short while taken up the philosophy of Herbert Spencer (1820-1903), an engineer turned autodidact philosopher who, in a series of publications, applied Darwin's theory of evolution to one field after another, arguing that evolution produced ever-greater diversity, greater complexity, and higher levels of organization in each field he studied. The Darwinian revolution had produced a naturalized conception of consciousness. Darwin's influence led thinkers to consider the human mind as a bodily organ (or as the immediate result of bodily processes) and the mind's activity, of forming knowledge, as an adaptive behaviour, as an agency of the drive to survive. Such thinkers, then, construed knowledge as a means to protect the organism in its struggle with the environment—to improve its chances of surviving to reproduce. Darwin's science thus led philosophers to argue that the 'truth' of a belief relates to its biological use—to whether it helps the organism in its efforts to survive—not to the belief's conformity to the world.

Edmund Husserl tried to counter Darwinian relativism by attempting to discover a pure subject of cognition unaffected by its biological, psychological, social, or historical contexts and to reveal its character. Bergson took a different tack. While he ceded to the Darwinian relativists that their claims held true for scientific knowledge, and for analytic thinking generally, Bergson proposed that there is a form of knowledge that rises above the limitations of situated existence and the struggle for survival. He called this form of knowledge intuition. Intuition enables us to commune with reality itself—with 'life' as he termed it. Of intuition's noetic value, Bergson wrote:

> To act and to know that we are acting, to come into touch with reality and even live it, but only in the measure in which it concerns the work that is being accomplished and the furrow that is being plowed, such is the function of human intelligence. Yet a beneficent fluid bathes us, whence we draw the very force to labor and to live. From this ocean of life, in which we are immersed, we are continually drawing something, and we feel that our being, or at least the intellect that guides it, has been formed therein by a kind of local concentration. Philosophy can only be an effort to dissolve again into the Whole. Intelligence, reabsorbed into its principle, may thus live back again its own genesis.[81]

It is one of Bergson's most explicit statements concerning the relation between intuition and primordial knowledge—a relation he considered to be one of identity.

Many of the artists who took up Bergson's philosophy as a cause had a conflicted relationship with science: They favoured, on the whole, a dynamic conception of reality, since (as many of them realized) a dynamic conception of reality was implied by the science of the period; Bergson's philosophy appealed to them, partly, because it, too, offered a dynamic conception of reality. Accordingly many thinkers connected the conception of consciousness as flux that Joyce's *Ulysses* presented to Einstein's physics—and this indeed not only by the literary critic Edmund Wilson (in *Axel's Castle*), but even by a person as learned in science as Alfred North Whitehead (in *Science and the Modern World*). Whitehead, whose writings (as we shall see) proved enormously influential on several of the most important artists of the second half of the twentieth century, also explained that poetry and science were developing towards a convergence, as contemporary science evolved towards the view that the Romantics had promulgated, that nature and our consciousness of nature constitute a unity.

Yet many of the leading ideas of Bergson's philosophy have the character of a counter-science. However strong their irrationalist bent might have seemed to artists of their day, these ideas were important for proposing ways to reconnect knowledge with the body—and this itself pitted them against the science of the period. Science had split sensation from proprioception by presenting sensation as a collection of visual representations reflected into the mind, which acts merely as a mirror of nature. Bergson's ideas about "life" and intuition related sensations and ideas back to the body by presenting experience as a somatic affair. Reason had separated humans from nature, he alleged. Intuition is the work of our total being, a participatory form of consciousness that reached into the life of circumambient beings. As such, it reconnects experience to the body from which reason had separated us. The basic tenet of Bergson's cosmology was that nature as a whole has the same form of the self, for the great stream of 'life' moves both and gives both their forms; among the reasons for the extraordinary popularity that Bergson's philosophy experienced was that it served as a rallying point for all those who longed to feel what the Romantics had proclaimed, that in engaging in action and in exhibiting creativity, they were manifesting a deep and irresistible cosmic impulse. Intuition allows us to connect with the fundamental pulse of life, the source of all creativity. Though Bergson did argue that consciousness surpasses the body, his descriptions of the internal experience of the body and his conception of intuition resemble the descriptions other philosophers have offered of bodily knowledge. Of greater, because more general, importance is that the resemblance that his descriptions of the life force have to descriptions that other thinkers have offered of our proprioceptive experience of the body—like many other twentieth-century thinkers, Bergson thought of the body as a stream of pulsating throbs.

Bergson's cosmology had a dualistic bent, though the opposing terms in his dualism are not, at least in a strict sense, matter and spirit (or matter and consciousness) as they are in most dualistic metaphysics. Rather, they are matter and what he called the *élan vital*, or life force, a notion that, for the popular mind, encapsulates the significance of Bergsonianism. These two forces, the material and the *élan vital*, struggle with each other constantly, as the active principle of life strives to overcome the obstacles that inert matter places in its paths. Thus, the opposing forces in Bergson's cosmology are really inertia and dynamism. Among Bergson's key discussions of the *élan vital* is *Creative Evolution*, a rather extraordinary book of philosophical biology. In *Creative Evolution*, Bergson likens the life force to the artistic impulse.[82] A creative force impels the artist to create, just as *élan vital* impels nature to produce new and varied forms. The life force works within nature in much the fashion of the creative urge that moves the artist, and, like the creative urge, the life force produces genuine novelty. In the First Introduction to *Creative Evolution*, Bergson makes the proposal that we undo the effects of the intellect that turn change into a series of frozen moments like those on a cinematographic film and "restore to movement its mobility, to change its fluidity, to time its duration. . . . Metaphysics will then become experience itself; and duration will be revealed as it really is—unceasing creation, the uninterrupted up-surge of novelty."[83] But philosophers, Bergson claims, because they have not understood the reality of change, and the necessity of understanding flux as an organic process whose basic reality is that of a flow, not the succession of novel but, nonetheless, static states like those recorded on a cinematographic film, cannot really understand the radically new and the unforeseeable conditions that emerge. Bergson describes the life force as "a current of consciousness" that has penetrated matter to produce living being. The *élan vital* is a principle of freedom for it works by "engraft[ing] on to the necessity of physical forces the largest possible amount of *indetermination*."[84] Its urge to generate novelty shapes the course of evolution. In its capacity to produce novelty and its characteristic organic manner of preserving the past, the *élan vital* resembles consciousness: "Continuity of change, preservation of the past in the present, real duration [*durée*]—the living being seems, then, to share these attributes with consciousness. Can we go further and say that life, like conscious activity, is invention, is unceasing creation?"[85] His answer, of course, was affirmative.

Though influenced by Darwin's theory of evolution, Bergson took exception to Darwin's materialism. Bergson accused Darwin of giving a too-rational, mechanistic, and deterministic picture of the evolutionary process. Bergson maintained that evolution was real exactly because time was real, and that we fail to understand that evolution produces novel properties that could not be predicted from its prior conditions (that is, that evolution really is what philosophers sometimes call "emergent evolution") for much the same reasons that we fail to understand that time and the flux of reality generate genuine novelty. Bergson considered our failure to distinguish "between an evolution and an unfurling, between the radically new and a rearrangement of the pre-existing, in fact, between creation and simple choice" damages our understanding of reality in much the very same way as our understanding of artmaking would be damaged by our failure to understand that a work of art exhibits genuine novelty because genuine creative originality emerges through time and does not pre-exist the process that evolves it.

> [W]e imagine that everything which occurs could have been foreseen by any sufficiently informed mind, and that, in the form of an idea, it was thus pre-existent to its realization; an absurd conception in the case of a work of art, for from the moment that the musician has the precise and complete idea of the symphony he means to compose, his symphony is done. Neither in the artist's thought nor, what is more, in any other thought comparable to ours, whether impersonal or even simply virtual, did the symphony exist in its quality of being possible before being real.[86]

We will see that the notion that artworks exhibit emergent features (that is, that they take on unforeseeable characteristics through the process by which they come into being) influenced T.E. Hulme, and through Hulme, Ezra Pound, and through Pound, the Projective Poets. The opposition between the notion of emergent form and the idea of "pre-existent form" is the fundamental contrast between the Projective Poets of the 1950s, who were so often spurned by the academic establishment, and the New Criticism (see glossary) of the poets that the academic establishment embraced; so Bergson's insight here has cardinal importance. Bergson's remarks enable us to trace the divergent aesthetic commitments of the two groups of poets all the way back to differences in the fundamental metaphysical assumptions. The New Critical idea of form draws upon the idea of pre-existent forms— upon the idea that reality is composed of perduring forms, some of which are actual at this moment, and some not, and that in making anything, we actualize one possible form. Such a conception of reality implies that if we knew enough about these possible existents, we would know if, and when, they would be become actual. The Projective Poets, however, have attempted to forge an aesthetic that takes full account of Bergson's strong insight that that time and change produce novel properties that could not be foreseen, that the process of artistic creation resembles emergent evolution.[87]

Bergson's cardinal point on the topic of evolution was that evolution produced both genuine novelty and directed variation. Under the influence of Spencer's evolutionary philosophy, Bergson proposed that, through evolution, the life force carries reality towards ever more complex organization. Like C.S. Peirce, Bergson alleged that Darwin's tychastic theory of evolution, because it is based on the belief that the processes that result in evolutionary change have no motivation (that is, no final cause), cannot explain why evolution produces ever-increasing complexity.[88] Bergson's ideas on evolution in fact reiterate many ideas Peirce had formulated earlier. Peirce, too, had argued that theories that explain evolution by chance variation are implausible and that there must be some higher form to evolution. Peirce called this higher form "agapastic evolution" or "evolutionary love." In agapastic evolution "advance takes place by virtue of a positive sympathy" among the created forms; this sympathy arises from what Peirce calls continuity of mind (and which is tantamount to what Hegel referred to as 'absolute mind').[89] This is an idea Bergson, too, arrived at when, late in his career, he wrote *The Two Sources of Morality and Religion*, and proposed that the primal energy at the heart of the universe is love. Furthermore, Bergson pointed out, the parts of any biological organization are mutually adapted to one another. A random variation in some part of the organism would affect the functioning of the whole; a change in some part of, say, the eye would impair the organism's visual functioning. Since evolution does occur, we must suppose that, if one part of the organism changes, other parts change along with it, to ensure effective functioning. Bergson alleged that the Darwinian account of evolution provides no way to explain the phenomenon of co-adapted variation. The notion of *élan vital* provides the basis for such an explanation: the life force is the vital impetus that produces the variations, ensures that these variations result in new species with increasingly complex organization, and co-ordinates those variations so as to maintain continuity of functioning across the evolving species.

Bergson's conception of 'life' was in keeping with the neo-Romantic spirit of the 1890s. Indeed, the term "life" had cardinal importance in the neo-Romantics' lexicon; 'life' was vital, free, and creative—and opposed to the scientific materialism and the determinism that, since the seventeenth century, had become such an important force. Reason itself fell under attack. As the early Romantics had, the neo-Romantics alleged that it was reason that had alienated us from nature. They criticized reason for its manner of cutting up the world instead of grasping it as an organic whole, for failing to consider that the organ through which we apprehend nature itself is part of nature, and for the mechanistic conclusions at which it inevitably arrives. Religious, metaphysical, and cosmological issues that the regime of modernity had rendered obsolete by judging them to be irrational (according, of course, to its concept of reason) again asserted their legitimacy, if only for a brief while, as the neo-Romantics came to see 'life' as a quasi-human spirit that pervades all of nature.

Under the influence of such notions, Bergson formulated a contrast between two different ways of knowing something, whether an object, an idea, or a person. We can know something either by circumambulating it or by delving into it, Bergson offered. When we circle around an object, we remain outside it, so our knowledge of it is perspectival. The knowledge we acquire by such methods is therefore relative. We can express such knowledge in symbols (which stand for general features that more than one object can possess or actions that more than one person or thing can engage in), but knowledge of this type affords no understanding of the individuality of any particular object of cognition. Knowledge of this sort is analytic—it decomposes the object into elements so that we can describe it in familiar terms. Our proclivity for isolating repeatable elements in experience keeps us from reaching down into reality's core. We apprehend an aspect that reality presents to our vantage point and shape what we perceive according to our interests and our previous experiences; but we do not apprehend what it is in itself. Through intuition, by contrast, we become empathically aware of its secret inner life. We grasp the object as it is in itself and acquire knowledge that is absolute, not relative.

Bergson attempted to clarify the difference between analytic knowledge and intuition with a familiar example.[90] When we move our hand, Bergson states, we apprehend our performance from the inside, as a simple whole. Perceiving this event from the outside affords us only incomplete knowledge, for it does not allow us to apprehend what moves the hand. Apprehending the event from the inside, by contrast, allows us to grasp the experience as a whole. But that of which we have certain knowledge through intuition is not an external object but oneself; the self is really the sole object of all our intuitions.

In *Matter and Memory*, Bergson extends this example to formulate a distinction similar to one that Schopenhauer made, between the body that one knows from the outside by perception and the body that one knows from the inside by proprioception and affection. Among all the bodies that occupy space there is but one of which I can have a dual awareness: that I can know from the outside by perception and that I can know from the inside by affect and proprioceptive sensation. There is only one body that I can experience internally, through a mode of awareness that resembles my intuition of the flux of reality: the body that I can know in this dual manner is my own body. I know this body as the centre of my actions.

Bergson alleged that philosophers have given inadequate thought to this mode of awareness. Instead, they have concerned themselves primarily with our sensations of the external world. Like Schopenhauer, again, Bergson claimed that the inner experience of the body—the body that we know through proprioception, will, and action—furnishes metaphysical insights in ultimate reality. Bergson critiqued the tradition philosophical position that proposed that sensations resemble reflections in the mind, which they consider to be like a mirror of nature. Actually, Bergson used a different analogy for the philosopher's conception of the perceptual process: he suggested that philosophers have considered our perception of the external world on the model of the photographic process for, on their model, perception produces a picture of what we perceive. They have envisaged the mind as a *camera obscura*, which forms the images that we perceive, and perception as an instrument of cognition, the aim of which is to produce knowledge. Bergson even drew a comparison to the intellect's "cinematographical method," for he likened the intellect to a movie camera that arrests the dynamism of the world in a series of still frames.[91] The intellect freezes that which is because it can deal only with that which is static, fixed, immobilized. Since it can comprehend change only as the rearrangement of already existing elements, it cannot account for any genuine novelty.

Bergson rejects the model of perception as pictorial representation, first, because the images that perception would produce would be spatially extended and so would have to be part of the external world, not our mind; and second, because perception and cognition do not give a pure image of the world but rather (like all which is produced by the faculties that evolution creates) a sense of the world germane to our interests, needs, and especially, as all the faculties that evolution produces are, to our actions. Perception does not create images, Bergson averred; rather the mind selects images from among the many available to it, those that have relevance to situation and the actions those emotions call forth.

Our perceptions of external objects are never pure and immediate, however. Perception combines the raw material produced by the impact that our environment has on our sensory mechanisms with memories that our minds furnish. The will selects, out of the many images available to it, those which are relevant to its interests at any given moment. The body contributes to this activity perceptual centres that respond to the influence of circumambient objects, while the mind, by supplying the raw material of our perceptions with memory images that stabilize the perceptual field, ensures that the world presented to us by the perceptual faculties is not a realm of flux. In perception, then, body and mind are united, for the body contributes the matter of perceptions (in the effects that environing objects have on the body), while the mind imposes a static form on this dynamic raw material. The resulting images, Bergson insisted, constitute the world.[92]

The intellect draws upon these pictorial perceptions in formulating its image of the world. Unlike many philosophers who write about intellectual activity as though it were self-rewarding, Bergson's commitment to evolutionary explanation led him to argue that the intellect is so designed as to be put to practical use. Accordingly, the products of the intellect do not reflect the world; rather they represent the world in a form that will be of practical use to us. Concepts are really pragmatic instruments, Bergson insisted, and their characteristics are shaped by human interests and by our evolutionary needs. Since science is the paradigm of conceptual knowledge, we can examine scientific knowledge in order to assess the characteristics of conceptual knowledge and to explore the nature of the intellect itself. And since scientific knowledge is reflected in technological implements, and since technology, inasmuch as it is directed towards the control of events and prediction, represents our practical needs, we can examine technological implements in order to discern the characteristics of scientific knowledge that evidence its value as *praxis*.

Bergson noted that scientific theories have what seems a telic disposition towards spatial thinking, just as ordinary language is pervaded by spatial metaphors. Furthermore, science (and, accordingly, the intellect itself) conceives of reality as composed of homogeneous units; it breaks wholes down into a collection of uniform parts. It prefers that which is immobile and unchanging, and so, when it considers motion, it deals with motion (as Zeno's paradoxes make evident) as being composed of many immobile units, like a strip of cinematographic film. Logic and mathematics, Bergson contended, furnish thinking with unchanging structures; it is this that accounts for their great appeal. The intellect understands change, including objects' coming into or going out of existence, as the rearrangement of these homogeneous units. From this analysis of the character of the intellect, Bergson concluded that the intellect is responsible for the world's being made up of stable, discrete entities.

Because our perceptions are stabilized by images from the past, they do not represent the reality that is simultaneous with perception; perception—or, at least, most perception—contains an admixture of memory. The mind's reservoir of images and its penchant for comparison notwithstanding, there is a mode of awareness that apprehends objects purely, without any involvement of memory images. Bergson identifies this sort of apprehension (perception with no admixture of memory) as 'intuition.' Reality is flux, Bergson affirmed, yet the world we know through picture perception is not, for memory images have imposed stability on them. So the greater portion of our thinking concerns matters that remain basically unchanged for long periods of time. It generally concerns things that are fixed in space, and have sharp outlines and well-defined properties. But reality is not fixed, and has no sharp outlines. This, Bergson averred, is what intuition reveals.

Bergson devotes much care to describing intuition, and what he describes is similar to what C.S. Peirce has described as abduction. Peirce attacked that proposition that the empiricists had made a part of philosophical orthodoxy, that all knowledge is the product either of induction or deduction. Another method of producing knowledge is the process he called "abduction," by which he meant, roughly, guessing or, more exactly, forming hypothesis. "[O]ur knowledge is never absolute," Peirce wrote, "but always swims, as it were, in a continuum of uncertainty and of indeterminancy."[93] Peirce's notions about abduction were, if anything, even more radical (though, admittedly, more logicist) than Bergson's ideas about intuition. Peirce argued that because we "swim . . . in a continuum of uncertainty and of indeterminacy," we must make conjectures about our situation that exceed whatever conclusions the methods of induction or deduction would warrant. The only way of determining whether the idea is a good one is to gamble on it. The idea that success in practice, and not conformity with reality, is the criterion of truth provided the basis of pragmatism, the philosophical doctrine that William James claimed he got from Peirce's writings; the enthusiasm with which so many picked up the idea indicates the popularity of *Lebensphilosophie* at the time.[94] Thus, the idea of a form of indeterminate awareness whose value is measured in practice is an idea that Bergson shared with Peirce. Bergson's similarities with Peirce become more striking later in his career, in the period after *Introduction to Metaphysics* (1903), when Bergson thought of intuition as a less immediate form of awareness than he had earlier, and came to understand it as an act requiring mental effort, more like a form of thinking than a flash of insight.

Bergson proposed that when we apprehend an object through an exercise of intuition, we identify with that object. Intuition is an act by which, Bergson says, "one is transported into the interior of an object in order to coincide with what there is unique and consequently inexpressible about it." Intuition is the product of immersion in an indivisible flow; it apprehends pure becoming and real duration. Through intuition, we know the world just as we know our own consciousness. Through intuition, we enter into the object through identification and we know the object as though inwardly. What we know through intuition, Bergson stated, has many features that the self or consciousness also possesses.

Bergson repeatedly pointed out that consciousness is a flux, arguing that since each state of consciousness is unique, consciousness itself cannot be identical in any two successive instants. But if consciousness is a flux, then, since the reality that intuition empathically reveals has many of the characteristics of consciousness, reality, too, must be flux. Like experience, the world has static and dynamic aspects, the one revealed by reason, the other by intuition. The world's temporal aspect is fluid, dynamic, and continuous.

These two ways of apprehending the world correlate with two sorts of time: time as we think about it and time as we experience it. The distinction between these two sorts of time is the conceptual groundwork of Bergson's philosophy. The time that we perceive in everyday life resembles the time that physicists discuss—Bergson described it as time apprehended as a concept. We apprehend this sort of time on the analogy to space, as a set of homogeneous segments strung together, composing a line of indefinite length. This scientific time, this time of chronometric instruments, this time represented by the letter *t* in scientific formulae and analyzed in mathematical systems, is an extended, homogeneous medium, made up of series of identical units. But this time is not real—it does not flow, neither does it act; it is passive, like a line drawn on a surface. Yet such time dominates our practical life.

By contrast, the time we apprehend through intuition—that time which Bergson called *durée* (a term only inadequately rendered by "duration"—is neither homogeneous nor divisible nor quantifiable. It is fluid, for we cannot distinguish between any two of its moments until they have receded into the past. *Durée*, according to Bergson's description, is time perceived as indivisible. When we turn our attention inward, we discover a time that flows—a time that is an irreversible succession of states that melt into one another without distinction. Every true *durée* is incomplete, dynamic (changing), and novel (unique); and every true *durée* is part of a continuum of successive but heterogeneous movements. Every new moment in *durée* possesses some degree of novelty, but every new moment also reflects some (but not all) of the past and some (but not all) of the future.[95]

Bergson pointed out the intensive character of the objects we apprehend through intuition: the realities we know through direct intuition, such as emotions, differ from each other in intensity, not in size. Because *durée* reveals itself through intuition, it has the nature of an intensity, not that of an object or property; *durée*, therefore, is not a property that we abstract from experience. There is a sort of time that we apprehend by abstracting from experience. By way of contrast with *durée*, abstract time, the time we constitute by abstraction, is composed of quantities of homogeneous units or segments that have only extrinsic relations with one another; accordingly, it is only a sign of the real *durée*, while *durée* itself is essentially indivisible and has no segments that are extrinsic to one another. *Durée* reveals itself when we turn away from the external world and concentrate on inner experience, when we eschew calculating utility and adopt an attitude of disinterested contemplation. It is, as Bergson described it, "the attention that the mind gives to itself, over and above, while it is fixed upon matter, its object."[96]

Contemplation reveals that *durée* is indivisible. It discloses that *durée* is not a succession of moments but flows in an indivisible continuity. This flowing is characteristic not only of time but of all experience: our experience is no more a set of demarcated, bounded, countable states than *durée* is; "In reality no one of them begins or ends, but all extend into each other."[97] Time flows, and each moment is organically and inextricably associated with all other moments; and like any organic whole, moments are accumulating beings, like snowballs, that always contain all of their ever-expanding past. One can know real time only through memory, for in memory moments are not distinct, nor are they juxtaposed in indifferent succession. In memory, as in time, there are no units of past and no units of present joined in extrinsic relations, like the *partes extra partes* relations among physical entities. In memory, as in time, each moment carries with it the past, and what it carries with it affects what it is, and what it becomes. Bergson highlighted these differences between the matter and memory by saying that while the matter of past vanishes, the memory of the past does not vanish.[98]

Bergson argued that the physical world is not really temporal, for a world without consciousness would be a world in which every moment is identical with all other moments. Time arises only in experience, through memory and specifically from the comparison of our present experiences with previous experiences. Even our sense that there is a continuum between "before" and "after" depends upon memory. Real time exists in memory and the temporality we attribute to the physical is only a projection that results from our experience of the world.

Time was central to the thought of the Vorticists on that most crucial of issues, rhythm. Indeed, that somewhat puzzling advice to "compose in the sequence of the musical phrase, not in sequence of a metronome"; the opposition between "the sequence of the musical phrase" and the "sequence of the metronome" is isomorphic with that between *durée* and the time with which science deals. Perhaps nothing in the Vorticists' legacy has been more influential than their belief in the primacy of rhythm. This belief affected Pound, for whom the poets' capacity to create rhythmic form is the primary index of their creative strength. Concerning the poets "design in TIME," i.e., rhythm, Pound writes:

> If [the poet] hasn't a sense of time and of the different qualities of sound, [his or her rhythm] will be clumsy and uninteresting just as a bad draughtsman's drawing will be without distinction.
> The bad draughtsman is bad because he does not perceive space and spatial relations, and cannot therefore deal with them.
> The writer of bad verse is a bore because he does not perceive time and time relations, and cannot therefore delimit them in an interesting manner, by means of longer and shorter, heavier and lighter syllables, and the varying qualities of sound inseparable from the words of his speech.[99]

Brakhage, following William Carlos Williams and Charles Olson (two poets whose works have had considerable influence on Brakhage's formulation of his ideas) has offered the view that the dance of its materials is central to poetry, indeed to any art of time. Brakhage takes as crucial the idea that the rhythmic flow of the poet's language describes a curve of thought;

these beliefs underlie Brakhage's ideas on artistic form.[100] After reading poet Michael McClure's sentence, "What is carved in air is blank as the finger touching it," Brakhage began to reflect on how one might capture one of its images on film; after much deliberation, he proposed to do it in this way:

> Give me a finger moving in air; and it will be picture of finger for *one frame only* (1/40th of a second), will become a carve of solid shape in air, thus: each frame is exposed full-time length needed for the movement (say: 20 seconds), and first frame finger is still at starting point, second frame finger has retained its position and then moved a fraction of an inch during the exposure, third frame finger returns to starting position and moves two fractions of an inch during exposure, and so on for 480 frames—finger carves solid shape OF itself in space of picture area . . . is finger-picture ONLY at time-source of itself, thus only in the referential mind of the viewer.[101]

Brakhage does not analyze the reasons McClure's image appealed to him; however, I believe that what excited him about it was that it provides a representation for his conception of artistic form (or, at least, of form in the arts of time). The form of a poem, a piece of music, or a film evolves through time, as does the curve traced by the moving finger; they are, consequently, as intangible and immaterial as the curve traced by the moving finger. Like the curve the moving finger describes, the form of a temporally extended artwork has existence only in the synoptic view of memory. Its form does not exist altogether, in a single place and at a single time, as an object's does. Its mode of existence is that of a form in evolution, not that of a concretely existing object that is fully given in a single instant. Brakhage conceives of artistic form (at least the forms the arts of time assume) as a trace of the process that evolved it. Moreover, the image suggests to Brakhage that the time-form of a poem (or a film) dematerializes its subject. Only the first frame, which contains no movement, actually depicts the finger. All the other frames show a "blur," the effect of motion. The use of open, evolving forms in artworks has a related effect—for it makes the movement internal to the work itself paramount and renders whatever the work refers to as secondary and indistinct.

His insights into the character of time provided Bergson with the basis for an argument for the ideality of evolution. Bergson argued that since real time has its basis in memory, that is, in the mind, and since the evolution of the universe occurs in real time, evolution must have properties similar to those of mind. Evolution must therefore have an essentially spiritual nature. Accordingly, it must be free and creative. Scientists have failed to acknowledge the spiritual nature of evolution, Bergson maintaned, simply because they are committed materialists. Materialists consider the course of the universe deterministically, primarily because they consider time in the analogy to space and believe that all events that will take place in the future were laid out as though they were images on a reel of film, and that time winds them by us just as a projector winds through a ribbon of film. However, Bergson averred, the essentially spiritual character of the evolutionary process makes this analogy false.

As we have seen, C.S. Peirce maintained that theories that explain evolution by chance variation are implausible. Bergson similarly maintained that the creative tendency, the *élan vital*, or life force, propels evolution. The *élan vital* is an original energy that, contending with the resistance of matter, bifurcated repeatedly, creating in the process all varieties of instinct and intelligence. Every species and every individual organism preserves some part of this original impulse. The *élan vital* strives towards realizing a goal, and it is the goal-directed nature of the *élan vital* that makes evolution more like a mental activity than like a mechanical process of eliminating organisms that are not well adapted to survive in their environment.

According to Bergson, life is a process whose singular, originary drive divides into an ever-increasing variety of forms. While this drive does not possess intentions (that is to say, mental representations that depict the goals it strives to achieve), it does have a basic tendency. The idea that the *élan vital* has inherent tendencies to move in certain directions is required in order to explain why similar forms appeared in unrelated (or very distantly related) plant and animal forms, or why similar variations appear in mutations on different branches of the evolutionary tree. Darwinian theories of evolution cannot explain it with their ideas about chance mutations and natural selection; and these are the only tools they have that might do the job. Bergson pointed out that it is most unlikely that similar sequences of chances could occur on several evolutionary branches. The idea that evolution has a set direction serves us better in explaining the common patterns that appear in different branches of the evolutionary tree and evolution's directed character. The force that counters inertia, and the tendencies towards increasing states of entropy, Bergson sometimes called God; in doing this, he suggested we can identify God with the creativity of the *élan vital*.

Bergson daringly proposed that, in knowing anything, what we really know is ourselves. But Bergson also believed that direct experience changes continually. If the experiences revealed in the immediacy of intuition are unlike even in two consecutive moments, and if what we know through direct experience is ourselves, then, Bergson concluded, the self or consciousness must undergo continual change. From this insight, Bergson concluded that it is memory that allows us to grasp the unity of self (or the unity of consciousness). Each of us is a physical being, a body among other bodies in the world. The self that correlates with this autoscopic body is the 'superficial self,' the self that we use to negotiate our way through the world and to obtain the wherewithal to survive. This self, Bergson said, must obey physical laws and belongs to the space of the world. However, there is another self, the 'profound self' (*le moi profond*) that is not an instrument of our practical concerns. Our experience of the superficial self is more closely associated with the means we use to analyze the world, while the profound self, which is usually only implicit in experience, is more intimately involved with the experience of reality as flux. But both selves, the superficial and the profound, are engaged in every feature and every moment of conscious experience, though we are ordinarily oblivious of the profound self. Hence, said Bergson, every aspect of our conscious life appears "under two aspects: the one clear and precise, but impersonal; the other confused, ever changing and inexpressible, because language cannot get hold of it without arresting its mobility."[102] For language, Bergson noted, is part of the apparatus that we use to divide up the world and to classify experience.

Language's way of operating relies on drawing comparisons among experiences and noting common features. In reality, however, experiences are never qualitatively identical. Every experience is an experience of the self— and the self is always in process, always undergoing transformation. For the self is intimately bound up with memory and memory is bound up with time. Memory changes with every passing moment, for memory can recall each successive instant after its coming-to-presence. If memory changes moment by moment, so must the self. The self, therefore, is never the same at two different moments. And if the self changes with every instant, so then must experience.

Determinists arrive at their position by comparing different moments— their argument relies on the proposition that if the same people found themselves in identical situations twice (or if people with very similar backgrounds found themselves in identical situations) their behaviours would remain the same. This repeatability is the minimum condition for the testing of scientific propositions about human consciousness (i.e., the propositions that so-called scientific psychology offers). However, Bergson stated, there are no repeatable psychological experiments, for no two people are alike; though their backgrounds may be similar, no two people have identical sets of experiences. Nor can individual experiences be the same at two different moments, since between the two moments they will have had other experiences that will have changed them.

Art, Bergson maintained, reveals the non-repeatability of objects and experience; in fact, to demonstrate the uniqueness of each experience and each object is art's principal purpose. Bergson's evolutionary convictions led him to conclude that our sensory faculties are adapted to our needs as an organism. Since our sensory faculties shape our perceptions, our physical needs, Bergson inferred, affect our perceptions. Our needs decide how we organize the world and the simplifications we impose upon it. And since our sensory faculties shape our perceptions according to principles of utility, we overlook the individuality and uniqueness of objects and events and attend only to their common features. We are, Bergson suggested, similarly oblivious of individuality in our apprehension of feelings, whether our own or those of other people; we attend only to repeating features of feelings and, consequently, our apprehension of emotions is also abstract.

If our intercourse with the world were not so practically abstract, we would have no need for art. However, considerations of utility do in fact inform our dealings with the world and, consequently, we do not encounter the world in its pristine purity. Art, Bergson states, is an attempt to overcome these considerations of utility, to get past the practical abstract and to uncover the world as it is in itself. Art presents objects and feelings in their individuality and uniqueness. Bergson's interest in the capacity of a work of art to testify to the absolute individuality of its maker influenced T.E. Hulme and, through Hulme, Ezra Pound and, through Pound, Stan Brakhage. Pound, for example, as early as *Blast* no. 2 (1915), quoted approvingly the Chinese dictum, "As a man's language is an unerring index to his nature, so the actual strokes of his brush in writing or painting betray him and announce either the freedom and nobility of his soul or its meanness and limitation."[103]

Analytic knowledge, Bergson states, is selective and serves practical ends. The mind focuses its efforts on those features of reality that have greatest use for us and discards all others. Analysis thus organizes the features of experiences into a hierarchy, according to their usefulness. Because the conceptual mechanisms that enable us to cut up and categorize experience have evolved to make it possible for us to survive in a very complex world, the analytic categories that we use to interpret experience have their basis in human needs. Bergson asserted that these abstract categories do not afford us direct knowledge of reality. Because of their abstractness, they furnish us with shadows, not substances.[104] Intuition, to the contrary, does reveal objects for what they really are. In the immediacy of intuition, we know objects directly, without the meditation of abstract categories that represent repeatable properties of experience. Intuition does not even distinguish subject from object, Bergson stated. Precisely because it is not a form of conceptual understanding, intuition furnishes us with knowledge of the unrepeatable, the unique, the truly real that is beyond the reach of analysis and that cannot be given symbolic representation. Because it operates beyond the purview of concepts that ensure our survival, intuition transports us to a realm free of utilitarian considerations.

Bergson accused the sciences, including psychology, of serving the ends of manipulation. It is in order to serve the ends of manipulation that scientists isolate qualities that events belonging to their domain of inquiry have in common, discover regularities among these occurrences, and immobilize these regularities by formulating laws. Psychology, to take that science as an example, breaks the whole of the personality into conceptual units. Although these conceptual units have the status of merely theoretical entities, psychologists treat them as if they were actual units and behave as though these units existed independently of their theoretical propositions. Yet every act of a person is the expression of a complete personality. In treating these conceptual entities as actual entities, psychology loses the concrete integrity of human existence. The 'ego' analyzed by psychology has little to do with the actuality of *durée* or with change, Bergson pointed out. Its method, like that of all the sciences, immobilizes the objects with which it deals. Bergson proposes a new empiricism to replace the empiricism that rested on pragmatic propositions. This new empiricism would feel the soul pulsating with life. It would dispense with old, general concepts and grasp life with a fresh vitality. It would reveal time and reality directly, in the utter simplicity of unmediated contact.

T.E. Hulme attached himself to Bergson's metaphysical theories. He did not arrive at the conclusion that Bergson's theories are true by a critical process, however; rather, he adopted them because of the emotional affinity he felt for them. He displayed little aptitude for philosophical analysis. What he did possess was a strong religious sense. He contrasted the religious attitude, which he averred was the only reasonable attitude to assume, with the position that, when he wrote, had recently come to dominate, which position he referred to as "humanism." Humanism, as Hulme used the term, is the theory that humans are good by nature, that they are perfectible, and that, throughout the course of history, they have approached this ideal of perfection ever more closely. Humanism expresses itself politically as liberalism, for liberalism teaches that, by reason of their inherent rights (their intrinsic value), people should be free of the shackles of authority and should be allowed to decide their own political destinies. The liberal's proposal, that individuals should have the widest possible latitude of self-governance, follows from the humanist's teaching that human nature is inherently good. In ethical theory, "humanism" expresses itself as the doctrine of relativism. Relativism teaches that there is no objective good in the order of nature that humans are suited to serve, that good and bad are relative to human desires, human pleasures, and the conventions and agreements of human societies. Hulme proposed (wrongly, I think) that humanism expresses itself in art as Romanticism, since Romanticism defines human feelings and the human imagination by considering them as manifestations of the immanent divine.

Theories of art as expression are caught between two unpalatable alternatives. They generally run into difficulty either because they provide no criterion for distinguishing between forming a work of art and howling with rage or, if they do provide some such criterion, such as 'significant form,' they fail to connect that criterion to activities of expression.[105] Bergson's philosophy offered Hulme the means necessary to develop a theory of art as expression that avoids this dilemma. The crucial Bergsonian idea that enabled Hulme to develop a viable theory of art as expression is the distinction between 'the superficial self' and 'the profound self' (*le moi profond*). The actions of the superficial self are analyzable, Bergson stated, because they are spatially and causally conditioned. The profound self's actions are not, however. The profound self has a more intimate relation to reality and so attains truths unavailable to the superficial self; and it is the insights (intuitions) of the profound self that art, and art alone, knows how to convey. Bergson's emphasis on the profound truths of the deeper self affected Hulme's thinking deeply and, through Hulme, that of an entire generation. Of all Bergson's ideas, the most influential was his conviction that poetry and art present truths of experience.

Experience as Energy: A Pattern for Thinking

Thought seeks inevitable limits—irreducibly stable patterns of energy— knowing that it prospers best within axiomatic perimeters that need never be patrolled or repaired.

I am told that, in 1927, a Louisiana lawmaker (haunted by the ghost of Pythagoras, no doubt) introduced into the legislature of that state a bill that would have made the value of *pi* equal to precisely three. No actual circle could pass unscathed through that equation. The Emperor Shih Huang Ti attempted an axiomatic decree of similar instability: his Great Wall, subject to entropy, never kept out an invader. Instead, the language and culture of China, an energy-pattern of appalling stability, simply engulfed one conqueror after another. Everyone who ventured South of the Wall became, in time, Chinese.

Marcel Duchamp is speaking: "Given: 1. the waterfall; 2. the illuminating gas." (Who listens and understands?)

A waterfall is not a 'thing,' nor is a flame of burning gas. Both are, rather, stable patterns of energy determining the boundaries of a characteristic sensible 'shape' in space and time. The waterfall is present to consciousness only so long as water flows through it, and the flame, only so long as the gas continues to burn. The water may be fresh or salt, full of fish, colored with blood; with gas, acetylene or the vapor of brandy.

You and I are semistable patterns of energy, maintaining in the very teeth of entropy a characteristic shape in space and time. I am a flame through which will eventually pass, according to Buckminster Fuller, thirty-seven tons of vegetables . . . among other things. Curiously enough, then, I continue to resemble myself (for the moment at least).[106]

The style is elegant, the tone ironic and witty—and identifiable immediately by anyone who has even a passing acquaintance with the filmmaker's prose style: it is by one of Pound's disciples, Hollis Frampton. The substance, however, is not original; this, by Hugh Kenner, makes that clear.

> Imagine, next, the metabolic flow that passes through a man and is not the man: some hundred tons of solids, liquids and gases serving to render a single man corporeal during the seventy years he persists, a patterned integrity, a knot through which pass the swift strands of simultaneous ecological cycles, recycling transformations of solar energy. At any given moment the knotted materials weigh perhaps 160 pounds. (And "Things," wrote Ernest Fenollosa about 1904, are "cross-sections cut through actions, snapshots.")
>
> So far Buckminster Fuller (1967). Now Ezra Pound (1914) on the poetic image: ". . . a radiant node or cluster; . . . what I can, and must perforce, call a VORTEX, from which, and through which, and into which, ideas are constantly rushing." A patterned integrity accessible to the mind; topologically stable; subject to variations of intensity; brought into the domain of the senses by a particular interaction of words. "In decency one can only call it a vortex. . . . *Nomina sunt consequentia rerum.*" For the vortex is not the water but a patterned energy made visible by the water.

*   *   *

> A patterned energy made visible by the water. Pound did not chance on such a conception lightly. . . . [H]e wrote in 1912 of "our kinship to the vital universe, to the tree and the living rock," having "about us the universe of fluid force, and below us the germinal universe of wood alive, of stone alive": man being "chemically speaking . . . a few buckets of water, tied up in a complicated sort of fig-leaf,". . . . "Energy creates pattern," he was writing three years later, explaining "Imagisme." "Emotion is an organizer of form." A magnet brings "order and vitality and thence beauty into a plate of iron filings," their design expressing "a confluence of energy." Thirty years later, in Pisa, he closed the 74th Canto with a double image of patterned energy: the magnet's "rose in the steel dust" and the fountain's sculptured flow through which passes renewing water, tossing a bright ball. The same passage mentions the winds of Zephyrus and Apeliota, moving energies so stable they have names, and cites Verlaine's comparison of the soul's life to the fountain's.[107]

Frampton was a self-aware and deliberate artist; *The Pound Era* is a well-known book. One can only surmise that he intended readers to notice the imitation. What might the point of the imitation be? The answer is simple: to confirm the truth of the passage it imitates by restating its key ideas.

> "Energy creates pattern." Like molecules of water in fountain or vortex, particulars of the pattern mutate; the pattern is stable, an enduring integrity, shaped by the movement, shaping it. This is a whole time's way of thinking. "Art never improves," wrote T.S. Eliot in 1919, "but the material of art is never quite the same": an Eliot aware, . . . of the mind of Europe persisting like the Cumaean Sibyl's, "a mind which changes" but "abandons

nothing *en route*":... A patterned integrity, the mind of Europe, or equally the poet's imagination where the greater mind is active here and now: where (suitably catalyzed) new objects of attention enter into new combinations ("really new") while the mind's identity (called Tradition) remains.

In Zürich James Joyce was drawing the 18 hours of Leopold Bloom through a patterned integrity defined by Homer: a tough self-interfering pattern through which, he discerned, Shakespeare had already drawn the skein called Hamlet (Telemachus, Stephen), and Mozart his Don Giovanni (Antinous, Boylan) and even the elder Dumas his Monte Cristo, returned avenger (Odysseus at Ithaca, the stone guest at the banquet, the ghost of Elsinore). Time, place and personnel alter; the pattern remains.[108]

Fuller, Kenner, and Frampton are not alone. William Carlos Williams joins them in drawing a relation between the crystalline, apparently stable, form assumed by its changing constituents and the transient contents that, moment by moment, constitute the matter that give that form its being, and in pointing out the illusory nature of fixity; here is a part of "Della Primavera Transportata Al Morale" (1930):

The forms
of the emotions are crystalline,
geometric-faceted. So we recognize
only in the white heat of
understanding, when a flame
runs through the gap made
by learning, the shapes of things—
the ovoid sun, the pointed trees

lashing branches

The wind is fierce, lashing

the long-limbed trees whose
branches
wildly toss—[109]

Consider the opposition between "crystalline,/ geometric-faceted" and "whose/ branches/ wildly toss—." Here, then, another semi-stable pattern of energy: Pound, Williams, Kenner, and Frampton exchange roles with one another while the conceptual principles they expound remain essentially the same. The pattern we have just identified is important enough to merit further perpension. For the energies that form and maintain this pattern, however fugitively, and the energies that it, in its turn, organizes, are the energies that vitalize modernism.

Frampton and Kenner's image of an energy formation represents something so immaterial that it can serve as a metaphor for consciousness. Thus Kenner: "the mind of ... [Sybil]," "the greater mind," and "objects of *attention*." And Frampton: "Who listens and understands?" Modernism did take the nature of consciousness as one of its central topics. Michael H. Levenson's synoptic history of English modernist literature, *A Genealogy of Modernism*, reveals that a concentration of artists' creative energies on the realm of consciousness figures among literary modernism's most significant characteristics. He offers the thesis that the interest the early modernists took in consciousness, and the attention they focused on it, led them to oppose the inner and outer worlds. Adopting an image from the science of thermodynamics as a metaphor for thinking, Kenner and Frampton attempt to reconcile the inner and outer realms that the modernists had driven apart. More important for our purposes, this condensed and overdetermined metaphor embodies a dialectic between an insubstantial but persistent form and the more concrete, but less determining particulars that it shapes. Their metaphor confirms a thesis that Sanford Schwartz offers in *The Matrix of Modernism: Pound, Eliot, and Early Twentieth Century Thought*.[110] According to Schwartz, the foundational ideas of aesthetic doctrines of the literary modernists concern the relation between form and flux in a work of art (recall the earlier comment that modernism relied on a notion of perduring potentials). The leading idea of this aesthetic doctrine maintains that a work of art has the unifying form that we can apprehend intellectually; yet, despite being an abstraction, this form does not suppress the differences among the flux particulars it incorporates.

Schwartz claims that many turn-of-the-century philosophers tried to expose a basic conceptual failure—an error that Nietzsche had called "the anthropomorphic error" and Whitehead "the fallacy of misplaced concreteness" (see glossary, concreteness). This fallacy mistakes the intellects' constructions for concrete reality. One of Schwartz's key examples of the effort to expose this philosophical error, which he claims has long presided over Western culture, is Ernst Cassirer's anti-Platonist tract, *Substanzbegriff und Funktionsbegriff* (1910). Cassirer's book appeared just shortly after Nietzsche's late work, around the time that A.N. Whitehead was working out the ontological and metaphysical consequences of the theory of relations he and Bertrand Russell had presented in *Principia Mathematica*, and about the same time that other major philosophers were working towards revising human understanding so that it might avoid this sort of error. Schwartz points out that, like Cassirer, T.E. Hulme turned the argument that many philosophical concepts exemplify the fallacy of misplaced concreteness in an anti-Platonic direction (the Spirit of the Time, it seems, conceived the relation between universal and particular in an anti-Platonic manner).

So it came to be that Hulme's ideas about the course of history also had anti-Platonic leanings. According to his historical schema, the ancients tried to escape the world's instability by building in their minds "things of permanence which would stand fast in the universe which frightened them." He saw this desire in Greek poetry (which attempted to embody, in a scant few lines, a thought in its perfected form), in the pyramids and above all in what he called "the hypostatized ideas of Plato." Because the idea of a dynamic, changing reality appalled them, they strove to create in their minds and their art an abidingly perfect reality in which change had no part. This, according to Hulme, was how the idea of perfection of form took on such an elevated importance in Greek aesthetics.

Hulme's schematized history of the West charted the progress from the denial of flux and change in Plato's philosophy to their acceptance in Henri Bergson's. Hulme claimed that the rise of modernism marked the point at which literary works evolved from denying to accepting flux. What defines modernist writing, he claimed, is its acceptance of the fundamental reality of flux. Because they accept flux, Hulme offered, modernist writers "no longer strive to attain the absolutely perfect form in poetry."[111] Modernism maintained that corresponding to every aesthetic form that an artist realizes there is a perduring potential, that represents that form's ideal. What led Hulme to reject this notion was the influence of Henri Bergson's metaphysics, for in *Creative Evolution* Bergson had demoted form from the lofty position to which philosophers had elevated it when he stated, *"form is only a snapshot view of a transition."*[112] Insistence upon "metre and a regular number of syllables" had disappeared because the regularity of metre is "cramping, jangling, meaningless, and out of place" for the present.[113] The poetry of earlier periods treated "big things" and "epic subjects" that fit well within traditional poetry's measured lines and regular metres. These subjects are not suitable for moderns, Hulme contended; and Pound complied with his suggestions by changing the metrical patterns of English verse, steering it away from constructions based on equidurational units. But it is, perhaps, the painting of James Whistler (1834-1903) that provided the paradigm of the subject matter appropriate to the new verse. Whistler was, along with Eliot and Pound, one of the American-expatriate founders of modernism and, like Pound, a brilliant controversialist and energetic polemicist on behalf of the new; and so he, too, was the subject of bitter attacks from people (like Ruskin) of more conservative disposition. Against such attacks from traditionalists, Hulme proclaimed that what has "found expression in painting as Impressionism will soon find expression in poetry as free verse."

One implication of Hulme's anti-Platonic thinking that neither Pound, nor Eliot, nor, so far as I am aware, any poet of their time, took up was that the form of the art work is not a transcendent entity. But, while the modernists continued to think of aesthetic form as Ideal, apprehended through pure, non-rational aesthetic intuition, the Open Form poets did not: they proposed instead that form was something felt on the nerves of the feeling body, a series of sensations, throbs, pulsations, surging, and waning energy. Thus they integrated aesthetic form into the field of being. Olson, as we shall see, worked out the implications of this by adopting concepts from A.N. Whitehead's philosophy.

Summing up his thoughts about the new poetry, Hulme asserted that it "has become definitely and finally introspective and deals with expression and communication of momentary phases in the poet's mind."[114] He stressed the formally disruptive implications of the modernists' concern with the interior life: "We are no longer concerned that stanzas shall be shaped and polished like gems, but rather that some vague mood shall be communicated. In all the arts, we seek for the maximum of individual and personal expression, rather than for the attainment of any absolute beauty."[115]

The statement announces Hulme's wish to turn the norms of art away from objective measure to the truths of inwardness—a turn that has since proved characteristic of modernist aesthetics.[116] The utopian project implicit in the writings of Antonin Artaud, the total *Book of Consciousness* that would contain every detail of his thoughts, called for similarly subjective standards. For Artaud's works imply that the standard by which we should judge a work of art is not how lucid and harmonious the arrangement of its elements is, but how closely it approaches the ideal of embodying the maximum of consciousness. Hulme shared Antonin Artaud's interest in having art convey qualities of its maker's consciousness, but he did not take up Artaud's totalizing aspiration. As conforms to Hulme's notion of subjectivism, modern art was to become tentative, modest, and Impressionistic, and was to avoid grand schemes or any effort to create grand schemes that construct an all-encompassing epic vision, whether that vision be based in philosophy, science, religion, or mythology.

Brakhage stands with Stein in the circle of exemplary artists who have devoted their efforts to this endeavour; Pound and Joyce were, with decidedly greater ambivalence, given to the same enterprise.[117] But emphasis on subjective experience is common in modern life. As Nietzsche foretold and the existentialists so cogently explained, with the waning of religion the traditional belief that values have objective grounding collapsed. Humans met starkly with the terrifying challenge to bring truth and value out of themselves, to create truth and value in a realm where none is given. When people rejected the belief that the natural world is God's creation, the external world lost its ground and melted into air—no, worse, it dissolved into nothingness. According to the traditional teachings, the cosmos has a design and serves an end and each existent has a role in the cosmic scheme, to which its nature fits it. The modern worldview rejected the interrelated ideas that nature has a purpose and that the values of individual existents are objective. Having lost certitude that values have an objective existence that follows from the order of reality, humans turned inward, to discover values in subjective intensity and creativity.

Brakhage's films exemplify the interest in subjectivity that Hulme proclaimed to be the future of art. Brakhage sometimes refers to his films as documents of consciousness. He considers them works that impart to their viewers the energies of the events that occur in the manifold of his vision. The scrupulous care with which he remembered (sometimes through a feat of imagination) and conveyed the evolution of his vision from earliest infancy to later childhood in *Scenes from Under Childhood* testifies to the importance he accords the study of subjective life.[118] *Scenes from Under Childhood* makes equally clear that he deems the scrutiny of consciousness to have moral importance. He began work on the film upon the birth of his first boy, when he realized he had a male rival for his wife Jane's love. To feel unalloyed love for the boy, he posited, he must empathize with him; and to empathize with him, he must strive to understand his inward life, so far as is possible. The qualification is cardinal: Brakhage's dedication to an individualism of the thoroughgoing Emersonian brand commits him to the belief that nobody has access to the contents of another's mind. The alternative he conceived to knowing his son's mind was to recollect how *he* saw at stages in his own childhood development, to reactivate, as far as that is possible, the visual mechanisms of his own childhood. He strove to see again as he had seen as a child. Through seeing as a child, he would come to understand one child's—his own—fears, delights, exhilarations, and despairs, and awareness of that child's fears and delights might enlarge his capacity for having sympathy with children.

Brakhage expounded his convictions about the three-termed relation among vision, individuality, and authenticity in remarks he made when he first exhibited his enormously troubled and enormously troubling 8mm film from 1966, *Song 23: 23ʳᵈ Psalm Branch*—one of the 8mm *Songs* series that was Brakhage's major effort of the mid- to late 1960s. The film embodies Brakhage's response to television's bringing the Vietnam War into his household. His discussion of the triangular relations among vision, individuality, and authenticity took the form of a recommendation. He explained that the particular size, colour, and pattern of dots in a television raster induce a form of self-reflection in which the viewer feels that he is watching his or her own memories being replayed in the theatre of the mind. As he puts it, the viewer comes en-meshed, or made-up-of, the television-scanning 'dots' which closely approximate his most private vision—his sense of his own optic nerve-end activity, seen as a grainy field of 'light'-particles when his eyes are closed, particles which seem to cluster into shapes in the act of memory and, thus, make-up the picture being re-membered [Brakhage often uses the word "remembered" as he does here, to suggest the way that memory re-members events or objects, i.e., pieces them back together from components.] as if it were a slide cast from the brain against closed eye-lids, particles which seem to explode into brilliant coloration and, often, geo-/sym-metrical patterns when the closed-eyes are rubbed.

He goes on to offer this counsel:

I ALSO suggest tilting your head while watching T.V.—an act which turns 'linear' to some verticality and, for some mysterious reason, makes the dots much less visible. But, these are finally only 'tricks' played on the machine itself and, as such, a too-simple patch-work against ultimate disaster. One must become aware of one's own inner-eye workings and thus, come to know television for what IT is, defeat ITS hyp-goggles at source in self.

ONE of the most useful meditations, in this respect, is the conscious act of remembering a T.V.-image—a careful and deliberate attention to the process of memory itself in calling forth a television scene . . . a seeing of it taking shape on the grainy-field of your own closed eyes, the pulse with which it comes back at you, the coloring it takes onto itself, et cetera . . . this, at least, restores the T.V. 'original' to your own physiological consciousness. I discovered the effectiveness of this process while making *23rd Psalm Branch*, a feature-length war film; and I found it to be the only way I could experience the newsreels of my childhood AND that 'staged' slaughter in Vietnam which T.V. brings daily into my home, in a creative way—that is, as an existent reality. Otherwise, it's just the old pea-and-the-nut trick: I somehow KNEW the pea was up the politician's sleeve; but I didn't know how it got there: and the politician's hand is faster than the preconditioned eye, but NOT faster than the inner eye's ability, thru memory, to play the whole trick back in extreme slow motion, with personally creative interpretation (in the mind's edit of the parts of the image re-membered, the order of objects called-forth having a meaningful continuity, or personal message, akin to any wordless comic strip or silent movie sequence) and 'colored' to suit, or express, your own deepest emotional response (the closed eyes flashing banks of color rhythmically in the act of memory thus, express the feelings of the person as surely as rhythmically structured 'tones' of music express a composer's feelings). TELEVISION dumped the implication of monstrous war guilt into my living room; and every conceivable hypnotic means of that medium seemed to imply its filthy (striptease/top-seek) pictures originated in ME and that its, thus, prophetic imperialism was/will-be an absolute necessity of my continued living. I was, thus, 'bugged' in the fullest sense of the word and had to go back, memory-wise to the sources of that trick in my life: the somewhat similar noose-reels of my World War II years under child's hood—1938 thru 1945 . . . : and the *23rd Psalm Branch*, the film I created OUT of these struggles, does illuminate the whole process of pictured war sufficiently to enable me to say, with Michael McClure (from "Poisoned

Wheat") "I AM NOT GUILTY. I AM A MEAT CREATURE": and to watch
my T.V. set from where I AM.[119]

Brakhage relates illusionism to failures in self-knowledge and failures in self-knowledge to moral failure. Illusionism draws one into another place and time and makes one take another's vision as one's own. To do this is to lose the source and ground of one's authentic (because individual) being. He goes on to correlate one's personal understanding with the fullness of one's subjective experience. The closer one comes to grasping and acknowledging the complete contents of one's subjective life, the more authentically one lives and the larger are one's capacities for empathy. Hulme, as far as I can discover, was the first to theorize the importance of subjectivity in terms that resemble Pound's and Brakhage's beliefs on the topic.

Brakhage's title for the film, and the concluding remark in the passage quoted from above—"the film . . . does illuminate the whole process of pictured war sufficiently to enable me to say, with Michael McClure . . . 'I AM NOT GUILTY. I AM A MEAT CREATURE': and to watch my T.V. set from where I AM"—evokes rich associations. The Twenty-third Psalm pays tribute to God's protection of, and goodness towards, the upright; the poem uses the images of the Good Shepherd and the banquet host to imply those qualities. Furthermore, the form or type represented by the Twenty-third Psalm has relevance to the character of Brakhage's *23rd Psalm Branch*. The founder of biblical form-criticism, Hermann Gunkel, classified Psalm 23 as one of the psalms of confidence (along with Psalms 4, 11, 16, 62, 161). The seed of this type of psalm (which, after all, like all psalm forms, is a type of song) is the motif of trust, a motif that also appears in the psalms of lament (in which, frequently, there is first an expression of unbridled personal agony, often expressed as a cry for help and concludes with the expression of certainty that the Lord has heard and answered the psalmist's prayer). Brakhage's *23rd Psalm Branch* wants to be a psalm of confidence (this is exactly what Brakhage stated in talk that I quoted from, and like its biblical model incorporates the motif of trust, but with this troubling difference: unlike the psalmist, Brakhage does not ever find the certainty that his cry of personal anguish is heard and answered. Like most psalms of confidence, it exhibits features of the psalms of lament; but unlike the biblical psalms of confidence, Brakhage's *23rd Psalm Branch* is overwhelmed by lamentation.

That *23rd Psalm Branch* wants to be work of the same type as the Twenty-third Psalm is one reason Brakhage titled the film as he did. There are more specific similarities that justify naming the film after the biblical source: the film is concerned about crossing "the valley of the shadow of death"—Brakhage concretizes his feelings about the travails of the situation in the comparisons between the landscapes of Colorado and Vietnam that first appear near the beginning of the film, and reappear several times subsequently. Furthermore, throughout *23rd Psalm Branch* Brakhage strives to engender the feeling that the Lord's comfort accompanies him in his journey, that the Lord's rod and staff shelter him from all adversity. But among the psalms of trust, the Twenty-third Psalm is remarkably restrained in its lack of exuberant expression of thanks for God's protection; nor is there any statement to reveal that the psalmist received an oracle of salvation. Its conclusions seem uncharacteristically (for the *Book of Psalms*) tentative; in this sense the Twenty-third Psalm represents a deviation—a branching off from— the other psalms, just as *23rd Psalm Branch*, by its length and its incorporation of social themes, deviates from the norm and pattern of Brakhage's *Songs*.

Walter Brueggemann revised Gunkel's classification of the psalms; the morphology he developed sheds further light on parallels between Brakhage's film and its biblical antecedent. Following up on a theme of Paul Ricoeur, Brueggemann distinguishes between what he calls: "psalms of orientation," such as Psalms 8, 33, and 104, which suggest that all is right with the world; "psalms of disorientation," laments such Psalms 13, 74, and 88; and "psalms of new orientation," which include, among others, Psalms 30 and 66, as well as the Twenty-third Psalm. The new orientation, to be sure, is not simply a psychological phenomenon, for it can result from God showing the nation, represented through metonymy in a single person, a new path. A new path—a path that can be trod by an innocent or can even accomplish the paradoxical feat of restoring innocence—is just what Brakhage searched for in making *23rd Psalm Branch*, and just what he proclaims he has found in the passage just quoted; what is more important, the film's travel motif, its depictions of Viennese streets, and even (peculiarly) its visit to the Old World, whose age might have inoculated it against America's callow barbarity, indicate its attempt to find "a new path." The attempt to discover a means to restore lost innocence that is the basis for Brueggemann's classification is a venerable theme of American literature, and relates to the theme of the American Adam, which finds exemplary expression in the extraordinary writings of Ralph Waldo Emerson.

Brakhage states that he desired what every decent, sentient non-Vietnamese desired during that miserable period of recent history—a desire to overcome feelings of war guilt, a desire to be able to say: "I am not guilty." Brakhage discusses the role of certain experiments with media— titling one's head while watching T.V. so that scan lines run vertically, against the horizontal direction of most eye movement—as well as that of confronting the source of one's terror and imaginatively transforming it through the creative process—but he does not discuss the role that, according to the implications of the film's form, the body plays.

Yet, the role the film assigns to the body is crucial. For one thing, as Gail Camhi (drawing on Brakhage's own claims that the film presents war as natural disaster) points out, the film depicts war as a natural phenomenon: "As a disease that has entered the bloodstream and is already a dynamic that one suffers, Brakhage's view of 'war as natural disease' finds resonance in a myriad of instances where through the collective tools of montage, paint, and, in several instances, insertions of language, he forges a run 'through the shadow of the valley of death [sic]."[120] Though she doesn't use the term, Camhi offers the insight that Brakhage uses painting on film and the other techniques she lists to create somagrammes. Immediately after the opening section (which combines monochrome blue shots of rocks, filmed to make them move erratically, domestic scenes and stock shots of World War II, edited to a rapid, insistent pulse), the film presents the images of piles of bodies that the German government produced in the first half of the fifth decade of the twentieth century. Brakhage paints over these images; and, while Camhi stresses both the integrative role of this painting over visual representations (in effecting a tensioned merger of the diegetic space of World War II footage and that of the Colorado imagery) and its representational role (in presenting alternative modes of vision to ordinary eyesight), and its subjectivizing effect (and the dialectic between inner and outer), the painting on film has another role as well: the painted forms are created as a result of pressures arising from the body and they impress somatic energies into the work's visual forms.[121] That, indeed, is why the first instance of painting on film appears when the piled up products of the death industry are presented—Brakhage answers the vision that sees human flesh as a industrial commodity by painting over the corpses, as though in an effort to imbue them with the animal body's vital energies.[122]

The images of the piled-up corpses, overlaid with painted somagrammes, are followed directly by frames uniformly filled with a single colour from frame edge to frame edge; these homogeneous colour frames remain on the screen only for a short time—in sequence they create a strong pulsing effect. This form of construction follows on Brakhage's conception of film form as an embodiment of energy; and in this regard, it resembles the principal strategy Brakhage deploys in a subsequent work in the same series, *American 30's Song (Song 30)*, 1969. In fact, the resemblances between the two songs (*Song 23* and *Song 30*) are many: both offer rather troubled depictions of the Colorado landscape, but invoke memories of the filmmaker's early years (of the Great Depression era in America and the era of World War II); both include aerial overviews of landscape; both make use of rapid montage. But the most important similarity is that both films rely on the extensive use of visual forms whose principal meaning is achieved not through semantic reference but through the material effect on the viewer's perceptual/somatic faculties of the energy they embody.

American 30's Song announces its reliance on such an actional conception of meaning by its use of pulsating geometric forms that Brakhage creates by filming tarmac, guardrails, etc., through airplane and automobile windows with a long lens. The abstraction created by the elimination of the contextualizing background and the hyperbolization of movement—both effects of using the most extreme telescopic settings of the zoom lens—serve to provoke a sense of rootlessness and the itinerancy so common in 1930s America (when unemployed people crisscrossed the country, as the film suggests Brakhage does). But they also have a significance that surpasses that disclosed by any hermeneutical endeavour—for they present themselves, simply, as kinetic forms. It is as though to counteract the threat of loss of home, of place, and, finally, of the reality of place—a loss that we can easily associate with the absence involved in representation—Brakhage summons up non-representational effects (whose reality is guaranteed by their effectivity) to serve as a ground.

Those visual forms of *23rd Psalm Branch*, whose principal meaning is most evidently achieved not through semantic reference but through their material effect on the viewer's perceptual/somatic faculties, are the pulsating colour frames and the black frames (which usually occur in pairs) between images. Gail Camhi interprets these interpolations as recreating the rhythmic pulse of video, a medium that is at the centre of the film's concerns, and as self-reflexive references to the black frames that filmmakers who work in 8mm use to conceal splice bars (a black or white horizontal line across the frame that indicates where two shots have been joined together).[123] The first notion of their use is almost certainly accurate, the second, right in all its essentials, though it is in need of elaboration, since Brakhage rarely attempts to conceal splice bars in either his 8mm or 16mm filmmaking. In fact he often makes the splice bar extremely pronounced by placing it in areas of the frame where it is sure to be noticed (a construction Brakhage used at several points in *23rd Psalm Branch*). Camhi's second suggestion for the role of the interpolated black frames simply needs to be refined. P. Adams Sitney introduces the necessary refinement in *Visionary Film*; he points out that the film is constructed from hundreds of shots, and that it is this highly constructed character that necessitated the interpolation of a pair of black frames between shots, in order to prevent an unmanageable torrent of visible splice bars.[124]

Additional roles for this form of construction suggest themselves: I have already pointed out that the pulsations created by the colour frames or by the interpolation of black frames separating shots have somatic effects that Brakhage evidently relates to the work's affective conditions; the interpolation of the black frames separating the shots has a similar effect. Second, these pulsating colour fields and black frames serve rhythmic purposes that Brakhage conceived for his entire *Songs* cycle. As the discussion after the April 22, 1967 screening of the film at New York's Film-makers' Cinematheque reveals, during the period in which he made the *Songs*, Brakhage took an intense interest in the music of the French composer Olivier Messiaen.[125] Messiaen propounded the theory of rhythm that made the concept of non-retrogradable (i.e., palindromic) rhythms central. When the theft of Brakhage's 16mm camera (and his impecuniousness, which made him unable to purchase new 16mm equipment) forced him into making the *Songs* on 8mm stock, he realized the applicability of Messiaen's ideas to (specifically) 8mm filmmaking: 8mm projectors run at a variety of speeds, and can be stopped and reversed while the film is loaded. Accordingly, Brakhage was concerned to create films that could stand up to being projected at various speeds, or could run forward or backward. Messiaen also insisted on the importance of using durative values that span the range from very small to very large, and that lack any sense of being created by repeating a module that marks out one unit of duration. The irregular, non-repetitive rhythmic structures that Brakhage uses in the *Songs* show Messiaen's influence, and the pairs of black frames may well represent the minimal unit, the importance of which is stressed in Messiaen's rhythmic theories.

Third, and perhaps most important, these black or homogeneously coloured frames indicate moments of negative hallucination (see glossary)—moments when excessively strong affects overwhelm consciousness and induce hiatuses into the manifold of awareness. That the negative hallucination has a role in our fear of the ultimate and terminal rent in awareness explains why Brakhage should have made use of this form of construction in a film about death. Even more, it explains why Brakhage inserted these chromatic interpolations at moments when the horror of the film's imagery seems to halt the film's forward thrust.

23rd Psalm Branch is evidently a film concerned with violence (Brakhage's commentary also makes that clear), and the extraordinary intricacy of its montage relates to this violence in a particularly fascinating manner. The British psychoanalyst Wilfred R. Bion is one among many of the object relations school who extended psychoanalytic methods towards an understanding of psychotic thinking. Bion developed in particular the Kleinian ideas of splitting and projective identification, the characteristic defense mechanisms of the paranoid-schizoid position. Taking as his starting point for this extension the idea that aggression can be turned inwards, Bion notes that hatred of reality can result in turning instinctive aggression inwards. This inversion of aggression has the effect of sabotaging the proper functioning of the

perceptual mechanisms, with the result that external reality is not acknowledged for what it is. One's capacity to sense external reality becomes disorganized, along with one's capacity for self-awareness. One's sense of
external reality becomes massively disorganized, and this sense of reality is
then projected onto reality in the form of myriad, minute fragments. And
because the inversion of aggression also undoes the capacity for linking concepts, the ability to transform reality into a coherent form in thought, or to
reintegrate the sundered world internally, is also lost, leaving the person
defenceless against the sundering of reality. It is the mechanics of this process that drives Brakhage's use of montage in *23rd Psalm Branch*.

The hiatus in the manifold of awareness, induced by the negative hallucination, provokes feelings of helplessness. *23rd Psalm Branch* focuses on
and, to a degree, concretizes this affect in its discourses concerning art's
impotence. The first of these discourses appears some time after Brakhage
has established the range of visual forms that constitute the film's principal
material: domestic images; images of the Colorado landscape; war images,
including images presenting the disaster of war; and overpainting. It consists of words scratched into black leaders: "Take back Beethoven's 9th,
then, he said." Presumably the remark (which alludes to Thomas Mann's
Dr. Faustus, and so to the Faustianism that has corrupted the Western
world in recent times, and even to Beethoven's Faustianism) offers a caus-
tic reference to the joyous conclusion of Beethoven's final symphony—any
hope that all humans will become siblings of one another (*Alle Menschen
werden Brüder*) in an ecstasy of joy must have seemed vain in face of the
carnage that was then taking place in Vietnam; an artist whose hopes are so
dashed can only take back his or her works in an act of defiance that,
although one knows it will be utterly futile, will at least spare the work the
mocking assaults perpetrated by the destructive animus of its philistinely
aggressive environment.

The despair concerning the role of art that *23rd Psalm Branch* conveys has
deep roots in the conceptual and affective content of the film, for it wells up
as the anguish that develops as the negative hallucination destroys all mental representations and creates a hiatus in the manifold of awareness; the
destruction wreaked by the negative hallucination threatens one of Brakhage's most cherished beliefs—the Romantic belief, expounded with
extraordinary force and beauty in his major mythopoeic film *Dog Star Man*—
that the imagination is capable of reintegrating a disassociate sensibility in
which reason and emotion have become separated and can merge human
consciousness and nature. For the negative hallucination can be fuelled by
the mechanism of identification with the aggressor, and it answers the
destructiveness of the external world with a destructiveness of its own (a

phenomenon that makes it all the more difficult for Brakhage to genuinely feel that he is not guilty of complicity in society's destructive bent); what is more, the process reveals the impotence of imagination—negative imagery insists on penetrating the inner recesses of consciousness, and the self cannot keep it out, nor can the imagination (the self's true activity) transform it, so forcefully and insistently does it impose itself on consciousness. And since the imagination cannot transform such brutally insistent material—cannot make the representations its own—it presents itself to consciousness as an alien entity, not as an image that accomplishes the ideal that the Romantics conceived for it, of fusing self and world. The terrible force with which the imagery of the Vietnam War impacts consciousness defeats the protections offered by the normal process of projection and introjection (see glossary), as it allows "bad objects" to enter the interior chamber of consciousness and fails to shelter "good objects" there; this is the meaning of the story of imagery of the Vietnam War entering the Brakhage household.

What is more, the Twenty-third Psalm in the Bible is a song of praise to successfully achieved introjection. The psalmist declares, "Yea, though I walk through the valley of the shadow of death, I will fear no evil: for Thou *art* with me; thy rod and thy staff they comfort me" (Psalm 23:4 AV). Internalizing love's comforting capacity is the very essence of introjection. One can be even more concrete about the psalm's allusion to the processes of projection and introjection: for the rod that the fourth verse refers to is a club shepherds used to fend off wild animals, while the staff is a crooked instrument they used to keep the sheep from wandering off. One kept the sheep within the protective fold; the other kept out beasts that threatened to attack and destroy the innocent creatures within the fold. The Twenty-third Psalm's image of the rod and staff relates to the opposition of inside and outside that structures *23rd Psalm Branch* and to the psychological defense mechanism of introjection and projection.

For a filmmaker who has celebrated the triumph of imagination, as Brakhage has, to feel that imagination is impotent is a threatening experience; the desperate acceleration of the pace of the film conveys the anxiety Brakhage felt to demonstrate that, in the end, the creative imagination can prevail even over destructive forces as strong and unrelenting as this blood-drenched century has unloosed. The strength of feeling that the sense of the impotence of imagination induced in Brakhage is also indicated by the centrality in *23rd Psalm Branch* of a dichotomizing structure, which opposes in a nearly schematized fashion several types of images: images from the past with images from the present; images from Brakhage's personal space (domestic scenes and the Colorado landscape) and the more distant, less personal spaces of the outside world; images of home and images of war;

forms painted by hand and historical footage. The structuring principle behind all these oppositions is the dialectic between personal space and an alien phenomenon that intrudes upon that personal space—a dialectic the imagination struggles (though at first without success) to resolve. What gives that principle its affective power is the feeling of the ineluctability facticity of the alien destructive forms of the outside world as they intrude into the space of consciousness that resembles the force with which television's images of the Vietnam War intruded into the Brakhage house, imposed themselves on the household, and created strife there—of the imagination's inability to make an alien phenomenon into its own. Among the tragic destructions that the film treats is that of the normal defences of projection and introjection necessary to give the imagination (the self) a safe place to be, for when the self feels exposed and vulnerable, the whole world becomes a place of terror and destruction. This is exactly the *imago mundi* that *23rd Psalm Branch* presents.

The text "Take back Beethoven's 9th, then, he said" is followed by a long panning shot of passing landscapes that are distinguished from those of the long prologue by being more legible. In keeping with the film's structure of opposition, Brakhage introduces many images of destruction into this lateral movement of the panning shot: a montage of explosions; then explosions combined with guns firing; the explosion of an atomic bomb; land submerged under a flood; a cannon firing; water bursting over a dam; more bombs; and a green-hued image of the façade of an apartment being brought down by wreckers; burning buildings; a boat sinking; and bombs exploding in the sky. That the film evolves its structure from the polarization of opposites, and from a desperate attempt to effect an imaginative reconciliation of those opposites, becomes even more evident as Brakhage brings together images of the Colorado landscape and images of destruction. Brakhage intercuts brief shots of the Colorado landscape with historical footage depicting a man working with a detonating device: the man establishes the necessary conditions, crouches near the device, and a bomb explodes in a landscape with mountains that resemble those near Brakhage's home.

A passage of pulsating colour frames follows, then an image of the filmmaker sitting in the sun with his shirt off, composing a letter. The shot is taken with a rapidly moving camera, so we cannot see very much of the letter he is composing; however, we can read its beginning: "Dear Jane, The checker boards and zig-zags of man" and, on the next line, the important word "Nature." The reference to zig-zags is signal: the psalmist, in the Twenty-third Psalm, declares that the Lord "leadeth me in the paths of righteousness for His name's sake" (Psalm 23:3 AV). For a more accurate (if less poetic) translation of the original, "paths of righteousness" would be "paths of rightness," and some less distinguished translations actually give it as "right paths." As an avid reader of Olson, Brakhage would be likely to connect "right" with "straight" and to conceive of "the zig-zags of man" as paths of errancy. God's mild kindness, testified to by the psalm's image of the Good Shepherd, is needed to keep humans on right paths, and it is that kindness which the film calls upon to restore a sense of innocence, of belonging to a flock of sheep tended to by the Good Shepherd.

After showing us these words, the camera whirls away from the letter (as though to confirm that humans are constantly on the go, without roots), and we see stones, the ground sweeping by, flashes of sun with a bluish cast (possibly to convey that the filmmaker is seeing the air as filled with orgonic energy), and then painted forms, applied to the film's emulsion, in a myriad of colours. The images of stones, dynamized ground, and the sun filling the air with orgonic energy suggest Brakhage's efforts to endow the alien world of Nature with attributes of consciousness; the painting-on-film, on the other hand, suggests the realm of the subject (as it so often does in Brakhage's films). True to the film's pattern of dichotomies, the images that follow present domestic scenes (i.e., of events belonging to the filmmaker's personal space): we see pictures of the home, images of his children playing naked and riding a sled, less rapid shots of laundry hung out to dry, which seem serene until one notices the ominous shadow—the ominousness of which the slower pace of these shots emphasizes—of trees on a sheet and several static images of a sculpture of human form, centring on a head that lacks facial features. These images are joined by very disruptive and aggressive splice bars (which again provide evidence of the filmmaker's complicity in acts of destruction). Soon after the faceless sculpted head, we see an image of a sleeping child, who reappears shortly afterwards with paint over her face; the relation between the child and the faceless sculpted head is that between a personalized and an impersonal imagery, another form of relation between personal and alien realms. In constructing this opposition Brakhage extends his despairing discourse on art.

There follow shots of clouds, taken from an airplane; these images are marked with a very pronounced frame line across the top of the screen—another form that indicates the destructive impulses the filmmaker experiences as the violent, alien world intrudes on his personal space. Violent bursts of clear leader strengthen the sense that Brakhage is engaging in acts of formal violence. Further, the shots taken from the airplane illustrate the idea of "zig-zigs" and "checker boards of man." The montage incorporates images of the wings of airplanes, of the dead, of crematoria.

Then the range of imagery expands somewhat, and the montage seems to hold a more dispersed set of images in a tentative unity. Night lights of a city appear, at first as superimposition. Then we see a newsreel image containing the name "NAGASAKI"; that image is met with another presenting the New York skyline. The relation between the two images is a relation between "here" and "there," between "America" and "the Far East"; it is, therefore, another version of the relation between personal space and the outside realm that provides the film with its central structuring principle.

Another passage of pulsating colour fields appears, then another passage of forms created by applying paint directly to the film. Then we see a book open on the table. It is Louis Zukofsky's *A*, and it lies open at the beginning of its eleventh section, a passage that declares the desire to raise grief to song; as P. Adams Sitney points out, to raise grief to song is the very aspiration of *23rd Song Branch*.[126] More images of explosions and bombs going off mark the end of this passage; thus, while the images in the immediately preceding passage belong to the personal realm, the images incorporated into this montage belong to the public realm.

The next images, of stick figures from 2500 B.C.E. that hint of violence, also relate to the intrusion of the outer world of violence into the inner recesses of consciousness and to the inability of imagination to triumph over the violent *données*; as if to insist that the childlike drawings belong to the inner realm, Brakhage intercuts them with images of his own face. The drawings drop out for a time and, to stress the references to interiority, he intercuts images of his face with intervals of black leader (which again signify the gap in consciousness that the negative hallucination creates). The montage continues as Brakhage returns to ancient graphics depicting warriors and to medieval drawings documenting war; these drawings and graphics constitute another instance of artists engaging, through narrative, in the violence of the world. The rhythm of this montage continues as these graphics transform into picture fragments presenting reproductions of ancient warriors in battle (the provenance of the representation is not clear to me). The transformation from graphic images to picture fragments again indicates how the violence of the outer realm imposes itself upon consciousness. A schematized, almost cartoonish, account—*narrative*—of battle follows (which, in its use of images to recount a narrative resembles a film). It presents one figure with a shield and spear, standing victoriously and grinding his opponent under his heel. The standing figure is white, and the figure ground under his heel is black, so Brakhage probably used it for its suggestion of the racial motivation for war—certainly it is an image that Brakhage took as indicating the psychological factors that lead humans to make war. This image of oppression breaks up in red flares (to signify violence); when an image returns, introduced as the camera draws away from its subject, it is the face of the poet Louis Zukofsky, and then, through another zoom, that of his wife, composer Celia Zukofsky. A series of images of wrecked buildings, interspersed with very convulsive flashes of homogeneously coloured frames, precedes a re-presentation of the poet's image, which presents him as a frail and deliberate-looking man. Zukofsky's deliberateness suggests the inner realm, so, in conformity with the film's fundamental structuring pattern, the film veers off into historical footage which, since it is introduced through the mediation of Zukofsky's Jewishness, presents images of products of the German death factories of World War II. The implication of bringing together the image of Zukofsky's face and the historical footage of the death factories shortly after the more insistent presentation of Brakhage's own face is that Brakhage is reflecting on the possibility that the great poet could so easily have been among the victims of the National Socialist tyranny. This implication, too, derives from central structuring opposition, for the victimization of imaginative people by a brutal polity lies on the same axis as the penetration of brutal images or, more generally, brutal representations into the more sensitive reaches of consciousness. But Zukofsky's face is calm and gentle, and is the first appearance in the film of an artist who does not engage with, or even promote, the violence of the circumambient world, but transcends its through his imagination; to use Brueggemann's term, Zukofsky's face shows the possibility of—or is a beacon light towards—the new path.

More black leader follows (again indicating that the effect of this violence is to produce a negative hallucination). Between these pulsating stretches of black leader, Brakhage presents images of himself sitting in front of Roy Lichtenstein's famous painting of man pointing a gun. The gun is pointed directly at the back of Brakhage's head; so the aggression that has been a central topic of the film is now turned inward, toward the filmmaker; this helps explains the film's melancholic tone. Camhi points out that the rhythm of black intervals here is similar to that which introduced images of individual victims in the German death factories.[127] This passage, therefore, is a sort of threnody for the victims of violence, a class that includes most of the art world in the present era of its degeneracy, in which it has been taken up by the spirit of the time and deploys images of violence without being troubled by them.

As though to counteract the violence of Lichtenstein's art, more images of Zukofsky follow, intercut with concentration camps. Then city traffic lights appear and, seemingly, zoom towards the picture plane and then off the screen. Then the lights move, so that when they reappear on the screen, they seem to zoom into the image's haptic space, only now mediated by a television screen. We see the poet Louis Zukofsky and his composer-wife, Celia, in a living room; in the room is a checkered tablecloth, recalling the phrase "The checker boards and zig-zags of man" (which, quite possibly, the movement of traffic lights illustrates).

The introduction of shots of cities, including an image of the New York sky-line, provides the basis for deliberation on the notion of the mass. Brakhage's examination of documentary and television footage of crowds, taken when they were especially inflamed, led him to the conclusion that crowds mass in distinctive configurations whose shapes reveal the violent feelings contained within the crowd. Brakhage presents the evidence for, and summarizes the results of, these deliberations in the form of a montage. We see: armies marching in rows; a large wedding celebration viewed from above; a ticker-tape parade; police engaged in the all-too-common behaviour of beating people; Hitler working a crowd into an apparent frenzy; then bombs bursting, some worthies (perhaps royalty) in a carriage in a procession; tanks firing.

Although Brakhage's meditation on the behaviour of the masses might seem tangential to the film's central concerns, the implicit association actually is anything but remote. Wilfred Bion hypothesized that paranoid-like anxieties provide the impetus for group formation; what Brakhage conjectures is that the configuration of crowds embodies the group dynamics, and that the expression of paranoid-like anxieties that fuel these group dynamics can be discerned in these configurations. What is more, Brakhage's introduction to *23rd Psalm Branch* expressed his longing for a protective, internalized *imago*—essentially for what Bion refers to as the maternal entity—while Bion also shows that the longing for the maternal entity is involved in the formation of groups. The idea that Brakhage formulates to relate the longing for the maternal entity and the dynamics of violence is that he himself possesses longings that can easily transmute into a paranoid-like form and in that form they can instigate the pathological formation of groups. This belief returns us to Brakhage's statement quoted at the beginning of this section, concerning his feelings of culpability. Of course, Brakhage himself would not likely set out the ideas in just this way, but they are amenable to being laid out in the form I have. The structure of the film and the statements he actually did make about it indicate Brakhage's powers to formulate psychological insights, at least implicitly; *23rd Psalm Branch* connects a cluster of psychological ideas that required a thinker as astute as Bion to relate.

At the end of the crowd scenes, the montage becomes hyperaccelerated, then comes to an arrest with the appearance of the third, handwritten text, "I can't go on." However, the montage does resume, immediately. We see heads of Western states, including Churchill, Roosevelt, Hitler, and Mussolini, passing a pen one to another and signing some document (as though to imply the equivalence of one head of state to another); over top of them Brakhage superimposes dots which graph their movements. The signing ceremony is intercut with additional war footage, to indicate that the actions in which the participants in the ceremony engage (both the historical incidents represented in the footage and the movements graphed by the patterns of moving dots) perpetrate violence.

The dots that were superimposed over the previous scene are now presented autonomously, in rigid straight lines. To these Brakhage adds dots drawn freehand, in black ink. The two sorts of dots seem at odds; then Brakhage adds a red background, likely to suggest blood. This construction is followed by an explosion of images that convey the destructive bent of the modern social order (and perhaps any social order): crowds, parades, airplanes, boats, official trains, tanks, bombs, weaponry, and assorted and sundry disasters. We next see a single airplane, on fire and in free fall, slowly plunging to its destruction, perhaps to convey the effect on specific individuals of the actions taken by the heads of state—the action is prolonged and made more tragic by the use of black leader. Brakhage's use of prolongation here makes us feel the individual's plight.

There follows a passage containing four images, one in each quadrant of the screen. The passage was created by photographing with a double-eight camera, which records two frames, one atop the other, on one half of the 16mm frame; then when the roll runs out, the film is turned over, and the other half of the 16mm frame is exposed. Because the roll is inverted (to make the second exposure by being flipped over to run tail to head), the images on one side are right side up and the images on the other are upside down and run backwards; ordinarily the 16mm roll is split at the lab, and the two halves reoriented to run consecutively. Brakhage, however, had the original printed as a 16mm frame, and so four images appear on the screen. This section's length and relative lack of fragmentation (at least so far as concerns its primary gestalt), at least in comparison with the hyperaccelerated montage that precedes it, provides a moment of calm. And, as P. Adams Sitney notes, its cyclical character (forward movement on one side, backward on the other) "dissolves the tension of the film by suggesting that the events depicted are cyclic while it reduces the illusion to cinematic physicality."[128] The comment is both judicious and, as far as it goes, accurate, though perhaps somewhat one-sided: while the passage does relax the tension somewhat, I do not think it dissolves all tension. For the circularity of the passage suggests to me that the convulsions of the time are part of the cycle of history—events that have come around before and will come around again; this, of course relates to the idea that war and violence are natural disasters that belong to the order of existence. Thus, the relaxation of tension is more the result of fatalism than of dispelling illusions about suffering and the concomitant evidencing of truths about film materials.

The film's tension rises again, but it is soon shattered as Brakhage returns to the letter he is writing (to indicate that the film records his personal thoughts, as a letter to an intimate friend ordinarily does). We see the words, "I must stop. The War *is* as thoughts (IDEAS, IMAGES), patterns . . . (RHYTHM) are—as endless as . . . precise as eyes' hell *is*!"

With this the first part of *23ʳᵈ Psalm Branch* ends. The second part, "To Source," presents Brakhage's further deliberations about war as he travelled to Eastern Europe. The division of film into two parts therefore conforms to the same pattern that has informed so many of the film's relations, for the first part presents the domestic (American) situation, the second part the situation of the world beyond America's borders—a division homologous with the opposition between the personal realm and the outside world. After the short prologue that begins Part 2, and shows a lamp superimposed over a landscape and night lights, the film presents two subsections, "Of Peter Kubelka's Vienna" and "My Vienna," the relation between which is evidently structured on the same opposition.

"Of Peter Kubelka's Vienna" intercuts five elements: Peter Kubelka playing his recorder in the warm light of an elegant chandelier; "Stop" and "Go" traffic lights (recalling the traffic lights in the Zukofsky section of Part 1); shots of buildings below; Kubelka walking the streets of Vienna with a child; and a statue in a square. The entire section conveys a sense of well-being, of a harmony not riven by violence. The film literalizes the metaphor of its biblical model, "Thou preparest a table before me in the presence of mine enemies: thou anointest my head with oil; my cup runneth over" (Psalm 23:5 AV). In this section, therefore, the filmmaker seems almost to rise, for once, above the feeling that the art has become complicit in the violence that has become a general feature of our time, and presents a very positive portrait of an artist. Like the Zukofsky figure of Part 1, Kubelka provides a positive figure with whom Brakhage can identify and, by that identification, dispel his feelings that he shares in the world's violent tendencies and so is as morally culpable as anyone.

The "My Vienna" section is four times longer than "Of Peter Kubelka's Vienna." As if to point up the relationship between the two sections, it begins with Brakhage at the same table where we previously saw Kubelka sitting and playing the recorder. At first he smokes a cigar ("a cigar is just a cigar"), but then adopts a posture and attitude that contrast with that of his Viennese colleague—he sits with his head resting on his arms, which are folded on the table, and he seems drunk. The image is fragmented by pulsating interruptions of black leader and, as with the image of the burning airplane, the use of these interruptions has the effect of prolonging the shot and of distending time. The importance of this temporal distension is Brakhage's gestures, for his hand keeps time with some music; both the distension and the gesture signify interiority—the artist is brooding on something, and the black pulsations may even indicate the filmmaker's intoxicated condition by embodying the insistent, thudding, rhythmic pulsation that is such a prominent feature of the experience of drunkenness.

The revelation of what he is brooding on is delayed slightly; before it is presented, we are shown images—of a china dish, from which someone scrapes up the few remaining crumbs of dessert—that convey a sense of the order and well-being of the Old World. They are taken with the camera gently circling around the dish, and the gentleness of movement and the constancy and perfection implied in the form it describes re-enforce this sense of the Old World. But the serenity is invaded by images (thoughts) of another place. However, "My Vienna" inverts the relation between the personal space (subjectivity) and the outside world (objectivity) that characterizes so much of the film's first part and, what is especially important, complicates it. For now images of home and images laden with personal import insist upon filling the filmmaker's mind—on entering this "other place," which the film treats as a place of serenity, harmony, and order. It is as if the image of "here" (Vienna) is also an image of "away" and the image of "home" is also an image of "there"; thus, the polarization at the heart of the film's form begins to break down, as each of the opposites takes on features of the other. We see images of his wife Jane, of his children, of the animals that others of his films have taught us to see as members of the Brakhage household. We see two young children (Neowyn and Bearthm) going about naked, inside and outside the house. The imagery turns into winter scenes and we see children playing on a sled. (The shots of the naked children and of the children playing with their sled are all quotations from one of the earlier *Songs*, a series of portraits that Brakhage did in 1965, entitled *XV Song Traits*.)

The quotations cease, but the images continue to be of Colorado scenes: the door to the house opens and we see a fire burning in the hearth, then Jane appears, in a red blouse, petting a dog. These scenes have a red tone, and so we associate them with similarly red-toned images of the interior of Kubelka's residence and, especially, of a Viennese woman with her children. Thus Brakhage continues to juxtapose images of "home" and "away"; and, indeed, the section proceeds by alternating images of Vienna and Colorado.

As the montage continues, the film seems again to recollect its past, as it did with the shots of the children playing from *XV Song Traits*; like images that invade and disturb the calm that "Of Peter Kubelka's Vienna" had created, these images introduce a new level of violence into the scene. War footage, of a sort familiar from the first part, begins to intrude; thus, the film's own form undergoes the same sort of invasion from the past that Brakhage's own mind does—an idea that provides further ground for the incorporation of the material from *XV Song Traits*, for it is as though that incorporation suggests that the twenty-third of the *Songs* series "remembers" the fifteenth of the series. We are also presented with shots of Brakhage's plaid shirt, an image that recalls the aerial shots of cities and farmland laid out in grids, which were also associated with turmoil and destruction.

The dialectical opposition/synthesis of "here/away" and "there/home" continues as we see first an image of a Viennese schoolgirl returning home, then of the Brakhage children getting into the family car, schoolbooks in hand. The film continues to remember itself, as it presents images of people walking the streets of Vienna reminiscent of those in "Of Peter Kubelka's Vienna," and of Brakhage at the table in Kubelka's home. The alternation of "here/away" images with "there/home" images continues as Brakhage intercuts the sculpture in the public square (also an image remembered from "Of Peter Kubelka's Vienna") to images of Hitler's marching troops taken from a documentary of the period, of the Brakhage children coming home from school, and of Viennese pedestrians. Projecting the dualities that structure the film onto a set of four terms provides the basis for a transformation in the film: from this point to near the end of the "My Vienna" section, there is, as P. Adams Sitney notes, "no fixed locale into which the montage cuts or from which it shifts. . . . Each second brings us to a different place and time."[129] A shot sweeping through the streets of Vienna turns into: a white Colorado landscape; a landscape seen through a car's rearview mirror; an art museum; depictions of equestrian soldiers taken from an illuminated manuscript; pedestrians walking in the streets of Vienna (some of the same streets we saw in the previous sequence); children's drawings; bombs exploding; fire destroying a street; and, from time to time over the length of the sequence, representations of a darker Egyptian warrior felling a lighter enemy warrior. Many of these images indicate again the complicity of contemporary art in the violence of the circumambient world.[130]

The lack of any diegetic space to comprise the images of this section of *23rd Psalm Branch* (which Sitney remarked upon) has a key effect: it shifts the film's contents into the filmmaker's mind so that, for example, the children's drawings in the section, which provide another instance of the film's remembering itself, present themselves as well as the filmmaker's own memories. The lack of a diegetic space for the images, and the consequent impression that the images belong to the interior realm, are key to the concluding sequence. It begins with an image of a stained glass window. The remainder of the sequence is constructed of a number of artistic depictions of Christ, with the central figure always placed in the same spot on the screen, and footage of dead bodies from historical documentaries; from these elements Brakhage constructs a montage that brings into a unity the opposites of the glory of the Crucifixion and the squalor of death in war in a universal image of torment and suffering. The images of Christ also indicate a possible religious basis for Western culture's fascination with suffering, its willingness to endure suffering, and to inflict it; that the representations of Christ Brakhage uses in this passage are artistic depictions indicates art's complicity in this deep involvement with suffering and violence.

The next section borrows for its name the title of H.D.'s famous memoir, *A Tribute to Freud*. The section shows Brakhage retracing the steps that Freud might have followed, going to and leaving from his Viennese home; the identification suggests that Brakhage is engaged in discovering the roots of human violence, as Freud was. The section retracing Freud's perambulations includes: nighttime images and flickering images of streetlights that create a sense of mystery or awe that we associate with Freud's research into the mysterious wellsprings of human behaviour; pure colour frames, pulsating at a rhythm we have come to associate with violence, answer the flicker of street lights and add to the intensity of the mystery. The filmmaker examines the windows of Freud's house and the weathered ironwork of a lantern box near the entrance. He sees a decorative work depicting equestrians, and he associates that sight with images of a monumental sculpture of war chariots. Once again, violent thoughts have invaded the filmmaker's mind, just as he was experiencing a still but mysterious awe. The "A Tribute to Freud" section ends with the camera circling around a statue as dawn seems to be breaking. The statue here, as in "Of Peter Kubelka's Vienna" section, seems to be a more positive cultural expression than is represented by the ancient or modern images that so often engage with violence.

The following section is entitled "Nietzsche's Lamb." The title evokes associations with ideas of the nineteenth-century philosopher's ideas, and specifically the idea of Europe sacrificed to the *Übermensch*. The section fuses, by its use of painting and by editing, images of the skinned lamb (from a performance by the Austrian performance artist Hermann Nitsche) and aerial images of land, maps, and pure painting on film. The identification articulates the idea of the earth being in travail and suffering, while the interpolated passages of painting on film again raise the idea of the negative hallucination.

The section opens with an image of a revolving airplane propeller, as seen from the side, which conveys menace, among other feelings. An array of black dots, similar to those seen towards the end of Part 1, all but overwhelms the photographed image. When the image emerges from the dense overpainting, it has transmuted into one of the lamb's eyes; its bluish form threads itself into the aerial views, boats, city maps (whose forms merge with the cracks in the overpainting), and the red, blue, and black painting-on-film; the fusion of photographed, diagrammed forms and forms created by applying paint to the film stock is particularly interesting for the implication that the photographed forms are emerging through cracks in the paint. This implication can be associated with Brakhage's belief that perceptual representations are formed in a number of stages and arise out of some more primordial mental contents that resemble raw energy—contents that Brakhage often likens to electrical sparkings in the brain that, presumably, resemble the cracks in the paint. The overpainting that dominates this section and the next makes these primordial mental activities manifest.

Further, like the "My Vienna" section, the "Nietzsche's Lamb" section remembers images from previous films in the *Songs*, especially *Song 19* (concerning women's rites). The incorporation of the images of women dancing associates women with the skinned lamb, and so with wounded innocence; but it does more than this, for it also implies that idea's opposite: it associates the women's rite with the ritual of slaughter. The dialectical fusion of those contraries again indicates that innocence (the interior self) is penetrated by violence.

"Nietzsche's Lamb" now seems to leave Europe behind and begin the flight home, for we see an airline flight attendant in the familiar, before take-off ritual, putting on an oxygen mask. No matter that the action is so familiar, the oxygen mask over her face (which many viewers undoubtedly associate with the gas masks of the two world wars) makes her look somewhat sinister. The potential for violence soon expresses itself, as a bomb appears to fall from the plane. The painting on film continues as the lamb's eye reappears (the past haunting the present), superimposed over the sky; the lamb's eye clearly becomes a metaphor for innocent vision. But, as both the filmmaker (through the narrative of the takeoff and the flight) and the lamb's eye are in the sky, the one is identified with the other. This conjunction implies that his vision is as innocent as that of lamb, and is moving towards the point when he can say, "I am not guilty." He is overcoming his terrible sense of the complicity of the artist in the violence of the world.

The identification of the filmmaker with the lamb's eye also implies that the filmmaker's visionary powers are under threat. As though a realization of this peril, there follows a long stretch of black leader, which leads into a very long interval of flares of the sort one finds at the end of reels of film when they come back from the processing laboratory. These flares return us to Europe, and so dispel our belief that the filmmaker was returning home and reveal that suggestion to be merely a wish. They lead into the "East Berlin" section. Through more flares, we see the night lights of a city; Brakhage pans his camera over the streets and shows, at one point, the neon signs of the shops and establishments around some downtown square. The camera

lights upon two women, leaning together as though to keep secrets; they finish up by furtively dragging something down the street.[131] Marching dots
reappear, as if to respond to this act which, of course, has a kinship with violence; these marching dots are soon replaced with overpainting.

The main body of the film comes to an end as we see, scratched into the
film's surface, the title, *23ʳᵈ Psalm Branch*. There is no resolution, however,
so another section, entitled "Coda," follows. It is so named not only because
it follows the film's apparent conclusion but also because it effects a nearly
complete rupture with the rest of the work. It starts off somewhat as a portrait, not unlike those of *15 Song Traits*. In the opening of the "Coda"
sequence, Brakhage makes extensive use of metonymy, presenting, all in a
bluish-tinted monochrome, a part of a man's face, hands, and, in his hands,
what appears to be electronic equipment. It turns out, however, to be a
stringed instrument, though we do not see it very clearly; the gestures that
the man engages in, however, make clear that he is playing a stringed instrument. Over top of the image of the man appears a superimposed image of a
hand waving a feather. The bluish-tinged monochrome gives way, after a few
more superimpositions, to colour footage. We are given, first, an image of a
tapping foot, then a more distant view, showing the whole figure of the
person holding the feather; the woman is playing harp in the woods, plucking
it with a feather. The image is idyllic, and again evokes the sense of the
redemptive power of art, and so provides a sort of refutation of claims about
the worthlessness of art or its complicity in violence. Then we see a close-
up of male hands playing the harp and a double portrait of the two, male and
female, making music.

Thus the section seems to close itself into a satisfying, idyllic circle. That
sense is destroyed when we see Jane and a group of children (presumably
either the Brakhage children, or, since we also see Robert and Bobbie
Creeley in this section, the Creeley children, or both) playing and dancing in
the woods, carrying sparklers that give their activities a menacing character;
over this an image of a donkey fades in and out several times. The passage
gives the sense of an ideal, harmonious world, the world of the first part of
Blake's "The Echoing Green." But there is an irony implicit here as well,
and it soon makes itself apparent. For the economy of the present world is
so structured that with every delight comes danger, and every festivity is
associated with war. We return to the theme of innocents under assault from
a violent, circumambient world. The image of the world as a place of terror
re-presents itself; "Coda" ends with an irresolution as troubling as that
which characterized the end of the work's main body.

Brakhage's *23ʳᵈ Psalm Branch*, then—and indeed all of Brakhage's films,
for *23ʳᵈ Psalm Branch* is quite typical of Brakhage's oeuvre in this respect—

suggests the triumph of subjectivity. Bergson and Hulme's aesthetic ideas exemplify the shift from an objective conception of value to a subjective conception that marked the transition from the pre-modern to the modern paradigm. From antiquity to the medieval period, philosophers had maintained that the values that guide humans in the conduct of their lives are external to the will; to be virtuous is to conform one's will to the Good, which establishes objective standards for the will. Modern philosophers disagreed. We can see the modern paradigm in the process of being formulated in Immanuel Kant's philosophy; but even so, Kant felt the need to defend aesthetic judgments against the accusation that they are merely subjective. He attempted to do this by showing that they are transpersonal. Hulme felt no such need, for in this matter he followed Friedrich Nietzsche. The common sense of modernity regarding goodness has found its most complete expression in the philosophy of Nietzsche, who was among the first to give explicit articulation to the proposition that defines modernity, that good and bad are not given objectively in the order of reality. He realized, too, that the notion of will encapsulates all the qualities that distinguish human from non-human nature. To will is to dictate to nature, to refashion the order of the given to make it accord with our desires. Non-human nature is morally indifferent; willing alone can realize value within a morally indifferent world. The historical process creates greater and greater goodness within the morally indifferent world; hence, it produces an ever-greater distinction between human and non-human nature. History, accordingly, is the domain of will.

This view is the core of the modern *Weltanschauung*. It places willing at the centre of the human universe, and depicts the will as engaged in the circular activity of endlessly bringing forth its own nature. For, as Nietzsche pointed out, what the will itself wants—the natural will, the will that is uncorrupted by those sickly, timid values of Christianity—is the power to choose whatever will enhance its own power. Nietzsche first identified this circuit of willing, and he named it "the Will to Power"; he also analyzed its self-enhancing logic. What the will wills is Power, and Power is simply the strength to realize one's desires; conversely, to realize one's desires is the role of the will. Therefore, the Will to Power is just the will to will. The will selects whatever will strengthen itself. Thus, the nature of willing is to will acts of will. Willing moves in a circular orbit. Like that with which Goethe's Mephistopheles seduces Faust, the pleasure it offers us is to strive without ceasing. The will elects to will and, since what it elects to will is, simply, to will, nothing outside its nature affects it. This is the self-aggrandizing, circular logic by which it operates.

So modernity presents its founding propositions. These ideas have important implications for aesthetics. Plato sometimes described the work of an artist as involving making a transcription from a pre-existing model (as a cabinetmaker does when making a cabinet or a statesperson when fashioning a polis or, even, a doctor in creating health and well-being).[132] The model the artist looks towards exemplifies the good of the things (or events) of the kind he or she makes. That good depends upon how well the object (or event) he or she makes is fitted to serve the ends that objects (or events) of its type are supposed to serve. Thus, the model that the cabinetmaker apprehends when making a cabinet manifests the form that an object must have to serve the purposes to which we put cabinets, of storing utensils or whatever. Similarly, the statesperson apprehends the form that the state must have if it is to serve the ends for which states exist, namely, of bringing forth human goodness by creating the conditions for developing human potentials. A doctor apprehends the form, or characteristics, that a heart, say, must have in order to move blood through the arteries and veins, and does what is necessary to ensure that the patient's heart meets those conditions. More generally, a maker transcribes from the forms that manifest the ends that objects of its type serve when making an object of a particular sort: when making real cabinets, or real states, for example, the cabinetmaker or statesperson examines the forms—that is, the purposes—of cabinets or states and then conforms the cabinet or state to the ideal.

Moderns rejected the applicability of this conception of *poesis* to the arts, and especially the proposition that an artist, in making an object, transcribes from pre-existing models for objects of its kind. The idea of a pre-existing poem that models the poem that a poet is about to write seemed absurd—as absurd as the idea of a pre-existing form for the walk I am about to embark upon, wherein I allow myself to follow my whims—to be drawn to that light shining over there, or that reflection on a patch of snow, or the sound in an alleyway that makes me curious. Some modern art theorists have distinguished art from craft on just these grounds. The objects that craftspeople make have a purpose, and craftspeople model the object they makes after deliberating on the functions that objects of its type serve—thus the slogan "form follows function." Artistic making, by contrast, is unconstrained by any deliberating about purpose, since art objects are non-functional.

This notion of the creative process proclaims that the form of a work of art emerges in the creative process, a proposition that Henri Bergson also stated. It is the fundamentum of Hulme's claim that there can be no objective measure of the value of a work of art, that the only measure that applies depends on the subjective intensity of its effects. He states that a work of art is not something its maker discovers or conforms to a prior existing purpose, but something he or she fashions in a process that depends upon the momentary urges of its maker. Hence, it has a form of existence that depends upon the process that brought it into being, not upon the purposes it serves.

The process of artistic creation changes with alterations in the maker's subjective states, and the artist's subjectivity is so highly developed that it responds to the slightest changes in environing conditions. When the process of artmaking and the forms it produces are open to change—when they are sufficiently adaptable to register all the shifts in feeling the artist undergoes—every change in the artist's subjective state will affect what he or she makes. The artist's every mark embodies a quality of feeling. From the vantage point of the receiver (the viewer or reader), the work of art displays marks of the process that brought it into existence, and these marks reveal the fluctuations in the artist's state as he or she created it. Because the finished work reveals the artist's subjective conditions, subjective considerations are germane when considering the aesthetic value of a work of art.

Since our assessment of a work of art must take into account all the feelings that it provokes, considerations of the states of mind we feel it conveys (regardless of the intentions of its maker) are also aesthetically relevant. Any object whose existence depends upon free creation (that is, does not depend upon our calculations of utility) is an object whose nature we cannot fully understand unless we have knowledge of its maker and of the conditions under which he or she made it—transitory subjective states included. We employ categories that depend on the condition of the maker at the time he or she engaged in the act of free creation when we analyze and assess the products of free creation. Take the simple example of my daily constitutional: I go for a stroll with no end in view. How would one go about forecasting the route I might take (or even go about analyzing it post facto)? Because it does not depend upon considerations of purpose, one cannot understand the path I trace out without considering who I am, what my energy level was when I started out, the rate at which I expend energy, what sorts of things attract me and what sorts of things do not, what I feel from moment to moment as I walk, the weather, the cloud formations that affect the play of light and shadow that draw my attention in one direction rather than another, and myriad other data. One must simply admit that fluctuation of interests, of which no teleological account can be given, is an intractable condition, and concede that no Platonic analysis can be given of the form my daily constitutional assumes.

These Hulmean ideas soon won allegiance from poets, though not from modernists (and especially Joyce, who maintained resolutely, when he insisted that the troubles he took were of the nature of adjusting each detail to conform with a pre-existing ideal, that there exists a transcendent perfect form that the writer strives to realize). The modernist poets were unable to make the radical move of rejecting Hulme's idea of a perfect form that exists beyond change, and the idea of the transcendent image. Open form poets (see glossary) proposed that accidents of the process of making a work of art determine its form—even down to the moment-to-moment variations in the creative process or in the feeling states that the artist undergoes while making the work and the myriad factors in the environing field that impact upon the artist and upon the creative process. This conception of the creative process—and of the myriad factors that affect it—proclaimed the crucial importance of process. Open form poetics proposed that all the factors that affect the creative process and that bring it into existence are relevant to artwork's nature and its value. This advocacy served a clear end. Art theorists, and no small number of artists, took the idea as offering the evidence necessary to prove that a work of art is a free creation.[133]

The idea that a work of art is a free creation leads directly to the ideas of open form and the field method of composition discussed in the next chapter. But a key consequence of this conception of open form demands mention here, viz., it expounds a notion of artmaking that depicts the work of art as being permeable to the world. Modernism denied that artworks possess that quality, by insisting that artworks have an autonomous, autotelic being; they argued that a work of art has an autotelic structure that isolates it from the world around it. The notion of open form prised open this closed conception of form by arguing that form arises from a creative process that is subject to myriad conditioning influences; advocates of open form poetry argued for the importance of considering the fact that poets are affected by an enormous number of features in their environing field and that whatever affects poets registers in the poems they create. Accordingly, exponents of open form often celebrate artists' sensitivity to conditions around them, claiming that as artists' sensitivities expand, they respond to more features of the environment; and as the number of features of the environment that they respond to grows, the register of their influence becomes more complex; and as the register of their influence becomes more complex, the works they produce become intricate. By such a line of thinking, a high degree of openness to circumambient conditions and an acute responsiveness to environing influences became hallmarks of the artistic sensibility. Among artists who have championed these ideas Stan Brakhage looms large.

Another germane aspect of open form composition demands comment here. Open form composition is a creative method in which raw impulses—one can just as well think of them as bodily impulses—shape the form that an artwork assumes. Because the words or images are propelled out of the body of the maker, they have a force that often seems primitive. This compositional practice resembles inspired speech, and the Bible gives us several examples that point out how potent and disturbing such speech can be, and how great an outrage to conventional knowledge and propriety it can create. On several occasions, the apostle Paul points out the subversive, anti-establishment nature of Jesus' teachings. He suggests something even more telling about the form in which Jesus' teachings were spread when he protests to Festus that he is not mad (Acts 26:25). Peter, too, was required to declare that he was not drunk of a morning (Acts 12:25). Paul protests against "speaking in tongues" in that great anti-Gnostic text, 1 Corinthians, when he declares that he would rather utter five words that make sense than ten thousand that do not (1 Corinthians 14:19). Taken together, these caveats and protestations convey much about how early Christian gatherings conducted themselves and about their use of inspired speech. Such use of language is a phenomenon that occurs in the religious practices of many groups, Christian and non-Christian alike. That state authorities have so often exercised their powers to stifle such language, and that "upstanding, decent folk" have so often taken offense at it, suggests something of its power. The relation between "open forms" and "words of power" is a topic we will return to in the next chapter.

Hulme states a more specific idea that Brakhage has adopted. Hulme suggests that the measure of a work of art is the "amount" of its "personal expression"; for art, he proclaims, "seek[s] for the maximum of individual and personal expression."[134] The idea that the intensity of his or her experience sets the artist apart from others, that we live life most creatively when we live it at the peak of its intensity, that the vitality and energy, the pulse and surge and throb of life are what matters are all ideas that Pound, and later Brakhage, drew from Hulme's Bergsonianism. Brakhage gives it expression at the beginning of *Metaphors on Vision* when he asks:

> How many colors are there in a field of grass to the crawling baby unaware of "Green?" How many rainbows can light create for the untutored eye? How aware of variations in heat waves can that eye be? Imagine a world alive with incomprehensible objects and shimmering with an endless variety of movement and innumerable gradations of color.[135]

All are questions about falling short of living life at the maximal intensity possible. Brakhage's film work has been true to the convictions these questions suggest. Films such as the *Duplicity* series (*Duplicity*, 1978, *Duplicity II*, 1978, and *Duplicity III*, 1980) are predicated upon the importance of being emotionally honest with oneself. Like many Romantic poets, Brakhage celebrates the imagination as evidence of the irrepressible vitality of humans' creative drive. In the *Duplicity* series, and especially in *Duplicity II* and *Duplicity III*, Brakhage uses superimposition to reveal how the imagination reworks experience to disguise our darker motives. The troubled emotional cast of the films in the *Duplicity* series reveals Brakhage's conviction that, no matter how unpalatable this self-knowledge may be, acquiring such self-understanding is a moral and spiritual imperative. Corollaries of this moral imperative are that an understanding of our inner nature is essential to our emotional, moral, and spiritual development, and that the intensity of our experience is an index of our sensitivity and our capacity for self-understanding. Thus, in *Tortured Dust* he comes to terms with his darker thoughts on the subjects of procreation and parenting and human frailty generally. Like several other of Brakhage's films, *Tortured Dust* presents the effort to come to terms fully with what one feels—the effort to repress nothing, but to know oneself in the deepest fibres of one's being—as a moral quest. In *The Loom*, similarly, the dreadful dramas we construct for ourselves, when domesticity makes us feel trapped, play themselves out in, of all things, the animal movements of the chickens that the Brakhages kept. Here again, Brakhage suggests that the unearthing of commonly repressed feelings and the effort to eliminate drama from our daily lives have positive moral implications.

Furthermore, Brakhage has devoted a considerable portion of his filmmaking to the quest to revivify and convey experiences to which most people have become oblivious. The paradigm of this aspiration is Brakhage's endeavour to convey what Andrew Lang called "hypnagogic imagery," those animated dots and swirls and moving fields of colour that result from physical stimulation of the retina. *Thigh Line Lyre Triangular*, the "Meat Jewel" section of *Dog Star Man: Part II*, and *The Process* exemplify the results of Brakhage's efforts to make a place for hypnagogic forms in film, to show us the character of these experiences that most of us "grow up" to neglect. He explained his use of painting on film to depict hypnagogic images in an exchange with P. Adams Sitney:

> [P.A.S.:] How was *Thigh Line Lyre Triangular* [1961] different, when it was finally edited, from *Window Water Baby Moving* [1959], the earlier birth film?
>
> [S.B.:] The main difference is the painting on film in *Thigh Line Lyre Triangular*. Only at a crisis do I see both the scene as I've been trained to see it (that is, with Renaissance perspective, three-dimensional logic,—color as we've been trained to call a color a color, and so forth) and patterns that move straight out from the inside of the mind through the optic nerves. In other words, an intensive crisis I can see from the inside out and the outside in.
>
> [P.A.S.:] You mean double exposure?
>
> [S.B.:] I see patterns moving that are the same patterns that I see when I close my eyes; and can also see the same kind of scene that I see when my eyes are open.
>
> [P.A.S.:] You mean you see color spots before your eyes?

[S.B.:] Right—spots before my eyes, so to speak . . . and it's a very intensive, disturbing, but joyful experience. I've seen that every time a child was born. Notice I use the word crisis. I don't mean crisis as a bad thing. At an extremely intensive moment I can see from the inside out and the outside in. Now none of that was in *Window Water Baby Moving*; and I wanted a childbirth film which expressed all of my seeing at such a time.

[P.A.S.:] And you added shots of animals too?

[S.B.:] That was because at moments like that I get flashes of what I call "brain movies." I'm taking Michael McClure's term there; he said, "When you get a solid structure image that you know is not out there, but is being recalled so intensively that you literally see it in a flash, that's a 'brain movie.'" Most people only get them with their eyes closed. They close their eyes and they see, in a flash, something from their childhood, or some person remembered, or something; and that should also be in the film experience. What I was seeing at the birth of Neowyn [Stan and Jane Brakhage's third daughter] most clearly, in terms of this "brain movie" recall process, were symbolic structures of an animal nature. This struck me as odd because I was working six ways sideways, day and night, to avoid symbolism. It was as if something had gotten backed up in my mind so that it could release symbolic terms at me as soon as it had a crisis. Curiously enough, those animal symbols were easily represented by taking material only out of *Anticipation of the Night*.

[P.A.S.:] Why are you never seen as father in this film?

[S.B.:] That's because I centered the occasion in my own eyes.[136]

The comments Brakhage makes in this passage reveal that his criterion of quality is the same as Antonin Artaud's: A work of art is good in the measure that it captures all the phenomena that occur within the manifold of consciousness, for Brakhage proposes that his art will capture a moment of consciousness whole.

Brakhage's remarks on symbolism are also telling. For one thing, they reveal that some of his reasons for opposing symbolism are aesthetic in character (i.e., they have to do with what fits with what). But the gist of the comments on symbolism here concerns a dual irony involved in his use of symbolic images in *Thigh Line Lyre Triangular*. One irony follows from the fact that, from the time he developed the lyrical film (see glossary)—that is, from about 1957—Brakhage disavowed symbolism, sometimes expressing the rejection in violent terms. His opposition to symbolism probably developed partly from a belief that visual symbolism reduces a visual image to a name and causes us to associate a verbal concept with an image.

But there is probably another source of Brakhage's distrust of symbolism, which derives from what the French literary and artistic moment Symbolisme (a name which, following convention, and tempting any confusion that the decision may invoke, we shall translate, and call "Symbolism," with a capital "S") owes to the literary device, symbolism.[137] For Symbolism provided the Open Form poets with one of their principal lessons, about the pernicious consequence of separation of the word (or, more generally, any signifier) from any connection to the world. In Symbolism we see, as Hegel had predicted, the Cartesian "I" uncoupling from Nature and History, and, in the process, the symbol (and, in fact, all language) undergoing *kenosis*: ultimately, their language became not symbols of Nature, or symbols of History, but simply symbols of other symbols, signs of other signs.[138] The Open Form poets Robert Duncan and Charles Olson wanted to restore the relation between the word and world, but not by reverting to reference; rather, they proposed that we think of words not as tokens that refer to categories of objects but as physical objects that act upon the other elements of physical reality (and, paradigmatically, upon the bodies of those who hear or see them); and similarly Stan Brakhage wanted to reconnect imagery, not by restoring it to its transcendental status, but by ensuring that it worked upon the bodies of those that see it. Like the Open Form poets, Brakhage wanted to avoid severing the word/image from the field that produces it, and to ensure that the deferral from word/image to word/image would not be endless, but would have a terminal point.

In the passage quoted above, Brakhage acknowledges the irony that he, who had so vigorously rejected symbolism, resorted to using symbolism in *Thigh Line Lyre Triangular*. Another irony has a more specific character that relates to the source of the symbolic images he experienced while watching the birth of his third daughter. The symbolic representations that came to his mind were images from a film about death and suicide, entitled *Anticipation of the Night*, which he finished about four years before making *Thigh Line Lyre Triangular*; so images from a film about death find a suitable place in a film about birth. Brakhage's point, in saying that, despite his aesthetic caveats about using symbolism, he incorporated symbolic forms in *Thigh Line Lyre Triangular*, is that he considers aesthetic principles to be of slight importance in comparison with the imperatives of capturing the manifold of experience in its entirety.

The lexical choices Brakhage made in expounding his ideas on symbolism are particularly telling. He speaks of centring his movies "in his eyes," of "brain movies," of images moving "out through the optic nerve." These choices indicate that his is a very physiological conception of vision. *Thigh Line Lyre Triangular* confirms these suggestions. While the film is very complex, its fundamental structure derives from a readily discernible rhythm that has a physiological basis. We can illustrate this basis best by comparing the painting-on-film and the visual distortions that appear in this film with the perceptual distortions that appear with autism. Psychologists have understood for years that autists strive to avoid experiencing people or objects in their environment, because they feel threatened by others. What autists experience as most threatening, usually, are other human beings. Recent work with autistic children has shown that perceptual phenomena play a role in the denial of threatening factors. An autist experiences kaleidoscope-like perceptual phenomena that fragment and distort the real world. (Actually, these distortions have neither the geometric forms nor the primary colours of kaleidoscopic forms, but they do fragment the world into continuously changing shapes as kaleidoscopic images do.) Sometimes autists' percepts resemble bright, fluffy spots that slowly change their shapes; they might see a skating rink as a sea of sparkles, all blue and pink, that whoosh by as they move, and thus they convert reality into an almost hallucinatory form. An autist's aural mechanisms serve a related function; they disassemble and rearrange sounds so that aural percepts have no meaning and convey no human messages. This process of fragmentation and disassociation keeps a threatening human presence from intruding on the autist's consciousness. Human speech becomes a mumbling jumble—sounds without meaning. Autists' speech echoes are simply a form of aural imitation—they return the sounds of the speech they hear because for them the speech has no meaning and is only an aural pattern.

When autists sit, apparently entranced, with eyes fixed, rocking slowly or engaged in some other repetitive motion, they have withdrawn from contact with the real world and are watching the forms changing in the internal world "in front of their eyes." Because these forms mutate continuously, their experiential world is a world that altogether lacks fixity. This very lack of stability is threatening itself. Therefore, they crave stability, to counteract the perceptual flux that the mechanisms of denial engender. Hence, autists insist on an unchanging, highly ordered environment; and when treating an autist, a caregiver has to take great pains to ensure that the environment in which he or she offers treatment undergoes little change between sessions. Furthermore, these kaleidoscopic distortions affect the figure/ground relations of both visual and aural perceptions. For autists, a person dressed in nearly the same colour as a room's wallpaper is indistinguishable from the environment: they will see the person as disappearing into the environment. Because the perception of figure/ground relations in aural phenomena is similarly disturbed, the aural environment strikes an autist with a painful intensity as the noise from the environment engulfs and overwhelms the signal. Even though the desire to repudiate the presence of another human plays a large role in this experience, the loss of the person to the environment can be terrifying for autists nonetheless. The tragedy of autism is that autists need to distort and deny a reality that is too threatening to bear. To deny reality, autists employ a process that they often find terrifyingly labile.

Thus they are trapped in a dilemma: either give up that process and experience the presence of people that seem too threatening to tolerate, or engage in the process and experience a perceptual reality that is terrifying because it is labile and fragmented.

Like the negative hallucination, the stream of kaleidoscopic images with which autists fill their minds destroys what they cannot bear to experience. The hypnagogic and anamorphic forms in *Thigh Line Lyre Triangular* appear in a sequence that derives from a similar process of denial, for they fragment and distort perceptions in order to disavow experiences that the filmmaker finds too intense to bear. *Thigh Line Lyre Triangular* is among the "messiest" and "grubbiest" of Brakhage's films; and its hypnagogic and anamorphic forms relate to its messiness. When the photographed subject becomes too intense—when the excitement it provokes becomes too great, or the scene becomes so biologically messy as to provoke a squeamish response—the hypnagogic forms overwhelm the cinematographic images. Then the urge to re-establish a relation with objective reality overwhelms the urge to deny and the cinematographic image re-emerges from behind the screen of the hypnagogic overlays. Predominantly white and egg-yolk yellow, dirty-blood red, and dark hypnagogic overlays appear in a related pattern of alternation. Further, Brakhage's use of anamorphosis results in flattened representations of his wife, Jane, in labour; by manipulating the anamorphic lens while shooting, he makes the image gyrate. These transformations of the conventional space of photographic representation also serve to deny an objective reality that is too intense to bear.

Though hypnagogic forms make up the most decisive item in the inventory of experiences that Brakhage strives to recover and incorporate in the complete book of consciousness, it is only one among many. Many of Brakhage's films convey a terror of the negative hallucination—of those gaps in consciousness of which Artaud complained with a bitterness that was undiminished by the frequency with which he uttered them. Brakhage, it seems, dreads those moments when visual representations disappear from consciousness. The speed and variety of his visual forms increase when the notion of death arises. This suggests that the proliferation of elements for which Brakhage's films are so famous is, at least sometimes, reactive. Brakhage seeks any visual form to dispel the terrifying nothingness that a gap in consciousness exposes. His efforts to acquire the mode of seeing angels (in *Angels'*, 1971), of animals (*The Domain of the Moment*, 1977), of children (*Kindering* 1987, *Scenes from Under Childhood*, 1967-70), of insects (*Mothlight*, 1963; *The Presence*, 1972), or of a businessman (*Dominion*, 1974) reflect his desire to have something, anything, undo the negative hallucination's death-threatening effects—to have something with which to fill the gap in consciousness that negative hallucination creates. Imagination, Brakhage's films point out repeatedly, is the faculty for producing images; these images testify to the imagination's vitality. Hence, when visual representations go missing from consciousness, we are as though dead. Similarly, throughout the 1980s Brakhage worked on and off at several series of "abstract" films, entitled the *Roman Numeral Series* (1979-81), the *Arabic Numeral Series* (1980-82), the *Egyptian Series* (1984), and the *Babylon Series* (1989-90), that convey the character of our experiences before they are sufficiently formed to come into most people's awareness. Brakhage began *The Text of Light* (1974) out of an urge to show us properties of light to which we have become insensate. In that film's case, his efforts were so painstaking, thorough, and revelatory that, once he began showing it, many people offered testimony that he had captured near-death experiences—experiences of the sort that Elisabeth Kübler-Ross describes better than anyone.[139]

Of all these films, it is, perhaps, *The Text of Light* that presents most insistently the triumph of the imagination in formulating an alternate mode of vision by synthesizing within itself numerous physiological attributes of perceptual experience that we ordinary neglect. In *Metaphors on Vision*, Brakhage proposed the possibility of a form of "visual communication [he later came regret the choice of the word 'communicate'], demanding a development of the optical mind, and dependent upon perception in the original and deepest sense of the word" and posits that "the Vision of the saint and the artist [involves] an increased ability to see," that, unlike the perception of the common run of humanity, acknowledges features of vision that "doesn't appear to be readily usable."[140]

The visual forms that populate *The Text of Light* really exemplify a world "before the beginning was the word." It was shot frame-by-frame (as animation is), through a crystal ashtray and prisms.[141] The method destroyed all sense of hapticity—the images thus produced engender little sense of depth, but (it is important to stress) not necessarily no sense of depth whatsoever. The effects are radical. Ordinarily we consider colour and shape to be distinct phenomena; however, when the boundaries that separate one object from another are blurred and reference eliminated from these boundary-less areas of colours, colour can become a shape-making function. Many recent artists, Hans Hofmann (1880-1966) for example, have taken an interest in the potential that colour possesses for creating shape and for locating shapes in space. The interest has often, as in Hofmann's work, taken the form of concern with discovering a shape that is appropriate for a particular colour (i.e., particular energy). Colours were seen as more or less expansive, more or less processive or recessive, more or less calm or agitated or violent, and the task of the painter became that of discovering a shape appropriate to the colours one used; thus the shape was determined internally by the colour, rather than imposed externally, by forms (whether mechanomorphic, or biomorphic, or of some other character entirely) that have nothing to do with that colour's nature.

The effect of the transformation in the relation between colour and shape was radical. Works that freed colours from shapes alien to their nature elicited a scanning mode of perception that is more primitive than our ordinary mode of perception, which operates by forming gestalts. This scanning mode of perception does not form a hierarchalized relation between figure and ground, but allows all elements of the form to interpenetrate one another. It does not distinguish light from colour or colour from light, just as it does not distinguish colour from shape or shape from colour. It does not even distinguish distance from shape or colour.

What *The Text of Light* does, exactly, is to elicit this mode of perception, and it does so by treating shape and colour in just that way that Hans Hofmann's teachings instruct us to. It promotes a regression to a more primitive mode of experience, "before the beginning was the word." Moreover, the film's duration makes us aware that when we watch the film, we engage in a different perceptual mode than our customary one—and, as importantly, it makes us aware that our usual mode of perception is customary, and that we are determined by our biological constitution to a particular mode of perception.

However, as we watch the film, our mind does sometimes try to interpret the visual forms we see by identifying their object matter; and, as I stressed, Brakhage's use of prisms in this film does not destroy all sense of the visual forms' hapticity. Thus, we see a form and interpret it as a landscape, for example. We impose preformulated interpretant notions on these visual forms: for example, we tend to interpret the areas at the top of the screen as sky and the lower areas as earth; our tendency to interpret a particular visual form as a landscape is stronger when the visual form is divided horizontally into two bands, a darker lower band and a lighter upper band. But the fit between the interpretant (see glossary) and the object is far from perfect, and so we become aware of the resistance that the object matter offers to such designative processes. What is more important, we become aware of the primacy, in the genesis of consciousness, of the experience of light as pure colour—aware that subsequent experience arises through the forming of light as colour and through naming the forms that result.

Brakhage's note for the film in the New York Film-makers' Cooperative catalogue begins with "All that is is light," a translation of the sentence *Omnia quae sunt lumina sunt* from Pound's *Cantos*.[142] The proposition that all things are lights, which is absolutely central to the Gnostic metaphysics of the *Cantos*, actually shifts the primacy of colour as light from the genesis of experience to the genesis of the cosmos, for it proposes that primordial experience—the experience of colour as light—discloses an ontological truth concerning light's reality as a metaphysical fundamental. The shapes and names that we impose on the experience of colour as light are secondary, and derive from our mental processes, but colour as a light remains an irreducible reality.

Like Hulme, Brakhage believes that the intensity of an individual's experience is a measure of his or her sensitivity. And, like Hulme, he longs for the self-understanding that such sensitivity brings. In *Metaphors on Vision*, Brakhage goes as far as to relate moral failure to lack of self-understanding. "This is an age which has no symbol for death other than the skull and bones of one stage of decomposition," he writes,

> and it is an age which lives in fear of total annihilation. It is a time haunted by sexual sterility yet almost universally incapable of perceiving the phallic nature of every destructive manifestation of itself. It is an age which artificially seeks to project itself materialistically into abstract space and to fulfill itself mechanically because it has blinded itself to almost all external reality within eyesight and to the organic awareness of even the physical movement properties of its own perceptibility.[143]

Brakhage's interests in recovering neglected aspects of vision overlap with Hulme's interests in personal, subjective, non-epic themes. Images and themes that reappear in several of Brakhage's films indicate another, and even larger area of overlapping interests. Some of the most intensely subjective passages in Brakhage's oeuvre take the form of responses to real or imagined deaths. *Sirius Remembered* (1959), *Flight* (1974), *The Weir-Falcon Saga* (1970), *Pasht* (1965), *The Act of Seeing with One's Own Eyes* (1971), *Deus Ex* (1971), *The Dead* (1960), and, in its own way, *Unconscious London Strata* (1981), are all responses to a real or imagined death. But his 1978 film, *Burial Path*, reveals more cogently the deeper reasons for Brakhage's returning time and again to the theme of death, for that film chronicles bereavement at the loss of mental representations (and specifically visual representations) that can summon a beloved object back to presence and, more importantly, that register one's own being. This conjecture finds confirmation in *Song 23: 23ʳᵈ Psalm Branch* in the fact that the physical and emotional violence that motivated Brakhage to make *Song 23: 23ʳᵈ Psalm Branch* (1966) portends death and destruction, and leads to frequent obliteration of representation, also inspires the most intense vortex of images that Brakhage has given us; indeed that film's imagery seems constantly on the verge of spluttering out of existence.

Antonin Artaud dreaded most those gaps in consciousness he experienced all too frequently; Brakhage's work seems haunted by a similar dread of loss—in his case, the loss he fears most is the absence of mental representations (and specifically visual representations). One of Brakhage's films thematizes absence—the experience of which some might consider a species of serenity (indeed, some people engage in meditative practices precisely in order to sweep away the contents of mind and to engender a state of no-consciousness). Brakhage clearly does not experience the absence of mental representations in this way—as evidence of this his program note for *Thot-Fal'n* (1978) reads:

> This film describes a psychological state 'kin to 'moon-struck,' its images emblems (not quite symbols) of suspension-of-self within consciousness and then that feeling of 'falling away' from conscious thought. The film can only be said to 'describe' or be emblematic of this state because I cannot imagine symbolizing or otherwise representing an equivalent of thoughtlessness itself. Thus the 'actors' in the film, Jane Brakhage, Tom and Gloria Bartek, William Burroughs, Allen Ginsberg, Peter Orlovsky and Phillip Whalen are figments of this Thought-Fallen PROCESS as are their images in the film to themselves being photographed.[144]

The note's style is uncharacteristic of Brakhage; not the least remarkable of its features is the ambivalence it evidences in Brakhage's thoughts about the status of *Thot-Fal'n*'s visual forms. He slips between calling them emblems, symbols, representations, and figments of some process. The verbal stress the passage displays hints at Brakhage's desperation to fill a gap in consciousness, a result he achieves only by invoking the idea of process, i.e., the mechanism that will fill the dreaded absence with simulacra, which, though illusory, are (as the idiom has it) better than nothing. Brakhage had dealt earlier with the process referred to in this note, in *The Process* (1972), a film that celebrates the capacities of the imagination. His program note for that film reveals that he conceives of the imagination in electrico-dynamic terms:

> LIGHT was primary in my consideration. All senses of 'process' are (to me) based primarily on 'thought-process'; and 'thought-process' is based primarily on 'memory-recall'; and that, as any memory process (all process finally) is electrical (firing of nerve connection) and expresses itself most clearly as a 'back-firing' of nerve endings in the eye which DO become visible to us (usually eyes closed) as 'brain-movies'—as Michael McClure calls them. When we are not re-constructing 'a scene' (re-calling something once seen), then we are watching (on the 'screen' of closed eye-lids) the very PROCESS itself. . . . [145]

Brakhage, in asserting that we can sense actual synaptic events, proposes a somatized notion of vision and imagination in this passage.[146]

Brakhage's art expands the notion of what it is to see. He has included in his films ordinary percepts, but also: memory images; images produced by anticipation; dream images (from both daydreams and night-dreams); hypnagogic images, either by themselves or mixed with percepts; phosphenes;

floaters (those dark specks that float in our field of vision); and percepts modified by intense emotion. Any sort of visual experience can claim a rightful place in film, simply by virtue of belonging to the register of vision. Because Brakhage continues to work in the paratactical mode that Pound bequeathed to the twentieth century, his films do not make distinctions of type between percepts and other types of vision; he simply presents a percept and juxtaposes it with a fragment of a nightmare, for example, making no distinction in type between the two.

The particular way Brakhage has expanded the concept of vision owes much to the Romanticism that dominates the poetics of the Black Mountain poets and their intellectual and spiritual descendants. Romanticism was principally an effort to restore a salutary identity between mind and nature. The Romantics cast reason as the enemy that had destroyed the salutary relation that had once existed and imagination as the faculty that would restore it (and this is even more true of American Romanticism than of other national forms). In the imagination they found evidence of a creative energy identical to that which produced natural forms. If the creative force that spurs humans on to engage in imaginative acts is the same as the creative force in nature that produces trees and clouds and animals, then the highest faculty of humans, the creative imagination, unites them with a force that runs through all of nature. That very Romantic poet Dylan Thomas noted, in what are probably his most famous lines, the identity of the life force in us and the creative force immanent in the whole of nature: "The force that through the green fuse drives the flower/ Drives my green age; . . . The force that drives the water through the rocks/ Drives my red blood." The Romantics identified this force as it manifested itself in humans with the creative imagination. And, since they claimed human imagination to be our defining feature, they thus identified human nature (or, at least, human being qua creature) with nature. "I do not represent nature, I am Nature," Jackson Pollock remarked. His comment was the inevitable product of the Romantic view of the imagination. What it makes wonderfully clear is how much of the rhetoric of spontaneity that artists from the Surrealists to Pollock's generation have produced expresses the desire to surrender consciousness altogether, and to be swept away by the blissful unself-consciousness of nature.

And Pound? As early as 1912, in "Psychology and Troubadours," he argued for the Romantic identification of human and natural creativity, using the Bergsonian idea of a fluid spirit.

> Let us consider the body as pure mechanism. Our kinship to the ox we have constantly thrust upon us; but beneath this is our kinship to the vital universe, to the tree and the living rock, and, because this is less obvious—and possibly more interesting—we forget it.

> We have about us the universe of fluid force, and below us the germinal universe of wood alive, of stone alive. Man is—the sensitive physical part of him—a mechanism, for the purpose of our further discussion a mechanism rather like an electric appliance, switches, wires, etc. Chemically speaking, he is *ut credo*, a few buckets of water, tied up in a complicated sort of fig-leaf. As to his consciousness, the consciousness of some seems to rest, or to have its centre more properly, in what the Greek psychologists called the *phantastikon*. Their minds are, that is, circumvolved about them like soap-bubbles reflecting sundry patches of the macrocosmos. And with certain others their consciousness is "germinal." Their thoughts are in them as their thought of the tree is in the seed, or in the grass, or the grain, or the blossom. And these minds are the more poetic, and they affect mind about them, and transmute it as the seed the earth. And this latter sort of mind is close on the vital universe; and the strength of the Greek beauty rests in this, that it is ever at the interpretation of this vital universe, by its signs of gods and godly attendants and oreads.[147]

The Romantics accorded very high value to all manifestations of that creative force, whether in human or in non-human nature. Hegel's philosophy makes clear that Romanticism was an effort to reconcile the traditional beliefs in Divine Goodness with the findings of modern science, to reconcile the substance of Christian faith with all that emerged from the Greek legacy of respect for acquiring learning through the scientific study of nature. Modern science seemed to present a threat to Christian faith, not primarily because its findings refuted basic Christian teachings or key points of dogma but because it toppled the hierarchical worldview that had developed from it and with which it had been associated throughout the era of its hegemony in the West.

Historians of ideas often call this hierarchical worldview the Great Chain of Being. Like so much of the Christian worldview, the idea of a Great Chain of Being was an amalgam of ideas from the neo-Platonism that Saint Augustine (354-430), Saint Bonaventure (1217-74), and Ibn Sina (980-1037) made central to Christian theology and, eventually, even to the characteristic worldview of the Christian Era based on the Peripatetic teachings on order and value that Saint Thomas Aquinas (1225-74) synthesized with neo-Platonism and the biblical teachings of Jesus and with Semitic transcendentalism. The Great Chain of Being depicted the cosmos as a hierarchical order of existents that starts with God, descends through orders of being characterized by diminishing simplicity and decreasing generality of their knowledge—through the realms of the angels, the Seraphim, the Cherubim, the Thrones, the Dominions, the Virtues, the Powers and the Principalities, the Archangels and the Angels, down through that unstable compound of matter and spirit we know of as human being, further down through the higher animals and the lower animals, further down yet to the vegetable kingdom, and finally to the mineral realm. The doctrine rested on the idea that every existent is a composite of an animating spirit and inertial matter. A decrease in the ratio between animating principle and inanimate matter marks each successive stage in the descent of the orders of being.

The cosmology associated with the Great Chain drew a basic distinction between the ontological, spiritual, and moral status of the sublunary realm and the superlunary realm. The superlunary realm is the realm of stasis, perfection, freedom, and immateriality; the sublunary realm is the realm of change, impermanence, imperfection, necessity, and materiality. This distinction between the two realms of being represented a synthesis of Aristotelian teachings concerning an Unmoved Mover and Judaic teachings concerning His transcendence. When Copernicus, Galileo, and Newton proved that the heavenly bodies not only do move, but move according to the same laws that govern the dynamics of bodies here below, this hierarchical worldview came into question. Their discoveries had the effect of extending the realm of materiality and law outward from earth to include the heavens. The cosmology that developed from their discoveries left no place where God could be, no place for an Unmoved Mover, or for a Being who creates freely. Thus, from the Early Modern to the Romantic Era, thinkers strove to carve out a place for the Divine. We get an inkling of the importance they accorded this endeavour when we read, in Kant's *Laying the Groundwork to a Metaphysics of Morals*, that the two supremely beautiful things in the universe are the starry heaven above and the moral law within. A single drive impelled Kant to create his entire philosophical system—to delineate the spheres of freedom and necessity and so to provide the foundation for reconciling the truths that Newtonian science revealed with the Pietist doctrines of his Lutheran faith by showing that an arena of freedom, an arena in which free creation is possible, actually exists.

Despite the strengths of its metaphysical and epistemological arguments, few believed that Kant's system provided an adequate scope for Divine activity or an intimate enough relation between human beings and God. Many thinkers of the period between Fichte and Hegel attempted to complete Kant's task, but the Romantics were the first to reconcile traditional Christian faith with modern science in a way that many people found satisfactory. Their reconciliation came at the cost of denying God's transcendence, however. The Romantics identified God with the creative force immanent in nature. Hegel's philosophy provides the paradigm case of immanentizing the Divine, for Hegel identified God with a principle that acts through history, that is, with a being that dynamizes the realm of change, the realm of transitory being, the realm of materiality and necessity. The Romantics extended Hegel's philosophy, for if Hegel brought the Divine into the realm of change, the Romantics went on to identify human creativity with this immanent divine. They deemed human creativity to be a divine (or, at least, almost divine) faculty, for human creativity is a natural force, an expression within human being of the same power that, in nature, produces trees and flowers and grass and clouds and people. The Romantics celebrated the imagination because, in their view, the imagination makes humans like God. A world that humans create is not a realm that is alien from human being; creativity bridges the gap between self and world that modern reason had opened, by creating—from the materials of given nature—objects, and indeed a world, marked with the evidence of human creativity. The Romantics associated language with reason, while they saw imagination as being what its etymology suggests—the faculty for producing images. The imagination creates a world that is integral with human being, a world in which objects do not stand over against us as alien beings, but are expressions or objectifications or outerings—or, to use Olson's telling term, projections—of our own character. Brakhage shares the Romantics' lofty conception of imagination. Nothing can produce a better understanding of Brakhage's poetics than reading *Metaphors on Vision* or some pieces in the *Brakhage Scrapbook* in the light of the Romantic conception of imagination (and there is no better place to acquire an understanding of the Romantic theory of imagination than in Northrop Frye's *A Study of English Romanticism*).

Brakhage's early films are particularly Romantic—and *Dog Star Man* (1961-64) is especially so. *Dog Star Man* portrays a solitary individual who, pitted against the forces of nature, struggles to reach the mountain top. This was the theme of countless Romantic paintings by German Romantic followers of Caspar Friedrich David. The Romantic character of the work is evident, too, in the shots that animate the mountainside, by shooting it either with a moving camera or with an anamorphic lens that Brakhage twisted while filming; such shots make it seem that a life force animates the mountain. The Romantic character of the work is evident, too, in the collage of scientific cinematography of solar flares (representing the macrocosmic dimension of existence), images of blood cells pushed first in one direction then the other, and of a pumping heart (which represents the microanthropotic dimension of existence). The collage of the solar flares and of the human circulatory system draws the macrocosmic and the microanthropotic dimensions of existence into an equivalence and so suggests that the same forces that animate the universe sustain the lives of human beings. The Dog Star Man appears at the beginning of *The Prelude* with a moon superimposed on his forehead. The trope suggests that the Dog Star Man creates the universe in his imagination. The same suggestion appears elsewhere in the film, and it reveals that *Dog Star Man* rests on the Romantic myth of cosmogenesis, according to which the human imagination is identical with a creative force immanent in nature.[148]

But Romanticism isn't all about enthusiasm; typically, there is as much scepticism in a Romantic work as there is enthusiasm.[149] Romantic artists, even while celebrating the creative process of life and the imagination's participation in this great *élan vital*, acknowledge too that the myths they construct will also pass away, and new myths, to be forged by artists to come, will be required. *Dog Star Man* expounds its myth of cosmogenesis with an irony of a sort typical of Romantic works. It depicts the struggle as a desperate battle of a potent individual, driven by the life force, to thwart all that would deny him the energies of being; but it also depicts the efforts as rather comic. The comic dimension emerges when Brakhage makes evident that the arduous ascent of the steep mountain slope is a trick, created by tilting the camera to increase the grade of the incline; and it expands as he includes his dog who delightedly frolics in the snow, appearing for all the world as if he was enjoying the best romp he had had in some time, though his master repeatedly stumbles and falls. Brakhage acknowledges the fictive nature of rendering of experience, by tilting the camera as he does in these scenes, and using what are evidently "effects," produced by: manipulating the anamorphic lens to produce gyrations in the image; conspicuous synthesis of films microanthropotic and macroanthropotic levels (juxtaposing solar cinematography and cinemicrophotography, which, when juxtaposed, produce the effect of an obvious analogizing); and the very abrupt interpolation of very ordinary, and far from edifying material (e.g., urinating) which brings the grandeur of the mythic cosmology into doubt. *Dog Star Man* thus becomes a work that shows itself as being simultaneously created and destroyed.[150]

Through all of this, we read the imagery as presenting the Dog Star Man's consciousness (or, more accurately, as presenting a vortex of visual forms that conveys an energy which provokes experiences in the viewer's mind that resemble the visual forms in the Dog Star Man's consciousness). As an example of mythopoeic cinema, it is as close to an epic work as Brakhage has given us, and it shares with Pound's great epic several crucial features. The most important, for our purposes, is an interiorizing impetus. Pound read Dante as presenting a subjective interior journey, one that incorporated both those who helped Dante or whom Dante admired and—who can forget— his adversaries, into a personal quest, and the religious and philosophical thought of the age into the poet's quest for the beatific vision. Pound set out to do likewise; thus, for him, at the centre of Dante's epic is the consciousness of The Poet and at the centre of Pound's epic is Pound's own consciousness. Consciousness has just as central a role in Brakhage's *Dog Star Man*. In this respect, Brakhage's epic, like Pound's, is really closer to such

Romantic epics as Wordsworth's *The Prelude*, which presents "The Growth of the Poet's Mind," and Whitman's *Leaves of Grass*, which Whitman could rightly claim to be a "Song of Myself," than it is to such works as *The Sea-farer* or *Sir Gawain and the Green Knight*. At the centre of Brakhage's works, as at the centre of Pound's, Wordsworth's, and Whitman's, is an all-inclusive, all-seeing subject.

A second feature *Dog Star Man* shares with Pound's *Cantos*, and probably because of the central role an all-inclusive, all-seeing subject has in both, is its compendiousness. The images of *Dog Star Man* range from the microscopic to the macrocosmic scale and the work constellates narrative (the Dog Star Man's story), myth (by connecting his story to a cosmic drama), personal statement (by including the birth film and domestic scenes), science, and religion. In this respect, it resembles Pound's integration of narrative, myth, economic theory, personal monologue, and religious speculation in the *Cantos*. Only Browning's *Sordello*, one of Pound's early models for the *Cantos*, even approaches the compendiousness of Pound's "poem including history."

A third common feature is that both have open forms. Pound stressed that there is no "Aquinas map" to provide a guide to the *Cantos*; and the openness of the *Cantos* to the circumstances of its composition is evidenced by Pound's inability, after the years of exile, of war, of incarceration in a cage and a madhouse, to lift the poem's concluding sequences into heaven. Brakhage's inclusion of domestic scenes highlights that *Dog Star Man* is also an open-form work. In this regard, the seaman's voyage in the *Cantos* and the Dog Star Man's adventures in Brakhage's film resemble the voyages of the Ancient Mariner and Ishmael—they embark into unknown waters, to experience they know not what.

First-Person Singular: Bergson, Hulme, and Brakhage on the Primacy of Individuality

Hulme followed Bergson in expounding the idea that the experience of every individual is unique and that the greatness of strong art derives from the power of art to recover forgotten features or neglected domains of the mind's perceptual contents and to reveal thereby the uniqueness of the individual mind: "The great aim is accurate, precise and definite description. . . . [E]ach man sees a little differently, and to get out clearly and exactly what he does see, he must have a terrific struggle with language."[151] And Brakhage:

> With every artist it's a case of trying to get something of what's really intrinsic to his being, and separable from all social senses of what other human beings are, out into the general air. I can't beat, as a basic maxim,

Robert Duncan's statement: I exercise my faculties at large. In the same way other men make war, some make love; I make poetry—to exercise my faculties at large. . . . Really what it means is that young men and women are faced with an impossible contradiction between their own intrinsic loneliness, and their own absolute dependence upon others. To make themselves *imaginable* within the general airs of all the other imaginations that others have accepted of themselves—they're forced to accept an equivalent. It's either that, or madness, or death, or total withdrawal, or a bitter eccentricity . . . and all the various other alternatives every artist toys with.

When I was a certain age, and when the glasses and the fat of me were a solid manifestation of my own removal from everything around me that I was so dependent on, I lost weight and threw away the glasses. When I threw away the glasses I literally could not see to cross the street safely. That meant I had accepted other persons' sense of sight—it didn't mean I couldn't see. I mean the ways in which I was seeing weren't acceptable, and therefore they weren't acceptable to me. I had no other equivalent for any of them in any of the books or pictures. Everyone else had an easy referential relation with Renaissance perspective.[152]

Brakhage speculates that the impulse to make art derives from our need to have other people recognize us as distinctive. Further, he relates individuality to physical being, to one's peculiar way of seeing. To highlight his efforts at individuating himself, he describes the efforts he made to assume the mode of vision (way of seeing) that was his by virtue of his physical constitution, not the result of his wearing "corrective" lenses that shape everyone's vision into the same mould (which accords with the Renaissance principles of geometric optics). Like William Carlos Williams, another poet who has exerted enormous influence on him, Brakhage has a penchant for considering tradition as threatening—as the individual must struggle against the legacy of the *tradita* that can obliterate all that is distinctive about a particular individual and, if not destroy, at least modify those authentic sensations that arise within the truths of personal experience, rendering them less distinctly individual.

These ideas are not unconflicted, however. Like Williams, Brakhage starts out by depicting creativity as a contested site, on which authentic individuals pit themselves against the smothering effects of history's legacy. However, Brakhage goes on to point out that his efforts to recover and maintain his own, personal way of seeing were made more difficult because he could not find "equivalents" to his way of seeing in the history of painting. Thus he offers the view that tradition could be liberating but, in concrete cases, is actually stifling. Like Carolee Schneemann, who could not find examples of female artists in recent Western art history whom she could take as role models, Brakhage complains that the tradition, which for other individuals might have the role of authenticating one's creativity, did not serve that function in his. He writes of the anxiety of finding himself unsupported in his creative endeavours and the longing to find predecessors who could under-write his own, individual ideas, his own, individual way of seeing, and his own, individual manner of experiencing.

This dual valuation of history is an aspect of William Carlos Williams's writings, too, as *In the American Grain* (1925) makes so clear.[153] Stephen Fredman, in *The Grounding of American Poetry: Charles Olson and the Emersonian Tradition*, suggests that this tension between two views of history, between the view that sees history as stifling (and adopts an oppositional stance to any regnant social structure, and demands one's own history, one's own works, laws, and faith) and the view that sees history as authenticating, is basic to American modernist and projectivist poetry.[154] He also shows that poets who have thought deeply about the American poet's relation to history have responded in two ways to the anxiety-inducing recognition that American poetry lacks a contextualizing tradition: on one hand, these poets celebrate the liberating effects of escaping tradition and celebrate the destructiveness of Americans' interest in all that is new for its capacity to clear the ground; on the other, they mourn the lack of tradition that might legitimate their endeavour. Fredman's remarks are apposite to Brakhage's works.

In any event, Brakhage's concerns with the subjective life of the individual thinker and, in particular, with the uniqueness of each person's experience, have their grounds in an individualistic conception of the person. The idea that the function of art is to allow an individual to speak in a fashion true to his or her deeper self is an idea that Brakhage has frequently expounded and consistently practised.

Brakhage's most forceful statement of his conviction that the artist must struggle to wrest the unique quality of his or her individual perception away from the corrupting influence of mass society appears in the opening pages of *Metaphors on Vision*, the first major statement of his artistic credo he issued. The prominent place this statement occupies in his writings and the eloquence with which he stated his beliefs have made the passage well known. In it, Brakhage insists the acquisition of language has deleterious effects on one's perceptual capacities, and especially on the faculty of sight. Brakhage's comments on the harm that language does to vision, offered on the first pages of *Metaphors on Vision*, resemble the commentary on vision and imagination that Hulme offered when contrasting poetry and prose.

Hulme depicts prose as a phase in the decline of language. Prose, Hulme states, uses "images that have died and become figures of speech." Drawing on an idea that was still quite new in his day, he says that when speaking or writing prose, we operate by a "reflex action," "almost without thinking," much as one does when lacing up one's boots, or engaged in any everyday action that we perform only half-aware to economize on effort. Thus Hulme critiques life lived at less than maximum intensity.

Hulme's criticism of language foretells Brakhage's aesthetics in an even more striking way. Hulme says that words in prose are simply "counters" used "to pass conclusions without thinking"—words that are "divorced from vision." Hulme thereby suggests that authentic thinking is concrete thinking, thinking about the objects and relations that words represent instead of thinking in words, by shuffling words about. Genuine thinking is therefore visual thinking, Hulme implies, and the real basis for knowing anyone or anything is seeing them clearly.

Brakhage propounds a similar position at the beginning of *Metaphors on Vision* (in a passage from which we have quoted previously).

> Imagine . . . an eye which does not respond to the name of everything but which must know each object encountered in life through an adventure of perception. How many colors are there in a field of grass to the crawling baby unaware of "Green?" How many rainbows can light create for the untutored eye? How aware of variations in heat waves can that eye be? Imagine a world alive with incomprehensible objects and shimmering with an endless variety of movement and innumerable gradations of color. Imagine a world before the "beginning was the word." . . . There is no need for the mind's eye to be deadened after infancy, yet in these times the development of visual understanding is almost universally forsaken.

> This is an age which has no symbol for death other than the skull and bones of one stage of decomposition . . . and it is an age which lives in fear of total annihilation. It is a time haunted by sexual sterility yet almost universally incapable of perceiving the phallic nature of every destructive manifestation of itself. It is an age which artificially seeks to project itself materialistically into abstract space and to fulfill itself mechanically because it has blinded itself to almost all external reality within eyesight and to the organic awareness of even the physical movement properties of its own perceptibility. The earliest cave paintings discovered demonstrate that primitive man had a greater understanding than we do that the object of fear must be objectified. The entire history of erotic magic is one of possession of fear thru holding it. The ultimate searching visualization has been directed toward God out of the deepest possible human understanding that there can be no ultimate love where there is fear. Yet in this contemporary time how many of us even struggle to deeply perceive our own children?[155]

Brakhage believes that the acquisition of language disturbs vision's natural relation to the body and disrupts the mind's relations with the world. Language makes us unaware of the "physical movement properties of its own perceptibility," i.e., of the saccadic movements and other movements of the eye. It destroys "organic awareness," i.e., the awareness of the natural organism, intimate with its own physiology. It damages both our relations with our own bodies and our bodies' relations with the world, by converting natural, healthy relations into relations mediated by language. In all this, Brakhage derives his ideas from the lesson that the Open Form poets learned from the Symbolists, that tokens (images or words), because they are all too internal, too subjective, become detached from concrete reference— become, really, symbols of symbols, signs of signs, signs whose only reference is to language itself. The text makes clear that Brakhage thinks of language itself as abstract, as being constituted through abstraction, and made up of tokens that lack concrete content. In acquiring language, children learn to think in these tokens; what is more, their subjectivity comes to be formed by language, and so lacks the concrete immediacy of the direct experience of particulars.

Brakhage and Hulme concur on the claim that the acquisition of language has deleterious effects on the sensibility. But before either Brakhage or Hulme, there was Bergson:

> This influence of language on sensation is deeper than is usually thought. Not only does language make us believe in the unchangeableness of our sensations, but it will sometimes deceive us as to the nature of the sensation felt. . . . In short, the word with well-defined outlines, the rough and ready word, which stores up the stable, common, and consequently impersonal element in the impressions of mankind, overwhelms or at least covers over the delicate and fugitive impressions of our individual consciousness.[156]

In his "Conclusion" to *Time and Free Will*, Bergson notes that this way of using language constrains us:

> The greater part of the time we live outside ourselves, hardly perceiving anything of ourselves but our own ghost, a colourless shadow which pure duration projects into homogeneous space. Hence our life unfolds in space rather than in time [for Bergson, this means it is structured by the principles of the outer world, not the inner world]; we live for the external world rather than for ourselves; we speak rather than think; we "are acted" rather than act ourselves.[157]

Or, as Brakhage suggests, the consensual language of the masses conditions our thinking and destroys our individuality.

Brakhage has expounded his ideas on language's influence on consciousness in quasi-poetic form. Recasting them into the prosaic form of philosophy fails to capture some of their qualities, and perhaps some of their thrust. Let us nevertheless tempt that disaster. Brakhage argues that language promotes categorical thinking, since language consists of nouns and qualifiers of nouns. (Predicates and verbs are qualifiers of nouns, he implies.) Common nouns (as distinct from proper names) are generic.[158] With the acquisition of language, a new form of mental activity develops that involves thinking in words and about words. This new process interposes itself between the self and the world, so all our subsequent thinking belongs to a realm divorced from reality (compare this assertion with the lesson that the Open Form poets drew from Symbolism). Thus, we think of the word "green," a categorical term, and this thought prevents us from directly experiencing a specific green tint.

Moreover, language is a social phenomenon. Accordingly, its terms represent the lowest common denominator of experience. When we learn the term "green," we acquire a token that not only does not distinguish one green tint from another, but that also does not distinguish between how I experience that green tint and how another person experiences it. Language creates experience, for once we learn language we begin to experience the world in terms of the features common to a number of objects and a number of people. Our thinking proceeds, as Bergson stated, in terms of "the word with well-defined outlines, the rough and ready word, which stores up the stable, common, and consequently impersonal element in the impressions of mankind, [that] overwhelms or at least covers over the delicate and fugitive impressions of our individual consciousness."[159] Art escapes this limitation of language, Brakhage suggests, because it allows an individual to convey the exact, individual qualities of his or her experience.

Hulme, Pound, and Brakhage have all proposed, each in his own way, that to see a thing clearly and distinctly is to apprehend its particularity and uniqueness and to be affected by the full power of its unique presence. The belief that to see something fully is to apprehend it in its complete individuality was Hulme's reason for asserting that the image, which we apprehend only through an act of vision, is the basis of poetry. Poetry is not, Hulme said, "a counter language, but a visual concrete one. It is a compromise for a language of intuition which would hand over sensations bodily."[160] The idea of "a language of intuition which would hand over sensations bodily" is likely Hulme's most important legacy to poets and filmmakers and has been indirectly influential on several of the most important artists of the century. Few know its source by first-hand acquaintance, however. Much of the remainder of this book is concerned with writers and filmmakers' efforts to minimize the compromise and to find more direct ways to "hand over sensations bodily."

While poetry, according to Hulme, is not a "counter language"—a language that treats words as tokens to be shuffled about like counters in board game—prose, because it trades in worn-out images is. Poetry is not so deleterious, because it is concrete and is a "visual" language. The function of poetry, Hulme proposes, is to revitalize a form of thinking in which the distinction between literal and figurative is yet unknown. A poet first sees a scene and recognizes in it an emotionally charged resemblance with some other object and then fashions a metaphor that expresses this vision. In time, however, the expression the poet forged becomes a phrase in the language, a token we use without having the concrete experience of the similarity of aspects of the two particulars that the metaphor identifies. It becomes a mere term of the language, or a *façon de parler*; it no longer conveys the actual experience of discovering an identity. Moreover, the phrase is too worn-out from overuse to provoke in the mind of one who hears it an image that shows the identity of features of the two relata.

> If I say the hill is *clothed* with trees your mind simply runs past the word "clothed," it is not pulled up in any way to visualise it. You have no distinct image of the trees covering the hill as garments clothe the body. But if the trees had made a distinct impression on you when you saw them,... you would probably not rest satisfied until you had got hold of some metaphor which did pull up the reader and make him visualise the thing. If there was only a narrow line of trees circling the hill near the top, you might say that it was *ruffed* with trees. I do not put this forward as a happy metaphor: I am only trying to get at the feeling which prompts this kind of expression.[161]

At the end of the statement, Hulme reiterates his belief that in matters of poetic form, experience has primacy. Like Hulme, Brakhage is concerned with the primacy of perception, with the way that the artists' unique perceptions recharge language and encourage them to form new metaphors that give precise expression to their way of seeing; and, like Hulme, Brakhage points to the way that a habitual use of metaphors (or even literal but habituated usage) drains language of power, by detaching the words from the experiences that engendered them. These beliefs underlie Brakhage's interest in etymology (as similar beliefs explain Heidegger's etymological interests)—for by tracing words back to their roots, he hopes to find evidence about the immediate perceptual experience that first brought the word into being and, in some measure, to recharge the word with its original sense.[162]

Hulme provided an argument to justify the important place in its repertoire of strategies that modern verse has given to the constatation of concrete particulars (to use Pound's phrase). In order for each distinct word and each distinct idea to have a maximum of energy, in order for a word to have the maximum power of giving itself to the reader as an immediately and forcefully present reality, the modern poet, Hulme suggests, uses a "piling-up and juxtaposition of distinct images in different lines."[163] Again, he derived the idea from Bergson; in *Introduction to Metaphysics* (of which Hulme was the official translator) Bergson pointed out that "many diverse images, borrowed from very different orders of things, may, by the convergence of their action [note that Bergson implies that he conceives of imagery as language with perlocutionary meanings], direct consciousness to the precise point where there is a certain intuition to be seized"; and the Vorticists, Pound, and Brakhage often have juxtaposed images of radically different sorts in an effort to stimulate a higher form of awareness, akin to Bergson's idea of intuition.[164] Hulme proposed that poets use personal and demotic subjects instead of the "epic subjects," the "big things" and the "heroic actions" of traditional literature in order to avoid conventionality and, more importantly, to overcome the forward impetus of the dramatic narrative that hurries the reader along from event to event without experiencing each event in the fullness of its presence. Instead of sliding over experience, Hulme wanted—to adopt Bergson's metaphor—to plumb its depths. He wanted, all in all, to create poems in the language of intuition.

Hulme's interest in the ordinary lives of ordinary people influenced Pound and, later, Brakhage (though the primary inspiration for this feature of Brakhage's work was Gertrude Stein and Marie Menken, not Pound's circle). Brakhage has spoken frequently of a utopian project that he will probably never make—a film concerned with quotidian existence, to be entitled *The Dailiness Film*. But Brakhage could have given that title to many films that he actually has made—to *Scenes from Under Childhood* (1967-70), *The Weir-Falcon Saga* (1970), *Fox Fire Child Watch* (1971), *Sexual Meditation: Open Field* (1972), *Star Garden* (1974), *Tortured Dust* (1984), *The Loom* (1986), *Flesh of Morning* (1956/1986) *Kindering* (1987), *Marilyn's Window* (1988), all the works from the *Sincerity* and *Duplicity* series (1978-80) and, paradigmatically, the entire *Songs* series (1964-69). *Western History* evolved from his wish to make an epic theme quotidian—to represent "the whole personal story of Westward Ho and Hoeing Man as He might attempt to remember it while watching a Pittsburgh basketball game," as Brakhage's program note for the film states.[165] The drive is similar to that which impelled Gertrude Stein to write *The Making of Americans* (written 1903-11, and first published in its entirety in 1925), though Brakhage's films have even more the span, scope, and texture of a "dailiness" film than Stein's novel has of a literary work dedicated to chronicling the type-forms of daily life, to putting down how each type of human being felt, to constructing an equivalent to the characteristic rhythm of each individual's type (of course, the notion of type was something that the author would have to bring into question). Most of the visual themes of *Dog Star Man* derive from everyday life, despite the film's grand theme; furthermore, that film parodies tragic irony, and the film's parodistic elements add weight to its quotidian quality.

Brakhage's views on basing artworks on epic subjects are closer to Hulme's than Pound's ever were. For Hulme's principles and practices opposed the epic form, which classical literature valued so very highly. Hulme, as we have noted, thought that the modern poem must be modest, impressionistic, "tentative and half-shy." It must not have any truck with attempts to encompass and to form the impressions that are the contents of ordinary mental life into a grand vision or overarching worldview. One can ascribe all these characteristics to Brakhage's filmmaking. Consider that *Dog Star Man*, even while striving to incorporate the commonplace within an an epic framework, keeps returning to—even collapsing into—the everyday; the film's final part, Part IV, offers sufficient evidence to support that claim: it not only keeps collapsing into the everyday, but also narratively falls back from the summer, which is that part's seasonal basis, to winter, and from the present into memory (with its recycled images from Parts I and II), and even shows the Dog Star Man, defeated, looking up at the sun (which is used as a symbol of the superior strength of nature, in comparison with that of human beings) putting down his axe, and amid several very brief cuts (showing branches, a baby, the sun's corona), falling backward in slow motion down the mountain. Pound, on the other hand, strove to construct an epic patterned after Homer's *Odyssey* and Dante's *Commedia*, an epic that would contain all that is important to know.

An anti-metaphysical and anti-heroic concern with subjectivity and with the struggle of the deeper self against language and convention are hallmarks of modern literature. The conviction, common in recent aesthetics, that art allows the individual to speak authentically, in a way that is true to his or her deeper self, is a notion that Bergson and Hulme were among the first to announce. Hulme's use of sincerity as a measure of the worth of a work of art, for all its Romantic echoes, was pioneering because, unlike the Romantics, Hulme did not present sincerity as the achievement of a hero, but as a possible feature of the ordinary spiritual life of the ordinary individual. We can find parallels for all these ideas in the work of both Pound and Brakhage, and that fact alone provides cogent testimony to Hulme's powers as a thinker.

Hulme's contrast between poetry and prose amounts to a critique of abstraction. Poetry aims "to arrest you, and to make you continuously see a physical thing, to prevent you from gliding through an abstract process." Pound shared Hulme's belief on this matter. "Go in fear of abstraction" was Pound's advice to young poets. The poet cuts through abstraction to get back to immediate experience. But Pound and Hulme simply modified Bergson's anti-abstractionist critique in order to arrive at these ideas. On the matter of what the poet might offer instead of the abstractions that prose trades in, Hulme differed from both Bergson and Pound. Hulme suggested that the concrete image rightfully had the place of highest privilege, while Pound was critical of Hulme's imagism for privileging the static over the dynamic, the timeless over flux. Having defined a virtue of poetry, phanopoeia, as "the throwing of an image against the mind's retina," Pound goes on to criticize the imagists (to whom Hulme served as an intellectual mentor).

The defect of earlier imagist propaganda was not in misstatement but in incomplete statement. The diluters [the lowest order of creators] took the handiest and easiest meaning and thought only of the STATIONARY image. If you can't think of imagism or phanopoeia as including the moving image, you will have to make a really needless division of fixed image and praxis or action.[166]

Bergson rejected imagery's static nature even more vigorously than Pound did, and was just as adamant as Pound on the matter of according rhythm pride of place.[167] He believed that the pulse of the poem unites the individual words in a poem into a whole, whose flowing movement reflects the essence of reality.

The words may then have been well chosen, they will not convey the whole of what we wish to make them say if we do not succeed by the rhythm, by the punctuation, by the relative lengths of the sentences and parts of the sentences, by a particular dancing of the sentence, in making the reader's mind, continually guided by a series of nascent movements, describe a curve of thought and feeling analogous to that we ourselves describe.... [T]he words, taken individually, no longer count: there is nothing left but the flow of meaning [*le sens mouvant*] which runs through the words, nothing but two minds which, without intermediary, seem to vibrate directly in unison with one another.[168]

Bergson goes on to stress the importance of rhythm: "The poet is he with whom feelings develop into images, and the images themselves into words which translate them while obeying the laws of rhythm. In seeing these images pass before our eyes we in our turn experience the feeling which was, so to speak, their emotional equivalent."[169]

Ideas on rhythm that Brakhage would later expound resemble Bergson's views more closely than they do Hulme's. Bergson laid the foundations for a presentational theory of poetic (or artistic) meaning, according to which poetry (or art generally), uses material forms that reawaken in the reader experiences equivalent to those that moved the writer to compose the verbal form. (We shall see that this is the basis of Brakhage's notion of artistic significance.) Furthermore, Bergson appealed to the temporal features of poetry—to the features that brought it close to music—and not its spatial resources that Hulme and the Imagists emphasized. Hulme spoke, for example, of the imagery of a poem, "endeavour[ing] to arrest you, and to make you continuously see a physical thing, to prevent you gliding through an abstract process."[170] Hulme believed the importance of poetry lies in its capacity to disturb our conventional ways of thinking and so to open us to a deeper truth: "Ordinary language communicates nothing of the individuality and freshness of things," while poetry, and poetry alone, can convey the "exhilaration" of direct and immediate communication—"unusual communication," Hulme calls it.[171] Aesthetic experience—the experience of what Hulme calls "unusual communication"—serves much the same function in Hulme's thought that intuition does in Bergson's. "Images in verse are not mere decoration, but the very essence of an intuitive language," Hulme declared.[172] What is most remarkable in all this, however, is that Hulme celebrated "the fixity of the image" for its capacity to engender an experience that lifts us out of mundane reality, while Bergson celebrated an artist's ability to identify with flux as the means to rise above conventional modes of experiencing. The fixity that Hulme extolled became the hallmark of modernist aesthetics and, as T.S. Eliot's poetry and James Joyce's prose evidence, gave modern art a place to preserve the transcendental values of its religious heritage. But it was Bergson's dynamism that was to win the loyalty of the poets and filmmakers of the 1960s and after.

Like Brakhage, Hulme believed the quintessential image is actually a metaphor. Again like Brakhage, Hulme believed that a metaphor is the product of an artist's intuition. The artist sees in a flash the similarity between two items in reality—or, sometimes, even between items in two different orders of reality. To use one of Hulme's examples, the artist sees the trees covering a hill as a mantle encloses a body and says that the trees "clothe" the hill. The metaphor juxtaposes different objects and, Hulme tells us, this juxtaposition, creates a "visual chord" (presumably because different sights blend in a harmony) that conveys an artist's perception of the object exactly as he or she sees it.

Hulme also anticipated the idea that the experiences that artworks elicit are noetic, and that the knowledge art furnishes is of a different sort than that which science provides. Brakhage declares a similar conviction: "there is a pursuit of knowledge foreign to language and founded upon visual communication, demanding a development of the optical mind, and dependent upon perception in the original and deepest sense of the word."[173] Hulme's belief in the noetic value of art rests upon his conception of the image. "Thought is the joining together of new analogies, and so inspiration is a matter of an accidentally seen analogy or unlooked-for resemblance," Hulme wrote.[174] Rather as a scientific model provides insight into the relations that exist among items in the world, artistic metaphors illuminate reality by furnishing us with new insights into the sensible flux of which we had hitherto been insensate. Like a scientist, then, an artist constructs models (the one in the form of scientific theories, the other in the forms of images and metaphors) that reveal hitherto undisclosed relations and associations; however, the artist cleaves more closely to concrete perception than the scientist does.

Hulme's conclusions on these topics contradict the fundamentals of Bergson's philosophy. Bergson took pains to distinguish the value that artworks have from those of scientific models. The very basis of knowledge is the real-ization we cannot grasp reality adequately using scientific models, but we can apprehend it in the immediacies of intuition. Bergson pointed to the limita-tions of concepts, arguing that concepts depend upon a spatial notion of exis-tence that denies the basic reality of time and change. Concepts abstract from reality and deal with features that several experiential items have in common. Only intuition can acknowledge the utter heterogeneity of reality. While many (but not all) of the early modernists followed Hulme on this matter, most of the principal later modernist writers (and, as we shall see, Stan Brakhage), arrived at notions that correspond to Bergson's thoughts on these topics.

Between Self and World: The Image in Hulme, Williams, Brakhage

The dispute over image and flux, fixity and change, has split the ranks of recent poets, filmmakers, literary theorists, and film critics. Brakhage has spoken for flux and change while others (some of whose work is in all other respects close to Brakhage's), have taken Hulme's side. Brakhage, espe-cially since the early 1980s, has been an outspoken opponent of imagery, insisting that images constitute a point at which energy goes dead. The most forceful call for cleaving to imagery to avoid the debilitating effects of using abstractions in art and poetry was issued by a poet to whom Brakhage and many of his poet friends were nonetheless close—the poet/doctor William Carlos Williams. Williams's poetics turns on a slogan that has made him famous (and a statement that Stan Brakhage is fond of quoting): "no ideas but in things." Behind this remark lies a metaphysics that resembles Hulme's in important ways, but is more extreme than his, since it rests on very American feelings of particularism. (Williams, for example, often expressed annoyance that Pound had gone off to Europe in search of art—though he might have recognized that Pound, in writing the *Cantos*, was pro-ducing an American epic, as Homer had produced an epic for the Greeks and Virgil an epic for the Romans.)[175]

American art has long been possessed by an aspiration to distinguish itself from European models. Several of the New England Transcendentalists, including Ralph Waldo Emerson and Henry David Thoreau, advanced claims that American art had distinctive characteristics. Consider Emerson's "The American Scholar": near the beginning, Emerson speculates that

> Perhaps the time is already come when ... the sluggard intellect of this continent will look from under its iron lids and fill the postponed expecta-tion of the world with something better than the exertions of mechanical skill. Our day of dependence, our long apprenticeship to the learning of

other lands, draws to a close. The millions that around us are rushing into life, cannot always be fed on the sere remains of foreign harvests.[176]

And near the end, he offers his listeners/readers this call to action:

We have listened too long to the courtly muses of Europe. The spirit of the American freeman is already suspected to be timid, imitative, tame. . . . The mind of this country, taught to aim at low objects, eats upon itself. There is no work for any but the decorous and the complaisant. . . . What is the remedy? . . . We will walk on our own feet; we will work with our own hands; we will speak our own minds. The study of letters shall be no longer a name for pity, for doubt, and for sensual indulgence. The dread of man and love of man shall be a wall of defence and a wreath of joy around all. A nation of men will for the first time exist, because each believes himself inspired by the Divine Soul which also inspires all men.[177]

The Gnostic doctrine that the American Republic of the Imagination would be one in which each individual would realize him—or herself through a self-reliance that involves nothing less than plumbing the depth of the self until one discovered the divine presence (spark) within, became the principal item of that polity's founding dogma. Thus the famous "Divinity School Address" (1838) casts the "appropriated and formal" language of catechismal instruction, the language that Europe taught America, as the enemy of inspiration and the agency that engenders obliviousness of the indwelling Supreme Spirit. Immediate experience, not secondhand learning, is the key to acquiring insight into the mystery. Thus, in "Self-Reliance," Emerson contends:

Our houses are built with foreign tastes; our shelves are garnished with foreign ornaments; our opinions, our tastes, our faculties, lean, and follow the Past and the Distant. The soul created the arts wherever they have flourished. It was in his own mind that the artist sought his model. It was an application of his own thought to the thing to be done and the conditions to be observed. And why need we copy the Doric or the Gothic model? Beauty, convenience, grandeur of thought and quaint expression are as near to us as to any, and if the American artist will study with hope and love the precise thing to be done by him, considering the climate, the soil, the length of day, the wants of the people, the habit and form of government, he will create a house in which all these will find themselves fitted, and taste and sentiment will be satisfied also.

Insist on yourself; never imitate. Your own gift you can present every moment with the cumulative force of a whole life's cultivation; but of the adopted talent of another you have only an extemporaneous half possession. That which each can do best, none but his Maker can teach him. No man yet knows what it is, nor can, till that person has exhibited it. Where is the master who could have taught Shakspeare [sic]. . . . Every great man is a unique. The Scipionism of Scipio is precisely that part he could not borrow. Shakspeare will never be made by the study of Shakspeare. . . . Abide in the simple and noble regions of thy life, obey thy heart, and thou shalt reproduce the Foreworld again.[178]

The civilized world impedes efforts to contact the self; withdrawing into the embrace of nature assists them. This proposition is the basis for the portrayal of humans' relationship with the natural world as redemptive and is a key theme of American documentary film. It is also the ground for the idea of the redemptive power of direct contact with the given thing, which one discovers anew once the deadening effects of historically induced preconceptions have been set aside.

Again, William Carlos Williams's celebration of the local realities is among the features of his oeuvre that made it a model for poets of the 1960s and 1970s who were concerned with immediate realities around them; Williams, too, believed that one must overcome the deleterious effects of history in order to open oneself to the exact condition of the local given thing which, because reality is flux (a Parmenidean conviction that Williams shared with Emerson), is made new with every passing instant. Thus, in his essay on Edgar Allan Poe, in the tellingly entitled *In the American Grain*, Williams asserts that

> The local causes shaping Poe's genius were two in character: the necessity for a fresh beginning, backed by a native vigor of extraordinary proportions,—with the corollary that all "colonial imitation" must be swept aside. This was the conscious force which rose in Poe as innumerable timeless insights resulting, by his genius, in firm statements on the character of form, profusely illustrated by his practices; and *second* the immediate effect of the locality upon the first, upon his nascent impulses, upon his original thrusts; tormenting the depths into a surface of bizarre designs by which he's known and which are *not at all* the major point in question. . . .
>
> The strong sense of a beginning in Poe is in *no one* else before him. What he says, being thoroughly local in origin, has some chance of being universal in application. . . . Made to fit a *place*, it will have that actual quality of *things* anti-metaphysical. . . .
>
> [H]e is the diametric opposite of Longfellow—to say the least. But Longfellow was the apotheosis of all that had preceded him in America, to this extent, that he brought over the *most* from "the other side." In *"Longfellow and Other Plagiarists,"* Poe looses himself to the full upon them. But what had they done? No more surely than five hundred architects are constantly practising. Longfellow did it without genius, perhaps, but he did no more and no less than to bring the tower of the Seville Cathedral to Madison Square. . . .
>
> Poe conceived the possibility, the sullen volcanic inevitability of the *place*. He was willing to go down and wrestle with its conditions, using every tool. . . . His greatness is in that he turned his back and faced inland, to originality, with the identical gesture of a Boone.[179]

Most know that the composer John Cage took great interest in the New England Transcendentalists, and especially in Emerson and Thoreau. So it should not be surprising that he developed similar ideas. In *Silence*, his famous statement of his aesthetic credo, he wrote:

[O]ne may give up the desire to control sound, clear his mind of music, and set about discovering means to let sounds be themselves rather than vehicles for man-made theories or expressions of human sentiments. . . . And what is the purpose of writing music? One is, of course, not dealing with purposes but dealing with sounds. Or the answer must take the form of paradox: a purposeful purposelessness or a purposeless play. This play, however, is an affirmation of life—not an attempt to bring order out of chaos nor to suggest improvements in creation, but simply a way of waking up to the very life we're living, which is so excellent once one gets one's mind and one's desires out of the way and lets it act of its accord.[180]

Such conceptions of American particularism are sometimes associated (as it is in the thought of Stan Brakhage) with the belief that language imposes a deadening weight of tradition on experience, and only the raw, unformed experience of the natural body is authentically related to the immediate conditions of living (i.e., related to what, in Williams's sense of the word, is "local"). Or it leads to the stress on the individual, autonomous existent and denial of the reality of relationships—to the belief that only individual sensations and the connections between them are real, to the uncompromising positivism that Leonard B. Meyer calls "transcendental particularism" or, better, "radical empiricism," in his great study, *Music, the Arts, and Ideas*.[181]

These ideas resonate through American avant-garde film. Emerson's teaching that "That which each can do best, none but his Maker can teach him. . . . Every great man is a unique. The Scipionism of Scipio is precisely that part he could not borrow" is precisely the ground of the individualist element of Stan Brakhage's aesthetic. Brakhage's aesthetic theory has its roots in the conviction that immediate experience is the ground of all truth and all value, and that constructing narrative relations between events depletes the experience of the concrete particular of intensity and, what is perhaps as bad, misrepresents the truth about reality. In this regard, Brakhage's aesthetic theories are consistent with that cluster of belief that Meyer terms "radical empricism."

In the Prologue to *Kora in Hell: Improvisations* (1920), Williams declared that "[t]he true value is that peculiarity which gives an object a character by itself. The associational or sentimental value is the false."[182] Metaphor debilitates, he averred, and so he castigated "[t]hose who permit their senses to be despoiled of the things under their noses by stories of all manner of things removed and unattainable" for being "of frail imagination."[183] However, he also proposed an alternative: "Much more keen is that power which discovers in things those inimitable particles of dissimilarity to all other things which are the peculiar perfections of the thing in question."[184] Further, he opined that artists must pay heed to the immediacy of their situations and recognize what is specific to their own time and place.

In the American Grain represents, above all else, Williams's struggle to establish a foundation on which American poetry could be raised or, to shift to Stephen Fredman's metaphor, to clear a ground for American poetry. Williams declares: "what has been morally, aesthetically worth while in America has rested upon peculiar and discoverable ground."[185] The firmest ground he could find was the uncorrupted character of the resolute, self-reliant individual (to use that Emersonian term). The true American poet must be a genuine individual, must be unique and, to use Williams's term, an original "in its legitimate sense of solidity which goes back to the ground, a conviction that he *can* judge within himself."[186] Brakhage shares with Williams (and, as we shall see, with Charles Olson) this idea that the character of a genuine original is the true source of creativity.

Gertrude Stein, too, committed herself to an ideal of American particularism. She attempted to distance herself from all those preconceptions that made up the "mind of Europe" which Pound and Eliot had so eagerly adopted; she particularly disliked Eliot's idea that the individual talent must absorb and transmute the strengths of the tradition of writing. What is more, Stein rejected the mystical element that the early modernists took from the French Symbolists. Rather than speaking for a repressed, occult tradition, as Yeats and Pound did, Stein spoke for what the individual can draw out of the concrete realities of his or her particular circumstances. So, like her predecessor Ralph Waldo Emerson, her contemporary William Carlos Williams, and her successor John Cage, Stein traced the particular virtue of America back to the Americans' openness to the specificity of the concrete particular in all its uniqueness.

Williams is the author of a work that is remarkable for the way it adopted and modified Cubist strategies for incorporating real world elements by decomposing and rearranging them. As a literary work, it could not incorporate real world elements per se, but it could—and did—use words that, because they derive from such close observation of objects and such scrupulous attention to how we see them, are near equivalents to them. That work, *Spring and All* (1923), alternates passages of prose and poetry; many of the prose passages offer Williams's views on art and poetry.[187] Williams states in *Spring and All* that "There is a constant barrier between the reader and his consciousness of immediate contact with the world"; and so the reader never knows "and never dares to know ... what he is at the exact moment that he is. And this moment is the only thing in which I am at all interested. . . . To refine, to clarify, to intensify that eternal moment in which we alone live" is the task of an artist.[188] The phenomenology of time consciousness that Williams adumbrated here resembles ideas concerning time that William James and Gertrude Stein offered, and, as we shall soon see, that Stan Brakhage offered as well.

The importance that Williams attached to immediacy, an importance to which his comments about *Spring and All* testify, inflects all phases of his poetic theory. That importance depended upon a belief that he shared with Hulme, Bergson, and with many of those who took up Bergson's philosophy: the belief that reality is flux. Williams did not read A.N. Whitehead's *Science and the Modern World* and *Four Lectures on Relativity and Space* until 1927, three years after writing *Spring and All*. Yet features of the work anticipate what he would later find in Whitehead (and which would become so important to him). *Spring and All* conveys a dynamic conception of reality, as Whitehead's system does; *Spring and All* celebrates continual rebirth, while Whitehead speaks of the universe being maintained in being by a continual process of creation; *Spring and All* celebrates the triumph of Imagination, while Whitehead discusses the all-pervading presence of Mind; and, most important of all, *Spring and All*, like *Process and Reality*, suggests that when one feels life vibrantly, one senses one's relation to all that is: here is *Spring and All* on the last theme, "The inevitable flux of the seeing eye toward measuring itself by the world it inhabits can only result in himself crushing humiliation [*sic*] unless the individual raise to some approximate co-extension with the universe. This is possible by aid of the imagination."[189]

All these similarities explain why, when Williams did read some of Whitehead's writings, he found them a philosophical system that fully developed many of the images of reality that had occupied him for several years; accordingly, by 1949, Williams acknowledged Whitehead, along with John Dewey and William James, as among those who taught him about the relation of content and form, process and reality, change and structure.[190] Whitehead presented the image of reality as a vast flux of relations, whose only permanence derived from Ideal Objects, that is, from a mind that permeates the entire field. Motion is everywhere and all reality really only a flow of events, he proclaimed; and the mind is everywhere and is in motion everywhere. For his part, Williams celebrated the object-like words on a page animated by a creative flux that reveals the creative power of a mind in motion. Just as Whitehead believed that reality is maintained in existence from one moment to the next by a creative power, so Williams believed flux is so pervasive that with each passing instant a world is destroyed and a new world created, so that it is constantly true to say, "THE WORLD IS NEW." It is as a countertendency to this flux that Williams used the fixity of the poetic image, that is, the poem's capacity to fix time and movement in a spatial arrangement; in doing this, Williams reaffirmed the modernists commitment to the Platonic ontology.[191] And just as Whitehead offered a neutral monism (see glossary), according to which mind and matter share in a common sort of being, Williams's poems provide a set of instances of the meeting of mind and matter, of the direct perception of objects that enlivens reality itself. The leaps of association that his poems contain evoke just this all-pervading subjectivity, without compromising the sense of the reality of objects they present.

Some of Williams's poems seem to be extraordinary objective: the very famous "Red Wheelbarrow" (which appeared first as "Poem XXII" in *Spring and All*) is as fine an example as any—but even in so seemingly objective a poem, we can discern a dialectic between subject and object, for the poem can be taken as eliciting feelings about so much depending on an exact, but accidental and variable condition. Others, for example, *Kora in Hell*, have almost the nature of free-association compositions. The best way to consider the relation between the seemingly objective aspect of the writer's output and its very American concern with subjectivity and the imagination—which relation really did, as Lisa M. Steinman shows in *Made In America: Science, Technology, and American Modernist Poets*, cause him consternation through-out his productive life—is after the manner of Whitehead: Whitehead pointed out (and Williams followed him on the matter) that the flow of energy is iden-tical throughout the universe, whether in the realm we commonly consider to be subjective or whether in the realm we commonly consider to be objec-tive. Such transfer of energy, and, more generally, movement, really is crucial for Williams; in "Della Primavera Transportata Al Morale" (1930) Williams offers the very Whiteheadian assertion,

> Moral
> it has never ceased
> to flow[192]

Of course, the ostensive deictic "it" is ambiguous, and its principal ambigu-ity concerns whether it refers to the subjective or the objective realm. One could, and should, resolve this ambiguity in a Whiteheadian fashion, by pointing out that the question whether "it" refers to something objective or something subjective is unanswerable, since the distinction between the two terms is a false one. What is important is what Williams termed the fluidity of all reality. In the "Introduction" to *The Wedge*, Williams opined that a poem is "a small (or large) machine made of words" and that "[i]t isn't what he [the poem] *says* that counts as a work of art, it's what he makes, with such intensity of perception that it lives with an intrinsic movement of its own to verify its authenticity."[193]

When Williams's poems are objective, they are objective as a machine is objective. When they seem to be free associational (as *Kora in Hell* some-times seems), it is the verbal energy carried in the stream of consciousness that has cardinal importance. A poem by Williams presents both an object and a process; and as Whitehead showed, those ontological categories are hardly distinct.

In *Spring and All* Williams expounds most fully one of the key themes of his oeuvre: his proposition that metaphors exercise debilitating effects, since they identify two beings with one another and, by doing so, fail to acknowledge the individual peculiarities of what they identify. "Everything that I have done in the past—except those parts which may be called excellent— by chance, have that quality about them. It is typified by use of the word 'like' or that 'evocation' of the 'image' which served us for a time."[194] As had the Romantics before him, Williams asserted that the faculty we use to discover whatever in our environing conditions is peculiar, and hence universally significant, is the imagination. "The only realism in art is of the imagination. It is only thus that the work escapes plagiarism after nature and becomes a creation."[195] And though the artist fashions a work of art using the materials of reality, the work itself is nonetheless an autonomous, autotelic entity. The imagination imposes a shape (or what Williams calls "a design") upon the material the artist uses, and so transmutes real matter into a new, independent entity. This transmutation, Williams realized, is just what the Cubists had achieved with their techniques of fragmentation and recombination.

Williams celebrated imagination to almost the same degree as Brakhage has. He addressed *Spring and All* to his goddess, imagination—the same figure, one presumes, whom Brakhage calls "the Muse." And Williams, like Brakhage, cast the imagination in the role of the producer of insight—to see a thing, to see *into* it with great clarity, is to imagine it. Williams testified to the power of the imagination when he pointed out that it has the capacity to destroy and to remake everything. In doing this, Williams claimed for the imagination the same powers that the modernists claimed for poetic irony— that imagination cuts words free from their bonds to meaning and transfers them to the aesthetic realm. Brakhage, as we shall soon see, makes similar claims for the powers of the imagination. Williams described the imagination by petitioning to the traditional Romantic view that the creative force in nature that drives evolution is the same force that in human subjectivity we call the imagination; imagination, like evolution, proceeds by copying existing objects and transforming them in the process.[196]

Williams's view on the imagination finally placed that faculty in a dialectical relation with direct seeing, which is immediate apprehension of concrete particulars set before one's mind; for in Williams's view, as in Brakhage's, direct seeing and imagination participate with one another in formulating the reality of the objects amongst which we live. Williams construed the relation between the two terms as a dialectical relation, because the faculty of seeing and the imagination have opposing characteristics, yet each requires its opposite to complete it: the interest one takes in a particular object is a form of self-abnegation in the face of reality, of emptying the self so that objective existence might reveal itself through the being that beholds it, yet they reveal the subject (for Williams maintained, somewhat as his compatriot T.S. Eliot, and T.E. Hulme also believed) that objects provide objective correlatives (see glossary) of the artist's emotion; by the meticulous observation of concrete particulars, artists find those objects whose lines, shape, textures, and volumes reflect their exact feelings. Where Williams's use of the particular object differs from Eliot's is that Williams's method does not convert the object into an objective correlative, i.e., a vehicle for conveying the artist's subjectivity, nor does his compositional process reduce it to a metaphor, or a symbol of some sort, of inwardness. The particular object remains autonomous, independent of, and indifferent to the feelings that its qualities suggest. It is, paradoxically, as utterly objective that these "correlatives" call upon subjectivity, and reveal its characteristics.

An image, in Williams's poetics (and in Brakhage's practice) is an ambiguous entity that spans the subjective and objective realms. The idea that there is a class of ontological entities (however broad that class may be) that straddles the realms of subjectivity and objectivity was one that late-nineteenth- and early-twentieth-century thinkers often expounded. William James, for example, opined that the contents of the stream of consciousness have that status: "The instant field of the present is at all times what I call 'pure' experience. It is only virtually or potentially either object or subject."[197] It is a crucial item in Eliot's thought from the time he formulated his exposition of and commentary on F.H. Bradley's epistemology (ca. 1911-16). In his doctoral thesis on Bradley, Eliot wrote this concerning Bradley's concept of "immediate experience" or "feeling":

> We have, or seem to have at the start a 'confusion' of feeling, out of which subject and object emerge. We stand before a beautiful painting, and if we are sufficiently carried away, our feeling is a whole which is not, in a sense, *our* feeling, since the painting, which is an object independent of us, is quite as truly a constituent as our consciousness or our soul. The feeling is neither here or anywhere: the painting is in the room and my 'feelings' about the picture are in my 'mind.' If this whole of feeling were complete and satisfactory, it would not expand into object, and subject with feelings about the object. . . . [198]

The first section of Eliot's doctoral thesis, on Bradley's metaphysics, was given over to demonstrating that immediate experience knows no distinction between subject and object, the second section to showing that there is no absolute distinction between real and ideal. From this, he proceeded to an Bradleyian critique of philosophical positions that implicitly have attempted to subtract the object from the subject or the subject from the object. He also propounded a version of the Brentano-Meinong thesis concerning the intentionality of consciousness, i.e., that all consciousness is "consciousness-of" something. He even postulated the idea of a "half-object" to deal with issues around intersubjectivity: he attributed the status of half-object to our perception of people, i.e., material bodies that we recognize and relate to as possessing subjectivity. Finally, Eliot's writings on poetry and art often criticized artists either for the excessive "subjectivity" (i.e., subjective affect that overwhelmed the object) or for excessive "objectivity."

Pound, too, was concerned with the interplay of subjectivity and objectivity, and with that class of entities whose ontological status straddles the objective and subjective realms. In his famous remarks on his equally famous "In a Station of the Metro," he notes that "[i]n a poem of this sort one is trying to record the precise instant when a thing outward and objective transforms itself, or darts into a thing inward and subjective."[199]

The popularity of the idea that there is a class of entities that straddles the subjective and objective among thinkers of Williams's time notwithstanding, that this idea, especially as Williams formulated it, has an ancestry in the Puritan tradition—a rather ironic ancestry, considering the poet's animosity towards the Puritans—is something that we simply must acknowledge. Puritans maintained a theory of language, based rather loosely on the hieroglyphic theory of langue that Frye presents in *The Great Code*. According to the Puritan theory, words that refer to external objects also constitute a code that signifies inner phenomena. A good part of Puritan efforts at textual interpretation aimed at revealing the inner truths that are allegorically presented as descriptions of the external world—but these texts, they acknowledge, are also actual descriptions of external reality, the truths of which must also be apprehended in the same interpretive act as apprehends their meaning as truths about the subjective world. Williams's conception of direct perception, Pound's conception of the ideogram, Olson's of the hieroglyphic, and Brakhage's of the film image (at least, as the form he conceived in the earlier phases of his career—up to, say, the mid-1980s, when he launched a critique of "picture" that in many ways resembles Bergson's commentary on the pictorial form of perception) are variant formulations of the idea that the poetic image illuminates inner and outer reality simultaneously. The imagery of most of Brakhage's films shares with Williams's imagery an ambiguous status—it seems both to derive from a specific place and yet to possess the qualities of the contents of mind; in sum, Brakhage's imagery, like Williams's, spans the domains of the objective and the subjective.[200] That is why, for example, Brakhage can offer photographically derived images to convey "moving visual thinking." The poetic image (or film image in

Brakhage's case) is a locus where the objective and the subjective realms intersect. Indeed, in Brakhage's work, as in Williams's and Pound's, the actual object, as revealed in intense concentration, becomes the meeting place of subjectivity and objectivity.

When Williams counseled that there must be no ideas but in things, he opened the converse possibility, that there can be ideas in things. An object revealed in direct perception brings the inner and outer world in alignment; this is why Williams and Brakhage both treat vision as redemptory. Robert Duncan conveys the sense exquisitely in my favourite of his poems:

> Often I am permitted to return to a meadow
> as if it were a scene made-up by the mind,
> that is not mine, but is a made place,
>
> that is mine, it is so near to the heart,
> an eternal pasture folded in all thought
> so that there is a hall therein
>
> that is a made place, created by light
> wherefrom the shadows that are forms fall.[201]

The meadow of Duncan's poem is, of course, the transitional area (see glossary) to the exploration of which the English paediatrician/psychoanalyst D.W. Winnicott devoted his work. And, as Duncan's poem indicates, there is no better representation for this ambiguous reality than light, which is both an energy in the external world and something so seemingly immaterial that it could be the contents of consciousness.

Williams offered a notion of place that enhances this dialectical relationship between the subjective and objective realms. Williams suggested that if people see into themselves and, as well, deeply into the place where they dwell, they will recognize qualities in the objects around them that, though they had passed over them previously, those objects have long possessed. Though these qualities belong to the objective order of existence, they reveal to us what we are, how we see, and how we feel. In sum, they have subjective value. They are, in fact, the wellspring of our spiritual being, since we fulfill ourselves in the complete and accurate perception of the objects in our surroundings.

Repudiating all the plans and schemes we usually bring to bear on the perception of objects is essential to seeing them completely and fully. Ordinarily, how we see an object is affected by the purposes we conceive for it; we do not see it for what it is in itself. To see an object truly and deeply we must put aside all our conceptions of what use value the object may have. We must set aside our interests and unburden ourselves of preconceptions—if we are to bring the object into full presence in consciousness and see it for what it is in itself. Hence Williams was somewhat sceptical of philosophical thinking; in *The Embodiment of Knowledge*, which Williams wrote between 1928 and 1930, he disparages science, technology, and philosophy (and especially John Dewey's philosophy of education) for their dogmatic character, and praises the "partial and tentative" insights that poets offer.[202] While philosophers offer fixed solutions (solutions they apply to a range of problems, introducing only minor modifications to accommodate variations among situations), poets and writers deal with ideas that arise in the immediacy of "in the act of writing."[203] Equally, Williams stressed that the object from which the poem arises must be free of any conceptions we might bring to it from an alien tradition.

To free poetry from an imposed tradition required liberating the poetic line from any imposed metric form that has little or nothing to do with the poem's content. From early in his career, Williams frequently constructed lengthy series of enjambed lines without regular metre or scansion; a result of this mode of construction was that the individual line became the poem's basic structural and metrical unit (there is no other form of segmentation that might be a candidate). Moreover, the line order of his poems frequently departs from the expected order of clauses in a sentence, and as a result, the tension the line arouses carries over line endings. Deviations from expected sentence order of this sort also make it evident that the language of a poem belongs to a different type than ordinary speech does, and that the precise difference between aesthetic language and other sorts of language is that aesthetic language is more dynamic. Such deviation from the expected grammatical order also allows the words to function as individual components of the poem which, since their sequence is not determined by syntactic laws, can be arranged in any array a poet cares to shape, just as freely as painters can decide upon arrangement of the daubs of paint they put onto canvas.

All these notions came to bear on the idea of the variable foot.[204] In Williams's later poems, those collected in *The Desert Music, Journey to Love*, and *Pictures from Brueghel and Other Poems*, Williams arranged the lines in, mostly, groups of three, with the second and third lines each further indented. Every line constitutes a metric unit; still, a line can have any number of syllables—hence he referred to the unit as the variable foot. A succession of lines can have different numbers of syllables or stresses, rather as a succession of bars of music can contain different numbers of notes, and yet reiterate the same metric unit (though the successive bars of music, unlike a series of Williams's variable feet, will usually have the same number of stresses).

What matters, simply, is that the successive lines have similar movement properties, so that the poem (or section of a poem) rhythmically repeats a basic module. What makes the line the metrical unit is its quality of motion, and this quality of motion does not depend on the number of stresses or the number of syllables in the line. The great advantage of the variable foot is that it maintains the pleasure we derive from the return of the same while allowing for variation from line to line; and this variation conveys the flux and fluidity of reality.

As much as freeing the line from an imposed metric, Williams's poetics are about freeing the American object from the grip of an alien European tradition (a tradition that valued discernment of likenesses among things and, consequently, esteemed metaphor, among all the poetic tropes, especially highly); it is equally about overcoming the deleterious effects of our habitually utilitarian manner of relating to objects. His enthusiasm for the particular existent, and, more generally, his ideas about locality, derived partly from John Dewey's essay "Americanism and Localism." Williams opined that the European tradition has been despoiled, and it threatens to corrupt America. He looked to the American earth itself to provide a more concrete, and therefore salutary basis of the true individual (a view Brakhage would later imply in his 1960 film *The Dead*). Nonetheless, the poet's cherishing of local values does imply that he believes the world of physical matter and ordinary objects to have ultimate value. Williams considered the most humble of perceived objects to have a place within the highest system of values, i.e., in the system that is reflected in the structure of aesthetic experience. Indeed, in his verse the perception of quotidian, local existents possesses an immediacy that elevates them to the highest epistemological value. The immediacy of such perception thwarts the inherited urge to divert its expression into similes and metaphors; in accepting the sensuality of the immediate image, the poet allows the natural to be itself, exactly; it is the force of such an act of perception that generates the individual line and the arrangement of lines on the page (always a key consideration regarding Williams's verse). And even humble objects, Williams states, can claim a place within the transcendent order of experience that is the aesthetic realm.

> the thing that stands eternally in the way of really good writing is always one: the virtual impossibility of lifting to the imagination those things which lie under the direct scrutiny of the senses, close to the nose. It is this difficulty that sets a value upon all works of art and makes them a necessity. The senses witnessing what is immediately before them in detail see a finality which they cling to in despair, not knowing which way to turn. Thus the so-called natural or scientific array becomes fixed, the walking devil of modern life. He who even nicks the solidity of this apparition does a piece of work superior to that of Hercules when he cleaned the Augean stables.[205]

So Williams wrote in the prologue to *Kora in Hell*. Williams shared with Gertrude Stein the attitude that cherishes each existent because its uniqueness imbues it with ultimate value. This is an attitude that Stan Brakhage, too, brings to bear on reality. Brakhage expresses his sense of the importance of having a ground in the humble objects of everyday experience in his films like *Scenes from Under Childhood* (1967-70), *The Machine of Eden* (1970), *Sexual Meditation: Open Field* (1972), *Star Garden* (1974), *Tortured Dust* (1984), the *Sincerity* (1973-78) and *Duplicity* (1978-80) series, and the extraordinary *Visions in Meditation* (1989-90) series—that ground themselves in quotidian reality. His photographed (as opposed to those created by applying paint directly, by hand, to the film's surface) films of 1990s, however, generally make Brakhage's convictions on the matter especially evident: to which does the imagery of *Unconscious London Strata* belong—is it of mind, or of world (or of neither)?

Perhaps it is *A Child's Garden and the Serious Sea* (1991) that makes most evident the ambiguous status the image has in Brakhage's film; it is not true, exactly, to say that a concrete particular is apprehended simply for itself, or that the concrete particular is used to convey the filmmaker's subjective state. This film returns to the themes that Brakhage outlined in *Metaphors on Vision* and dealt with in such films as *Anticipation of the Night* (1958), *The Weir-Falcon Saga* (1970), and *Star Garden* (1974), among others. However, it is *Scenes from Under Childhood* (1967-70) that, among all of Brakhage's previous films, *A Child's Garden and the Serious Sea* most resembles. Brakhage shot the film in Victoria, British Columbia, the birthplace of his second wife Marilyn; the garden that the film's title refers to is the garden in the backyard of her home. Like *Scenes from Under Childhood*, *A Child's Garden and the Serious Sea* is an affirmation of love as a quest for a deeper understanding of the loved one, and like *Scenes from Under Childhood*, the search for deeper understanding takes the form of efforts to imagine how the loved one sees—or, in this case, saw—as the film tries to "re-member" the vision of the child which provided the basis for the loved one's subsequent experience. Brakhage has described *A Child's Garden and the Serious Sea* as a film about the tragedy of a child losing her unique vision and developing a socialized mode of seeing. His commentary is accurate, as far as it goes, but it is partial. The film does contain visual forms that represent a theme park (reminiscent of representation of the sculpture of a gigantic hand that appears in *Faust 4*), which show how civilization corrupts nature. Thus, *A Child's Garden* provides an equivalent that suggests the corruption of the self's world. While this story of corruption is a dimension of the film, the conflict between the personal and the social realms, and between nature and civilization, seem mitigated by the demonstration of the imagination's undiminished power to see reality—of whatever form—in a fresh, more profound way. Every item in the perceptual inventory he constructs possesses extraordinary beauty, and the extraordinary beauty of each fleeting moment of perception, whether socialized or not, attenuates the tragedy the film charts.

A Child's Garden and the Serious Sea shows Brakhage in full maturity, making work unsurpassed in all of cinema. The obvious comparison would be to Monet at Giverny. The comparison is not superficial: there is a real Impressionist quality to *A Child's Garden and the Serious Sea*. Like the subject matter of so much Impressionist art—for example, the fleeting appearance of light on the façade of the Rouen cathedral or the momentary configuration of smoke in the Gare St. Lazare—the subject matter of *A Child's Garden* has only transitory existence; indeed Brakhage could hardly have found a better subject for depicting flux than the ocean waves that are the subject of this film (and of *Made Manifest*, 1980). Like Impressionist painting, *A Child's Garden* isolates and calls to our attention the perceptual contents of our quotidian existence and, by doing so, encourages us to understand them in a new way. Like Impressionist painting generally, but even more in the manner of Monet's late paintings, *A Child's Garden* lifts the fleeting appearances of demotic objects to an aesthetic transcendental by an act of attention that goes over into their being.[206] In Monet's later work, beauty charges each evanescent effect of light on the ponds and rivers surrounding his house with ultimate value. It was because he saw that every moment in vision possesses ultimate worth that Monet could conceive of producing a series of paintings that collectively represent the appearance of objects at many times of day.

The values that *A Child's Garden* reflects are close to those maintained by William Carlos Williams. The primary object matter of *A Child's Garden* is water—and the film's prolonged concentration on such a simple element makes the film an extraordinary display of Brakhage's capacity to create many (seemingly endless) variations from a single visual form, and thus of the strength and fecundity of his imagination.[207]

The structures of Williams's poems sometimes mirror the ambiguous status of the image in his poetry, straddling the division between subject and object. For although his poems often relate to a concrete situation, their strength does not derive from a portrait that the words in the poem paint; rather their strength depends on their creating a structural equivalent to the situation or object to which the poem relates. Thus we can discern in Williams's writings—both his expository and his creative writings—the key ideas of the objectism that Charles Olson was to propound four decades later.

As an example of how the forms of Williams's poems provide a structural equivalent for experience of the particular object, and, so as a object, through its structure, invites us to have an experience similar to that which the poet underwent in scrutinizing the object, take the early poem "Young Sycamore" from 1927:

> I must tell you
> this young tree
> whose round and firm trunk
> between the wet
>
> pavement and the gutter
> (where water
> is trickling) rises
> bodily
>
> into the air with
> one undulant
> thrust half its height—
> and then
>
> dividing and waning
> sending out
> young branches on
> all sides—
>
> hung with cocoons—
> it thins
> till nothing is left of it
> but two
>
> eccentric knotted
> twigs
> bending forward
> hornlike at the top[208]

The poem concerns feelings of movement evoked as the eye travels up a tree, first along a solid trunk, then following one of the many branches that split off the trunk, till the branch thins out into two twigs. However, the poem evokes the sensation of the eye moving over the object not by presenting a full, detailed description of the sensations in all their complex variety; rather it does so by presenting a verbal structure that we experience analogously to way the poet experiences the tree. The poet wishes to evoke the sensation of the eye in movement; consequently, the poem includes terms suggesting movement. More importantly, its structure encourages us to feel movement. The firm trunk stretches "between the wet," Williams writes—and then breaks the stanza. Consequently we feel the eye travelling across some expanse until it reaches . . . what? (We don't find out immediately.)

    The second verse operates similarly. We are told the tree stretches "between the wet/ pavement and the gutter/ (where water/ is trickling) rises/ bodily." Note the break within the parenthetical participle phrase which segregates the verb phrase "is trickling," and separates it from the subject. The use of enjambed lines, and of interpolated phrases evoke the sense of action.

The verb form "is trickling" is followed by another, "rises." Such a succession of verb phrases is unconventional; one likely purpose for the poet's using such an unconventional construction was to further stress the sensation of movement. More importantly yet, the parenthetical interpolation suspends the forward movement of the principal clause, so that when the principal verb—"rises"—appears, an interrupted movement resumes, since the verb reaches all the way back to the poem's second line for its subject. The extent of the verb reaches back—through three lines and across a stanza break—to convey the feeling of crossing over an interval of some considerable extent. Thus the poem's structure corresponds to its content— the poem refers to a tree that reaches from the gutter into the air, and the verb reaches back across a number of lines for its subject. Consequently the reader experiences the poem's structure in a manner similar to the way the poet responds to the form of the tree. The poem does not describe the tree, but provides a verbal structure that elicits an equivalent experience—an experience of the tree not as a static object, set over against the poets, but an experience of dynamism.

One is reminded that later in life, and very much under the influence of A.N. Whitehead, Williams would compose an essay under the very Olsonian title, "The Poem as a Field of Action." But something Williams had written earlier, in 1919, reflects on his sense of the importance of engendering feelings of movement. "Poets have written of the big leaves and the little leaves, leaves that are red, green, yellow and the one thing they have never seen about a leaf is that it is a little engine. It is one of the things that makes a plant GO."[209] (By the same token, in *Gertrude Stein: Meditative Literature and Film*, Brakhage quoted Olson, and then a distinguished Westerner poet friend: "'Keep it moving,' like they say, and/or 'Shoot first, and ask questions later,' as poet Ed Dorn puts it.")[210] The dynamic conception of the poem that Williams presents here stretches back to the Vorticists and forward to the Projective Poets who emerged at mid-century.

Furthermore, the language in the opening stanza is weighty and precise: the trunk is described as being round and firm. The poet's use of digressive interpolations thickens the poem's texture even more. The heft of the language of the first stanza evokes a response similar to the response the sycamore's trunk engenders in the poet. As the poem progresses, the language loses some of its strength and power, and becomes more delicate. Thus the third stanza conveys the feeling of the trunk rising bodily "into the air with/ one undulant/ thrust." The contrast between the relatively weak, "undulant" and the beginning of the following line, which starts with the strong, monosyllabic word "thrust"—a word that begins with a speedy, unvoiced fricative and ends, as though braking, with a sibilant and clipped consonant—evokes a feeling of the strength we feel as the eye travels along an object that seems strong and powerful, and of the resolution we feel when there are no alternative paths to follow. The contrast also foreshadows the dissipation of energies, which here regroup themselves (with "thrust"), but soon dissipate again.

The poem continues with another relatively weak conjunctive phrase, "and then." Thus the stanza ends, and we are left in suspense, rather like that which the poet feels as his eye travels to the end of the trunk and hesitates, not knowing which branch to follow. Here again, the poem's structure elicits from the reader an experience similar to that which the poet undergoes as he observes the tree. We expect such a stock phrase will be followed by one that possesses more strength and power. It is not; rather it is followed by "dividing and waning/ sending out/ young branches/ on all sides—." The aural thinness of the words "dividing and waning," which are composed entirely of short vowels and consonants, evokes the feeling that the power the tree exerts on the poet's eye/mind is waning, and that, when the eye moves upward above the trunk, which we experience as a single, solid, strong mass, the eye's movement is no longer so strong and resolute. As well, the details that the poem presents thin out—consider, for example, that the entire last third of the poem is occupied with saying that the branch that the poet's eye travels along splits into two small twigs. The repeated *i* sound in the last third of the poem elicits similarly delicate feelings. So the poem's structure thins out and disappears, just as the sycamore tree does.

The arrangement of line breaks is always one of the most important factors to consider when studying a poem by Williams—even in those poems he wrote long before he had developed the idea of the variable foot, it was clear that each line in a poem by Williams constituted a rhythmic unit, however many stresses it might have. A fine exercise to learn about the poet's metric practices is to experiment with "The Red Wheelbarrow"—write it out as a single sentence and try dividing its line differently than Williams did, and you notice just how very much depends on the particular configuration that Williams devised. You will notice, on top of that, that the poem has a splendid intricacy, for the number of syllables per line, in order, is 4,2,3,2,3,2,4,2—a pattern consisting of two interlocking series, one a series of duples and the other a symmetric 4,3,3,4 series, i.e., two lines that increment the most insistent module, the duple, by one count, and two that increment it by two counts.

The reader experiences the poem's structure in a similar way to that in which the poet experiences the tree. The poem itself offers, in its caesuras, and in its use of the long u and of the a and o in the first third and of the short i in the final third, a structure that we can experience similarly to the manner in which we experience a tree, with its strong lower half and considerably more delicate upper half.

The features of the poem determine our response to it; that they do helps us to see just how rich Williams's dictum "No ideas but in things" really is. "Young Sycamore" does not represent the tree's structure by offering a precise description of all its details; rather it presents precisely a few observed details within a structure that, because it is homologous with the poet's experience of the sycamore, we respond to in much the same way that the poet responded to the tree. What is more, the poem does not propose reflections on the tree's structure (about, say, how the tree spans heaven and earth), nor does it offer ruminations on the human condition that the tree inspires (as Shelley or Keats, or even the Imagists, might have). The mode of experience is entirely different (and it was this difference that made Williams's poetry so radical): the content of the poem is its shape, for what it evokes, it evokes by its structure, by its pauses and hesitancies, and forward movement. The experience the poem evokes, it evokes not through what it describes, but through being what it is, i.e., through having the structure that it does. The poem is as much presentation as it is representation; it is not a linguistic artifact that describes the world, but an object, with an autotelic structure, that claims the right to be experienced as any object in the world (say a tree) might be. The form allows the poem to be experienced as any other object in the world might be; like any other object, the poem can make the mind go.

A poem by Williams does not represent nature; it is not set over against nature, but juxtaposed to it. But some precision on this topic is required. For though the poem is not set over against nature, nonetheless it does belong to the same order of being as nature. It is a reality of a different sort, because it is dynamized by our perception that it has a peculiar sort of significance. To create a poem, a poet first receives a dynamic impression from nature; but the poetic act reverses the vector of this exchange. The poet constructs a verbal equivalent for the dynamic impression he or she received by acting in the world (in adding something to the world). That the object the poet constructed bears evidence of its making distinguishes it from other objects in the world, for it alerts us that it has been imbued with a different sort of energy than other objects. Nonetheless, the poem becomes an object in the world, that the reader, if sufficiently open, experiences dynamically.

Williams highlighted the presentational nature of the poem in the first line, by emphasizing that the poem is a speech act ("I must tell you") and by using an ambiguous deictic marker in the second (*"this* young tree")—"this" is ambiguous because it can be taken as referring to the actual sycamore ("this tree that I am looking at through my front window in Paterson") or the poem ("this tree structure that I am setting out for you here, on this very page"). The poem picks up the action in the eighth line, which consists of the single word "bodily," and here too the character of the action is such as to reaffirm a three-termed homology among the dynamic experience that originated the poem, the poem's structure, and the reader's experience. The word's isolation lends it weight, and so invites us to consider the body's involvement in the work of writing.

Williams raised the question of the sort of consideration his poems invite in a comment he made in "How to Write" (1936). There he tells us that the compositional process takes its impetus from "the very muscles and bones of the body itself speaking."[211] Throughout the poem, we are encouraged to consider the poem as a speech act ("I must tell you"). Consider the inversion of the customary sentence order that begins on the fourth line: The third line mentions the tree's trunk, the seventh line presents the verb for that subject, stating that the tree "rises." We expect subject and verb to be adjacent to one another and that, after the verb is presented, we would be told from where the tree rises and to where it reaches. However, the subject and verb are not adjacent to each other—the description of the space through which the trunk rises is transposed so as to precede the verb. The transposition, as well as encouraging us to feel the span through which the tree rises, also lends the poem a quality of speech, for such transpositions are commonplace in ordinary conversations. The transposition also puts stress on "bodily"—as its stark simplicity and its being on a line of its own contrasts with the rather elaborate texture created by the transposition; yet, despite that emphasis, and all the intricacy of construction that analysis reveals, the word's appearance seems, because of the poem's active character, almost an afterthought. And for all the emphasis that results from putting the single word on its own line, the reason for its being segregated does not obtrude upon the objective order of the poem in such a way that it might give too forceful evidence of the operations of a shaping intelligence that bends syntax out of shape; the poem retains the character of a speech act.

The remainder of the poem is similarly speech-like. Consider the fourth quatrain: While the sixth quatrain uses verb forms (and so seem stronger), the fourth quatrain uses exclusively participles, not verb forms. I commented above on the (deliberately) weak character of this verse, which we experience as the thinning out of the tree's thrust. By this use of participles, Williams weakens the thrust of the poem's forward movement (in analogy with the diffusing of the tree's upward thrust), for the triad of participles spreads out the reader's attention (the use of a single, strong verb form, by way of contrast, would have concentrated the reader's attention). But the sentences we use in daily life also tend to slide into a string of participle phrases, as the energy that prompted us to speak splutters out. Thus Williams's use of participles also gives the poem some of the qualities of ordinary speech, and so makes its construction seems all the more natural. This quality, in its turn, gives the poem a more objective character.

By highlighting the poem's character as speech, Williams draws attention to the creative process which brings the poem into being. Thus he creates a three-termed equivalence among the movement (the tensions and relaxations) the reader experiences when reading the poem, the movement of the eye and changes in sensation the sycamore tree induces, and the creative activity that brings the poem into being. The equivalence between the last two terms spans the objective and subjective realms; hence, in forging that identity, Williams gives new life to the Romantics' claims concerning the identity of subject and object.

We have noted that Williams does not offer propositions that describe a tree; rather he creates a form—an *object*—that has structural similarities with the structure of the tree, and so invites an experience similar to the poet's experience of the tree we experience; the reader experiences the poem as a form (an object) that unfolds through time and, hence, possesses movement. Qualities of this movement resemble the qualities of movement of the eye up the tree and the transformations of sensation that accompany the eye's movement. Brakhage likewise constructs film forms that have analogous features to Williams's poetic forms. A film of his that has many similarities with "Young Sycamore" is *Made Manifest*. Rhythm is the primary determinant of that film's form. Brakhage presents three shots in rapid succession at the film's opening; they are segregated from the remainder of the film, as though to emphasize their importance. And they are important—or, rather, succession is important—for the rest of the film is based on repetitions, prolongations, and augmentations of the rhythm that succession established. The film creates tension by delaying expected recurrences, and then creating a splutter of activity when that resolution takes place. But the experience of waves in an ocean evokes just the same experience—we are impressed by the regular periodicity of the wave's movement, and experience tension when we expect a wave to break, but there is a delay.

The film's ability to provoke the experience of its subject goes farther. It is not just that the flux is also metaphoric—though it is that, for the energy of the sea is the energy of the mind, and the movement of the water the stirring of the mind.[212] Rather it is that film evokes the quality of mind through its formal construction. We don't need to know that the sea is almost a *topos* (see glossary), a conventional, ready-to-hand metaphor for the mind, or for the experiences that flow through it. The film creates its meanings through our experience of its concrete structures; its concrete structures make manifest how formed images emerge out of that primordiality for which the rolling ocean waves provide an equivalent. The film is based on the contrast between two types of visual forms. First, there are shots in which a mass of water swells to form a crest, or breaker; these shots are somewhat "realistic," as they are give a fairly wide-angle view of their object matter, and present some illusion of depth (though, to be sure, that illusion is of a rather shallow space). Secondly, there are shots that create no spatial illusion, that are really just streaks of light over a dimensionally flat, but tonally modulated, surface. (Brakhage created the shots of the latter sort by rapidly panning the camera, which was adjusted to present a close-up image). Most often shots are arranged in groups of three, with one shot of the first (more "realistic") sort followed by two shots of the second ("light-streaks") sort. Quite commonly (but not without exception) the last two shots in a group present contrasting motion, through the degree of that contrast various among the pairs differ. But whatever the relation between the two shots, a rhythm of alternation, a strong swell, followed by two weak shots, evokes the experience of a wave swelling and then, after breaking, spreading in different, often opposite directions.

But there is a deeper, more formal pleasure. I mentioned that the two "light-streak" shots that follow a more "realistic" shot usually present contrasting motions: what that remark failed to address was the relation between the first of the "light-streak" shots and the more "realistic" shot. For sometimes the first "light-streak" shot after a more "realistic" shot will continue the direction of movement contained in the more "realistic" shot, sometimes it will have the opposite vector, and sometimes the two vectors will have some other relation. This means the tacti of successive triads vary—sometimes a triad is made up of a strong stress, a medium stress, and light stress (and, of course, "strong," "medium," and "light" all come in degrees (sometimes of a strong stress, a light stress, and a medium stress). The tactus fluctuates, and our experience of that fluctuation resembles our experience of the flux of water.

What is more, the more "realistic" shots present movement as occuring in a shallow space. The very fact of the wave action swelling up within a space that is so very close to the picture plane is a principal source of the film's tension. Bringing the swelling water up so close to the picture plane invests the swelling with great power; it also reduces its apparent distance from us, which makes it seem all the more powerful. What is more, by reducing the apparent distance of the wave from the observer, it retards its movement, and its retardation further heightens the tension the shot provokes. The pair of "light-streak" shots that usually follow this more "realistic" shot serve to reduce to the tension; but they do not generally provide a complete resolution, since they are rapid, and weak, in comparison with the long, slow, powerful swell that precedes them. The contrast between the strength of the first shot in each of the triads and the relative weakness of the two, rapid "light-streak" shots that follow provides Brakhage with a challenge, against which we gauge his performance. For the triad of shots constitutes a template of sorts, on which Brakhage will produce variants; but there is risk in using this template (beyond that of stultifying repetition, which no one who is acquainted with Brakhage's oeuvre would ever suspect he might fall into): the triad, consisting of a slow, strong swell, followed by two rapid, and comparatively weak movements, could very easily degenerate into a heavy beat followed by two spluttering beats. The challenge Brakhage confronted (in addition to producing fresh variants of the template) was to strengthen the two "light-streak" shots, and to do so without altering their basic character. Brakhage does this by extending the duration of these hyperaccelerated shots, and by altering the relation of their direction. To experience the continuously altering relations between those shots, to feel the different pulses that result, is not only to witness an extraordinary feat of virtuosity (in bringing forth such variety from such a limited range of materials)—it is also to experience a nearly regular, yet nonetheless fluctuating rhythm, a rhythm that is exactly like that of waves, in which the relative emphasis of beats, and the duration between the beats, change continuously.

Furthermore, most of the film's montage modulates directions of movement. One of the great pleasures of the film results from Brakhage's orchestration of movement: movement is halted, deflected into a different direction, accelerated, retarded, and arranged in contrasting patterns. But we get a similar pleasure from watching waters, whose movements are also various yet patterned.

Finally, Brakhage does not adhere slavishly to the template. Sometimes the grouping are extended by adding a shot, or contracted by eliminating a shot; sometimes the triadic pattern is broken, as two shots of swelling waves will follow another, or more radically, the shot will be truncated (or will seem truncated, judging from the expectations we develop). Another form of extension that Brakhage uses is more extreme yet—a few times Brakhage incorporates a different sort into one of these groupings. As though to heighten our awareness of the virtuosic nature of his performance (in making the film), the material that Brakhage incorporates is material that we can sense ought to resist being incorporated into these groupings. The images interpolated into these triadic groupings are of two sorts: first, shots of the back of a woman's head, looking over water; and, second, blue-toned shots of hills. These depictions are far outside the range of images that the film establishes, at the outset, as its subject matter. The shots of the back of the woman's head abruptly obtrudes a human presence into a film of astonishingly superhuman power, and what is more, breaks with the quality of the shots adjacent to them: they are nearly static, while the gestalt field around them is dynamic. The images of the hills are even more static, so, despite their blue tone (which nearly matches that of the water), their two-dimensionality, and the similarity of their rolling shapes to those of waves, we feel that they, too, ought to resist being incorporated into the film. That material of which the film is constituted belongs to such a narrow range that we feel they ought to establish a norm for the film's construction should make it all the more difficult to integrate these shots into the film. Yet Brakhage manages to do exactly that.

Finally, though, we ask what purpose the inclusion of these static shots serves. A part of the answer has already been given. But another part of the answer depends upon the fundamental analogy on which the film is based (which analogy helps to explain the film's title), between the rolling ocean and the turbulent mind. The film makes manifest how formed images emerge out of that primordiality for which the rolling ocean waves provide an equivalent, while these static images are brief manifestations, a flickering realization, of what results from later stages in this process of bringing images from the primordial depths of experience into a highly resolved, stable image. They indicate well that the earlier phases of the process know no distinction between subject and object, while the later phases of the experience result in the objectification (the externalization) of the experienced object.

In an essay published in the November 1917 *Poetry Journal* (vol. 8) Williams related his particularist ontology to the American spirit, as Emerson had in his famous "Divinity School Address." The dialogue between the poetry and the prose of *Spring and All* reflects the contrast he had described in the essay, for it creates tensions by interrelating the abstract forms of thinking that Europe had bequeathed to America and the more concrete manner of seeing that is indigenous to Americans. Throughout his career, Williams returned frequently to the Emersonian theme of the importance of the American experience. The poet's interest in the American way of experiencing was essentially a concern with experiencing truthfully and with experiencing what is immediately present, not what one wishes or hopes or believes is present. In his major statement on poetics, *In the American Grain*, Williams declares, "unless everything that is, proclaim a ground on which it stand, it has no worth."[213] Further, Williams conceived of a poem (as

Olson was later to conceive it) as a fluxing field of energy that generates a charge in the reader. He entitled the magazine he produced *Contact* because, as he noted on the opening page, a contact is "a vast discharge of energy forced by the impact of experience into form."[214] His earlier poems sometimes adopted a rolling, Whitmanesque line, to suggest dynamism, and his use of the variable foot in his poems was a means for conveying a changing field of energy; he even stated in a letter that he considered that the structure of the poetic line "is where aesthetics is mated with physics"; elsewhere, he proposed that "[t]he line must be pliable with speech, for speech, for thought. . . ."[215] As well, Williams sometimes celebrated American technology for its capacity to engender the experience of movement and energy; indeed his polemical writings sometimes tip over almost into the vitalist (see glossary) cult doctrine of process and change (just as Bergson's philosophical writings sometimes do). As late as 1940, in "Writer's Prologue to a Play in Verse," Williams continued to expound a dynamic conception of reality, a dynamism with which he continued to make ambivalent associations— associating it sometimes with the reality described by the new physics, but more often with the movement of mind (as when he describes the mind moving "after a pattern/ which is the mind itself, turning/ and twisting the theme" and "We are not here, you understand,/ but in the mind, that circumstance/ of which the speech is poetry").[216]

The poet's comments about the need Americans have to establish a new relation with the immediate reality of their situation derive from his analysis of their history and the firm grasp he had of its essential contours. Williams claims that Americans had never really experienced their land and their place as it really is, because America did not pass through a stage of childhood wonder and discovery. America was born old, he alleged, for the nation was born with the mental dispositions inherited from Europe. As Charles Olson was to do later, Williams accused the Puritans of being the real culprits, the contagion that had infected and sickened the noble American character.[217] "If the "puritan" in them could have ended with their entry into the New World and the subtle changes of growth at once have started," he alleged, "everything would have been different."[218] However, they did not respond to the truths of their senses; they did not open themselves up to experience the land as it was given them. Rather they experienced an "otherwhere" of religion, as they sought a place that embodied their idea of what their dwelling place should be, "terrifying unknown image" based on Puritan religion.[219] "All that they saw they lived by but denied," Williams states.[220] Consequently, they "befouled" America and distorted the American character.

When Williams formulated his commentary on American history, many intellectuals still regarded the Puritans as a severe, life-denying, punishing, soul-destroying group of pleasure-haters. These conceptions were the grounds of the poet's hostility towards them. However, over time, Williams did develop a somewhat more complex understanding of one matter concerning the Puritans. "The Puritan," he says, "finding one thing like another in a world destined for blossom only in 'Eternity,' all soul, all 'emptiness' then here, was precluded from SEEING the Indian. They never realized the Indian in the least save as an unformed PURITAN."[221]

Here Williams relates the Puritans' alleged incapacity to see people from the continent's first nations to the Puritan conception of history, which furnished them with an ideal type of humanity—the Puritan himself. Williams understood that the Puritans' way of seeing reality had its basis in a hermeneutical tradition, according to which events that occur in the Old Testament ("types," as such events were known) foreshadow other similar events in the New Testament (their "anti-types"). Though this hermeneutical method was originally a method for understanding the events in the Bible, the Puritans extended the interpretative strategy, which became known as typological criticism, into the realm of historical understanding. According to this method of understanding history, earlier events foreshadow similar later events and give them their meaning. The problem of historical understanding is essentially one of deciding which historical events anticipate that historical event which requires being interpreted. For example, the Puritans understood their leaving England, the land of their persecution, as the anti-type whose type is the Israelites' exodus from Pharaoh's Egypt and their coming to American as the anti-type whose type is the Israelites' migration to the Promised Land. The return to the Promised Land in turn gets its significance from the biblical account of Adam and Eve's expulsion from the garden. Their method of historical interpretation really does involve what Williams claimed—noticing resemblances between past and present—and it does tend to make people see the present in terms of the past. It encourages us to see one event or one place or one object as like another—as a metaphor for something else. And we have already seen that Williams considered all hermeneutical methods based on historical comparisons, and especially metaphor, to be the principal culprits in the whole affair. So Williams, too, even before the Open Form poets, took the lesson of Symbolism: that the sign is an abstractive agent, that, in the end, cleaves the mind and the world apart, and when the mind is so isolated it cannot reach the things of the world.

Consequently Williams, like Emerson, dedicated his art to the essentially phenomenological project of re-establishing our relation with our situation in the immediacies of embodied consciousness. Williams accuses metaphoric or symbolic thinking of encoiling a person in thought and of closing one off from the environment. Embodied consciousness would establish a salutary relation with the environment and so would undo the deleterious effects of metaphoric and symbolic thinking.

Brakhage shares the poet's tendency to valorize direct perception. Like Williams, Brakhage believes that in the act of "pure seeing" an individual discovers both the truth of her relatedness to her situation and the truth of her own being. Like Williams, too, Brakhage maintains a dialectical position on seeing, as he claims that seeing reveals both the object and the self—both the contexts within which imaginative acts emerge and the force of the imagination that propels those acts. Like Williams and Olson—and for that matter, like several English Romantics—Brakhage believes that direct vision may help us transcend the distinction between subject and object that has bedeviled moderns. Direct seeing will lead us towards realizing the dialectical unity between the seen object and the imagination; this dialectical unity, Brakhage repeatedly stresses, reflects into the aesthetic realm as the relation between form and content. Furthermore, like Williams, Brakhage conceives history as a constricting influence that diminishes our capacity for direct perception (consider *The Dead, Western History*, or the struggle for vision that *Unconscious London Strata* conveys).[222] And, again like Williams, he offers us the promise of an American artist who will be able to overcome the effects of Western history and show us the way that leads us toward recovering the pristine truth of pure vision.

Countering the anti-historical strain of the poet's thinking is another tendency, exemplified by *In the American Grain*. Williams averred that this second strain is not a counter-tradition and, indeed, that America lacks an authentic poetic tradition. He believed that he had, in fact, only one real forebear, Edgar Allen Poe. Lacking such a tradition, all one can do, Williams concluded, is to set out to construct a usable history for oneself, to create a ground on which to stand. Brakhage acts similarly, for like Williams he has attempted to construct a serviceable history for himself by searching for antecedents for his art—often in the works of earlier painters who, against all odds, found ways to convey the character of primordial perception that is the true basis for Brakhage's work. The remarkable persistence of primordial modes of apprehension, even in cultures that hardly acknowledge them, and their insistence on being expressed, even when there are no forms available for conveying them, is, for Brakhage, evidence of their strength—of a force the persistence and insistence of which suggest that these modes of apprehension derive from nature itself, and, specifically, from the body.

Another topic on which Brakhage and Williams agree closely is the inhumanity of technology. As with the topic of the Puritan conception of history, on this topic Williams's grasp of Puritan thought is evident. Williams, as we noted, accused the Puritans of failing to see deeply their immediate situation. Williams claimed this failure splits human beings from the circumstances within which they live out their lives. He suggests that, as a consequence, the Puritans' world contracted into themselves and so their experiential relations were to a "smaller, narrower, protective thing and not to the great, New World."[223] As did Max Weber and, more recently, George Grant, Williams thought that the Puritan concern to be industrious, their notions of progress, and their lack of openness to the beauties of what is given in experience resulted in their great emphasis on willing. They valued more highly the creative remaking of nature than the delight we can take in the gift of what manifests itself to us. Hence, they had a proclivity toward developing technologies for the transformation of nature. It was the culture that Puritanism shaped that transformed science from an inquiry, motivated by wonder, into the order and beauty of the cosmos, and became the foundation of technologies for enriching our material existence.

Machines put a distance between human and non-human nature, Williams alleged. "Machines were not so much to save time as to save dignity that fears the animate touch." Puritans' fear of having a corporal—an *animal*—contact with nature produced their (and later all Americans') diligence in inventing machinery. "It is miraculous energy that goes into inventions here," Williams remarked. He suggested that the feeling that generates such energy is a "fear that robs the emotions; a mechanism to increase the gap between touch and thing, *not* to have a contact."[224] The poet's comments on this matter constitute a prophetic analysis of the fear of and contempt for the body that has become so pervasive. At another point, Williams stated, "men are trained never to possess fully but just to SEE. This makes scientists and it makes the masochist.... Our life drives us apart and forces us upon science and invention—away from touch."[225] If fear of being in direct contact with reality, of touching it directly, is what Americans feel, then, Williams concluded (as Bergson had earlier), the obvious solution is to get back in touch with the body and with immediate reality. Williams's commentary on the role of touch has parallels, too, with that of Merleau-Ponty; in fact the importance of touch in putting one in contact with reality is a topic that the philosophers Henri Bergson and Maurice Merleau-Ponty stressed as strongly as the physician/literary theorist/poet William Carlos Williams.

For an artist, Williams stated, "[t]he only world that exists is the world of the senses."[226] He continues: "If I succeed in keeping myself objective enough, sensual enough, I can produce the factors, the concretions of materials by which others shall understand and so be led to use—that they may the better see, touch, taste, enjoy—their own world *differing as it may* from mine."[227] Brakhage, too, has advanced the propositions that "the concretions of materials" that make up works of art can evoke in those who attend to them nearly the same sensory experience that the artists who created the work experienced, and that it is this experience that a work of art is really about. He stated in *Gertrude Stein: Meditative Literature and Film*:

> For it is in the nature of Image that it is received as a clustering of object-shapes to be individual perceived. . . .
> And if a film be, rather, illustrative—a series of pictures of nameable forms—WHAT on earth might alleviate the inaesthetic burden of referential nomenclature?
> My answer is (as inspired by hers [Stein's]) a freeing of each image (as her each-and-every word) to its un-owned self-life within the continuities (rather than context) of the work.[228]

His belief that "the concretions of materials" in a poem provide the material cause of the experience that is the poem's real subject matter led Williams to think of the poem as an object with an ontological status similar to (but, as I pointed out above, not identical with) that of other objects in the world. That he maintained this belief about the ontological status of a poem is the primary reason the Objectivist poets of the 1930s and the Objectist poets who emerged in the 1950s (poets whose work Brakhage has taken a great interest in) regarded Williams as their forerunner. He insisted that a poem is a thing in its own right, and that the reader should regard it as he or she would any other object—for its shapes, volumes, masses, textures, and colours. Words are the poet's primary pigment (to seize upon Pound's term) and their arrangement on the page is every bit as important as the arrangement of masses and colours in a painting. In *Spring and All*, Williams went so far as to assert (a claim that I suspect Brakhage would agree with) that each word in a poem should appear as a quasi-independent object. Williams recognized, too, that the dissociative and paratactical forms of construction that Pound was in the process of developing had the effect of separating a word from its conventional contexts, and of making it assert itself as a quasi-independent entity. In an essay on Pound, Williams comments on Pound's method of "piling up and juxtaposition of distinct images": "the word has been used in its plain sense to represent a thing—remaining thus loose in its context—not gummy—(when at its best)—an objective unit in the design—but alive."[229] Stein shared with Williams a conviction in the importance of having the letter of the text assert itself in its concreteness, of doing away with remembered, and often pernicious, conventions, to liberate every phoneme and every grapheme so that each might allow its effects to be felt; similarly, as we have just seen, Brakhage proposed to unshackle "images" (i.e., visual forms) from reference, and from the bonds of narrative structure—"a freeing of each image . . . to its un-owned self-life with the continuities (rather than context) of the work." Williams later developed this theme:

> When a man makes a poem, makes it, mind you, he takes words as he finds them interrelated about him and composes them—without distortion which would mar their exact significances—into an intense expression of his perceptions and ardors that they may constitute a revelation in the speech that he uses. It isn't what he *says* that counts as a work of art, it's what he makes, with such intensity of perception that it lives with an intrinsic movement of its own to verify its authenticity.[230]

Brakhage shares the poet's sense that creative making depends on giving oneself over to the immediate moment and on taking guidance from its energies. In a letter to Ronna Page concerning music, originally published in Toronto's 1960s "underground" newspaper *Guerrilla*, Brakhage speculates:

> I'm somehow now wanting to get deeper into my concept of music as sound equivalent of the mind's moving, which is becoming so real to me that I'm coming to believe the study of the history of music would reveal more of the changing thought processes of a given culture than perhaps any other means—not of thought shaped and/or Thoughts but of the *Taking shape*, physiology of thought or some such. . . . [231]

This might invite being interpreted as a declaration of the familiar aspiration to have a film register the process of its coming-into-being—or it would but for the reference to the "physiology of thought or some such." Brakhage and the Open Form poets (whom we shall discuss in Chapter 2) certainly do believe that a work of art should register the energies that produce it. But the passage just quoted does not actually declare that intention: rather it states Brakhage's concern with the primitive elements of experience—elements that one might well think of as Bion's alpha or beta elements (see glossary)—and with how those somatic effects which are the most elemental registrations of energy on the body become experience. As he puts it in another text, "IT IS MIND MOVEMENT which finally, vitally, concerns me IN another man's art," that is, with the kinetic features of experience (which Brakhage identifies with experience itself) and how the energies of somatic/mental dynamics (for Brakhage also identifies body and mind) become experience.[232]

The idea that art captures the process by which thoughts form in the mind and the course by which they evolve or turn into other thoughts is a key to Brakhage's creative method. Brakhage's films attempt to collapse the time of making and the time of viewing into one. He strives to create forms that suggest that the thought forming in the viewer's mind is still incomplete in the maker's (or, at least, it was when the maker made the film). The mode of construction that Brakhage favours for creating this sense of time was also one of the modes of construction that William Carlos Williams preferred—the constatation of concrete particulars.

Undoing the illusion of seamless continuity is a hallmark of modern art. A primary means artists have used to dismantle that illusion is to create forms based on parataxis; Pound uses it ellipses, tmesis (see glossary), the repetition of phrases, or repetition with augmentation, and associates phrases on the basis of their rhythms to a high degree of disjuncture. One of Brakhage's most inspired and original pieces of writing, a dense, phonetically titled concrete, "S.A.," exemplifies the disruptive effects of taking a medium as material and creating sense through juxtaposing material items. Here is a fragment, in which we see at work a mind dismantling and turning over the aural components of "facts," to the end of displaying the nature of a document.

F Acts

I make IF of it . . .

As I make It of it . . .

As IF I make It . . .

As if "as" were "A-Z" . . .

As "it" "is" . . .

"Is" "As" . . .

and so for THE: Axe:
AXE: :the

S A won, mind moving now axiomatically, viz: . . . [233]

Brakhage shares the poet's sense that it is through the local and the specific that an artist reaches the universal. Williams said about Edgar Allen Poe, "[W]hat he says, being thoroughly local in origin, has some chance of being universal in application. . . ."[234] It was, however, when he came to write on Stein that he stated these beliefs most cogently.

> To be democratic, local (in the sense of being attached with integrity to actual experience), Stein, or any other artist, must for subtlety ascend to a plane of almost abstract design to keep alive. To writing, then, as an art in itself. Yet what actually impinges on the senses must be rendered as it appears, by use of which, only, and under which, untouched, the significance has to be disclosed.[235]

Here we find Williams referring again to the tension between abstract design and concrete embodiment so prevalent in his own thought, and in that of Ezra Pound, Gertrude Stein, Charles Olson, and Stan Brakhage.

The influence Bergson, Hulme, and Williams have had on recent poetics in English-speaking countries is enormous and, while not completely unrecognized, definitely underestimated. Together, they propelled poetry away from the epic sweep and that grand, all-encompassing vision that provided a norm for traditional poetry and moved it in the direction of greater emotional intimacy. They furthered the Romantics' mission of valorizing sincerity and authenticity and of discrediting lofty, poetic statement and the ringing state- ment of high-blown sentiments of the sort that we now label rhetorical. They brought metrical rigidity into disrepute and celebrated a flexibility of rhythm appropriate to the "vague moods" that Hulme believed to be the proper inspiration for poetry. They continued the Romantics' efforts to dis- lodge from the centre of critical discourse those criteria of beauty grounded in absolute mathematical principles of harmony and proportion and to install in their place criteria based in ideas of personal expression and the genuine- ness of emotion.[236]

They were not wholly Romantic, however. Pound expounded Vorticist principles, and Vorticism was staunchly anti-Romantic—indeed Vorticism represented the beginning of Pound's reaction against what he considered as the emotional excesses of imagism and *vers libre* (see glossary). T.E. Hulme, once the intellectual force behind Imagism, found the conceptual tools Pound subsequently took up, for his critique of Imagism, in the works of Wilhelm Worringer, Julien Benda, and Pierre Lasserre. Julien Benda was a highly regarded social theorist, and the author of *Le Trahaison des Clercs* (a denun- ciation of the decadence French intellectual life). Pierre Lasserre was a well- known art theorist and the author of *Le Romantisme français: essai sur la révolution dans les sentiments et dans les idées au XIXième siècle*, a right-wing text attacking France's cultural decadence (which he traced back to a Rous- seauesque individualism and as an antidote for which he prescribed classi- cism); Lasserre was also the author of an attack on Bergson, entitled *La Philosophie de Bergson* (which identifies Bergson's thought as Romantic and chastises his philosophy for individualism, its emphasis on sensation, its irrationalism, and for being of Jewish origin). T.E. Hulme met Lasserre and published an interview with him (*New Age* 10 [1911]) that included a condem- nation of Bergson on many grounds, but especially for the anti-conservative implication of the view that history is perpetual novelty and does not instruct us about the best social order for the present.

Equally important was the arch-conservative Julien Benda, who, in the signal year 1912, published *Le Bergsonisme*, a diatribe that enjoyed enor- mous popularity. Benda celebrated the contemplative life above the life of action, considered himself the defender of logic and reason, and believed humankind's highest intellectual achievement was science. Benda attacked Bergson as a Jew subversive to the French spirit—in fact, according to one of the book's cardinal distinctions, not a severe, moralistic Jew of Spinoza's ilk but a sensation-loving, "Carthaginian" Jew; Bergson's Carthaginianism is especially evident in his emphasis on time and intuition, Benda asserted. But, Benda pointed out, it was not Bergson's Carthaginianism that was the reason for his popularity; rather it was his contempt for the accomplishments of science, and his promise that there is a way to reach the absolute that had great appeal to the bourgeoisie—an irrationalist enthusiasm that such "voices of reason" as Benda found troubling. Above all, though, what distressed the conservative critics was Bergson's Romanticism.

Reactionary French circles of the time associated Romanticism, alongside Jewishness, with the feminine: Romantic art, reactionary cultural critics complained, exhibits a lack of general ideas; is concerned with the concrete and the particular; celebrates intuition and swift, intuitive perception; is absorbed in the inner world and sentiment; and is given to indulgence of the emotions. The discovery of these features in Bergson's philosophy turned not only Lasserre and Benda against it, but also T.E. Hulme and the Vorticists.[237]

An issue that has troubled Brakhage's ruminations on art concerns the question how private perceptions—for the highly individuated characteristics of which he makes grand claims—can nonetheless move others deeply. Why should one individual feel that his or her unique way of feeling and seeing can affect others? And why should she or he feel that they can recognize the character of the artist in those alien perceptions? If different individuals' ways of seeing and feeling are so different, how can one person recognize his or her qualities in another's manner of seeing? Why are their different systems of representation not incommensurate with one another?

A similar problem haunted Hulme's aesthetics.

> [A]n individual way of looking at things ... does not mean something which is peculiar to an individual, for in that case it would be quite valueless. It means that a certain individual artist was able ... to pick out one element which is really in all of us, but which before he had disentangled it, we were unable to perceive.[238]

Hulme comes to a conclusion with which Brakhage agrees, that the uniqueness of an artist's perception depends on his or her unusual perceptual intensity and that anyone can recognize and respond sympathetically to artwork's intensity. As Brakhage puts it near the beginning of *Metaphors on Vision*, "Suppose that the ability of the artist and a saint be the increased ability to see."

Brakhage considers this so important that he deems the efforts to expand the sensory faculties the essential training an artist must undertake. Poets or musicians hold themselves open to the varieties of sounds; painters or filmmakers hold themselves open to the varieties of seeing. Thus, Brakhage told the filmmaker Hollis Frampton:

I see so many qualities of light, so many things that seem to *be* light but aren't anywhere categorized as such or spoken of as such or referred to by other people as such. I always have, and as I get older I see more and more. I see so many qualities of light continually, every day constantly new ones and new aspects of old ones, that it's become a normal condition. At this time in my life it is the variety of the quality of light that I see, and live with daily, that removes me most from feeling I share sight with other people. . . . [I]t was a long time ago that I was startled by Scotus Erigena's, "All things that are, are light." Along with all the many gifts of Ezra Pound, this was certainly one of the most startling and immediately mean- ingful to me. . . . It comes back to me at a time when I really *need* it because slowly and gradually over the years my attention to the world in relationship to light has increased my seeing of all kinds of things that other people either don't see, or don't admit they see . . . or don't have any *way* to admit they see. . . . Year after year more and more things began to seem to me to *glow*. . . . [O]ne day I knew rain was coming. I asked myself how I knew. . . . And then I *saw* it. I saw streaks of whitish lines, almost as if drawn, or as if comic-strip drawn, very quickly coming down on a slant into the ground. There was a feeling that this was being *sucked* into the ground, that these were actually being pulled, as if by gravity. . . . I see light that appears to pool. It appears to be a glow that's as if it had weight and liquid substance. It doesn't pool in holes in the ground, necessarily, or any depression. But it pools *as if* there were some hole there. And it is of a glow that's all of what we call light, as we extend that term to phosphores- cence. It happens quite normally. And there's also a quality of light that streams over the ground; and I've seen it running absolutely counter to the blow of the wind. Just streaming, in all senses as if it were a charged or phosphorescent mass of floating liquid. In fact, it looks very much like a mountain stream.[239]

Brakhage goes on to claim that, like any artist, what he has tried to do is to create equivalents for sights of different kinds, including those which—like the experiences he mentions in this passage—lie outside the range of con- ventional perceptions. Film is not sensitive to all the frequencies of light that a sensitive human eye responds to, however. So Brakhage has had to invent ways to construct equivalences, by painting on film, for example, or scratching it to mar its surface, using double exposures, putting film stocks to uses other than those for which it is stipulated, or, as he did in *The Wold- Shadow* (1972), interposing a glass plate between the camera and the scene he is filming and painting over parts of it, altering it frame by frame to render the changes in colour that he cannot film.

   That the techniques I have mentioned figure among the best-known fea- tures of Brakhage's work is testimony to the importance of Hulme and Pound's influence on Brakhage. The slowly altering "grain" patterns and the subtle colours of shadows in *Scenes from Under Childhood*, whose peculiari- ties only very close attention reveals, provide additional evidence that Brakhage accepts Hulme's claim that modern poets will concern themselves with the unique qualities of their perception. Brakhage's commitment to maintaining the individuality of his percepts and to creating equivalents for them on film is also born out by films such as *Thigh Line Lyre Triangular*, *Star Garden*, and *The Peaceable Kingdom*, all of which reveal a highly developed sensitivity to the qualities of light. *The Peaceable Kingdom*, for example, lays out the varieties of light, while the masterful *The Text of Light* reveals more comprehensively than any other film the characteristics of pure light, light as it is in itself, light that, to use the notions of the emanationist (see glossary) metaphysicians, has not yet joined with matter and been turned into objects—or, if one prefers to consider the issue in developmental terms, that resembles primordial, preverbal precepts.

The advice Pound offered in "A Retrospect," to allow lines and even phrases to follow the rhythm "of the musical phrase, not of the metronome," has been of cardinal important to Brakhage (as it has been to other filmmakers). It is empty counsel, in a sense, for even musical phrases can, and most often do, follow a strict metre that is as inflexible as the tick of the metronome. The Canadian pianist Glenn Gould provided splendid evidence that Bach's metres and tempi should be strictly kept and that rubato is out of place in performances of J.S. Bach's compositions. Even more important, Gould's performances have allowed us to glimpse the reason for that strictness—viz., that the strictness of the music's form, as precise and unyielding as the order of numbers, reflects the Order of Being.

One can put this cavil aside, however, when one considers the historical context in which Pound offered his counsel. His edict to avoid using strict metres, was offered polemically, probably in response to the practice of the period just before his own, a period that resonated with the hoof-beat of Algernon Charles Swinburne's (a poet he admired and I detest) thumping rhythms:

> Before the beginning of years,
>   There came to the making of man
> Time, with a gift of tears;
>   Grief, with a glass that ran;
> Pleasure, with pain for leaven;
>   Summer, with flowers that fell;
> Remembrance fallen from heaven,
>   And madness risen from hell;
> Strength without hands to smite;
>   Love that endures for a breath;
> Night, the shadow of light,
>   And life, the shadow of death.[240]

ta-BOOM-ta-ta BOOM-ta-ta BOOM-ta/ BOOM-ta-ta BOOM-ta-ta BOOM—the Swinburne stomp, I call it. The rhythm is firm, the stresses heavy. Ten out of twelve lines begin with a noun (or "and" along with a noun) followed

by an adjectival phrase. This sameness reinforces the heavy bass-drum
"BOOM-ta-ta" metre, hardly alleviated by the mixing of dactyls and trochees,
or by the fact that rhythm almost bears being scanned as all trochees).

How far Swinburne's rhythms are from Pound's!

> Thus was it in time.
> And the small stars now fall from the olive branch,
> Forked shadow falls dark on the terrace
> More black than the floating martin
>   that has no care for your presence,
> His wing-print is black on the roof tiles
> And the print is gone with his cry.
> So light is thy weight on Tellus
> Thy notch no deeper indented
> Thy weight less than the shadow
> Yet hast thou gnawed through the mountain, . . . [241]

Here we hear no hoof-beat echo, no thumping foot. Even when his song was
furious, he avoided stomping out the metre.

> Thus saith Kabir: "Politically" said Rabindranath
>   "they are inactive. They think, but then there is
> climate, they think but it is warm or there are flies or
> some insects"
>
> "And with the return of the gold standard" wrote Sir Montagu
> "every peasant had to pay twice as much grain
>   to cover his taxes and interest"
>
> It is true that the interest is now legally lower
> but the banks lend to the bunya
> who can thus lend more to his victims
> and the snot press and periodical tosh does not notice this
> thus saith Kabir, by hypostasis
> if they can take Hancock's wharf they can take your cow
>   or my barn
> and the Kohinoor and the rajah's emerald etc.
>
> and Tom wore a tin disc, a circular can-lid
>   with his name on it, solely:
> for Wanjina has lost his mouth, . . . [242]

And when he wishes subtle melancholy:

> And Brancusi repeating: je peux commencer
>   une chose tous les jours, mais
>   fiiniiiir[243]

How gently that sad sigh slides from the first, doubled *i* to the quadrupled *i*!
How heavy the regret over the work still undone that slide conveys! Yet
there is no heavy thumping.

When one examines Pound's edict to "follow the meter of the musical phrase, not of the metronome" together with examples of Pound's own use of rhetorical stress, one finds that, far from being empty, his counsel makes a great deal of sense. It asserts the value of using a pulse that modulates from one textual fragment to the next. If one applies Pound's dictum to making a film, each segment or even each image, takes a high degree of autonomy. This autonomy subjectivizes the elements the film incorporates at the same time as it gives each phrase enough independence that it presents itself as a quasi-autonomous cluster of energies.

The flexibility of Pound's rhythms is not due to Pound's metric system being quantitative or to his using conversational forms. He could, and sometimes did, maintain strongly stressed accents over long passages:

> But for the clearest head in the congress
> 1774 and thereafter
> pater patriae
> the man who at certain points
> made us
> at certain points
> saved us
> by fairness, honesty and straight moving[244]

Sometimes Pound fractures the rhythms:

> This liquid is certainly a
> property of the mind
> nec accidens est   but an element
> in the mind's make-up
> est agens and functions   dust to a fountain pan otherwise
> Hast 'ou seen the rose in the steel dust
> (or swansdown ever?)
> so light is the urging, so ordered the dark petals of iron
> we who have passed over Lethe.[245]

This passage provides a masterful example of the use of a rapidly modulating pulse, a pulse that changes from one textual element to the next. It furnishes evidence that Pound saw the mind as a part of reality and our memories as responses to a gentle force that emanates from reality, a force that is like the magnetic field which, though unseen, pulls iron filings ("steel dust") into an exquisite order. Reality, as the poem figures it, is the Tradition and the Order of Being that orders ideas within its force field. Pound extends the idea in a late canto:

> Guido C. had read "Monologion"
> vera imago
> and via mind is the nearest you'll get to it,

"rationalem"
            said Anselm.
                        Guido: "intenzione."
Ratio,
            luna,
                        speculum non est imago
                                    mirrour, not image;
Sapor, the flavour,
            pulchritudo
                        ne divisibilis intellectu
                not to be split by syllogization
        to the blessed isles (insulis fortunatis)[246]

Pound's use of a flexible, modulating rhythm is highly overdetermined. Ultimately, it took its inspiration from nothing less grand than an entire conception of reality. Considered more technically and restrictively, it drew on Pound's knowledge of Anglo-Saxon prosody. Anglo-Saxon metre was not based on syllable counts but on the number of stresses (or lifts) per line— the Anglo-Saxon poem had to have four stresses per line, but so long as this fact was respected the poet could, within reason, put variable numbers of unstressed syllables between the stresses. Thus Anglo-Saxon poetry used not a syllabic, but a quantitative metre.[247] Just for its basic flexibility, quantitative metre has had an enormous influence upon twentieth-century verse, influencing both Ezra Pound and Charles Olson and their many followers; a related understanding of the structure of the line undergirds William Carlos Williams's idea of the variable foot.

There are several standard metres in Anglo-Saxon. Type A is the rising falling metre, which proceeds from stressed to unstressed (from a lift to a dip); its basic schema is HEAVY-light HEAVY-light. Type B is the falling metre, which proceeds from unstressed to stressed (from a dip to a lift); its basic schema is light-HEAVY light-HEAVY. Type C is the rising/falling metre, and it combines a Type B unit and a Type A unit; its basic schema is light-HEAVY HEAVY-light (dip-lift lift-dip). The reader can easily see how such a principle of combination can result in the juxtaposition of two stresses; a similar principle produces the spondee (two stressed syllables in sequence) that Pound often used to end a segment of the *Cantos*.

On the other hand, two unstressed syllables coming together do not constitute a distinctive type, for the unstressed syllables form, collectively, a single dip between two lifts; however, the variable length of the unit between stresses can be (and was) used to delay the appearance of the stress (somewhat as a good jazz drummer occasionally "lags the beat"), thereby creating tension. Furthermore, by introducing a stress intermediate between heavy and light, called a half-lift, Anglo-Saxon poetry was able to juxtapose two distinct non-lift elements. It did so in two forms. Type D follows two stresses with an unstressed element and a medium stress (two lifts with a dip and a half-lift): its basic schemas are HEAVY-HEAVY-light-medium (lift lift dip half-lift) and HEAVY-HEAVY-medium-light (lift lift half-lift dip). Type E follows a stress with a medium-stress and an unstressed element and completes the pattern with a stress (a lift, a half-lift, a dip and then another lift); its basic schemas are HEAVY-medium-light-HEAVY (lift half-lift dip lift) and HEAVY-light-medium-HEAVY (lift dip half-lift lift). One can easily see how such use of marked, semi-marked, and unmarked units, in combination with the use of varying lengths between the marked and semi-marked units, can produce a pattern of fluctuating pulses. Each line in an Anglo-Saxon poem, moreover, was divided in two, and the first half of the line could be in a different metre than the second—and indeed it usually was. This division made the pulse of the Anglo-Saxon poem even more fluid. The overall effect is of a highly changeable pulse, quite unlike that created by strict alternation of heavy and light units of fixed length that was the common basis of English metre from the Renaissance until the Pound era. Pound had considerable experience with verse based on such a prosody (he translated *The Seafarer* from the Anglo-Saxon) and Anglo-Saxon's fluid pulse had an enormous influence on his prosodic principles.

An even better example than we have provided until now of the subtlety and flexibility of Pound's rhythmic construction appears in his *homage* to the seventeenth-century masque song and, more particularly, to Jonson's "Have you seene but a bright Lillie grow?" While Pound was kept in the cage at a US Army Detention Training Center in Italy, the thought dawned on him of an imprisoned poet of another century, Richard Lovelace, and of the renowned poem he wrote to Althea from jail. The thought the poem begins with led to a good example of counterrhythm ("Yet/ Ere the season died a-cold") that scans both as iambic and as trochaic tetrameter. Its second line ("Borne upon a zephyr's shoulder") is definitely trochaic. From here on, though, the only instances of tetrameter are in the rhyming refrain: "*Lawes and Jenkyns guard thy rest/ Dolmetsch ever be thy guest.*" After that, it turns briefly anapaestic—though with some iambs admixed, creating hemiola:

> I rose through the aureate sky
> > *Lawes and Jenkyns guard thy rest*
> > *Dolmetsch ever be thy guest,*
> Has he tempered the viol's wood
> To enforce   both the grave   and the acute?
> Has he curved us the bowl of the lute?[248]

Right after the refrain, the poem continues with anapests, but then, in mid-line, it shifts to iambs with "airy a mood."

> Hast 'ou fashioned so airy a mood
>   To draw up leaf from the root?
> Hast 'ou found   a cloud   so light
>   As seemed neither mist nor shade?
>
>   Then resolve me, tell me aright
>   If Waller sang or Dowland played.[249]

Then, quoting from "Merciles Beauté," the poem shifts into Chaucerian iambic pentameter:

> Your eyen two wol sleye me sodenly
> I may the beauté of hem nat susteyne[250]

The next line expresses Pound's idea that after Chaucer, the art of poetry went into decline: "And for 180 years almost nothing." The line has a prosy rhythm, to convey the collapse of poetry into prose. Then follows that very affecting line that seems as though Dante himself would have been its author, but is actually a Poundian invention (only a most magnificent ear for language enabled him to do the imitation so well): *Ed ascoltando al leggier mormorio*. Then, picking up on Chaucer's "eyen two":

> there came new subtlety of eyes into my tent,
> whether of spirit or hypostasis,
>   but what the blindfold hides
> or at carneval
>   nor any pair showed anger
>   Saw but the eyes and stance between the eyes,
> colour, diastasis,
>   careless or unaware it had not the
>   whole tent's room[251]

Pound made formidable claims for the powers of rhythm:

> I believe in an 'absolute rhythm', a rhythm, that is, in poetry which corresponds exactly to the emotion or shade of emotion to be expressed. A man's rhythm must be interpretative, it will be, therefore, in the end, his own, uncounterfeiting, uncounterfeitable.[252]

Two points the text raises are especially important. The first is that the proper relation between emotion and idea in an artwork is one of identity. The second is that when the relation between words and rhythms (or between their equivalents for a filmmaker, viz., visual forms and rhythms) is perfected, the emotions and ideas they evoke will be at one. In another text, his introduction to his first translations of Guido Calvacanti (1910), Pound speculated that

Rhythm is perhaps the most primal of all things known to us. It is basic in poetry and music mutually, their melodies depending on a variation of tone quality and of pitch respectively, as is commonly said, but if we look more closely we will see that music is, by further analysis, pure rhythm; rhythm and nothing else, for the variation of pitch is the variation in rhythms of the individual notes, and harmony the blending of these varied rhythms. When we know more of overtones we will see that the tempo of every masterpiece is absolute, and is exactly set by some further law of rhythmic accord. Whence it should be possible to show that any given rhythm implies about it a complete musical form—fugue, sonata, I cannot say what form, but a form, perfect, complete. Ergo, the rhythm set in a line of poetry connotes its symphony, which, had we a little more skill, we could score for orchestra. *Sequitur*, or rather *inest*: the rhythm of any poetic line corresponds to emotion.

It is the poet's business that this correspondence be exact, i.e., that it be the emotion which surrounds the thought expressed.[253]

Pound's teachings that musical dynamics carry both the emotional and the conceptual freight of a work of art, and that all musical dynamics originate in rhythm, have been fine lessons for poets and filmmakers alike. Pound understood that the problem of finding the exact rhythm to convey the desired emotion/idea is THE primary consideration in making poems (a comment that holds true for film as well). Rhythm, Pound pointed out, has the power to remind us of "the most primal of all things known to us." Brakhage would agree (the non-inclusive language aside) that "a man's rhythm . . . will be . . . his own, uncounterfeiting, uncounterfeitable"; this conviction is the keystone of his ideas on art and expression.

In Pound's thought, the two points, rhythm and emotion, together with the measure of the vector of rhythm's power, triangulate a third: time. In the "Treatise on Metre" (appended to *ABC of Reading*, Pound states, "Rhythm is a form cut into TIME, as a design is determined SPACE." The medium wherewith the filmmaker cuts his design in time is not the "articulate sounds" of language but the kinetics of the shot, including those which derive from its design that conducts the eye through space, placing impeding obstacles and complexities in its way to slow the eye down or obviating impediments to movement to speed the eye in its movement through space, and the various gravities (i.e., weights-of-movements) of its colours. The primary failing of bad poems and bad films alike results from the poet's or filmmaker's wanting for a keen sense of time, and a bad poet or filmmaker is a bore because he or she does not perceive time and time relations subtly and cannot therefore delimit them interestingly—by gentler or sharper movements, by more ponderous or more sprightly colour, and by using the various other qualities of movement that are inseparable from images. It is from Pound that we have learned to understand the primary consideration in writing poems or making films is that of creating a design in time that is absolutely accurate to the emotion/idea that the poet or filmmaker strives to convey. Brakhage has grasped these propositions intuitively.

Pound's use of forms in which the metre can change almost line by line, and his use, inspired by his interest in Anglo-Saxon and Early English poetry, of quantitive metres results in his poems having a different sort of temporal construction from that which dominated English verse for the five hundred years before him. A regular, qualitative metre became the hegemonic form at about the time when the modern paradigm was in its infancy (just shortly after the time of, say, Nicolas of Cusa). It suggests that view of time which was the cardinal topic of Bergson accusations against the philosophies that preceded his: the view that time is composed of equidurational quanta laid out on a single line. To be sure, the varying lengths of the vowels in qualitative verse do advance and delay the accented syllables, but the form itself exerts considerable pressure towards isochrony—we really want to place the accents at regular intervals when we read the lines, so we lengthen or shorten, slur, and sometimes even omit syllables, to create more nearly equidurational units—and this pressure becomes greater as the accents become heavier. The temporal constructions of Pound's verse accord more closely with the view of time that Bergson's philosophy expounded. The same is true of the temporal constructions of Brakhage's films. Behind this is a very different view of reality than that which maps entities into a geometrically conceived space-time.[254] It is a view of reality that accords more closely with the proprioceptive body's knowledge—it is something felt on the nerves of the feeling body, an series of sensations, throbs, pulsations, and surging and waning energy (it was this that Open Form poets took up, to bring poetry and art into the present age and to make them a part of present reality).

Pound's aesthetics rests on a dynamic metaphysics, one that senses the differing qualities of the motion of different orders of entities. Among those who swayed Pound towards this metaphysics was Ernest Fenollosa, a Harvard-trained professor who spent many years teaching philosophy in Japan. Like Pound, Fenollosa was an ambitious synthesizer who attempted to draw together metaphysics, science, and literary criticism. His writing drew from the ideas of Ralph Waldo Emerson, Hegel, esoteric Buddhism, and James Clerk Maxwell's thermodynamics. His favourite intellectual trope was also one of Pound's own habits of mind, for it is characteristic of syncretic thinkers. Fenellosa delighted in taking an idea from one context and introducing it into another, thereby transforming both the idea and the context into which he introduced it. Accordingly, his writing leaps in arcs that span poetic theory, philosophy, religion, and modern scientific theories.

Fenollosa was the author of an extravagant and basically unreliable treatise on Chinese written characters; in it, he argued that the Chinese way of writing had effects on the Chinese conception of reality.[255] He believed this form of writing ultimately gave great strength to the Chinese worldview. According to Fenollosa, the Chinese written character is a compound of pictures that represent actions or "transferences of force."[256]

> All truth has to be expressed in sentences because all truth is the *transference of power*. The type of sentence in nature is a flash of lightning. It passes between two terms, a cloud and the earth. No unit of natural process can be less than this. . . . Light, heat, gravity, chemical affinity, human will have this in common, that they redistribute force.[257]

Fenollosa applies the central ideas of the Bergsonian metaphysics in his analysis of language. The theory of language that resulted from this endeavour resembles Brakhage's conception of language, both in its general outline and in most of its specific details.

> A true noun, an isolated thing, does not exist in nature. Things are only the terminal points, or rather the meeting points of actions, cross-sections cut through actions, snap-shots. Neither can a pure verb, an abstract motion, be possible in nature. The eye sees noun and verb as one: things in motion, motion in things [How like Bergson!]. . . .
>   The sun underlying the bursting forth of plants = spring.
>   The sun sign tangled in the branches of the tree sign = east. . . .
>   [N]o full sentence really completes a thought. The man who sees and the horse which is seen will not stand still. The man was planning a ride before he looked. The horse kicked when the man tried to catch him. . . . And though we may string never so many clauses into a single compound sentence, motion leaks everywhere, like electricity from an exposed wire. All processes in nature are inter-related [Again, how like Bergson!]. . . . [258]

Fenollosa noted that the basic distinction in Western languages, between nouns and verbs, does not exist in Chinese. The eye "sees noun and verb as one" in the Chinese character—sees, "things in motion, motion in things." The Chinese conception of reality is more true than the Western, Fenollosa proclaimed, because events are what the Chinese conceive them to be, "the meeting points of actions." Though many have claimed that the fundamental influence of the Fenollosa essay had on Pound was to steer him toward the idea that a poem could be composed through the juxtaposition of concrete elements, this is not the key to Fenollosa's influence on Pound (many prior influences had steered him towards the constation of concrete particulars)—rather it was the idea that "[a] 'part of speech' is only *what it does*."[259] This conception of artistic meaning is one that, as we shall see, Stan Brakhage reformulated for cinema.

Hulme's Bergsonianism had prepared Pound to accept the metaphysics that Fenollosa expounded in "The Chinese Written Character." In his Vorticist period, Pound had proposed that a poem is made up of words that rotate through a force field that radiates out from a single axis and organizes the whole. This conception of a poem made Fenollosa's notion that the Chinese written character engages in "transferences of forces" very attractive to him. Fenollosa also reawakened for Pound the idea that language can have a vital relation with organic processes. Pound described Fenollosa's manuscript as "the big essay on verbs, mostly verbs," and from Fenollosa Pound drew new ideas about how he could fashion his poems into constructs of energy and force. Thus, in "The Serious Artist" Pound writes, "We might come to believe that the thing that matters in art is a sort of energy, something more or less like electricity or radio-activity, a force transfusing, welding, and unifying. A force rather like water when it spurts up through very bright sand and sets it in swift motion."[260] Brakhage proposed a similar idea in a lecture on Sergej Ejzenstejn that he delivered to participants in the first course in film history that he gave at the Art Institute of Chicago. It is also a Fenollosian idea.

Furthermore, the concrete character of the images from which the ideogram is compounded exists, so that there is a relation between these visual representations (or their referents). But it is left to the eye and mind of the reader to discern that relation's character—an extremely attractive notion to a writer who was advocating that a poet should use no unnecessary word. More than that, the concreteness of the elements of the Chinese lexicon make them resistant to corruption, as the Chinese ideogram accurately mirrors the actual forces of nature that are responsible for meaning in the first place. Thus, by its nature Chinese is, like the language that American poets had long dreamt of, an Adamic language; by reason of its concrete pictorial nature, it avoids abstraction and the tendency to fashion metaphors (to substitute inaccurate terms for more accurate terms), or comparisons of any sort, which abstract away individuating features of particular objects—that tendency which both Emerson and Williams had identified as language's most debilitating characteristic, and that characteristic which demands language's reformulation. This effort, as we shall see, is an outgrowth of Romanticism's founding myth.

Pound took Fenollosa's essay at its best, as an *ars poetica*. The poetic theory Pound discerned in "The Chinese Written Character as a Medium for Poetry" had monumental impact on the composition of the *Cantos*.[261] Fenollosa had described the Chinese ideogram as a "thought picture," as a "continuous moving picture," as a *"verbal idea of action"* and as a "vivid shorthand picture of the operations of nature."[262] It is worth noting that Fenollosa's description of the Chinese ideogram possesses the same ambiguity in regard to the objective or subjective existence of its referent as Pound's *Cantos*—and not only Pound's *Cantos* but also Hulme's idea of the image, Williams's poetry and Brakhage's films. Further, the ideogram combines the function of noun and verb in one, Fenollosa implied. This combination undoes all Western ideas of parts of speech, and thus syntax and grammatical function. As a result, Fenollosa believed the Chinese language lacks a grammatical structure comparable to that of Western languages; and a principal difference between Chinese and Western languages, he claimed, is that the Chinese language does not engage in the business of arranging phrases and clauses in hierarchies. These ideas provided an impetus for Pound's paratactical practices.

Furthermore, because the Chinese language lacks grammatical rules that map experience onto the spatial structures of syntax, it promotes the experience of "the fundamental reality of *time*."[263] This claim, too, had cardinal importance for the *Cantos*, for at the point of embarking on the *Cantos*, Pound was learning to make the transition from writing Imagist and Vorticist poems, which emphasized dynamism in space, to composing a long poem, where time would be a key factor. The Chinese language has the advantage over Western languages of presenting a series of pictographs depicting object-events arranged according to their proper temporal sequence. This idea provided Pound with an important clue as to how to include time in a poem composed of concrete images, and so it is key to the *Cantos*. Previously, Pound's images had presented "a frozen moment," as "In a Station of the Metro" did, and such images resist being shaped into a long poem. The dynamic image, presenting a process unfolding over time, and presenting it in its proper sequence, is not similarly resistant—indeed it invites being incorporated into forms that make time palpable, and so into longer and more complex structures. Creating a similarly complex mythopoeic structure was also Brakhage's ambition for *Dog Star Man*; the formulation of such an ambition marks the transformation of the lyrical film into the mythopoeic film.

Fenollosa taught Pound to read Chinese written characters as pictures—pictures that rendered not so much things as the transferences of forces between things. Fenollosa encapulated the relational ontology that underlies his linguistic theory in a statement that resonates through American poetics of the twentieth century.

> But the primitive metaphors do not spring from arbitrary subjective processes. They are possible only because they follow objective lines of relations in nature herself. Relations are more real and more important than the things which they relate. . . . This is more than analogy, it is identity of structure. Nature furnishes her own clues. Had the world not been full of homologies, sympathies, and identities, thought would have been starved and language chained to the obvious. There would have been no bridge whereby to cross from the minor truth of the seen to the major truth of the unseen.[264]

One could read the statement that "[r]elations are more real and more impor-tant than the things which they relate" as the founding principle of the New Critics program; one can also read "nature furnishes her own clues" as the founding principle of William Carlos Williams's poetic theory and practice.

For an example of the written character as a picture of the transference of forces between things, we can take the first Chinese character that appears in the *Cantos*, the Chinese character for "sincerity."[265] The character con-sists of two parts: to the left, the familiar figure that looks a little like a stick-figure person; and to the right, two forms arranged one on top of the other. On the bottom, there is a box-like form, and on the top, four dashes (that, in a stretch, one might see as suggesting something ephemeral rising out of the box).

All Chinese characters consist either of a radical or of a radical and a sec-ond part. The radical, of which there are 214 basic forms, make up the left part of the character The other part of the character, for which the Chinese language contains no name, but F.W. Baller (in his introduction to that great book of my young adulthood, *Mathews' Chinese-English Dictionary*) refers to it as "a phonetic" when it suggests how one should pronounce the character and "a primitive" when it does not. The phonetic itself generally consists of two sub-parts, another radical and a phonetic. The character for "sincerity" is composed as many Chinese characters are: the form that makes up its left half is the radical, the form that constitutes its right half is a phonetic that itself is made up in the typical manner, of a radical on the bottom and pho-netic on the top. The character's radical, the form that makes up its left half, has an independent meaning, as radicals always do—it is the character for "person." The radical that forms the bottom half of the character's right-hand part, we might suppose, depicts a mouth. It is a small (though not nec-essarily correct) step from identifying these components to surmising that the strokes above the box represent words issuing from the mouth. Thus, Fenollosa and Pound infer, the Chinese character for "sincerity" literally depicts a person standing beside his or her word.

Pound took the idea farther—he claimed that the components of the char-acter are not depictions of static entities. In fact, they really are not depic-tions of anything; rather, he claimed, they embody and convey energies. About the Chinese character for "sincerity" (to return to that example), he remarked that the figure on the right depicts words rising from the box and so, he claimed, indicates fire/air. Throughout his work, when interpreting Chinese characters, Pound resorted to images of fire, light, electricity, and illumination, as Fenollosa had done in his essay on the Chinese written char-acter. Part of the attraction Fenollosa exerted on Pound resulted from the way Fenollosa had extended his method of interpreting Chinese characters until it had become a general theory of language—one that has resonances with ideas about language that Artaud proposed around the same time, and similarities with ideas about language that Olson and Brakhage would later propose. Words, Fenollosa insists, are not inert. They have charges, and so they are active. "[M]otion leaks everywhere, like electricity from an exposed wire" was Fenollosa most basic characterization of Chinese characters.[266] A poem, Pound avers, is similar, for it brings words together in such way that a charge passes between them; and this idea is the basis of Brakhage's ideas on editing (as it was the basis for the conception of montage that Ejzenstejn raised to the status of a general theory of aesthetics). Fenollosa described the ways the words in a poem interact with one another in the deservedly famous sentence, "Thus in all poetry a word is like a sun, with its corona and chromosphere; words crowd upon words, and enwrap each other in their luminous envelopes until sentences become clear, continuous light-bands."[267] A Chinese written character, in Fenollosa's view, is like a poem in miniature, for both embody "entangled lines of forces as they pulse through things."[268]

Fenollosa's proposals for what a poem could be describe the *Cantos* rather well. The micro-structures of that epic poem consist of words brought closely together until sparks flow between them. Its macro-structure consists of a giant line, beginning in mid-sentence and continuing through a nearly uncountable number of phrases joined by "and," or by no connective at all, that in the end reaches an incomplete infinitive phrase; thus, it is a massive sentence fragment bringing together all the forces of nature that would, as Fenollosa had it, "take all time to pronounce."[269] Open the *Cantos* where you will, and begin reading with a view toward parsing the composition—before long you will find parts that would scramble any machine in existence for analyzing grammar.

The *Cantos* does not have the linear form of an extended grammatical construct. Pound's composition is much better described in Fenollosa's terms, as "continuous light-bands" created by the sum of the radiation from differently charged words brought sufficiently close to each other that energy flows between them. From these ideas it follows that Pound's famous statement that the *Cantos* would be a "poem containing history" has a dialectical thrust that commentators have missed. He wanted to take "phalanxes of particulars"—concrete, time-bound entities—and raise them to the realm of the eternal. To achieve this end, Pound composed a poem that combined all times into a grand sentence fragment that would take all time to pronounce; it is an effort that I endorse with my own practice.

Fenollosa criticized the Western tradition's celebration of metaphor, which he considered to have been fostered by medieval logic. As the agency to counteract the deleterious effects of metaphor, Fenollosa proposed direct, immediate perception of things. All one need do to generate a position that ends by valorizing the film medium is to replace, as the central topic of one's advocacy, Fenollosa's direct presentation of things with the direct presentation of actions. This is exactly what Brakhage (under the influence of Charles Olson, an influence commented on in Chapter 2) did.

Fenollosa's essay, "The Chinese Written Character as a Medium for Poetry," pointed out as well that syntagmatic sequences in Chinese possess many of the same features as the individual written character. There are few connectives in Chinese—no copula verbs, transitive verbs, or co-ordinate conjunctions—and connectives are rarely used. When Chinese authors write "a man sees a horse," they write three characters: the character for "man," a character that looks like a stick person with two legs; the character that conveys the idea of seeing, which consists of a square containing two horizontal strokes surmounting two marks that begin vertically but are elongated forwards and backwards; and the character for "horse," a square with three lines through it surmounting a line that encloses, at the front, four vertical strokes. Fenollosa offers brief descriptions of the three written characters as ideographs: "First stands the man on his two legs. Second, his eye moves through space: a bold figure represented by running legs under an eye, a modified picture of an eye, a modified picture of running legs. . . . Third stands the horse on his four legs."[270] The Chinese version is not only ideographic, it is also highly condensed. The sentence, "A man sees a horse" is rendered, roughly, as "Standing man running eye horse." The condensed and very concrete character of the "ideograms" led Fenollosa to remark that when reading Chinese, "we do not seem to be juggling mental counters, but to be watching *things* work out their own fate."[271]

This last comment provides the basis for a reasonably adequate understanding of Pound's signal achievement. It *is* possible to discuss the *Cantos* as Allen Ginsberg does, as presenting a graph of thoughts arising in the author's consciousness. None of the *Cantos* can be discussed profitably without taking this dimension of them into account (and what is left out if we do not take it into account becomes proportionally greater as we leave the Chinese and John Adams cantos (Cantos LII-LXXI) and move through the *Pisan Cantos, Section: Rock-Drill de los Cantares*, and the *Thrones 96-106 de los Cantares*). That acknowledged, it is also true to say that any description of Pound's achievement must also recognize that Pound does not always present the internal world as an enclosed, private world, as a separate reality to the world of objective reality. Notwithstanding that some passages in the *Cantos* do seem to present a private, inner space utterly isolated from objective reality, there are others, the *Cantos'* most sublime moments among them, that seem egoless—moments in which mind and nature seem to merge and in which the text presents us with direct perceptions of the natural world.

His desire to record these moments of revelation was at the very heart of his endeavour from nearly the beginning of his career. In 1916, commenting on his famous three-line poem,

IN A STATION OF THE METRO

The apparition of these faces in the crowd;
Petals on a wet, black bough.[272]

Pound highlighted the subjective nature of this apparently objective presentation with the comment (already quoted): "I dare say it is meaningless *unless one has drifted into a certain vein of thought*. In a poem of this sort one is trying to record the precise instant when a thing outward and objective transforms itself, or darts into a thing inward and subjective."[273] And later in life, as a man "already old," "a man on whom the sun has gone down," held in a US Army Detention Training Center, he receives the charity of nature, and writes:

When the mind swings by a grass-blade
    an ant's forefoot shall save you
the clover leaf smells and tastes as its flower[274]

It is a state that children know well, when they stare empty-headedly at an object and identify with what they see to the point that they feel themselves transported on the wind that lifts the grass-blade or entirely taken up with examining the wondrous forms of nature—with an ant's forefoot, for example. The moments in the *Cantos* when Pound achieves such a state of mind are the *Cantos'* moments of instruction (for example, "Learn of the green world what can be thy place/ In scaled invention or true artistry" in Canto LXXXI).

How different this is from Eliot. Reading Eliot, we do feel that we are seeing into a mind—we sense that a "lyrical ego," as Charles Olson called it, intervenes to transform the world of things imaginatively.

The yellow fog that rubs its back upon the window-panes,
The yellow smoke that rubs its muzzle on the window-panes,
Licked its tongue into the corners of the evening,
Lingered upon the pools that stand in drains,
Let fall upon its back the soot that falls from chimneys,
Slipped by the terrace, made a sudden leap,
And seeing that it was a soft October night,
Curled once about the house, and fell asleep.[275]

The lines have many of the features of Pound's own verse (though, in syllable count they are much less free). There is a similar tension between conclusion and *enjambment* at the line endings. And the effect of having a quasi-conclusion at each line break is to convert the overall form of the poem into a list of perceived particulars. Yet we know we are seeing the world through a sensibility. Similarly:

> The morning comes to consciousness
> Of faint stale smells of beer
> From the sawdust-trampled street
> With all its muddy feet that press
> To early coffee-stands.
>
> With the other masquerades
> That time resumes,
> One thinks of all the hands
> That are raising dingy shades
> In a thousand furnished rooms.[276]

"One thinks of . . ." is just the point. With Pound, on the other hand, we feel that the writing presents us, at least sometimes, with the direct perception of the objective world:

> And before hell mouth; dry plain
>   and two mountains;
>   On the one mountain, a running form,
>   and another
> In the turn of the hill; in hard steel
> The road like a slow screw's thread,
> The angle almost imperceptible[277]

Even moments as neo-Platonic as those recorded in Canto LXXXIII climb down from their enclosure in subjectivity to meet with the actual world of the concrete particular. There Pound, a prisoner in a US Army Detention Training Center, describes what he sees one morning through the thinning mist as he looks off towards a distant mountain (which, because it reminds him of a mountain he read of in a Chinese poem, he calls Taishan):

> Heliads lift the mist from the young willows
> there is no base seen under Taishan
>   but the brightness of 'udor   ὕδωρ
> the poplar tips float in brightness
> only the stockade posts stand
>
> And now the ants seem to stagger
>   as the dawn sun has trapped their shadows,
> this breath wholly covers the mountains
>   it shines and divides[278]

Quite a contrast to Eliot's morning scene!

Yet for all their quality of presenting direct perception, we never forget—not even for a moment—that the *Cantos* chronicle the education of one person's sensibility. We are always aware that with each new element presented, we are following a shift in that person's attention. The conflict of interpretations that lines such as these evoke—lines that present direct seeing and moments in the education of a man's soul (and there are many in the *Cantos*)—suggests a peculiar indeterminacy in the status of what they describe. We cannot come down firmly on either side of the question of whether these lines present the objective or the subjective world.

A similar indeterminacy surrounds no small portion of Japanese and Chinese poetry, from those of the great poet Tu Fu:

> Tumult, weeping, many new ghosts.
> Heartbroken, aging, alone, I sing
> To myself. Ragged mist settles
> In the spreading dusk. Snow skurries
> In the coiling wind. The wineglass
> Is spilled. The bottle is empty.
> The fire has gone out in the stove.
> Everywhere men speak in whispers.
> I brood on the uselessness of letters.[279]

to most haiku, for example, Basho's:

> First winter rain:
> The monkey also seems
> To want a small straw cloak.[280]

We have seen earlier that a similar indeterminateness characterizes Williams's poetry. Such indeterminancy is an attribute of Brakhage's films as well. Take *The Weir-Falcon Saga* as an example. Its opening section includes: children at play, often performing child-dances; flares, of red and gold and their complements, green and blue; representations of objects; and, perhaps most impressively, images of fire. Retrospectively, we can interpret these representations of fire as associations to the theme of fever, but this significance is not clear when they are first presented. Even their ontological status is unclear. We do not know if we should see them as the visual content of the children's mind, as the visual content of the filmmaker's mind, or as presentations of the objective world (of something actually on fire).

Sometime after the end of this opening section, we see the smaller of Brakhage's boys (Rarc) playing with a gun and then, shortly after, fallen and panting. There follows a series of shots of trees, of Brakhage's wife, Jane, naked from the waist up, of sheets flapping in front of a window, of water droplets on an evergreen tree. We cannot say with any certainty who is the subject for these representations, that is, who (if anyone) perceives them. We can just as well consider them direct presentations of the objective world as representations in somebody's mind. Furthermore, because Brakhage makes connections among visual forms based on their intrinsic properties, we cannot interpret them as associations around some theme (say, given the sequence that precedes them, the theme of danger). We cannot consider the flow of visual forms as purely subjective, and that impossibility adds to the ambiguity surrounding their status.

The same ambiguity about the ontological status of what it represents characterizes the entire work. The ambiguity becomes obvious in the section where the boy is taken to a clinic. The film cuts between representations of the naked little boy in the examining room and images presenting the anatomic details of a building—a naked lightbulb, pipes exposed to view, wiring, basement corridors, and, later, rippled glass.[281] We could attempt a metaphoric reading, claiming, perhaps, that the shots examine internal elements of the building's substructure, just as the doctor examines the boy's internal organs, or that the naked lightbulb or pipes offer a metaphor to a naked boy—or even, if we deem that an awkward and too-literal metaphor, that the botched effort at constructing a metaphor conveys Brakhage's desperation to tell us what he thinks and feels. If there is any truth in such an interpretation, it is only a small quantity; for what *The Weir-Falcon Saga* presents is really direct perception. "This is what was there, in all its bleakness," the visual forms suggest.

One does know that the film presents a crisis seen principally through Brakhage's eyes. We can take the same example cited above—intercutting shots of pipes and a naked lightbulb in the building's basement and shots of the doctor examining Rarc, whom Brakhage photographed in an uncharacteristically static and, therefore, anxiety-inducing manner, lying on the examination table, just the sweetest, naked little boy. Most viewers, I think, would take it that this crosscutting joins what the anxious father saw as he paced about, fretting over his little boy, with the cause of his anxiety. However, another quality of the work balances the work's subjective nature: the film seems to render the objective world directly. Brakhage established this quality early in the work, by using a series of shots that we cannot ascribe to any subject.[282] In sum, like Pound's paratactical constructions, the forms Brakhage constructs in *The Weir-Falcon Saga* render undecidable the question whether its visual forms belong to the objective or subjective realm. The images in Pound's poetry, as in Brakhage's film, occupy a zone intermediate between objectivity and subjectivity.

Fenollosa's contribution to Pound's poetry, partly, was to strengthen its objective character. Fenollosa's influence on Pound was so great that Pound began referring to his compositional practice, on the analogy to the Chinese character, as the ideogramic method. He accepted Fenollosa's claim that the Chinese written character was a poem in miniature which, by its juxtaposition of elements, causes energies to circulate among its parts and in doing so reveals truths about the make-up of nature which the science of his day was only just approaching. This conception of a poem as elements in juxtaposition that pass charges between them led Pound to create a form that relies on simply presenting concrete particulars, with few connectives between them, resulting in extreme condensation. Pound described the method as "a form of super-position, that is to say, it is one idea set on top of another."[283] It is the basic method of the *Cantos*, so any passage chosen at random could serve to illustrate it. A splendid example appears in Canto LII:

> This month is the reign of Autumn
> Heaven is active in metals, now gather millet
>   and finish the flood-walls
> Orion at sunrise.
>   Horses now with black manes.
> Eat dog meat. This is the month of ramparts.
> Beans are the tribute, September is end of thunder
> The hibernants go into their caves.
>   Tolls lowered, now sparrows, they say, turn into oysters
> The wolf now offers his sacrifice.
>   Men hunt with five weapons,
> They cut wood for charcoal.
>   New rice with your dog meat.
> First month of winter is now
>   sun is in Scorpio's tail
> at sunrise in Hydra, ice starting
> The pheasant plunges into Houai (great water)
>   and turns to an oyster
> Rainbow is hidden awhile.
>   Heaven's Son feeds on roast pork and millet,
> Steel gray are stallion.
>   This month winter ruleth.
> The sun is in archer's shoulder
>   in crow's head at sunrise
> Ice thickens. Earth cracks. And the tigers now move to mating.[284]

The juxtaposition of charged particles is Pound's method. It is also Brakhage's. It would be unfair to Brakhage to say that one could generate a work basically similar to *Dog Star Man* by taking each element in Pound's poem and translating it into a cinematogaphic representation, while making sure that just as Pound's word choice throws the material of language into relief, so some cinematographic device (slow-motion or fast-motion, under- or overexposure, graininess of the visual form, or superimposition, for examples) would throw the material of film into relief. It would be unfair—but it would not be risibly far off the mark. Imagine the film section that would correspond to the last line of the section: a shot of ice, overexposed; and of a crack in the ground, filmed by an accelerated camera moving along it; two tigers in a green, green field, etc.

Pound hoped that paratactical constructions would release an exciting force, that the interaction of the elements brought into proximity would produce an impulse that would incite the reader's mind to an epiphany. Pound himself came to understand that he harboured a curious mixture of ambitions for the *Cantos*: on the one hand, he proposed to write a long epic work, a poem whose scope comprised the whole of history and all that was important to know; while, on the other, he wanted to create a work of extreme concentration, dedicated to the quest for sudden epiphany—to the quest for the revelation of the immediate moment that would annihilate time.

The envelope of a work that contains history can only be metahistorical, and a work that contains, simultaneously, all times, can only be timeless. The aspiration to rise above time and to accede to the realm of the timeless is also implicit in Pound's desire to overcome abstraction and Aristotelian logic through a method that deployed "a phalanx of particulars." Pound, like Fenollosa, held a hierophantic conception of reality, on which the ascent to higher levels of reality preserves the reality of all the lower levels. The Chinese written character provided Pound with a splendid example of how particulars can be preserved in relations that convey something as abstract as "sincerity."

Fenollosa's "The Chinese Written Character" offered comments about the importance of metaphor. The notion of metaphor that underlies them resembles Brakhage's conception of that trope, in some respects at least. Fenollosa believed that an experience lies at the core of any written character (even an abstract term) and that the core experience can be uncovered by discerning the structure of the sign. Brakhage believes much the same about language. (For Brakhage, as for Charles Olson, that structure depends on the term's etymology; for Fenollosa, it depends upon the combination of radicals in the written character.) Furthermore, Brakhage and Fenollosa agree that the experience that one can discover at the core of any term is an experience of action: "The whole delicate substance of speech is built upon substrata of metaphor. Abstract terms, pressed by etymology, reveal their ancient roots still embedded in direct action."[285] At another point, Fenollosa alluded to light to convey the lasting importance of the root meaning of words. He writes that the original metaphors buried in words "stand as a kind of luminous background."[286] Pound concurs. Speaking of what has been lost to moderns—lost partly through language's reifying effects—he writes:

> We appear to have lost the radiant world where one thought cuts through another with clean edge, a world of moving energies *'mezzo oscuro rade'*, *'risplende in sè perpetuale effecto'*, magnetisms that take form, that are seen,

> or that border the visible, the matter of Dante's *paradiso*, the glass under
> water, the form that seems a form seen in a mirror, these realities percep-
> tible to the sense, interacting, *'a lui si tiri'*. . . . [287]

Pound concludes the paragraph with proleptic comments that distinguish his
notion of how the energies of words disclose a mysterious, luminous world
from the ideas of the Symbolists, whom (along with Unitarians, Wordsworth-
ians, and all adherents of the Perennial Philosophy) he despised as vague
and woolly dreamers. His conception was something as hard as crystal and
as definite as the *'section d'or'* that gives churches like Saint Hilaire, San
Zeno, and the Duomo di Modena their clear lines and proportions. The energies he was after produced the " 'harmony in the sentience' or harmony *of*
the sentient, where the thought has its demarcation, the substance its *virtu*,
where stupid men have not reduced all 'energy' to unbounded undistin-
guished abstraction."[288]

Through the combined influences of Bergson, Hulme, and Fenollosa,
Pound came to adopt the view that poetry is a matter of energy. In 1911, he
described a collection of pictures as "an array of engines each designed 'to
gather the latent energy of Nature and focus it on a certain resistance. The
latent energy is made dynamic or "revealed" to the engineer in control, and
placed at his disposal.' "[289] Questions about the picture's being pretty or not
have little importance. What counts is how these picture-machines gather,
concentrate, transform, and convey energy. The rhetoric is reminiscent of
that of Wyndham Lewis, perhaps, but the conception itself has nonetheless
had enormous influence. Brakhage, for example, adopted this dynamic conception of a work of art.

Brakhage came to the idea that poetry is not representation, that it does
not offer propositions, but transmits energies, in an endearing way. In high
school, he fell in with a group of anti-sportsminded boys, who called themselves the Gadflies and who, incredibly, included both the renowned avant-
garde animator Larry Jordan and the distinguished composer James Tenney.
Brakhage had already gained a reputation for his ability to understand poetry
that others found difficult. So, as a joke, the Gadflies gave him as a birthday
present a book of poems that seemed completely indecipherable—it was
written in several languages, including Chinese, and populated with gods
from every mythological system imaginable. Brakhage recounts the episode
in a lecture/question period at the University of North Carolina at Chapel
Hill:

> This [book] of course was Ezra Pound's *Cantos*, which is, if I must choose
> one book, the single most important book in my life. Indeed I couldn't read
> it and they had their good laugh. I could only put together three words in a
> row and then stumble over a lot I couldn't understand and then three more

words that I could understand. But right off the bat, because I was too desperate not to be defeated in the teeth of my friends who were getting too
much of a laugh out of this, I started the book and it starts "And then went
down to the ship." Right there (writes on board) I noticed something:
"And." To start off a book like this with "and!" I am very concerned with
the beginning and endings of books—"and"—that was thrilling. And
immediately it moved all the emotions this way (writes on board "⇒")—so
powerful. I remember it brought tears to my eyes, which no doubt
increased the laughter of my friends. And the next word which hit me was
"down," "and then went *down*." "Set forth" was there too. And within
those lines you also get "up." In those first two lines the mind splits, the
mind moving, going in two directions and very powerfully and very reinforced. That kind of thing is where the relationship between my sense of
poetry and what film can do begins, and that is like the first level set of
meaning: direction! The poem has the capacity beyond just its rhythm to
make reference to the process of thinking itself. If you set that in a
model—that's forward and back. Poetry is having to do with the actual process of thought, as absolutely distinct from what I don't regard as poetry at
all, the writer telling you his mind.[290]

Here Brakhage reveals his sense of the poem (a sense bolstered by the
resistance to interpretation passages of the *Cantos* offered) as an organization of forces and vectors—"direction," he explains, is what first and most
affects us when we read a poem; the movements the poem organizes are
movements of the mind. Later, from the mid-1980s, Brakhage was to
expound a conception of a film based on the idea that film's distinctive
virtue, the quality that distinguishes film from all the other arts, is that it can
convey what he calls "moving visual thinking." Interest in the dynamics of
thinking remains a constant in Brakhage's thought and in his art. We can
locate its point of origin in Pound's vortex.

Writing = Composing Sound's Energies,
Filmmaking = Composing Light's Energies:
Gertrude Stein and Stan Brakhage's
Conceptions of Their Media

Brakhage's admiration for Gertrude Stein is well known, for he has frequently expounded on her importance for him. Of all the literary influences
on Brakhage, Stein is likely the most difficult to penetrate; so today, nearly
one hundred and fifty years after her birth, she keeps Louis Zukofsky company as the least read, least discussed, and least assimilated of the great literary modernists. Stein is famous for developing a style based on repetition.
It is well known that Stein's use of repetition depends on the principle that
no two elements in a literary work, even repeated elements, are ever phenomenologically identical; when an element occurs the second time it is

different because it follows a previous appearance, and when it appears a third time, it is different because it follows two previous instances.[291] The debt Stein owes to her teacher, William James, on this account is less well known. Like Bergson, James wanted to show that novelty is a reality, that there is real change in the world. He intensely disliked philosophies of the absolute that propose that everything ultimately belongs to the One, thereby eliminating variety. He had an equally strong distaste for the views of mechanistic materialists who see change simply as the rearrangement of already existing particles of matter.[292] In "The Notion of Reality as Changing," James points out that "[t]he common objection to admitting novelties is that by jumping abruptly in, *ex nihilo*, they shatter the world's rational continuity."[293] To counter this view, James argued that change is continuous and develops from previous situations. "Novelty, as empirically found, doesn't arrive by jumps and jolts, it leaks in insensibly," he states. His theory of consciousness argues similarly for the reality of novelty.

> Does not the same piano-key, struck with the same force, make us hear in the same way? Does not the same grass give us the same feeling of green...? It seems a piece of metaphysical sophistry to suggest that we do not; and yet a close attention to the matter shows that *there is no proof that the same bodily sensation is ever got by us twice.*
> *What is got twice is the same* OBJECT.[294]

Stein used repetition to show, among other things, that "novelty leaks in insensibly" and that "the same sensation is [n]ever got by us twice."

The most famous example of Stein's use of repetition is the most often quoted and alluded to line in American English, perhaps in all English. Though often offered as humour, it is much more than that. The line is "(A) rose is a rose is a rose."[295] This little poem serves as a demonstration of the modernists' basic teaching, that context so thoroughly transforms any lexical element that enters an artistic work that it retains only vestiges of the meaning it has in everyday use. What is more, Stein's demonstration proceeds in a rigorous, indeed almost scientific manner that might have been approved by her mentor, William James.[296]

The first instance of "R/rose" states the subject of the sentence and arouses the expectation that the sentence will go on to ascribe an action or quality to the rose. One of Stein's principal ambitions was to defeat the sense of expectation, to make us take each item she presents in its full immediacy. So we might well expect that Stein would do something to defeat our expectations, likely by doing something unconventional, such as constructing a phrase like "a rose is not a trifling matter" or "a rose of willing seen in the bird day." Given those expectations, the most unexpected thing that she could do is to follow "(A) rose is" with "a rose." However, the sec-

ond "a rose" is very different from the first (and this difference is emphasized in those variants in which Stein drops the indefinite article). While its
first use, as a subject and to begin a sentence, "a rose" elicited expectations,
its use as a predicate closes down those expectations, creating a sense of
finality. "(A) rose is a rose" is a statement roughly equivalent to "It is what
it is" or "What else can you say?" When the second "is a rose" joins the
first, the quality changes again, into an almost metaphysical statement.
Thus, each occurence of "rose" is affectively distinct and each has a different
function. These differences create variety where none seemed to exist.

This is one of the major lessons that Brakhage has drawn from Stein's
example. Thus, when P. Adams Sitney, discussing *Sirius Remembered* (a film
that shows the corpse of a beloved dog decomposing in the forest) with
Brakhage, asked about his interests in Stein, Brakhage replied:

> I would say that the greatest influence that she had on *Sirius Remembered*
> was by way of my realization that there is no repetition; that every time a
> word is "repeated" it is a new word by virtue of what word precedes it and
> follows it, etc. This freed me to "repeat" the same kind of movements. So
> I could literally move back and forth over the animal in repeated patterns.
> There are three parts to the film: first there is the animal seen in the fall as
> just having died, second there are the winter shots in which he's become a
> statue covered with snow, and third there's the thaw and decay. That third
> section is all REmembered [*sic*] where his members are put together
> again. All previous periods of his existence as a corpse, in the fall, the
> snow, and the thaw are gone back and forth over, recapitulated and inter-
> related. Gertrude Stein gave me the courage to let images recur in this
> fashion and in such a manner that there was no sense of repetition.[297]

Brakhage acknowledges two crucial features of Stein's modernism. The
first is her use of simplified constructions to throw form into relief. Previously, when writers or composers used repetition, they associated it with
embellishment or variation. Most artists (and art theorists) would have
thought exact repetition could not be countenanced; repetition of similar
(but not identical) elements was possible, for such repetition relates diverse
elements. In her famous miniature poem, Stein attenuated diversity to
whatever difference resulted from the use of simple repetition of an unvaried
element. She recognized that when an element is simply repeated, it is not
the same, since its context is inevitably different. By using simple repetition, she made its effects evident. Stein takes a small difference, a difference
as small as small can be—simply that the second instance of "(a) R/rose"
appears after "(A) R/rose is" had already appeared once, and that its third
instance appears after "(a) R/rose is" had already appeared twice—and
makes it seem momentous. Because the actual differences are so small, the
change is very apparent.

Second, Brakhage points out that Stein's work demonstrates that we do not necessarily experience the repetition of a simple element as a succession of elements. He points out that Stein's work evidences that context so deeply affects the meaning of a repeated element that a passage composed strictly of repeated elements can elicit the experience of the continual coming-on of novelty (to borrow an expression from William James). We experience every new repetition as novel, if only because it presents itself as belonging to a new moment of presence. By composing passages of a few, simple repeated elements, that alternate with one another, or vary slightly, Stein reshapes the sequential temporality of writings into a prolonged, but nonetheless immediate "now"—the now that William James referred to as the "specious present" (quite intending the pun).

Stein was aware of these features of her writing. In her famous *Composition as Explanation*, Stein looked back over her career to 1926 and remarked:

> In beginning writing I wrote a book called *Three Lives* this was written in 1905. I wrote a negro story called *Melanctha*. In that there was constant recurring and beginning there was a marked direction in the direction of being in the present although naturally I had been accustomed to past present and future, and why, because the composition forming around me was a prolonged present. A composition of a prolonged present is a natural composition in the world as it has been these thirty years it was more and more a prolonged present. I created then a prolonged present naturally I knew nothing of a continuous present but it came naturally to me to make one, it was simple it was clear to me and nobody knew why it was done like that, I did not myself although naturally, it was natural.[298]

Later, in "How Writing Is Written," Stein points out the effect this produces, of "present immediacy" and explains that she creates this sense though substituting present participles for nouns. In "Composition as Explanation" she points out her use of "perpetually regenerating forms" (see glossary; she refers to this as "beginning again and again") and the quotidian character of her interests (which she refers to as "using everything").

Brakhage has commented often on Stein's famous rose single, and sometimes he has ventured far in his commentary on the phenomenal transformations (the transformations in the consciousness of a receptive reader) that the basic constituent module, "(a) R/rose is," undergoes in this poem. When giving a lecture at the University of North Carolina at Chapel Hill, Brakhage went to the blackboard, wrote "A ROSE IS A ROSE IS A ROSE" in capital letters and arranged it in a circle with an "A" in the 12 o'clock position and then delivered this commentary:

> That's the way Gertrude Stein originally wrote in a child's book called *The World Is Round*. It's written this way [in a circle] because Rose, the little heroine, carves it in a tree. I think it arose that simply in Gertrude's life,

because very shortly she was using it on her stationery. But suddenly Gertrude had the sense that she had been given a great gift. First of all it's a wonderful centrepiece of arguments for her great teacher, William James, about the nature of being and nothingness before it got obfuscated into that, in my opinion, by the existentialists. It looks like a silly thing—ok, we got it—a rose is a rose is a rose. It means it is only and ever a rose. That's something to brood on, and we could say that's kind of a silly poem. After it sprang from her subconscious mind into this child's book, she must have come to realize the incredible puns that move through it. There is a reference that [shows] she was aware of those, though she wouldn't be as academic as I am to lay it all out here. Someone was once attacking the poem in Chicago, and she said "all I have to say is that the rose has not bloomed so sweetly in English poetry in 200 years." Which meant that she had come to recognize what that whole tradition of English poetry is; so poetry always has a tradition, a whole lattice of meaning. So the rose, if having looked at the whole history of English poetry as a history, is used in three basic symbol places: birth, sex, death. (AROSE) Here we have a nice pun for birth, for something coming up; here we have his Eros, sex; and with a slight slur, we can get sorrows; with another slight slur we can get the connective, the thing that relates symbolically, arrows. What springs magically if you start feeling it with the tongue, as distinct from just taking it along with the clichés of everyday language, birth, sex, death is represented back thru the Greek, and perhaps earlier, by the three sisters. The three sisters are in there. She glorified that sense of the forest by laying it out in a line, not always putting it in a circle. So it's a meditation piece as a poem which has to do certainly with the whole history of English toying with these particular words, and these qualities of meaning. There are other kinds of spring-off from it, like for an English garden, that is planted in *rows*.[299]

What is fascinating is to see how Brakhage locates an allusion to the life cycle (birth/sex/death) within such an apparently modest piece of writing; and more interesting still is his emphasis on the idea of death.

Brakhage is correct to point out that Stein's use of repetition rests on Jamesian ideas, though actually their provenance is more broadly in the philosophy of pragmatism. Stein seems to have held a somewhat Peircean conception of significance. Peirce maintained that meaning does not inhere in individual concepts, but in the relations among concepts. A desire to work out the means for analyzing meaning drove Peirce's work in the logic of relations (a logico-mathematical field he helped to found). Stein might have had some familiarity with Peirce's ideas, either directly or indirectly through her mentor William James, who claimed to have derived the foundations of his pragmatism from Peirce's writing; but in any case, Stein's conception of meaning must have been similar, for one of her fundamental interests is in showing that the meanings of terms undergo change as they take on new relations. This concern is a major part of her interest both in repetition and, as we shall soon see, in anacoluthon (see glossary).

The pictures of reality that Peirce and Stein present coincide with one another remarkably well. Peirce too wanted to refute that item of philosophic orthodoxy which maintains that reality is made up of fixed substances. He maintained, to the contrary, that objects are constituted exclusively by the laws that determine their behaviour in all possible situations. This ontological principle is the foundation piece of his pragmatism. Its semiotic equivalent is the proposition that meaning is unstable for it does not inhere in individual signs; rather meaning depends on the effects that signs have, and their meaning alters with their effects (and effects alter according to circumstances.) This "pragmatic" theory of meaning is exactly what Stein's practice implies. It also provides a basis for the conception of meaning that undergirds Stan Brakhage's work; Brakhage's films—especially the hand-painted and "imagnostic" (see glossary) films, but really his entire body of work—suggest that he, too, believes that reality is dynamic and that this dynamism makes all fixed representations implausible.

Put this way, however, the ideas seem metaphysical. Another of Stein's points is that this "pragmatic" difference (i.e., difference in perlocutionary [see glossary] effect) is felt somatically. We can achieve some insight into the bodily effects entailed by the principle that there can be no exact repetition in a literary work by reconsidering the piece under our noses, for we could not imagine a more forceful demonstration of context establishing a lexeme's significance than Stein's famous miniature composed by compounding a single module, "R/rose (is)"—indeed, the miniature's paradigmatic simplicity gives the demonstration its force.

The miniature uses repetition to create rhythm, and rhythm is corporal in its effects. The repetition of a single, simple element throws the sentence's rhythm into relief, and the rhythm is ingenious. Taking the variant that begins with the indefinite article and scanning it, we get: "A róse is a róse is a róse—or, "Ta DOOM tada DOOM tada DOOM." Basically, the metre is anapaestic—a waltz-like rhythm with the accent on the third beat. It starts with an iambic foot, however. Since the iambic metre is the most common English metre, beginning with an iambic foot creates the expectation that the poem's basic metre will be iambic. The two anapaestic feet that follow thwart that expectation. The pattern of eliciting expectation, then thwarting it, is the same pattern we noted above in connection with the miniature's syntactic and semantic elements.

But its rhythmic complexity is even greater. When we consider the passage retrospectively—or when we take it as whole—we realize that we can consider it as three anapaestic feet, the first of which is truncated, so that it starts on the second beat, not the third. Use of an abbreviated first bar is a common device in musical compositions, and Stein may have been using the device of anacrusis (see glossary) as a linguistic equivalent to that construction in order to highlight its aural properties, including its rhythm. Whether or not that is so, Stein's single provides a marvellous demonstration that an item (an iambic foot) changes as it forms relations with other elements (when an iambic foot is followed by two anapaestic feet).

Even this description underestimates the sentence's rhythmic intricacy. It would be more correct to say that if the common teachings of prosody were universally applicable, we would consider the sentence as three anapaestic feet, the first truncated. However, Stein bedevils the common teachings of literary studies. She opposed the subordination of individual parts to the whole, and of retrospectively altering our understanding of the one foot by what comes after. She insists that each item be taken on its own. "(A) R/rose is a rose is a rose," makes each noun phrase a phenomenologically distinct element. So we scan the sentence as one iambic foot followed by two anapaestic feet; or we can scan it as three anapests (one of which is truncated). The clash between these two scansions means that the sentence starts with the effect of hemiola. Furthermore, we can scan the lines as two dactyls followed by a spondee. A spondee is a common means for creating line closure, and the spondaic foot at the end of this line serves that typical function. Thus, Stein highlights why the presentation of three instances of "a rose seems so satisfying." The third instance is much different from the previous two. Moreover, as though confirming the difference, "rose" is unaccented in the two dactyls but accented in the spondee.

We still have not exhausted the miniature's complexity. The construction into which Stein inserted the first "a rose" consists of two more instances of the same item, the three joined by two copulas. The effect of the series of copulas joining identical phrases makes the first item appear as a quasi-independent element in a modular construction. Thus this construction gives evidence that the general context does shape our interpretation of its metre—in fact, the context of relations so thoroughly reshapes the metrical units that each (one dimetric unit followed by two dimetric units) appears almost independent. This independence makes each seem distinct, isolated, and, paradoxically, unaffected by its context. This distinctness creates variety that makes apparent that the items *are* both affected by and dependent on their context. So it goes, around and around, just like the sentence, which also has a circular form.

And there is still more: Stein maintained that the nouns were the culprit that held literature back from entering the American Century; in this respect, her views resembled those of Fenollosa, who thought that nouns were responsible for the undoing of Western metaphysics. Like Fenollosa, Stein believed that nouns present the world as fixed, while she, like her mentor William James, believed that everything is in motion. However, her response was only partly to turn nouns into verbal forms, as Fenollosa extolled the Chinese written character for doing (and as Guy Davenport claims that she did, as we have seen). Her response was mostly intended to displace the emphasis in her writing, away from type words (nouns) and towards aggregates of words, where repeated sounds (assonance and alliteration), rhythm, and other aural structures could play a role—where sound could become a material agent, i.e., meaning. "(A) R/rose is a rose is a rose" is a sentence about nouns, and it manifests just what nouns do—they fix the real and render its face unchanging. The sentence is an object lesson in the effects of naming.

This very simple example makes clear that Stein's interest focused on language; of all the great literary modernists, only Louis Zukofsky matches her in the single-minded devotion to discovering the conditions that make language distinct from any other artistic medium. Stein (perhaps inspired by William James) realized that she should attend to the pragmatics of writing, that she should heed the effects of word-sounds and word-shapes rather than their conventional "representational significance," the role of which she did everything in her power to lessen. She understood that if she was to create works that are presentational rather than representational, that if her works were to evoke a sense of present immediacy, they would have to be about language, and not simply about the world. The tautological form of "(A) rose is a rose is a rose" makes it a manifestation of facts of language, not a statement about the world.

Stein later commented on her famous miniature in an essay entitled "Poetry and Grammar," collected in *Lectures in America*.

> When I said.
> A rose is a rose is a rose is a rose
> And then later made that into a ring I made poetry and what did I do I caressed completely caressed and addressed a noun.[300]

While the commentary (to use the term very loosely) raises many interesting points, one point that it does not raise is crucial. An aspect of the miniature's achievement is that the repetition produces the effect of movement. We can easily read the sentence as saying "(A) R/rose is arose. . . ." What is compelling about the ease with which we formulate this version is that the verb phrase suggests the miniature's movement—its rising action. One of the effects of the circular form of the miniature relates to the paradoxical status of the impression of movement that literary works evoke. For presenting the sentence in a circular form compels the reader's eye to move around the sentence, and this forced deviation from the eye's normal, rectilinear movement makes the dynamism of the eye evident. Yet the movement around the circle closes back on itself; it is a movement that returns to where it started, a movement that goes nowhere and so, in a sense, is not movement. And since this is movement that is not real movement (in the sense that it does not progress towards an outcome), it is ceaseless.

One of the probable reasons for Stein's affection for this miniature is that it suggests the dynamics of a literary work. All reading is dynamic; all reading involves movement—movement of the eye and of the imagination through a text—but movement that is virtual, not real. Furthermore, while most literary works, because their forms have the purpose of articulating conflict, produce the illusion that the movement they embody is teleologically oriented and progresses to a state qualitatively different from that initiated at the outset by the development of the conflict that the work embodies, Stein overturns that illusion by demonstrating that the movement is always one of words leading to words leading to words leading to words.

Still, what Stein actually does say in her commentary on her famous miniature is as interesting and important as what she does not—her commentary stresses that a writer has a physical relation with the materials she uses, that is, with words. Stein goes so far as to distinguish poetry from prose on the basis of poetry's greater love for the actual, material word, evidenced in the poet's greater use of repetition. She elaborates on this idea with another point in the same essay:

> But and that is a thing to be remembered you can love a name and if you love a name then saying that name any number of times only makes you love it more, more violently more persistently more tormentedly. Anybody knows how anybody calls out the name of anybody one loves. And so that is poetry really loving the name of anything and that is not prose. Yes any of you can know that.[301]

A poet understands that a word is a palpable, material thing, and establishes physical relations with its physical properties. Each successive instance of "rose" is a qualitatively different phrase, and the differences among the instances, highlighted by the proximity of their occurrences, throws the word's material properties into relief. This has the effect of pushing its referential or signifying function into the background, while the physical properties of the signifier—the elements actually presented in the work—comes to the fore. Stein names this interest in the words' physical characteristics love, love that is no different from one human's interest in another person's physical characteristics and his agreement to being caressed. The freshness with which a phrase appears each time that it is repeated is both a cause and an index of our love for it and is in every way similar to the renewed enthusiasm with which we greet each appearance of our lovers; hardly surprising, then, that we should enjoy caressing those phrases—and those names—that we love.

A poet is a person who awakens to the love that names evoke, and finds forms that contain those nouns in such a way that those who read them also feel love for the actually present, material word. The poet reanimates the sensation of the lovely liveliness of the word.

> Naturally, and one may say that is what made Walt Whitman naturally that made the change in the form of poetry, that we who had known the names so long did not get a thrill from just knowing them. We that is any human being living has inevitably to feel the thing anything being existing, but the name of that thing of that anything is no longer anything to thrill any one except children. So as everybody has to be a poet, what was there to do.[302]

The word "know" has an important role in this passage. Stein suggests that there is a way of knowing a word (knowing what it means, but not knowing it intimately, for what it is in itself) that does not engender any thrill. On the other hand there is also a way of knowing that poets respond to, that does engender pleasure. One suspects that the distinction between knowledge as a form of dispassionate cognition and knowledge in the famous biblical sense underlies Stein's distinction between these two ways of knowing language. The ease with which our minds leap to that association indicates just how deeply ideas about corporeality are implicated in Stein's conception of language.

There is a more intimate relation between multiplicity and pleasure than Stein allows in this passage—one that relates more closely to the urge to evoke the sensation of things by words other than their names. By avoiding conventional nominal reference, Stein frees the signifier from a too-close bond with the signified. The signifier becomes a floating signifier, though one that provokes sensations equivalent to those produced by the experience of an actual object; thus, contrary to what conventional practice would have us believe, the free-floating signifier, purged of reference, evokes a more precise impression of the object than does an accurate description of that object. What is more, when words are too closely aligned with their referential functions, we don't feel them the same way or caress them in the same way. They possess less levity than when they do float free of their referential function and so they provoke less merriment. Our mind enjoys playing in the spaces opened up by polysemia. Brakhage's remark that this famous poem first appeared in a book for children is interesting, for the rhymes and rhythms of children's stories and poems are surely built into the fibre of our bodies.

Stein realized, too, that close attention to observed objects strengthens language's capacity to present the actual object vividly or, at least, to recreate the actual effects of the object. In *Everybody's Autobiography*, in a statement that now echoes with her famous last words before dying, Stein remarks that William James had taught her that "science is not a solution and not a problem it is a statement of the observation of things."[303] The recognition opened up for her the understanding that composition is not simply an act through which a writer presents a completed conception but a process that displays the growth of the form that the work renders—a process in which statement and observation occur simultaneously. Rendering the process which evolves the work collapses the time of reading, the time of writing, and diegetic time into the single moment of presence. Bringing the work into the present does much to eliminate the threat of expository writing's dullness, which she attributed to its being remembered.[304] The general lack of attention to Stein's writing meant that the idea of embodying form-in-evolution emerged into prominence long after Stein first pronounced it, in the Open Form poetics of Charles Olson and Robert Duncan; but once this occurred, Stein's interest in consciousness-in-time and in individual consciousness could be shared with other early modernists, several of whom reworked narrative to embody these new ideas about subjective time. Among those whom it influenced most profoundly is Stan Brakhage, many, perhaps most, of whose works embody, and evoke, that struggle-for-form that brings them into being. Of all Brakhage's films, it is perhaps the first part of *My Mountain: Song 27: Rivers* that most cogently conveys the struggle-for-form. The mountain in the film stands as an example of the object that resists being transformed by imagination and assimilated into the space of subjectivity, that resolutely remains outside of, and alien to, consciousness; the "My Mountain" section of *Song 27* presents the filmmaker's struggle to overcome the mountain's otherness, to transform the mountain imaginatively so that it might be brought within the sphere of the self. Thus, it presents a struggle to display the acts through which imagination triumphs over the sheer givenness of things, a struggle that ultimately fails.

Further intricacies of "(A) R/rose is a rose is a rose" emerge as we consider its relation to Cubist painting, and this relation becomes somewhat clearer when we recall that "(A) R/rose is a rose is a rose" was not the first piece that Stein composed using (among other elements) iterations of the term "rose." A passage from her 1922 poem "Oval" goes:

Rose
Rose.
Rose up.
Rose.
Rose.
Rose up.
Rose.
Rose up.
Able in stand.
Able ink stand.

Rose.
Rose.
Able in ink stand.
Rose up.[305]

The passage plays with various sounds and meaning of the sound sequence "rose." It includes the noun "rose," the verb "rose (up)." In addition, it contains implicitly, "Rosabelle," "Rosa," "belle," "a bel," and "able." The entire passage operates somewhat as the ninth and tenth lines ("Able in stand./ Able ink stand.") do, showing us how a slight difference in form can create a great difference in meaning. The poem iterates a term to create an identity which is not an identity, and the extent that separates the different instances from perfect identity is a measure of the difference among the iterated terms. Furthermore, the overall shape of the passage, that of a column, is more referential than the terms it incorporates (when it is the terms that it incorporates that, in more conventional constructions, would be the primary sememes).

The passage highlights its tautology. It is, in fact, this tautological quality that allows for the free play of the compositional terms, for it releases those terms from orthodox syntactical and semantic strictures, and this freedom makes Brakhage's remark that this famous poem first appeared in a book for children interesting, for the rhymes and rhythms of children's stories and poems are built into the fibre of our bodies. Structural tautology is also the necessary condition of Stein's most fundamental and radical accomplishment—and the quality of her work most similar to any feature that Cubist artworks display. For her use of tautological formulations voids the lexical elements of nearly—but not quite all—the referential meaning she incorporates into the structures she creates; and this reduction of semantic meaning is necessary to create the effect of collage. Collage involves overlaying one system of relations upon a second. In most strong collage pieces, including all the well-known Cubist examples, the new systems of relations involve intrinsic rather than representational relations. The differences among the iterations of the single term "rose" similarly result from overlaying a system of referential relations upon a system of purely intrinsic relations. The reference of terms is fixed (we can apprise ourselves of terms' reference by consulting a dictionary); therefore the referential system holds all the iterations of a term against a single paradigm of which they are all identical copies. The material system, by way of contrast, presents each iteration as a new item, unconnected to any paradigm. Within the material system, all likeness, whether between the terms in a syntagma or between word and referent, is an illusion constructed on a plane of difference.[306]

Stein, as we have noted, used repetition to show that each instance of the repeated element appears as new and different. Stein's interest in Cubism led her to another interest in repetition, an interest that creates a balanced tension with the first. Among the most widespread of Cubism's formal devices were visual and verbal puns that often took the form of what Juan Gris, and most commentators on art after him, have called "rhymes." Like rhymes in a poem, visual rhymes highlight identity within difference. Thus an artist depicts two forms, often of different sizes, that share a common, or similar, shape: the painter might, for example, "rhyme" the outline of a guitar with the outline of a bottle of Bordeaux wine, a pear, or a woman's bottom, and thereby establish an equivalence—if not an identity, then at least a relation close to it—between two objects.[307] But a penchant for aural and visual rhymes is a feature of Stein's writing as well. "In every action we can take he knows that if the hair is there and the ears hear and the Caesars share and they linger and if they linger and finger if they finger their pair, if they finger the pair and care to be more hesitant than before if they are to partake in this action, the action is memorable."[308] To point out just a few of the implicit and explicit rhymes in the passage: We start with head, the site of knowledge, so there is hair there. (This association of hair with the head is a metonymic relation.) Near the hair are the ears, so the passage associates "hair" and "ears" metonymically, in the fashion of analytical Cubism. This association made, the text goes to join "ears" and "hears" both through actual rhyme and through a variant of metonymic association that involves referring to an object by its function. If we say "hear" we might think of "see." So the passage moves on to the Caesars (the "sees—are"—and the "sees" are—just as the hair is there and there are ears). Further, a very famous (and therefore likely to be recalled) passage in English literature is Mark Antony's funeral oration in Act 3, scene 2 of Shakespeare's *Julius Caesar*, "Friends, Romans, countrymen, lend me your ears!/ I come to bury Caesar, not to praise him." Moreover Shakespeare's passage concerns endurance ("The evil that men do lives after them,/ The good is oft interred with their bones"), so Stein's passage goes on to refer to "lingering." But there is a conceptual rhyme here too, for when the eyes take their share they linger; hence the use of "linger" is overdetermined. Then, by an obvious rhyme we get finger. And when one contemplates something (lingers on it), one often fingers one's hair. But instead of saying "hair," Stein substitutes "pair," relying on an aural rhyme and on condensing "hair" and "pair" (the latter term appears because ears and eyes come in pairs and because, when we contemplate, we sometimes rub our eyes). Then, if they look more closely (if they finger the pair with care—another rhyme—that is, if they finger it more hesitantly) than before, then they see what they observe well and can remember it. Thus Stein creates a play of equivalence and equivocation by constructing homonymic relations.

Her use of visual and verbal rhymes throws light on another significance of Stein's use of repetition—to uncover identity within difference. Stein's use of repetition aims not simply at the discovery of difference and the presentation of continual novelty, as it is commonly said to do, but also at revealing similarity with diversity. As well as highlighting the diversity that exists within apparent identity, Stein's use of repetition aims at creating and throwing into relief the sameness within what is apparently diverse. Stein's writing, then, conjoins an interest in repetition as difference with an interest in difference as repetition of similar (call them identical) elements.

William James influenced Stein's thinking on this topic as well. In his writings after the *Principles of Psychology*, James argued that a single sort of stuff makes up reality—the stuff he calls pure experience. Like Hume, James supposed that all we can know is experience; however, James insisted, the mistake that earlier empiricists such as Hume had made was to suppose that experience consists of isolated sensations and impressions. James protested that "Consciousness does not appear to be chopped up into bits. . . . It is nothing jointed. It flows." James discussed our tendency to seize upon the "substantive" facts of experience and to neglect the "transitive," i.e., to consider existential above relational claims in experience. James was convinced, even as early as the *Principles of Psychology*, that consciousness is a stream or flow of moments in which later moments grasp and own their predecessors.

Stein's formal devices elicit experiences that confirm James's assertions. She went as far as to thematize James's notions about flow and about the indivisibility of certain phenomena in her literary works: "You do see that halve rivers and harbors, halve rivers and harbors, you do see that halve rivers and harbors makes halve rivers and harbors and you do see, you do see that you that you do not have rivers and harbors when you halve rivers and harbors, you do see that you can halve rivers and harbors."[309]

Stein's use of repetition highlights another feature that her compositions share with Cubist paintings. The forms of analytical Cubism, just as much as those of Henri Matisse, inhabit a space that is bimorphic, i.e., that we can see as both two-dimensional and three-dimensional. Stein's compositions occupy an analogous space of significance. Sometimes the meanings of the words come to the fore and sometimes their material properties—their sound and design—assert themselves more strongly. Stein's work depends on this apophantic relation between material and sense (a relation in which, as one term moves to the fore, the other recedes). The alternating procession and recession of material and sense in Stein's work mirrors the apophantic relation between geometric shapes and representations in analytic Cubist painting, for the relation between both pairs of terms is one of mutual disclosure and concealment. Further, Stein's work offers evidence that the procession or recession of either sense or material is a noetic-noematic construct, that it is our attention to the one or the other feature that brings it to the fore. Because it is a phenomenon created by attention, this apophantic procession and recession is only possible when the material structures and the structures of meaning are equally rewarding; achieving a balance between material and sense is one of Stein's greatest achievements. But Brakhage's films sometimes do essentially the same, for they can reward attention that is directed either to their material properties (the light-colour of the visual forms, their grain, their resolution, or, above all, their dynamic properties) or to their representational features. While this feature characterizes many of Brakhage's photographed films, it has become especially prominent in the photographed films of the late 1990s (such as *The Cat of Worm's Green Realm*, *Self Song*, and *Death Song*, all made in 1997); parts of all these films were done using macro-cinematography (extreme close-up shooting) that makes it extremely attractive for us to consider the images as pure texture, yet at the same time, we know that visual forms of the film derive from the real, and we strive to apprehend them as representations and to identify the correlations between the visual form and reality.

By opening up the possibility of creating intrinsic relations among the material features of a composition, Stein established a new order for literature. Furthermore, she took measure of its scope. A plausible index of this measure would be the span of the types of terms such relations can comprehend. Stein provided demonstrations of its breadth by linking both utterly heterogeneous and utterly homogeneous terms in structures that engender such apophantic procession and recession. She provided examples of this process at work in passages consisting of heterogeneous terms in *Stanzas in Meditation* and *Tender Buttons*. An example:

A CARAFE, THAT IS A BLIND GLASS

A kind in glass and a cousin, a spectacle and nothing strange
a single hurt color and an arrangement in a system to pointing.
All this and not ordinary, not unordered in not resembling.
The difference is spreading.[310]

At the other extreme her "rose" poem, shows the process at work in a passage that consists of maximally homogeneous terms, viz., iterations of a single term. Stein shows that it is possible to link even apparently heterogeneous terms in such a way as to create a unified (homogeneous) meaning while, conversely, homogeneous terms can be linked in such a way as to make them seem heterogeneous. And since differential relations arise within a series of iterations of a single term, we can say, with Stein, that the difference is spreading.

Stein's writing is a motherlode of ideas about literature and art that Brakhage has mined, enriching himself at that source more than any other artist. Brakhage's major exposition of his reflections on art in the 1980s is the aforementioned *Gertrude Stein: Meditative Literature and Film*. The lecture deliberates on Stein's writing at length; that he used the occasion of being appointed Distinguished Professor as an opportunity to deliberate on Stein's writing supports the claim he has long made—that Stein is *the* major influence on his filmmaking (and especially, I believe, on his later films, while Ezra Pound was the stronger influence in the period from the beginning of his lyrical period in 1957 to *The Text of Light* in 1974). Further confirmation, if it is needed, is the fact that, when he delivered this address, Brakhage was finishing a series of films entitled *Visions in Meditation* in homage to Stein's *Stanzas in Meditation*, which inspired them.

The text of the address, published by the University of Colorado, is a dense, rich, and forceful summary of Brakhage's film aesthetics as they developed in the 1980s. In it Brakhage reaffirms something that he proposed in his commentary on Marie Menken nearly a decade and half earlier, that Menken and Stein together had impelled him towards an interest in quotidian aspects of life—in "dailiness," as he terms it.[311] In the earlier piece, when describing the influence that Stein and Menken had on him, that of steering him towards taking a livelier and deeper interest in everyday events and everyday objects, he characterized their influence in moral terms. In the more recent lecture, he explains their importance in more aesthetic terms, of encouraging him to forswear drama and to develop a sensuous appreciation of unconflicted reality and of forms that forgo conflict. At least, he describes their influence in *primarily* aesthetic terms—for he also provides a secondary description, by claiming that the interest in everyday reality they encouraged him to adopt has paid cognitive dividends. He says that Stein had

> inspired much daily filmmaking of mine, a whole oeuvre of autobiographical cinematography in non-repetitive variations. [The idea that there is no such thing as exact repetition in real art; elsewhere in the text he argues that perceiving "an exactitude of repetition" results either from sloppy writing or from inattention—a truth he claims to have learned from Stein's example.]
>
> But I then was, as was she, infected with Drama as an assumption; and assumptions always pre-suppose *some* sense of repetition. . . . All writers who eschew Story *altogether* are essentially aspiring to the philosophical.[312]

He grounds his notion of philosophy in metaphor:

> Metaphor can be said to have been born as an evasion of "straight talk" or what's known as The Simple Truth.
>
> It can also, as such, be said to have come into Human Consciousness in order to resolve Dualities.

("The Simple Truth" is bound to be a lie, considering the complex nature of Being.

Thus Humans evolved puns and all multiple levels of The Paradoxical, or a way to get at Complex Truth.)[313]

The underlying conception of reality is similar to that which undergirds Keats's statement that the special ability of strong artists is their "negative capability" (see glossary), for negative capability adapts the artist to the all-too-frequently denied perplexity induced by the realization that reality is inherently contradictory; negative capability, then, enables the artist to tolerate reality's antithetical character. Knowing this, one might suspect that the argument Brakhage is about to present at this point is that metaphor yokes multiple meanings in a single phrase and that we require polysemic signification to capture a reality whose most prominent attribute is that it is replete with contradiction. The argument Brakhage actually goes on to present is even more extreme. He introduces it by commenting again on that most famous of Stein's poems, "A rose is a rose is a rose" (using that variant):

Though this work of Stein's is most usually invoked as a joke, it is, nevertheless, the most oft' quoted poem in the English language.

It is a demonstration of the utter other-worldliness of language constructs—the rrrrr-o-sis/buzz print-and-paper rose ROSE is.[314]

Here he characterizes the truly real as being akin to sound energy. But what are we to make of the echoes of New England Transcendentalism (see glossary) we hear in this claim?

Digressive Interpolation: The Persistence of Emerson's Vision in Stein's Writing and Brakhage's Filmmaking

In his perspicacious commentary on American modernism, entitled *Modernist Montage*, P. Adams Sitney points out that American modernism, from its origin to the present, has had an Emersonian character. Sitney's analysis of the role that vision (and its correlative, the blank in vision that I refer to as the negative hallucination) plays in Stein's writing relates her most famous single, "(A) rose is a rose is a rose," to Emerson's writing, and specifically to a well-known passage from "Self-Reliance." Sitney goes as far as proposing that Stein's entire prolific and prodigious literary project simply expands on this passage.

These roses under my window make no reference to former roses or to better ones; they are for what they are; they exist with God to-day. There is no time to them. There is simply the rose; it is perfect in every moment of its existence. Before a leaf-bud has burst, its whole life acts; in the full-blown flower there is no more; in the leafless root there is no less. Its nature is satisfied and it satisfies nature in all moments alike. But man postpones or remembers; he does not live in the present, but with reverted eye laments the past, or, heedless of the riches that surround him, stands on tiptoe to foresee the future. He cannot be happy and strong until he too lives with nature in the present, above time.[315]

Emerson's text invokes a religious conception of time and its transcendence. It further proposes that when we accede to the experience of the eternal 'Now,' we perceive things as perfect—as existing with God; for then we accept all things as perfect "in all [their] moments alike." Emerson presents Being-in-the-present as the ideal mode of experience and memory or anticipation as agents that corrupt consciousness. Stein and Brakhage share these convictions and, by underwriting these ideas, they have given them a place among the most important influences that Emerson has had on American poetics.

Brakhage is even more Emersonian than Stein in one respect: While both Stein and Brakhage share Emerson's sense that every object of quotidian reality possesses ultimate worth and appears as marvellous, Stein does not share in the visionary character of Emerson's ideal. What is more, Emerson longed to become a pure eye that responded equally to each perceptual reality (and, in *Nature*, claimed to have experienced that transformation when in ecstatic states conditioned by having formed a particularly intimate relation with the natural world). Brakhage too gives his allegiance to vision (and, simply, sight) as an ideal—just consider his desire to respond to each sight as an adventure in perception and his extraordinary celebration of the visual modality at the opening of *Metaphors On Vision*; Stein, on the other hand, celebrates sound and touch above sight.[316]

Implicit, but nonetheless crucial, in Emerson's passage about the roses that bloom under his window are larger issues concerning the artist's mission. Sitney points out astutely that Emerson reworked the traditional Protestant theology of election, to fashion from it the notion of artistic vocation.[317] But (and Sitney would agree) the idea of election is not the only Protestant filiation evident in Emerson's work, or in the Emersonian tradition as a whole. The paradoxical combination of radical subjectivity with a form of "objectivism" (see glossary) and with a mediumistically based impersonality that we find in both Stein's and Brakhage's work is also a part of the legacy of Emersonian Protestantism.[318] Emerson's *Journals and Miscellaneous Notebooks*, like the confessions of his Puritan forebears, are extraordinarily objective yet intensely personal and introspective documents. Furthermore, it is their place within the Emersonian tradition that gives Brakhage's ideas about vision their most profound significance.

Furthermore, Emerson opined that every age and place needs a distinctive culture, and set about the task of creating a distinctive American poetry and American language that could convey the genuine experience of America's denizens. "The American Scholar," which Emerson originally delivered in 1837 as the Phi Beta Kappa Lecturer at Harvard University, is tantamount to a declaration of the rights and freedoms of a new American poetry, forged out of the experience of the inhabitants of the New World. Stein later echoed Emerson's comments in her proposals for a form of writing true to what twentieth-century Americans experience. And Brakhage's art, as *The Dead* (1960) makes clear, is permeated by a similar attitude; remarks he delivered at Millennium in 1976 confirm this, for he described iambic pentameter as appropriate for a time when horses still filled the streets, but utterly inappropriate to the American present; he went on to offer analogous comments about the sonnet, then expanded his critique of that form to include all pre-established forms that cannot take account of contemporary realities but, rather, reflect antiquated modes of response. Brakhage then radicalized his critique to encompass forms that are fixed before the work is completed, and so prevent any spur-of-the-moment intervention that the artist might be prompted to make—forms that don't remain in flux until the moment when the work is completed.

The remarks suggest the notion implicit in Emerson's and Stein's advocacy, that constructions artists create have an intimate relation with their sensibility, and one's sensibility develops in the course of the experiences one has, so that when the world of experience undergoes change (and American culture is different from European culture, just as the twentieth century is different from nineteenth-century culture), people's sensibility undergoes a change, and as the sensibilities of artists undergo changes, the forms they create to convey that experience also change.[319]

Furthermore, Stein's writings and Brakhage's films are introspective and highly personal in just the same way that Emerson's work is. In a self-assessment, the candidness of which has contributed to its renown, Emerson set out his reasons for deciding to become a minister: "My reasoning faculty is proportionably weak, nor can I ever hope to write a Butler's Analogy or an Essay of Hume ... [but] the preaching most in vogue at the present day depends chiefly on imagination for its success, and asks those accomplishments which I believe are most within my grasp."[320] The assessment is too modest, of course, but it foreshadows the central role that the concept of imagination would play in his later philosophy—and in Brakhage's filmmaking. Brakhage's conception of the artist rests on a notion of the imagination. Furthermore, Emerson was a radical individualist and given to beliefs about the primacy of personality, as Brakhage is; further, in their admiration of genius, Emerson and Brakhage join with Fichte and Carlyle. Emerson's assessment of mass society was as negative as Brakhage's has been—he considered the mass a calamity (as Brakhage, too, seems to have believed when he made *Song 23: 23rd Psalm Branch*, which depicts the gathering of masses as the gathering of a horde bent on violence).

One index of people's individuation is the strength of their imagination. Emerson presented his thoughts on imagination in "The Poet," and what he offers there are ideas that Henri Bergson and William James were later to endorse regarding reality's nature as flux.

> But the quality of the imagination is to flow, and not to freeze. The poet did not stop at the color or the form, but read their meaning; neither may he rest in this meaning, but he makes the same objects exponents of his new thought. Here is the difference betwixt the poet and the mystic, that the last nails a symbol to one sense, which was a true sense for a moment, but soon becomes old and false. For all symbols are fluxional; all language is vehicular and transitive, and is good, as ferries and horses are, for conveyance, not as farms and houses are, for homestead.[321]

The ideas that "symbols are fluxional" and "language is vehicular" are ideas we traced through the writings of Ezra Pound, Ernest Fenollosa, and Gertrude Stein, and which we shall find in the writings of Charles Olson and the Projective Poets. It is also a key to Brakhage's filmwork and, indeed, to the reason why he is a filmmaker (rather than, say, a poet or a painter).

Another index of people's individuation is the individuality of their language, Emerson offered. Emerson associated the development of a distinctive, grounded, individuated personality with the creation of a distinctive mode of speaking and writing. The idea that an individuated person has a special insight into language that makes his or her language more authentic and truly distinctive counts as one of Emerson's principal contributions to the radical strand of America *poesis*, of which Pound, Williams, Stein, and Brakhage are all practitioners. He writes:

> A man's power to connect his thought with its proper symbol, and so to utter it, depends on the simplicity of his character, that is, upon his love of truth and his desire to communicate it without loss. The corruption of man is followed by the corruption of language. When simplicity of character and the sovereignty of ideas is broken up by the prevalence of secondary desires,— the desire of riches, of pleasure, of power, and of praise,—and duplicity and falsehood take place of simplicity and truth, the power over nature as an interpreter of the will is in a degree lost; new imagery ceases to be created, and old words are perverted to stand for things which are not; a paper currency is employed, when there is no bullion in the vaults. In due time the fraud is manifest, and words lose all power to stimulate the understanding or the affections. . . .
>
> But wise men pierce this rotten diction and fasten words again to visible things; so that picturesque language is at once a commanding certificate that he who employs it is a man in alliance with truth and God.[322]

Emerson's ideas that authenticity certifies truth, that people whose characters are corrupted fall out of alliance with truth and, when they do so, they corrupt language, that the warrant of true speech is conformity with observed facts (and this postulate's correlative, that excessive speculation nearly always leads to mental error), and that inspired speech engenders visual experience are all ideas that Brakhage would endorse (and, in fact he has repeated most of them).

Emerson's conception of individuality (which, as we have just seen, is associated with ideas about language) has a religious foundation, in the belief that the relation between the individual soul and a divine, universal Presence that Emerson termed the "Over-Soul" is an intimate, one-to-one relationship. That relationship, Emerson averred, can be corrupted by introducing the established church or ecclesiastical authority, or some other extrinsic agency into it. The idea that an artist's individuality develops from and is supported by a relation to higher agency, a relation between the self and the Over-Soul which involves no extrinsic elements and which grants one a special form of knowledge (which, outside the artistic tradition, is often called "gnosis"), is one that Brakhage, too, has expounded in his discussions of the Muse.

What is more, Emerson's ideas about individuality are grounded in his concept of self-reliance, and that concept of self-reliance is central to the American religion (which, as Harold Bloom points out in his extraordinary book *The American Religion*, is really Gnosticism and not Christianity).[323] Emerson expounded his assessment of Christian thought and morality in his anti-doctrinal tract, "Divinity School Address," and it was not very flattering—what he proposes, in doctrinal Christianity's stead, is Gnosticism pure and simple, for he states that what humans bring forth out of themselves is what is needed to save them. The church simply interposed itself between the individual soul and the Divinity, and in doing so made itself not just useless, but downright harmful.

It is this idea of the absolute uniqueness of every authentic person that is Emerson's principal legacy to the life of the American Mind and his most profound influence on Brakhage. Emerson's notions about individuality, identity, and personhood formed into a coherent conception only after discussions with Wordsworth, Thomas Carlyle, and Samuel Taylor Coleridge, whose ideas (and particularly his distinction between understanding and reason) became especially important in the formation of Emerson's system of thought. Emerson had embarked upon the trip for therapeutic reasons—his wife of less than two years, Ellen Louisa Tucker, had died of tuberculosis shortly before. The English eminences confirmed for Emerson what he already believed, and gave him the strength to state it. While sailing back to

America, he recorded his thoughts, sometimes in forms of maxims (which still make themselves felt in the aphoristic style of Emerson's first major publication, *Nature*) on individuality, God, the correspondence between the soul and the world, self-reliance, the doubleness of the cosmos, and compensation. Emerson continued to work out the implications of these conceptions across the remainder of his life.

By the time he came to formulate his philosophical ideas in a systematic fashion, Emerson had long been a reader of Zoroaster, the neo-Platonists, Jakob Boehme, Madame de Staël (creator of *De l'Allemagne*) and, especially, the Scandinavian mystic Emanuel Swedenborg, whom he deemed a veritable religious genius; and so he first worked out the problematic of the self in emanationist terms. It is perhaps regrettable that his most famous piece of writing is his 1836 manifesto, *Nature*, and that essay hardly typifies his thinking. It is certainly a splendidly written, and exuberantly optimistic work, that evidently captured the spirit of the time and place of its origin. Its qualities not withstanding, however, its fame rests largely in the impact it had in Emerson's own time, for it became the bible of the New England Transcendentalist movement. But it is an early work; in his later work he combined, in a unique manner, the idealistic conclusions of the American Hegelians (with whose house organ, *The Journal of Speculative Philosophy*, Emerson was closely associated in the 1870s) and a down-to-earth interest in the affairs of ordinary life. Furthermore, *Nature* is a rather ecstatic work that excitedly presents Emerson's discoveries concerning the relation of self to nature, while his later essays are imbued with a scepticism about the possibility of knowing higher things that becomes ever deeper. But despite its relative immaturity (in comparison with his later works), *Nature* does present many religious tenets that Emerson never abandoned: his acknowledgment of our relationship to nature is important to our spiritual development, and in fact, nature's life and vitality is integral with our own; that the material world is an inferior copy of the spiritual; the Coleridgean idea that what we call intuition is really a form of Reason; and the essential doubleness of cosmos, i.e., the idea that the cosmos is split in half, divided between nature and the soul (Emerson later expanded on this notion when he expounded the ideas of Polarity, i.e., that the cosmos alternates between paired conditions—spirit/matter, man/woman, subjective/objective, even/odd).

Emerson's notion of the doubleness of the cosmos plays much the same role in his system that the tension between thesis and antithesis plays in Hegel's system: it furnishes the terms that undergo dialectical unification as a mind attains higher insight. One notion Emerson developed to explain the unification of the opposing "doubles" was "Correspondence." By correspondence Emerson meant that the two terms were like one another in some respects and different in some other respects—Nature and human being, for example, are like each other in some respects, and different in others, just as the universe and a drop of water are like each other in some respects (both contain the principle of the whole) and different in others (one is large, the other small). And, as the course of dialectical progress led in Hegel's philosophy to the unity of the Absolute, so in Emerson's thought it led to the Over-Soul—Emerson's term for the final, universal spiritual principle, an all-encompassing heart of the universe that contains the principle of each individual's being. As his career developed, Emerson increasingly treated the Over-Soul as a personal support that buttresses each person's individuality.

Emerson elaborated on the framework of the Hegelian dialectic, developing it into a theodicy rather different from that which Hegel's system offered. Emerson maintained that the purpose of this alternation between opposites is to maintain balance and unity and to effect what he called "Compensation," the inevitable reward ensured by divine order that compensates every human for every suffering he or she may endure.

A fundamental concept in Emerson's religious thought is that of a lustre—an illuminating incident or phrase, or an epiphany of some sort. Emerson was especially concerned to identify the general principles or universal laws that these lustres revealed; he was concerned, then, to discern the general meanings that attach to these particular experiences. The idea that particular experiences open human reason towards universal laws is another element in the Hegelian legacy to Emerson's thought.

The Hegelian features of Emerson's thought result from something deeper than a shared commitment to Romanticism's founding tenets. As Hegel's philosophy represented a reaction to Kant's Enlightenment philosophy, so Emerson's thought represented a reaction to the American Enlightenment tradition of Benjamin Franklin et al. and its religious progeny, Unitarianism. Emerson's idea of correspondence (i.e., that there exists a radical correspondence between visible things and human thoughts), that language becomes more pictorial as we trace it back to its roots (an idea that Charles Olson was later to expound with great force), and that the spiritual facts are best represented by natural symbols (an idea that Ezra Pound and William Carlos Williams would later adopt and modify) are all anti-Enlightenment notions that entered the central tradition of American poetry and art through Ralph Waldo Emerson; and all them of can be traced, either directly or indirectly, back to Hegel.

Central to Emerson's later and more mature formulations of his convictions about the self was the idea that many of the distinctions that trouble both life and thought are mistaken—those between reality and illusion; natural law and moral law; the eternal and the temporal; in sum, the transcendental ideal and the banal actual. In common with Hegelians of every stripe, Emerson claimed that these dichotomies reflect earlier stages in the development of the Absolute.

But whatever the period in Emerson's career we choose to draw from, the idea that we should have regard for the self (in both senses of "regard") is central. The key feature of the Emersonian tradition in American literature is the belief that self-regard enables authentic discourse. Both Stan Brakhage and Gertrude Stein have expounded variants of this central belief.

Furthermore Emerson, like Stein and Brakhage, asserted the absolute primacy of perception. He celebrates those moments when the eye becomes all and the mind gives way to direct seeing. He also spoke for a childlike enthusiasm—an advocacy that drove Olson to barely contained anger whenever the topic of Emerson came up.[324] But if one considers enthusiasm as the state of mind that opens the self to the world in childlike wonder and leads to embracing the world with love, the sort of state that James Broughton's films convey, then this celebration of childlike enthusiasm becomes easier to accept. And Brakhage, after all, extols the virtues of the untutored eye in his writings and celebrates the child who accepts each experience as an adventure in perception.

Many of these Emersonian ideas are evident in Brakhage's film *The Dead*. The film concerns Europe. Brakhage's note on the film reads:

> Europe, weighted down so much with that past, was The Dead.... The graveyard could stand for all my view of Europe, for all the concerns with past art, for involvement with symbol. *The Dead* became my first work in which things that might very easily be taken as symbols were so photographed as to destroy all their symbolic potential. The action of making *The Dead* kept me alive.[325]

The connection between death and the symbol that the text implies is one that can be better explained after considering Charles Olson's ideas on the image. Its conceptual context is nonetheless Emersonian; and it is a film heavily influence by Gertrude Stein.

P. Adams Sitney identifies the source material that went into making *The Dead*: first, there was black-and-white footage of Père Lachaise cemetery; second, there was colour footage of people walking along the Seine; and, third, there was a black-and-white shot of filmmaker and Luciferian Kenneth Anger sitting in a Paris café. He also describes the genesis of the film: when he returned to America he associated the footage of Europe and Kenneth Anger, and two *topoi*, the river and the tomb (and that each is a *topos* might alert the reader to Olson's idea, which we will discuss later, that an image—Brakhage, I believe, would use the word "symbol"—is a dead-spot), with death.[326]

Brakhage acknowledged that the problem he confronted when he made *The Dead* was not that of conveying one's responses as one watches a loved one die, but of imagining the answer to the question, "What is death like?" The problem that one confronts when attempting to answer the question is that none of us have any idea of what death is like, since, as Ludwig Wittgenstein put it, death is not an event that we live through.[327] Brakhage uses Wittgenstein's famous remark to cover over an achingly personal trauma—that attempting to imagine death produces a blank in consciousness. Experiencing a gap in consciousness is terrifying, and one's response to the experience is generally to try desperately to fill it up. This is just what Brakhage's response was.

Consequently, *The Dead* consists in an excess of images. The most important sort of construction that it uses is the superimposition, as Sitney points. One effect of the superimposition is to make the superimposed forms appear shadowy or, one might say, ghostly—to surround people and things with an auric envelope.

The film opens with a frozen form, a Gothic statue. Its Gothic provenance elicits an association with violence. Perhaps because of those associations with violence, but more likely because it is static (and so elicits association with death), Brakhage seems desperate to animate it, just as he animated, with a moving camera, the shots of the decaying dog in *Sirius Remembered* (1959): he tilts the camera up the statute; he splices short bursts of negative into the shot (which not only suggests bursts of energy, of animation—though the efforts at animation seem to lead nowhere—but also presents a ghostly effect).[328] The footage of statue was shot on black-and-white, but printed on colour stock, so the image takes on a very faint (could one say, "ghostly"?) tint.

We soon see the image of Anger, sitting at the café table. The sense of desperation engendered by the gap in consciousness prompts Brakhage to elaborate the image. He prints the negative overlay, reversed left-for-right, over the positive image, to produce an embossed, bas-relief look.[329] The film then brings in an impressive montage of fragments of black-and-white shots, taken with a rocking camera, panning along crypts and gravestones. Bursts of superimposition appear from time to time, but because they do not seem to connect with one another, they seem almost fruitless (as the interpolated negative did in the shot of the statue that opens the film); the superimpositions seem the product of desperation that cannot form the image adequate to its needs. Throughout this passage several bas-relief images also appear (produced through printing positive and negative together).

The camera lurches towards a crypt—and blackness follows. This blackness stands in for the gap in consciousness that one confronts when one attempts to imagine what death is like. The shot is replaced with an accelerated montage of dark blue images of the Seine. Brakhage often identifies water as the primal element, and this shot seems another example of such an identification (for to confront death, the blank, is to prepare oneself to learn about first and last things). Or, rather, we might make such an interpretation, if the image of water were not so much the character of a *topos*—if were not such a conventionalized image that we are inclined to view it as a desperate attempt (the desperation is registered in the rapidity of the montage) to fill up the void with anything ready at hand. The sense that this is a ready-to-hand image is confirmed with the next shot, a slow pan, in monochrome, in the cemetery. The trap the filmmaker finds himself in relates to the Emersonian problematic we are tracing: his characteristic response would be to go back to first things, to re-establish a connection with nature, or with the grisly roots of existence. But he cannot—he is trapped in a city, in history, in a place that he does not experience as "local" (in the sense in which William Carlos Williams used the word), and that, accordingly, does not engage the imagination. Only the *topos* (which itself acknowledges that it carries a history with it), an image from what T.E. Hulme called a "counter language," comes to hand. The character of a *topos* is what Brakhage intends when he refers to "all the concerns with past art, . . . [and] involvement with symbol." And the task, as he acknowledges it, is to use objects that might very easily be taken as symbols and to photograph them so as to destroy all their symbolic potential.

This shot is followed by a variation on the opening (once more involving a gothic statue and Kenneth Anger) as though to close this section of the film into a circular form and, thus, to bring everything into a form where nothing ever passes, where everything belongs to the present. The circularity of the form is picked up in the next section, as Brakhage superimposes coloured shots (only the reds and blues are strong, because of the printing technique Brakhage used) of people walking along the Seine with shots inside the tombs, many of them inverted. The people seem to be walking in the land of the dead. We recognize that rightside-up/upside-down inversions match the left-for-right transposition we have seen in some of the bas-relief shots (notably the shot of Kenneth Anger sitting at a café table), and the relation these left/right-up/down inversions have to circle.

In this section of the film Brakhage also radicalizes the "short burst" construction that appeared right at the film's opening. The radical of the construction is a staccato rhythmic form. The tempo of the film switches from leisurely to accelerated, then to stuttering pace, then to slow, then to stuttering again. It involves a great deal of variety, but the variety seems unproductive—or desperate.

The people walking along the Seine, in the land of the dead, disappear, and the film gives us superimposition, a few frames out of register, of negative footage of the cemetery with the same positive footage, so that what we see are moving forms in bas-relief. These forms present, all in all, a very spectral appearance. They have a whitish cast, as do some very overexposed images of graves; and white is a colour, as we know, that Brakhage associates with death.

An example of an intensely white (overexposed) shot of graves soon appears. This shot follows an assemblage of water shots, and is superimposed over another similar shot. This introduces a passage that cross-cuts shots of the water and (whitish) shots of the graves, contrasting the qualities of the movement in the two shots. The tension that results from this contrast breaks the film apart, so that the image gives way, at first in short bursts, then in much longer passages of white. Here is even a stronger (and stronger just because it is so spectrally clear) suggestion of the gap in consciousness.

The white bursts give way to negative, acidly white trees against a black sky and dark crypts that seem, because they are in negative, to be emitting light from their mortar joints.[330] These negative images are, again, intercut with a passage of black leader (that, once again, stands for the gap in consciousness). Everything seems to be tipping over, first in one direction, then, after a passage of black leader, in the opposite. The film goes black for such a long time that one imagines that the film might have ended, but it does continue with more whitish. bas-relief images. The film ends with an image of the Seine and a shot of the marble wall along the riverbank which brings together the river and the cemetery.

In addition to the Emersonian ideas we have discussed so far, other of Emerson's ideas are echoed in Gertrude Stein's and in Stan Brakhage's ideas about art. One such notion is Emerson's belief "that picturesque language is at once a commanding certificate that he who employs it is a man in alliance with truth and God." This belief expresses a core notion of Romanticism's founding myth. We have already pointed out that with the transition from the pre-modern paradigm of medieval Christianity (which synthesized the cosmological principles implied by biblical teachings and the worldview of the Classical Greeks) to the modern paradigm, humans lost the sense of nature as evidence of the Creator's beneficence and the belief that the objects of the natural world belong to a network of divinely ordained interlocking purposes that have the character of objectively given values. The existence of humans and natural objects thus became ungrounded. This, as we have previously noted, resulted in a turn towards subjectivity: humans act to bring values out of themselves when none is given in the order of existents. From this comes the view that has been so common in modernity, that the good life is a life lived at fullest intensity. But intensity alone does not satisfy the spirit, and the longing for connection with something beyond, and indeed above, remains. The contemporary interest in the body is part of this, in a way Bergson's philosophy makes clear: the dynamics of the body (Bergson was more inclined to say "the body's sense of time as *durée*") unites the active subject with the dynamism of reality. Emerson's views on language—and generally the wish for an Adamic language (including Fenollosa's wishful speculations on the Chinese character)—also reflect the desire to bring the human in intimate contact with nature (indeed, to forge a unity between the human and the natural realms): when symbols are identified with things, then the anthropogenetic faculty of language is identified with nature, and humans and natural objects are encompassed in one embrace. This is also the deep meaning of Emerson's idea of correspondence, one of the leading ideas of system.

All this reflects the Romantic view of meaning, expounded paradigmatically in the writings of Elias Lévi (Zahed), the nearly homophonic nom de plume of the writer Alphonse Louis Constant, which posits an era when there was a transparent relation between earthly phenomena and their cosmic meanings. However, these meanings have been lost, but they will be recovered with the Messiah's Second Coming. This commonplace concerning a language of nature whose meanings were lost with humankind's fall from grace was frequently a basis for thinkers condemning all present languages as corrupt. The Romantic notion of a "hieroglyphic" language (as Elias Lévi called it) is reflected in Emerson's ideas about Adamic language (as it is in notions about meaning that Charles Olson and Stan Brakhage would advance in a later era).

But Emerson's ideas on language were even more radical than the passage just quoted from indicates, for Emerson actually formulated a version of perlocutionary theory of poetic meaning that, we maintain, Gertrude Stein held, and that Stan Brakhage also holds. In his inspired essay "The Poet," Emerson writes, "Words and deeds are quite indifferent modes of the divine energy. Words are also actions, and actions are a kind of words."[331] How Emerson arrived at this insight so early is equally extraordinary; he leads up to the conclusion just cited by the following remarkable deduction:

> For poetry was all written before time was, and whenever we are so finely organized that we can penetrate into that region where the air is music, we hear those primal warblings and attempt to write them down, but we lose ever and anon a word or a verse and substitute something of our own, and thus miswrite the poem. The men of more delicate ear write down these cadences more faithfully, and these transcripts, though imperfect, become the songs of the nations.[332]

Brakhage's frequent comments on the Muse, and on being given his films, repeat ideas similar to those Emerson sets out here. In fact, Emerson's ideas go a long way towards explaining that peculiar dual status that images have in Brakhage's work (and in the poetry of Ezra Pound, T.S. Eliot, and William Carlos Williams)—of being at once both subjective and objective. For Nature in Emerson's system is (as an emanation) an expression of the Over-Soul: "The Universe is the externization [sic] of the soul," Emerson writes.[333] Consequently,

> we are apprised of the divineness of this superior use of things, whereby the world is a temple whose walls are covered with emblems, pictures and commandments of the Deity,—in this, that there is no fact in nature which does not carry the whole sense of nature; and the distinctions which we make in events and in affairs, of low and high, honest and base, disappear when nature is used as a symbol. Thought makes everything fit for use. The vocabulary of an omniscient man would embrace words and images excluded from polite conversation. . . . Small and mean things serve as well as great symbols. . . . Why covet a knowledge of new facts? Day and night, house and garden, a few books, a few actions, serve us as well as would all trades and all spectacles. We are far from having exhausted the significance of the few symbols we use. We can come to use them yet with a terrible simplicity.[334]

This, of course, states the principle behind Gertrude Stein's and Stan Brakhage's use of quotidian and domestic material. But it offers more than just that—in fact, it presents the assumptions behind the use of external objects as "objective correlatives" or "emblems" or "equivalents" or whatever term we use to designate an image, or other form of evocation, of an external thing that is presented as possessing subjective significance or even as belonging to the artist's interior world.[335] For the passage (in its context, which I have not fully presented) asserts that the world is the externalization of the Divine Mind (the Over-Soul), so the objects of the world are the contents of the Divine Mind. However, the human mind participates in the Divine Mind; hence there are no contents of any human mind that do not also belong to the Divine Mind. The objects of the world therefore are really subjective. When we photograph the world, we are making pictures that represent (or, as Brakhage revises the idea, conveys the energies of) the soul.

Out of Stein: A Theory of Meaning for Stan Brakhage's Films

In a particularly telling passage, Stein draws a relation between the act of seeing and melody.

I began to wonder at at [sic] about this time just what one saw when one looked at anything really looked at anything. Did one see sound, and what was the relation between color and sound, did it make itself by description by a word that meant it or did it make itself by a word in itself. . . . I became more and more excited about how words which were the words that made whatever I looked at look like itself were not the words that had in them any quality of description.[336]

There are two cardinal points in this passage: the first, to which P. Adam Sitney draws attention, a distinction between two possible relations that words/sounds can have to colours: the relation between a colour and "a word that meant it" and the relation between a colour and a "word in itself."[337] One relation is that which obtains between a colour and its name; and a second, a possibility, raised in the form of a question, that one might "see sound." The latter strikes me as the crucial point, for it asks how word/sounds work, i.e., how they engender experience; and the way that Stein formulates the question ("Did one see sound?") raises the possibility of synaesthetic experience which provides a basis on which tokens from one sensory modality can mean (i.e., arouse a mental representation) something belonging to another mental sensory modality. The importance of this is that it reveals the key assumption of the passage; that words mean by engendering mental representations (or, more broadly, experience of some sort, perhaps that has no reference to the world), and the meaning is mental representation (or, more broadly, the experience). This is what the passage's allusions to making colour imply: that words make colours (in the mind).[338] The passages ask how words/sounds have this power, how they can make colours. Stein speculates there could be two possibilities (and one turns out to be the conventional way, which she implies has less potential for creating the experience of colour using sound) and Stein's new way (which she of course suggests has greater potential, since what she is doing here is tracing the reasons that she has for writing as she does). The distinction in the relations between words/sounds and colours is cryptic. But Stein's characterization of one relation between a colour and a word/sound is "by description by a word that meant it"; and this description seems to assimilate colour's names to reference, so the relation between a colour and "a word that meant it" seems to be that of naming. That she connected naming with description suggests she accepted a traditional idea that names and things are related to one another through resemblance (for descriptions resemble what they describe)—the notion that there is a name that is proper to each type of thing because it resembles the thing.[339]

The other possible relation that a word may have to colour is more difficult to discern. Sitney offers the helpful observation that Stein's poetics of "the word in itself" reformulates ideas of Symbolist poetics, and in particular

Mallarmé's definition of poetic magic: "la merveille de transposer un fait de nature en sa presque disparition vibratoire selon le jeu de la parole" ("The wonder of transposing a natural fact in its almost vibratory disappearance according to the play of the word.")[340] The suggestion is astute. For, I believe, the other relation that Stein describes is between a colour and any sound (of a word or of a series of words, that is) that evokes the colour—that calls to mind or prompts us to experience the colour. In relations of the latter sort, Stein tells us, the "word in itself" evokes the sensation of colour.

The difficulty of the passage makes any interpretation of it conjectural, but it is likely that, in saying "words that made whatever I looked at look like itself," Stein is claiming that sounds posssess the capacity to elicit a primordial, synaesthetic (see glossary) form of sensation by their vibratory and rhythmic properties—primordial synaesthetic sensations that finally become visual. Composing with words produces a sound structure that can elicit such a primordial form of sensation. A verbal relation that has the second sort of relation to its object (say, a colour) does not simply make reference to an object of experience (in this example, a colour); rather, it produces the actual experience—engenders the sensation of the colour red, say, by the action of its aural properties. It evokes the object experienced by the actions of language itself, and this evocation occurs through language's material properties. The energies embodied in the flow of sounding consonants and vowels produce experience—actually create the experience of the intended colour. This conjecture regarding Stein's claim here finds support in her reference to "seeing sound." Stein tells us that she wondered whether the system of reference more exactly brings into existence the precise phenomenological event that the writer intended, or whether the aural properties of words that are used, not to refer to something, but for their own sake (just for their aural properties) can better elicit that phenomenological event. She comes down on the side of the latter.

We can discover in Stein's commentary traces of another theological notion that the Romantics (including the Emersonians) transformed by, first, secularizing it, and then re-sacralizing it, before passing it along as a keystone of modernist doctrine. The beliefs about language and its force that Stein expounds here rework the traditional conception of the *kerygma* (see glossary). In *Words with Power*, Northrop Frye brilliantly demonstrates the enduring power of that conception by relating important literary forms of construction back to the biblical conception of the power of the word.

Frye lays the basis for that discussion in *Words with Power*'s companion volume, *The Great Code: The Bible and Literature*. There he discusses what he calls "hieroglyphic" language, an early conception of language that has its basis in the feeling that a common power links words and things and, hence, a subject who possesses a word also possesses (or, at least, has intimate knowledge of) the object to which it refers. On this view of language, a word does not have an arbitrary relation with the object it refers to, nor does it refer to the object by virtue of representational qualities (for example, having an appearance similar in some respects to what it represents). The bond between a word and its referent is much stronger than either of those conceptions imply: as a word is associated with some object because it shares a power with it. But, as with Heidegger's idea about the relation between language and being, on this view, the power that links words and things does not exist prior to language and outside language. Words bring this power into being. Words create the powers that link them with things by bringing the very essence of referents into being. This view of language, like Heidegger's, sees language as world-forming and ontogenic. A magic develops, in which the verbal elements, "spell," and "charm,"and their kin play a central role. This notion of language proposes that there may be a potential magic in any use of words. Words, then, are words of power—they are dynamic forces.

Northrop Frye offers examples of the force of words—of what, according to this conception, can be achieved by the powers words possess:

> Thus knowing the name of a god or elemental spirit may give the knower some control over it; puns and popular etymologies involved in the naming of people and places affect the character of whatever thing or person is given the name. Warriors begin battles with boasts that may be words of power for them: boasting is most objectionable to the gods for a corresponding reason: the possibility of man's acquiring through his words the power that he clearly wants. . . . Jephthah's "I have opened my mouth unto the Lord, and I cannot go back" (Judges 11:35), again expresses the sense of quasi-physical power released by the utterance of words. . . . [W]here the subject and the object are not clearly separated, and there are forms of energy common to both, a controlled and articulated expression of words may have repercussions in the natural order.[341]

Charles Olson, another poet whom Fenollosa's essay influenced, argued similarly, regarding Mayan "glyphs." The Mayans, he claimed, "invented a system of written record, now called hieroglyphs, which, on its very face, is verse [note the echo of Fenollosa and Pound], the signs were so clearly and densely chosen that, cut in stone, they retain the power of the objects of which they are the images."[342] Significantly, Olson, like Fenollosa, associated this manner of writing with habits of mind, viz., a focusing of attention. He conceived as a purpose for his own poetry to open readers to the circumambient field, and he believed the way one opens oneself to the environment is to concentrate one's attention on it. Frye, too, we have seen, associated hieroglyphic language ("hieroglyphic language" used in his idiolexical sense of the term) with specific mental attitudes.

Frye goes on to say that Homer's language (that so inspired Pound) is language still at the hieroglyphic stage, and so has, for its basis, physical representations connected with bodily processes or specific objects. He then provides a telling description of the structures that suit words of power: "The operations of the human mind are also controlled by words of power, formulas that become a focus of mental activity. Prose in this phase is discontinuous, a series of gnarled epigrammatic and oracular statements."[343]

This conception of language is alive in Jewish notions of sacred language.[344] More generally, it is kept alive in our culture by sacred scripture. For in scripture, too, a highly discontinuous manner of speaking and writing hold sway. The scriptures contain whole passages where every line is like a discrete unit, and others where each pair of lines forms a nearly independent unit. Sometimes parallelism between lines (and especially between two paired lines) creates an utterly predictable rhythm of return, and so emphasizes the closure that strongly marks the end of each unit. The general effect is not so very different from one we examined at the beginning of the chapter, of parallel lines in end-stopped couplets producing a sense of finality or closure at their end.

> Cast thy bread upon the waters:
> for thou shalt find it after many days.
>
> Give a portion to seven, and also to eight;
> for thou knowest not what evil shall be upon the earth.
>
> If the clouds be full of rain, they empty *themselves* upon the earth:
> and if the tree fall toward the south, or toward the north,
> in the place where the tree falleth, there it shall be.
> (Ecclesiastes 11:1-3 AV)

Or:

> Behold, the LORD maketh the earth empty, and maketh it waste,
> and turneth it upside down, and scattereth abroad the inhabitants thereof.
> And it shall be, as with the people, so with the priest;
> as with the servant, so with his master;
> as with the maid, so with her mistress;
> as with the buyer, so with the seller;
> as with the lender, so with the borrower;
> as with the taker of usury, so with the giver of usury to him.
> (Isaiah 24:1-2 AV)

Here, anaphora leads the poet to the list form, and the list form leads him to employ paratactical constructions.

Frye points out that passages of sacred scripture have the form of a series of commands from God, because this sort of form is simple, and because it conveys God's authority over us. Frye also points out that a list of commands has a paratactical form.[345]

> And they shall make an ark of shittim [acacia] wood: two cubits and a half *shall be* the length thereof, and a cubit and a half the breadth thereof, and a cubit and a half the height thereof. And thou shalt overlay it with pure gold, within and without shalt thou overlay it, and shalt make upon it a crown of gold round about. And thou shalt cast four rings of gold for it, and put *them* in the four corners thereof; and two rings *shall be* in the one side of it, and two rings in the other side of it. And thou shalt make staves *of* shittim wood, and overlay them with gold. And thou shalt put the staves into the rings by the sides of the ark, that the ark may be borne with them. The staves shall be in the rings of the ark: they shall not be taken from it. (Exodus 25:10-15 AV)

Similar linguistic forms appear in the New Testament, for they have the effect of making language seem oracular. "Or what man is there of you, whom if his son ask bread, will he give him a stone? Or if he ask a fish, will he give him a serpent?" (Matthew 7:9-10 AV).

The usefulness of such a simple, discontinuous manner of construction for conveying oracular utterance testifies to its force. The function derives from our belief that the energies of words have as real effects in the world of nature as they do in humans' minds. The rhythmic use of repetition creates a high degree of discontinuity, and so gives each item a high degree of independence. This discontinuity and independence exerts a centrifugal force that threatens to break the text apart into myriad small fragments.[346] The rhythmic use of repetition, and the consequent discontinuity the text exhibits, invest each element with a life of its own and, by that, threaten to destroy its relation to the central unity that gives the text its overall shape. Stein's verbal constructions release powerful centrifugal forces of just this sort. The clearest evidence of this is the ease with which we can excerpt fragments from her texts that stand alone as independent objects. Of course, we can do the same with the Bible—but Stein was a penetrating Old Testament reader, and her sense of language seems to have roots in a conception of language that pervades those scriptures.

Stein reflected on her penchant for lists. In 1922 or 1923 she wrote a short play entitled *A List* that actually is a list, with punctuating phrases, which makes evident that Stein's compositional forms depend upon serial variation.[347] In "Composition as Explanation," Stein offers

> In this natural way of creating it then that it was simply different everything being alike it was simply different, this kept on leading one to lists. Lists naturally for awhile and by lists I mean a series. More and more in going back over what was done at this time I find that I naturally kept simply different as an intention. Whether there was or whether there was not a continuous present did not then any longer trouble me there was or there was not, and using

everything no longer troubled me if everything is alike using everything could
no longer trouble me and beginning again and again could no longer trouble
me because if lists were inevitable if series were inevitable and the whole of it
was inevitable beginning again and again could not trouble me so then with
nothing to trouble me I very completely began naturally since everything is
alike making it as simply different naturally as simply different as possible.[348]

There is a considerable irony about Stein's passage concerning how
"colour words" mean, an irony that concerns the means language uses to
evoke a colour experience. Stein asks whether colour names (e.g., "red,"
"green," "blue," etc.) or "words in themselves" (i.e., the aural properties of
words that are not necessarily—nor even likely to be—names of colours)
better evoke the sensation of colour. That irony has to do with the phenomenon that the more words detach themselves from reference, the more
they exert their own autonomous powers, and the more they exert their
autonomous powers—powers that depend upon their sound and their construction—the greater is their capacity to deliver us "the thing" to which
they relate. In sum, the more words detach themselves from reference, the
better they deliver objects—and not just the sound objects actually inherent
in the work (or, more exactly, represented in a script which, when performed, actualizes them) but also to extra-poetic objects.

This paradox turns upon the distinction between presentational and representational modes of art; that same distinction helps resolve the paradox.
Both Brakhage and Stein argue that good art is presentational, not representational. This belief is a part of the modernist credo, and their underwriting
of this belief is a part of what makes them modernist artists. Stein realized
the importance of the distinction, and deliberated upon it. Her most profound
comment on the issue appears in "If I Told Him: A Completed Portrait of
Picasso": "Exact resemblance. To exact resemblance the exact resemblance
as exact as a resemblance, exactly as resembling, exactly resembling,
exactly in resemblance, exactly a resemblance, exactly and resemblance. For
this is so. Because."[349] The significance of her use of the verb "to exact"
comes through its referring to the power of certain visual forms to create
the impression of giving "the thing itself." That such forms can render phenomenologically actual the objects, events, properties, or persons that they
refer to is the basis for Stein's distinguishing (in the interval between the
second and third iterations of the word "resemblance," and through the
phrasing that interval contains) between the exact resemblance and the
resemblance that it is as exact as. To exact resemblance—accurate, exact
resemblance—one must do away with all remembered conventions and all
previously constituted ideas of the thing.

Stein's ideas about the value of the particular existent, and doing away
with all memories of the object, and with all preconceptions about it, and

seeing it in the immediate moment, directly, exactly for what it is in itself, are germane even to the set of miniatures concerning a rose ("(A) R/r is a rose is a rose"). That famous set of miniatures alludes to another very famous comment, Juliet's speech in Act 2, scene 2, of *Romeo and Juliet*: "What's in a name? That which we call a rose by any other word would smell as sweet."[350] The arbitrary relation between a noun and that to which it refers—that we could "doff [the] name," "which is no part of" the flower, and were it not a rose called, it would still retain that dear odorous "perfection which it owes without that title," that that which we call a rose would have the same the odorous features, even if it were referred to by some other token—must have bothered Stein. Exactly what she wanted to do is to unleash the energy that's "in a name," to show that the relation is not arbitrary, but, to the contrary, that there is a perlocutionary reason why anything is called what it is—a reason wherefore roses art roses, or a reason why "a rose is a rose": it would not smell so sweetly (on the page) were it not a rose. That is why the rose has not smelled so sweetly *in literature*, in the two hundred years before Stein: in that period of time, writers had not allowed words to provoke the direct experience of the thing itself.

Stein's interest in the particular explains the concrete quality her writing possesses. Brakhage found an analogue for this concreteness in the cinematograph's specificity. Brakhage has formulated several constructions that emphasize the concrete, specific, and material characteristics of his medium. In his earlier work, he emphasized the particularity of the quotidian reality he filmed; more recently he has emphasized the material properties, and has frequently created non-representational forms to serve as the content of his work. However, Stein, as a writer, was somewhat disadvantaged in this regard, for language trades in general concepts—in general rather than specific terms—and its words embody an already formulated understanding of how reality can be sliced up and categorized.[351] The paradox that Stein faced, of working concretely with language, the terms of which are abstract, Brakhage did not encounter. However, he did meet up with another paradox that is not unrelated—that of working non-representationally with a medium the essence of which is to present a likeness of the outer world formulated according to principles of geometric optics and other conventional means for creating mimetic forms and mimetic effects. Brakhage's interest in Stein is due partly to her showing how to resolve this apparent paradox—her notions of meaning and representation eliminate any vestigial viciousness from the paradox; further, they resemble Brakhage's own intuitions on the matter, for they, too, depend on the material effects of language and representation. Stein showed that by using the concrete, material, sensuous effects of language an artist can overcome the generality of language. Brakhage interpreted Stein's example as a lesson in how the material, concrete, sensuous effects of any visual form (including representational forms) may be used to eclipse their referential sense. Brakhage drew another conclusion from Stein's apophantic constructions: he recognized that, like the Cubists, Stein moulded forms determined by material factors over top of a referential system, and used it to balance the effects of the representational system; so Brakhage, too, superimposes materially based and representational systems, and uses the effects of each to balance the effects of the other.

Stein points towards another, more extraordinary paradox—that these visual forms exact resemblance by an inherent potency-in-action. What exactly is this potency-in-action? It is resembling. A convoluted conception of the relation between representation and presentation, between words as signs of denotational meanings and words as things—in sum, between text and vision—characterizes Brakhage's thinking on art as much as it does Stein's. The essence of their conception of the relation is that the ideal documentary medium is presentational, that art best documents things (and for Stein and even more for Brakhage, what the contents of artworks make present are the phenomena of consciousness[352] not by attempting to form the documenting media into simulacra of the reality it refers to, but by attending to powers inherent in the medium used, and by deploying its powers to call forth the phenomenal qualities of objects. Stein's art, like Brakhage's, strives to awaken in the reader/viewer's body and mind sensations which closely resemble those which prompted the creative activity that produced the poem or film. Stein maintained that there are close relations between words and thoughts/sensations, just as Brakhage maintains there are close relations between a flow of moving visual forms and the contents of the stream of consciousness, but that relation is not the iconic relation of a representational resemblance. Rather Stein and Brakhage focus their interest in the materials of their media on their perlocutionary capacities—their capacities to engender a response in the reader/viewer's body and mind. Furthermore, their focus on the sign's perlocutionary effects brings the grain of the medium into evidence and encourages the reader or viewer to an awareness of his or her role in the act of reading or viewing; this, in its turn, brings the reader or view to consider the semiotic protocols and conventions that play such an important part in all our semiotic experiences (whether artistic or ordinary), though we seldom acknowledge their function.

Interest in the perlocutionary force of the media in which they work is the basis for Stein and Brakhage's antipathy towards representation. Insofar as the object has a stand-in—is *represented* by a stand-in—the work fails to achieve its full potential as a presentational medium. This insight into representation is the core of their conception of the ideal relation (for artworks) between representing medium and the represented object, event, property, or person. Their understanding of that relation is so intricate and so complex, however, that we must pursue it further if we are to comprehend Brakhage's beliefs about rhythm or to appreciate his metrical innovations.

Brakhage points out that Stein, so far as is possible, eschews using meanings that arise from denotation. The insight is central to his own creative work; he seems to have formulated the idea that representation has deleterious aesthetic effects near the beginning of his career, and once he had, he too was disposed to embrace an approach that resembles Stein's in many significant ways. Divorcing a word from its representational meaning, Brakhage understood, is the key to Stein's creative practice. Commentators on twentieth-century writing have made much of Stein's interest in Cubist and post-Cubist painters. They are not wrong in this. Like the Cubists, Stein's work contains references to quotidian objects; and, like the Cubists, Stein treats these quotidian objects in such a way as to thoroughly defamiliarize them.[353] Stein achieves this defamiliarization with asyntax (see glossary, asyntactic)—linguistic constructs that are highly disjunctive; that use grammatical abnormalities; frequent anaphoric irresolution that destabilizes a term's reference and so makes the grammatical construction of sentences uncertain; repetition that emphasizes sound over meaning and allows for radical shifts of thought and reference even while the linguistic texture of the verbal construct remains unaltered; and, most generally, ideational parataxis. A trope that has special importance in Stein's work is amphibolous anacoluthon—the failure to complete a sentence according to the structural form that began it, due to a shift in apparent structural form that turns upon an ambiguity in grammatical function. A splendid example of Stein's use of amphibolous anacoluthon appears in "A Portrait of Mabel Dodge": "A plank that was dry was not disturbing the smell of burning and altogether there was the best kind of sitting there could never be all the edging that the largest chair was having."[354] The phrase "there could never be" has an ambiguous grammatical role: First it completes the expression, "there was the best kind of sitting [there could never be]"; but it has a different syntactical function in the expression, "there never could be all the edging that the largest chair was having." The expression's function alters in mid-course. Such doubling of a word or phrase's grammatical function is what makes amphibolous anacoluthon possible. This duple function, because of its ambiguity, produces an uncertain reading of the word or phrase. The effect that this has—of destabilizing language—connects amphibolous anacoluthon with several other devices that Stein uses, such as the incorporation (or creation) of homonyms and homophones and puns that often cross English and French words ("Guillaume Apollinaire" provides excellent examples of both); such unstable verbal constructions show that a writer need not allow referential relations to fix a term's significations, and (of more fundamental importance) that linguistic terms are not securely fixed by reference.[355]

An instance of amphibolous anacoluthon appears in the famous "(A) R/rose is a rose is a rose," for the second "a rose" plays a dual role: it appears first as a tautological predicate, and then as the subject of the second instance of predication in the line. Another set of examples of Stein's use of amphibolous anacoluthon occur as variations around the Cartesian theme *cogito ergo sum*, "I think, therefore I am." Harriet Scott Chessman points out that Stein started to use the famous Cartesian statement as a sort of template in the 1930s. Chessman ties the origins of Stein's interest in the Cartesian dictum to the fact that in the 1930s questions about identity became more pressing for Stein.[356]

Stein produced several pieces on the despairing theme of needing to have one's identity verified (and its obverse, fear of losing one's identity). One variant is: "What is a sentence for if I am I then my little dog knows me."[357] We can consider the word "for" to have two different syntactical roles, one defined by the initial form, "What is a sentence for?" and the second defined by a second form, "For, if I am I, then my little dog knows me"; an attenuated amphibolous anacoluthon occurs with the dual use of the second "I" in the structural unit "I am I." By using amphibolous anacoluthon in texts expressing concern over identity, Stein provides an example of what is troubling her (and, more, creates linguistic structures that elicit the troubling experience), because amphibolous anacoluthon is a trope in which a linguistic element has no fixed identity (it takes on two or more incompatible functions).

A second variant of the Cartesian phrase appears in *Four in America* as:

> I am I not any longer when I see.
> This sentence is at the bottom of all creative activity. It is just the
> exact opposite of I am I because my little dog knows me.[358]

The second "I" in the first sentence wavers in function as its beginning slides from "I am I not any longer ..." to "I am not I any longer ..." to "I am not any longer. ..." A third variant appears in "Identity A Poem" as: "I am I because my little dog knows me."

Chessman also points out that Stein's motif, "I am I because my little dog knows me," contains an allusion to a popular English rhyme, "Lawkamercyme."

> When this old woman first did wake,
> She began to shiver, and she began to shake;
> She began to wonder, and she began to cry—
> "Lawkamercyme, this is none of I!"

"But if it be I, as I do hope it be,
I've a little dog at home, and he'll know me;
If it be I, he'll wag his little tail,
And if it be not I, he'll loudly bark and wail."

Home went the little woman, all in the dark;
Up got the little dog, and he began to bark;
He began to bark, so she began to cry—
"Lawkamercyme, this is none of I!"[359]

The multiple allusions in Stein's texts often create pressures to consider the terms the texts comprise in different ways. This enhances the effect of anacoluthon. We noted above that amphibolous anacoluthon elicits an experience similar to that of loss of identity—a element of the sentences appears first as one thing, then as another.[360] When we read an instance of amphibolous anacoluthon, we look at a word first in one way, then in another. There is a shift in perspective—not entirely unlike that which occurs when we look at Cubist paintings and see, for example, a forehead and eyes from one vantage point, and the nose from another. What is more, the grammatically ambiguous expression in amphibolous anacoluthon can link apparently incongruous elements; consequently instances of amphibolous anacoluthon accolate verbal terms in a way similar to the way Cubist paintings accolate incongruous aspects of an object. Just as a Cubist painting, by showing us the same object (or more radically, the same visual module) in variant forms of perspective, encourages us to see the repeated element differently, so amphibolous anacoluthon encourages us to see a syntactic element from different perspectives.

Further, in Stein's writings, as in Cubist painting, the represented object recedes as the method of treating the object and actual material that depicts it comes to the fore. Poet Michael Davidson points out that the effect of Stein's compositional method is to make her readers aware of the difference between object and representation—to make them aware that, like a Cubist painting, a verbal artifact relates to a quotidian object, but it does not resemble it. He delineates the implications that follow from repudiating representation.

> What this implies for the act of reading is that there are no longer any privileged semantic centers by which we can reach through the language to a self-sufficient, permanent world of objects, foodstuffs or rooms. We must learn to read *writing*, not read *meanings*, we must learn to interrogate the spaces around words as much as the words themselves; we must discover language as an active 'exchange' of meanings, rather than a static paradigm of rules and features.[361]

Stein commented on what she took from paintings by Cézanne and the Cubists by contrasting their work with Courbet's. "Courbet bothered me," she wrote.

He did really use the color that nature looked like that any landscape looked like when it was just like itself as you saw it in passing. Courbet really did use the colors that nature looked like to anybody, that a water-fall in the woods looked like to anybody.

And what had that to do with anything, in fact did it not destroy a little of the reality of the oil painting. The paintings of Courbet were very real as oil paintings, they existed very really as oil painting, but did the colors that were the colors anybody could see trees and water-falls naturally were, did these colors add or did they detract from the reality of the oil painting as oil painting.[362]

Brakhage shares Stein's distaste for forms that detract from the reality of the medium as medium. Stein contrasts Courbet's use of colour with Cézanne's:

And then slowly through all this and looking at many many pictures I came to Cezanne.... The landscape looked like a landscape that is to say what is yellow in the landscape looked yellow in the oil painting, and what was blue in the landscape looked blue in the oil painting and if it did not there still was the oil painting, the oil painting by Cezanne. The same thing was true of the people there was no reason why it should be but it was, the same thing was true of the chairs, the same thing was true of the apples. The apples looked like apples the chairs looked like chairs and it all had nothing to do with anything because if they did not look like apples or chairs or landscape or people they were apples and chairs and landscape and people. They were so entirely these things that they were not an oil painting and yet that is just what the Cezannes were they were an oil painting. They were so entirely an oil painting that it was all there whether they were finished, ... or whether they were not finished.... [I]t always was what it looked like the very essence of an oil painting because everything was always there, really there.[363]

Stein suggested (as the pre-eminent Canadian artist Michael Snow has also) that Cézanne tried to create a balance between the material reality of the painting itself and the material reality of the objects the painting depicts.[364] She meant, I think, that Cézanne and the Cubists strove to create works that, though they refer to objects in the everyday world, we can appreciate for their formal construction. This really is the Cubist method—the Cubists painters dissolved the appearances of the everyday world into basic formal elements (the rod, the cylinder, and the cone) and then recombined these elements into a composition whose values depended on the formal organization of intrinsic properties. Stein worked similarly: she opened herself to visible reality until she caught its rhythmic essence, and then found words that, when combined, created a rhythmic equivalent to what she had felt.

Brakhage, too, strives to attune himself, bodily, to the rhythms of the events he films, and then to construct equivalents to his experience of those rhythms, using film materials. But this is not the only feature of Brakhage's films that derive from Cubism (or from Stein's interest in Cubism and her desire to create analogous structures to those she found in Cubist paintings). Brakhage has had a profound interest in Sergej Ejzenstejn's films. Ejzenstejn insisted that film is an art form that relies on dissolving reality into fragments and recombining these fragments into a new order determined by formal principles. The vigour with which he insists on the point reflects his enthusiasm for Cubist painting. When we look at a Cubist paintings that belongs to the high analytic mode, we see first a formal composition that only slowly gives up evidence of what it refers to. It is the same when we read Stein's writing—we respond first to the pattern of rhythm and repetition and movement and only later discern what the rhythm and repetition intend. Structure does not subserve representation in Cubist painting; rather, in Cubist painting, structure and representation are two systems that interact to create a stimulating tension. Cubists recognized the impossibility of reconciling the solidity of objects with the two-dimensional surface—or, what is more important, they realized the impossibility of depicting, on a single flat surface, the entire perceptual *process*, including the roles that memory and anticipation play in forming percepts. But, they concluded that if they could not display the solidity of objects or the processes that form perceptions, they should forsake verisimilitude altogether and, instead, try to create a new order *equivalent* to the phenomenal forms that a perceptual process produces.

Furthermore, the Cubists chose the common objects we experience daily as the object matter of their paintings (to use Meyer Shapiro's famous phrase). They did this partly to ensure that the object matters of their paintings would not evoke the intense feelings that strange, exotic, marvellous, or grand objects can elicit; and so, by cleaving to the quotidian, they ensured that if their paintings elicited a sense of wonder (as, surely, they often do) it would be clear that our wonder and fascination result from interests aroused by their works' forms, and what they represent. They also used quotidian object matter to eliminate emotional associations from them and to restrict the interest we take in them to purely visual concerns. Subject matter that strongly affects the viewer unbalances the relation between the reality of the painting—the goo on the canvas's surface—and the reality of what it represents. By using familiar, everyday objects, Cubist painters could dissolve the visual appearance of the world into fragments that they then recombined into a new order that depended partly on the fragments' formal principles and partly on the demands of preserving some recognizability for the objects, i.e., representational demands. The familiarity of the everyday objects their paintings depict allowed them to carry this program of fragmenting visual appearances very far, since it allowed the Cubists to resolve them into basic visual forms without making them unrecognizable.

Stein used demotic objects for similar reasons. But Brakhage, too, has generally used everyday objects and situations as the subject matter for his films.[365] *The Riddle of Lumen* is an example from Brakhage's oeuvre of a film largely devoted to the effort to defamiliarize everyday objects—and of a film whose pleasure depends on the new order that he created through recombining the visual elements. Unlike Stein and the Cubists, Brakhage often uses objects and situations that carry considerable emotional freight. Not all his films use highly charged imagery, however: *Scenes from Under Childhood* relates to quotidian reality in a characteristically Steinian manner. And, while the content of *Unconscious London Strata* carries greater emotional freight, it is nonetheless a fine example of decomposing visual reality into basic elements, then recombining it according to formal principles. In *Unconscious London Strata*, those formal principles concern rhythmic construction, for the film uses uneven rhythms that Brakhage created by repeating elements at durations of inharmonious length. But it is characteristic of Brakhage to decompose reality into rhythmic rather than geometric modules, for the biological basis of his aesthetics gives him a distaste for geometric, and generally non-biomorphic forms.[366] The decomposition of visual reality in *Unconscious London Strata* is so thorough that individual frames bear a strong resemblance to some paintings in Monet's *Rouen Cathedral* series. At points in the film, Brakhage so completely abstracts the object matter of his shots by rapidly moving the camera that the buildings he photographed for the film (the Houses of Parliament, Westminster Abbey, etc.) dematerialize into traces of movement that he later forms into dynamic constructions based on musical principles.

Unconscious London Strata begins in fact with ambiguous, abstracted soft close-ups, initially indoor scenes, and often of windows, composed into sequences of blue, red, yellow, and green. The viewers' response to this opening section is similar to the readers' initial response when they encounter a text of Stein: at first the elements of composition seem ambiguous, and the principles that determine the composition of these elements difficult to discern. The film gradually, through a form of repetition with augmentation (a type of construction Stein often used), moves from interior to exterior. The elements of the composition remain very dynamic, however—often the object-matter is blurred by camera movement, and the colour pulsates. Over time, these brief, very fragmentary elements give way to longer shots, of streets, the Thames river, and the night sky.

At this point, the filmmaker contrives the film's most daring means for creating tension: the buildings that he photographs become more identifiable (we see the Houses of Parliament, Big Ben, etc.), but, as a counterbalance to our familiarity with these sources, uses abstractive means that, while they leave the buildings identifiable, transform them into nearly autonomous aesthetic constructions. He uses prisms and shifts of focus, and enhances the grain of the film, so as to draw our attention to the facts of film, to its character as moving coloured light. The tension between familiar object and abstractive form is gripping. Such tension is characteristic of Cubist painting.

Efforts to arouse a similar tension determines the montage of this passage. At one point, the camera pans by Westminster, rendering its walls and rooftop, and their reflections in the river, with light-streaked, impressionistic forms. It then switches to a sequence of pure blue and red forms. The montage then fuses these different sorts of images—there are some pure red forms, then an image of houses, then of water, then another of pure colour. Viewers watching this section of the film respond rather as readers do when they are becoming familiar with a passage by Stein: gradually representational meanings emerge out of the swirl of perlocutionary meaning—though, from time to time, the representative meaning vanishes briefly, submerged by perlocutionary force, only to return again.

Unconscious London Strata has many similarities to *The Dead*. Both treat the city as the material embodiment of history and tradition (in *Unconscious London Strata* this is evident in the allusions to Turner and to Monet). More importantly, both *The Dead* and *Unconscious London Strata* treat the film medium as something whose meaning is opaque, something that does not surrender its significance to the register of the visual (in *The Dead* that is made apparent by the passages of leader, and in *Unconscious London Strata* it is made evident in the use of prisms, of out-of-focus shooting, of blurry close-ups, and of rapid camera movement).

Tortured Dust, Brakhage's major film project of the 1980s, is also constructed in much the same way as text by Gertrude Stein is. That film consists of four parts. The first part, and, perhaps, the most Steinian part, opens with a shot looking out through a window, onto a snowscape. The Brakhages' two teenage sons, Beartham and Rarc, are tramping, in slow motion through the snow. The contrast between the two couldn't be more striking: the older lad is tall, dark, self-possessed; the younger, troublingly awkward, heavy, and wears an outsized cowboy hat.

The section turns into a montage, principally of quick shots, taken inside the house, interwoven with rapid shots of the landscape. The construction has a strikingly Steinian/Cubist character: quotidian objects—a glass pane, a piece of wood, plants, the type of objects that Gertrude Stein often wrote about—are presented from different angles, so there is considerable repetition and repetition with variation in this section of the film. Here Brakhage treats the human form just as he does the quotidian objects, fragmenting them, and looking at them from many different angles.

A key motif in this section of the film is the window. Brakhage probably uses it as he often does in his films, as a metaphor of seeing, of the lens, and of a frame. But in this part of *Tortured Dust* it seems to have another significance: the window separates the filmmaker from what he observes. Thus, we see the filmmaker looking through a pane of glass as Jane talks with the children. This sense of alienation is extended by the device of using rooms as separate spaces on the screen (so the door, too, is a prominent visual motif in this film).

The montage is sometimes radical: at times a series of very short images, from, I estimate, three to eight frames long, interrupt a longer passages (of, for example, the boys reading, or doing their chores, or playing). This construction is an elaboration of the interruptive flash-frame, a technique that Brakhage developed when he made *Cat's Cradle* (and which I commented on earlier). Further, pure colour frames appear, superimposed over, or interposed between, family scenes (especially family, or family and friends sitting around the table). To strengthen the interruptive effect of these colours, Brakhage sometimes uses hues that contrast with the dominant tone of the scene. For example, the dominant tone of much of the first part of *Tortured Dust* is blue, and at one point, a bluish image is interrupted by sudden red burst (a red image that depicts double windows); the intense effect of the interruption is prolonged as Brakhage then goes on to alter the colour of the image.

An even more Steinian aspect of the montage is the manner in which Brakhage sometimes treats simple, everyday actions. At one point, one of the boys stands up: at another, somebody passes a cup. Brakhage radically fragments both these actions and repeats them, reshuffling the pieces of the action about, just as Stein rearranged clusters of words to create repetition with variation. Brakhage accomplishes much the same in the manner that he photographs a conversation between Jane and the boys—resolving the scene, after the fashion of the Cubist, into many elements, amongst which he creates a variety of relationships. In this scene, a figure, who at first seems isolated, is later integrated into the conversation by re-editing. The technique not only shows Brakhage's impressive command of this Steinian mode of construction, it also provides a compelling demonstration of the imagination's capacity to triumph over the given, even as it operates with real material. Further, because of the scope this Cubist method of fragmentation and recombination gives to the imagination, it also provides scope for wish-fulfillment (as the example I cited demonstrates).

Even the details of the manner that Brakhage uses to reassemble the elements into which he resolves reality are telling. The transposition of a close-up of a person's face turns what is seemingly an expression of anticipation into a response. This, of course, simply rehearses V. Pudovkin's famous experiment with the actor Mosjukhine; or it would be simply that, were it not for the fact that the co-ordinates that define the space of the experiment are so very different. I have pointed out earlier that Gertrude Stein's writing demonstrates how context inflects meaning, and showed how she uses repetition to make her case. Brakhage here repeats a shot, placing it in different contexts to establish exactly the same point.

The intricate montage of the first part of *Tortured Dust* also takes simple everyday actions—cooking, eating, talking—breaks them into fragments, and recombines them dynamically, to create an intricate flow of kinetic sensations. We shall see in the next section that this is also a very Steinian strategy.

The second part of *Tortured Dust* has most of the same stylistic features of the first part; what sets apart the beginning of the second part from the first is that monochrome and negative and out-of-focus forms appear in this part. Soon, however, it invents its own characteristic modes: the pace slows, and film begins to pulsate. The dominant colours of the passage switch to blue and orange. The object matter out of which the imagery is formed remains similar: we see domestic scenes: Beartham and Rarc go for a walk, a group of people work on a car, the boys sit about, looking vaguely resentful (perhaps because of the camera's constant intrusion). One difference betweeen this part of the film and the first part is in the pacing: while the movement of the first was rather intense, this part is considerably slower. Furthermore, in this section of the film, Brakhage uses many long fade-ins and fade-outs. These fades emphasize the difference in this part's pacing, but it also evokes a sense of sadness, as it makes what we see seem so very evanescent.

Brakhage even indicates his own role in this: we see him in the mirror, operating the camera. He adjusts the shutter on the camera, and the scene plunges into darkness. Thus Brakhage identifies himself with the force that at least transports all that is around him into obscurity. Thus Brakhage acknowledges his role in the dark mood of the film of those around him.

Like the third part of the *Faust Series*, the third part of *Tortured Dust* reworks a classic form of the American avant-garde cinema of the 1950s, the psychodrama. This part of the film begins with soft colours that slowly change hues; intermixed with these slowly changing colours are a few inverted shots. Out of this matrix of colours (which surely stand for what we have called primordial experience) emerge the forms of the Brakhages' grown daughters, Myrenna, Crystal, and Neowyn. Almost the entire section is soft, the impression being that what we are seeing is an equivalent for night thought, and so this part of film conveys a dreamer's consciousness. (That the third part of the film deals with night thought helps explain why Brakhage made the fade the key trope of *Tortured Dust*'s second part.)

The montage accelerates: there are shots of a boy playing in the snow with his dog, of children, of a person chopping wood, and much shadowplay. The still point of the vortex of images is the sleeping youths, images of whom appear repeatedly. Intermittently, we see soft, dreamy film images, of the wedding of one of Brakhage's daughters, being projected on a wall. The projection has a oneric quality that integrates it into the texture of this part of the film; but it also portends the dispersal of the family unit (which, we surmise, must haunt the dreamer/filmmaker/father).

A shot of one of the boys, awakening in a burst of light, confirms that what we have been seeing is intended as a equivalent of a dream: the shot also represents an abrupt transition from one form of experience (night experience) into another form of experience (waking experience). In a later film, *I . . . dreaming*, Brakhage was to make much of the disturbances that these transitions precipitate. The abruptness of the transition ensures that the dream from which the dreamer awakened suddenly will structure the following day.

The final part of the film confirms our suspicion. The fourth part begins with intensely coloured frames of pure colour; their colours occupy a fairly limited range on the spectrum (they are orange, green, turquoise, purple, and red)—the warmer part. These gently transitioning, pure colour fields are interrupted by a number of different shots: we see, first, a shot of the married daughter, breastfeeding and playing with her baby, and shots of rooms and gardens. With a shot of the family taking the sun on the terrace, these colour fields subside. We see a small girl, old enough to walk easily, among the family group. We recognize with a start that this girl was the baby we saw being fed moments ago. What transpired in the years between, the elision suggests, is something beyond the filmmaker's ken. The family unit has been rent.

I have pointed out that Stein's and Brakhage's concerns with the formal principles of composition coincide with those of the Cubists. The area where this coincidence occurs lies within the domain of sensation, that is to say, in the domain of somatic effects. The Cubists caught the visual rhythms of reality; another way of expressing this would be to say that they captured the relation between the objects that belong to visual reality and the body. They captured how the body feels these objects—not in their optical appearance, but how they impress themselves on the body. The Cubists, Stein, and Brakhage all made rhythm (and often rhythm created through repetition) central to their work, and rhythm, as any teenager can testify, has somatic effects. The body held another interest for the Cubists. Cubists based their artistic ideas partly on scientific theories about perception that led them to understand that perceiving is not a passive affair. The mind is active in perceiving; it synthesizes a percept from a number of fragments. When we look at an object, the mental representation we form of it does not conform strictly to the laws of geometric optics that describe mathematically the shapes that objects project onto a limited surface whose centre is our vantage point. Our previous experience with objects of its type, and the memories and anticipations those previous experiences furnish, become part of the experience of the object immediately before us. When I look at a box straight on (so that the axis along which I view it is orthogonal to one of its surfaces), I do not see a square, as projective geometry would imply. I see this three-dimensional box against a horizon of previous, remembered experiences that tell me what the box would look like from the side, from above, etc. This horizon of expectations, furnished by memory and by my corporal knowledge of three-dimensional space, structures the percept presented to my mind. Because I have had other experiences of cubes and I know what it would look like from the side, from above, etc.; when I look at a cube I see a box in a three-dimensional space.

All the paradoxes in which Cubist painting became involved turned on the difficulty of representing the synthetic character of the perceptual process—of capturing its dynamics in a static form. In this regard, Stein had the advantage, for hers was an art of time. The formation of complex unity through the accumulation of small differences is the essence of the perpetual processes (right down to the minuscule differences created by the eye's tremoring, to constantly refresh the cones in the retina) and of Stein's writing alike. As well, Stein's writing offers many structural homologies to the process by which the body forms perceptions—it is not too much of an exaggeration to say that in some of Stein's works (e.g., "Susie Asado") the rhythms constitute somagrams—graphs representing the body's states over time—for, in the example given, she uses rhythm to imitate the physical sensations of intercourse. But if Stein had the advantage over the Cubist painters, Brakhage has the advantage over Stein, for his is an art of dynamic visual forms (not language) that includes a temporal dimension; thus, Brakhage could combine the strengths that resulted from the Cubist's use of the material of seeing with the strengths that resulted from Stein's use of temporally extended homologies to the structure of the perceptual process. The combination of his openness to film's medium-based potentials and his exquisite sensitivity to proprioception and, more generally, to the nuances of internal awareness, has enabled Brakhage to give us the most detailed evocations of the process by which the body forms perceptions that any artist has ever made. He has been especially good at conveying the subtleties of how that process feels from the inside.

In recent years Brakhage has argued that Stein is a more radical, and more crucial, writer than Pound. His assessment is not one I can assent to: Stein's span is narrower than Pound's and her writing, at its weakest, too mannered.[367] Her self is less labile than Pound's and she lacks Pound's ability to assume several personae, and so the range of her verbal constructions is more limited. I also miss in Stein the heart-rending testimony of a sundered personality, speaking directly out of the various parts of himself, to heal the world. She seems, by comparison with Pound, wilfully difficult, as though her writing were a code constructed to conceal as much as it reveals. Perhaps the play of revealing/concealing that is so characteristic of her writing is the result of wanting to testify to the importance of her relation with Alice B. Toklas, a tribute she could not offer openly at the time. Her writing at its weakest seems to play with some secret (likely involving her relation with Toklas)—and to refuse to identify, name, describe, or locate itself in real space and time, as though she is playing with something we want to know, but she will not divulge. At such times, the formal properties of Stein's writing present themselves as signs that require decoding; and then they seem more like an enigma to be solved than a construction to be savoured. Confronted with references that appear almost *sous rature*, we await for some insight to come to us that will fill the confounding absence and provide us with a satisfying plenitude of meaning.

But that the aesthetic implications of Stein's method are far more radical than any of Pound's pronouncements on poets and poetry seems even to me to be a defensible claim. Pound, at least much of the time, maintained the empiricism that forms the core of American philosophy and the heart of the American spirit.[368] He maintained, at least much of the time, faith in the existence of the world of natural objects, whose existence is innocent of the corrupting taint of those interests that structure human knowledge. For Pound as for Williams, getting to know things as they truly are is a redemptive spiritual act. Pound's imagism preached the direct presentation of the natural object in its immediacy—Pound's essay "A Retrospect" shows that the Imagists believed the natural object is always "the adequate symbol." The Imagists and the Objectivists generally, and Pound and Williams specifically, argued that cognitive processes distort our understanding of the actual world, because our vested interests in certain domains distort the flux that is our psychological life. But we can strive to see objects as they are and, in epiphanic moments, we can make direct contact with the natural world. Pound modeled the process of understanding objects on the visual process, which he contrasts with the associative process that is the essence of thinking. The truths of pure cognition, i.e., pure seeing, overcome the falsehoods bred in the mind.

Stein's aesthetics puts these simplicities behind it. She saw through the claim that direct treatment could lead to the thing itself. Language cannot directly present "the thing itself," for what writing gives us is not "the thing," but words. Writing does not represent an accurate likeness to a reader, let alone the essential nature of anything. But it can evoke the object with a verbal equivalent—a series of sounds whose energies produce the sensation of the thing. This is a way in which one who believes that the *feeling* body grants a better form of consciousness writes.

The Paradox of a Perlocutionary Semantics: Brakhage and Stein on Artistic Meaning

Let us attempt to formulate a more definite and precise understanding of what Brakhage might have learned from Gertrude Stein's writings. To do so, let us consider some examples. Let us take for our first example the Stein single quoted above:

A CARAFE, THAT IS A BLIND GLASS

A kind in glass and a cousin, a spectacle and nothing strange
a single hurt color and an arrangement in a system to pointing.
All this and not ordinary, not unordered in not resembling.
The difference is spreading.[369]

Most critics regard *Tender Buttons* (in which this single appears) as Stein's most Cubist work, and this inkling of meaning we get when first reading it through accords with that view. What analogies to Cubist painting does this single offer? One involves an interplay between representation (however attenuated) and form; and that Stein draws attention to such an interplay justifies using methods that rely on the experiences that arise from attempting to identify her object matter.

The passage thwarts attempts to interpret it semantically (i.e., through its reference). What, for example, is "a system to pointing"? One can get an inkling of how to go about interpreting the passage from the obviousness of its topic: it is surely writing about writing; so one would conjecture that in it, Stein offers some insight into her creative method. Surely for Stein, the point in using phrases such as "an arrangement in a system" and "not unordered in not resembling" is to draw attention to the way that the carafe makes her think about systems of representation and the representational and formal characteristics of art objects. Furthermore, this carafe that is not unordered in not resembling is also "not ordinary." Why? One thinks immediately of the carafes in so many Cubist paintings that are defamiliarized, "but not unordered in not resembling."

Cubist painting developed from the attempt to create an object that was faithful not to surface appearances of things in the world, but to the process through which we apprehend the world. Such interests in process were widespread in the early years of the twentieth century; in particular, attention to cognition as process—to the manner in which the mind apprehends reality—was fuelled partly by Bergson's philosophical studies, partly by Einstein's theories of motion and, later, as well, by the atomic models of Neils Bohr et al. By superimposing a variety of vantage points of an object or scene onto a single surface, the Cubists intended to show the contributions that memory and previous acquaintance with objects of the types being represented make to the formation of percepts. However, the piling up of forms upon forms had the almost paradoxical effect of attracting attention to the surface of the canvas, as the multiplicity of represented vantage points in the work undid any sort of organization that centred on the single vanishing point—that is, any of the range of compositional methods that had proved so useful in creating a sense of depth. The attenuation of contrast and the dismemberment of spatial homogeneity further distanced the painting's appearance from the appearance of reality. Altogether, these features produced a remarkably tense dialectical relation between the painting's dual aspects—as an image and as an autonomous, non-referential object.[370]

Thus many Cubist paintings provide examples of a splendid tension between the painting as an image and the painting as an autonomous object. Stein's single from the opening of *Tender Buttons* plays on the similarly dual status of all artistic forms. First, its prima facie inscrutability draws attention to the language itself, to the verbal artifact, while its mention of its "topic," a carafe, elicits expectations that the passage will provide an image of a carafe similar to those which so many Impressionist and Cubist paintings present. But the various terms of the description possess a similar tension. "A kind in glass" probably seems to most readers, on first consideration, to refer to "a glassy object." However, the nature of the object as an image becomes evident when we consider that a "glass" can also be a mirror (or any reflecting surface), so "a kind in glass" can be a reflection in a mirror; the allusion to a mirror (or any sort of reflecting glass) is strengthened by Stein's having included in the title line (actually a title that is not a title): "A CARAFE, THAT IS A BLIND GLASS," for the word "blind" can be taken as conveying that the glass is not reflective.[371] The term "cousin" has a similarly indirect reference (as almost all the terms in this collection do), for it refers to a particular person not by direct reference, i.e., not by reference to that person's intrinsic properties but indirectly, by reference to her or his relations with some other person. Furthermore, the conjunction of the two terms, "A kind in glass and a cousin" juxtaposes a term whose primary reference is to something objective—something which the passage's objectivity foregrounds—and a term whose primary reference is to someone whose meaning/being is not intrinsic but depends on his or her relation to some other person.

The next term, "a spectacle" possesses a similar ambiguity. For a spectacle is something in its own right—even something that attracts attention to itself (as people admonish a child, "Now don't make a spectacle of yourself" when the child threatens to embarrass them by drawing attention to herself). However a spectacle is also a play—a performance that presents the illusion of being something other that it is. But though a spectacle seems other than it is, Stein goes on to affirm that it is nothing strange, i.e., nothing out of its sort, nothing alienated from its own nature. Furthermore, the term "strange" compares one object with others, for we define "strangeness" by reference to the common run of objects we encounter in our experiences— when we say that an object is strange, we mean that it is out of the ordinary. Simply by being unusual and out of the ordinary, an object becomes a spectacle. However, the nature of a spectacle (and now, although, through ambiguity, "spectacle" preserves the sense of "anything out of the ordinary," the primary referent of "spectacle" shifts to become a play or show of some sort, so the construction involves amphibolous anacoluthon) is to be out of the ordinary, so for a play to be out of the ordinary is nothing out of the ordinary—it is nothing strange, for that is just what a play is.

"A single hurt color" again suggests the objective nature of whatever the text intends, as does the first part of the next phrase, "an arrangement in a system." However, Stein's construction of the phrase "a system to pointing" once again creates a virtual amphibolous anacoluthon, for the single transforms itself from being one that intends an autonomous object to one that intends an object the significance of which depends upon its reference to something besides itself. "All this" foregrounds the actual presence of the objects, while "and not ordinary" bolsters this sense of presence by emphasizing the particular nature of the composite "all this" forms and the extraordinary nature of its composition. Since they do not appear ordinary, they do not resemble the objects of the everyday world. Their composition is therefore autotelic; yet, Stein asserts, this system "is not unordered in not resembling," i.e., it possess an autonomous structure, it is still a thing with a self-contained structure that does not depend on resemblance.

We realize, then, that the passage turns on a distinction between resembling and pointing, a distinction which all forms of realism fail to draw. A painting or verbal construct does not have to resemble some object in order to pick out that object for us—it can do so by creating an impression that corresponds to the object in any of a number of ways. Stein's statement that "the difference is spreading" involves a similar interplay between self-identity and difference. For when some characteristic spreads, it turns the

entire field through which it spreads into a collection of objects that are identical with one another. Hence "The difference is spreading" should, paradoxically, entail homogeneity. Yet the passage does not, for by juxtaposing words
whose differences with one another are unusually great, it makes us feel the
individuality of each particular word. Truly, Stein's writing makes difference
spread, and the effect of this speading is not to create homogeneity, but individuality.

Stein's single also reflects on the conditions of visual forms in Cubist
paintings. We can take every phrase in it as offering an equivalent to a carafe
in a Cubist painting. The carafe is "a blind glass" because it is opaque—
because it is a glass that we cannot see through, perhaps because it is filled
with a robust red wine. The visual form suggests a carafe (though it does not
resemble it all that much) so it is "a kind in glass"; that is, it is like (it is "a
kind") something made of glass, but is not glass. Furthermore it is "a
cousin" to the glass object, for it relates to it. It offers itself for viewing;
hence it is "a spectacle." It refers (or points) to a quotidian object; hence it is
"nothing strange." It consists of "a single hurt color," because it is a simplified, unmodelled form, as forms in Cubist paintings often are, articulated
with a single, orange-brown wine tone. As a thing in itself (what it consists
of) it involves "an arrangement in a system" whose end is partly to indicate
something in the real world; however its systematic arrangement makes it
something in itself, even though it does indicate something in the real world.
The conflicted status of the visual forms in Cubist painting are mirrored in
Stein's disrupted and unstable syntax.

Still, what figures in a Cubist painting in one sense is not unusual, Stein
says. Despite this ("All this [granted]"), what appears in a Cubist painting is
"not ordinary"; this paradox is explained by the fact that the structure the
painter gives the painting does not resemble the structure of real world
objects. In spite of this lack of resemblance, in spite of the Cubist painting's
unordinariness, the form of the work is not unordered. The best evidence
that it possesses an order is that it still indicates something about the real
world—its system still points towards the world.

In "How Writing Is Written" Stein explains that getting rid of nouns
helped to make her writing contemporary and give it an American character.

> The other thing which I accomplished was the getting rid of nouns. In the
> Twentieth Century you feel like movement. The Nineteenth Century didn't
> feel that way. The element of movement was not the predominating thing that
> they felt. You know that in your lives movement is the thing that occupies you
> most—you feel movement all the time. And the United States had the first
> instance of what I call Twentieth Century writing. You see it first in Walt
> Whitman. He was the beginning of the movement. He didn't see it very
> clearly, but there was a sense of movement that the European was much influ-

enced by, because the Twentieth Century has become the American Century. That is what I mean when I say that each generation has its own literature.[372]

The contrast between Stein's anti-Aristotelian declaration and a remark by T.S. Eliot could not be more signal. In an early writing devoted to the Absolutist philosophy of F.H. Bradley (a formidable English Idealist who lived between 1846-1924), Eliot comments on the essential role that nouns play in forming knowledge: "Try to think of what anything would be if you refrained from naming it altogether, and it will dissolve into sensations which are not objects, and it will not be that particular object which it is, until you have found the right name for it."[373]

Here Eliot rehearses the common Idealist view of the role the Concept plays in producing the world that we apprehend, according to which the world is not something that is given to us in the making of which we have no part. Eliot restates the point Hegel made in *The Phenomenology of Spirit*, in the section in which he offers his analysis and critique of sense-certainty. In that section, Hegel questions the conception that empiricists hold so dear, that objects can be directly presented to consciousness through a process in which consciousness plays no active role. In sensation of this sort, the impressions by which an object makes itself known to us are bare particulars, not really objects (things set over against us), but sensa—bare appearances, raw impressions that do not much more than acknowledge the presence of "this" in one's consciousness. In his rejoinder to the empiricists, Hegel points out that all experience is brought under the determination of the universal. There can be no experience unless the categories that make experience possible subsume the sensuous manifold. There is no such thing as the experience of a raw particular—a pure *ecceitas or haecceitas* (a pure "there-it-is-ness" or a pure "this-here-ness"), to adopt the terms Duns Scotus used. For all experience involves relation. It is only by virtue of its relation to other times that I can identify this immediate moment as now, as not past and not future. Similarly, I can never recognize myself as an individual or as a subject of experience except by comparing myself with other individuals.

Compare these ideas with Stein's. In "How Writing Is Written," Stein offered a useful, statement of her intent:

> I was trying to get this present immediacy without trying to drag in anything else. I had to use present participles, new constructions of grammar. The grammar-constructions are correct, but they are changed, in order to get this immediacy. In short, from that time I have been trying in every possible way to get the sense of immediacy, and practically all the work I have done has been in that direction.[374]

Stein's ideal of a writing of presence is interesting for a number of reasons, not the least important of which concerns its psychological background. For the period during which all an infant's mental contents are experienced as belonging to a mode of immediate presence coincides with that of pre-Symbolic thinking—and, more specifically, with that stage which the French psychoanalyst Jacques Lacan calls "the Real"—the time before any gap in consciousness has opened, the time when the infant enjoys the raw immediacy of presence of his or her mother's body. Stein's work involves two ways of constructing language (each of which elicits a distinctive mode of experience). One way of constructing language relates to pre-Symbolic experience; it treats words concretely, for its forms of construction are based on the sound meaning of language. The other way of constructing language develops after the child's entry into the Imaginary realm, i.e., after the child acknowledges not only the separateness of the mother but also the impossibility that he or she will ever again enjoy the mother so immediately, and so alleviates its own feelings of separation through a literally self-denying identification with its image in the mirror (or in some virtual space). The gap between the inherently labile self and the prosthetic images that bring it coherence is reflected in those forms of thinking that belongs to Imaginary and Symbolic realms, for those forms of thinking treat words as having only arbitrary relations with the objects to which they refer and, more generally, the ubiquity of dyadic relations. Stein's most profound relation with the Cubists is that her writing attempts to bring these two ways of constructing language into relation, and to provide pleasure by developing and reconciling tensions between the two orders.[375]

The distinction between these two orders of language figures among Stein's major interests. It inflects even her use of repetition. For Stein, as we have noted, uses repetition to show that there is no such thing as exact identity across a temporal span, that something which appears on two separate occasions will be perceived differently each time. Exact repetition (e.g., "is a rose is a rose") suggests identity at the same time as it highlights the non-identity of the repeated elements. The relation here between identity and non-identity is homologous with the relation between the pre-Imaginary awareness's apprehension of reference as immediate presence and the experience of reference as involving difference and absence that develops with the child's self-alienating entry into the Imaginary—that is, the relation between identity and non-identity is homologous with the relation between with experience of language as presence and the experience of language as representation.

Stein contrasts the nineteenth century, "the Englishman's Century," with the twentieth century, the American Century.

The United States, instead of having the feeling of beginning at one end and ending at another, had the conception of assembling the whole thing out of its parts, the whole thing which made the Twentieth Century productive. The Twentieth Century conceived an automobile as a whole, so to speak, and then created it, built it up out of its parts. It was an entirely different point of view from the Nineteenth Century's. The Nineteenth Century would have seen the parts, and worked towards the automobile through them.[376]

She explains:

You see, I had this new conception: I had this conception of the whole paragraph, and in *The Making of Americans* I had this idea of a whole thing. But if you think of contemporary English writers, it doesn't work like that at all. They conceive of it as pieces put together to make a whole, and I conceived it as a whole made up of its parts. . . . So the element of punctuation was very vital. The comma was just a nuisance. If you got the thing as a whole, the comma kept irritating you all along the line. If you think of a thing as a whole, and the comma keeps sticking out, it gets on your nerves; because, after all, it destroys the reality of the whole. So I got rid more and more of commas. Not because I had any prejudice against commas; but the comma was a stumbling block. When you were conceiving a sentence, the comma stopped you. That is the illustration of the question of grammar and parts of speech, as part of the daily life as we live it.[377]

Stein drew an important conclusion from this. She wanted to capture how we know what we know. She outlines two conclusions:

[I]n *The Making of Americans*, . . . I gradually and slowly found out that there were two things I had to think about; the fact that knowledge is acquired, so to speak, by memory; but that when you know anything, memory doesn't come in. At any moment that you are conscious of knowing anything, memory plays no part. When any of you feels anybody else, memory doesn't come into it. You have the sense of the immediate.[378]

Bergson's thought provided another basis for Stein's belief that the key to creating a twentieth-century literature is dynamism—the twentieth-century writer must convey the flux of reality. Bergson had contrasted the two means by which humans apprehend the world: analysis, which considers objects as though they stand outside us in space, and which freezes reality into a series of static snapshots; and intuition, which alone can apprehend the flux and movement of reality and the inward reality of a thing.

Our eye perceives the features of the living being, merely as assembled, not as mutually organized. The intention of life, the simple movement that runs through the lines, that binds them together and gives them significance, escapes it. This intention is just what the artist tries to regain, in placing himself back within the object by a kind of sympathy, in breaking down, by an effort of intuition, the barrier that space puts up between him and his model.[379]

Bergson's principal epistemological theme was that only intuition can comprehend life, that "life transcends the intellect" since the intellect only considers the "outside" of life, while intuition gets inside. In striving to capture the movement of reality, Stein's practice conforms to Bergson's teaching, for this effort amounts to the attempt to find the "intention of life, the simple movement that runs through the lines, that binds them together and gives them significance."[380] Even the idea that Stein is most frequently identified with, the idea that there is no exact repetition within the dynamic temporality of our psychic life, figures among Bergson's key themes.

> Now, if duration [*durée*] is what we say, deep-seated psychic states are radically heterogeneous to each other, and it is impossible that any two of them should be quite alike, since they are two different moments of a life-story. While the external object does not bear the mark of the time that has elapsed and thus, in spite of the difference of time, the physicist can again encounter identical elementary conditions, duration is something real for the consciousness which preserves the trace of it, and we cannot here speak of identical conditions, because the same moment does not occur twice.[381]

Bergson contended that the continual coming-on of concrete novelty characterizes our experience of reality. But Bergson was not alone in this: the claim that reality is a process that continually brings on novelty was also fundamental in the philosophy of William James—and not only his view of the world, but that of the entire Emersonian tradition (indeed Emerson states the principle, by asserting that every moment authorizes an new state of mind).[382] Retrospection isolates consciousness from reality's flow (as it involves an image of something not present—not *real*—occupying the mind and taking up its energies); but stepping into the continuous present immerses one in nature's temporality, Emerson suggested. It was precisely to elicit a sense of the continual coming-on of novelty (to borrow an expression from William James) that Stein used the constatation of concrete particulars. And what Bergson described as a psychic reality, *durée*, is really the time of the body as we experience it from within.

Bergson understood, as Stein and Brakhage have, that each individual's experience is unique.

> I smell a rose and immediately confused recollections of childhood come back to my memory. In truth, these recollections have not been called up by the perfume of the rose: I breathe them in with the very scent; it means all that to me. To others it will smell differently.—It is always the same scent you will say, but associated with different ideas.—I am quite willing that you should express yourself in this way; but do not forget that you have first removed the personal element from the different impressions which the rose makes on each one of us; you have retained only the objective aspect, that part of the scent of the rose which is public property.[383]

Brakhage uses the very same argument to show that meaning is unique for each subject. Bergson's rejection of the associationalist's claim that the mind associates experiences from the past with the contemporary experience of the rose has relevance to Brakhage's ideas about perception. Bergson insists that we breathe childhood experiences "in with the very scent" of the flowers, and that these childhood experiences are part of the meaning of the rose for that individual; Brakhage offers the same argument about meaning, though unlike Bergson, he refuses to isolate a core of common experience and to call that the sensation's public meaning. For Brakhage, the sensation's meaning consists in the entirety of the personal experience towards which it points, including all the so-called associations that come along with it.

It is exactly this belief that enables Brakhage to fuse visual representations from memory, imagination, perception, hallucination, and closed-eye vision seamlessly, as though they were all part of contemporary experience. He proclaims such a capacious notion of seeing near the beginning of *Metaphors on Vision*.

> Allow so-called hallucination to enter the realm of perception, allowing that mankind always finds derogatory terminology for that which doesn't appear to be readily usable, accept dream visions, day-dreams or night-dreams, as you would so-called real scenes, even allowing that the abstractions which move so dynamically when closed eyelids are pressed are actually perceived.[384]

What is primary, for Brakhage, is vision—everyday seeing, memory, cogitation, hallucination, reverie are simply aspects of the visionary experience. Vision is different from perception. There is something very Emersonian about this claim. Both Brakhage and Emerson agree that all seeing is a form of imagining, and that any analysis of seeing begins with an understanding of the role of the mind/imagination in constituting what we see.[385] We must recognize that mind/imagination's role in forming what we see, for otherwise we fall prey to one of two errors: On the one hand, the mind can turn, towards introversion, and so falls victim to the Symbolist's syndrome, in which the mind becomes so self-involved that it becomes entirely abstract, entirely separated from the world; and if does so, it withdraws from the world and takes self-consciousness as the subject of its rumination.[386] Having no other, it reifies its own self-consciousness as object; but that object is too immediate to bring forth knowledge of the other. Taking self-consciousness as its object, especially a self-consciousness that has emptied itself of concrete content by thinking in abstractions, means turning away from the world of the other (and even the capital 'O' other). It cleaves mind and object, and does not recognize the limitations that constrain the mind's capacity to create the objects it experiences by according too slight a role to the phenomena of objectivity and givenness.[387] On the other hand, consciousness can deny its active role, and consider that the objects of the world are reflected into the glassy essence that is the mind. This gambit, rather than taking self-consciousness as everything, accords it no role whatsoever. The eye that knows itself only as perceiving, and has no understanding of the role of the imagination in perception, is a mind that believes in the absolute givenness, and so the absolute otherness of nature. Again, the vital contact between mind and nature is broken.

A salutary relation between mind and world develops when the mind is aware of its own divinity—when the mind understands its role in creating what it beholds. It is repetition, lack of energy, and the decline of individual vision into mass sensation that reduces the role the mind plays in forming the contents of vision. But a mind that knows its own divinity, that shuns all preconceptions, that does not settle upon a single, fixed image (a "representation") experiences a vivifying interplay of mind and world, a humanizing energy of the self conforming to a humanized nature to the individual self. It draws the power of the other into itself, and enfolds the other within the sphere of the imagination.

It is a universally acknowledged truth that the use of the continuous present is among the most important features of Stein's writing. It derives from Stein's sense of the absolute importance of each existent. Her writing suggests that the immediate, existing individual, not some featureless Absolute, is the final reality. Just as Stein developed a way of using repetition that shows clearly that each time a word occurs, it appears differently, so she created a temporal modality in which each moment appears as distinct, each complete in itself, and each presenting itself in a continuous present, neither looking back toward a previous moment, nor forward toward a succeeding moment. Her writing creates a precise sense of the distinctiveness of each moment, of the total character of the moment that makes that moment different from any other moment. This compositional method, which juxtaposes words that maintain their independence, reflects Stein's conception of experience, on which any moment is likely to hold disparate phenomenological features in a tenuous unity—to include different smells and tastes and textures in an odd combination. To reflect the fact that every experience has many dimensions, Stein often combines in a single passage terms that refer many sensuous particulars, which sometimes even belong to different sensory modalities. The accolation of a variety of concrete particulars formed the basis of her paratactical constructions. A passage from "A Portrait of Mabel Dodge," a part of which we quoted previously, offers a fine example.

> A plank that was dry was not disturbing the smell of burning and altogether there was the best kind of sitting there could never be all the edging that the largest chair was having. It was not pushed. It moved then. And there was not that lifting. There was that which was not any contradiction and there was

not the bland fight that did not have that regulation. The contents were not darkening. There was not that hesitation. It was occupied. There was not occupying any exception. Any one had come. There was that distribution.[388]

This feature of Stein's writing, of conveying the continual coming-on of novelty, also characterizes Stan Brakhage's films. His films, too, elicit the sense of a continuous presence. Most of his earlier, and many of his more recent works in longer forms, use perpetually regenerating forms—forms that appear always on the brink of collapse but regenerate themselves at the beginning of each cut—to engender this sense. Brakhage's primary means for creating perpetually regenerating forms is to use diversity (so the films seem to alter character from moment to moment—from a representation of forms in an illusory deep space, to an abstract, monochrome, all-over (see glossary), two-dimensional form, and then to a hypnogogic skein), parataxis (so that each cut seems abrupt, at least when measured against conventional norms) and present immediacy (which makes each moment seem completely autonomous and self-contained). Brakhage takes risks in his filmmaking; the testimony to this fact often takes the form of evidence that he engages in open field composition—a method of composition employing no pre-established forms, but forms that evolve during the process of making the work. This emphasis on "open form" conveys that no pre-established structure protects them against the threat of failure; indeed they often seem to teeter on the verge of collapse. I noted that *Made Manifest* invokes the idea of performance, but it is not unique among Brakhage's films in that regard—almost all of Brakhage's films claim to evolve out of an implied performance; so we rely on a performance aesthetic to appreciate them. As we watch the welter of too-disparate elements, we wonder (as we do when we listen to a risk-taking jazz improvisation) if the filmmaker has the strength of imagination to forge this diversity into a simple unity—we wonder whether Brakhage can pull off what he appears to want to do, and when he does, we marvel at his inventiveness.

Further evidence of Brakhage's interest in risk appears not only in use of an almost unfathomable diversity of visual forms (use of which arouses the threat of disunity, and so valorizes the imagination of the filmmaker who can unify this welter of diversity) but also in its opposite, the extreme use of repetition (which, as Stein's use of repetition does, threatens to slacken tension unpalatably).[389] Sometimes Brakhage's film forms seem to totter on the brink of degenerating into the powerless repetition of a small set of elements.[390] This emphasis on risk suggests the rootlessness of the individual moment, the groundless of the artistic work, and the artist's effort to create value out of the depths of his self, to intensify (and usually by using repetition) the groundlessness moment until it takes on ultimate value.

But it is not only the physical object evoked that seems rootless, it is also the phantasmagoric element (indeed, their phantasmagoric character relates to their rootlessness). A viewer, watching one of Brakhage's films, is acutely aware that the visual forms are shaped by an intense sensibility—that they are products of imagination, not perception in Emerson's sense of that word. The viewer is aware that they are the products of a "representative" artist, aware of his mind's "divinity." These visual forms also have the quality of the contents of the fascinated consciousness's phantasmagoria, so rapid is their movement, so elliptical their phrasing, so paratactical their construction, and so fluxing their content; thus they suggest a consciousness that goes over entirely into its object. So they appear as the work of self that never appears—of the transcendental self that Kant and Husserl suggested is the very condition of experience.

Or they would call forth that idea, but for one major quality of the imagery. Because there is often little consistency either in the content or in the visual forms that Brakhage presses into a single, integrated work, we sometimes have the impression, while watching one of his films, that any sort of image could follow any other sort—that a piece of scratching on film (presenting hypnagogic forms) could follow a shot made with an anamorphic lens, or a cosmic shot of solar flares could follow a realistic image with quotidian content, or a narrativized representation of a man climbing a snowy mountain could follow a shot of almost unrecognizable content that emphasizes texture. In short, we feel radical uncertainty about even the most basic features of ensuing visual forms. Just as when we read Stein's writings we cannot predict what phrase will follow another, when watching one of Brakhage's films we often cannot form expectations about what shot will follow next. Every successive shot appears as new and independent of those that preceded it. Each new shot, moreover, seems a triumph as it marks a new beginning. Such perpetually regenerating forms are a very Steinian sort of construction—Stein refers to its effect, which she also strove to achieve, as "beginning again and again." But because each shot is evidently the imagining of a "representative" individual, and, at the same time, because these visual forms also have the quality of the contents of the fascinated consciousness's phantasmagoria, they suggest a consciousness that goes over entirely into into its object. Hence with every collapse of one visual and its replacement by another, the self—the transcendental ego—hangs in the balance, for we fear it has not the power to constitute a visual form of yet another sort. Yet it does, in a triumph that we feel is the equivalent of rebirth.

Nonetheless, the reconstituted self is not identical to the self that collapsed a moment before. Brakhage's films often evoke a sense of threatened transcendental ego, which, because it is constantly being fissured, is barely able to sustain powers of imagination from moment to moment (and yet, usually, in triumph that is testimony to the mind's divinity, does manage to do so). And because collapse and regeneration occur from moment to moment, the treat seems a continual one, a condition of the imagination's activity. Since the quality of the imagery changes so drastically moment by moment, and since it is the quality of the imagery that gives evidence of the self's character, we do not feel them as belonging to a single self, that remains self-identical throughout the process. Rather we feel the self undergoes complete transformation, moment by moment, with every change in experiential mode. Some of Brakhage's films make continual vanishing of the self seem rather menacing.[391]

The performative dimension of Brakhage's work has other characteristics that show Stein's influence. The first relates to their lyric character. Because the elements of his films are often very diverse, because their rhythms are variable and uneven, because his films seem constantly to be on the brink of collapsing and to be continually renewing themselves, Brakhage's visual forms have a heightened presence. That is, we are always aware of the act of enunciation. Emile Benveniste has pointed out that the time of enunciation is the "unceasing present" and that is certainly the temporal modality within which Brakhage's films transpire.

People watching a film by Brakhage identify with the maker since they must create a coherent whole from the many diverse visual forms they confront. But they identify, too, with the film—they enter into its images, and so sense their changes viscerally—and by this identification they come to feel they participate in revealing the imaginary realm the film puts on display and (this "and" is the cardinal point) elicits. Viewers thus feel that they have a role in the film's enunciatory acts. Furthermore, the temporal qualities of Brakhage's films and the temporal qualities of enunciation are very similar, for the temporality of both is that of the present tense; this identity strengthens the identification and makes viewers feel more strongly that they play a role in the enunciatory process. Brakhage likely derived the idea for creating a work based on homologies among the forms of artistic works, the structures of conscious acts, and acts of enunciation from Stein, for her work depends on similar homologies. Stein proposed that

> The time of the composition is a natural thing and the time in the composition is a natural thing it is a natural thing and it is a contemporary thing.
>
> The time of the composition is the time of the composition. It has been at times a present thing it has been at times a past thing it has been at times a future thing it has been at times an endeavor at parts or all of these things. In my beginning it was a continuous present a beginning again and again and again and again, it was a series it was a list it was a similarity and everything different it was a distribution and an equilibration. This is all of the time

some of the time of the composition. . . . In the beginning there was the time in the composition that naturally was in the composition but time in the composition comes now and this is what is now troubling every one the time in the composition is now a part of distribution and equilibrium. . . . There is at present there is distribution, by this I mean expression and time, and in this way at present composition is time that is the reason that at present the time-sense is troubling that is the reason why at present the time-sense in the composition is the composition that is making what there is in composition.[392]

In this passage, Stein reveals how fundamental were her concerns with distribution and equilibrium. Brakhage evinces a similarly deep concern with those same matters. Stein's conception of distribution and balance pushed her towards non-teleological structures. She realized that teleological structures involve a transitive sense of time—according to which a moment is not valuable in itself but only because it leads towards something else (that leads towards something else that eventually leads to a climax). Stein's sense of the preciousness of each concrete particular inflects the temporal attributes of her work, for that sense aroused in her the desire to make each moment in time appear equally precious as the next. Teleological structures, she realized, attenuate, or even eliminate, that sense of time. Accordingly, Stein contrived non-teleological structures for her writing, so as to convey a sense of time as a series of moments, or, more exactly, as a flow of differentiated, but not normatively distinguished moments. Brakhage's forms are also non-teleological and non-hierarchical. Stein tilted against forms that subordinate clauses one to another and against narrative forms, since they involve the domination of one element by another. An analogous drive motivates Brakhage's use of perpetually regenerating forms. Futhermore, Stein strives to eliminate hierarchy, univocity, linearity, narrative, and closure in favour of multiplicity and open-endedness, while Brakhage similarly seeks to create works that can engender an unlimited semiotic activity. Such forms, furthermore, by furnishing a plethora of signs that cannot be reduced to a single meaning—that, in fact, resist all semiotic reduction and remain stubbornly multiple—provide evidence of the arbitrariness of significance.

The poet Robert Duncan (a close friend of Brakhage) acutely recognized the implications that Stein's methods had both for Open Form work and for the conception of the self on which the practices of the Open Form poets rest. He remarked about Gertrude Stein's conception of "composition":

But now the Composition and we too are never finished, centered, perfected. We are in motion and our meaning lies not in some last or lasting judgment, in some evolution or dialectic toward a higher force or consciousness, but in the content of the whole of us as Adam—the totality of mankind's experience in which our moment, this vision of universal possibility, plays its part; and beyond, the totality of life experience in which

Man plays His part, not central, but in every living moment creating a new
crisis in the equilibrium of the whole.[393]

He could have drawn the implication from Brakhage's film forms.
Brakhage's visual forms convey the energies out of which images and ideas
emerge. They are not pictures, for they are presentational (and not representational) forms. Consequently, their relation to what they signify is not
arbitrary. While watching Brakhage's films, we do not feel bound by convention or by meaning. We experience freedom from meaning as pleasure (nonsense verse or nonsense chants—"Rah, rah, sis boom bah!"—make evident
the pleasure that results from escaping meaning). This pleasure becomes
even more intense when the delights of kinesis accompany the joys of being
liberated from meaning. Brakhage's films provide many examples that invite
us to revel in the combined effect of kinetic *jouissance* and the delight in
being released from iron laws of meaning. The pleasure we feel in being
released from meaning and our enjoyment of the pure visual kinesis that
Brakhage's films afford is not unlike what we derive from some of Gertrude
Stein's more audacious constructions:

> Can thinking will or well or now a well.
> Wells are not used any more now
> It is not only just why this is much
> That not one can add it to adding main
> For never or to never.
> Suppose I add I like to
> I can should show choose go or not any more not so
> This is how any one could be in no hope
> Of which no hope they did or did not
> There is no difference between having in or not only not this
> Could it be thought did would
> By it a name.[394]

Roland Barthes, a pre-eminent theorist of textual pleasure offered the following comment about readerly writing (writing that is characterized by an
excess of meaning—meaning that exceeds semiotic coherence and semiotic
closure and that, consequently, we cannot form into a definite assertion):
"We needn't plough through [this writing] at all. We need pay attention only
as long as the thrill lasts, the tantalizing pleasure of the flood of meaning of
which we cannot quite make sense." Stein's writings, like Brakhage's films,
are elusive exactly because they produce a semiotic process that seems to
lack bounds. They consequently elicit just that sort of pleasure that Barthes
alluded to in this passage.

Barthes's comment also helps to explain the temporal features of Stein's
writings and Brakhage's films. We do not plough through such writing;
rather we enjoy "the flood of meaning"—or, what is more to the point, the

flood of sensation. The pleasure we feel evokes no sense of anticipation; rather we submit to experiencing the mode of immediacy as we succumb to the feeling that what we experience belongs fully to the present. The unceasing present is also the time of internal somatic awareness. The exchange of semiotic energies without sense has the same character as the dynamic exchanges of energy that occur within the body, and is felt with the same immediacy. The body, as felt from within, is energy. Hence, in internal time-consciousness, each new moment is a distinct intensity. Internal time-consciousness is a succession of throbs, each of which we feel as a distinct, autonomous sensation—and discerning the relations among these throbs is a matter for the intellect and for the understanding. But that is the intellect's only role in time consciousness; otherwise time-consciousness is a somatic, or at least a non-intellectual, process. Stein's ideas for creating a sense of time as a succession of texturally distinguished "nows" have attracted many followers, and the reason for this is that the experience of time is a primal— it lies at the core of human experience, for it is the experience of the body from within.

Brakhage's ideas on rhythm are also at one with the actualities of the time-sense he tries to elicit, and the time-sense he strives to evoke is the body's time-sense. Thus, Brakhage's ideas on rhythm, which are so important to his compositional practices, have a somatic basis. Also, the disembodied movement—the movement contained within itself that films involve— captures the quality of movement not of an objective order, but of the ebb and flow of somatic energies just emerging into feeling. On the other hand, the mind is always, to a greater or lesser extent, concerned with meaning. The time of Brakhage's films, like that of Gertrude Stein's compositions, is somatic, not mental time.

But there is something of an irony connected with this: both Stein's writings and Brakhage's films, while they are constructions that affect the reader's/viewer's body, often strike us as discorporate beings—as bodiless phenomena.[395] "Mabel Dodge" is renowned for its use of "disembodied movement"—movement that, as Stein described it, is "something that is completely contained within itself and being contained within itself is moving. Not moving in relation to any thing not moving in relation to itself but just moving." Stein pointed out that she used fewer nouns and more present participles than previous writers; by doing so, she captured the impression of happening itself—not of someone or something doing something to someone or something, but the dynamics of an event itself. This sense of disembodied movement characterizes Brakhage's films, too. Brakhage has developed a powerful set of devices for emphasizing motion and, especially, for disembodying movement: Only in a small portion of the shots that appear

in his films is the camera static (or nearly static) and often his camera movement is very rapid; he employs various means (among which hand-cranking
is pre-eminent) to create a difference between successive frames we perceive as a "jitter"; he sometimes uses multiple layers of images that give
the objects in the film a "ghostly" appearance, as though they are not solid
objects; he sometimes blurs objects, either by defocusing or by swish-
panning, to the end of de-realizing objects and presenting pure motion, an
effect analogous to that produced as Stein replaced nouns with present participles; he sometimes composes his frames so that large areas are dark,
with just a small portion illuminated; sometimes, either because the shooting is done from very close up, or because so much of the photographed
object lies in the dark, the exposed object matter, too, is such a small portion
of the whole object that we cannot identify it, and so we see the frame as a
modulator of coloured light rather than as an image. These devices have the
effect of converting film from a representational to a presentational medium—
from a medium that represents objects to a medium that presents movement—that we experience first visually and then, because of the paucity of
our actual kinaesthetic sensations the movie theatre situation forces on us,
as virtual kinaesthetic phenomena. The *Arabic Numeral, Roman Numeral,
Egyptian*, and *Babylon Series* of films carry this tendency of Brakhage's work
to its destination.

If in Stein's writing, each unit is complete in itself, then she could not avail
herself of any of the traditional means for creating organic unity to bring
them together in a whole. For the relations that obtain in an organically unified work of art alter the internal nature of the elements that enter into
those relations—they are "internal," rather than "external relations." Other
sorts of relations were required: a simple and endlessly flexible means for
creating relations between such self-contained units is juxtaposition. Stein's
method, especially in her middle period, relied on juxtaposition as the primary means of relating completely, or almost completely, self-contained elements. Passages that simply juxtapose quasi-independent elements have a
characteristic lumpy texture, for parataxis does nothing by itself to create a
smooth transition from one element to the next. Moreover, as both Sergej
Ejzenstejn and Ezra Pound realized, parataxis is a flexible means, for it
allows a writer to assemble elements that are startlingly different one from
another; indeed, a high degree of difference among the juxtaposed elements
can produce effective contrasts among them, and this contrast can engender
a sense of "a continuous coming-on of concrete novelty." Furthermore, a
high degree of contrast among juxtaposed elements increases the likelihood
that those elements will have tensional relations with one another. What is
more, contrasts among juxtaposed elements create jolts, of various intensi-

ties, that resemble the throbs of internal sensations. Stein realized all of this, and so she developed a method of juxtaposing elements that did nothing to smooth out the contrasts and differences among the units that she put together. Thus, in *A Long Gay Book*, for example, Stein often strung together a series of quite different elements: *"All the pudding has the same flow and the sauce is painful, the tunes are played, the crinkling paper is burning, the pot has a cover and the standard is excellence."*[396]

The passage is fascinating for how different the elements are one from the next. It is characteristically dense and employs her characteristic word plays: the painful sauce is, of course, a *sauce piquante* (unless it was a Spanish dessert, in which case it was a *salsa picante*—and then the wordplay is even better)—but whoever would serve pudding with a *sauce piquante*, or even with *salsa picante*? (That one would not likely have pudding with *sauce piquante* which reveals that the terms the imagination arrives at to interpret this passage are incongrous, as the spatial elements in a Cubist painting are; what is more important, this incongruity destabilizes the image.) Furthermore, some paper, especially the less pliable varieties of paper, when crinkled does make a crackling noise, so perhaps it was a dinner party that Stein was preparing, and a guest brought a wrapped gift—perhaps a bottle of wine like those one sees in many Cubist paintings; and if the gift was wrapped, then it was covered and so what it contained was a surprise, just as the pot itself contains a surprise—and, for a dinner guest, the best surprise of all is a delicious dessert, one prepared according to standards of excellence; and a sweet treat with a piquant, even painful sauce, and gifts, and perhaps a bottle of wine can be pretty enticing. No wonder, then, that the pot had a cover and has to be stopped from boiling; so maybe it was not a guest she was having for dinner, but Alice B. Toklas after dinner. The passage animates—sets into motion—such interpretative activities. Because it does so, the image the passage evokes is no static thing. It is dynamic.

The critic Donald Sutherland points out the most important thing about this passage:

> [I]n any given immediate scene, no matter how commonplace, there is bound to be an association of disparate elements, which exist very vividly to a perception persuaded of the equal importance of all phenomena, even if they are largely irrelevant to the main gist of the scene. Instead of letting things go at "I had a good pudding with sauce piquante for supper" she gives an equable list of concomitant phenomena, some relevant, some not, to the main practical event, but all of them equally and simultaneously existing in perceptual fact.[397]

Stein herself offered an interviewer a similar remark about the influence that Cézanne had on her work.

> Everything I have done has been influenced by Flaubert and Cézanne, and this gave me a new feeling about composition. Up to that time composition had consisted of a central idea, to which everything else was an accompaniment and separate but was not an end in itself, and Cézanne conceived the idea that in composition one thing was as important as another thing. Each part is as important as the whole, and that impressed me enormously.[398]

When Robert Bartlett Haas asked Gertrude Stein to sum up "what she was trying to do" in her writing, she offered, in the middle of a long answer in which she gave an account of her work according to three periods, the following statement about her paratactical method:

> I took individual words and thought about them until I got their weight and volume complete and put them next to another word, and at this same time I found out very soon that there is no such thing as putting them together without sense. It is impossible to put them together without sense. I made innumerable efforts to make words write without sense and found it impossible. Any human being putting down words had to make sense out of them.[399]

Stein states that she paid attention to the material qualities of words—to their sound, their heft, and their thrust—and how she juxtaposed words in a composition depended upon those material factors. Although the verbal artifacts she created took account only of properties inherent in the words she used, and did not depend upon the words' conventional, referential relations with objects extrinsic to language, they nonetheless have some sense—they still pointed towards something in the world. As she suggested in the single from *Tender Buttons*, the words are arrangements in accord with a system and the arrangement results in pointing—an ostensive act that does not result from resemblance.

Stein's predecessor in this was the French Symbolist poet Stephane Mallarmé (1842-98). In "Crise de vers," Mallarmé had written:

> The pure work implies the elocutory disappearance of the poet who abandons the initiative to words mobilized by the shock of their inequality; they light one another up with mutual reflections like a virtual trail of fire upon precious stones, replacing the breathing perceptible in the old lyrical blast or the enthusiastic personal direction of the phrase.[400]

Keeping the narrator out and allowing words a maximum of free play are characteristics of Stein's writing as well (just as they are characteristics of Charles Olson's poetry, as we shall see).

One feature of paratactical constructions in particular has made them attractive to artists of this century: the juxtaposition of self-contained elements does not result in a hierarchy of superordinate and subordinate structures. English grammar, as taught in schools, produces sentences that have one principal clause and, if a sentence has other clauses besides the principal clause, those clauses are subordinate to the principal clause. Such teaching instructs us how to use subordination to make one's principal point clear. Further, school grammar teaches us how to subordinate all the sentences in a paragraph to the topic sentence and simultaneously to create another hierarchy in which each sentence leads to the concluding sentence of the paragraph that will have special force or, at least, a sense of finality. This manner of composing linguistic terms is reflected in the equally conventional manner of composing narratives, for novels' narrative macrostructures likewise exhibit the microstructural hierarchy of superordinate and subordinate elements. The conventional design of a novel depends on identifying the principal plot and throwing it into relief by subordinating subplots to the principal plot.

The method of composition by juxtaposition is a powerful corrosive to these principles of design—and to all design norms based on hierarchy. Juxtaposition does not produce hypotactical structures; nor does it organize elements into a hierarchy of greater and lesser importance, or form relations of superordination and subordination. Instead, the juxtaposed elements maintain the weight and volume they have as independent entities. Stein commented on the "evenness" of Cézanne's paintings—the evenness of the brush-strokes over the entire canvas, the equivalence of the values he accorded different blocks of colours and different hues, the equal weight he gave to the centre of the canvas and to its corners. The effect of this equivalence was to spread our eye over the entire canvas (so that in his case, equivalence, not difference, is spreading). The method of juxtaposition can produce something equivalent for a verbal artifact, for the result of this method is a structure in which all the elements have nearly the same weight. Composition by juxtaposition favours treating all elements as though they had equal weight and equal value, for the forms one produces by juxtaposing elements are not hierarchic. Furthermore, a series of successive items, all of nearly equal importance and unsubordinated one to another, produce the impression that Stein sought for, of "the continual coming-on of concrete novelty."

The impetus to create anti-hierarchic forms spread out from the microstructures of parataxis to the macrostructures that constitute the global design of her work; "The difference is spreading," as Stein said. It even spreads into a conception of reality. For the possibility of creating such a structure of equivalents depends on the elements having nearly equal weight as independent entities, and that fact goes a good way towards furnishing an account of the role that Stein's adherence to a theophanic conception of reality played in shaping her compositional methods. Furthermore, Stein's use of non-hierarchical forms of composition represents a further

stage in the modernists' efforts to dehierarchalizing composition—exemplified in painters eschewing perspective, especially linear perspective, play-
wrights ridding drama of climax, novelists eliminating main plot/subplot
parallelism from narrative, and composers adopting atonal methods of composition are other early manifestations of the drive to create non-hierarchical
forms. The same objections apply to creating paintings that lead towards a
vanishing point, dramas that lead towards a climax, and musical compositions that lead towards a tonally determined consonance—all employ central,
focusing elements instead of giving equal weight to all the elements that
make up a work. The conviction that the formal possibilities of a system in
which all elements have the same weight are much greater than they are in a
system of predetermined hierarchical relations was basic to modernist practice. Thus, using the interval that goes from the dominant to the tonic has a
particular quality (and a particular—and almost predetermined—significance) in tonal music, while the succession of the same two notes in a piece
of atonal music can have many different qualities, according to context.
Atonality, therefore, releases the interval from a fixed meaning, destabilizes
it, and in destabilizing it, imbues it with greater potential. Modernists
wanted to make those greater resources available.

Stein shared those modernist convictions. However, Stein's practice
implies even more. Stein's paratactical composition had the effect of pointing
out a series of objects and events in reality, as though inviting us now to look
at this and now at this and now at this. Stein presents them not as parts of a
whole, even though, like the "one, and one and one, and one . . . up to one
hundred ones" that she offers in *Useful Knowledge*, they do belong to a
whole. She presents each singly and separately, to give the impression that
each is separate and absolute in itself. Each "one," joined with the next
"one" by the conjunction "and" is equal to every other, and each is self-
contained. Thus, she accords respect to the absolute integrity of each component. This is how one presents things if one loves them. Stein's efforts to
accord all particulars the same weight, like those of Pound, Fenollosa, and
Emerson, developed from conceptions about the constitution of reality. All
these writers harbour a belief that the concrete particular has ultimate value.
Like Emerson's comment about roses—"they are what they are"—Stein's
"a rose is a rose" proposes a conception of reality that is based on the
Romantic idea that God makes himself evident in the objects of nature, as
the One who defines Himself through His self-being, through being the "I
am who I am" who comes into contact with the world of concrete particulars.
Stan Brakhage, too, contrives forms that convey such theophantic beliefs.
This is nowhere more evident than in Brakhage's most Steinian films, *For
Marilyn* (1992) and the *Visions in Meditation* series (*#1, #2: Mesa Verde,*

#3: Plato's Cave, and *#4: D.H. Lawrence,* 1989-90), a series inspired by Stein's monumentally difficult *Stanzas in Meditation.* All these works synthesize elements that are remarkably different from one another into "an equitable list of . . . phenomena . . . all of them equally and simultaneously existing in perceptual fact."

A few pages ago we cited a passage from *A Long Gay Book* that started out, "All the pudding has the same flow and the sauce is painful." That passage raises some further issues concerning what Stan Brakhage drew from Gertrude Stein. Stein devoted her work largely to describing those raw sensations that, as Eliot stated, "are not objects" but a primordial form of awareness. This choice of subject matter was one means Stein used to avoid having language do the instrumental work of naming. It is understandable, given her interest in sensations that are not objects, that Stein devoted great attention to the imagined sensations of taste that the sight of foodstuffs elicits. These passages also hint at the synthaesthetic character of primordial forms of awareness. Stein gave over a large portion of *Tender Buttons,* around twenty pages, to food. One long passage in this section deals with roast beef. Here is an excerpt from that passage: "Lovely snipe and tender turn, excellent vapor and slender butter, all the splinter and the trunk, all the poisonous darkening drunk, all the joy in weak success, all the joyful tenderness, all the section and the tea, all the stouter symmetry."[401]

The passage displays remarkable symmetry and regularity in its form. The caesurae occur almost periodically, after seven syllables or so: *all the splinter and the trunk* (seven syllables)/ *all the poisonous darkening drunk* (nine syllables if read "properly," but seven if, for the sake of isochrony, one elides "poisonous" and "darkening" into two—thus, the use of "poisonous" and "darkening" in such a highly metrical-periodic passage creates tension through hemiola) / *all the joy in weak success* (seven syllables)/ *all the joyful tenderness* (seven syllables) / *all the section and the tea* (seven syllables)/ *all the stouter symmetry* (seven syllables).

Furthermore, the passage makes extensive use of internal rhyme to mark these periodic caesurae: "all the splinter and the *trunk,* all the poisonous darkening *drunk*"; and "all the joy in weak suc*cess,* all the joyful tender*ness*"; and "all the section and the *tea,* all the stouter symme*try.*" Stein makes extensive use of alliteration, too: "*t*ender *t*urn" and *d*eadening *d*runk" and "*s*touter *s*ymmetry" as well as assonance: "t*u*rn," "b*u*tter," "dr*u*nk," "tr*u*nk," and "st*ou*t" as well as: "*s*nipe," "e*x*cellent," "*s*lender, "*s*plinter," "*s*uccess, "tenderne*ss*," "*s*ection," "*s*touter," and "*s*ymmetry." A principal device of the passage is the interweaving, by nearly strict alternation, of sibilants and voiced or aspirated 't' sounds. To write with such concern for sound—to compose language in terms of sound—is to write with a view towards the effect of sound on the body, and it is to understand the intimate relation between sound, language, and feeling. It is not to use language representationally, or to use it to offer abstract propositions to the detached intellect. Stein wrote to compose language in terms of sound, and it is sound's intimate relation to the internal dynamics of proprioceptive body, the body as feeling, that is one of the reasons why an artist who is as deeply concerned with the proprioceptive body as is Brakhage would have such a deep interest in Stein's writing. It also explains the presence in Stein's oeuvre of works given over to capturing the rhythms and feelings of (lesbian) sexual encounters.

Brakhage shares Stein's anti-Idealist interest in those contents of consciousness that we cannot name. His statements on Stein's influence stress the capacity of her writing to evoke experience that has not yet formed into nameable objects and events. One such statement appeared in one of his regular contributions to the Canadian periodical *Musicworks*. Brakhage introduces the topic not with commentary on Stein's writing, but rather, first, on Olson's and then on Chaucer's:

> The very afternoon of his dismissal [from the circle that had gathered around Pound at Saint Elizabeth's], returning to his room in a state of dejection, Olson had a dream in which Pound appeared to him and gave him (what was to be a major cornerstone of Olson's aesthetic) the following:
>
> > Of rhythm is image.
> > Of image is knowing
> > And of knowing there is a construct.[402]
>
> What does this *mean*?
>
> Taking it simply 'as one poet to another,' we can get a gloss of some of the aesthetic limits of Poetry—that imagery, for example, is dependent on rhythm, at scratch . . . (i.e. that that's the first impression one can be having of viable *picture* invoked by language).[403]

Brakhage continues with an example that is apposite to his own work:

> In "The Nun's Priest's Tale" Chaucer gives us Chauntecleer (and some of *all* rooster) thus:
>
> > In al the land, of crowyng nas his peer.
> > His voys was murier than the murie orgon
> > On messe-dayes that in the chirche gon.
> >
> > His coomb was redder than the fyn coral,
> > And batailled as it were a castel wal;
> > His byle was blak, and as the jeet it shoon;
> > Lyk asure were his legges and his toon;
> > His nayles whitter than the lylye flour,
> > And lyk the burned gold was his colour.

> The particularities of the strut of the cock, incorporated with the back/
> forth trip-rhythms of his counter-balancing neck movements, are 'at one'
> with the writ, so that Chautecleer can be *felt* as if seen *in motion*, as well as
> occasionally poised, throughout.[404]

Here Brakhage expounds his belief that language (i.e., according to this statement, a system of nominal reference) evokes pictures, and that the picturing capacities of rhythm far outstrip those of nominal reference. In stating this, Brakhage reworks the Bergsonian conviction, which he probably got through Stein, that analytical knowledge produces snapshots of reality—frozen pictures of objects arrayed outside us, in space—that capture only the static appearance of the outer surfaces of objects, not the inward dynamic that is their life; only intuition, which apprehends the flux and movement of reality, can reveal its deeper life.

Brakhage makes a more extreme point about naming; as extreme as the point seems, it finds support in Stein's own commentary on her work. In *Lectures in America* Stein reported that in her *Tender Buttons* period she strived to fashion a form of "naming things that would not invent names, but mean names without naming them" and she compares this with what Shakespeare had done in *A Midsummer Night's Dream*, for "in the forest of Arden [he] had created a forest without mentioning the things that make a forest. You feel it all but he does not name its names."[405] The forest of Arden, of course, represents a pristine site, and so the language to which Stein (and according to Stein, Shakespeare) aspires is an Adamic language. Shakespeare depicts Arden wood as a world antipodal to our own, a world where imagination prevails (if only for a spell) over Theseus's sad dream of reason, and where (as Bottom's frequent and egregious linguistic errors highlight) the falsities of conventional language no longer proliferate; the forest, then, lies closer to paradisiacal realm.

The paradisiacal nature of the play's setting (which Stein explicitly evokes) and the utopian cast of her declaration make clear that Stein's linguistic interests here are essentially a form of interest in Adamic language. Stein's interest in Adamic language relates her to Emerson (and, more broadly, with all those US writers who have offered the image of an American Adam). But there is this important difference between Stein and Emerson: Emerson's ideas about Adamic language preserved vestiges of the pre-modern doctrine of correspondences. So Emerson maintained that the language of the new American Adam was pre-ordained, for the authentic nouns that would make up a class of the terms of the language would contain in their being essential attributes of that to which they refer; the relationship between signifier and signified in this Adamic language would be natural, not arbitrary—indeed, the relation would ideally be analogous to the "hieroglyphic" relation between a natural object and its cosmic meaning that Elias Lévi Zahed discussed. Such an Adamic language, Emerson maintained, would restore language to its authentic potential, the potential it possessed when nouns had been properly aligned with the objects to which, by their nature, they rightfully refer. Stein did not subscribe to the doctrine of correspondences, yet she maintained, nonetheless that the Adamic language must be constituted by natural relations between signifiers and that which they signify (the tendency to stake naturalizing claims for one's mode of discourse is one Brakhage shares with Stein, as his commentary on the relationship between the visual forms of his painted films and their synaptic signifieds confirms). So for Stein the restoration of Adamic language would represent a triumph of bodily imagination—a triumph achieved by sufficiently cathecting the actual physical properties of words. Features of her ideas on language and meaning resemble those of the German aesthetician Gotthold Ephraim Lessing (1729-81), for like Lessing she believed that poetic (or, more generally, literary) language elevates signs from arbitrary to natural relations, and that it achieves this by the sounds of the words and their orders, the length of the syllables that compose them, and, more generally, the composite effect of the composition of all their material features. Unlike Lessing's, however, Stein's version of this conception of the direct, natural relation between words and things is not dependent on any presupposition that the natural relation between the words and their referents has an iconic character.

A belief on the topic of Adamic language that Stein and Emerson share is that any language of absence—any language the properties of which are determined entirely by convention (that is, by arbitrary relations between words and things)—cannot be the language of the new Adam. Both Emerson and Stein believed that only a language of presence can bring a world into presence. However, while both celebrated a language of presence, Emerson's valorization of that sort of language whose founding idea of presence depended on the pre-modern doctrine of correspondences, while Stein held the more orthodox Romantic belief in the creative potential of the word.

So in his *Musicworks* article devoted to Stein and her impact on his filmmaking, Brakhage reaffirms the conviction Stein held in her *Tender Buttons* period—that the resources of rhythm, cadence, intonation, and gesture are the materials out of which sound objects, such as poems, are fashioned, and that it is through the arrangements of these sound materials that a poem produces meaning; a poem does not import meaning from the pre-existing semantic relations possessed by the terms that it incorporates into itself, but effectuates meaning in what it does to the reader's body and mind. Its meaning, then, belongs to the natural order of cause and effect. Stein probably would not have understood the concept in these terms, and Brakhage certainly does not, but such a conception of language can be related to an infant's consciousness of the Real—a stage in the development of consciousness before any gap has opened in consciousness, when a person not know the difference between self and world, a stage of raw, immediate perception; the pleasurable rhythmic sensations of the flow of pre-symbolic sounds recreates the pleasant place formed through the infant's relations with his or her mother's body.[406]

We have seen that Brakhage insists that Olson's meanings, like Chaucer's—indeed, we may suppose, all poetic meaning, since Olson seems to represent The Poet for Brakhage—relates to its capacity to evoke dynamic sensation: "The particularities of the strut of the cock, incorporated with the back/ forth trip-rhythms of his counter-balancing neck movements, are 'at one' with the writ, so that Chautecleer can be *felt* as if seen *in motion*, as well as occasionally poised, throughout." This is the ground of all knowledge, Brakhage suggests, by quoting Olson's "of rhythm is image/ of image is knowing" (a conviction that, of course, makes filmmaking a privileged medium for Brakhage). He suggests, in sum, that Olson conceived of real knowledge as the apprehension of movement, for movement belongs to a more profound realm than the static world to which conventional signs refer; this claim is consistent with Gertrude Stein's Bergsonian view of understanding. Brakhage's art, like Stein's, strives to reanimate our primordial awareness of the Real—of what pre-existed language and symbolic reference—and the Real is a realm of lability and change.

So it should not be surprising, then, that Brakhage also displays a Steinian antipathy towards nouns and nominal reference (an antipathy he expressed in this *Musicworks* column). Brakhage goes even farther than Stein, however, in dissociating rhythm from reference, since he sees the meaning of the word as irrelevant to the flow of dynamic sensation that poetry engenders.

> It is imagery-as-*movement* which rhythm invokes, as *distinct* from such symbols as "Stop," "Go," soforth. The mind's flow of (thus) moving images, transformative images which are metamorphosing and (thereby) reflective of the sensed 'world,' is (as Olson's dream has it) designate of "knowing."[407]

So unbending is Brakhage's conviction that the words that form a poem are not nominal that he goes to great lengths to explain that, in the poem-fragment Olson conceived after being dismissed from Pound's circle, the word "construct" is not really a noun.

> [The word "construct" as used by Olson] [is] one with metaphorical bounce inasmuch as "construct" (as distinct from the word "construction") strongly implies the mnemonic end-process of coming-into-existence, therefore of movement, of Time, then/therefore timing; but it is

verbal [i.e., a verb form] (despite the prefix "a") and 'slides loose of' becoming a noun, a sign, symbol, soforth.[408]

Thus, Brakhage denies that the word "construct" has a denotative function in Olson's poem-fragment. Accordingly, he goes on to expound on the function he believes it serves: "[It] does clash its two-syllables, in the thought patterns of reading, so as to reverberate back/forth across the dream poem itself to reverse the imagined continuity of coming-to a construction."[409]

Thus, its sound structure alone determines the function it serves; its function depends only on the aural relations between its two syllables and the reverberation that the clash between the sounds of the two syllables produces, both throughout the poem itself and the reader's experience of it (these two things are not distinct in Brakhage's aesthetic, for Brakhage suggests that the actual poem *is* the reader's experience of it—a claim concerning the ontological status of a work that follows from Brakhage's conception of meaning).

Brakhage goes as far as proposing that the phenomenal (phantasmagoric) appearances the poem creates in its readers' minds—the poem itself, according to his artistic theory, and which he characterizes as "imagery-as-movement"—have noetic importance. He propounds this conviction by first posing a question:

> [A]nd of knowing IS there, then, such a 'full stop' as the word "construct," thusly rhythmed, would suggest?: yes!, because "construct" is an 'end tempo' in that rhythm pattern.[410]

In other words, rhythm circumscribes and delimits knowledge. This is, admittedly, an extravagant hypothesis, but it is not wholly original. An item in the Romantic credo claimed that there is a type of knowledge that we can get from poetry, but not by any other means. For the Romantics, the epistemological privilege of poetry resulted from the fact that a poem conveyed images that were the products of imagination, and the imagination knows truths that reason cannot discover. Brakhage has simply revised that tenet. As he states in *Metaphors on Vision*:

> Yet I suggest that there is a pursuit of knowledge foreign to language and founded upon visual communication, demanding a development of the optical mind, and dependent upon perception in the original and deepest sense of the word.
> Suppose the Vision of the saint and the artist to be an increased ability to see—vision.[411]

Brakhage's notions about the creative process overlap with Stein's at another key point. Stein considered that her writing arose from a state of trance or deep meditation, a state of mind that can engender more profound,

less habituated visions than normal consciousness can. Ulla E. Dydo
unearthed these comments that Mabel Dodge made about Gertrude Stein's
creative method:

> Her habit of working is methodical and deliberate. She . . . brings all her
> willpower to bear upon the banishment of preconceived images. Concen-
> trating upon the impression she has received and which she wishes to
> transmit, she suspends her selective faculty, waiting for the word or group
> of words that will perfectly interpret her meaning, to rise from her sub-
> consciousness to the surface of her mind.
>
> Then and then only does she bring her reason to bear upon them, exam-
> ining, weighing and gauging their ability to express meaning. . . . She does
> not go after words—she waits and lets them come to her, and they do.[412]

It was almost certainly her interest in this mode of consciousness that led
to Stein's efforts to create a sense of the moving present, just as Brakhage's
interest in trance led to his efforts to evoke a similar temporal modality. In
both their cases, this trance or meditative character is associated with the
use of extreme fragmentation and the construction of series, of open-ended
forms-in-evolution, and with the use of capacious structures to create a
sense of pure flux.

I have already shown that the forms of Brakhage's films leave no place for
the transcendental ego. In a similar way, Stein's meditative practices led her
to the point where she could decreate the self and become a pure, unself-
reflective consciousness. She expresses this in a text I have quoted previously:

> I am I not any longer when I see.
> This sentence is at the bottom of all creative activity. It is just the
> exact opposite of I am I because my little dog knows me.[413]

The second sentence tells us that meditation is as central to Stein's creative method as trance is to Brakhage's. All her famous innovations relate to
the temporal qualities of the meditative experience: the sense of the continuous present relates to focusing on the present and eliminating anticipation
and recollection—important properties of meditative experience. The emphasis on verbs and the reduction of the noun's role in her writing relates to
the notion that reality is a process that meditators often offer, and that follows from the derealizing of objective reality and the elevation of energy to a
status where it can claim ontological priority over objecthood. The capa-
ciousness of her prose, the desire to allow in anything, relates to the loss of
wilfulness and the acceptance of all things that mystics often proclaim to be
the highest form of existence.

Though all Stein's writing relates to the experience of meditation, that
experience is especially important to *Stanzas in Meditation*. In fact, as

Ulla E. Dydo points out, Stein offered *Meditation in Stanzas* as an alternative title. Both titles suggest action and process, for Stein conceived of thinking as dynamic, even in meditation. She always maintained that "real thinking is conceptions aiming again and again always getting fuller, that is the difference between creative thinking and theorising."[414] She saw reformulating and reworking as essentially involved in thinking. That is, as Charles Caramello points out, "not only the meaning of the thing being observed but also the meaning of the manner of observation and the meaning of the mode of its presentation" are significant.[415] Stein strove to perceive in a fashion that was free of the debilitating effects of habituation and, in fact, of pernicious conventions of any sort; she strove indeed to perceive in the present. She strove to dispense with everything from the past, to ensure that nothing remembered be brought to bear on observation, so as to perceive in the immediate moment, just as Brakhage does.

Furthermore, Stein believed that the formulation of a verbal equivalent of observation is an essential aspect of the process of observation. No doubt Stein derived this pragmatic belief from her former teacher, William James, who also considered practice and result to be aspects of a single, integral process. Because she accepted this aspect of James's pragmatism, Stein saw writing not as the product of observation at a distance, but as a concrete experience in which she observed, theorized, and composed all at once, in a sort of experiment in which the result, the observation of experimental result, and the reflection on experimental method are aspects of a single process. Thus, Stein's compositions are always and at the same time representational (with respect to their relations to the real world objects and events that moved her to write), presentational (with respect to the process of formulating observations), and self-reflexive (with respect to the acts of creation and observation). Thus,

> Premeditated meditation concerns analysis.
> Now this is a sentence but it might not be.
> Premeditated. That is meditated before meditation.
> Meditation. Means reserved the right to meditate.
> Concerns. This cannot be a word in a sentence.
> Because it is not of use in itself.
> Analysis is a womanly word. It means that they discover there
> are laws.[416]

This passage represents the act of meditation, presents the activity of formulating a thought in meditation, and (as self-reflexive) embodies the activity of meditation. It consists of an attempt at analyzing the first sentence or, more exactly, constitutes a demonstration of its inability to be analyzed. That is, in this passage Stein shows that what appears to be the first sentence really is not a sentence. She attempts to make a sentence by developing on the term "premeditated meditation,"—a plausible candidate to describe her method of writing—but she cannot. Then she shows that "concerns" does not denote an entity that exists in itself, but only a relation that links the ideas of premeditated meditation and analysis. And since "concerns" cannot be a word in a sentence, the verbal structure in which it appears cannot be a sentence. The next sentence offers another implausibility through conjoining real words to constitute a remark on a real world. The words state that analysis is a womanly word. However, words are neither manly nor womanly (even though conventions teach us they are). After offering this absurdity in sensible words, Stein proposes another absurdity, that we discover laws by a process of analysis. The absurdity here is that general laws are not real laws. They cannot be laws because to be a law they must apply to a real domain and any real domain contains only actual particulars, not abstract generalities. Only the observation of particulars has importance. But this is an absurdity that is not an absurdity, for through her meditation she discovers something lawful, something regular (perhaps a sentence, as Ulla E. Dydo suggests). This is her premeditated meditation on the impossible phenomenon of premeditated meditation. The phenomenon is impossible because language is essential to observation and to meditation. But a meditation on an impossible form of meditation is itself a meditation—and, in fact, is an instance of that impossible form.

In shifting among representation, presentation, and self-reflexivity, Stein imitates and extends the method of the Cubists, whose works occupy a similarly complex space that spans both representation and self-reflexive construction. Of all Stein's writings, it is *How to Write* that slips from representation to presentation, from presentation to self-reflexive construction, and from self-reflexive construction to representation most frequently. But Stan Brakhage's films have a similarly plural character, for most of the visual forms that appear in his films, whether photographed or hand-painted, refer to some real world experience that prompts them, reactivate the energies that are the essence of that experience, and are self-reflexive inasmuch as they acknowledge their status as both representations and objects.

Neither Stein's work nor Brakhage's presents its maker as a full personality.[417] Rather they present their makers primarily as perceiving, that is to say, world-forming, consciousnesses. Their meditations are exercises in vision, worked out in their respective media, that refine and develop the vision that inspires them to compose an equivalent to it (an equivalent that, to be sure, undergoes change in the compositional process). The refinement and development of particular perceptions in a specific work, and more generally of the perceptual faculties in the artist's practice of his or her vocation, enables the artist to discover ordinarily unseen depths in quotidian reality. Brakhage and Stein share these notions about the value of art and artmaking—if Brakhage's beliefs on these matters differ in any way from Stein's, it is only insofar as he holds them more tenaciously, more passionately, and asserts them more forcefully in his lectures on art and artists. Jamesian influences on both give their work a phenomenological cast.[418]

But there is more to it than that. We can get at the additional something that needs saying by considering a remarkable discovery that William James made through introspection. Like Hume, James looked within, searching for the central, active self, only to find that

> *Whenever my introspective glance succeeds in turning round quickly enough to catch one of these manifestations of spontaneity in the act, all it can ever feel distinctly is some bodily process, for the most part taking place within the head* . . . the acts of attending, assenting, negating, making an effort, are felt as movements of something in the head . . . I cannot think in visual terms . . . without feeling a fluctuating play of pressures, convergences, divergences, and accommodations in my eyeballs. . . . In consenting and negating . . . the opening and closing of the glottis play a great role. . . . In a sense, then, it may be truly said that . . . *the "Self of selves," when carefully examined, is found to consist mainly of the collection of these peculiar motions in the head or between the head and the throat.*[419]

James asserts, then, that the only experience of the self available in experience is in the experience of embodiment; the body thus carries the burden of anxiety. Both Brakhage and Stein, in true Jamesian manner, represent "pure experience" as the primary—indeed as the *sole*—reality. So, they seem to be idealists (of some sort). Nonetheless, the experiences they portray are always seen as belonging to a body—though this body be the autoscopic body, that is, the internally sensed, proprioceptive self, the corporeal self that senses itself inwardly, to which all that one experiences belongs. The most prominent quality of Brakhage's film style, the assertive physicality of Brakhage's camera handling, constantly suggests that all that we experience in his films is a projection of the proprioceptive body. Thus it is that the proprioceptive body is what allows us to apprehend the unified forms of Brakhage's films; the performative dimension of Brakhage's films suggest the struggle to make contact with the proprioceptive body, to access the resources for forging a unified formed for his film.[420]

Stanzas in Meditation, more than any other work by Stein, conveys the struggle to make contact with the proprioceptive body, in order to access the resources for forging a unified form *Stanzas in Meditation* also shows more completely than any of Stein's other writings the capacity of meditation to engender a highly focused, highly individuated perception of ordinary objects. Ulla E. Dydo comments:

> Throughout the *Stanzas [in Meditation]*, which are filled with commonplace
> troubles and ordinary daily life, she attempts always to say what she sees, to
> state what is what and who is who in situations where everything is mixed
> up and where one is not always one but sometimes two and sometimes three
> and sometimes nothing. It is at times as if the stanzas hovered on the border
> of a no-man's-land where words become inaccessible and where identity dis-
> solves and the visible world disappears from sight and from words. Disem-
> bodied and abstract kaleidoscopic patterns, her stanzas sometimes appear cut
> loose from the referential world. Yet these disembodied stanzas always begin
> with the events and objects of daily life. The process of meditation removes
> words from immediate referential connection with private experience only in
> order to make them speak their meaning more absolutely.[421]

Stein herself has provided confirmation of Ulla Dydo's hypothesis about the
role that common, ordinary objects and events had in inspiring the *Stanzas
in Meditation*, for in the *Autobiography of Alice B. Toklas* (composed within
months of the *Stanzas in Meditation*) she offered this description of the state
of mind in which she composed the *Stanzas*:

> She began at this time to describe landscape as if anything she saw was a
> natural phenomenon, a thing existent in itself, ... I am trying to be as
> commonplace as I can be, she used to say to me. And then sometimes a lit-
> tle worried, it is not too commonplace. The last thing that she had finished,
> Stanzas of Meditation, and which I am now typewriting, she considers her
> real achievement of the commonplace.[422]

As it is with Stein, so it is with Brakhage. Like Stein, Brakhage takes special interest in objects that are, at once, both typical and unique. He strives
to see typical objects in their unique particularity. He tries to see them
freshly, as though discovering them for the first time. This accounts for his
interest in the mode of perception characteristic of early childhood, when
one encounters each object as "an adventure of perception."[423] Furthermore,
Brakhage's way of conveying vivified perceptions of ordinary objects resembles Stein's, for in order to dynamize the forms he uses as equivalents of
percepts, Brakhage loosens the relation between visual forms and their
models, just as Stein loosened the relation between words and things. Stein
accomplished this by refusing to use the words that habit provides (the conventional words we use to describe an object), and by refusing to link words
into conventional syntagmatic patterns. Conventional syntax follows its own
laws for succession in presentation, and these laws are incompatible with the
order in which phenomena present themselves in consciousness. Grammar,
Stein avers, lies with the writer's (or speaker's) power, a view implicit in the
anti-Platonic, and generally anti-transcendentalist, thrust of postmodernist
writing, which does not consent to the modern/modernist belief that rational
structures are eternal, and that artists improve as they understand these
eternal forms more clearly and realize them with greater fidelity; grammar

lies within the province of the living, and it must be integral with living.[424] Readers and writers are responsible for the codes that govern language, not some eternal law, given from on high. Stein states the argument for using unconventional syntagmatic constructions and asyntax in *Tender Buttons*: "A sentence is a vagueness that is violence is authority and a mission and stumbling and also certainly a prison."[425] On the basis of the comments Brakhage makes at the beginning of *Metaphors on Vision*, one could surmise that Brakhage would agree entirely, even down to the manner in which Stein formulated it (for the dehierarchalized structure of this sentence, in which no part is subordinate to any other, imitates the manner in which objects appear in consciousness).

Stein does not distinguish between reality and reality-in-the-moment—and that she does not draw the distinction implies her acceptance of that position which Leonard B. Meyer calls "radical empiricism." The identity between those two terms explains why she must contrive syntax that breaks with the conventional linear order of presentation. Stein's use of repetition, like her use of syntagmatic disaffiliation, has the purpose of capturing the flux of reality, for her repetitions insistently re-enact, as consciousness does, the perpetual reformation of noetic-noematic structures that reveal consciousness to be a function prior to objective experience and reveal conscious process to be as James believed them to be, i.e., "subjective and objective both at once" and "entirely impersonal . . . pure experience."[426] Like Hume before him, James conducted experiments in introspection that led him to reject any egological conception of consciousness and to formulate a notion of the self remarkably like that of Hume's radical empiricism.

> [C]onsciousness . . . can be fully described without supposing any other agent than a succession of perishing thoughts, endowed with the functions of appropriation and rejection, and of which some can know and appropriate or reject objects already known, appropriated, or rejected by the rest.[427]

The self of William James's philosophy is also the self of Stein and Brakhage's practice; for in the works of both artists we feel the process of identification with a fluxing perceptual reality to be so complete that the continual coming-on of novelty involves the moment-by-moment eradication of the existing self and the constitution of a new self.

Stein's manner of systematically dashing expectation until expectations arise no longer relates to her efforts at syntagmatic disaffiliation and syntactic defamiliarization, at revivifying experience by casting it in a startlingly new manner. What is special about the syntactical forms that Stein creates is that they are not based strictly on the material order of language, as so many modernist forms are, but on the experiential process (though we must admit this process itself relates to the material through which the experience comes to be) and on the phenomenal, phantasmagoric effects of language's material powers. The syntagmatic disaffiliation that characterizes Stein's verbal constructions both evokes and reflects a sense of the shifting, unstable, labile self. According to the theory of consciousness that William James expounded, the self continually arises anew, with its changing objects (since consciousness is defined by its object). Stein's work shares in this sense of the self as labile (while Brakhage's use of what I have termed perpetually regenerating forms conveys a similar sense of the self). In Stein's work it is evoked by parataxis, diversity, and, especially, amphibolous anacoluthon. Here is an example of Stein's use of diversity for this end: "Startling a starving husband is not disagreeable. The reason that nothing is hidden is that there is no suggestion of silence. No song is sad."[428]

The artistic constructions Stein and Brakhage have created evoke a sense of the self as undergoing continual transformation; and for both (as for James) the body becomes the real nucleus of individual being since, as the forms they use make evident, there is no stable ego underlying experience (or, if there is one, it is a very sparse self and anyway hardly apprehensible). Accordingly, the passage just cited "means" not so much through its material construction, nor through the self-reflexivity of its form (for it is only marginally self-reflexive), but through its phenomenological effects—effects that depend ultimately on the passage's somatic effects. Most of Brakhage's films exhibit a similar tension between the use of cinematic representations as conveyors of subjective reality and as material forms. Furthermore, any Brakhage film furnishes examples of his Steinian avoidance of the visual representations that we conventionally use to depict an event or situation, but his use of animal images in *Thigh Line Lyre Triangular* provides a splendid example of reaching beyond conventional representations to render the mental impact of seeing a child being born. His use of flattened space, anamorphosis, and overpainting in that film contributes to the same end. His use of juxtaposition (and even, at times, of associational montage) loosens the conventional relations between objects by overlaying the system of representation that typifies the classic realist text with another that engenders experiences of how the mind recasts objects and events so that they might be perceived as though for the first time. In short, he uses these defamiliarizing devices to construct equivalents for fresh and vital experience.

Furthermore, Brakhage's style involves paratactical, non-hierarchical modes of construction similar to Stein's. And like Stein's, Brakhage's paratactical style refuses to distinguish among the types of phenomena within consciousness; all are, simply, phantasmagoric.[429] *Dog Star Man*, just to take the most famous example, presents memories, perceptions, imaginings, and hypnagogic forms making no distinctions in type among them. As that film illustrates, Brakhage uses repetition in a Steinian fashion, to formulate structures in which all the elements have equal importance. Brakhage's paratactical style, a form of "starting again and again," and his agrammaticism generally, sometimes become so extreme that passages in his film seem to be examples of what Jakobson described as a contiguity disorder, a type of aphasia that results in producing "heaps of words/images," or what we colloquially call a "word salad." Thus, detractors commonly condemn Brakhage's films for being "a jumble of images." The combined effect of these devices is that Brakhage's films, like Stein's writings, convey a sense of consciousness as being the product of a process of continual self-appropriation—i.e., they convey the activities of a consciousness that is never self-identical between any two distinct moments, but nevertheless engages in continually appropriating the new for itself; they convey, that is to say, a pulse of consciousness that, though it surpasses itself anew with every new instant, claims each new pulse for its own and reconciles it to a stream which, by virtue of a prethematic relation to a singular body, apprehends the identity that pervades this flux. And just as *Stanzas in Meditation* carry these features of Stein's writing to their most fully developed form, so the *Visions in Meditation* present Brakhage's fullest achievement in this area.

The Romanticism of Brakhage's Conception of Meaning

Brakhage's artistic beliefs valorize the image. His concept of imagination is that of the Romantics: the imagination is the faculty that gives birth to images; it is also, as Kant's philosophy intimated, a faculty responsible for shaping the world with which we are acquainted. Romantic philosophers subsequently developed Kant's analysis of the imagination's creative role in perception into systems which proposed that the imagination is cosmogenetic, and that is an idea which, as *Dog Star Man* so vividly shows, Brakhage took up. The imagination's cosmogenetic role develops out of the nature of the image and the form of cognition by which, Romantic philosophers (and subsequently, Romantic artists) believed, we apprehend images. We grasp an image, they suggested, through an immediate, intuitive, non-rational act. No distance separates the knowing subject from the object of knowledge in such acts of immediate intuition, for this form of cognition effects an identification of the subject and the object of knowledge (while reason, to the contrary, opens up a distance between the subject and object). So the visionary experience is important in that vast, difficult complex of ideas that we call Romanticism, but it is equally true that the Romantics modeled their notion of Imagination, as the divine-like faculty in humans, on the faculty of sight.

That the Romantics prized vision above language, and that they exhibited a massive scepticism about the effects on human consciousness of acquiring language, are also true.

Brakhage expounds similar Romantic ideas. Yet despite his valorization of the role of the image, the doctrines that are the provenance of Brakhage's poetics are teachings that identify poetry with music—teachings that are both venerable and persuasive. Pseudo-Longinus (212-273) was the first to identify and announce the central tenets of this position:

> We hold, then, that composition, which is a kind of melody in words— words which are part of man's nature and reach not his ears only but his very soul—stirring as it does myriad ideas of words, thoughts, things, beauty, melody, all of which are born and bred in us; while, moreover, by the blending of its own manifold tones it brings into the hearts of the bystanders the speaker's actual emotion so that all who hear him share in it, and by piling phrase on phrase builds up one majestic whole—we hold, I say, that by these very means it casts a spell on us and always turns *our* thoughts towards what is majestic and dignified and sublime and all else that it embraces, winning a complete mastery over our minds.[430]

Though seminal, the passage is not without its difficulties. Its primary *hiatus* is its failure to address music's structural properties. Commentators on music and art since Boethius have attempted to rectify this failure by distinguishing two aspects of the aesthetics of music. The first, which Boethius called *musica mundana*, deals with musical structure and has little concern with the effects that sounds have on the listener. The other, Boethius's *musica humana*, concerns the psychological and moral effects of hearing music and has little concern with music's formal and material basis. The one branch of musical aesthetics concentrates on the structure of musical works (or of works of art generally), the other on their effects. Because they are complementary domains of inquiry throughout the history of aesthetics, these two viewpoints have alternated with one another.

The distinction separates two concerns: structure and effect. The distinction has been very fruitful in the field of musical aesthetics; on the other hand, developing an aesthetic of poetry that separates structure and effect has calamitous consequences, for it makes it difficult to discern how the two interact. The interaction of structure and meaning (effect) in poetry has great importance. The propositions that sound is the material of poetry and that, in literary language, the properties inherent in sound and the manner of their organization carry the work's meaning help to bridge the gap that separates the two aesthetic domains.

The means of organizing musical sounds into unified structures are well understood—at least as well as any process involved in making art is understood—partly because composers have worked on the issue for centuries, partly because music is such a pure medium (the basic components of films, viz., photographs, on the other hand are denotational), and, perhaps, partly because music theorists have been quicker to understand these matters than theorists working on other media. Or it may be the fact that sound seems to be an internal sense that has made the inquiry into musical structure more pressing—certainly sometimes it seems that sound has the capacity both to reflect and to influence the soul's dynamics. Wordsworth offered a poetic version of something like that last proposition:

> ... And a Spirit aerial
> Informs the cell of Hearing, dark and blind;
> Intricate labyrinth, more dread for thought
> To enter than oracular cave;
> Strict passage, through which sighs are brought,
> And whispers for the heart, their slave;
> And shrieks, that revel in abuse
> Of shivering flesh; and warbled air,
> Whose piercing sweetness can unloose
> The chains of frenzy, or entice a smile
> Into the ambush of despair ... [431]

The passage is from Wordsworth's "On the Power of Sound"; I have quoted it at some length here to dispel the belief that Romantics celebrated vision above hearing.

At the same time, the Romantics rendered their description of many of their epiphanic experiences in aural terms. The eye seems to give way to the ear in moments of heightened experience. Thus, Wordsworth's description of that intense moment in which he heard

> ... the roar of waters, torrents, streams
> Innumerable, roaring with one voice!
> Heard over earth and sea, and, in that hour,
> For so it seemed, felt by the starry heavens.[432]

attributes to hearing the status of a sense receptive to cosmic harmonies. Blake's "London" shifts its descriptors from the visual to the aural realm as the experience that the poem describes becomes more elevated,

> How the Chimney-sweeper's cry
> Every black'ning Church appalls;
> And the hapless Soldier's sigh
> Runs in blood down Palace walls.[433]

The verse calls upon synaesthetic process: the misery of the chimney-sweeper's cry and the hapless soldier's sigh turn to soot and blood as they strike the church and palace walls. Nevertheless, the simplest way to understand the transformation in perceptual modality, and the way most consistent

298 The Films of Stan Brakhage

with the ontological commitments of the tradition to which it belongs, is to think of the emotion as an energy (or even as a vibratory power) that condenses into different forms as they variously impinge on other bodies, including, most importantly, the sensory organs, but other real objects as well. Their wave motions excite activities in the bodies they strike that manifest themselves as soot and blood.

The crucial matter is to consider the cry as an expression of the same power that produces the soot on the blackening church, and the sigh as an expression of the same power that "runs in blood down Palace walls." The chimney-sweeper's misery—indeed, his very being—is so wrapped up with the soot on the church wall that we can well refer to this blackness as the form of his life. (By associating the blackness on the church wall with blood, Blake relates that horror of the chimney-sweeper's life with the institutionalized religions that worshipped Urizen instead of Jesus.) Similarly, the blood on the palace wall (blood that has flowed because of the monarch's antidemocratic edicts) is the form of the soldier's life—the form of his being. Thus, Blake associates the forms that lives assume with this animating force; the power that produces the soot on the blackening church also creates the forms that humans' lives assume. And this power resembles emotion.

Further support for our conjecture concerning the powers Romantics believed sound to have can be found in the German Romantics' belief that music is the highest form of poetry. Schopenhauer, in his most famous remark, that "music expresses in an exceedingly universal language, in a homogeneous material, that is, in mere tones, and with the greatest distinctness and truth, the inner being, the in-itself, of the world," declares his conviction that music conveys as no other art can the striving of the Will, and "the Will" is Schopenhauer's term for the true reality—for what is "really real" unlike that which the senses present, which is mere appearance.[434] Thus, Schopenhauer avers his belief that sound can elevate our thought so it can apprehend a higher realm. To demonstrate the persistence of the belief that music and sound surpass the image in conveying the noumenal, here is a passage from W.H. Auden's "The Composer":

> All the others translate: the painter sketches
> A visible world to love or reject;
> Rummaging into his living, the poet fetches
> The images out that hurt and connect,
>
> From Life to Art by painstaking adaption,
> Relying on us to cover the rift;
> Only your notes are pure contraption,
> Only your song is an absolute gift.[435]

The traditional view of poetry and rhetoric had held their virtue to be the product of an intricate interpenetration of *melos*, *opsis*, and *lexis*. The Romantic views that I have been discussing cede a privileged place to *melos* or, at least, to sound. We can find the reason for their doing so in their conviction that the power of the word resides in its sounding properties.

Brakhage has offered similar views: contrary to contemporary taste and fashion, and far removed from his celebration of Stein and Olson, Brakhage has recently lauded the poetry of Alfred Lord Tennyson. Though he has not articulated the reasons for admiring Tennyson's verse so, we might assume the reason that Tennyson's poetry appeals to Brakhage is that he finds in Tennyson's poetry a similar aesthetic principle as undergirds his own film-making. And Tennyson (*pace* Northrop Frye) is an essentially musical poet.

We can see now why Brakhage would take Olson's assertion "of rhythm is image" so literally.[436] The next line in Olson's poetically expressed declaration, "of image is knowing," Brakhage takes as stating ideas similar to those we discussed in relation to the fragment from Blake—that the realm of visible phenomena, brought forth by the power of rhythm/sound, provides the clearest manifestation of the creative powers that bring them into being, and afford us our primary means of access to them. The Scholastics averred that knowledge involves a conformity of the intellect to the object of knowledge. Brakhage revises this conception of the relation between language and reality so as to have it suggest that for poetic language (at least), truth depends upon perluctionary effect (rather than conformity to represented fact). Thus Brakhage insists that Olson, in this famous pronouncement, used the word "construct" as a verb form (i.e., that knowledge is process) because it must convey a process if it is to conform to, and reawaken, the experience of its object—an experience which is as dynamic as the vibratory powers of sound/rhythm. Behind this claim lies the conviction that for a poetic construction to have poetic truth, it must not simply represent the energies and powers of reality—in fact, such representational concerns are not properly part of the task and, moreover, likely have a deleterious effect—but must impart them to the reader/viewer; and to impart them to the reader/viewer, it must contain those actual energies in its own material forms.

Thus, reality has the nature of energy, and sound evidences reality's essentially ludic character. Brakhage has stated another, perhaps competing, belief—that light is the character of ultimate reality. Following Hollis Frampton, who used the text in the third section of *Zorn's Lemma*, Brakhage has cited the work of Robert Grosseteste (1168-1253), the bishop/philosopher for whom "the form and perfection of all things is light," as he stated in "The Ingression of Forms." Quotations from, and references to, this work appear several times in the canon of avant-grade films, partly because of the force of Frampton and Brakhage's reputations, and partly because it expounds an emanationist metaphysical principle that filmmakers easily find attractive, according to which Light is the first principle of being. Brakhage used a similar statement in his note for *The Text of Light*, attributing to John Scotus Erigena, a ninth-century philosopher whom students are said to have murdered with their pens while he was lecturing, (and which Pound also quotes several times in the *Cantos*, attributing it "John the Oirishman"): *"omnia quae sunt lumina sunt* [all things that are, are light]."[437] And the privilege that Brakhage sometimes accords film depends upon the close relation that the film has with what he senses might be ultimately real—viz., light.

The idea that sound constitutes ultimate reality and that reality is light are not really as opposed as they seem, prima facie, to be. For light, like sound, is an oscillatory energy, a wave power and wave energy. Because they are vibratory energy, they have a close relation with the body and with the emotions; and this vibratory energy is the object of true knowledge, according to Robert Grosseteste, Richard St. Victor (?-1173), the great Scottish mystic and scholastic philosopher, and others who have expounded a light-metaphysics (as well according to those, like Stan Brakhage and Jack Chambers, who, if only for affective reasons, have embraced the fundamental principles of light-metaphysics). At times, Brakhage, like Williams and Merleau-Ponty, speaks of this energy as being revealed, directly and immediately, through sensation—indeed as the object that is apprehended through the most basic, and therefore most reliable sort of cognition; at times he speaks of this energy as though it were sound (consider his *Musicworks* comments on Olson and Stein) and at other times he refers to it as light. The crux of the matter, though, is that for primordial awareness, sight, sound, and touch are not differentiated—they are all energies alike. This primordial awareness is what Brakhage seeks to impart, and the visual/verbal equivalents he creates to convey these experiences, though they are formed in the terms of the various sensory modalities, are all compromise formations. The underlying primordial sensation, like the underlying primordial reality, is neither specifically aural, nor specifically visual, nor specifically tactile, but something prior to all these modalities.[438]

Though Brakhage concurs with Olson that knowing is "of image," I believe that, again like Blake, Brakhage would hold that the sort of human experience that this knowledge is closest to—closest both as a cognitive faculty and as an object of knowledge—is emotion, or, just for that reason, that it is feeling that comes closest to informing us about this ever-changing reality that primordial awareness discloses. Furthermore, because this primordial form of cognition has a self-reflexive structure—it is (e)motion in the viewer/reader apprehending (e)motion in so-called external reality—it bridges the rift that Western epistemology has erected between the knowing agent and the object of knowledge.

Brakhage's interest in primordial awareness explains his famous insistence that real knowledge is preverbal. His claims regarding primordial awareness resemble those of such early modernist dancers as Isadora Duncan; this co-incidence of beliefs alone should indicate how corporeal primordial awareness is. The conformity of rhythm and feeling makes sound and movement the clearest manifestations of this reality.[439] If our knowledge is primarily "of rhythm," it is because, as Blake's verse about the chimney-sweeper suggests, the objects and events that we see are manifestations of an underlying power whose nature is rhythm; all rhythmic and aural phenomena are modalities of an underlying power that sensation, among all the human faculties, most readily comprehends. The point is really epistemological, not metaphysical—it concerns what humans can know about the reality's expression of itself, and not about the fundamental nature of reality. In this regard, the famous poetic declaration that Olson offered in "Equal, That Is, to the Real Itself"—"of rhythm is image/ of image is knowing/ of knowing there is/ a construct"—as Brakhage interprets it, resembles Spinoza's famous distinction between substance and attributes. If Gilles Deleuze's book *Expressionism in Philosophy: Spinoza* is right (and I believe that some elements of it are) then Spinoza's conception of substance is not so very different from Brakhage's conception of reality.

> [T]his triad occupies the whole concluding section of Part One of the *Ethics*. It takes the following form: the essence of substance as an absolutely infinite power of existing; substance as *ens realissimum* existing of itself; a capacity to be affected in an *infinity of ways*, corresponding to this power, and necessarily exercised in affections of which substance is itself the active cause.... [M]odes themselves present us with the following triad: a mode's essence as a power; an existing mode defined by its quantity of reality or perfection; the capacity to be affected in a *great number* of ways.[440]

Or, perhaps even more similar to Brakhage's mode of thinking is the comment Deleuze offers in *Spinoza: Practical Philosophy* concerning Spinoza's identification of God with infinite power (*potentia*): "All *potentia* is act, active and actual. The identity of power and action is explained by the following: all power is inseparable from a capacity for being affected, and this capacity for being affected is constantly and necessarily filled by affections that realize it."[441] Brakhage could well agree with Spinoza's claim (so beloved by Deleuze that he founds his entire interpretation of Spinoza on it) that the power to act and to be acted upon defines reality—that all power is "act, active, and actual," so that, in the end, the terms "the act," "the active," and "the actual" are co-extensive. Perhaps this explains Brakhage's frequently expressed admiration for the writings of Spinoza (an admiration that Gertrude Stein shared)—which, considering the mathematical form that Spinoza uses to prove his beliefs, and Brakhage's general distaste for calculative thinking, is a most unlikely admiration. It is the intimate resemblance between the powers of sound and this dynamic reality that explains why poets like Blake and filmmakers like Brakhage resort to aural terms when they come to describe moments of heightened consciousness.

Stan Brakhage's conception of film, like Stein's poetics, is characterized by a grand ambiguity around the concept of representation. Brakhage sometimes suggests, as he does in the interview with P. Adams Sitney that appears at the beginning of *Metaphors on Vision*, that his films are documentary films—indeed the most truthful documentary films that have ever been made since they admit to the subjectivity that informs them instead of pretending to an unattainable objectivity.[442] They are documentary films because they do what the cinéma-vérité filmmaker Ricky Leacock claimed to be doing—presenting "aspects of the filmmaker's perception of an event." However, because Brakhage's documentaries foreground their first-person point of view as Ricky Leacock's do not—by incorporating "memory images" and hypnagogic forms in his films, Brakhage includes more of the filmmaker's consciousness in his films than Leacock's stylistics allow him to include in his films. Only through their use of the hand-held camera and the odd angles on events that the camera sometimes adopts do Leacock's cinéma-vérité films convey that fact that we are seeing through the film-maker's eyes. Brakhage's films are true documentaries of consciousness for they present the whole truth about what occurs in the visual consciousness of the filmmaker.

Brakhage had antecedents in the Emersonian tradition in American art who asserted that the truthfulness of their works had a basis in the evidence they gave of the artist's personal encounter with reality. Thoreau, for example, complained of documentary that elides the self and vowed to do differently.

> In most books, the *I*, or first person, is omitted; in this it will be retained. . . . We commonly do not remember that it is, after all, always the first person that is speaking. I should not talk so much about myself if there were any body else whom I knew as well. Unfortunately, I am confined to this theme by the narrowness of my experience. Moreover, I, on my side, require of every writer, first or last, a simple and sincere account of his own life, and not merely what he has heard of other men's lives.[443]

Like Thoreau, like Charles Olson, and (as we shall see) like Merleau-Ponty, Brakhage accepts the importance of acknowledging that we live within limits, that limits apply to everyone, that none of us can adopt a vantage point that surveys the universe, nor any vantage point located anywhere but where we actually are—"Limits/ are what any of us/ are inside of," Olson writes in *Maximus* 25. Acknowledging that truth means acknowledging the inevitably perspectival character of our knowledge and perception. Brakhage insists on this with his invariably first-person point of view.

When expounding on the documentary character of his films, Brakhage sometimes seems to imply that his films are mimetic, that the flow of visual forms in film accurately represents the stream of visual representation in consciousness. Yet Brakhage also goes to lengths to disavow any claims that his films are mimetic and, as *The Domain of Aura* (a major, but as yet unpublished, text) makes clear, he opposes the picturing function of representational art, going as far as to propose that it is a potential source of evil (and that, in this regard, representational forms resemble dramatic forms). Of course, if primordial reality is something that no picture can present, then the use of words or pictures to convey ideas about higher things would invite a confusion between these unworthy "stand-in/representatives" and those entities or elements that actually belong to a primordial, preverbal reality, and so would prompt people to believe that they had real knowledge of these higher things when they are acquainted only with these inaccurate and misleading representatives. In fact, much of *The Domain of Aura* offers a critique of "picture" similar to Bergson's commentary on the picture form of perception, and celebrates another mode of awareness akin to what Bergson called intuition. Where it differs from Bergson's analysis is in its extending a point already present in Bergson's thought, which is that intuition resembles our inner awareness of our bodies. Brakhage extends this notion considerably, by arguing that we become aware of all those features of reality that Bergson claimed are disclosed by intuition exactly though developing a profound inner awareness of our bodily states.[444]

Brakhage's commentary in *Musicworks* on Olson's famous pronouncement provides us with a way of reconciling his statements about picturing. Brakhage seems to believe that film embodies the energies—forces clashing rhythmically—that engender whatever we see, whether in nature (as independent of consciousness) or the mind. The rhythms embodied in a work of art engender in consciousness a resemblance (they "exact resemblance to exact resemblance") which is "as exact as a resemblance" can be "exactly as resembling," since the dynamics of consciousness reveal the *process* of the resemblance's coming-into-being[445] "exact resemblance to exact resemblance the exact resemblance as exact as a resemblance, exactly as resembling," as Stein had put it in "If I Told Him: A Completed Portrait of Picasso." Surely many of the films Brakhage has created by applying paint directly, by hand, to the film stock (for example, *The Dante Quartet, Rage Net, Loud Visual Noises, The Glaze of Cathexis,* and *Night Music*) present something equivalent of that field of energy that "exact[s] [a] resemblance the exact resemblance as exact as a resemblance."

These ideas allow us to formulate a more profound understanding of the influences that Pound's metrical innovations had on Brakhage. But before turning to this topic, I must make a more general statement on Pound's importance as a thinker and as a poet. The Western metaphysical tradition has been a dichotomizing one. Its primary approach to the key problems of philosophy has been to draw a distinction between opposing modes of being and assign to one of the modes a greater value and to the other a lesser value; a term's position on a table of opposites determines the value it possesses. The implications of this have not really been adequately worked through, since many of the distinctions can be shown to lead to contradiction.

Ezra Pound, too, tended sometimes to think in terms of opposites: past/present, permanence/change, identity/difference, unity/multiplicity, concept/feeling, abstract/concrete; but the most significant of the oppositions that inform Pound's poetry is the opposition between sensory flux and conceptual fixity. Sometimes, however, Pound aspires to overcome opposition, and to discover unities that will hold these contrasting pairs together in a productive tension.

The dichotomizing tendency of Pound's thought and his habit of seeking for unities both have a provenance in the metaphysical tradition, for they are both fueled by a belief that considers the particulars of manifesting underlying realities to have superior ontological and epistemological value. In Pound's case, both habits of thought were driven, Pound believed, by the desire the ancient mystery cults, such as that at Eleusis, celebrated—to unite the chthonic and the celestial.

The desire to discover the reality underlying illusory particulars exemplifies the traditional side of modernism, the side for which T.S. Eliot (the author of a thesis on F.H. Bradley's metaphysics, it should be remembered) is the paradigm. This desire to discover the reality underlying illusory particulars, the traditional side of modernism, is modernism still under the sway of the Western metaphysical tradition. The other side, the anti-traditionalist celebration of the new, has Stein as its exemplar. It does not wish to create unity; it possesses no totalizing drive—rather it accepts the absolute independence of every existing atom. It is the side of modernism that Leonard B. Meyer characterizes as radical empiricism.

Pound lived and worked at the cusp of a major intellectual transformation, when these totalizing aspirations were at the point of being dismissed. Thus, while a dichotomizing method sometimes restricted his thinking to conventional forms, at other times, he managed to escape the pernicious influence of the Western metaphysical tradition, for he could not accept its devaluation of change, multiplicity, and difference. His thinking strained to hold the tension between a traditional, dichotomizing vision of reality that attributed maximal reality to what perdures beyond change on the one hand and, on the other, a dynamic vision that accepted both change and the irreducibility of existents in a precarious, and often unachievable, stable state. The way Pound thought about permanence and change is instructive: on the one hand, Pound celebrated the dynamism of the present. Vorticism, the movement Pound most conspicuously associated with, had many similarities with Futurism, including an enthusiasm for energy, machines, and the dynamic image. Pound's poetics made a personal aesthetico-ethical edict out of the Vorticist/Futurist slogan "Make it new!" The slogan perhaps makes it seem that Pound attached special value to what is new and so devalued the old; but really he did not. On the other hand, Pound balanced his interest in the contemporaneous with deeply conservative ambitions. He wanted his *Cantos* to be a compendium that collected all that was useful to preserve and relearn from the past. His highly polemical, and aggressively modern critical writing had as a principal purpose the reawakening of interest in Provençal poetry, Guido Calvacanti's writing, the wisdom of Eleusian mystery religions, and Vivaldi's music—in sum, of handing the tradition of great literature, art, and religion down to those who will bother to read him. What Pound meant by "Make it new!" was that artists and writers should recharge the tradition with fresh energy, so it will have impact on the modern mind. What is more, he aspired to create poems that would marshal "a phalanx of particulars"; and not (or at least not always) to create forms that would subsume these particulars in an all-embracing aesthetic totality, but forms that would result from their simple constatation.

The basic tension that charges his poetry is that between the desire to recover and revitalize forms of experience that suppression has vitiated, even extinguished, and the competing desire to break out of outmoded forms of experience so as to experience the immediacy of concrete reality (i.e., sensory flux). This tension strains the *Cantos'* formal unity to near their breaking point. On the one hand, Pound tried to create the great poem of the modern era—its *Pagana Commedia*, as he declared. This form of unity annuls the differences between the fragments that make up the poem; they all become part of the declaration of a modern sensibility. The *Cantos* is also a compendious work, and the form of unity appropriate for the archive that Pound spoke of assembling would have to be much different from that of a *Pagana Commedia*, for it would have to preserve the differences among the fragments. But it was Pound's desire to preserve the truth of the individual fragment (and of the unique quality of each author's manner of stating these truths) that provided his motivation for developing the paratactical forms for which his writing is renowned.

Thus, two antithetical interests compete with one another to determine the form of the *Cantos*. The tension between the two threatens at every turn to break the poem apart. Somehow Pound manages in the main to keep the tension in a state of equilibrium.[446] But when he fails poetically, it is because the disintegrating forces win out. When he fails in his political thinking, on the other hand, it is the forces of integration and of the denial of difference that prevail. This gives evidence that differing impulses drive his making poems and his pamphleteering; the differing impulses in his verbal art and in his political thinking are the basis for separating his enormous failure as an intellectual and his greatness as a poet.[447]

The fundamental tension that charges Pound's poetry—between the desire to accept the realm of particulars in flux (and to establish a direct relation with the energy that drives that flux) and the desire to subsume particulars within a timeless, perfect, unchanging realm—was not unique to his poetry. It animated the writings of several of Pound's contemporaries and successors as well. Stephen Fredman argues, in *The Grounding of American Poetry: Charles Olson and the Emersonian Tradition*, that a related tension is fundamental to the work of the major American modernists and the projectivist poets we discuss in the next chapter. According to Fredman, these poets came up against the fact that American poetry lacks a tradition, since American history begins with a divorce from the European traditions. They have responded to this rupture in two ways, and these two ways we have discovered in Pound's work. The first response is to embrace the unsettling and destructive thrust of the new, to destroy traditional poetic contexts and to create new forms of unity, based on new means, such as collage, that provide their component elements greater degrees of autonomy. The second is to attempt "to ground" their work, to discover the basis of a tradition that will provide a context for their work. They do this by turning to movements and ideas that antedate the West's descent from classical Greece—such as the Eleusian mystery religion that provides the *Cantos* with its basic ground or the Mayan and pre-Socratic cultures that provide one of the foundations for Olson's *The Maximus Poems*. Many American poets have attempted to erect an alterative to the orthodox history of the West—a history that would be of personal, if idiosyncratic, importance, a usable past that would, paradoxically, sustain the poet in his/her rupture from the tradition. This effort is central both to the *Cantos* and *The Maximus Poems*, but the *Cantos* are especially important in this regard, for they depict the suppression of a counter-tradition, based in the Eleusian mysteries and handed down from generation to generation of the enlightened, sometimes flourishing, as it did in the south of France before the Crusades, but usually despised and suppressed by the established religions.

In this regard, Stein is more radical than Pound, for she manages to escape the desire to establish a ground (as Fredman calls for) for American literature. Her commitment is singular—to the new alone. In this regard, Brakhage's work more closely resembles Pound's than Stein's, for like Pound, he attempts to create for himself a usable tradition. This is evident in his writings on film history which, though exquisitely accurate, are nonetheless highly idiosyncratic, in the mode of Williams in *In the American Grain* (cf. Williams on Poe and Brakhage on Méliès).[448]

The ideas, and the methods, of Pound and Stein dominated advanced thinking about literary composition in the 1940s and 1950s. So the next urgent task for poetics was to form a synthesis of what was crucial in the work of each. This task fell to Charles Olson. It is to Olson we therefore must now turn, for he too, as we have intimated so often, had an enormous influence on Stan Brakhage.

Chapter 2

The Conception of the Body in Open Form Poetics and Its Influence on Stan Brakhage's Filmmaking

D.H. Lawrence and the Poetics of Energy

David Herbert Lawrence was many things. One thing he was not was an astute political thinker. Like many great thinkers and artists, he was anything but cosmopolitan—in fact, like many great thinkers and artists he was a provincial, and his thinking displays the best and the worst features of provincialism. He persisted in the foolishness that England was an uptight, anti-sex state long after debauchery had reached, in high places if not among common folk, levels unprecedented since the last days of the Roman Empire. He preached a religion of sexuality and the body that make the worldly-wise giggle. Take a look at some reproductions of his paintings— they are simply ridiculous, not because of the iconography of women with huge bottoms and gigantic, sex-hungry, autochthonic males, nor even because they are so inept as paintings (which they are), but because they are products of a sexual fantasy more unreal than the wet dreams of the most sheltered and socially inept adolescents. Whenever he systematized his ideas and contrasted his beliefs with the ways of the world, he became obnoxious. Worse yet, his emotional make-up was that of a fascist. The phantasms of Pound's distraught and sundered intelligence led him to propose a

---

Notes to Chapter 2 are on pp. 512-31.

mound of hideous claptrap, but when the true self prevailed, his writing was lyrical, serene, charitable, and even wise. Lawrence was just the opposite. He worshipped the *Geist* (see glossary) and lacked humanity. When people of his sort allow the real self to show, the world becomes a worse place. But he was a great novelist, an even greater poet, and an important poetic theorist. Read any college literary magazine from the twenties and thirties or any penny-a-rhymer of the time and compare its language with that of Lawrence's verse and you will get a sense of how revolutionary his verse was. "Bavarian Gentians" is likely the finest Imagist poem—certainly the equal of anything that William Carlos Williams wrote around the same time.

But it is Lawrence the poetic theorist that is of interest in this text. A key to D.H. Lawrence's poetic theory is his insistence that the intense experience of the moment of sheer, immediate presence can restore the broken harmony between the self and the world. This new harmony, Lawrence recognized, would be of a different sort than that which preceded it. The earlier harmony had relied on the belief, basic to the Judaeo-Christian tradition, that there is a purposive force in the world. Lawrence believed that Walt Whitman established the possibility for the ego to embrace the whole of reality and for consciousness to become the creator of the world. Robert Duncan's opinion of Walt Whitman was Lawrence's: "In Whitman there is no ambiguity about the source of *meaning*. It flows from a "Me myself" that exists in the authenticity of the universe."[449] Self exists in the world itself and encompasses it completely.

By 1926 Lawrence had conceived of an open form of poetry, a "poetry of the instant present," a poetry of "the sheer appreciation of the instant moment, life surging itself into utterance at its very well-head."[450] Lawrence had even arrived at the Nietzschean idea that religion, in promising us our rewards in a hereafter, devalued the here and now. Against the teleological conception of history that the Judaeo-Christian tradition espouses, Lawrence argued, "there is no goal. Consciousness is an end in itself. We torture ourselves getting somewhere, and when we get there it is nowhere, for there is nowhere to get to."[451]

Lawrence conceived of reality as dynamic, as "the rapid momentaneous association of things which meet and pass on the for ever incalculable journey of creation: everything left in its own rapid, fluid relationship with the rest of things."[452] Accordingly, Lawrence proposed that "[t]here must be mutation, swifter than iridescence, haste, not rest, come-and-go, not fixity, inconclusiveness, immediacy, the quality of life itself, without dénouement or close."[453] He advocated the use of paratactical forms of construction as a means to achieve such an end; to do so, he contrasted "the modern process of progressive thought" with "the old pagan process of rotary image-thought" in which "Every image fulfills its own little cycle of action and meaning, then is superseded by another image. . . . Every image is a picture-graph, and the connection between the images will be made more or less differently by every reader."[454] He spoke for a poetic form that would be flexible and open, with each new statement following the previous on its own terms. Images would flicker through this verse, suggesting the supreme mutability of reality and the power of change. Lawrence suggested that we attempt to return to earlier ideas of language, on which a word embodies an "existing entity" and so have instrumental, not referential, value. Lawrence praised those of earlier times (and, by implication, of times to come) for believing that words "were things in themselves, realities, gods, *theoi*. And they *did things*."[455]

Lawrence's idea that action was the essence of the new, open form poetry led him to alter, among other features of traditional English poetry, its rhyme forms. Lawrence's rhymes are often hard and anti-literary. In a splendid introduction to an anthology of Lawrence's poems he had assembled, and as a pre-eminent poet writing with an insider's sense of the creative process, Kenneth Rexroth made these comments on Lawrence's rhyme forms:

> His "hard" rhymes, for instance, "quick-kick, rushes-pushes, sheepdip-soft lip, gudgeon-run on." I don't imagine that when Lawrence came to "soft lip" he remembered that bees had always sipped at soft lips and that, as a representative of a new tendency it was up to him to do something about it. I think his mind just moved in regions not covered by the standard associations of standard British rhyme patterns. At the end of his life he was still talking about the old sheep dip, with its steep soft lip of turf, in the village where he was born. Why, once he even rhymed wind and thinned, in the most unaware manner imaginable. That is something that, to the best of my knowledge, has never been done before or since in the British Isles.

Rexroth arrives at a description of the genesis of Lawrence's notion of open form, starting from within the creative process:

> The hard metric, contorted and distorted, and generally banged around, doesn't sound made up, either. Compulsive neurotics like Hopkins and querulous old gentlemen like Bridges made quite an art of metrical eccentricity. You turned an iamb into a trochee here, and an anapest into a hard spondee there, and pretty soon you got something that sounded difficult and tortured and intense. I think Lawrence was simply very sensitive to quantity and to the cadenced pulses of verse. In the back of his head was a stock of sundry standard English verse patterns. He started humming a poem, hu hu hum, hum hum, hu hu hum hu, adjusted it as best might be to the remembered accentual patterns, and let it go at that. I don't think he was unconscious of the new qualities which emerged, but I don't think he went about it deliberately, either.[456]

Rexroth's insight that Lawrence's rhythmic forms developed from his sensitivity to quantity is important. We shall see that it was his concern with quantity in verse that led Olson to reject accentual metre and to develop the idea of Projective Verse—verse whose metres arise from the poet's physiology, as they reflect the flow of breath into and out of the body.

Furthermore, D.H. Lawrence was ordinarily as acutely attuned to the complete reality of the demotic particular as ever William Carlos Williams and Gertrude Stein were. And, like Olson and Brakhage, Lawrence committed himself to bringing us the news of what he knew first-hand. Poems like "Piano" present a concrete situation with such accuracy, particularity, and intensity that it lifts it into the order of an aesthetic transcendental. Lawrence's poetry presents objects as complete, self-sufficient entities existing within a complete, perfect aesthetic order; it does not subsume the individual object in aesthetic structure in any way that lessens its reality. Medieval writers and philosophers pointed out that the beautiful stands forth, luminous in a resplendence of form; but in Lawrence the luminous particular is not beautiful because it participates in divine beauty as medieval thinkers believed—it is resplendent in itself. And while in Surrealist painting, the resplendent appearance of the demotic object often seems a trick, Lawrence's poetry gives us the real thing. So, too, do Brakhage's films. In Brakhage's films, each observed thing is "valued absolutely, totally, beyond time and place, in the minute particular," as Rexroth writes about Lawrence's poem from his Rhine journey with Frieda.[457] *For Marilyn* (1992) even suggests, as Lawrence's poems of the period of the Rhine journey do, that the light of the Holy Sacrament of Marriage illuminates all that the eyes of the seer sees, in much the same way as a devotee brings the god to presence in a statue. For Brakhage, as for Lawrence, the craft of making is identical with the art of vision.

That identity, more than anything else, is responsible for open form. Rexroth, with characteristic brilliance, recognized this fact, and offered the following comments by way of contrasting Lawrence's working methods with those of T.S. Eliot and Charles Baudelaire, who spent long periods in quiescence, producing nothing, but brooding on the substance of their visions:

> Lawrence meditated pen in hand. His contemplation was always active, flowing out in a continuous stream of creativity which he seemed to have been able to open practically every day. He seldom reversed himself, seldom went back to re-work the same manuscript. Instead, he would lay aside a work that dissatisfied him and re-write it all from the beginning. In his poetry he would move about a theme, enveloping it in constantly growing spheres of significance. It is the old antithesis: centrifugal versus centripetal.[458]

No one who is aware of how prolific Brakhage is can fail to be impressed by the speed and spontaneity of his production. His works, like Lawrence's, possess a magnificent vitality that comes from being created at electric speed. More that any other filmmaker's, Brakhage's working methods are centrifugal. Another word for it would be "projective."

Two Crucial Influences on Embodied Poetics: A.N. Whitehead and Maurice Merleau-Ponty

With Whitehead we come to a central figure of our age, but one whose writing style is so dense and so fraught with neologisms that most people know his work only secondhand. This is really a pity, since getting past the challenges is really only a matter of getting over an initial period of discomfort, and when that discomfort has passed, his writing has a marvellous Victorian charm all its own. His metaphysical system is among the most beautiful of modern times. Poets such as Robert Duncan and Charles Olson (1910-70) studied his original texts—Olson, for example, first went to San Francisco to deliver a series of lectures on Whitehead's magnum opus, *Process and Reality* (1929), at Duncan's house.

Both the density and the idiosyncrasy of Whitehead's writing style have created enormous problems for his interpreters as well as many misunderstandings regarding his metaphysical system. Unfortunately, few commentators have attempted to link his metaphysics with the theory of relations he developed in collaboration with Bertrand Russell.[459] Not to make that link, however, is to neglect the synoptic cast of Whitehead's metaphysics, which holds that being is a relation between entities. The central categories of Whitehead's metaphysics—prehension (see glossary), ingression (see glossary), patterning, concrescence (see glossary), mutual sensitivity—are all relational categories. Conversely, his attacks on various forms of ontological reification—on the Aristotelian idea of substance, on the fallacy of misplaced concreteness (see glossary), on the conception of matter as particles that occupy points in space at moments in times—criticize them for being non-relational ideas or for being based on incoherent conceptions of relation. There is a strong Aristotelian strain in Whitehead's philosophy; and one way into the dense web of ideas that Whitehead weaves is to consider what form Aristotle's metaphysics would assume if one were to replace the category of substance with the category of relation.

One side of Whitehead's metaphysics is formed by a set of Heraclitean notions about the world being in a continuous state of flux and the entities that make up the world constantly coming into being and passing away.[460] He argued that the experienced world of stable objects is merely an appearance that belies reality, where all things are transient. According to Whitehead, the universe is made up of what he calls "actual entities" or "actual

occasions" (or, occasionally, "epochal occasions" or "occasions of experience").[461] These "actual entities" (see glossary) are not inert bits of matter but organisms that grow, mature, and perish—in fact, they are the
primary organisms of actuality and the primary unit from which the actual
world (see glossary) is built. In their collective unity, they compose the
evolving universe. The life of each actual entity consists in striving to attain
a specified end or goal, a goal which Whitehead terms the "subjective aim"
of the actual occasion. The subjective aim is the ideal of what an actual entity
could become. Whitehead referred to these ideals or patterns of action which
actual entities or actual occasions are capable of becoming as "ideal objects."
He described them as forms of definiteness that specify the characteristics
of actual entities (and furnish the universe with values). Thus, Whitehead
viewed an entity's process of becoming as one of acquiring definiteness: an
actual entity becomes more definite through its participation in a series of
occasions in which it takes on or rejects various forms of definiteness. By
engaging in such a process, an entity satisfies some of its aims but leaves
others unfulfilled, for in becoming definite, it chooses one goal and sacrifices
others. Thus, Whitehead stated, an actual entity, in becoming itself, solves
the question of what it is to be.[462] More radically, Whitehead asserted a
"principle of process" which identified "how" with "what"—that is, identifies the manner through which an actual entity becomes definite with the
nature of that entity, and conversely, identifies what an identity is with how
that entity came to be.[463] Or, to put the idea otherwise, Whitehead identified
an entity's being with the process through which it comes to be—its being
with its becoming. For an actual entity then (though not for all sorts of
being), process and reality are identical; an actual entity is a "becoming-
ness," Whitehead stated, and not something substantial.[464]

Like almost every great philosopher since Kant, Whitehead opposed
Cartesian metaphysics for depicting subject and object as radically different
sorts of beings. Against that view, Whitehead offered a neutral monism,
according to which all entities possess a common nature. Everything—"matter" and "consciousness" alike—is composed of actual entities. Whitehead
described these actual entities, which themselves are nexûs, societies that
grow, mature, and perish as "drops of experience, complex and interdependent."[465] Whitehead did not intend that remark to imply some sort of panpsychism, but rather that complex societies consist of hierarchies of other
societies composed of hierarchies of further subordinate groups and, of
these, consciousness qualifies only extremely complex societies or nexûs.
Whitehead's monist principles derived not from panpsychism, but from an
evolutionary view of mind that sees consciousness as evolving out of matter.
He believed that we can best explain this evolution by conceiving of actual

entities not as bits of matter like Democritus' atoms, nor as tiny souls like Leibniz's monads, but as units of process that can be linked, in one form of organization, into temporal strands of matter or, in another form of organization, with other complex actual entities to form the route of inheritance of the complex society that we recognize as a conscious soul. These units of process are the final reality, Whitehead says—"There is no going behind actual entities to find anything more real."[466] Whitehead expounded that idea most fully in *Process and Reality*, but he stated the same idea for a more popular audience in *Science and the Modern World*:

> The point to be made for the purpose of the present discussion is that a philosophy of nature as organic [Whitehead claimed that his was an organicist metaphysics] must start at the opposite end to that requisite for a materialistic philosophy. The materialistic starting point is from independently existing substances, matter and mind. [Whitehead believed that both empiricism and rationalism started from this point.] The matter suffers modifications of its external relations of locomotion, and the mind suffers modifications of its contemplated objects. There are, in this materialistic theory, two sorts of independent substances, each qualified by their appropriate passions. The organic starting point is from the analysis of process as the realisation of events disposed in an interlocked community. The event is the unit of things real. The emergent enduring pattern is the stabilisation of the emergent achievement so as to become a fact which retains its identity throughout the process.[467]

Whitehead acknowledged the similarity of some of his ideas with the tenets of Bergson's philosophy in *Science and the Modern World:* there he pointed out that it is an error for which the Ionian thinkers are responsible that we conceive of reality as the succession of instantaneous configurations of matter (or some fundamental material factor) and that the idea of the simple location (see glossary) of instantaneous configurations was what Bergson protested against.[468]

The unity of an actual entity results from "a particular instance of concrescence," that is, a growing together of the remnants of the perishing past to form the vibrant immediacy of novel, present unity. It endures only an instant—the instant of becoming, the instant when it creates itself out of the elements of the perishing past—and then perishes and becomes part of the ever-accumulating past out of which new actual entities can form themselves.

The concrescence of an actual entity occurs in stages, Whitehead suggests. The first phase is a passive moment in which the given past thrusts itself upon the emerging actual entity. The second and later phases are creative, in which the actualizing entity adjusts, integrates, and modifies the data given to it. Simple actual entities merely store the given data; writing about inorganic entities (which are simpler forms of actual entities), Whitehead asserted that they are merely "vehicles for receiving, for storing in a napkin, and for restoring without loss or gain."[469] More complex actual entities engender originality in the supplemental phases (their second and later phases) in order to enjoy integration and unity.

Whitehead believed consciousness to be neither subjective nor objective—or, more precisely, he believed that consciousness does not have exclusively the characteristics that the subject in Cartesian philosophy has, nor simply the characteristics that material has. Consciousness is really both subject and "superject" at once. Any "actual entity is to be conceived both as a subject presiding over its own immediacy of becoming and a superject which is the atomic creature exercising its function of objective immortality."[470] Whitehead's description of any actual entity is two-sided, for he considers any actual entity to have both subjective and superjective features, depending upon how we consider it, rather as Spinoza's modes do. An actual entity is a "subject-superject," Whitehead says, "and neither half of this description can for a moment be lost sight of. . . . '[S]ubject' is always to be construed as an abbreviation of 'subject-superject.' "[471] The superjective character of an actual entity "is the pragmatic value of its specific satisfaction qualifying the transcendent creativity."[472] That is, the subjective character of an actual entity is that of dead data, that belong to the past and function as nexûs of data for subsequent generations of actual entities—data that affect them in their process of concrescence.[473] While the Cartesian and Kantian philosophies accorded primacy to the subject, Whitehead's philosophy construed the "subject" as a superject, an emergent and a posteriori entity, a historical trajectory, and not as something that is simply in-itself and for-itself.

Cartesianism has proved to be the philosophical bogeyman of late modernity—so much so that nearly every major philosopher of the last hundred and fifty years has announced anti-Cartesian doctrines. It should not be surprising, then, that Whitehead would share an anti-Cartesian animus with Merleau-Ponty—pick whichever philosophers of the twentieth century you want, and they, too, would probably all avow anti-Cartesian beliefs. However, Whitehead and Merleau-Ponty do have much in common: for one thing, both were interested in Bergson's thought (Merleau-Ponty makes frequent reference to Bergson in *The Structure of Behavior*); and, for another, both were interested in the body's role in knowledge and believed that the tradition held the role of the senses in too-low esteem. The area where their beliefs on knowledge and the body overlap is worth looking into—both for what that inquiry will tell us about Whitehead's philosophy and for what it will reveal about the poetics of embodiment.[474]

Merleau-Ponty was the paradigmatic philosopher of embodiment. Merleau-Ponty's philosophical endeavours spanned several stages and, because he died young, and suddenly (in 1961 at age fifty-three), his life work was left uncompleted. Merleau-Ponty's first field of study, in the mid-to late-1930s, was phenomenological psychology, which he used principally to attack the neo-Kantianism that was still widespread at the time. Husserl's *Crisis of the European Sciences and Transcendental Phenomenology* first opened the phenomenological alternative to him. He followed this with a study of Husserl's other works, including unpublished papers kept at Louvain; and he engaged in a crucial, formative study of Martin Heidegger's philosophy. His first works, on phenomenological psychology and heavily influenced by Köhler, Koffka, and Wertheimer's gestalt ideas, were *The Structure of Behavior* (1942) and *Phenomenology of Perception* (1945).[475] He then turned to writing on history and politics; only in the late 1950s did he return to issues of perception that had interested him at the outset of his philosophical career. Essays that expound his later philosophy of perception are "Eye and Mind," a major source that appears in a collection of essays entitled *The Primacy of Perception and Other Essays* (1964) and several essays collected under the title *Signs*. One uncompleted philosophical manuscript appeared posthumously, under the title *The Visible and the Invisible*, in 1964, and another, even rougher and more incomplete, *The Prose of the World*, appeared in 1973. Various collections and occasional writings have appeared in English as well.

Merleau-Ponty's most profound thoughts on embodiment appear in his unfinished manuscripts—the posthumous *The Visible and the Invisible*, which collects these unfinished writings, is likely Merleau-Ponty's most important work. This creates much difficulty for those who wish to apprise themselves of Merleau-Ponty's ideas, as his writing style here is somewhat obscure, probably because Merleau-Ponty had not finished working through the issues the manuscripts address. However, the thrust of Merleau-Ponty's argument is undiminished by the wooliness of some of its details. The essay "Eye and Mind" is helpful (among other ways) as a summary statement of some of the principle themes of *The Visible and the Invisible*. That essay starts with the contrast between the scientist's and the painter's relation with the world. Merleau-Ponty states that scientists look on things as from above, while painters immerse themselves, and their viewers, in the world that their paintings put on view. Painters do not present mental representations that pre-exist the work they are painting; rather, painters paint with their bodies, and a person's body mingles with the perceived world. Hence, the self that reveals itself in a painting is "not a self through transparence, like thought, which only thinks its object by assimilating it, by constituting it, by transforming it into thought. It is a self through confusion, narcissism, through inherence of the one who sees in that which he sees."[476] The self, what the self sees, and what the self makes are not distinct from one another. Merleau-Ponty concluded that "the one who sees" inheres in "that which he sees." Mikel Dufrenne, the philosopher who has worked out the most interesting extensions of Merleau-Ponty's ideas expands on the idea of the inherence of "the one who sees" in "that which he sees":

> Merleau-Ponty thinks of the savage in vision according to the Husserlian model of passive synthesis. This vision does not organize the visible, nor does it bestow a meaning upon it or constitute it as readable and express-ible in words. It receives the visible, rising from an invisible that still clings to it; one can say at the very most that vision opens itself to the visible which is given to it. This act of giving is an event in the visual field.[477]

The path Merleau-Ponty followed to reach this conclusion concerning the inherence of "the one who sees" in "that which he sees" was a long one, but the ideas that perception is an active process, that a primordial form of per-ception precedes intentional awareness, and that the "outside spectator" of realist epistemologies is a bankrupt notion were thoughts that Merleau-Ponty propounded right from the beginning of his philosophical career (even in his first book, *The Structure of Behavior*).[478] The idea of there being a pri-mordial form of perception prior to sight came to Merleau-Ponty by way of Heidegger; and at first, in *The Structure of Behavior*, Merleau-Ponty ad-vanced the idea somewhat uncertainly (in a footnote that appears near the end of the text). The idea became central in his later work. In the *Phe-nomenology of Perception*, Merleau-Ponty attacks the prejudices about per-ception that empiricists and intellectuals harbour on the ground that they do not take into account our primordial, pre-reflexive perceptual relation in the world.

Merleau-Ponty takes up in that work a question that had remained unsolved since the time of the English empiricist philosopher John Locke (1632-1704). William Molyneux (1656-98), a Dublin lawyer and member of the English parliament, doubted the empiricists' claim that all knowledge derived from experience; in particular he questioned whether we might not have innate knowledge of space. Molyneux wrote Locke a letter which became quite famous—and which Locke himself found sufficiently interest-ing to insert into the second edition of his *Essay Concerning Human Under-standing*—in which he hypothesized a man who had been blind all his life and who suddenly developed the capacity to see. Molyneux questioned whether "that man's visual perception of space [would] accord with the space that he learned about through touch and movement." Molyneux proposed the ques-tion in a specific form, concerning a child, who had been born blind but who had learned to distinguish, by relying on the sense of touch, between a cube and a sphere made of the same metal "and nighly of the same bigness"—"If the cube and sphere were placed on a table, and the blind child made to see, would he or she be able, before touching the objects, to tell which was the globe and which was the cube?" Molyneux asked. Sighted mobile feelers might have learned from an early age how to correlate the spatial data that the different sensory modalities present and how to form all those impressions into the idea of a single space that is the source of all those different sensory data. But what about the blind man who has just developed sight— does he understand how to correlate the spatial data that comes through sight with the spatial data that comes through touch and movement?

Molyneux's question (as it has come to be called) puzzled philosophers for centuries. Merleau-Ponty suggests that philosophers found it intractable because it overlooked crucial facts about the nature of perception. There is a corporeal form of awareness anterior to the differentiation of the senses, a primary layer of intersensory experience that is primordial. The senses do not require an interpreter to translate experience from one sensory modality to another, exactly because this primordial awareness comprehends all the sensory modalities.[479] Each sense, including touch—a sensory modality Merleau-Ponty considered neglected—contributes to a single, highly textured experience of the world. Such primordial awareness is the awareness of the lived body (*le corps vécu*). It is also the sort of awareness that attracted Ejzenstejn to James Joyce's writings despite the persecution this brought down upon him—he held Joyce's writings to be special because they impart that sort of awareness which Ejzenstejn celebrated in his expositions of his ideas about pathos, ecstasy, and synaesthesia. And experience of the lived body was the sort experience that Bergson made central to his philosophical writings, a fact that accounts for the many similarities one notes between the writings of the two philosophers; like Bergson, Merleau-Ponty argued that the experience of the lived body brought one into closer contact with reality than does spectatorial reasoning.

Furthermore, Merleau-Ponty asserted, the lived body's relation to the world is reciprocal. Like Whitehead, Merleau-Ponty had a profound interest in what he called a "chiasmus" in experience. Merleau-Ponty objected to Sartre's too-sharp distinction between the *pour-soi* (see glossary) and *en-soi* (see glossary)—between the *pour-soi* (for-itself) who in the act of seeing forgets it has a body and becomes an abstract, discorporate consciousness and the *en-soi* (in-itself) that the seer sees as an absolute positivity replete with being. Merleau-Ponty's style of thinking reminds one somewhat of Bergson's, for his purpose in raising an accepted antithesis is usually to discredit it. The problem with Sartre's philosophy, Merleau-Ponty claimed, was that Sartre made the distinction between being and nothingness a knife-cut distinction.[480] Merleau-Ponty considered such ideas in *The Visible and the Invisible* and, against them, he proposed that every perception has a reciprocal structure. ". . . [T]he idea of *chiasm*, that is: every relation with being is *simultaneously* a taking and a being taken, the hold is held, it is *inscribed* and inscribed in the same being that it takes hold of."[481] He elaborated on the chiasmatic structure of experience by commenting on Hegel's famous expression, the *an sich oder für uns* (the in-itself or for-us, as opposed to the for-itself). Merleau-Ponty exfoliated the truth that Hegel's expression encapsulates into the insight that every attempt at grasping things as they are "in themselves" ends by "retiring into oneself" and that every attempt at apprehending things as they are "for us" casts us back into the world of things in themselves.[482] Cognition of self and world are mutually implicated with one another. Knowledge of the world involves knowledge of the knower while knowledge of the knower involves knowing how the world affects the knower.

In both *The Phenomenology of Perception* and *The Visible and the Invisible*, Merleau-Ponty illustrated these ideas with an Escherian example of a person's left hand touching the right while the right hand, the hand being touched, itself touches something else. Merleau-Ponty used the example as the basis for a critique of Sartre. Sartre's phenomenological enterprise had convinced him that to touch and to be touched are radically distinct phenomena that exist on "incommunicable levels."[483] Merleau-Ponty objects.

> I can identify the hand touched as the same one which will in a moment be touching. . . . [I]n this bundle of bones and muscles which my right hand presents to my left, I can anticipate for an instant the integument or incarnation of that other right hand, alive and mobile, which I thrust towards things in order to explore them. The body catches itself from the outside engaged in a cognitive process; it tries to touch itself while being touched, and initiates 'a kind of reflection' which is sufficient to distinguish it from objects.[484]

Merleau-Ponty draws an eidetic and so apodictic conclusion: This is one of the "*structural* characteristics of the body itself"; the body is always and at once subject and object, capable of both "seeing" and "suffering."[485] The apodicity announced here introduces an important modification to Schopenhauer's distinction between two bodies of experience as much as it corrects Sartre's belief that consciousness and its objects belong to different orders of being. It is an essential aspect of our knowledge of our bodies that we are conscious of them as something that can be consciousness, that we sense them as something that can sense. This chiasmatic structure is central to the argument that Merleau-Ponty offers in *The Phenomenology of Perception*, that primary consciousness is incarnate consciousness—that consciousness knows itself first as an embodied subject.[486] A body, whether one's own or another's, is never simply an object among other objects in the world.

Whitehead's neutral monism, his characterization of actual entities as "drops of experience, complex and interdependent," and his conception of experience as exchange have similarities to Merleau-Ponty's theory of embodiment. And both Whitehead's neutral monism and Merleau-Ponty's served the same end—of overcoming the sharp distinction that Western philosophy has maintained since Plato, between the mind that experiences and the objects it experiences. Merleau-Ponty argued that the philosophy of experience must not forget that the philosopher has a body that belongs to the world, a body that puts him or her in immediate contact with being. Merleau-Ponty's archrival, Jean-Paul Sartre, had depicted the interaction of self and other as one of struggle. The other seizes an image of me and takes it as my self; however this image represents me as an *en-soi*, not as a *pour-soi* (as an object in the world, not a subject). Merleau-Ponty criticized this account, claiming that Sartre's commentary neglects important aspects of what occurs in an exchange of regards—it leaves out much of what the other reveals of himself and much of what I reveal of myself to the gaze of the other. Sartre knew only the rivalry between self and other; but, Merleau-Ponty pointed out, there is also the co-functioning of self and other in mutual recognition. The distinction here is not between beings with wholly different ontological features. It is not a distinction between two orders of being—there is no for-itself that is ontologically opposed to an in-itself. Rather, each is simply the obverse of the other; hence the two beings are non-identical, but not ontologically independent. Sartre failed to understand the interrelation of these two realms of experience because his viewpoint was too lofty, Merleau-Ponty alleged.

The intertwining of self and world that occurs in such an exchange of regards characterizes all our relations with the world. All our perceptual experiences open us onto a world that exceeds what our understanding apprehends from its limited, momentary perspective. Still, all knowledge is corporal, for it comes through our bodies' interactions with the flesh of the world. All our knowledge is therefore perspectival. Accordingly, we must not attempt to universalize knowledge. This is a proposition that Olson, too, would expound as the basis for his instruction that humans must learn to live with their limits and to accept the individuality of their experience: in "Against Wisdom as Such" (an open letter to Robert Duncan attacking, explicitly, Duncan's esoteric interests, but, implicitly, the hermeticism that formed the heart of early English modernism), Olson refers to "the third of the civilized pleasures . . . 'Perspective'—which is everywhere and every thing, 'when it is contained.' "[487] Failure to acknowledge the perspectival nature of all awareness splits consciousness from the body, and produces unfortunate claims to universality. This is exactly the dynamic we observe at work in Sartre's thinking, Merleau-Ponty suggested. Sartre's thought is, as Merleau-Ponty accused Descartes's of being, a breviary of thought that wants to remain no longer in the domain of the visible.

But there is no vantage point we can have that is removed so high above the world as the philosophy of Sartre suggests, no panoramic viewpoint, no abstract, disembodied consciousness that is a pure for-itself that can clearly distinguish between being and nothingness, oblivious of the interpenetration of the two. The philosopher is no *kosmostheoros*—a seer whose synoptic purview encompasses the entire universe. Rather the philosopher, like everyone else, explores the world from within its midst. Merleau-Ponty persistently searched out those referential or self-transcending characteristics of consciousness that make experience different from conceptual thought; and he persistently accorded primacy to our perceptual encounters with the world, in preference to the knowledge we have of it.

The consciousness that knows and the world that is known are not identical, any more than the hand that touches and the hand that is touched are identical. The hand that touches always eludes us; or more generally, the body through which we know always escapes us. Just as touching and being touched never exactly coincide, so the body's activity of knowing never brings the body into identity with the objects that it knows. Still, no abyss separates one's body and the flesh of the world. They have a chiasmatic relation, and the relata bound in a chiasmatic relation belong to the same ontological category. That they belong to the same ontological category is what makes it possible to describe our self-reflexive acquaintance with consciousness as the means by which the world comes to knowledge of itself, rather like when hands join across a corporal space they form one organ of experience. We are thus prevented from understanding our relation with the world by our unthematized belief that we observe the world as one peering out a window onto a scene below.

> We have to reject the age-old assumptions that put the body in the world and the seer in the body, or, conversely, the world and the body in the seer as in a box. Where are we to put the limit between the body and the world, since the world is flesh? Where in the body are we to put the seer, since evidently there is in the body only "shadows stuffed with organs," that is, more of the visible? The world seen is not "in" my body, and my body is not "in" the visible world ultimately: as flesh applied to a flesh, the world neither surrounds it nor is surrounded by it. A participation in and kinship with the visible, the vision neither envelops it nor is enveloped by it.[488]

Thus, Merleau-Ponty rejected the tradition of observation and the notion of "the outside spectator." He pointed out that vision unites the seer with the flesh of the world. Vision is an act of a *voyant-visible* [seeing-visible], an act of a seer who belongs to the very realm that he or she sees. Sensibility possesses a reflexive structure, Merleau-Ponty pointed out repeatedly. Space is not something that exists in some Cartesian grid, viewed with a geometer's eye from high above. Space starts with subject. The space we live in is "a space reckoned starting from me as the zero point or degree zero of spatiality. I do not see it according to its exterior envelope; I live in it from the inside; I am immersed in it. After all, the world is all around me, not in front of me."[489]

Dufrenne has considered incisively the implications of Merleau-Ponty's putting into question the idea of the outside observer. In exfoliating those implications, he arrived at ideas concerning language and its relation to vision that are remarkably close to Brakhage's.

> Perhaps what one calls "totalizing thought" (la pensée de survol) is the vocation of thinking, whenever the subject stands at a distance with respect to the object in order to become its "master and possessor." This is precisely the purpose of language whenever it allows for the passage from presence to representation. This thought is, however, never fully realized, as it is always sustained by perceptual faith that anchors us in the truth of the sensuous. The eye, said Breton, exists in a savage state, and it may be that it is never completely tamed, even when it is employed by understanding; no more than when vision, instructed by language, becomes the utilitarian and assuring (sécurisante) vision of a prosaic reality.[490]

One could go a good distance towards framing an understanding of Brakhage's film work by considering it the attempt to make evident the "perceptual faith that anchors us in the truth of the sensuous" that underlies all thinking.

Dufrenne also extends Merleau-Ponty's phenomenology of perception by focusing more sharply on the nature of the subject's relation to the world that develops through aesthetic perception

> what the work [of art] says insofar as it speaks, what painting renders visible, as Klee says, and music audible, is also another genesis—one of a world brought about by the genesis of the sensuous. We say a world and not the world because today art forgoes imitating appearances, and perhaps it always has, despite certain catchwords. What it produces is an apparition, thereby revealing the power of appearing. And what appears is what Klee calls the Urbildliche: the upheaval of the sensuous. The aesthetic object, returning perception to its beginning, leads the subject back to presence. But this sensuous [sic] is not meaningless—it is of little importance if the work represents the real or not, for it always opens a world to us and promotes its genesis.[491]

The idea that a work of art manifests its own coming-into-being through the agency of creative energy is not an uncommon idea in twentieth-century art; it is, in fact, the more common reason that twentieth-century artists have wanted to incorporate the process through which a work of art comes into being than the reason that is commonly given, i.e., the desire to foreground the material of which the work is made. In *Spring and All*, his composition that most closely approaches a statement of his aesthetic credo, William Carlos Williams proposed an idea even closer to Dufrenne's. He writes: "we are beginning to discover the truth that in great works of the imagination A CREATIVE FORCE IS SHOWN AT WORK MAKING OBJECTS WHICH ALONE COMPLETE SCIENCE."[492]

Brakhage shares many of Merleau-Ponty's ideas. Dufrenne comments that "[i]t is not the body that gives access to originary being, it is originary being that gives access to the body."[493] Like Merleau-Ponty and Dufrenne, Brakhage maintains that a primordial body awareness precedes the differentiation of the various sensory modalities, and like them he considers such a mode of awareness to be embodiment's great gift. Brakhage's hand-painted films (or, at least, most of those done before 1992, and a few since), attempt to capture moving visual thinking, a kinetic sense of something before it has come to thematized intentional awareness, and are renowned for their extraordinary dynamism and tactility.

These properties are very telling, for Merleau-Ponty characterized primordial perception largely in dynamic and kinaesthetic terms. Dufrenne expanded on this aspect of Merleau-Ponty's work when he claimed that artworks reveal "the power of appearing," and certainly Brakhage's films (consider *Dog Star Man* or most of the painted films done from 1992 onwards) present a world coming-to-appearance, or if not exactly that, then what Spinoza, in *Short Treatise of God, Man and His Well-being*, calls Providence. Merleau-Ponty's hypotheses on primordial awareness of the lived body (*le corps vécu*) go a good way towards elucidating the character of the experience that Brakhage's hand-painted films thematize.

Furthermore, like Merleau-Ponty, Brakhage maintains that vision is the work of something larger than the isolated subject, that vision is an activity of the world that takes place in us and through us. Merleau-Ponty was a deeply Romantic thinker, as Brakhage is a deeply Romantic artist—and the Romantics identified the imagination with the creativity of nature manifesting itself in nature. In doing so they suggested that human subjectivity—or at least human imagination and vision—belong to nature. Ideas about the primordial awareness of the lived body, about revealing "the power of appearing," and about vision belonging to the flesh, and ultimately to the body of nature, inform almost all of Brakhage's filmmaking. For it is not just the films that Brakhage created by applying paint directly, by hand, onto the film's surface that suggest this: and even *Dog Star Man* gives visible form to Merleau-Ponty's assertion that "it is not *I* who sees, not *he* who sees, because an anonymous visibility inhabits both of us, a vision in general, in virtue of that primordial property that belongs to the flesh, being here and now, of radiating everywhere and forever, being an individual, of being also a dimension and a universal."[494]

Like Merleau-Ponty, Brakhage reproaches the philosophers of reflection for the *imago humanis* they bequeathed us, an image that presents the reflecting subject as simply thought; like Merleau-Ponty, he offers in the place of the *imago humanis* of the philosophers of reflection (and most forcefully in *Dog Star Man*) a picture of the subject who is involved in the world, whose vision is the act of the world seeing itself. Like Merleau-Ponty's, Brakhage's comments on seeing and light sometimes sound as though he is describing a mystical flash of all-consuming brilliance. But he is not. Rather his view, like Merleau-Ponty's, suggests an ecstatic decentring of the subject and the recognition that vision, though active, is not the work of the will, but a form of submission to what is given—that when we release our selves we allow the flesh of the world to see itself in us and through us. This conception of vision was fundamental to Brakhage's films from the time he made *Anticipation of the Night* (1958), but he has never presented it with such beauty as in the *Visions in Meditation* series of the early 1990s.

A.N. Whitehead's Project: Reconciling Permanence and Flux

Whitehead used the notions of actual entities and ideal entities to reconcile the notions of permanence and whatever it is that creates our impression of change, for change (*stricto sensu*—change in a concrete entity), Whitehead argued, is impossible—to change, an entity would have to both remain the same (only an entity that preseves all its essential characteristics could be said to endure through change) and become something different (for it would have to assume new characteristics through the change, and so would, according to Whitehead's metaphysics, assume a new identity and become a new entity). There can be no real change to concrete entity, only supersession, Whitehead averred. He realized that a philosophy of creative evolution would be untenable if it is true that (as the old Aristotelian concept of substance has it) that reality is composed of elements that are permanent and maintain their identity throughout all the changes that it undergoes or all the relations into which it enters. Yet, to reject entities in favour of flux, to reject permanence for change (in the modified sense introduced above, of supersession) is to deny the patterns of order in experience. His solution was to propose that the ontologically fundamental reality is process, and that entities (of a sort) emerge from process.[495] The category of entity is not the most fundamental category for ontology because, according to Whitehead's metaphysics, entities derive from process. The entities of Whitehead's metaphysics come into being and pass away; so, Whitehead suggested, there must be something from which they emerge and to which they return.

Furthermore, each existent unifies the multiplicity of the world since, according to Whitehead's philosophy of relation, each element of nature receives its identity from all others. There is in nature no being-in-itself that possesses permanent qualities which it lends to all the relations into which it enters. The universe, as Whitehead's metaphysics presents it, is a network of actual entities, and these actual entities are throbs of feeling that, through making a series of choices, have taken on forms of definiteness. Each of the actual occasions in the network that forms the universe calls upon all the others in order to come into being as the thing it is—that is, in order to acquire its character. Each actual entity is an occasion in the creative process and perishes as soon as it has "expressed itself." But its nature constitutes the basis and establishes the conditions that determine succeeding actual occasions. Hence, the network of relations is active, the nodes of the network are themselves active, and the pattern of the whole changes ceaselessly.

Whitehead's choice of actual entities (or actual occasions) as the ontological basis for his philosophy of organism was really a consequence of his theory of perception (which, as a theory of perception, is a theory concerning relations) that is the true *fundamentum* of his philosophy. His philosophy is one of experience; among the primary tasks he set it was to overcome what he called "the bifurcation of Nature," that is, the Galilean-Lockean distinction between the world of sensations, of colours, sounds, smells, feels, etc., and the colourless, odourless world of scientific abstraction, of particles moving in space and time, the bifurcation of the ontological universe into logical abstractions and material particulars (that Charles Olson, too, protested so vigorously). Right from the beginning of his philosophical work, long before he developed the impressive system of his later years, Whitehead maintained that the classical conception of the material world, with its sharp distinction between entities of three sorts—instants in time, points in space, and particles of matter—could not give an adequate description of change.

The classical way of conceiving the make-up of reality implied that the relation between a particle and a point in space was completely arbitrary; it was the arbitrariness of this relation in particular that perturbed Whitehead about this conception of the world. Whitehead attacked the Newtonian conception of the universe which divides the world into two neat categories, matter and space, as resting on an example of what he termed "The Fallacy of Simple Location." For one thing, Whitehead realized the essential truth that Hume's analysis of causality exfoliated, that nothing in the classical conception of reality allows us to connect two successive instants in any fashion that involves either physical or logical necessity. But, Whitehead pointed out as well, Hume's analysis fails to take into account that no entity is self-determined, that its relations to all other objects determine the nature of any actual object.

One can make similar arguments concerning the "classical concept of the material world," Whitehead proposed. The ontology that undergirds modern physics distinguished three types of entities: points of space, instants of time, and the particles that occupy space and time. The theory is an elegant mathematical abstraction, but it fails as a basis for physics because it cannot provide an adequate account of change. Since fixed points in space cannot change, any account of change that is based on this ontology is going to wind up with an unresolvable duality of unchanging points in space and their changing contents. This duality makes the fact that the particle occupies a certain point in space at a particular instant in time wholly arbitrary—a fact that can be deduced neither from the nature of the particle, nor from the nature of the point, nor from the nature of the instant, nor from any combination of them. Schopenhauer offers the story of a man who finds himself, to his own great astonishment, suddenly existing, after thousands and thousands of years of non-existence; then existing for awhile; and then once again, not existing during an equally long period. By this story, Schopenhauer ridiculed partly the arbitrariness inherent in the ordinary concept of coming-into-being, but more the unfathomability of existence. Whitehead's point of attack was more strictly the arbitrariness of the process of coming-into-existence, but he found this arbitrariness equally unacceptable, for as he explained in *The Concept of Nature*, the ideal of philosophy is "the attainment of some unifying concept which will set in assigned relationships within itself all that there is for knowledge, for feeling, and for emotion."[496]

Whitehead dismissed the Cartesian belief in an existent that requires nothing but itself to exist; to expound his objection to it Whitehead proposed what he called the Principle of Relativity, according to which a change in any entity affects all others. The world simply is not what Bertrand Russell's logical atomism depicts it as being: a heap of separate things as, say, a pile of marbles is. It is, rather, an organically interrelated whole whose constituent relations are internal relations, i.e., relations that determine the nature of its relata (at least insofar as events are concerned, though actual events of course do not affect the Eternal Objects [see glossary] that are ingredient upon their concrescence). Thus Whitehead, in his admirably popular *Science and the Modern World*:

> The theory of the relationship between events at which we have now arrived is based first upon the doctrine that the relatednesses of an event are all internal relations. . . . This internal relatedness is the reason why an event can be found only just where it is and how it is,—that is to say, in just one set of definite relationships. For each relationship enters into the essence of the event; so that, apart from that relationship, the event would not be itself.[497]

Process and Reality reinforces this assertion:

> an actual entity cannot be a member of a 'common world,' except in the sense that the 'common world' is a constituent of its own constitution. It follows that every item in the universe, including all the other actual entities, is a constituent in the constitution of any one actual entity. This conclusion has already been employed under the title of the 'principle of relativity.'[498]

Or again: "We diverge from Descartes by holding that what he has described as primary *attributes* of physical bodies are really the forms of internal relationships *between* actual occasions, and *within* actual occasions." And he continued by encapsulating the fundamental importance of this divergence: "Such a change of thought is the shift from materialism to organism, as the basic idea of physical science."[499]

In opposition to the bifurcation of Nature, Whitehead proposed that philosophy should begin with accepting our experience of the world. Accordingly, his philosophy of organism accepted what he called the subjectivist bias of modern philosophy, i.e., the idea that the universe consists in elements disclosed in subjects' experiences. Whitehead's concept of prehension is fundamental to this dimension of his philosophy. By prehension Whitehead means the grasping by an organism of part of its environment, an apprehension which may or may not be cognitive. The verb "to prehend" actually means both to engulf and to transform; and both meanings are relevant to Whitehead's theory of feeling and perception, for according to that theory, in prehending its environment, an organism takes it over and transmutes it. Whitehead described the soul of anything—and in his philosophy everything, from rocks to trees to humans is ensouled—as a sequence of prehensions, each of which in succession prehends all its predecessors. A prehension involves three factors: the prehending organism; the data it prehends; and the form of the relation between the prehending subject and the prehended data, which Whitehead described as the "subjective form" or the manner in which the subject prehends that data. The prehended data may be of two sorts, actual entities or eternal objects. Whitehead terms prehensions of actual entities "physical prehensions" and prehensions of eternal objects he terms "conceptual prehensions."

However, Whitehead expanded his notion of feeling to cover more than we conventionally refer to by the term. Whitehead's system acknowledges several varieties of feelings. To one category belong what he calls "physical feelings" and these come in two types, simple and complex. Simple physical feelings concern the transmission of energy from one event that belongs to the physical to another. Even the transmission of energies has an experiential aspect in Whitehead's philosophy, for he used the expression "the transference of throbs of emotional energy" to refer to the transference of quanta of energy between events.[500] Whitehead believed that these energies and processes were the prototypes of feelings that more complex organisms have. He went so far as to write, "The key notion, from which [a systematic cosmology] should start, is that the energetic activity considered in physics is the emotional intensity entertained in life."[501] This philosophical principle formed the basis for Whitehead's challenge to the manner of philosophical thinking exemplified both in the Rationalist tradition that stems from Descartes's analysis of the *cogito* and in the Empiricist tradition that stems from Berkeley's exfoliation of the entailments of *esse est percipi*. Whitehead did not do what thinkers of this ilk did, viz., to define subjective reality at the outset (to make attributes of what is generally considered ideal the foundation of their system) and then to go on to describe reality in terms of consciousness, thought, and sensation, thereby making it relative to subjectivity. Instead, Whitehead began his philosophical system by considering reality—both physical reality and mental reality—in terms of enjoyment, feeling, urge, appetite, and yearning. Thus, he took as the starting point for his philosophical system principles that apply to all forms of existence, whether they are the subject matter of physics, physiology, psychology, biology, or ethics—to all entities, ranging from so-called "inert" objects like stones to human beings.

Prehensions are like microcosmic sensations that become macrocosmic perceptions through a process that Whitehead called transmutation. For example, the perception of a table supersedes the prehension of a welter of actual entities through transmutation. If there is an identity of pattern among a series of pure feelings (that is, among the feelings of the individual members of the nexus that makes up an actual entity), then, in the first stage of concrescence, that pattern will be reinforced by reason of being relevant to all the members of the emerging actual entities. Then, in a second stage of transmutation, that pattern becomes the basis of a single conceptual feeling shared by the series of pure physical feelings. In a third phase, this single conceptual feeling becomes established within the context of the nexus (see glossary) as a whole. Whitehead stated that when the external object that characterizes the nexus in a physical feeling characterizes the analogous physical feelings of some or all members of the nexus, "the nexus as a whole derives a character which in some way belongs to its various members."[502] The transmuted physical feeling of the whole nexus substitutes for the several feelings of the various actual entities in the nexus. That is, in our example, the perception of a table substitutes for the prehension of the many actual entities that make up the table.

The concept of prehension serves several roles in Whitehead's philosophy. For one, Whitehead used the concept of prehension to combat the hoary idea of British empiricism, that perception furnishes isolated or separable sensations (the so-called "sense data," or "sensa"). He used the concept, too, to show how embedded in the world consciousness really is. We do not apprehend the world as observers, but as participants. Thus Whitehead's concept of prehension serves a role in overcoming Cartesian dualism.

Whitehead's notion of prehension had considerable influence on many poets and filmmakers who came to intellectual maturity in the 1950s and 1960s. *Maximus III*, 145, reveals that his idea that we do not apprehend the world as observers but as participants was a principal reason for Olson's interest in Whitehead's philosophy. While Whitehead would likely not have endorsed their claim, Olson and many of those to whom he passed down his metaphysical views, also believed that we can get back to "raw feels"— really to the prehension of actual entities. When, for example, Charles Olson considered the possibility of realizing the Emersonian dream of a natural language, a language that will possess "the actual character and structure of the real itself," he wrote as though he longed for a language that can describe prehensions.[503] Or, to take another example, Brakhage's description of our experience of synaptic events shares many features with Whitehead's characterizations of prehension.

Whitehead's analysis of the make-up of reality culminated with the proposition that the basic processes in the physical world are similar to perceptual processes, for the former are simple physical feelings, the latter, complex physical feelings. An important consequence of this proposition is that there is no ontological gulf that separates perceptual processes and physical processes. "[A] simple physical feeling," Whitehead wrote, "is the most primitive type of an act of perception, devoid of consciousness."[504] Or again:

> There is thus an analogy between the transference of energy from particular occasion to particular occasion in physical nature and the transference of affective tone, with its emotional energy, from one occasion to another in any human personality. The object-to-subject structure of human experience is reproduced in physical nature by this vector relation of particular to particular.[505]

Whitehead thus refuted the idea of the bifurcation of Nature that has plagued modern consciousness since the early modern period. His philosophy of organism is a monist theory that maintains that only one basic type of reality exists—process.

Whitehead understood simple physical feeling as a cause that transmits a physical characteristic from a past into the future. A feeling is therefore to be understood as a stream of influence. Whitehead's analysis of physical transmission is pertinent to his theory of experience, for Whitehead claimed that physical organisms respond to their environments in analogous ways to those in which human sensory organs respond. A magnet acting on iron filings or a physical object acting on the eye exerts similar influences. A simple prehension in essence is just the transmission of influence from one event to another. Thus, simple prehensions lack a subjective dimension, while more complex prehensions, simply by virtue of their complexity, do have a subjective dimension. A self or, as Whitehead preferred to call it, a "personal society" emerges in the process of prehension, since a personal society (a self) is no more than a sequence of prehensions, each of which comprehends all of its predecessors. According to Whitehead, then, the soul grows in time. The soul is not an eternal entity which antedates birth, survives death, and remains eternally unchanged, as the Pythagoreans, Plato, the Gnostics, the neo-Platonists, and a variety of later Hermetic sects believed it to be. It is in process. It fluxes.

Beside those societies or nexûs that require only sequence, Whitehead recognized another sort which require extension as well. A collection of things (say marbles) is such a society and so is an individual object (an object, in fact, is a collection of particles unified into a society). Whitehead insisted that all societies possess some qualities of mental phenomena because they are all societies of actual occasions, and every actual occasion is characterized by ardour, yearning, striving after delight. However, non-animal (or at least non-living) societies exhibit no spontaneous behaviour, since the mental desires of their constituent members and the choices they make cancel each other out. Living societies, and especially personal societies, are more highly integrated, and the desires and choices of their constituent members act more in concert, co-operating with each other in a more highly co-ordinated manner.

Whitehead enumerated three factors that determine the nature of a prehension: the subject who prehends; the datum prehended; and the occasion of the experience. He stressed that the affective tone of any prehension derives initially from the datum of the prehension. Thus, Whitehead stresses the objectivity—i.e., the fundamentally physical—origin of experience. One of the most important purposes Whitehead set for his philosophy was to show that the emotional aspects of experience resemble the basic elements of physical experience; his neutral monism and the parallels he draws between simple and complex prehensions help fulfil this purpose.

Whitehead realized that his views about similarity between the elements and processes that constitute natural events and human experience imply that human experience exhibits all the properties that qualify actuality. That realization led him to claim that we can discover much about the nature of the external world by examining one's visceral sensations. That proposition had enormous influence on the generation of poets, painters, and filmmakers that emerged in the 1940s and 1950s.

Whitehead thought of every event (and of every object, which can be understood as a route of events) as a force field with a focal centre from which influence radiates. Whitehead concluded that it followed from this that the proper definition of being is simply power. Every focal centre consists of many overlapping aspects—indeed each quality of every focal centre overlaps aspects of all other events in the universe. This concrescence of aspects of events, this process which unites disparate features in the actual event, is the primary topic of Whitehead's theory of process. Creativity, one of Whitehead's principal topics, presupposes the categories of the many and the one. Whitehead argued that the universe consists at any instant of a disjunctively diverse many, and that these many form a complex unity. In forming a complex unity, the many which disjunctively are the primary constituents of the universe become the actual occasion which is the universe conjunctively. A novel *one* results from this unification or, as Whitehead calls it, this concrescence.

This unity is truly novel in the sense that it is qualitatively distinguishable from and stands over against what has been unified through this concrescence; as Whitehead put it, the many become one and are increased by one. Whitehead thus depicts creativity as the force driving emergent evolution. There could be no genuine novelty if all there were to change was the rearrangement of matter, Whitehead noted; evolution requires organic systems that are capable of selecting and grading elements from their environment— and that, he knew, requires the co-operation of an organism with the multitude of other organisms that constitute its environment. Emergent evolution requires the evolution of structures that act as complex centres of activities, and this is the role that complex societies have in Whitehead's philosophy.

The evolutionary process proceeds by continually generating new forms of novelty, for once the many have become one and been increased by one, there then exists a new diversity, a new many, from which another novel unification may arise. Thus the existence of actual entities is characterized by nearly perpetual perishing, as actual entities lose subjective existence and are transmuted into objects that exert influence on subsequent emergent occasions; or, one could say, considering that the future alone is real (the present being merely actual, and the past an immortal nexus of actualities) that the coming into existence of entities is characterized by a nearly continuous transition in which the merely real is colonized by the actual.

It should be emphasized that this transition is not really continuous (but only nearly so), for time itself is not really a continuum; rather it is—as some contemporary physicists have described it—granular. For if it were continuous, each entity or occasion would have to be perpetually superseding itself. Time, Whitehead claimed, is "epochal," that is, it is not a continuum. Time comes in discrete occasions, each of which (like William James's specious present) has a finite duration.

Creativity drives this supersession, Whitehead proposed. Whitehead describes creativity as a ceaseless activity, or energy, that underlies all emergent occasions. Creativity is responsible for reality being process, for its being characterized by ceaseless change. Creativity is responsible, too, for reality's being a process and for the nearly continuous transition by which the merely real is colonized by the actual. Creativity, through this process by which actual entities lose subjective existence and are transmuted into objects that exert influence on subsequent emergent occasions, brings about an "organic" community of occasions. All process, finally, is creative.

Whitehead's theory of creativity reconciles the many and the one, as well as change (the actual entity) and permanence (the entity transmuted into objective existence in the realm of Eternal Objects).[506] A work of art, too, reconciles unity and diversity and, at least when it is conceived as a kinetic object, it reconciles change and permanence. So it is not surprising that Whitehead's manner of discussing reality as made up of perishing subjective moments that pass into eternal existence should have excited poets such as Charles Olson. For example, Olson made a clear reference to Whitehead's idea of concrescence in "A Later Note on Letter #15" (*The Maximus Poems II*, 79):

> ... the dream being
> self-action with Whitehead's important corollary: that no event
>
> is not penetrated, in intersection or collision with, an eternal
> event
>
>   The poetics of such a situation
> are yet to be found out[507]

That Olson connects the idea of the intersection of the eternal object (permanence) and actual event (change) to the proposition that history's role is to discover the permanent that underlies change, and that he associates the endeavour of the new poetics with a new understanding of the relation between permanence and change, testify to the importance Whitehead had in Olson's life and thought.

But the concepts of permanence and change were not the only pairs of prima facie opposites that Whitehead's philosophy reconciled. Whitehead's conception of creativity reconciled the categories of freedom and determination. For, while Whitehead's philosophy allows that any concrescent occasion experiences objective definition at the hands of other entities, it does not follow from this fact that actual entities lack freedom. For every actual entity is an individual, for its own sake, a *causa sui* (to use that Spinozist phrase); yet at the same time, every actual entity (including God) is transcended by a creativity which it qualifies. Whitehead expended much effort in showing that freedom can be reconciled with science; he wrote of an entity's "self-realization," "self-creation," "self-constitution," "self-completion." These advances, Whitehead insisted, produce a felt response, so Whitehead stated that God's purpose in creative advance is the evocation of intensities. One aspect of Whitehead's reconciliation of freedom and determination depends on a distinction between extrinsic and intrinsic experience. Whitehead argued that every concrescence is internally determined, though externally free.[508] This description of creativity, too, must have appealed to the Projective Poets, for it indicates how we can reconcile the idea that the world internal to a poem is precise, definite, and determinate (since it tolerates no change without being lessened) and, at the same time, is a product of a free creativity—the elements of the poem are internally determined but externally free, in the sense that nothing in the world extrinsic to the poem determines their nature.

But Whitehead offered a more precise description of creativity's ability to reconcile determination and freedom, and this more precise description would too have appealed to the Open Form poets. Whitehead extended his description by introducing the distinction between objective and subjective factors. Whitehead claimed that every concrescence has a subjective aim. The subjective aim of the concrescent actual entity is the ideal of what that subject could become—"ideal" because, were it to be actualized, the maximum ordered complexity would be realized in the world. This is God's mode of operating in the world, for God acts so as to create the kind of world that, when prehended by His consequent nature (that is, the physical prehensions of actual entities in the actual world, which endow God with the nature of a process [see glossary, consequent nature of God]), produces the maximal intensity of satisfaction. Whitehead saw God as the source of an actual entity's subjective aim and the way that God operates in the world. Insofar as we consider the actual entity as a subject that possesses subjective aims, we conceive it as being free, as being limited only by logical possibility. But insofar as we consider the entity in its relation with previous and contemporary actual entities, it is limited and subject to determination, since the available data do not fully prescribe the exact manner that one actual entity prehends other actual entities and Eternal Objects. Whitehead summarized his thoughts on how the concepts of contingency and necessity can be reconciled in the following passage from a more popular work, *Adventures of Ideas*:

> This process of the synthesis of subjective forms ... is not settled by the antecedent fact of the data. For these data in their own separate natures do not carry any regulative principle for their synthesis. The regulative principle is derived from the novel unity which is imposed on them by the novel creature in process of constitution. Thus the immediate occasion from the spontaneity of its own essence must supply the missing determination for the synthesis.... Thus the future of the Universe, though conditioned by the immanence of its past, awaits for its complete determination the spontaneity of the novel individual occasions as in their season they come into being.[509]

If the universe simply produced endless novelty, without regard to any principles of order, the result would be sheer chaos. Whitehead introduced the idea that there are limitations on the novelty the universe creates—both limitations that result from the logic of the relations (or, what is the same, that derive from the Realm of Eternal Objects) and limitations that result from prior conditions. Since the source of order was traditionally understood to be God, Whitehead identifies God with this benevolent principle of limitation. Furthermore, the unity of the Divine ensures the internal consistency of the Realm of Eternal Objects: without the Divine there would be simply "a disjunction of eternal objects unrealized in the temporal world"—by which Whitehead means that the various Eternal Objects (which represent forms of relation that possess the potential, i.e., the logical possibility, for becoming actual)—would be mutually exclusive. It follows, then, that God is the source of novelty as well as the source of order, for His unity establishes the possibility that a variety of Eternal Objects can be realized.

But despite the existence of these limits, creativity involves genuine novelty, for Whitehead asserted the probability of foreseeing that a particular novelty will be evolved is slight, though there can be some non-inductive intuition of this probability (based upon the judgments about the degree of 'intensive relevance' of selected Eternal Objects to the primary physical data of experience).[510] Whitehead's idea that the emergence of the novel occasion involves spontaneity even though, at the same time it is limited—limited both by logical necessity (eternal occasions) and by prior conditions—offered the Projective Poets a valuable model for their aesthetic doctrine, for it showed them how to go about reconciling their recognition that a completed work is necessarily an integrated whole that tolerates no changes to any of its parts with their idea that a poetic form could emerge through spontaneous creativity. They found even more appealing Whitehead's idea that a benevolent principle is the source of order in the universe and guides the process of spontaneous creativity through which novelty emerges, by luring it towards Harmony which is the Good Itself. They would also have been impressed by the way that Whitehead's theory of concrescence ensures that thought and the world have an intimate relation to one another. Whitehead did not embrace the idea, so fundamental to American art and philosophy, of the redemptive potential inherent in awareness of the concrete particular in all its details.[511] Whitehead understood that generalization is a necessary part of knowledge; experience gives us no access to brute fact; the issue abstraction raises, and the criterion of their value, according to Whitehead, is relevance. The philosophers' idea that we must always be able to exchange a generalization for the particular facts that it generalizes is false, because general ideas (represented by Eternal Objects) go into the very constitution of actual events. But when our understanding of some actual occasion involves prehension, the same Eternal Objects that constitute the actual event, our generalizations have relevance to the world.

Whitehead's philosophy of organism proposes that the universe oscillates between the Many and the One—with the points on the path traced out by its oscillations representing various phases in various parts of the universe, thus giving the illusion of an ongoing semi-stable order. However, Whitehead placed his emphasis on the novelty that arises in this creative process. His stress on the creation of the One from the Many, his belief that an event is composed both of the pattern of aspects of all other events integrated into its unity in the "here and now" and of the pattern of influences it exerts on neighbouring events, and his insistence upon the continual coming into being of novelty were among the features of Whitehead's philosophy that appealed to many artists and so merits further comment.

Every metaphysician must answer the question: What are the ultimate categories in terms of which one can construct an adequate account of reality? Whitehead named just three members of what he called the Category of the Ultimate: Creativity, the Many, and the One. "Creativity" is ultimately his word for "process." It is the impulse to enjoy something new, the desire to advance toward something more beautiful. It is formless ardour, pure desire without any specific aim. It is restlessness, curiosity, yearning, but without shape or direction. Whitehead likened creativity to Aristotelian *materia prima* for, he stated, it has no character of its own but is simply the vitality that quickens the universe.

Whitehead realized that just as the Aristotelian *materia prima* was pure potentiality that needs some accident (i.e., quality) to give it form and actualize it, so too that which belongs to his ultimate category, creativity, would also lack actuality unless it possessed some accidental characteristics, or took on features through some accident. Whitehead claimed that creativity's "primordial, non-temporal accident" is God; and by this he meant that God is the form or pattern that the universe strives to embody. Neither is the world a part of God nor is God apart from the world—God and the world are both aspects of the yearning for novelty, the world being the aspect of unformed yearning, of desire without shape or aim, and God being the aim towards which the endless forming and ever anew reforming of the universe strives. The primordial aspect of God comprehends the Realm of Eternal Objects, and Eternal Objects are really forms of definiteness which actual objects can take on (Whitehead refers to them as "transcendent entities," "ideal objects," "ideal forms," "abstract forms," and "possibilities").[512] These are abstract forms or ideal forms because their conceptual recognition does not involve any reference to specific actual entities; they do not require reference to any occasion of experience in order to be understood; any entity whose conceptual recognition involves no necessary reference to any definite, actual entity Whitehead calls "an Eternal Object." The Primordial Nature of God therefore represents the general potentialities of the universe. Because these possibilities are eternal and unchanging, this aspect of God is atemporal and resides in the unchanging Primordial Mind of God. It consists, in short, of the unlimited recognition of the wealth of possibility that arises from the timeless prehension of every eternal object.

Whitehead's philosophy attempts to reconcile permanence and change (or, more strictly, supersession), and the Realm of Eternal Objects is a key notion that Whitehead used to explain permanence. Eternal Objects somewhat resemble Plato's Forms, especially the Forms as Plato described them in his later, and more mathematical, philosophy. For Eternal Objects are unchanging patterns of relations that establish the possibility of concrescence; one might consider Eternal Objects as establishing the logical compatibility (the "consistency and coherence") of certain relata—as showing that such and such a feature can coexist with some other feature in some specified relation. Thus they are "Pure Potentials for the Specific Determination of Fact" or "Forms of Definiteness," as Whitehead describes them in his outline of the Categories of Existence.[513] There are no novel eternal objects since such "logical compossibilities" neither come into existence nor pass away, but are unchanging for all time. And, while they are not themselves actual, they are exemplified in everything that is actual, for no actual entity can exist unless the relations instantiated in its concrescence be possible. Considered in terms of an actual occasion's prehending Eternal Objects, therefore, the process of concrescence involves the selection of which range of possibilities will be actualized. Considered in terms of an actual occasion's prehending other actual entities, prehension is a process of acquiring definiteness, of becoming a stubborn fact with consequences for subsequent emergent entities. Hence, God and the world enjoy a relation of mutual dependence, as Creativity would remain unactualized *potential* if Eternal Objects (which are the primordial aspect of God) did not exist, and God could not exist with any *potential* to actualize.[514]

And at what does creativity aim? Whitehead is unequivocal in his answer: The universe is directed toward the production of Beauty and the evocation of intensities. Whitehead offered this characterization of Beauty in *Adventures of Ideas*: Beauty is the mutual adaptation of the several factors in an occasion of experience, a character that comes into being when the members of a society of occasions conform harmoniously with each other's purposes in a manner that enriches their contrasts. The term "contrast," as Whitehead used it, is a part of his idiolect (see glossary) and refers to the unity that comprises the several diverse components of a complex datum. Whitehead's use of the term can be quite misleading if one does not keep this in mind, for according to Whitehead's manner of expressing himself "to set in contrast with" means "to put in unity with." Because of the conformal (see glossary) relation among members of any society that involves contrasts, the parts of such a society contribute to the feeling of the whole and the whole contributes to the intensity of feelings of its parts. To create beauty is the final cause of every society. Thus, art serves the purpose that every society serves, but in a specific way, for art is the ongoing, never-ending, human effort to produce the appearance of truthful beauty.

Beauty results from the strength of many feelings mutually reinforcing one another as they meet in a novel unity. The realization of beauty is good in itself. However, Whitehead points out, beauty is unstable exactly because it involves novel unities, which, as the continually novel can only be, are utterly fleeting. But though there are no stable, unchanging patterns in the production of beauty, it is nevertheless possible to maintain order in the midst of change for, feeling the surge of life moving upwards towards the production of novel beauty, we can recognize certain emergent patterns and subject them to modification. It is not difficult to discern how the Open Form poets interpreted Whitehead's analysis of beauty as the surge of life manifesting itself in the emergent patterns of novel concrescences.

The Primordial Nature of God is Whitehead's conceptual valuation of Eternal Objects; it is the timeless nature of His Primordial Nature that is the basis for Whitehead's referring to God as a non-temporal actual entity. But God has a Consequent Nature as well as a Primordial Nature. This symmetry is required by the structure of Whitehead's resolution of the problem of the relation between permanence and change (or, as Whitehead said, also reversing the order of the terms, between 'fluency and permanence'). Or rather, the more complex, but more crucial problem, that is generally reduced to the question of the relation between 'fluency and permanence.'

[C]ivilized intuition has always, although obscurely, grasped the problem as double and not single. There is not the mere problem of fluency *and* permanence. There is the double problem: actuality with permanence, requiring fluency as its completion; and actuality with fluency, requiring permanence as its completion. The first half of the problem concerns the completion of God's primordial nature by the derivation of his consequent nature from the temporal world. The second half concerns the completion of each fluent actual occasion by its function of objective immortality, devoid of 'perpetual perishing,' that is to say, 'everlasting.'[515]

God's Consequent Nature, then, represents the reaction that the temporal world creates in God. It is the physical prehension by God of the evolving realm of actual occasions. Thus, Whitehead's God, unlike Aristotle's, is not entirely timeless; to the contrary, He is also affected by the time-bound reality of fleeting occasions. Whitehead's idea that God undergoes evolution (in a sense a radicalization of the Hegelian historicization of the Absolute) inspired process theologians, such as Charles Hartshorne.

Thus while actual entities proceed from physical prehensions to conceptual prehensions, God moves in reverse: while his primary prehensions are conceptual, he moves to engage with actual entities by forming physical prehensions of them. These physical prehensions constitute his Consequent Nature. This is not all there is to God's Consequent Nature, however, for at a later stage in the process that evolves God, the physical feelings of His Consequent Nature become integrated with the conceptual feelings of His Primordial Nature. Thus, God's Consequent Nature integrates primordial prehensions of Eternal Objects with prehensions of actual events; hence Whitehead stated that the Consequent Nature of God represents "the weaving of God's physical feelings upon his primordial concepts."[516] In this way, each actual occasion is confronted with its potential.

Furthermore, Whitehead's God has, as actual entities do, a "superjective character" i.e., its character as a dead datum which serves as a *donnée* for the concrescence of subsequent generations. Like all beings, God is an emergent entity, for He is the sum of all the brute facts that the objects and creatures of the world lay down along the pathways of their existence. He takes up the facts we leave behind, unites them within His primordial realm of value and grants us in return the intuition that the deeds we offer Him may become beautiful in the light of His providence. His envisionment of the potential for the world becomes an aspect of what an emergent actual occasion prehends. Thus, through God's superjective character, God's envisionment of the potential of the actual entity—of what it could be ideally—passes back into the temporal realm and qualifies each emergent actual occasion. So God is the source of order as well as of novelty in the realm of actual existents.

Working out the analogies that Whitehead likely drew between "actuality with permanence requiring fluency," (which fluency Whitehead refers to as "God's Consequent Nature") and "actuality with fluency requiring permanence as its completion" to the poetic work, we might suppose that what is permanent is the form of poem. Then this principle says that the form of the poem needs to be completed by fluency; that is, the permanent form must be completed, brought into contact with the realm of the actual. It is therefore not wholly transcendent, wholly other than the world, for it has to be completed by the world. And Olson likely construed that "actuality with fluency requiring permanence as completion" was the poem itself, still in the open field, in the process of being composed, needing to have its various vectors brought into a balance, so as to be perfected (completed); this relation to the Eternal ensures that the evolving poem is not a haphazard, inharmonious thing.

Working out the details by which throbs of physical energy (which, according to Whitehead, have the same nature as the intensities of energy involved in emotional experience) connect with sensory qualities is an extremely complex part of Whitehead's philosophy. Suffice it to say this: as the throbs of physical energy are transmitted into and through the body of the perceiver, they are transformed into sensory qualities which characterize regions of space. Whitehead's own way of stating this point was to say that "causal efficacy" (the transmission of affectively toned energies, see glossary) transmutes into "presentational immediacy" (see glossary) by undergoing some "qualification of their affective tone."

Whitehead's distinction between these two modes of prehension, "causal efficacy" and "presentational immediacy" arose as a consequence of his admitting that experience is more diverse than the atomistic psychology of Locke or Hume or their many followers allows. Experience is not always the result of clear-cut data presented to us by the senses. We sometimes experience as well vague, diffuse, all-comprehending feelings that come through no specific sense at all (anxiety and nostalgia are prime examples); and more of experience than we care to admit possesses something of this vagueness and indefiniteness. Bergson had discussed the way that intellect presents the continuous flux of matter as discrete and simple objects. We respond to a stream of vibrations and our mind interprets this as a patch of colour in a specific part of space. Whitehead made a similar point, and named the error that the intellect commits in doing this the "fallacy of simple location."[517] The fallacy of simple location alone accounts for the widespread but erroneous conviction that the senses only present discrete, well-defined qualities and entities. Whitehead referred to that mode of prehension which, though vague, ill-defined, and inarticulate, nonetheless transmits data that are massive in emotion and felt as the efficaciousness of the past, as "causal efficacy." "Presentational immediacy," on the other hand, is the mode of prehension that transmits data that are discrete, sharply defined, isolated, spatially bounded, and temporally self-contained. As self-contained, they have no power of being continued.

Prehension in the mode of presentational immediacy results from the development of features of the perceptual process that are already present in prehensions belonging to the mode of causal efficacy. For prehensions in the later mode occur in the initial phase of prehensive concrescence (the growing together of the many elements that form the unity of a prehension), while those in the former occur in later phases, and so presume the earlier stages (those involved in causal efficacy). Presentational immediacy seizes upon the massive and vague feelings involved in prehension in the mode of causal efficacy and transforms them into sharp qualities. The experience "Grey, there" is a typical perception in the mode of presentational immediacy. (It is experience in the mode of causal efficacy that is the basis of the sensationalist theory of perception.) In this mode, all we are aware of when we sense a grey stone is the sight of a grey shape contemporaneous (see glossary) with the act of prehension. In ordinary perception, a causal influence operates in concert with this bare sight and makes us recognize that the object (the grey stone) we see has a history and, likely, a future. The vague massiveness of the presence of the past that we derive from prehension in the mode of causal efficacy we project onto the spatial region that we experience—experience in the mode of presentational immediacy, that is— the stone as occupying. The resulting mixed mode of perception involves seeing the stone not only as clearly located in a contemporaneous time and well-defined spatial region but also as a persisting entity with a past and a future. Thus Whitehead's elaboration of the concept of the specious present became the core of Whitehead's rebuttal of the atomization of temporality that forms the basis of Hume's critique of causal efficacy.

These sensory qualities and even the spatial regions that they characterize are "projected" into events. Whitehead claimed this projection results from emphasizing particular features of experience. Thus it is that we think in terms of symbols (that is, in terms of signs by which one can know or infer something), for the shapes and sounds that we perceive, which are the product of the process of reduction, are taken as the primitive elements of the feelings that underlie our experience; it is, however, the primitive elements of the feelings that underlie our experience that really give us direct connection with the physical world.[518] Whitehead described the perceived colours, shapes, and forms of our perceptual world as symbols of the underlying world of throbbing physical activity.

According to Whitehead's account, sense perception occurs through a process of simplification in which many individual events fuse into a single sensory quality which is then integrated with a spatial region.[519] During their transmission along neural paths, impulses of nervous energy become simplified into the various modalities of sense: sight, touch, taste, hearing, and smell. Whitehead believed this bodily excitement itself is sometimes pleasurable. "In their most primitive form of functioning, a sensum is felt physically with emotional enjoyment of its sheer individual essence . . ." of, to use that example, "its sheer redness."[520] Whitehead stated that these energies are the basis of all feeling and emotion. In saying this he claims that what, from one vantage point, we can understand as the transmission of feelings, i.e., throbs of energies, from another point of view we can understand as the basis of all affectively toned sensation. For the gradual modification of sensa results in their being transformed into affectively toned sensory qualities characterizing regions of space that appear in the mode of presentational immediacy.

In the realm of physics, the prehension of occasion B, which, like all actual events, entertains energy, by occasion A, an antecedent subject, is felt as the transmission of a form of energy. Of the bodily transmission from occasion to occasion within the "high-grade" animal body, Whitehead wrote: "In their most primitive functioning for the initial occasions within the animal body, they are qualifications of emotion—types of energy, in the language of physics; in their final functioning for the high-grade experient occasion at the end of the route, they are qualities 'inherent' in a presented, contemporary nexus."[521] Whitehead described the subjective form of a conceptual prehension as a valuation since, he stated, a conceptual prehension is the mental pole of feeling which involves the recognition of what might be. Thus, Whitehead stated, conceptual prehensions allow the Primordial Nature of God to reach our decisions and, reciprocally, allow us to have contact with the Divine. If we were not able to grasp the values volunteered by God, we could not make sense of our experiences, for our ability to interpret experience depends upon our ability to comprehend the eternal values of the "what might have been" or the "what might be."

Whitehead considered that experience is more varied than philosophers have generally acknowledged. But he valued especially highly prehension in the mode of causal efficacy, for that mode of prehension, he believed, provides the experiences that give life meaning. Whitehead's acceptance of different kinds of experiences enabled him to rebut the prevalent scepticism about induction, about our knowledge of the external world and about our awareness of other minds. Whitehead saw that everything is constituted of the same sort of reality, namely process. We know the world because we are made of the same stuff as it is and we are aware of other people because our souls and theirs are made of the identical stuff. This knowledge is certain—for even if we do not apprehend things in discrete, localized definite awareness, that fact does not imply that we have no knowledge of them.

Whitehead modelled his understanding of the stream of experience on the scientific understanding of the transmission of energy within electrical systems. Whitehead's notion that there is a close resemblance between the fluxes of energy described in physics texts and throbs of emotional intensity experienced within the body—and between physical energy and affective sensation—appealed to a generation of poets, painters, and filmmakers. But above all else in his philosophy, artists who took an interest in Whitehead's ideas were intrigued with his notion that in reality, energy clothes itself in many forms, among which are emotional intensities. Whitehead summarized the concept of energy, a key to his philosophy; thus: "The science of physics conceives a natural occasion as a locus of energy. . . . The words electron, proton, photon . . . all point to the fact that physical science recognizes qualitative differences between occasions in respect to the way in which each occasion entertains its energy."[522]

Among Whitehead's greatest contributions to philosophy was his revision of the concept of causation and the associated concepts of agency and action. The Aristotelian analysis of causation had dominated Western philosophy since the close of the classical era. That analysis depicted causality as a power of an agent to actualize potentialities latent in the object it affects. David Hume, in his critical reflections on the idea of causality, took this analysis as its basis; he simply showed that our belief that causal agents possess powers to affect other bodies has no basis in observation. A power of a sort can be felt in mental life in the form of intention that leads to action, but no analogous power can be found in the physical realm.

Hume's despairing conclusion, that echoes even in Immanuel Kant's stern depiction of the noumenal realm as something utterly unknowable, has its point of origin in Descartes's strict division of reality into mental and physical substances. It was on the platform provided by the Cartesian separation of mind and matter that Hume erected the argument that, while we can experience productive power in mental life, we cannot observe it in the physical realm. The very notion that our knowledge of the physical realm comes from the detached observation—a notion so common in modern philosophy and absolutely fundamental to Hume's critique—suggests this division. But Whitehead was no dualist, and to defend his neutral monism he had to recast the conception of causation.

Whitehead's revision of the traditional concept of causation involved a brilliant stroke—the insight to invert the conventional notions of what is active and what is passive in causation. Action is not something that an agent exercises, Whitehead argued. Whitehead charged the idea of action, as philosophers had developed it from the time of classical antiquity, with being incoherent. Modern philosophy rests on a conception of substance as units of corporal extension. According to this conception, Whitehead pointed out, to be is to be "simply located," that is, in Whitehead's lexicon, to be independent of other simply located units; it is to exist within its own space and time and never anywhere else in space or time. This conception of substance makes it impossible to understand how one entity can act on any other, for a medium of transmission is required if such action is to occur. Furthermore, in order to interact with the medium of transmission, the entity would have to have some feature in common with it—which feature it would have to have in common with the entity upon which it acts. Whitehead concluded that it follows from the philosophers' conception of substance that one entity cannot act directly on another entity, and that is absurd.

Thus Whitehead performed a *reductio ad absurdum* on the philosophical conception of substance (though, as we shall see, Whitehead accepted a remarkably large portion of the argument that no action can directly act upon any entity). Whitehead noted, further, that philosophers concocted the theory of substance primarily to explain causal activity. That the purpose of the philosophers' conception of substance was to explain causal efficacy, and that it failed in this purpose, brought the theory of substance under suspicion. Working through to such anti-Cartesian conclusions brought Whitehead to reject the traditional concept of substance.

To counter the traditional concepts of substance and causality, Whitehead proposed that an action is the emergence of an actual occasion; and that it is this very emergence of an actual occasion that constitutes agency. This concept of agency has a remarkable implication, one that seems to contravene common sense, but which Whitehead nonetheless accepted, viz., that an agent cannot be active because an agent is something that already belongs to the past as soon as it emerges. Indeed, Whitehead concluded, nothing that is actual can be active, since anything that is actual belongs to the past and the past cannot be active.

However the past does constitute data, a set of givens, or conditions, out of which the novel occasion emerges. Any actual occasion's present is a genetic process through which the actual entity becomes a completed thing. Although the completed actual entity is not active, it does form an occasion that can affect, through its relation with the emergent entity, the formation of a new occasion. These initial occasions do not actually exert causal influence on consequent occasions. Rather, they make up the conditions or limits on what other conditions can arise; but they do not exercise power on other subsequent occasions. Whitehead summarized the process:

'Creativity' . . . is that ultimate principle by which the many, which are the universe disjunctively, become the one actual occasion, which is the universe conjunctively. It lies in the nature of things that the many enter into complex unity.

. . . The 'creative advance' is the application of this ultimate principle of creativity to each novel situation which it originates.

. . . The ultimate metaphysical principle is the advance from disjunction to conjunction, creating a novel entity other than the entities given in disjunction. . . . The many become one, and are increased by one. In their natures, entities are disjunctively 'many' in process of passage into conjunctive unity. This Category of the Ultimate replaces Aristotle's category of 'primary substance.'[523]

Whitehead formulated his theory of prehension to explain the emergence of actual entities, i.e., how the emergent unity of one actual entity influences the concrescence of subsequent entities. Whitehead proposed that the end of the activity of experiencing is to order data so as to form a coherent individual occasion. The process of constituting an individual occasion involves both positive and negative prehensions—positive prehensions, which Whitehead also termed 'feelings,' are prehensions that incorporate the prehended occasion into the emergent entity and negative prehensions are prehensions that exclude it; Whitehead called positive prehensions 'feelings' to suggest "that functioning through which the concrescent actuality appropriates the datum so as to make it its own."[524] Thus, when an actual entity perishes, its actuality loses only subjective existence. Objectively, it transcends itself to gain objective immortality as it becomes a factor in the concrescence of subsequent actual occasions. Its activity changes from one of 'self-formation' to one of 'other-formation.'

There are two forms of negative prehensions: the first involves the exclusion of the data from any role in the emergent occasion; the second, the dismemberment of data and their recombination into new forms. Both negative and positive prehensions create orders that grade the prehended data according to their importance for the emerging occasion. Some data are accorded such importance that their structures establish conditions to which all other data to be co-ordinated in the emergent occasion must conform. The grading of data relegates whole masses of these *données* to triviality.

The grading of data that form an actual entity reflects that entity's need for definiteness. Whitehead saw this need for definiteness as a striving for value. The value of any actual entity results from the conditions it sets for subsequent occasions. Whitehead's actual entities are not like Leibniz's isolated monads, for they do have windows.[525] Each actual occasion opens onto the world. Any actual entity is a co-ordinated nexus of past elements. Its formation takes place in a manner that gives the actual entity a definite, unique perspective on the conditioning past, and constitutes a being whose density reflects the complexity of its environing occasions.

In constituting its perspective, each actual occasion accords value to all the past occasions that it co-ordinated in its emergence. Thus, we can consider an actual entity as the sum of the values of the past occasions it incorporated into the the pattern formed in its evolving concrescence. Furthermore, every actual entity, though fleeting, possesses enduring value as it forms the condition for the emergence of other actual entities. Any actual entity contributes its worth to whatever it affects.

An emergent occasion might accept completely the worth of an entity, and then the emerging occasion will incorporate the entity wholly, using it as a condition with which data must co-ordinate if they are to become a part of the evolving concrescence. This is what happens with positive prehension. Or, as is the case with one form of negative prehension, the emergent occasion might reject outright the worth of some entity. Or, as is the case with a second sort of negative prehension, the emergent occasion might dismember and transmute the entity, thereby denying its integral value.

Actual entities attain their actuality through the ingression (see glossary) into their forms of Eternal Objects (see glossary)—that is, according to Whitehead's terminology, into patterns of connection that come, through ingression, to characterize actual entities. The process though which entities are actualized involves what Whitehead called "decisions," i.e., determinations regarding what will enter into the concrescence of the actual entity and what will not. Such decisions concern which antecedent occasions, from among all those prehended, can be so harmonized as to create the definiteness and determinateness of a satisfied occasion. With the completion of this decision making, the actual entity slips away into the potentiality of influencing subsequent novel occasions. In making this claim, Whitehead inverted the conventional relation between definiteness and actuality. Traditional philosophy associated an object's coming into being with its becoming determinate. Whitehead, to the contrary, associated an entity's becoming determinate with its entering the past, and, so, with its ceasing to be actual and, what is the same, with its becoming nothing but a potential for influencing subsequent entities.

Experience arises as an experiencer integrates data into a single, coherent experience. This process of integration occurs by synthesis, dismemberment, and reorganization, and by the elimination of aspects of antecedent occasions that the experiencer cannot co-ordinate with the conditioning features that the emergent occasion incorporates into itself. Significant experiences are clusters of moments, united by common values, into what Whitehead called societies. The simplest explanation of a society in Whitehead's metaphysics is that it is a historical route pervaded by a specific character, thus constituting an enduring object. Thus, for Whitehead, "[a]n ordinary physical object, which has temporal endurance, is a society."[526] In fact, he specifies 'an enduring object,' or 'enduring creature' is a society whose social order has taken the special form of a personal order; by this he means that it is a society whose genetic relatedness involves a serial ordering (that is, an order such that any member of the order except the first and last inherit from earlier members in the ordering, but not the later members). Accordingly, only a single line of inheritance constitutes an enduring object.[527] Enduring objects, therefore, are strands (i.e., linked transitions) possessing a self-identical pattern. Whitehead told us this about the order that characterizes such a 'social order' or society:

> (i) there is a common element of form illustrated in the definiteness of each of its included actual entities, and (ii) this common element of form arises in each member of the nexus by reason of the conditions imposed upon it by its prehensions of some other members of the nexus, and (iii) these prehensions impose that condition of reproduction by reason of their inclusion of positive feelings of that common form.[528]

Olson conceived of the actual world as a field of energies and of the poet (like every human—and in fact every existent, all of which we might consider in Whiteheadian terms, as actual entities) as a route of concretions which preserves individual character by grading the energies that act upon it (an activity that, according to Whitehead, requires Eternal Objects). Thus one of his most Whiteheadian remarks states:

> I am not able to satisfy myself that these so-called inner things are so separable from the objects, persons, events which are the content of them and by which man represents or re-enacts them despite the suck of symbol which has increased and increased since the great Greeks first promoted the idea of a transcendent world of forms. What I do see is that each man does make his own special selection from the phenomenal field, and it is thus that we begin to speak of personality, however I remain unaware that this particular act of individuation is peculiar to man, observable as it is in individuals of other species of nature's making (it behooves man now not to separate himself too jauntily from any of nature's creatures).[529]

The Projective Poets admired Whitehead's idea that an actual entity responds to the environing field of occasions and develops through its complex co-ordination of the influences of that field. Take the emerging actual occasion Whitehead speaks of to be a poem and you get an inkling of what the Projective Poets took from Olson. He gave a concrete, definite, and philosophically respectable form to the idea that a sensibility or perspective is constituted by its place within an aesthetic field and the relations it possesses by virtue of that location. Furthermore, he showed how this perspective noted the value, the aesthetic worth, of each occasion within this field and co-ordinates it within its own being. Olson's idea of a circuit in poetry, of the poet

taking in energy, incorporating into it his or her own being, and then projecting that value outward, is very close to Whitehead's ideas on the formation of
actual entities. Olson's idea that the poem is a field of energy resembles one
of the fundamental ideas of Whitehead's system. Furthermore, Whitehead's
description of a society as a historical route, that is, as a series of linked transitions, provided an extremely valuable model for Projective poetics' conception of the open form poem as an entity whose features emerge from the
process by which it comes into being. So we shall turn to these ideas and
examine the way that Olson developed a corporeal poetics from them.

Olson's Energetics of Embodied Existence

The basis of Charles Olson's manifesto "Projective Verse" (1950) was a concept of energy similar in character and role to the concept of energy in A.N.
Whitehead's system. He proposed that poets not think in terms of time or
rhyme or symmetry or form, but in terms of the complete field (a notion that
in most respects is analogous to Whitehead's conception of the electro-
dynamic field). About his method of "composition by field," Olson proposed
this as the first "simplicity":

> the *kinetics* of the thing. A poem is energy transferred from where the poet
> got it (he will have some several causations), by way of the poem itself to,
> all the way over to, the reader. Okay. Then the poem itself must, at all
> points, be a high energy-construct and, at all points, an energy-discharge.
> So: how is the poet to accomplish same energy, how is he, what is the pro-
> cess by which a poet gets in, at all points energy at least the equivalent of
> the energy which propelled him in the first place, yet an energy which is
> peculiar to verse alone and which will be, obviously, also different from the
> energy which the reader, because he is a third term, will take away?
>   This is the problem which any poet who departs from closed form is
> specially confronted by.[530]

A poem, then, should have the force of a verb, the universal form of action
and effect, and the reader should be "the receiver of the impact."[531] Some
years after Olson delineated his beliefs concerning the special importance of
verbs in language and poetry, Brakhage arrived at similar ideas. Drawing a
contrast between the character of Ejzenstejn's still and moving images for
his students in the first course in film history he gave at the Art Institute of
Chicago, Brakhage stated that

> *moving* images, edited in juxtaposition, cast spells of mood—make one long
> visual verb . . . a choreograph—thus: the peacock-statue on the imperial
> office door becomes a creature of the assumption-of-power in its spread-
> of-tail . . . the act of boasting which Pride engenders; and it becomes sym-
> bol of Pride and power-noun again only when 'still'-prideful.[532]

Olson's ideas on poetry as a vehicle for conveying force is profound, rich, and independently worked out; but it is not without antecedents. In fact, Ralph Waldo Emerson had proposed a similar idea in "The Poet," an essay that served its time somewhat as Olson's "Projective Verse" essay did in the 1950s and 1960s.

> But the quality of the imagination is to flow, and not to freeze. . . . Here is the difference betwixt the poet and the mystic, that the last nails a symbol to one sense, which was a true sense for a moment, but soon becomes old and false. For all symbols are fluxional; all language is vehicular and transitive, and is good, as ferries and horses are, for conveyance, not as farms and houses are, for homestead.[533]

Emerson's statement also provides a basis in similarity for American poetics to merge with the Bergsonian ideas that Hulme expounded. The poetic theory of postmodernism emerged from this synthesis. Thus Robert Duncan comments, in "The Self in Postmodern Poetry," that "reading that essay [Emerson's famous "Self-Reliance"], I find again how Emersonian my spirit is."[534] Then, quoting and discussing that passage in "Self-Reliance" in which Emerson states that his inquiry about the aboriginal Self "leads us to that source, at once the essence of genius, of virtue, and of life, which we call Spontaneity or Instinct. . . . We first share the life by which things exist and afterwards see them as appearances in nature and forget that we have shared their cause. Here is the fountain of action and of thought."[535] About this passage, Duncan remarks: "As Emerson concludes this passage he seems to speak directly for the poetic practice of open form, for the importance of whatever happens in the course of writing as revelation. . . . In this am I "modern"? Am I "postmodern"? I am, in any event, Emersonian."[536]

A poem that remains open to the "some several forces" and that follows whatever "track . . . the poem under hand declares" must be disjunctive. Instead of looking for patterns of symmetry, readers of Projective Verse should open themselves to the poem's transitive energy, to how one moment leads, or leaps, to another. Olson's stress on the transference of energy suggests that his ideal for a poem is that it be able to communicate without loss of "speech-force." Walter J. Ong offers some fine insights into the nature of speech-force. Among his observations is:

> All sensation takes place in time, but sound has a special relationship to time unlike that of the other fields that register in human sensation. Sound exists only when it is going out of existence. It is not simply perishable but essentially evanescent, and it is sensed as evanescent. . . .
> There is no way to stop sound and have sound. I can stop a moving picture camera and hold one frame fixed on the screen. If I stop the movement of sound, I have nothing—only silence, no sound at all. All sensation takes place in time, but no other sensory field totally resists a holding

action, stabilization, in quite this way. Vision can register motion, but it can also register immobility. . . . There is no equivalent of a still shot for sound. An oscillogram is silent. It lies outside the sound world.[537]

From these observations, Ong draws the conclusion that pre-literate oral cultures sensed the word as power and action. This is exactly what Olson was after; his theory of the sounding syllable and his theory of kinetics thus reveals itself to be all of a piece.

Ong also observes:

> Protracted orally based thought . . . tends to be highly rhythmic, for rhythm aids recall, even physiologically. Jousse . . . has shown the intimate linkage between rhythmic oral patterns, the breathing process, gesture, and the bilateral symmetry of the human body in ancient Aramaic and Hellenic targums, and thus also in ancient Hebrew.[538]

Olson agreed that rhythm constitutes a poem and that rhythm is linked to breath patterns and to gesture.

Ong goes on to point out that oral expression favours additive over subordinate forms (or, to put it in the terms we have used, favours paratactical over hypotactical forms),[539] tends to be copious and capacious,[540] to be done to the human life world[541] and to be empathetic and participatory rather than objectively distanced.[542] Olson could not have hoped for a more complete confirmation of his theories; then again, Olson was no slouch as an anthropologist.

Similarly, Ong's theological interests reappear in Olson's writing—in what some critics have described as its "vatic" character (see glossary, vates)—and I would prefer to call kerygmatic character.[543] The force of oral speech makes it congenial to the prophetic mode. The historian of religion, Hans Jonas, offers this comment about Martin Heidegger, but it applies just as well to Charles Olson:

> He brings to the fore precisely what the philosophical tradition had ignored or withheld—the moment of call over against that of form, of mission over against presence, of being grasped over against surveying, of event over against object, of response over against concept, even the humility of reception over against the pride of autonomous reason, and generally the stance of piety over against the self-assertion of the subject.

Jonas makes clear that Pound's distinction between receiving and conceiving artists represents the Western tradition's valorization of techne; the radicality he attributes to Heidegger applies just as well to Charles Olson, for Olson too celebrated moments when the creator is released from willing.

Jonas continues by relating these qualities of Heidegger's thinking to speaking/hearing: "At last, to resume the Philonic cue, the suppressed side of "hearing" gets a hearing after the long ascendency of "seeing" and the spell of objectification which it cast upon thought."[544]

It might seem that the verbal basis for Olson's interest in speech-force and in the immediate temporality of hearing would preclude Brakhage's sharing it. This is not really so, however. For one thing, Brakhage's interest in abstract expressionism seemed directed more to the poets who belonged to that broad movement than to the painters, though he has a deep interest in both. Further, film is a medium of time as well as space, and some of Brakhage's most important achievements have been in the ways he has contrived to form time; and Brakhage's reformation of cinematic temporality has been largely to the end of making it more immediate. The key to his making cinematic temporality more immediate has been an effort to overcome the deleterious post hoc mode of temporal construction that characterizes narrative and—as often in mental life as much as in literary narratives—substitutes disastrously for causal succession.

A more compelling reason that Brakhage could share these ideas is that not all ways of seeing have the characteristics that Jonas attributes to vision; some ways of seeing more closely resemble hearing. David Michael Levin draws a cardinal distinction in *The Opening of Vision: Nihilism and the Postmodern Situation* between the "assertoric" and the "aletheic gaze." The former is monocular, singular, exclusionary, rigid, unmoving, inflexible, abstracted, and ego-logical, while the latter is multiple, inclusive, aware of its context, and caring. Brakhage conceives vision in a manner similar to Merleau-Ponty, as aletheic and therefore close to speech and hearing. The difference between the two is analogous in most respects to the difference between reducing movement to static frames or events (as Marey's chronophotography did) and actually experiencing motion in the lived world. The former strives for a synoptic view that denies time and change, while the latter opts for the life world. While the former attempts to tame time by achieving a panoramic point of view outside experience, the latter enjoys a narcissism of vision, for it knows that the world consists of the same sort of material as the body, the agent who sees. It understands that in all experience the flesh of the world reveals itself in the flesh of the body. Because the body belongs to the world, all experience is really an experience of the flesh of the world sensing itself. This integral relation of self and world, the notion that world experiences itself through human consciousness, is part of what Olson intends by the term "field."

The "simplicities" that follow in Olson's famous 1950 essay "Projective Verse" are equally Whiteheadian as the first. There Olson proposed, for example, something very close to Whitehead's idea that actual occasions possess an internal, organic line of development: "the law which presides conspicuously over such composition [composition by field], and, when obeyed, is the reason why a projective poem can come into being. It is this: FORM IS NEVER MORE THAN AN EXTENSION OF CONTENT."[545]

In adopting Robert Creeley's formula prescribing the proper relation between form and content—"Form is never more than an extension of content"—Olson proposed that the poet must not impose a form upon a poem's content like a wrapper that tidies up a gift, but must allow the poem's form to grow out of its content. More specifically, a poet can ensure that this relation between form and content obtain by allowing the poem's form to develop out of the urgencies of the moment of composition and by permitting the poem's form to change as those energies shift direction or alter in intensity. In his preface to *For Love: Poems 1950-1960*, Creeley wrote, "Wherever it is one stumbles (to get to wherever) at least some way will exist, so to speak, as and when a man takes this or that step—for which, god bless him."

The San Francisco poet Jack Spicer made this comment on Robert Duncan's instruction that the form of a poem evolves in the compositional process: "the trick naturally is what Duncan learned years ago and tried to teach us—not to search for the perfect poem but to let your way of writing of the moment go along its own paths, explore and retreat but never be fully realized (confined) within the boundaries of one poem."[546]

Olson echoes Whitehead's claims that reality is made up not of permanent, individual entities but of processes by which individual entities come into being and pass away. Like Whitehead, too, Olson argued that reality's principal attribute is innovative becoming, only Olson extended this proposition, to assert that the innovative becoming is also the poem's principal attribute, for according to Olson, the features of a true poem reflect the attributes of reality. Olson expressed his belief in the dynamic character of both the poem and reality in many ways, but often with the slogan "What does not change/ is the will to change" or, more tellingly, "If there is any absolute, it is never more than this one, you, this instant, in action."[547] His most famous statement of the idea appears, however, in "Projective Verse," a formulation that Brakhage made the centrepiece of his film aesthetics:

> Now ... the *process* of the thing, how the principle can be made so to shape the energies that the form is accomplished. And I think it can be boiled down to one statement (first pounded into my head by Edward Dahlberg): ONE PERCEPTION MUST IMMEDIATELY AND DIRECTLY LEAD TO A FURTHER PERCEPTION. It means exactly what it says, is a matter of, at *all* points (even, I should say, of our management of daily reality as of the daily work) get on with it, keep moving, keep in, speed, the nerves, their speed, the perceptions, theirs, the acts, the split second acts, the whole business, keep it moving as fast as you can, citizen. And if you also set up as poet, USE USE USE the process at all points, in any given poem always, always one perception must must must MOVE, INSTANTER, ON ANOTHER![548]

For Olson, a poem displays the activity by which thought develops, streams, and courses. It is not—must not be—retrospective.[549] It must not be, for example, emotion recollected in tranquillity.

The passage given above is uncharacteristic of Olson in one way, however. As Fredman points out, in it Olson allows Dahlberg's term "perception" to stand, rather than changing it to his own more characteristic term, "recognition."[550] Olson, as his practice shows, did not intend that Projective Verse would convey a fast-moving stream of perceptions. Brakhage, however, took Olson at his word, and has evolved a form that concatenates a stream of immediate visionary experiences. Thus, while Olson makes extensive use of quotation, allusion, intertextual reference, and, perhaps despite himself, intellectual abstraction, Brakhage's work remains resolutely concrete, specific, and focused on the register of what immediately presents itself in vision, for Brakhage is even more deeply committed than Olson to the value of cleaving to the concrete particular. But while it is important to acknowledge this crucial difference, it is equally important to acknowledge that Brakhage does not restrict himself to "perceptions" in the traditional sense of the word and that, like Olson—and somewhat like Robert Creeley, Robert Duncan, and Ed Dorn (poets on whom Olson had major influence)— Brakhage creates works that present the widest imaginable spectrum of "recognitions," from percepts, through dream images and eidetic images, through memories and hallucinations, to aperçus and insights.[551]

Olson's idea of poetic form evolving in the process of being composed has similarities with Pound's idea of the *periplum* (see glossary), the "image of successive discoveries breaking upon the consciousness of the voyager," as Hugh Kenner defined it. Both Olson's idea of open form and Pound's of the *periplum* entail using the poem's sequence of presentations to suggest the movement of the mind. What distinguishes Pound's ideas of the *periplum* from Olson's ideas about form-in-evolution and about Projective Verse generally is that Olson insists that language is a form of action that externalizes the psyche. The new poetic language does not present pictures of things, Olson suggests, nor does it evoke the presence of objects by speaking their names. Rather, it is like the gesture of the action painter, an exteriorization of the artist's psychic state, that leaves a mark that kinaesthetically induces a similar dynamic in the viewer or reader by imparting to him/her energy that has similar dynamic and functional properties in his/her mental universe as the energy that initially motivated the poet's writing had in the poet's mental universe. The poet opens him- or herself to as many influences as possible—to as many forces active in the circumambient field from within which he or she makes the composition. What distinguishes the poet from other humans is a more highly developed sensitivity that allows the poet to be aware of elements in the circumambient field that other people overlook. Poets opens themselves to the effects of forces to which others close themselves or, through floating attention, value more strongly, and hence experience more strongly, dynamic activities the importance of which other people greatly diminish by lack of attention. Artists' receptiveness opens them to forces and energies that others diminish, or even deny outright. The energy poets take in they then project back into reality, in the form of a poem whose energy can stimulate the reader.

Though Olson's idea of open form resembles Pound's idea of the *periplum*, it has even closer similarities with Whitehead's revised version of causation, according to which entities do not harbour causal powers and are not the source of causal agency, but, rather, an actual entity emerges through prehending and interrelating antecedent and environing occasions. Olson's stress on the poem as a field of energies rather than as a perfect, constructed object mirrors Whitehead's efforts at replacing the common philosophic conception of reality as made up of inert, simply located objects with a conception of reality as active, as the process through which actual occasions emerge. Even Olson's extreme individualism, his insistence on the uniqueness of each individual, reflects Whitehead's ideas that integration of actual occasions is located within a specific perspective and that each actual occasion integrates what it prehends in a way that is specific to itself and that depends largely on its specific perspective.

Furthermore, Olson's conception that a poem completes a circuit of energy that began with the environing field affecting the poet and concludes with the poet reprojecting that energy back into the field resembles Whitehead's conception of experience as an expression of the relatedness of the experiencing consciousness to whatever that consciousness experiences. Cartesian metaphysics had left consciousness as a sort of homunculus, peering out the windows the senses provide, and observing the world around it (and sometimes turning the gaze to the glassy sensory medium that transmits the impressions it receives of the world). Whitehead objected, and, against that common philosophic conception of consciousness, offered the idea that perception is self-reflexive for it arises within, and belongs to, the system of nature—the idea, then, that our experience is really a process through which nature experiences itself. And what nature knows in knowing is the whole of nature from one of its perspectives. Thus, like Merleau-Ponty, Whitehead considered the experiential structure of cognition to be continuous with the processive structure of reality, just as Olson considered the dynamic structures of creativity to be continuous with the energetic structures of reality. The ideas of the poet and the philosophy on this topic exhibit further similarity: just as Whitehead proposed that knowledge is possible because the process of cognition participates with the fundamental dynamics of reality, Olson argued that non-egoic creativity is somatic (i.e., natural) because such creativity participates in reality's energetics. Just as Whitehead's epistemology rests on a biological (i.e., non-mentalistic) understanding of perception, Olson's poetics rests on a biological conception of "representation becoming projection." And just as Whitehead's epistemology depicts the perceiver as a natural organism that is an organic part of a world and responds to its flux, Olson's poetics depicts the poet as a biological organism that is an integral part of nature (not above it) and responds to its dynamics and its energy.

Like others of his generation, Olson formulated a poetics that valorized what Keats had called negative capability. Keats had asked whether any philosopher ever constructs a system without ignoring objections that he or she cannot answer, or ignoring features of reality that cannot be reconciled to the system. In asking the question, he was pointing out human's liking for intellectual systems and their aversion to contradiction. One key ability of the poet, Keats argued, is what he called negative capability, by which he meant the capacity to endure contradiction and the doubts that contradictions raise. Exponents of open form poetry evinced a similar loathing of exclusion as Keats had and a similar belief that the strong poet is one who can endure multiplicity, contradiction, and doubt, and they frequently invoked Keats's name when they expounded their beliefs. If reality is an infinite dynamic process, then a poet who opens himself or herself to as much reality as possible must accept that the senses will present reality as contingent, inconsistent, changing, and uninterpretable. Most humans systematize their perceptions, and in doing so, they eliminate doubt, inconsistency, and incomprehensibility. The strong poet, on the other hand, accepts contradictions and ambiguities of reality. The method of composition by the open field demands the capacity to live with indeterminacy and contradiction, since indeterminacy and contradiction are inevitable features of any method for comprehending anything more than a small part of reality.

Nor did the Open Form poets care to create smooth transitions from item to item in their work. To create such transition is to forge an artificial link where none really exists, and so to be untruthful to reality. The poet must have the strength of Keats's negative capability, to live with doubt and uncertainty and to live through to the discovery of truth. Olson recognized that the discovery of truth is a disclosure in immediate experience which relies on one's being open to process. The poet must be ready to get on with it, prepared to move in whatever direction the next recognition carries her. The poet that possesses negative capability does not impose categories on experience to tidy it up; he or she follows nature rather than dictating to it. Thus

Olson's poems, like many of Brakhage's films, involve continuous change, fragments, discontinuities, and abrupt shifts in direction and tone.

The Open Form poets were willing, therefore, to incorporate widely dissimilar items in their poems. Olson had taught Pound's *Cantos* at Black Mountain College and dwelt extensively on the sudden juxtapositions of images in that work, using them as a model for poetic composition. Even though Pound strove for a comprehensive order and, as Robert Duncan shrewdly remarked, seemed to show distress at the "complexity and heterogeneity" of the world, it is easy to see how the *Cantos* might inspire ideas of an open form in which each successive juxtaposition presents itself as a fresh, and even startling beginning that turns away from the previous moment. Each new element in a paratactical series is a vividly independent moment, different from all others and possessed with a vital energy all its own. Robert Duncan, who shared Charles Olson's interest in paratactical constructions, wrote in his introduction to *Bending the Bow*:

> [T]he phrase within its line, the adjoining pulse in silence, the new phrase—each part is a thing in itself; the junctures not binding but freeing the elements of configuration so that they participate in more than one figure. . . . [The poet] strives not for a disintegration of syntax but for a complication within syntax, overlapping structures, so that words are freed, having bounds out of bound.[552]

A poem that incorporates a paratactical series is constantly changing, and each change instills new life and fresh energy into the poem. The appearance of each successive element in series enacts a sudden turning of feeling and thought, a rapid reversal of opinion, an instantaneous formation of an association, or an unexpected leap of comparison. Thus, the series of juxtapositions externalizes the mental activities of the poet while composing them.

Nor did ideas of the ineluctable modality of the visible and of the impossibility of knowing reality trouble these poets the way that it troubled their predecessors (especially, and famously, James Joyce). The earlier modernists, as I have already pointed out, remained committed to a Platonic ontology, that included the belief that the intellect seeks to apprehend ideal, unchanging forms that underlie sensible objects, and that artists seek to realize the structures (purposes) of the ideals in the works they make. The Open Form poets rejected this belief; their attitude seemed to be that if the intellect cannot comprehend reality, too bad for the intellect. But we must not trouble ourselves over the intellect's incapacities, for the intellect is just an instrument for exercising control over reality. Instead of trying to comprehend reality within some grand system, poets and poetic theorists with an allegiance to the notion of open form propose that we should concentrate on the moment of experience, on what *this* very instant of experience reveals. Complete openness to everything that belongs to every moment of experience can reveal much more about reality than any overarching system can. The Projective Poet's ideal, accordingly, was complete responsiveness to the entire content of each moment—a responsiveness that allows him or her to go wherever it seems to be leading. They strove to experience life with what Olson characterized as "point by point vividness." "Every moment of life is an attempt to come to life," Olson taught. We must open ourselves to the throb of life that every moment of experience conveys. These proposals expound the radical empiricism's core belief, that openness to the particularities of the concrete existent is redemptory.

Olson's ideas on poetic form stressed as well the importance of personal rhythm. The true end of poetry is to create an object that contains verbal energies projected from the self's dynamics and that transmits that verbal energy to anyone who reads it. Pound still maintained the Romantic belief that moments of ecstasy can transport us out of ourselves and enable us to experience something impersonal; he continued to believe that transcendence of the self was the state that great poetry strives for, because it is the state that great spirits seek. Olson maintained no such beliefs. Rather he thought that to make a poem is to create an external equivalent of the feeling self. His constant effort was to get as much of the process of composition into the finished poem as possible. In this way, his efforts resembled those of the Action Painters.

The open, ideogrammic form permits such a display, for it allows the many elements cast up by movement of thought to be held together in a field of tensions. As Allen Ginsberg put it, it allows the poem to be the "exfoliation, on the page organically, showing the shape of the thought."[553] A poem exposes the movement of thought, and what makes such a poem an important poem is the magnitude of its field, the number and complexity of elements (perceptions) it holds in a tension. Poets and readers persuaded by these claims considered Pound to be a great poet, not for the ideas and aspiration he harboured but because he managed to achieve what Robert Duncan called composition by the phrase: each phrase in the *Cantos* is a quasi-independent element, yet, as evidence of his power, Pound manages to hold all these discontinuous entities within a field.

Furthermore, Olson declared

> that every element in an open poem . . . must be taken up as participants in the kinetic of the poem just as solidly as we are accustomed to take what we call the objects of reality; and that these elements are to be seen as creating the tensions of a poem just as totally as do those other objects create what we know as the world.
>
> The objects which occur at every given moment of composition (of recognition, we can call it) are, can be, must be treated exactly as they do

> occur therein and not by any ideas or preconceptions from outside the
> poem, must be handled as a series of objects in field in such a way that a
> series of tensions (which they also are) are made to *hold*, and to hold
> exactly inside the content and the context of the poem which has forced
> itself, through the poet and them, into being.[554]

Nor are the objects to be brought into a uniform accord: "[Y]et each of these
elements of a poem can be allowed to have the play of their separate energies and can be allowed, once the poem is well composed, to keep, as those
other objects do, their proper confusions.[555] And:

> (wow, that you capitalize it makes *sense*: it is *all* we had (post-circum *The
> Two Noble Kinsmen*), as we had a sterile grammar (an insufficient "sen-
> tence") we had analogy only: images, no matter how learned or how sim-
> ple: even Burns say, allowing etc and including Frost! Comparison. Thus
> representation was never off the dead-spot of description. Nothing was
> *happening* as of the poem itself—ding and zing or something. It was refer-
> ential to reality. And that a p. poor crawling actuarial "real"—good enough
> to keep banks and insurance companies, plus mediocre governments etc.
> But now Poetry's *Truth* like my friends from the American Underground
> cry and spit in the face of "Time."[556]

Olson used the term "projective verse" in its etymological sense, to indicate his belief in the possibility of creating verse that consists of sounds projected from the body, that is, of verse that is propelled out of the body;
"Speech-force" means "projective" or "projectile," Olson suggested. Or,
rather, by "projective verse" Olson intended verse that propels the energy
that caused the poem to be written in the first place over to the reader. It
must not have escaped him that "projective" can also mean "propelling forward," for "projective verse" evolves out of the force that propels the poet
forward through the composition. Every word that a poet writes down
exerts a push. This push—this force—is what the poet must attend to while
writing, and not what he or she wanted to say: a poet should write a poem by
listening to the poem that he is she is creating (or by attending to it some
other way), by opening oneself to the anti-inertial push of the movement of
all the syllables and all the lines so far put down and to the interrelations
among these forces (i.e., to the entire field of the poem) and by heeding
where the forces generated by those interrelations are leading.

A trouble Olson found with writing is that it tends to assume linear form.
A poet when writing a poem is not subjected to a simple succession of singular, isolated impulses; he or she is influenced, moment by moment, by the
total environing occasion, which includes the entire circumambient universe.
Olson's ideas on this matter resemble Whitehead's. From his first philosophical work, *Treatise on Universal Algebra* (1898), Whitehead argued that most
existents have complex relations with other entities. Much of the trouble

with science, he insisted, is the result of its attempting to model the relation between material objects and space as a two-termed relation, rather than as the polyadic relation it actually is. Later, in the period in which he produced *Process and Reality*, Whitehead argued that each actual occasion relates, either positively or negatively, to the entire antecedent universe. Exfoliating the complex structure of relations that existents possess, showing that ultimately everything relates to everything else, was the fundamental point of Whitehead's theory of prehension. Every actual entity takes account of, or prehends, every prior antecedent occasion, either positively or negatively. If it prehends the other occasion positively, the emergent actual occasion incorporates the prehended occasion into its complex nature, harmonizing characteristics of the prehended occasion with other characteristics of the emerging entity. If, however, the emergent occasion prehends an existing actual occasion negatively, the negatively prehended object does not become a part of the emergent occasion. The solidity of the universe requires that negative prehensions influence the emergent entity in this way; that is, it requires that the elimination of negatively prehended occasions play a role in constituting the nexus that is the emergent actual occasion. Thus, the emergent actual entity reflects the entire universe from its own perspective.

Olson wanted to capture speech that moved with the speed of synaptical triggering. He strove, too, to fashion in the poem a field that could hold together a lifetime of experience—in Olson's case from the Worcester tenement he lived in as a child to the fantasy of the present moment. Stan Brakhage, at least in his lyrical period, shared this Olsonian (and Steinian) ambition of creating a work of art that can contain everything. Such a poem (or film) can be thought of as conjecture, since it takes its form from the electrical discharges of the synapses, or from all that is thrown together—all that is simultaneously pitched into—the force field of the poetic work. Such poems will incorporate paratactical constructions, as Pound's did. But unlike Pound's paratactical constructions, Olson's do not suggest the simultaneity of the particulars the poem presents; rather they suggest the shifts of thinking that leave ideas uncompleted. Olson wrote to Elaine Feinstein concerning that key idea concerning the identity of form and content he claims to have taken from Robert Creeley:

> The basic idea anyway for me is that one, that form is never any more than an extension of content—a non-literary sense, certainly. I believe in Truth! (Wahrheit) My sense is that beauty (Schönheit) better stay in the thingitself: das Ding—Ja!—macht ring (the attack, I suppose, on the "completed thought," or the Idea, yes? Thus the syntax question: what is the sentence?)[557]

Along with these ideas came the idea that traditional poetic forms, closed forms, broke the relation that art has with life—or, more exactly, with the life force. The closed form poem is limited in scope because it is selective, and it imposes meaning on experience. Life, though, is unselective—it presents everything that comes along in an undiscriminating flow. In life nothing exists as a completed entity and nothing is isolated, nothing set apart for special attention. Moreover, events in life do not bring their interpretation along with them: they just are, and we make of them what we can. If we cannot discern their significance, then so much the worse for meaning.

Exponents of open form poetics often rejected the idea that each composition should be a separate object, complete in itself. Instead, they strived to bring the poem into the organic flow and pulse of life. Instead of the perfect poem, they proposed to create compositions that are best regarded as fragments of an ongoing composition, a serial poem that will take years to produce. Olson's *Maximus Poems* and Robert Duncan's *Passages* were just that— ongoing, open form, evolving, never-ending works. And so, for that matter, is Jonas Mekas's great film autobiography, *Diaries, Notes, Sketches*. The idea has a central place in recent poetic theory and practice.

Olson's emphasis on language as action led him to reject notions of poetry as representation, and thus to reject the Romantic celebration of the poetic image. In the same letter he wrote: "Which gets me to yr 1st question—'the use of the Image.' 'the Image'. . . . Image, therefore, is vector."[558] Or it could be, but mostly isn't. For, Olson alleged, the image, because it is representational, is a dead-spot. Olson certainly took his understanding of what a vector is from Olson's *Process and Reality*. At the end of a chapter entitled, "Flat Loci" (recall Olson's ideas of place) Whitehead asserts:

> In the language of physical science, the change from materialism to 'organic realism'—as the new outlook may be termed—is the displacement of the notion of static stuff by the notion of fluent energy. Such energy has its structure of action and flow [cf. a poem], and is inconceivable apart from such structure. . . . Mathematical physics translates the saying of Heraclitus, 'All things flow,' into its own language. It then becomes, All things are vectors. . . .
> But what has vanished from the field of ultimate scientific conceptions is the notion of vacuous material existence with passive endurance, with primary individual attributes, and with accidental adventures.[559]

Olson says that the true, poetic image is a vector; he must mean that it is a dynamic affair—that it is "fluent energy." The representational image lacks the energy; for, if it had energy, the energy would be present in the poem and the term would not be a mere representation, a dead-spot that points to something that has energy, but would be something that in itself was dynamic, and would convey the energy that it actually possesses. A representational image has "a vacuous . . . existence [and endures] with passive endurance." Since it lacks energy, it does not cause anything to happen. The Projective Poet, therefore, will reject the image.

Brakhage is of two minds about this. On the one hand, Brakhage shares Olson's ideas about the importance of the dynamics of artworks. Brakhage believes that the sound energy of a poem's language—the actual buzz and roar and hiss of words (and I think we can infer, by analogy, colour properties and the dynamics of his visual forms)—carries the thought of the poem (or the thought of the film) and, thus, that a poem actually embodies the energy of consciousness and conveys that energy to a sensitive, open reader (viewer). Accordingly, a poem or a film is presentational, not representational, for its dynamics actually embody the energies of thinking. On the other hand, Brakhage considers the imagination to be the faculty for producing images and, in common with the Romantics, valorizes the image because imagery provides us with a form of knowledge that words cannot impart. Brakhage conceives meaning as an action, a force, or an energy, as Olson did. Like Olson, he believes that the significance of artistic forms depends on their effects, not on what they represent, and so an understanding critic will probe their perlocutionary aspects—will inquire into their actual pragmatic effects, not into their conventional, denotational aspects, which anyway, in film, operate primarily through magic thinking, or identification.[560] Rather like Sergej Ejzenstejn, Stan Brakhage proposes that the measure of work is its effect on sensation, its capacity to dynamize perception, to efface conventional ways of responding to the world and to convey the unique sensory reality of a completed human being by inducing similar effects in the viewer's or reader's own sensory system. But Brakhage goes even farther, for he maintains that the physical (corporal) phenomenology of the object the artist experiences—the way the object affects the maker's body—must be re-enacted while filming and editing (or in writing), and the work produced must be equal in effect to the real itself. Thus, neither Brakhage nor Olson wholly rejects realism, though the realism they expound is very different from that of the classic realist text. Their brand of realism—a realism that consists in creating a work that is "equal to the real itself"—justifies the efforts of both to claim for their art the status of documentary.

Olson's claims here are very Emersonian. For Emerson, too (especially in his essay "Experience"), decried those moments when objects are rendered inert, when the urge for propositional truth immobilizes reality so as to ensure correspondence, when thinking becomes a treadmill. But every solid can be liquified and made to flux and, as he suggested in "Fate," the power to make it flux belongs to mind itself.[561] One's mind, after all, is always in transit, for it treats every truth as merely provisional, and its active powers affect everything that we know.

Olson's remarks on the identity of form and content, together with his remark that an image is (or should be) vector, raises another important issue in Olson's poetics. It concerns the distinction between meaning as action generated by the material of language and meaning as description—that is, between perlocutionary effect and denotation. Olson repeatedly instructed anyone who cared to listen that meaning is a self-actualizing power. In the famous lecture he delivered to the Berkeley Poetry Conference on July 20, 1963, Olson stated, at the outset, that *"that which exists through itself is what is called meaning."*[562] What does he mean by this? A clue to answering this question appears in his essay, "Human Universe," in the rejection of what he calls "description."

> [W]e do not find ways to hew to experience as it is, in our definition and expression of it, in other words, find ways to stay in the human universe, and not be led to partition reality at any point, in any way. . . . It is the function, *comparison*, or, its bigger name, *symbology*. These are the false faces, too much seen, which hide and keep from use the active intellectual states, metaphor and performance, [*sic*] All that comparison ever does is to set up a series of *reference* points: to compare is to take one thing and try to understand it by marking its similarities to or differences from another thing. Right here is the trouble, that each thing is not so much like or different from another thing (these likenesses and differences are apparent) but that such an analysis only accomplishes a *description*, does not come to grips with what really matters: that a thing, any thing, impinges on us by a more important fact, its self-existence, without reference to any other thing, in short, the very character of it which calls our attention to it, which wants us to know more about it, its particularity.[563]

In this passage we can hear echoes of Emerson's "Divinity School Address," and specifically of Emerson's remarks about the importance of the direct perception of the immediate particular. William Carlos Williams averred that metaphor has deleterious effects on cognition because it results in comparing one thing to be like another. Olson reiterated this claim. "To exist in and through itself," is partly to have a self-contained existence, to exist as a concrete particular. What has meaning, in Olson's view, is the concrete particular. Olson must have recognized, especially given the coinage, *muthologos*, that a being that exists through itself, that has self-actualizing power, is the classical conception of divinity, the conception which fused with the Semitic conception of a Transcendent Creator to produce the Christian conception of God. By likening the concrete particular to the classical divine, he suggests that the concrete particular has ultimate value. Thus, Olson expounds a version of the American doctrine of particularism (what Leonard Meyer called "radical empiricism"), a doctrine that Stein, as we saw in the previous chapter, also maintained.

But the claim that *"that which exists through itself is what is called meaning"* has yet another significance, one that relates to the method of composition by the field. For the method of composition by the field treats the poem (or artwork) evolved as a self-generating region (to use Whitehead's term, and which, as P. Adams Sitney very usefully points out, Olson construed as having the same character as a poem), which, though embedded in a larger field, is nonetheless completely bounded. It exists, in a sense (that would have to be defined) in and through itself, for it has self-constituting powers denied to what surrounds it but remains only potential; that is, its actuality is evidence of its self-constituting powers.[564] Olson's proposition that meaning is that which exists in and through itself ties meaning to what is actual: a poem is meaningful—is, indeed, meaning—because it is (as practise of composition by the field assures) self-constitutive. The aesthetic form does not draw away from world; its actuality is its meaning.

Whitehead's philosophy, which Olson cites as the formative influence on his work, is a philosophy of organicism. We have already remarked that his metaphysical theory developed from his early work in the logic of relations, and explicates the relatedness of each existent to all others. Olson's notion of the "field" provides the means by which he, as a poetic theorist, works out a similar metaphysical and aesthetic organicism. Hence, unless Olson is simply inconsistent on the matter—a possibility we should never discount when considering a theorist who celebrates Keats's idea of negative capability—this particularism cannot imply that each existent is an isolated, self-contained monad. What then can Olson's remarks on meaning entail, and how can we reconcile the idea of an entity existing in and through itself with the idea of field (which construes points in the field relationally, and not as absolute existents).

Fredman devotes considerable attention in *The Grounding of American Poetry* to Olson's idea that meaning is that which exists through itself, and proves that we need not resort to the proposition that Olson held inconsistent views about the nature of meaning. He shows, by following up on the work of George Butterick, that this famous claim about meaning—that meaning is that which exists through itself—developed from Olson's reading of a Daoist text, *The Secret of the Golden Flower*, in which Lu Tzu is quoted as saying, in Richard Wilhelm's translation, "That which exists through itself is called Meaning (*Tao* [according to the orthographic conventions of an earlier transliteration, but *Dao* according to current orthographic conventions]). Meaning has neither name nor force. It is the one essence, the one primordial spirit."[565] Olson interpreted this in a Whiteheadian manner, to mean that each existent comes into existence within an all-encompassing field by reducing its unique potential (which depends on its relations to previously and contemporaneously existing entities) to a determinate actuality. Each existent is unique, irreplaceable, and incommensurate with any other concrete particular, since it can be referred only to the relational field itself—

which, in this context, Olson calls Meaning. Fredman quotes Olson's text "Experience and Measurement": "everything does issue from the Black Chrysanthemum [the *Dao*, as Fredman shows] & *therefore* nothing is anything but itself." Relating this to Olson's ideas about "the third of the civilized pleasures ... 'Perspective'—which," like the *Dao* or the field of relations, "is everywhere and every thing," we note that Olson's cosmological beliefs (which coincide remarkably with Whitehead's) imply that everything emerges within a field of relations and is nothing but collocation of those relations; therefore nothing is anything but itself, since no other being can possess the same perspectival conditions or, consequently, the identical set of relations.[566] To know an object in its uniqueness, we must not compare it with any other, but must penetrate it deeply enough to appreciate its uniqueness. Bringing the lesson home to the individual knower, Olson puts it (somewhat opaquely): "we like everything else are only anything because everything is itself only ... we ... become ourselves itself as all is anyway, direct from the Black Gold Flower."[567] Thus Olson suggests that each particular becomes meaningful through an act of self-creation; thus, despite its provenance in a relational theory of existence, Olson goes on (though with dubious consistency) to develop this relational theory of existence into nothing less than a celebration of the human being's creative self-making.

Like Whitehead and Merleau-Ponty, Olson considered the ontogenetic relations that form a person in a dialectical fashion. Of course, the anthropogenetic potentials of relations were not primary in Olson's mind—Olson developed his ideas concerning the ontogenetic potential of relations primarily as a basis for his open form conception of poetic creation. Nonetheless, his ruminations on poetics involved him in considering the nature of objects and a poem's relation to the world. Olson tried to avoid drawing too sharp a distinction between the self that experiences and the objects it experiences. For Olson, poetic forms mirror the structure of reality, and the interrelatedness of all the evolving forms in a poem mirrors the interrelatedness of all the evolving forms existing at all points in the universe as a whole; he wanted, in sum, to show how the poem, the self, and the world advance together into creative novelty, each making and being reciprocally influenced by the other. Whitehead's philosophy provided a model on how to work out this problematic, for Whitehead avoided isolating some parts of reality from others by claiming that actual entities are everywhere complex and composed of the same sort of stuff-in-process, and that they differ locally only in the degree of complexity their organization exhibits; Whitehead, after all, had taught that the subject inheres in the process of its production, and that God and the world jointly make up the character of the initial, physical phase of a novel concrescence that eventuates in the subject/superject.

Merleau-Ponty offered similar ideas in *The Structure of Behavior*; the theory of interrelatedness he worked out there, especially, has parallels with Olson's. Merleau-Ponty turned to the Romantic conception of unity for the founding idea for this theory of behaviour and experience (which Romantic influence explains the Hegelian cast of his argument). The most common conception of part-part and part-whole relations in philosophy (the conception that, as Merleau-Ponty repeatedly pointed out, Jean-Paul Sartre accepted) derived from the Cartesian idea of *partes extra partes*—that parts are exterior to one another and that the forms that unify these parts result from their being arranged in a sort of constellation, a complex whose make-up can be reduced to the parts that it comprises. Against this common philosophical view, Merleau-Ponty, on the other hand, maintained the Romantic/ Idealist understanding of unity (the Romantic conception proposed that the whole is more than the sum of its parts, i.e., that the elements that constitute the final unity change internally as they form relations with other elements). He offered, then, what is essentially a theory of internal relations, the Bradleyian version of which Whitehead's collaborator Bertrand Russell (and G.E. Moore) attacked earlier in their philosophical careers. The theory of internal relations proposes the unity of a whole cannot be reduced to the sum of its contextual factors, because the elements that form the whole have different characteristics as independent elements and as parts of a whole.

Comportement, a term that translates as "behaviour"—and especially "behaviour" as the behaviourist psychologists used the term—is such a whole. The behaviourists modelled behaviour on the causal relation, maintaining that stimuli produce behaviours in the same manner as causes produce effects. But behaviour is not a product of a quasi-causal relation, Merleau-Ponty averred. Because we can consider behaviour more properly to be a response elicited by a situation, we should view the nature of the situation as being integral to the nature of the response as much as is the nature of the organism that responds. Behaviour is not the response of an organism to its milieu but a dialectical relation between organism and milieu formed both by factors that derive from the organism and by factors that derive from the milieu. Behavioural patterns therefore have a meaning: they respond to the significance that the milieu has for the organism.[568] Merleau-Ponty points out that like everything in nature, behaviour is a structure, by which characterization he meant that behaviour possesses a gestalt form. Nature presents a hierarchical 'universe of forms.' Hence, in the most Hegelian of his analyses, Merleau-Ponty describes physical forms (i.e., the forms of supposedly inert matter) as imperfectly formal, while non-human living forms are more complex, and human forms yet more so. He stated: "[M]atter, life and mind must participate unequally in the nature of form;

they must represent different degrees of integration and, finally, must constitute a hierarchy in which individuality is progressively achieved."[569]

Whitehead could have written this statement, for Whitehead, too, believed that reality is a hierarchically ordered complex, a unity in which every part consists of similar stuff but different parts of which are unequally complex. Again, like Merleau-Ponty, Whitehead believed an organization's degree of complexity, not the stuff that makes it up, determines what sorts of experiences that organization can have. Furthermore, Whitehead, like Merleau-Ponty, conceived of experience as a complex formed out of the interaction of experiencer and experienced.

Whitehead had direct influence on Olson—in March 1966, Olson described Whitehead to a National Educational Television crew as "my great master and the companion of my poem," and George Butterick notes that *Process and Reality* is among the most heavily annotated books in Olson's library.[570] The key idea Olson took from Whitehead is that reality is an energy field (see glossary, field) in which all elements have organic links with one another, with each state influencing the successive state to create an organic form whose nature evolves from within; that idea forms the backdrop of Olson's famous pronouncement that Brakhage has frequently repeated: "Form is never more than the extension of content." The idea of the identity of mind and syllable (energy) so fundamental to Olson's prosody and poetics is equally Whiteheadian. So too is the belief that there is an essential continuity between the throbbing energy of the physical world, characterized by the continual generation of novelty, and the stream of experience which, likewise, is in continual flux and, when not under the stultifying regulation of a static, life-denying logic, is charged with tension and conflict. Awareness of this continuity of body/self and world comes by

> getting rid of the lyrical interference of the individual as ego, of the "subject" and his soul, that peculiar presumption by which western man has interposed himself between what he is as a creature of nature (with certain instructions to carry out) and those other creations of nature which we may, with no derogation, call objects. For a man is himself an object.[571]

Whitehead attempted to overcome the "bifurcation of Nature" that had plagued Western philosophy by basing his metaphysical theory on concepts of physical nature (rather than psychological structures or psychological phenomena, as had the foundationalist tradition, which took epistemological concerns as central), and by describing physical nature as characterized by the precursors and prototypes of feeling. Olson adopted a similar strategy in the passage immediately above, for he reinserts consciousness back into nature, but, simultaneously, characterizes nature as throbs of energy that resemble feelings. Olson realized that the reification of logical categories had been primarily responsible for the bifurcation of nature, for when logical abstractions are taken as the content of thought (and the meanings of words), then thought withdraws from the world and into itself; eventually it loses all contact with reality. This, after all, was the great lesson of Symbolism, which the earlier modernists had been unable to take, but whose instruction Olson accepted. That lesson brought Olson to adopt a variant of Whitehead's philosophy of organicism as an alternative to the traditional, deleterious metaphysic based on the reification of logical categories and logical division.

> But if [a man] stays inside himself, if he is contained within his nature as he is participant in the larger force, he will be able to listen, and his hearing through himself will give him secrets objects share. And by an inverse law his shapes will make their own way. It is in this sense that the projective act, which is the artist's act in the larger field of objects, leads to dimensions larger the man.[572]

Or, according to an even more Whiteheadian formulation,

> For this metaphor of the senses—of the literal speed of light by which a man absorbs, instant on instant, all that phenomenon presents to him—is a fair image as well, my experience tells me, of the ways of his inner energy, of the ways of those other things which are usually, for some reason, separated from the external pick-ups—his dreams, for example, his thoughts (to speak as the predecessors spoke), his desires, sins, hopes, fears, faiths, loves. I am not able to satisfy myself that these so-called inner things are so separable from the objects, persons, events which are the content of them.[573]

This longing for immediate contact with the circumambient world we have traced back to modernity's founding myth. While the pre-modern paradigm (really the synthesis of the Classical and Christian paradigms in the world-view of medieval Christianity) conceived of the order of nature as evidence of God's beneficence and the objects of nature as His creations, the modern paradigm represents the objects of nature as ungrounded—as the product of simply natural processes for which no higher explanation can be given (and possibly the result of a cluster of statistical probabilities). One result of this change was just what we have seen in Olson's writings: a turn towards subjectivity and the idea that the good life is life lived at its fullest intensity (a conception of life not remarkably welcoming to the goods of contemplation and "inactivity." But humans long for contact with something beyond themselves, and so sheer intensity can never fully satisfy the spirit. Another response, therefore, is the one that Olson expressed in the passages just quoted: to make contact with a world that might enfold one—to "act in the larger field of objects" in order to make contact with "dimensions larger than the man." The philosophies of Alfred North Whitehead, and especially, his predecessor Henri Bergson, show how this can be done without abandoning the conviction of the merely fluxional character of reality and the importance of intensity: the internal dynamics of the proprioceptive body (Bergson would be inclined to say the body's sense of time as *durée*) puts us in touch with the dynamics of reality. A similar wish to get into contact with fluxional reality animated Emerson's writings.

Olson shared with Whitehead (and with Merleau-Ponty) the idea that experience is of the world and in the world—that we cannot attain a panoramic view of experience, nor can we transcend the world in experience. Thus, in *A Special View of History*, Olson described his project as "re-setting man in his field" and says that he is "doing no more than giving him back his 'time.'"[574] Olson even adopted the phenomenologist's tendency to reduce time to the living present, in which the past is present as a spacious legacy and which, being totalized at every new moment of presence, provides a place for consciousness to dwell. A similar aspiration fuels Olson's archaeological interests as motivates the phenomenologist's researches: the desire to get back *zur den Sachen selbst* (to the thing itself) by stripping away the accretions of history and convention to reach the primordial conditions that produce the artifact of experience we now live within.[575] It was this very desire that inspired Maurice Merleau-Ponty in his research into the ground of being, and Mikel Dufrenne to carry Merleau-Ponty's project further, by extending Merleau-Ponty's deliberations around primordial and embodied experience. Dufrenne worked out the implications of one aspect of Merleau-Ponty's project that Merleau-Ponty himself had left uncompleted, for he focused on aesthetic experience, asking of it what insight it might provide concerning the primordial experience, that is, the experience of embodiment. He writes that in aesthetic experience

> the eye attempts to attain a fuller presence, to somehow coincide with the painting, and, as we said, to become lost in it. This effort is required for the eye to gather what is expressed in the painting, and also for the simultaneous genesis of the seer and the visible to be effected. Both must discover a kind of communication more primordial than the real, and join together, in order to be paradoxically reborn, in what can be called the pre-real, what Merleau-Ponty calls "savage being"—the orgasmic union in one and the same flesh of the subject and object. *Pre-real* and *non-real*: such is the visible when the gaze is made one with it (such also is the seer when he yields to the fascination of the visible).[576]

Brakhage's project could well be described as rendering the pre-real present.

Like Olson, Brakhage strives to cut through conventional experience and to recover a potentially authenticating, but mostly forgotten mode of experience. This similar desire motivated Olson's etymological explorations (and, for that matter, Brakhage's as well). Olson's and Brakhage's etymological endeavours aim alike at uncovering the way words were used at their origin, at the privileged first encounter with something that prompted the experiencer to name it, at the pristine perception that the sociolect later diminished. The effort at purifying experience and language by finding the originary, intense, and utterly authentic moment of encounter with things drives Olson's efforts to find the first stone carved with a caphole, the first bracelet, the first shaped clay, the first statue of a woman, etc. It also drives Brakhage's interest in childhood perception, so beautifully realized in *Anticipation of the Night, Scenes from Under Childhood* and, perhaps most exquisitely, *A Child's Garden and the Serious Sea*. It stands behind his imaginary archaeology of visual types in the *Roman Numeral Series*, the *Arabic Numeral Series*, and *The Babylon Series* as well. Like Olson, Brakhage longs to recover an authentic, individual, and primordial consciousness.

The desire to establish an authentic, individualized relation with one's situation is a longstanding tradition in American literature—we can find it, for example, in Thoreau's *Walden*, in that section in "Where I Lived and What I Lived For" in which Thoreau discusses his efforts to learn the actual depth of a pond that was rumoured to be bottomless. The thrust of that discussion is to expound Thoreau's conviction that to live authentically, and to be in touch with the reality of our actual situation, we must cut through rumour and innuendo, dispense with hearsay evidence, and ground ourselves in experiential certainties. He is chary of notions received on hearsay evidence, and proposes to replace them with focused, attentive perception and rigorous personal examination of evidence (which necessarily involves a component of rigorous self-examination). These very American ideas which, as we saw in the previous chapter Williams also expounded, are central to both Olson's and Brakhage's practices. Olson frequently valorized Herodotus as the historian who demanded evidence based on personal encounter. About Herodotus, Olson wrote, "'*istorin* in him appears to mean 'finding out for oneself,' instead of depending on hearsay. The word had already been used by the philosophers. 'But while they were looking for truth, Herodotus is looking for the evidence.'"[577] History, in Olson's system, came to mean the knowledge that one acquires by adopting a special stance toward reality, a stance that sets one against the dominant philosophical tradition, since it commits one to the effort to apprehend reality directly, without the mediation of the general categories through which discursive thinking operates. While philosophers were looking for truth in language's airy abstractions, "Herodotus," Olson pointed out, was "looking for the evidence." Similarly, Brakhage's cinema of crisis, the cinema he practised insistently until the early eighties, rests on the importance of the act of seeing with one's own eyes, as the title of one of his films puts it.

Olson recognized, too, that consciousness has what Merleau-Ponty called a chiasmatic structure. Since the birth of the human sciences, man has been both "the instrument of discovery and the instrument of definition," Olson states.[578] Humans are both subject and object within the human universe. Indeed Olson, like Whitehead, claims that the terms "subject" and "object" make no real distinction within the human realm, for here the perceiving subject is "now inside, and now down under his own eye as microscopic or probe." Olson used this example, as Merleau-Ponty used his example of a hand touching a hand touching an object, as proof that bodily experience cannot be neatly divided up into subjective and objective aspects. The subject is immersed in the world; from this proposition concerning subjectivity's relation to the world follows the claim (which is actually only implicit in Olson's poetic theory) that there is no transcendental vantage above experience from which we can experience.

In Brakhage's artistic work Olson's efforts to reinsert the subject back into the world of process are transmuted into the quest to invent film forms that provide no place for the transcendental subject, no place beyond experience where an experiencing subject might exist. Brakhage's films, like Olson's poems, convey the experience of a subject immersed in the flux of experience. Brakhage accomplishes this especially by using what in the previous chapter I called "perpetually regenerating forms."

Olson goes on to relate language and experience to the body:

> [B]reath is man's special qualification as animal. Sound is a dimension he has extended. Language is one of his proudest acts. And when a poet rests in these as they are in himself (in his physiology, if you like, but the life in him, for all that) then he, if he chooses to speak from these roots, works in that area where nature has given him size, projective size.[579]

Olson went as far as to relate breath, and in particular its projective thrust, to the phallus. As he wrote in a letter to Robert Creeley:

> [I]f you hide, or otherwise duck THE ORAL as profoundly phallic—if you try to ignore the pile of bones . . . you leave out the true animal bearing of the species and in the end . . . you pay for it by sex, and sex alone, becoming the only ORAL, and thus, the very inversion of the whole PHALLIC base—you get the present ultimate DELINQUENCE (example, Hitler, who, was a copralagnist [sic]).[580]

The philosopher William James had understood the deep meaning of breath. He proposed in fact that breath is the physiological substrate of the illusory notion of consciousness, and that we would do well to substitute the idea of this persistent process for the Kantian transcendental unity of apperception.

I am as confident as I am of anything that, in myself, the stream of thinking (which I recognize emphatically as a phenomenon) is only a careless name for what, when scrutinized, reveals itself to consist chiefly of the stream of my breathing. The "I think" which Kant said must be able to accompany all my objects, is the "I breath" which actually does accompany them. There are other internal factors besides breathing ... and these increase the assets of "consciousness," so far as the latter is subject to immediate perception; but breath, which was ever the original of "spirit," breath moving outwards between the glottis and the nostrils, is, I am persuaded, the essence of which philosophers have constructed the entity known to them as consciousness. That entity is fictitious, while thoughts in the concrete are fully real. But thoughts in the concrete are made of the same stuff as things are.[581]

James, then, proposes a neutral monist position on the relation of consciousness to matter, as do Schopenhauer and Whitehead (a position that Brakhage's intuitions endorse, for he has made assertions that we must take as implying that he too accepts neutral monism). The reason that so many recent thinkers, including Olson, have found neutral monism attractive is that the neutral monist view has the effect of integrating humans into the field of being, as having a being like that of all other beings. A key implication of views that see humans as integrated into field of being, as having a being like that of all other beings, is that humans should not lord it over other beings. The idea that humans belong wholly to nature, that nothing in human nature puts human being beyond nature, spells the end of the voluntarist philosophies such as Kant's Second Critique expounded—philosophies that, to be sure, have exfoliated the inner kernal of modernity. To forge the perfect object that, like Wallace Stevens's jar, stands out from the world around demands an active will; but to create open form work demands "getting with it" "going with it," participating will-lessly in the dynamic that envelops the creator.

Olson sought in studies of pre-Socratic and pre-Columbian cultures for a new language that would be vital, that would be "language as the act of the instant ... [as distinguished from] language as the act of thought about the instant."[582] Olson's interest in the power of the spoken word derives partly from what he discovered through these studies. His study of the Hopi language convinced him that it would be possible to reorganize tenses, to "drive all nouns, the abstract most of all, back to process—to act" and so to revitalize the kinetics of a language based in the body's dynamics.[583] He conceived of a poem as a sort of biogram and he wrote as though he wished he could dispatch the body into the work. Brakhage holds a similar conception of film as sort of biogram and the various evidences of facture—the shaky, hand-held camera, the hand-made visual form, the visible, hand-made splice, no less than the swirl of movement within the image that suggests the response of the nervous system—all serve to project the body into the visual form. Such devices serve Brakhage's corporeal poetics much more than they do the materialist/formalist interests that most commentators on his work suggest they do—and as Brakhage himself indicated they do in his early text *Metaphors on Vision*. His working methods enable his body to impart energy to his shooting and this forces the cinematograph (that so commonly is a conventionally constructed artifact) back into the realm of natural phenomena—it drives it "back to process." The body is constantly present in Brakhage's films, just as it is in Olson's poetry. The word or image in their works consequently lack the effect of the delay that ordinarily arises because of the gap between experience and formulation: the effect is instantaneous, because it is visceral. These qualities of instantaneity and somatic vitality result from Brakhage's having greatly reduced the sphere over which the transcendental subject holds sway. The philosophically astute might want to respond, "But that would be impossible. The transcendental subject is the condition of all experience—the condition that ensures that all my experiences are mine. Without the transcendental subject experience would be nothing more than a series of raw feelings unconnected with any subject." But such non-egological perception is exactly what Brakhage aims at, and this helps explain his use of perpetually regenerating forms: the constant collapse and recreation of form in his work make for a considerable discontinuity of experience, as Pound's use of paratactical forms similarly does.

Brakhage takes the idea the work of art registers its maker's nervous system to its *terminus ad quem*. He believes that there is fundamental tension between two forms of vision. One form is geometric; it is a learned manner of seeing. The other is non-geometric and has its origins in the body itself. The body produces images that, in their raw form, are non-geometic—in fact, they resemble closely the hypnagogic forms (such as those that children enjoy when they rub their eyes). Their space is not three-dimensional, nor do they assume geometrical shapes. They do not even possess clear and distinct boundaries. And they change constantly, with every alteration in any part of the body.

These raw, fleshy visual forms are the *material prima* of visual representations of nameable things. Social conditioning gives these images more definite, distinct, precise, and geometric shapes. The result is tantamount to repression of the body's natural vision. An ongoing struggle results between this structured vision and the body's natural way of seeing. Some people surrender their natural vision completely, by successfully repressing it. Artists do not. They remain true to their bodies and to their bodies' modes of awareness. Many artworks reflect this struggle between these two modes of vision and the urge to outer the private, somatic mode of vision. Brakhage believes that the trajectory of his artistic endeavours has brought him ever

closer to realizing the visual forms produced by primordial, corporeal awareness, or what he usually calls "moving visual thinking." He believes that
film is ideally suited to render this mode of thinking.

Brakhage began an article in the Canadian periodical *Musicworks* by pointing out that the eye and the brain are the only two organs in the body that
extend identical cellular links to one another and from this he draws the
inference that the eye therefore is really a part of the brain—its outer surface, so to say. The importance of this point for him is that it suggests that all
events in the brain/nervous system will have effects on the visual field,
though we may learn to suppress some of those effects. He goes on to speculate on foetal vision, tying it directly to the activity of the nervous system
and referring to it as the "ur-consciousness."

> It seems only reasonable to assume that [in the womb] the optic nerve-
> ends are sparked by direct cellular electrical synapse, that the resultant
> hypnagogic (or "closed eye") patterns optically would be affected by the
> very synapting cells themselves, shaped by the process of synapse and
> perhaps the shapes and conformities of optic nerve ends *as well as* by the
> cells of the interactive brain . . . [his ellipsis] and the biological designa-
> tions of brain process—cellular "firing": the reciprocity of these foetally
> "seen" hypnagogs and their prompting cell-sparking affecting the brain
> (and thus the whole nervous system) must constitute ur-cathexis or "the
> first investment" in what comes later to be known as memory.[584]

The "ur-consciousness" Brakhage refers to in this passage, I believe, is
what I have been calling the "prime matter" of vision (or primordial awareness).

Brakhage continues by commenting on the way later perceptual developments reduce the imagery that arises directly from the nervous system to
conventional symbolic forms. He also offers proposals for developing a
notion of the nature of ur-consciousness and some understanding, however
rudimentary, of how the biological mechanisms that transmit the *materia
prima* of consciousness to consciousness affect the messages of the nervous
system:

> [E]xact electrical "cookie-shapes" of cells, for example, transform (in the
> passages of connective process) to "representative" or symbolic shapes
> (which may be thought of as "compromise shapes") embodying, as they
> inevitably do, (1) the various brain-cell forms, (2) the inter-connective tis-
> sue formation, (3) the optic-cell receptor shapes as well as (4) the trans-
> formative shape-shifting which is implicit in the entire feed-forth-and-back
> process.[585]

Brakhage's analysis of the organic tissues of vision leads him to conclude
that the foetus must really see and, during the months *in utero*, must construct an increasingly complex representation of a world:

Previous to external light lighting eyes, the foetus can be thought of as lighting itself up eye-wise inside out and "reflecting" back to the source/mind
the optic effect: the connective tissue . . . is reciprocally operational, constantly (one might say "insistently") shuffling an increasingly compound
"world" of purely internal "vision" . . . a moving picturization, then, of continuously transformed and transformative apparitions, always juggling effect
of the cell-starters of each pulse of inner light between brain and eye.

Some ur-consciousness also then must be inferred—each cell *both
shaper and carrier* [emphasis mine] of every spark struck from and through
it, affected by each impulse-backlash and in synaptical montage with each
previous and following impulse: the whole organism feeding its varieties-
of-fires into this interplay between brain and eye, as finally each cell of the
foetal body can be intuited to be "telling" its "story" interactive with
every [other part] . . . the developing body, over-ridden by some entirety of
rhythming light (as every individual heart-cell is conjoined to the dominat-
ing beat of each heart-part's over-riding beat) in the conglomerate rhythm
of the whole heat-light of any given organ . . . of which each cell is a radical
part compromised by every other cell's variable interaction, all contribu-
tory to the organic "tales" of these cells in concert.[586]

These ideas are certainly unorthodox; nonetheless, Whitehead would
have concurred with many of the assertions that Brakhage offers here. He
too argued that perception is a complex phenomenon that co-ordinates responses to an array of influences; that every part of the complex society that
makes up the brain responds to every other part of its environment; that the
act of perception forms a world by compounding complex organizations of
responses to the huge array of inputs that come in the form of bodily sensations; and that the individual projects the form of the world he or she fashions from bodily experiences out onto the surrounding space are all claims
that Whitehead would have found familiar.

Alfred North Whitehead realized the conceptual violence perpetrated by the
distinction our language draws between subject and predicate and by the cate-
gorization that language imposes on experience through segregating its basic
terms into nouns and verbs. This violence results from language prescribing a
morphology of experience that is out of true with our real experience, because
it is based on the assumption that the world can be described in sentences of
subject-predicate form and so in terms of substances and qualities.

The result always does violence to that immediate experience which we
express in our actions, our hopes, our sympathies, our purposes, and which
we enjoy in spite of our lack of phrases for its verbal analysis. We find ourselves in a buzzing world, amid a democracy of fellow creatures; whereas,
under some disguise or other, orthodox philosophy can only introduce us
to solitary substances, each enjoying an illusory experience.[587]

Olson undoubtedly was familiar with Whitehead's critique of language, and
he drew the obvious conclusion: if we could align language with the pro-

cesses of nature so that language did not impose its own order—which derives strictly from its own morphology—on experience, then we could say what we experience and mean what we say. A new linguistic order must replace the mimetic mode of our present language; a new language must replace our present language that is based on faulty abstraction from the world of objects. This new language must be, before all else, kinetic. Language must be used as action and speech acts themselves must become equal to the real by taking on the same energy.

Olson found in the Pre-Socratics a model for a non-mimetic discourse that avoids the discontinuities between the subjective and objective order embedded in our present language. More exactly, he found his model in the discussion of the Pre-Socratics that the Canadian philosopher and literary theorist Eric Havelock presented in his great work, *Preface to Plato*. In a review of that book Olson extols pre-Socratic syntax as an antidote to the present order of language and, more specifically, to the periodic sentence and its debilitating effects. Olson states that the poetry of Homer and Hesiod was based on

> a wholly different syntax, to which Notopoulos (1949) has applied the word *parataxis* in which the words and actions reported are set down side by side in the order of their occurrence in nature, instead of by an order of discourse, or 'grammar,' as we have called it, the prior an actual resting on vulgar experience and event.[588]

Olson recognized as well that pre-Socratic writing implied a different mode of temporal experience. In the same piece he writes:

> There is no while back at the farm sequence possible. The epic action is a stream and you are not free to play around jump as though you was [sic] on the bank or the other [sic] or in the water—at your choice or privilege or pleasure, that you either is or you isn't, definitely.[589]

These two passages, taken together, state some basic reasons why so many twentieth-century artists have shown interest in dynamic parataxis—just to take as examples that are relevant to the present subject of discussion: feelings of transit, turbulence, and stir shaped Charles Olson's mature poetry; they also had a role in motivating Brakhage's hand-held camera, his rapid editing, and his frequent overlaying of visual forms.

Furthermore, Olson's interests in a language whose attributes corresponded to the dynamics of experience and his concern with the temporal modality of flux led him to conceive of a manner of speaking and writing that would engender attention synchronous with the experienced event—a form of attention that is given over to an experience that is actually occuring (in reality, not through memory or anticipation) at the very instant of apprehension—a manner of writing that would eliminate all temporal contradictions in

376   The Films of Stan Brakhage

an uninterrupted, complete presence.[590] This moving, ecstatic "now" is the time of Olson's later poetry. It is also the time of Brakhage's films.

Olson turned to sites other than pre-Socratic Greece to garner ideas about the new linguistic order he envisioned. His efforts to replace "the Classic-representational by the primitive-abstract" (as he, following Worringer, characterized it) led him to the Yan-Hopi alternative. To formulate his ideas about the character of that alternative, he drew on the work of Edward Sapir and his student Benjamin Whorf—linguists who claimed to have shown that different languages present differently structured worlds and, on that basis, to have described how language shapes experience. Olson accepted Whorf's proposition that the Hopi language does less violence to the actual structure of space-time than our own language, which segments and classifies reality into one temporal and three spatial dimensions. Moreover, the Hopi language favoured nouns-in-action and avoided separating of terms into nouns and verbs. Olson offered this metaphrasis of Hopi in *Maximus*.

"And past-I-go
Gloucester-insides
being Fosterwise of
Charley-once-boy
insides"[591]

Olson's anthropological/linguistic explorations took other forms; for example, he searched the Yucatan for Mayan inscriptions that gave evidence of a natural, even Adamic, pictorial language with a salutary relation to the real. Olson believed that the Mayans had a truer relation with the real because their pictorial language aligned more accurately with the real, just as Fenollosa and Pound believed the Chinese people conceived reality more truly because the Chinese ideogram more accurately depicts reality. Olson wrote that "these people [the Mayans and the Sumers] & their workers had forms which unfolded directly from content (sd [*sic*] content itself a disposition toward reality which understood man as only force in field of force containing multiple other expressions."[592] Olson believed, then, that humans have become "estranged from that with which [they are] most familiar" and holds out the possibility for a more salutary language that would have the effect of returning humans to more genuine, more authentic epistemological space, and of stimulating cognitive processes that are more in keeping with the multivalent, fluxing nature of reality than the currently normative forms of cognition.[593] Brakhage holds out the same possibility regarding "visual language" (as he calls it) in the first pages of *Metaphors on Vision*.

Brakhage and Olson share these beliefs partly because both descend from the Emersonian tradition. Olson's efforts to develop a method that would allow him to compose with the materials of reality (i.e., fashion linguistic forms that convey fields of energy by inducing corresponding organizations of energies in those to whom they are addressed), and to create works that possess the actual structure and character of the real, have filiations with Emerson's ideas about natural language. Like Emerson and the Puritan reformists with whom Emerson shared so much, Olson proselytized for a new, redemptive language that would rescue Americans from the inherited sin of Western European culture. In a letter to an editor of an academic journal, protesting (what seems to have been) an egregiously silly, overly academic article on William Carlos Williams, Olson exposed how its author uses words slyly, to derogate "the whole of the American push to find out an alternative discourse to the inherited one, to the one implicit in the language from Chaucer to Browning, to try, by some means other than "pattern" and the "rational," to cause discourse to cover—as it only ever best can—the real."[594] What is most remarkable about this passage is that Olson expounds a radical belief that Brakhage, too, has offered—that language corrupts our relation with things. Brakhage's alternative was to adopt "a visual language," whose imaginative nature (i.e., whose nature relates to images and is engendered by the creative forces that bring forth all that is) guarantees that we have a direct relation with its objects. For in the imagination, the opposition between representing form and represented object collapses; for the imagination there is a perfect identity between image and object. Olson, as a poet, could not adopt this alternative (even though it was the view of the Romantic poets), so he proposed instead to renew language, to imbue it with the authenticity of American being and thereby to crack it out of its European mould, in which it had gone stale.

Olson's investigation of hieroglyphic writing was propaedeutic to reconstructing language. Olson commented about the glyphs on Mayan stellae that "the signs were so clearly and densely chosen that, cut in stone, they retain the power of the objects of which they are the images."[595] Because they have the power of the objects of which they are the images, they are poems in miniature. Here language does not float free of the world, nor does it substitute for the world (which was the fate of representational language); rather, the world constitutes the meaning of language. Olson's comment that glyphs on Mayan stellae are miniature poems reflects Olson's desire to find "a way which bears *in* instead of away, which meets head on what goes on each split second, a way which does not—in order to define—prevent, deter, distract, and so cease the act of, discovering."[596] Direct contact with the concrete particular was the thing. European languages, since Plato, have traded in abstractions: Western thinking has accorded special importance to the conceived relation between the universal and the particular, and in doing so has diminished the importance of the concrete particular in itself.[597] After learning a European language, people begin to think in abstractions—to think in words and about words.[598] Olson formulated this idea by saying that after acquiring language, one begins to think in descriptions. Further, he suggested that when one thinks in abstractions—that is, in words—one directs one's mental energies towards apprehending the similarities and differences between the object one currently observes (i.e., one word) and other objects one has experienced (i.e., other words). Against this, Olson adopted what Williams had advocated, that there be "no ideas but in things" (which Olson renders "not in ideas but in things," perhaps to stress that ideas/signs now are isolated from things).[599] Language doesn't constitute meanings on its own (as logocentrism has it); only the objects of the real world make up its meaning, Olson insisted.

The Symbolists had provided a great lesson, that symbol, especially, but all signs (whether verbal or not) too readily withdraw into the inwardness of the Cartesian subject, and so becomes isolated from the world. When signs lose their connection with an objective referent, they become (in a fashion that Jacques Derrida's writing has done much to explain) signs of signs, and signs about signs. Olson, working in the wake of Symbolism (and early modernists, who for various reasons were unable to take the Symbolists' lesson), identified the principal problem of language as its having lost its connection with the real.[600] Olson's proposal for an Emersonian "natural" or "absolute language" turns on the contrast between presentation and representation. Whitehead's philosophy gave Olson the idea (or confirmed his idea) that reality is not made up of fixed forms (i.e., objects); he concurred with Whitehead's idea that reality is a field of dynamic energy. Colour is not a property that inheres in an object—colour is rather the product of quanta, particles of energy that excite our nervous system as they impact upon it. We can find words (which themselves are bundles of energy) that, arranged appropriately, stimulate the nervous system of those to whom they are addressed in the same way that the poet's environing field—in our example, the colour— excited the poet in the first place. Olson is never precise enough, when proposing this, to analyze how an arrangement of words might have such an effect, or to describe how we might go about finding the words that will have this effect: what he does offer amounts to no more than a set of metaphors for the process. Perhaps the most interesting of those metaphors is the modern (post-Lobachevski, post-Cayley, and post-Klein) understanding of congruence.[601] Earlier centuries understood congruence through spatial intuition involving the superpositioning of fixed forms; but, following Lobachevski's, Cayley's, and Klein's lead, Olson pointed out that a more recent topological conception does not consider congruence as the coincidence of static forms in Euclidean/Cartesian space. Rather, "As it developed in his [Melville's] century, congruence, which had been the measure of the space a solid fills in two of its positions, became a point-by-point mapping power of such flexibility that anything which stays the same, no matter where it goes and into whatever varying conditions (it can suffer deformation), it can be followed, and, if it is art, led, including, what is so important to prose, such physical quantities as velocity, force and field strength."[602] The mathematical metaphor that Olson used here, of a point-to-point mapping is a function that correlates each element in the domain of the function with a different element in its range: given two sets of elements that can be correlated with one another by a function that meets these conditions, then any set drawn from the range of the function is said to form an image of the set drawn from its domain; congruence is maintained as long as certain orderings are.[603] Olson used this mathematical metaphor to suggest that the force that each corpuscle of energy in the poet's field (each actual entity in the poet's environing field) possesses a corresponding force in the poem itself; and though there may be some distortion, some expansion or contraction of the force's energies, the relations among various forces that make up the event that registers in the poem are preserved by the forces inherent in the poem. A poem's verbal constructs actually possess energy and force.

Hence, the poem does not represent the energies that inspired it, but actually *presents* them. Olson rejects mimeticism—he proclaims that he wants to re-enact reality, not reproduce it. Since the poem (as a conformal mapping of the energy of the original) contains the similar energies of the event, and since reality is nothing but a field of energy, the poem is "equal ... to the real itself." Each quantum of energy in the circumstance that prompted the writer to write the poem has a corresponding quantum of energy in the poet's responsive body (though, of course, the quantum might differ in magnitude) and the relations between the quanta in the poem resemble the relations between quanta in the original. Furthermore, each quantum of energy in the poet's responsive body is propelled outward as a quantum of energy in the poem he or she creates in such a way as to homologically preserve the forms of relations among quanta of energy in the poet's body. Hence, each quantum of energy in the precipitating event has a corresponding quantum of energy in the resulting work of art.

That it possesses the energy of objects makes a poem an object, just as much as a foot that kicks is, so Olson called his poetic theory "objectism." This poetic theory maintains that a poem should be presentational, not representational. The metaphysics of energy, which Olson got from Whitehead's *Process and Reality*, is the basis for this proposition. Brakhage uses a dynamic conception of reality, and the associated view that sensation results from the discharge of electrical energy, to a similar end.

Olson's metaphysics of energy serves another purpose: it grounds his claim that the actual relation between a subject and world is much different than what European metaphysics depicts it as being. European metaphysics has traditionally portrayed the subject as a kind of "outside spectator," above the world and looking in on it; in truth, Olson maintains, the spectator is immersed in the world of flux.

> Nothing was now inert fact, all things were there for feeling, to promote it, and be felt; and man, in the midst of it, knowing well how he was folded in, as well as how suddenly and strikingly he could extend himself, spring or, without even moving, go, to far, the farthest—he was suddenly possessed or reposessed of a character of being, a thing among things, which I shall call his physicality. It made a re-entry of or to the universe. Reality was without interruption, and we are still in the business of finding out how all action, and thought, have to be refounded.[604]

Brakhage's rapidly evolving, perpetually regenerating forms suggest the same surrender of the ego, the same felt relation to the world, the same imbeddedness in flux, and the same sense that one's sensations really are the experiences of the universe experiencing itself from a particular vantage point. In this "human universe," humans are both the instruments and the objects of discovery; here the invidious distinction between subject and object has no purchase on reality. Reality articulates itself in experience, without the intervention of the effects of subjectivity[605] does so somatically or, as Olson puts it, in "the skin itself, the meeting edge of man and external reality."[606] Furthermore, both Olson and Brakhage suggest that immersion in the world and close attention to experiential events annihilate anticipation and recollection and bring the spectator into James's specious present, or what we could better call the living present.

Olson contrasted forms that depend on the mind alone with forms that derive from that place where the ear and the mind are at one—from the place "where the breath comes from"—the source of energy that connects mind and body and world. In doing this, Olson corporealized the conceptions of rhythm, breath, dynamism—dimensions of art that traditional metaphysics tended to depict as spiritual. Brakhage picked up on Olson's corporealizing turn in poetics and carried it to its logical conclusion, in identifying vision with electrical discharges of the synapses.

To get rid of subjective effects is to give energies over to the body instead of the mind. The mind controls, the body impels. Hence, to experience bodily is to experience immediately, directly, naturally, to open oneself to the energy of event-objects. To speak bodily is to invest every word with force, to compose with words with power. The body imparts a blow to the letter of the word and empowers the otherwise inert terms of language; the dynamic force of enunciating body tears words away from abstractions and converts them into actual energies. Olson's term for the force of the enunciating body is "resistance," a term he chose because what "resistance" refers to is a life force mobilized primarily against death, but also against the categorical, detached thinking that dominates Western cultures: "In this intricate structure [our body] are we based, now more certainly than ever (besieged, overthrown), for its power is bone muscle nerve blood brain   [space in original] a man, its fragile mortal force its old eternity, resistance."[607]

Olson framed "The Resistance" (the essay Creeley selected as the opening piece for his collection of Olson's *Selected Writings*) in the wake of Auschwitz and Hiroshima; more than commentators generally consider, these events really did exert a shaping influence on Olson's poetic theory. Olson believed these terrible events had drastically reduced human existence, and resistance is the urge to struggle against these life-denying forces. To have the strength to stand against history's monumental force, a person must stand on solid ground. But that same process that lead to Auschwitz and Hiroshima had, as those very events evidenced, shattered all certainties and all systems of value. The only way one can tolerably inhabit the present is to find a ground in the human body. In a time that has reduced humans to fat for soap and to superphosphates for fertilizing soil, then "[i]t is his own physiology he is forced to arrive at." The basis of resistance is the physical body. By connecting with the physical body we focus ourselves in the present moment. We contract attention to a foreshortened span. We abolish layer upon layer of false self-images and dispel the deceits engendered by living out the social roles assigned to us. Finally, after disabusing ourselves of all false self-images, we reach bedrock, in the body itself, firmly situated in a particular setting and aware, in its fibres, of its connection with that setting. When one situates oneself in the resistance, one's stance takes on moral force, for the body gives one a solid foundation upon which to confront the world.

These, too, are ideas that undergird Brakhage's filmmaking. Resistance means living inside one's own fleshy casing, graciously living within one's own limits rather than sprawling over the whole face of the world, for by living within one's own flesh one attunes oneself with others by recognizing what one has in common them. Discussing the Yucatan Maya, Olson commented on the sort of being that emerges through living graciously within one's own flesh. The Maya, Olson stated,

> do one thing no modern knows the secret of . . . : they wear their flesh with that difference which the understanding that it is common leads to. When [riding in one of those wondrous Mexican buses] I am rocked by the roads against any of them—kids, women, men—their flesh is most gentle, is granted, touch is in no sense anything but the natural law of flesh, there is

> none of that pull-away which, in the States, causes a man for all the years
> of his life the deepest sort of questioning of the rights of himself to the
> wild reachings of his own organism. The admission these people give me
> and one another is direct, and the individual who peers out from that flesh
> is precisely himself, is a curious wandering animal like me—it is so very
> beautiful how animal human eyes are when the flesh is not worn so close it
> chokes, how human and individuated the look comes out of a human eye
> when the house of it is not exaggerated.[608]

Like William Carlos Williams and Maurice Merleau-Ponty, Olson considers
the contempt that moderns have for the sense for touch. Like them, he
believes that a spectatorial relation to reality has hypertrophied the sense of
sight, which results in detached relations with other human beings and with
the world. Sight separates consciousness from the world, while touch connects subject and object in a unified field. The Mayans acknowledge, with
simple and straightforward grace, that the flesh craves to touch and to be
touched, and by acknowledging this desire rather than recoiling from it, they
accept the common human condition.

We affirm the force of resistance, or we fall victim to civilization's fraud.

> It is his body that is his answer, his body intact and fought for, the absolute
> of his organism in its simplest terms, this structure evolved by nature,
> repeated in each act of birth, the animal man; the house he is, this house
> that moves, breathes, acts, this house where his life is, where he dwells
> against the enemy, against the beast.
>   Or the fraud. . . . [609]

The body is what makes it possible for "man [to be] that participant thing,
[and] to take up, straight, nature's, live nature's force."[610] Olson extended
this notion of having a somatic relation with nature to the sexual energies,
saying that we might know nature most immediately through nature's sexual
powers. Writing about the Mayans, he speculated, "[M]y assumption is that
they took the phallus—& sex—as simply man's most immediate way of
knowing nature's powers—and the handiest image of that power."[611] The
implication of this is that language becomes revivified when it comes into
proximity to phallic (perhaps one might want to say, more generally, sexual)
powers. Olson believed that the body provides, in the lungs, the physical
machinery of poetic inspiration and poetic aspiration but, as the remark he
made to Creeley about phallic/sexual powers reveals, he also maintained
that orality, at the same time, is also profoundly sexual/phallic. Olson maintained that the body mobilizes unity and power against the divisive and inert
categorizations of subjectivity; consequently, it furnishes the grounds for a
natural and therefore authentic language. Olson felt strongly enough about
the body's redemptive potentials that he proposed (but did not undertake)
two writing projects: the one, a book on the body, "[a] record in the per-

fectest language I can manage of the HEART, BRAIN, LIVER, KIDNEY, the organs, to body them forth, to give a full sense of the instrument of the organism, approached on the simplest of premises," that would have served as a prolegomenon to the second, which was to be "fables of organs."[612]

Like Lawrence, Olson advocated the use of paratactical forms of constructions that present each object or each moment in experience in its full particularized intensity. He outlines the experiential basis of this advocacy:

> [A]nalysis only accomplishes a *description*, does not come to grips with what really matters: that a thing, any thing, impinges on us by a more important fact, its self-existence, without reference to any other thing, in short, the very character of it which calls our attention to it, which wants us to know more about it, its particularity. This is what we are confronted by, not the thing's "class," any hierarchy, of quality or quantity, but the thing itself, and its *relevance* to ourselves who are the experience of it (whatever it may mean to someone else, or whatever other relations it may have).[613]

Like Lawrence again, Olson praised such forms for their ability to convey corporeal energy. Lawrence's idea of an open form of poetry, of a poetry of the immediate present, the essence of which (to repeat the point) would lie in "the sheer appreciation of the instant moment, life surging itself into utterance at its very well-head," conformed remarkably well to Whitehead's view of reality. Olson's ideas on open form have important similarities to Lawrence's. Both Olson and Lawrence conceived of reality in a Whiteheadian manner, as a process, and both strove to create a poetic form which (to repeat Lawrence's assertion) could convey a sense of "the rapid, momentaneous association of things which meet and pass on the for ever incalculable journey of creation: everything left in its own rapid, fluid relationship with the rest of things."[614] Olson even went a ways towards accepting Lawrence's prescription that, to overcome the Faustian desire to control nature, one must integrate oneself into it, by acknowledging, as we noted earlier, those "primordial & phallic energies & methodologies which ... make it possible for man, that participant thing, to take up, straight, nature's, live nature's force."[615] Further, Olson underwrote, too, the Whiteheadian idea that the shape of any living thing is fluid, changing, and to a degree indefinite, and that, when it becomes definite and completely formed, it loses its actuality and becomes only the potential for influencing subsequent concrete actualities. This belief led him to a Lawrentian idea of open form, a form that is actual as long as it is in evolution.

Olson also had a predilection for forms that allow instantaneous shifts in tone, syntax, diction, metre, rhythm, or whatever.[616] Hence, the length of successive lines in Olson's poems often varies widely. Following on Lawrence's dictum that a free verse is the "direct utterance of the instant whole man," Olson found a physiological justification for where he put line breaks. The division of a poem into lines should follow the poet's breathing, Olson counselled. Line breaks occur where the voice pauses for breath: the line "comes (I swear it) from the breath, from the breathing of the man who writes, at the moment that he writes," Olson proclaimed.[617]

Olson strove to develop forms that allow the transitory conditions of the poet's physiology to decide the rhythm of the poem. If a poet is in touch with his physiology, he or she feels rhythm, and "Whoever has rhythm has the universe," Olson averred. Being centred in one's physiology, one's *being*, is a key feature of the poet's make-up.

> [T]he use of a man, by himself and thus by others, lies in how he conceives his relation to nature, that force to which he owes his somewhat small existence. If he sprawl, he shall find little to sing but himself, and shall sing, nature has such paradoxical ways, by way of artificial forms outside himself. But if he stays inside himself, if he is contained within his nature as he is participant in the larger force, he will be able to listen, and his hearing through himself will give him secrets objects share.[618]

Olson's idea of *tropos*—which he variously (and somewhat obscurely) characterizes as a tropistic drive, a dynamic energy, energy that is our response to the influx of cosmic energies, but generally means by it a sense of place and of the creative role of one's environing field—also reflects the idea that human beings are participants in nature's life force. Olson maintained that, in obeying one's own urges, one complies with cosmic desire. The very possibility of human action depends upon the world's eliciting the desire for action in the individual; consequently, Olson claims that "the actionable is larger than the individual." The cosmos, working through the body, impresses the intention to act upon the individual.

Life surging through the body registers the whole of reality. In the true poem, reality expresses its relevance to us through the poem's capacity to elicit and modulate the coursing and flowing, the ebbing and surging, of somatic energies. Contrary to the Romantics and the Symbolists, who conceived of the image as a transcendent ideal, Olson considers it a vector, i.e., as directed energy—and energy that the poem can re-enact, but cannot describe precisely. For, he points out, description attempts a false separation between the image, the instrument of the description, and the object of the description and, ultimately, leaves out the dynamics of their object:

> Here again, as throughout experience, the law remains, form is not isolated from content. The error of all other metaphysic is descriptive, is the profound error that Heisenberg had the intelligence to admit in his principle that a thing can be measured in its mass only by arbitrarily assuming a stopping of its motion, or in its motion only by neglecting, for the moment of the measuring, its mass. And either way, you are failing to get what you are after—so

far as a human being goes, his life. There is only one thing you can do about kinetic, re-enact it. Which is why the man said, he who possesses rhythm possesses the universe. And why art is the only twin life has—its only valid metaphysic. Art does not seek to describe but to enact. And if man is once more to possess intent in his life, and to take up the responsibility implicit in his life, he has to comprehend his own process as intact, from outside, by way of his skin, in, and by his own powers of conversion, out again.[619]

The ideas that the image is a vector, that human beings live in a field of energies, and that rhythm is primary are all poetic notions that Olson drew from Pound, and especially from the poetics Pound expounded during his Vorticist years, and especially, from Whitehead.[620] From the proposition that artists live in a field of energies to which they must open themselves, and the conviction that true poetry must have deep roots in a sense of place and must be brought out of artists by their responsiveness to the place where they live, Olson drew the conclusion that space is the distinctive feature of American culture: "I take SPACE to be the central fact to man born in America, from Folsom cave to now," Olson declared at the beginning of *Call me Ishmael*. "I spell it large because it comes large here. Large, and without mercy."[621] When he says "space," he means space as opposed to time: if you live in time, then you know in every moment of your existence that the past both conditions and limits your present experience, while if you live in space, every point is a point you can move from, to begin anew. Olson praised Pound's *Cantos* for treating time and history as space and for the way he leaps from one point in that space to another. Brakhage's perpetually regenerating forms are, in this sense, spatial rather than temporal forms, for they allow Brakhage to cut from one condition to another, and to begin over and over again.

Olson perspicaciously connected his ideas on the role that space played in shaping American culture to his understanding of Americans' beliefs about technology and the illusions they harbour about its liberatory potential:

> Americans still fancy themselves such democrats. But their triumphs are of the machine. It is the only master of space the average person ever knows, oxwheel to piston, muscle to jet. It gives trajectory.
> To Melville it was not the will to be free but the will to overwhelm nature that lies at the bottom of us as individuals and as people. Ahab is no democrat. Moby-Dick, antagonist, is only king of natural force, resource.[622]

Olson believed that wilfulness, which he saw as the downfall of contemporary humankind, was a consequence of our failing to recognize the essential continuity between the dynamic of the world and that of the inner realm of experience. The failure to recognize that continuity, which the Romantics so celebrated, results in our conception that Nature is bifurcated. Olson argued, too, that humans often overvalue human action, and that when human action is good, it is the equal of all intake plus all transposing. It deserves this word, that it is the equal of its cause only when it proceeds unbroken from the threshold of a man through him and back out again, without loss of quality, to the external world from which it came.... In other words, the proposition here is that man at his peril breaks the full circuit of object, image, action at any point. The meeting edge of man and the world is also his cutting edge. If man is active, it is exactly here where experience comes in that it is delivered back, and if he stays fresh at the coming in he will be fresh at his going out. If he does not, all that he does inside his house is stale, more and more stale as he is less and less acute at the door.... Man does influence external reality.... If man chooses to treat external reality any differently than as part of his own process, in other words as anything other than relevant to his own inner life, then he will ... use it otherwise. He will use it just exactly as he has used it now for too long, for arbitrary and willful purposes which, in their effects, not only change the face of nature but actually arrest and divert her force until man turns it even against herself, he is so powerful, this little thing.[623]

Here Olson suggests the importance of recognizing that we belong to the field, that we are not above the world, but a part of the world, that our flesh is one with the flesh of world—the skin only the region of contact between the fused bodies. So in Olson's poetics, as in Robert Duncan's, care for the body is important. A poet must be able to sense her process from within, intact within the body, and then, through powers of concentration, project it out again. He argues in the passage above for the need for care of the body, the skin, and the senses, and for the poet to open the skin (the senses) to the world in order to refresh and revivify the contents held within the skin. Olson stressed that the skin, the surface of the human body, maintains the relation between the self and the world; the skin, after all, is only a porous membrane, not an inviolate frontier.

Olson extends the above by articulating a paradox that is right at the heart of Stan Brakhage's oeuvre; in fact, it is germane to any artist whose work rests on the premise that alterations in our bodily state are the source of our knowledge of reality. The paradox depends upon the relation between two methods for incorporating analogues of reality's flux and change in a work of art, and more specifically, upon the relation between two non-narrative means of "narrating." Underlying the paradox is the principle that a work of art must re-enact the energy that drives reality's flux. The narrator may have two sorts of relation to that "outer energy," and these two relations lead to two narrative methods. One method is

what I call DOCUMENT simply to emphasize that the events alone do the work, that the narrator stays OUT, functions as pressure not as interpreting person, illuminates not by argument or "creativity" but by master of force ... the art, to make his meanings clear by how he juxtaposes, correlates, and causes to interact whatever events and persons he chooses to set in motion. In other words his ego or person is NOT of the story whatsoever. He is, if he makes it, light from outside, the thing itself doing the casting of what shadows;[624]

The other technique, which Olson discovered in Creeley's stories, relies on just the opposite—on the total subjectivity of the narrator.

> [T]he exact opposite, the NARRATOR IN, the total IN to the above total OUT, ... the narrator taking on himself the job of making clear by way of his own person that life *is* preoccupation with itself, ... so powerful inside the story that he makes the story swing on him, his eye the eye of nature INSIDE (as is the same eye, outside) a light-maker.[625]

Many commentators have described Brakhage's cinema in paradoxical terms, both as a first-person cinema and as an objective document that registers the energies of the time of its making: we can consider *Dog Star Man*, in these terms, first, as a record of what Romantics called the Imagination, but also as an instantaneously constructed cosmology based on energetics, for it provides a record of the surge of energies through the subjective body. The difficulty we experience in attempting to reconcile these two ways of considering *Dog Star Man* (or almost any of the films Brakhage made up to the late 1970s) evidences the conceptual difficulties arising from what Whitehead called "the bifurcation of Nature." Olson escaped that modern understanding of nature and so, like Whitehead, he could see the reconcilability—indeed the essential identity—of these two methods. Both drive toward the same end, of letting reality speak for itself, "so to re-enact experience that a story has what an object or person has: energy and instant.... And the writer, though he is the control (or art is nothing) is, still, no more than—but just as much as—another "thing," and as such, is in, inside or out."[626]

There are American precedents for artworks that simultaneously turn inward and outward: Thoreau, too, characterized the discipline of self-examination as reflecting on ourselves as we encounter the world; thus in his view, self-examination, which is necessary to a good life, is a discipline that involves turning one eye inward and one eye outward. Facts have the same ambiguous ontological status in Olson's writings, in Brakhage's cinema, and in the Emersonian tradition as a whole: on the one hand, facts provide the ground one stands on, the certainties upon which authentic being rests—for lacking a tradition that has the strength to authenticate one's being, the artist validates his or her efforts by making contact with the immediate realities of one's objective situation; while on the other hand, facts would remain "mere facts" were it not for the artists' subjective powers, for their capacity to break through the received convictions that enclose and entrap consciousness and force us to revise our beliefs. To open oneself to facts is to put our seeming certainties about the self on the line, to expose our self-conceptions to the risk of rejection, to render our self-image vulnerable to assault by the hard, stern force of reality. Emerson, Thoreau, Olson, and Brakhage all suggest that "knowing the facts" is an achievement we win only by arduous effort. Such efforts ground us in the realities of our environing circumstances. They put us in touch with reality—this is how such artists explain the rewards their works provide. On the other hand, Emerson, Thoreau, Olson, and Brakhage emphasize the subjective benefits of those efforts. Getting to know the facts overwhelms our complacently held but false self-certainties, and so affords us an opportunity to get to know ourselves better. Facts break through the enclosures that we erect to protect ourselves from the world, and which we use to separate ourselves from the world so as to control it. Getting to know the facts destroys the tame, complacent beliefs we hold and renders the world and ourselves strange and marvellous.

The ambiguous status of Brakhage's visual forms reflects the Emersonian tradition's dual conception of a fact as reflecting simultaneous internal and external reality. Nothing reveals this more strongly than the extraordinary efforts that Brakhage has made to yoke films composed of photographic images and films with painted forms to a common cause. He has presented both the photographic images and the painted forms as conveying the contents of consciousness, and he conceived the primary difference between the two modes to relate to the different types of consciousness they present: the photographed films present a more superficial mode of awareness, inasmuch as they present a level of consciousness that forms pictures of things. These pictures, to be sure, are not completely formed by the photographic conventions of representation—the extraordinary amount of superimposition, out-of-focus shooting, blurs produced by rapid camera movement, the intensification of qualities of colour that make his films so sensuously appealing (e.g., *Creation* and *Made Manifest*), the cutting that does not respect the serial chronology of material reality, wrest his visual forms away from being representations of the objective world, imbue them with emotional force, and most importantly, subjectivize them. However, we still identify and respond to the visual form's represented content—the darling little boy of *The Weir-Falcon Saga* still affects us as a darling little boy; that no one likes to see things come to the point where children need to be attended to by doctors is a part of what shapes our response. And, while the photographed films present a later, more developed (and therefore more superficial) mode of consciousness, most (though not all) of the films Brakhage has created by applying painting directly to the film's surface, and the imagnostic films, present more archaic levels of consciousness—primordial levels that do not form stimuli into picture, levels for which the dynamic character of proprioception is central and that responds to all sensory stimuli kinaesthetically. The archaic character of their contents is, after all, the reason why Brakhage

titled his imagnostic films after more and more archaic strata of Western civilization, regression from the Arabic phase to the Roman, to the Egyptian,
and finally to the Babylonian—by titling the series of imagnostic films after
each of these strata Brakhage offers a schema that implies that ontogeny
repeats history.

However great the differences between the photographed and the painted
films, both consist of, literally, projections of Brakhage's consciousness.
Thus, Brakhage has made films that combine photographic images and forms
created by applying paint and dyes directly to the film's surface, to represent
different levels of consciousness. Examples of this include: *Dog Star Man,
Thigh Line Lyre Triangular, Through Wounded Eyes* (1996, with Joel
Haertling) and, the film that goes furthest in this, *Yggdrasill, Whose Roots
Are Stars in the Human Mind* (1997). The primary meaning of neither
depends on what real-world events they depict (though the photographed
films also derive secondary meanings and secondary affective properties
from what they depict). Nor do their meanings depend, at least immediately,
on the cultural or conventional meanings of their visual forms, for if anything
is evident, it is that these films are truly idiolexical.

The fact that two minor film modes mediate between these two principal
modes provides a remarkable demonstration of his belief in the continuities
between these two modes of his cinema. One of these modes is the "collage
film," exemplified by *Mothlight* (1963) and *The Garden of Earthly Delights*
(1981), which, like the photographed films—even more than the photographed films—incorporate real world elements. *Mothlight* consists of moth
wings and other evidences of the insect kingdom, pasted onto clear leader to
form a three-part musical structure, while *The Garden of Earthly Delights*
consists of petals of alpine flowers, grass, and fragments of leaves pasted
onto clear leader to form patterns of alternating movement. Although these
films are composed of real materials, their dynamic qualities are closer to
those of the painted films, as the entire contents of each frame varies from
the next. Furthermore, although the materials that compose their visual
forms are drawn from the real world, these films, even more than the photographed films, are formally autonomous from the outside world inasmuch
as one cannot map the space within the frame into the space of the outside
world (though certain textures do seem familiar).[627]

The second minor mode that mediates between the two principal modes
(of the photographed and the painted films) is exemplified by films such as
The Arabic Numeral Series (1980-82), *The Roman Numeral Series* (1979-81),
The Egyptian Series (1984) and parts of the *Babylon Series* (1989-90). These
films consist of visual forms produced by shooting through prisms, "imper-
fect" lenses, and other such refracting devices. They are clearly photo-

graphed films, but their meaning does not derive from what their visual forms depict, or from any representational features. The rhythm of these films reveals that what we see derives from shooting continuously (since they don't exaggerate the flicker effect), and their optical qualities reveal that what we see has a photographic basis. But nothing in the films is nameable, aside from a few forms that seem to echo the numeral forms that mark off the sections of the films and that we could identify as numeral (if we wished to be so perverse). Because the frame contains no nameable objects, what we see on the screen is radically discontinuous with the world beyond the frame—or, at least, with the objective world, though perhaps not with the world that primordial awareness discloses. Films of the late 1990s, *Commingled Containers* (1997), *The Cat of the Worm's Green Realm* (1997), *Self Song* (1997), and *Death Song* (1997) constitute a variant subform of these photographed abstracts, for they are works whose object matter is recognizable, but has been extremely distanced, by macro-cinematography (shooting with a "macro lens," which creates an extreme form, the photographic analogon of synecdoche), and pushed rather far in the direction of abstraction.[628]

Brakhage's efforts to hold these various modes of filmmaking together in a continuum reveals that the principal significance of his films generally derives from primordial awareness. For in all these different modes of cinema, meaning depends upon how the dynamics of the visual forms affect us kinaesthetically and proprioceptively—or more exactly, through a primitive form of movement awareness that requires no concept of external spaces or any form of conceptual mediation, but is known strictly inwardly, through simple, direct awareness. The isolation of the forms of his painted films, his collage films, and his "photographed abstracts" reveal that his visual forms have autonomous meanings, i.e., meanings that are fully disclosed in what they present—meanings inherent in their forms, considered apart from their relation to anything outside themselves. Some of his photographed films have a secondary level of meaning that derives from what they depict, but even in them it is still the significance that derives from the pace of shooting and of the shot exchanges, from the intensity of the colour or the quality of the camera-movement, or the rhythm of the cutting—in sum, from the ensemble of the films' intrinsic qualities and relations which, by reason of the kinetic intensity that is such an outstanding characteristic of Brakhage's films, relate to our primordial kinaesthetic awareness—that constitute the films' primary meanings.

The continuity among these various modes of cinema also suggests the fusion of self and world that is the true end of direct perception. Adapting Hopkins's terminology, they show that the apprehension of inscape produces revelations about the self. The continuity thus reinforces the ambiguous status of Brakhage's visual forms. This ambiguity also characterizes Olson's notion of a document, just as it characterizes the poetry of William Carlos Williams.

Olson believed that by getting to know the facts, we break through the ego, that unbounded subjectivity that sprawls across the world and hampers us from seeing things as they really are. This has the salutary effect of establishing a parity between the self and objective world which the lyrical ego, in the absence of such of relation to the world, derogates. Olson stresses this dual role of getting to know the facts in his famous open letter entitled "A Bibliography on America for Ed Dorn." (Dorn had been a student of Olson's and went on to become an important poet in his own right.) In this letter Olson argues for the importance of engagement with the facts, with primary documents and facts.

> "PRIMARY DOCUMENTS. And to hook on here is a lifetime of assiduity. Best thing to do is *to dig one thing or place or man* until you yourself know more abt that than is possible to any other man. It doesn't matter whether it's Barbed Wire or Pemmican or Paterson or Iowa. But *exhaust* it. Saturate it. Beat it. / And then U KNOW everything else very fast: one saturation job (it might take 14 years). And you're in, forever."[629]

A complexity of Olson's thought that can easily escape notice becomes conspicuous when one considers the relationship between these two methods of narration—or, for that matter, when one considers Olson's thoughts on the more general matter of the relationship between artistic control and chance or—what is perhaps a better a way of understanding the matter—between artistic control and self-surrender. At the very basis of Olson's poetics is the contention that the new poetry must be *open*; and, as we have seen earlier, by this he meant that the form of the poem must derive from—must never be anything more than the expression of—content, that it is the energy transactions occuring in the vicinity of the poet at the time of composition, some of them released in the very act of composition, which must give the poem its shape. This proposition might seem to be exactly what Olson called it—a simplicity. After all, Olson used it to combat the use of those preconceived metre-stanza-rhyme-scheme forms that had been turned out from their position of dominance long before Projective Verse was written. However, the juxtaposition of a few more quotations will show that Olson had something more profound and more complex in mind than the principles of *vers libre*:

> In any given instance, because there is a choice of words, the choice, if a man is in there [N.B.], will be, spontaneously, the obedience of his ear to the syllables. . . .
>   Let me put it baldly. The two halves are:
>   the HEAD, by way of the EAR, to the SYLLABLE

the HEART, by way of the BREATH, to the LINE
And the joker? that it is in the 1st half of the proposition that, in composing, one lets-it-rip; and that it is in the 2nd half, surprise, it is the LINE
that's the baby that gets, as the poem is getting made, the attention, the
control, that it is right here, in the line, that the shaping takes place, each
moment of the going.
  ... [T]he projective act, which is the artist's act in the larger field of
objects, leads to dimensions larger than the man.
  ... [A] projective poet will, down through the workings of his own throat
to that place where breath comes from, where breath has its beginnings,
where drama has to come from, where, the coincidence is, all act springs.[630]

Thus Olson suggests that the poet must be attentive to the act of composition itself, and must respond to feelings that arise from it as though to an act
of nature. To this end, he advocates using a compositional method that
resembles the creative methods practised by his contemporary, the abstract
expressionist painter, Jackson Pollock who, too, believed that painting was
an activity that involved entering into and being controlled by the energies of
a natural process.

Whitehead's metaphysics undoubtedly influenced Olson in formulating his
poetics. In *Science and the Modern World*, Whitehead summarizes how the
picture of reality he draws differs from that of seventeenth-century science
(which he believed had its conceptual foundations in materialist philosophy
and which, in its turn, founded modernity). As against seventeenth-century
science's conception of an empty event (i.e., an event in empty space, devoid
of electrons, protons, or any other form of electric charge) as a habitat of
energy, Whitehead notes "that there is no individual discrimination of an
individual bit of energy, either as statically located, or as an element in the
stream. There is simply a quantitative determination of activity, without individualisation of the activity in itself."[631] Setting aside "the lyrical ego" and
entering into a stream of energy, allowing oneself to become "the quantitative determination of activity, without individualisation of the activity," is
exactly the triumph of creativity according to Olson and Brakhage; Brakhage's description of efforts to embody the flux of electical (synaptic energies) has evident relations to these Whiteheadian principles.

Whitehead goes on to show how an organicist philosophy construes
events in occupied spaces (i.e., spaces containing electrons, protons, or any
other form of electrical charge).

When we look into the function of the electric charge, we note that its rôle
is to mark the origination of a pattern which is transmitted through space
and time. It is the key of some particular pattern. For example, the field of
force in any event is to be constructed by attention to the adventures of
electrons and protons, and so also are the streams and distributions of
energy. Further, the electric waves find their origin in the vibratory adven-

tures of these charges. [This was a point Bergson also made.] Thus the transmitted pattern is to be conceived as the flux of aspects throughout space and time derived from the life history of the atomic charge.[632]

And Olson proposed that as the words that make up a poem (or, by an implication that Brakhage in fact made, the visual forms that make up a film) are effected by the field in which they originated, that they transmit pattern through space and time, that we should construe projected words or projected moving visual forms as adventures of charged monads that form a stream of energy, and that the poem (or film) represents the flux of aspects on the field of energies registered by a sentient energy.

Olson's propositions about creative method and the relation between the creator subject and nature implies that the creative process endows its product, the work of art, with the status of a natural object leads to the view that, as Olson put it, "the thing [the artist] makes to try to take its place alongside the things of nature."[633] The conclusion that artworks aspire to the same status as natural objects figures among Olson's motivations for making the comment that the elements that enter a poem must be taken up "as participants in the kinetic of the poem just as solidly as we are accustomed to take what we call the objects of reality."[634] Projective Verse offered a method for overcoming the classical realist effort to reflect or reproduce reality as it is: rather than being a derivative of the real, the poem will be equal to the real itself. It will have the "actual character and structure of the real itself," by which Olson means that it will have the fluxing, changing, relational, experiential character of reality as Whitehead described it.[635] His concern with the object-like nature of the elements that enter a poem and of the poem itself and with the ability of a poet to overcome the ego, that hideous construct which humans have interposed between themselves and nature, and with getting in touch with "real objects" (i.e., with temporary patterns of relation between fields of energy, on the model of Whitehead's actual objects) were undoubtedly (along with his belief that a human being is an object that takes its place alongside other objects) among the motivations for Olson to choose "objectism" as the name for his poetic theory. The term also declares Olson's reaction against "objectivism" (of which Pound was an early advocate), a term which Olson interpreted as suggesting a dichotomy between objective and subjective aspects of existence and a detached and contemplative, rather than participatory and highly charged, consciousness. At the same time, the modernist idea of the objecthood of a work of art, which the term also invokes, was part of the polemic waged against mimeticism.

Though Olson was committed to the modernist belief in the objecthood of a work (for, as we have seen, he insisted that a work of art has the same status as a natural object), Olson was no orthodox modernist. What distinguishes his poetics from much of modernist art theory was his concept of "open form," a concept that acts as a dialectical dual of the modernist idea that the work of art has an autotelic character. This openness is the formal analogue, and perhaps the consequence, of the type of experience Olson wants poetry to engender, perhaps best characterized as "ecstatic," for it involves "standing outside" (Gr. *ek*, out, *histanai* place) oneself, of being lifted out of the quotidian ways of experiencing and coming to the realization that "the projective act . . . leads to dimensions larger than man" and that the Projective Poet, in going down into the workings of breath, will enter into that place from which "all acts spring."

This celebration of ecstasy is an effort to reach beyond the comfortable half-truths of conventional knowledge and to get in touch with the actual reality of one's situation. The American poet, after all, lacks a tradition which might validate his or her achievements. Lacking such a tradition, poets seek to ground themselves in the immediate reality of the present situation. Olson's theory expounds these propositions, and Brakhage's filmmaking puts them into practice. Brakhage's emphasis on dailiness, with achieving a hard-won insight into the actual character of his immediate circumstances, derives as much from these Emersonian beliefs that Olson passed on to him as they do from Stein's notions of the preciousness of every object and every moment (notions that, to be sure, are every bit as Emersonian). Olson reiterated Heraclitus' statement that "Man is estranged from that with which he is most familiar," and searched for poetic means to overcome this estrangement; the purpose of Brakhage's creative method is similarly to put himself—and perhaps all humans—back in touch with the reality that lies the nearest in daily living. And just as Olson's epistemology accords facts a dual function, so Brakhage's aesthetics maintains a dual conception of "that with which [we] are most familiar." Sometimes, especially in his earlier work, Brakhage takes his domestic situation as that reality, while at other times, especially in his work of the late 1980s and the 1990s, he gives his own thoughts and perceptions that status. His earlier works especially engage with objective reality (admittedly transformed by subjectivity) and in these works, Brakhage strove to establish a direct and genuine relation to the immediate circumstances of his life. This feature of his work, too, has antecedents in New England Transcendentalism: Thoreau described himself as an "[e]xpert in home cosmology"; Brakhage's earlier films show that he had acquired expertise in the same domain. As Thoreau embarked on many exploratory journeys in Concord, so Brakhage engaged in endless adventures in perception and imagination in the backyard of his mountain home near Rollinsville, Colorado. In his later works, Brakhage has taken a more radical interest in subjectivity—the radical nature of the enterprise is indicated by the fact that the progression from each series of imagnostic films to the next is represented as a sort of archaeological excavation, digging towards ever deeper, and more primitive layers of consciousness—Brakhage has attempted to rediscover the real nature of perception—with the raw material of perception that has not yet been shaped into conventional forms.

The desire for a spontaneous compositional method commits him to allowing himself to be carried wherever the force field that impels this creative activity might take him—to following along a line of energy. This compositional method aims not at producing works that fit into traditional forms and possess the traditional values of timelessness, autonomy, and intricacy, but at allowing a work's form to evolve through the process of creation, in an interaction between the creator and the evolving form; a spontaneous compositional method that respects—indeed celebrates—the continual coming-on of novelty has become common in American art since mid-century. We can observe its influence in Action Painting, in the movement in documentary filmmaking of the late 1950s and early 1960s known as cinéma-vérité, and especially in improvised music (e.g., that of John Coltrane (1926-67), Ornette Coleman (1930-) Pharoah Sanders (1940-), Archie Shepp (1937-), and the Art Ensemble of Chicago).

Despite his not sharing Olson's anti-mimeticism, cinéma-vérité filmmaker Ricky Leacock's declared intentions have some similarities to those of Charles Olson and other exponents of "projective art." He advocated an "uncontrolled cinema," a cinema that does not depend upon the filmmaker's exerting control over an event but upon following the event's "natural" course of development. Leacock denounced the use of preconceived forms and advocated a cinema free of pre-conceptions, that simply tracked the course of an evolving event. Leacock's beliefs about the ideal form for the interaction among an artist, the grand dynamic of nature, and the artistic form evolving in the creative processes, establish the most significant point where his thought and Olson's converge. For Leacock insisted that cinéma-vérité filmmakers must not formulate plans for their works, or otherwise dictate to reality, nor should they impose relations on their material after the shooting that misrepresent the actual chronology by which the event unfolded. They must invent forms whilst the events being documented are taking place. So, as Stephen Mamber showed in his *Cinéma-Vérité in America: Studies in Uncontrolled Documentary*, the cinéma-vérité filmmaker usually contrives to invent a form that is homologous with the evolving form of the event itself. In short, cinéma-vérité filmmakers must immerse themselves in the events they document and become sufficiently engaged that they develop a sense for how events are going to evolve. Strong documentarians must possess a special, perhaps even intuitive, sensitivity to the flow of reality which allows the film to evolve and grow with the event, and this sensitivity is the basis of their creative methods. The conjoint operation of the artistic will-to-form and nature—a mixture of spontaneity and artifice in which spontaneous features of reality give the artifact its shape and the artifact opens itself to the spontaneity of real processes—produces the narrative structure of cinéma-vérité films. Such a process ensures that the film as it evolves will have an organic form quite different from the mechanical, functionally determined narratives of classical fiction.

Given these affinities, it should not be too surprising that Brakhage has described Leacock as "a supreme artist," and praised his work in Olsonian terms, as working clearly and directly with the "document."[636] However, despite himself, Leacock did impose closure on his works, for he chose as his subjects events that would lead up to and culminate in a contest situation, thus guaranteeing conflict and its resolution (usually with one character triumphing over another). Had he avoided this and launched into an exploration of the multiple indeterminacy of everyday reality, had he filled his films with excursions into tangentially related reality and associative connections and included digressions and fascinations and obsessions in his work, he would have created a form of cinema that would have resembled Olson's poetry; of course, his films then would have looked like Brakhage's *Pittsburgh Trilogy* (*eyes, Deus Ex, The Act of Seeing with One's Own Eyes*, 1971).[637]

What Brakhage includes in his spontaneously evolved documents that Leacock leaves out provides insight into what Brakhage, and Olson, mean by a document. Take *eyes*, Brakhage's "documentary" on the Pittsburgh police. One clear difference between *eyes* and any film that Ricky Leacock has done is that Brakhage's film is far more concerned with the interplay between the self and the world—what one sees and how one sees are much more of a piece in Brakhage's film. This is not to say that Leacock's films are wholly subjective. They are not—they present, as Leacock stated, "aspects of the filmmaker's perception of reality." But Leacock's films do rely on what Emerson called "perception," in which consciousness does not play a key role in shaping the percept, but registers it passively. Brakhage's films rely much more on what Emerson referred to as "imagination," a process in which self and world interact to produce the contents of the perceptual manifold.

Brakhage associates the word "police" with "polis," and then accepts Olson's questionable etymological proposal that "polis" derives from a root that also yielded the Greek word for "eyes." Thus, Brakhage concludes, " 'polis' is 'eyes'." So, 'police,' too, is cognate with "eyes"—the police watch over a city. Whatever the etymological extravagances on which these associations are based, they provided Brakhage with an idea for his film which would allow him to mobilize all his usual strengths, the idea for a film that conveys (transmits) something of the nature of police work by creating an equivalent to a way of seeing (that is, according to one of the basic assumptions that undergirds Brakhage's creative approach, a mode of vision).

A fundamental dichotomy structures the film: while the people with whom the police deal (Brakhage did the film by accompanying two policemen as they went about their duties) appear at least once in full figure—we are shown a bleeding corpse lying in the street, an angry prostitute, traffic-code violators, and disaffected youth—the policemen are never shown full figure. They are always fragmented: we see their midriffs, with police belts, police holsters, and handcuffs; we see wristwatches; we see thumbs hooked, gun-slinger style, into pocket-tops; we see fingers lovingly handling guns, lighting cigarettes, pointing directions, handing out tickets, adjusting their squad car's rearview mirror; we see the policemen (though not in full view) preening and polishing up their caps; and we see, in close-up, badges, chevrons, pop cans. We catch only a glimpse of only one of the policemen's faces, though that face (with sideburns) is shown several times.

The reason for the dichotomy relates to Brakhage's efforts to foreground the work of the imagination; more specifically it relates to the distinction between bodies ("selves") that are seen from the outside and the body (the "self") as it is experienced from within. The filmmaker clearly identified with the police—or, more accurately, with the mode of vision that he imagines is theirs; fathoming that mode of vision, actually imagining (bringing to life) for oneself another's mode of vision so that one might better understand the reality behind the mythological personae (the lifeless representation) embodied in the public's conception of these people, is the very goal of the film. Since Brakhage sets out to imagine/see for himself what being a policeman is like, the policemen are presented as though their place—their "selves"—were being experienced in the manner that each of us experiences his or her own body. The people the police encounter in their daily rounds are presented as one experiences another's "self," from the outside.

The title of another film in Brakhage's Pittsburgh trilogy, *The Act of Seeing with One's Own Eyes*, draws on Olson's etymology of the word historian.[638] In constructing that allusion, Brakhage acknowledges that the entire Pittsburgh trilogy, and, in fact, much of his oeuvre, has the character of a historical document. Each film Brakhage has photographed is a record of evidence that forms the ever-accumulating historical legacy of civilization; hence they could be used by future commentators, from centuries to come, to say, "And this [film] shows what one person in time saw when he observed the Pittsburgh police at work, or the doctors in an emergency ward in Pittsburgh at work, or the pathologist in the Pittsburgh morgue at work. This is evidence, both of how twentieth-century America policed itself, and of the attitudes of one individual towards that." That evidence is exactly what Olson means by "document"; and that Brakhage's films have this character is why he insists on being considered a documentary filmmaker. In considering Olson's idea that each spontaneous recording of how a person saw his or her world contributes to the historical legacy, one should recall Whitehead's idea that every actual occasion moves on to qualify a transcendent creativity.

However, as its title suggests, of all Brakhage's films, it is *The Act of Seeing with One's Own Eyes* that makes most evident the filmmaker's role as historian. When he completed the film, Brakhage acknowledged that its quality was a bit different from his other films, by characterizing his other works as "baroque." Certainly *The Act of Seeing with One's Own Eyes* is a much less lush, mythopoeic film than most of Brakhage's other films, and does not make the same hyperbolic use of superimpositions, for example, that *Dog Star Man* does.[639] It is still, however, recognizable as a work by Brakhage.

The most obvious difference between *The Act of Seeing with One's Own Eyes* and Brakhage's other films is the importance that this film accords to its object matter. *The Act of Seeing with One's Own Eyes* was shot in the Pittsburgh morgue, and depicts pathologists going about their work of performing autopsies on corpses.[640] And it is unflinching, largely because of its repudiation of "baroque" devices. Because the shooting is straight, because we know that it records direct perceptions, because it has all the marks of a spontaneous composition, and because we know that film by and large respects the injunction of the cinéma-vérité filmmakers that the editor must respect chronology (must present shots in the order in which they are made), we are forced to acknowledge the reality of what we see.

The fundamental tension the film modulates is the tension between responding with horror at the images, and responding to the real beauty of the images (for they are astoundingly beautiful); that this is the character of the film's central tension suggests that beauty and horror lie close to one another, an idea that has long been a key to radical aspiration in the arts.[641] Modulating that tension involves, primarily, modulating the viewer's distance from the image (and that Brakhage can bring us to step back from such highly charged imagery, and to see it as beautiful, is testimony to his remarkable skills).

The Act of Seeing with One's Own Eyes mobilizes a set of devices for increasing the emotional power of the images. Besides those listed above, the most notable is the use of a slightly trembling camera: the camera is not completely fixed, but its movements are not large and bold, as so often they are in Brakhage's films. Essentially, the trembling camera embodies the pulse of Brakhage's body as he holds it; confronted with death, it registers a life's vitality, its breath, and its heartbeat.

The Act of Seeing with One's Own Eyes also mobilizes a set of devices for distancing what we are seeing. One we might characterize as "iconographic conversion," distancing an image by turning it into an allusion to a familiar image, which evokes a much less troubled, less intense response. An example occurs early in the film: a heavy, male body lies on the table, an identification tag on its toe. Brakhage shoots the cadaver from a low angle, and turns the image into a Renaissance study in perspective.[642] A related device is what might be termed "motivic conversion": by creating visual rhymes among shots, Brakhage lifts our attention somewhat from what we are seeing, and directs it towards the film's construction. One example would be the use the film makes of images of hands, which is established right at the beginning of the film, when we see first a close-up of gloved hands, then another close-up of hands. Another example is the use of white cloth—white sheets, white uniforms—that are brought right up to the picture plane. The elements of this last motif are used both for themselves, kinetically, and to make transitions.

Another device for creating distance is the use of the close-up (indeed most images belonging to the white leitmotiv are shot mostly in close-up). Levoff points out an irony in this use of close-up: close-ups are used ordinarily to increase an image's emotional impact—a child is sobbing, we see a close-up of the child's hurt expression, and our hearts break.[643] Brakhage, in *The Act of Seeing with One's Own Eyes* uses close-up to reduce the emotional impact of the image; we see a luminscent eyelid meeting eyelashes as composition in light and dark. He does this by hyperbolizing the close-up, so that it becomes virtually an abstraction, a pure colour composition. Indeed, abstraction is another of the devices that Brakhage uses to create greater distance for the viewer.

Finally, there is extremely rhythmic construction of the film. I have commented early on the way Brakhage's complex rhythms braid together rhythmic elements from the object matter's movement, from the cutting, form the movement of the camera, and from the alternation of colours. *The Act of Seeing with One's Own Eyes* is typical of Brakhage's films in this way; in this case, the alternation of colours is between blue-white and various shades of red (which parallels the modulation between more distanced images and more engaging images). However, I must point out that I am underestimating the complexity of the film when I describe the colour exchanges by this polarity, for in fact Brakhage used many different film stocks when shooting, to create a variety of colour values. As a result the rhythm of the modulations from colour to colour is more like that of a fluxing thing. The intricacy with which Brakhage braids together this complex of rhythms here, as in so many of Brakhage's films, makes evident that *The Act of Seeing with One's Own Eyes* presents the way a singular person, with a highly developed sensibility, saw, and imag(in)ed, what he saw.

Leacock, by way of contrast with the historian/filmmaker Brakhage, wants to direct our attention towards the so-called "outer world." Because he is concerned with what Emerson called perception and not with imagination, because he is not concerned to make manifest the work of the imagination through which we form our images of the circumambient world, he does not include this more primordial form of experience in his work. Because he wants to include it, Brakhage has developed a more capacious film form that can accommodate both—indeed many—ways of seeing. Brakhage therefore uses a more lyrical form, one that can contain a greater diversity of elements, bringing them together in such a way that does not elicit any sense that these diverse elements are implausibly or inappropriately conjoined (as similar bindings would seem in Leacock's more rhetorical films). They do so principally by using the associative rhythms that are characteristic of the lyrical—rhythms that, as Northrop Frye has pointed out, avoid the demands of conforming to the conditions of waking consciousness and of adapting themselves to the propositional meanings of assertive language.[644]

Frye also points to where the lyric, which associates words on the basis of the sounds (*melos*) and the images they conjure up (*opsis*), leads. The radical of *melos* is *charm*, Frye states, while the radical of *opsis* is *riddle*.[645] The word "charm," Frye points out, derives from "carmen," Latin for "song," and the oracular (I have used the term "kerygmatic") quality of lyrical works hints at their spell-inducing powers; these powers are physical, or, as I have been saying, perlocutionary. Brakhage, through his use of associative rhythms, fascinates consciousness, calls forth an experience akin to trance. Riddle, Frye states, depends on the fusion of sensation and reflection (I have suggested the ambiguous status of image in Williams's and Olson's poetry and in Stan Brakhage's films); the object of sense experience is used to stimulate mental activity, Frye suggests (as I have suggested that, for Brakhage, occasions of sensation are used to trigger imaginative activity).[646] Riddle, Frye proposes, involves constructing equivalents (Frye does not actually use the term, but it is apposite), that must be plumbed for meaning. Brakhage has created an actual riddle film, *The Riddle of Lumen* (1972), modelled on the riddle-poems of Old English, but that work simply hypostasizes the issue that is a common method to most of Brakhage's films—discerning the import of his equivalents. Frye again points out that riddling is never far from a sense of enchantment or magical capture, and Brakhage's method of equivalents evokes exactly that response.[647]

The form Brakhage creates for the film carries *eyes* towards the radicals of *melos* and *opsis*, that is, towards charm and riddle. The lyric's associative form, and the associative rhythm that animates its primary unifying force, encourages Brakhage to create a work that is a flow of highly dynamic visual elements, many of which are initially unidentifiable ("riddling") and yet, as riddles, do coalesce into meaning; the film is a flow of repeated elements or element-types: badges, chevrons, refreshments, fingers, etc.[648] Meaning—that which we also term "coherence"—emerges out of a flux of repeated shapes, repeated movements, and repeated rhythms, as out of something elemental (a similarity Brakhage characteristically alludes to by making use of self-reflexive forms of construction, and in *eyes'* case by including many flash frames, a single-frame, long flash of pure light). What is remarkable is that despite the film's character as a riddle (and this is characteristic of most of Brakhage's films), the film appears no less riddling, no less mysterious, and no less wondrous after we've identified many of the images and discerned some of their meanings as equivalents. It is surely the awesome alienness of the mode of response his films elicit that accounts for this. And it is the fact that meanings that continue to fascinate (charm) us when watching Brakhage's films repeatedly are dynamic, perlocutionary meanings, not propositional meanings, that accounts for the alienness of this mode of response.

The passages of eyes that Brakhage shot while he accompanied police on their rounds are framed by a curious—a riddling—device. At the beginning there is a passage of clouds (as though from a plane taking off) and, at the end, of sea. The enigmatic preface and conclusion, of course, raise the film from the level of the concrete particular to, as Frye notes that riddles always do, the level of the universal.

Brakhage contrived a similarly riddling form, with a similar conclusion, for *Western History*, another film he made in Pittsburgh in the same year. Near the end of that film, the bodies of the basketball players (who furnish the film's principal object matter) go out of focus. Other out-of-focus shots have appeared in this film. Fred Camper points out their effect, describing it in a manner that recalls Fenollosa's characterization of the metaphysics conveyed by the Chinese written character: it makes shape and motion hardly distinguishable.[649] Two shots of clouds taken from an aerial vantage point, which create an illusion of depth unprecedented in the film, follow. Then, breaking again with the style of the film, which had been made up mostly of short, and often close-up shots, there is a long pan across a red evening sky. This shot is then subjected to a form of fragmentation, as pans of this sort are intercut with shots of erratically careening city lights. This assemblage of fragmentary elements is terminated by static shots that show the city and sky above it. The static shots begin trembling, with the characteristic jitter of pixillation (exposing a single frame at a time) or of manually cranking a Bolex camera with the tiny rewind-handle (a means Brakhage employed relatively often in 1970, usually to create frame-by-frame variations in the image and, so, to embue with energy shots, like this one, that would otherwise be static); then the space of the images thrusts towards and away from the picture plane, with a series of zooms on distant buildings.

Western History, as Fred Camper points out, also fragments the profilmic scene (a Pittsburgh basketball game), so that the results present a continuous associative flow, or what he perceptively describes as "a continuous process."[650] Camper enumerates the devices Brakhage used to create the associative flow: the shots usually begin and end within movement or action, and not as movement or action begins or ends; sequences built up of such actions conjoin images with different dynamic qualities, generally from different subjects: the fragmentation of the human form; the occlusion of faces; the fragmentation of action. The montage of such fragments creates a flow of dynamic elements.

But the film revolves around the contrapositioning of two elements of two sorts. There are "actuality" shots that involve a great deal of action, and "history" shots that are almost static. This opposition is established near the beginning of the film: after several, brief, fast shots of basketball players, we see a static image of a statue. The film includes several static or nearly static images of paintings and sculptures, counterpoised to dynamic images of the basketball game (and often, in fact, to assemblages of fragmentary images, which give the impression of a flow of dynamic elements).

To describe the structuring opposition that gives the film its form in this way is far too simple. Paraphrasing Whitehead, we might say that the issue of the film is not the mere problem of integrating fluency and stillness. There is the double problem, in fact, of discerning: that fluency requires stillness (atemporality) as its completion, or it vanishes without trace; and that stillness, to become actual, requires stillness. The viewer comes to recognize that the filmmaker is striving to embue some of the static shots with movements: the camera moves in circles over a painting; in another shot of painting, we see the room the painting is in and minute actions, reflected in the glass covering; and Brakhage frequently zooms in on the statues or racks focus. Similarly, the viewer comes to recognize that Brakhage is shooting the basketball court so as to make it seem static; sometimes, for example, Brakhage shoots the floor, with the players legs visible just at the very top of the screen.

Furthermore, the film includes shots that seem to mediate between the "history" and the "actuality" shots. These are of two main sorts: first, there are the shots of night lights, which Brakhage's dynamizes through camera movement, though the results of this effort seem relatively feeble; and shots of people in a store, which resemble the actuality images of the basketball game, but are much more static (i.e., they resemble the dynamic shots, but they are more static).

By associating "historical" shots (shots of the paintings and statues) with live action shots (the basketball game), on the basis of the conjoined shots having similar shapes or similar dynamic qualities, Brakhage implies a relation between past and present. The constructions Brakhage uses to dynamize stasis (the past) and to still the moving present suggests something similar. But what is this relation between past and present that Brakhage's use of these forms implies? The answer is somewhat complex, but it has to do with the tragic nature of Brakhage's vision—and by "tragic" I intend not a loss of innocence (though that is an aspect of Brakhage's tragic vision), but rather that Brakhage sees human life as caught in an impossible situation (impossible insofar as it has a contradictory structure). On the one hand, Brakhage depicts the interaction of history and actuality in Western history as a negative force—history dominates actuality, and humans must struggle out from under that domination. History, as *The Dead* disclosed, furnishes only *topoi*. This is what is implied by the near emptiness of some of the shots of the basketball game, of people in the store, of night lights, and the concluding sky images. On the other hand, Brakhage, like Olson, longs for the fleeting moment to produce a form that endures (as Whitehead has it doing). The clash between the two attitudes constitutes another source of the film's tension.

As influential as the idea of spontaneous creation was among visual artists and filmmakers, it was among jazz musicians that we find the closest parallels to Olson's poetic ideas; the parallel is especially strongly marked among the exponents of the "New Thing," a type of jazz that developed in the early 1960s as a reaction to bebop and the styles that descended from bop, and that flourished regnant for a decade: the New Thing made extensive use of polyrhythms and complex patterns of interaction between different metres played simultaneously and that eschewed pre-set chord progressions established by the harmonic structure of pre-set pieces that jazz improvisation, until bop, depended on. Thus, of drummer Elvin Jones, like John Coltrane (a player whose work spanned the transition from post-bebop styles to the New Thing), the critic David C. Hunt wrote:

> Preliminary evaluations of the New Thing indicate that the standards of jazz in the 1960s changed dramatically as a result of a new aesthetic philosophy. The process of acquiring, developing, and knowledgeably utilizing technique ... became subordinate to the raw physical act of music cre-

ation. For the contemporary drummer, the new emphasis on "action," or released energy, mirrors an enactment of the drummer's own psyche and allows other players and listeners to have a direct and immediately accessible path into the deepest recesses of his creative individuality.[651]

These resemble claims Olson made on behalf of Projective Poetry. Further, Hunt's commentary on Elvin Jones's music, like Olson's discourses on Projective Poetry, focuses on the overall flow of energy among polyrhythmic elements. And like Olson, Hunt takes this concern to imply the identity of content and form. Hunt also realized that the condition for responsiveness to compositional imperatives of the moment, to tracking the several energies under hand at any particular moment, resulted in continually altering forms (not unlike those that I have called "perpetually regenerating forms").[652]

Adopting claims first put forward by LeRoi Jones (the name poet and playwright Amiri Baraka used before he became a Muslim), Hunt also proposes a notion that resembles Olson's and Duncan's conception of open form. Hunt quotes from Jones's linear notes for *Coltrane at Birdland*: "You feel when this is finished, amidst the crashing cymbals, bombarded tom-toms, and above it all Coltrane's soprano [saxophone] singing like any song you can remember, that it really did not have to end at all, that this music could have gone on and on like the wild pulse of all living."[653]

LeRoi Jones, in his own famous socio-political commentary on jazz history, *Black Music*, developed further these claims for the physical nature of New Thing music. He comments on Sunny Murray, perhaps the greatest of the New Thing drummers:

> [I]t is immediate, his body-ness, his physicality in the music. Not just as a drum beater but as a conductor of energies, directing them this way and that way. . . . Sunny['s] . . . accents are from immediate emotional necessity rather than the sometimes hackneyed demands of a prestated meter. . . . [Sunny] wants "natural" sounds, natural rhythms. [Here Jones Baraka is referring to Murray's practice of trying to focus, virtually in meditation, on the sounds of the natural environment—birds, car engines, doors, screeches—so as to be able to incorporate their resonances in his playing. Such ambitions resemble those of Olson's objectism.] The drums as a reactor and manifestor of energies coursing through and pouring out of his body. Rhythm as occurence.[654]

Awareness of the body's energy, Olson avers, is the only basis of knowledge, the only ground of metaphysical thinking, the basis of the "only valid metaphysic." Earlier, we glossed Olson's endorsement of the Pythagorean claim that "he who possesses rhythm possesses the universe," and for Olson, rhythm is "a pumping of the real" as breath is evidence of our oneness with the rhythms of things.[655] By turning ourselves over to the rhythms of reality, by learning to feel them in the body, we become participants in the real, rather than masters set above it.

Olson's attention to bodily knowledge likely followed from, and certainly was involved in, his interest in dance. He was a professionally trained dancer and among the first to recognize (around 1951) the greatness of Merce Cunningham. He performed with Cunningham in one of the first happenings, a dance/performance inspired partly by Olson's research among "primitive" cultures. The performance dealt with a fictive tribe of the Upper Nile that Olson called the Gumnoi or Nakeds, and their rituals he characterized as having "taken up direct from energy ... [from] daemonial nature in anything, including ourselves."[656] Among the features of Cunningham's dance that impressed Olson was its non-representational nature—that it aimed not at describing events but of re-enacting the energies that drive an event. Dance generally was Olson's favourite projective form. Olson set out his ideas on the paradigmatic importance of dance for the contemporary writer in a series of letters written to the Indian dancer Nataraj Vashi (collected in "Syllabary for a Dancer"). Comparing the writer and the dancer, he states that the writer

> has been forced, today, to re-make his attention to the kinetics of words, to syllables as the eyes and fingers of his medium, to the nouns & verbs in the torso and limbs, to the connections in the ankles and the wrists of speech and to his total use in any given go as more than the sum of any of those parts, or of their relevances to each other, as a dance which has achieved its implicit form is more than the body and its movements, is, actually, the thing we used to call the beauty of it.[657]

Olson took sufficient interest in dance that he felt justified in referring to dance as the base of his discipline. Dance's syllabary is the source of any other, he proclaimed. His respect for dance suggests the importance he accorded to recognizing the kinetic as the action of life—to being owned by the life force, to being operated by it, to belonging to life; and the forms of his films would suggest that Brakhage adopted the idea that kinesis integrates one with the field of being. What is more, Olson appreciated dance because it returns us to our bodies, because in dance, "we use ourselves." It brings the whole of the intelligence—body, mind, and soul—into participation in the present, as Action Painting and jazz improvisation do. It brings our body into relationship with the whole field of being.

Olson was unquestionably a seminal figure in the movement of American art that began at mid-century and that endeavoured to ground artistic truth in the body—and in particular the body as experienced from within, the body that links us to the rest of reality. Not only did he accord the body a central role in his poetic theory, he suggested that our culture had devalued the body, at a horrifying cost. That devaluation had gone so far that a reaction would develop—one that accorded the body pride of place. In a passage (part of which I quoted earlier) Olson declared:

When man is reduced to so much fat for soap, superphosphate for soil, fillings and shoes for sale, he has, to begin again, one answer, one point of resistance only to such fragmentation, one organized ground, a ground he comes to by a way the precise contrary of the cross, of spirit in the old sense, in old mouths. It is his own physiology he is forced to arrive at. And the way—the way of the beast, of man and the Beast.

It is his body that is his answer, his body intact and fought for, the absolute of his organism in its simplest terms, this structure evolved by nature, repeated in each act of birth, the animal man; the house he is, this house that moves, breathes, acts, this house where his life is, where he dwells against the enemy, against the beast.

Or the fraud. This organism now our citadel never was cathedral, draughty tenement of soul, was what it is: ground, stone, wall, cannon, tower. In this intricate structure are we based, now more certainly than ever (besieged, overthrown), for its power is bone muscle nerve blood brain   a man, its fragile mortal force its old eternity, resistance.[658]

Olson's interest in non-Western cultures—the aboriginal peoples of the Americas, the Sumerians, Hittites, and the Egyptians—and in the source of Western culture, the Greeks, reflected his belief that, with the bombing of Hiroshima, Western culture came to end. Ours is a "post-historical age," he said; the apocalyptic event that ended the war with Japan broke our continuity with the past. We must begin again, amidst the ruins. We must go back, beyond history, to a "primitive" state of mind, and rebuild an immediate bodily, and hence timeless and mythical relation with the world. Olson valued the body so highly, probably, because his sense of embodiment was so strong that he believed it could found in the new, redemptive relation that we, moderns, must build with nature if we are ever to escape the crushing wilfulness of technology. His sense of nature's energy was similar to Lawrence's, and so like Lawrence, he strove to reawaken a sense of the power in nature. The body provides the source of our sense of energy's force, Olson averred. The body teaches us that human being is no more than one among many forms of life in nature and that we, humans, have no special status in nature.

As a poet, Olson was profoundly antagonistic to the idea that there is a single, static tradition. He insisted on taking a personal look at "the facts of the matter," of doing away, as much as possible, with historical influences on the sensibility and understanding, on ridding oneself of inherited perceptions and inherited ways of writing. Olson managed to convince himself that the root meaning of *historein* is to "discover for oneself"; that this was what Herodotus understood by "history"; and that he (Olson) was a Herodotian historian of American life, but a historian only in the sense of one who forges a useful tradition for oneself, and at most, for the citizens of one local polity. But tradition figures in Olson's writings mostly as it does in Brakhage's—as a logomachy that denigrates individual perceptions. The irony in all this, as

P. Adams Sitney points out in his essay on Olson in *Modernist Montage*, is that poets or filmmakers who insist on starting from scratch, on going back to the evidential, and dealing immediately with concrete realities is thereby declaring their allegiance to the Emersonian tradition in American art and letters.

Unlike Tate, Eliot, Brooks, Yeats, or Pound, who attempted to establish an alternative tradition to that of the modern (whether based in the church, the Hermetic tradition, or Fascism), Olson avoided the desire to provide a replacement for the discredited, still-decaying civilization of modernity. Rather than a fixed, static tradition, Olson sought an epistemology, a metaphysics, and a society that would accept a more radical sense of history and that would recognize change and novelty as the only real constants, that would allow seeing for oneself, that would be more vital, more generative than that of the accepted social canons.

Olson's antagonism for stasis accounts for his vilification of logic which, he claimed, prohibits change and growth. Too, logic eliminates the contraries which are usually present in experience. At the very base of Olson's antagonism for logic is his recognition that our hypervaluation of logical form depends on a bifurcated view of nature—a view that denigrates the outer world as a realm of process, change, instability, and chaos and valorizes the inner world as a realm of stasis and stability, the order of which (at least according to the New Critics) is the source of value. Olson was utterly antagonistic to that New Critical proclivity to celebrate the mind's capacity to impose an order on the poem whose coherence and stability transcends the chaos of everyday reality.

In place of "the old discourse," which trades in the tyranny of abstractions, Olson proposed "a new discourse" which would be permeable to the fugitive interactions of real, concrete things. Olson associated "the old discourse" with Europe; "the new discourse" he associated with America. American poets should listen to the speech of their streets, rather than read things European. Olson averred (as Emerson had before him) that America had the responsiblity to renew language by reformulating it so as to bring it into accordance with claims that Emerson had made for natural language. The conviction that America would be the site of a renewal of language is another belief Olson shared with Gertrude Stein. The abstract expressionist painters and Stan Brakhage, at least for the first several years of his career, also believed that America was to be the agent of a renewal of the arts, a break with dead European traditions and the start of something new and individual.[659]

Olson's efforts at reconstructing language resembled not just Emerson's proposals concerning natural language: they exhibited, too, the reformist zeal that entered American life through the Puritans. As I remarked above,

Olson himself described his efforts as a part of "the American push to find out an alternative discourse to the inherited one, to the one implicit in the language from Chaucer to Browning, to try, by some other means than 'pattern' and the 'rational,' to cause discourse to cover—as it only ever best can—the real."[660] Like Stein before him, and like the abstractionist painters who were his contemporaries, and like Brakhage after him, Olson believed that America, by cutting free from domination by a historical tradition, pitched people back upon themselves. Americans must speak of "ONE'S SELF AND ONE'S RELATIONS," Olson stated, because "We Americans have nothing but our personal details."[661] Like most American Romantics from Emerson to the present, Olson celebrated the primacy of experience. He strived for a poetic line that would externalize the pulse of an actual person's thinking. Olson told his friend and fellow poet Cid Corman, "The revolution that I am responsible for is this one, of the identity of a person and his expression." Olson advocated what Brakhage consistently practises (both in his public speaking and, what is more important, in his filmmaking), viz., replacing the conventional sociolect with a personal idiolect: "there is point now to speak of a syntax which is, ultimately, dependent upon the authority of a completed man, might I say, in this sense, that the syntax is of the man's own making, not something accepted as a canon of the language in its history and the society."[662] Brakhage offers identical arguments in the second and third pages of *Metaphors on Vision*, in which he argues against conventional syntax and the conventional film style and for an idiolexical cinema that draws upon the completed self.

Olson proposed what Brakhage's practice (both as a writer and filmmaker) also implies, that completed humans will possess linguistic and imaginative powers beyond those inherited from the social order of communication, and, what is more telling, that only discourse that is so thoroughly idiosyncratic as to be idiolexical can reveal those powers. To fall into speaking the conventional language of one's society is to lose one's being in inauthenticity; consequently, making oneself complete and authentic means formulating a discourse that every point in its creation bucks against all conventions. The authentic discourse of a completed person, instead of following conventions, is shaped, at every turn, by an individualized and localized imaginative act. Poet Cid Corman commented on the force of such speech, using the example of Olson's language to typify it: "Olson's language is thrown back at him as if it were impossible. But the meaning is in the motion of it. And what is impossible is to read him consecutively and fail to grasp, or be grasped by, what he is driving at. For the 'end' arrives at every moment and is 'co-substantive.' "[663] One could make the same the point concerning Brakhage's films that Corman makes of Olson's language—that the meaning of Brakhage's films is in their dynamics, and even if one opens oneself to their dynamics, and allows one's animation to be affected by the energies they impart, it is impossible to fail to grasp, or be grasped by, what he is driving at.

Corman spoke on behalf of an action poetry whose founding ideas resemble the ideas that ground Action Painting. While many critics have traced Brakhage's aesthetic declarations (and particularly those in *Metaphors on Vision*) to the influence of the theory and practice of Action Painting, the evidence of Brakhage's own references suggests that action poets such as Charles Olson, Cid Corman, and Michael McClure had a greater influence. The aesthetics of dynamism that underlies action poetry derives from Whitehead's idea of presentational immediacy. Whitehead believed that perception in the mode of presentational immediacy is more primitive than our ordinary mode of experience, which he calls symbolic reference, since symbolic reference is a mixed mode of perception that combines the two pure modes, causal efficacy and presentational immediacy. Whitehead's analysis of perception in the mode of causal efficacy showed it to be a crude form of perception, for it involves the inheritance of feeling from past data. Perception in the mode of causal efficacy, which pervades any actual entity, has no need of consciousness or life. Perception in the mode of presentational immediacy is more complex, as it does demand consciousness. It is the perceptive mode "in which there is clear, distinct consciousness of the 'extensive' relations of the world. . . . In this 'mode' the contemporary world [the world existing in the instant] is consciously prehended as a continuum of extensive relations."[664] Causal efficacy transmits into the present the inheritance from the past; these data are massive in emotional power, but vague and inarticulate. Presentational immediacy, on the other hand, transmits data that are sharp and precise. Too, the data that presentational immediacy transmits have spatial location—they resemble the sensa that ground the empirical and analytic philosopher's analysis of experience (i.e., an immediate and almost uninterpreted sensation such as "green there"). And, unlike the data that causal efficacy transmits, the data of presentational immediacy are self-contained temporally and unconnected with any inheritance.

The two pure modes of perception amount to a functional separation of the two forms of location, temporal and spatial. Whitehead, as I pointed out above, maintains that causal efficacy, by transmitting data from the past, enables an actual entity to form temporal relations. Presentational immediacy, by transmitting data from the world contemporaneous with the instant of prehension (that is, the world constituted by actual entities that have no causal connection to the prehending entities), enables an actual entity to have extensive relations, but lacks any power of continuity. To conceive of perception in the mode of presentational immediacy only in this way would be too simplistic, for there is interaction between these two functionally distinct modes of perception. Because perception in the mode of causal efficacy occurs in the first phase of concrescence, it presents only ill-defined sensa. Perception in the mode of presentational immediacy, because it occurs in later phases of concrescence, seizes upon these vague emotional feelings and transmutes them into well-defined qualities that are then projected onto the region of experience contemporaneous with the percipient occasion. Thus the two modes of perception, by reason of their functional differentiation, complement one another.

These ideas, though perhaps a bit abstract, really are close to ideas that Olson advanced, and their influence on Olson's manner of formulating his ideas was direct. Whitehead argued that contemporaneous actual entities are not mutually prehensive—that they do not prehend one another follows from his analysis of the concepts of prehension and concrescence, and especially what he called the principle of universal relativity, that is, the principle that every item in an actual entity's universe affects its concrescence (or, to state the principle otherwise, it belongs to the nature of any "being" that it is a potential for future "becoming"). Any entity contributes to the general process of becoming, but does not affect other contemporaneous occasions.

Olson must have found the principle of universal relativity extremely attractive, for it has the strength to explain the relation of every element to every other in the open form creative process. But it had an even more definite influence; to understand that influence, we must ask Whitehead's philosophy the important question, "If contemporaneous actual entities cannot prehend one another, then how can an actual entity prehend a contemporaneous actual entity in the mode of presentational immediacy?"[665] Whitehead answers that it cannot. People who are conscious of some entity located in contemporary space do not really perceive the nexus of contemporaneous actual entities—in fact, they do not even derive their sensations from contemporaneous events. Rather they derive them from antecedent states of their own bodies (and indirectly from the world, as it affects their bodies) and then project those sensations into contemporary space. The idea that organisms take energy in through the body and project it out into the environment influenced Olson's idea of Projective Poetry at its very bases.

It is important not to confuse perception in the mode of presentational immediacy with prehension in the mode of presentational immediacy. Perception is a more complex society than prehension, for in any perception, a mind (i.e., a series of complexes of actual entities that share a common pattern through their temporal span) prehends the contents of a series of multiple entities that also share an evolving pattern in their temporal path; when a mind experiences something in the mode of presentational immediacy, each entity in that mind experiences reality as made-up of multiple series of prehensions. Whitehead maintains that we require the serial nature of perception to explain how a perception can be sustained. Whitehead's idea that perception involves a changing subject knowing a changing object through its body is another of his epistemologico-metaphysical notions that Olson probably would have found attractive.

The desire to create works that exist wholly in the present, that import no influence from the past, was part of what drove the action poets (i.e., the poets associated with the aesthetics of abstract expression) to use "spontaneous, irregular, guerrilla forms."[666] The action poets aspired to create works that belong wholly to the present in order to recreate the pure perceptual mode that Whitehead refers to as presentational immediacy; that is, they strove to create poetry that was as much of the nature of process as reality is, to "get on with it" by getting with it, whatever it was that it was going.[667] Yet at the same time, they desired to reawaken the primitive mode of awareness, with attributes of perception in the mode of causal efficacy.[668] This accounts for their being chary of hypotaxis, of sentence forms involving relative clauses (consider the contrast between Olson's poetry and Swinburne's), and of extended qualifiers, since sentences that do not employ those constructions can better convey the flux of reality and the sense that change comes as so many discrete impulses. The action poets wanted to create a totally synchronic experience, in which anticipation and recollection play no part. All these features of action poetry have analogues in Stan Brakhage's films. Brakhage's use of rapid montage, of frequent broad changes in visual forms, of flattened space and extreme changes in colour, intensity, or speed from visual form to visual form also suggests reality in flux. And, like action poems, Brakhage's films thwart anticipation and recollection, preferring instead to create experience that transpires in the immediate instant, the unconflicted and non-contradictory time of *Dasein*, a time that is manifest in the living, moving present which transmutes and totalizes the past into a space for subjectivity.

The idea that authentic language expresses the being of the person who speaks is the basis of a fundamental challenge to the poetics of the New Criticism. Following Eliot's distinction between the person who suffers and the mind that creates, New Critics had argued that the "I" of the lyrical poem is a fictional *persona*, not the actual poet. This distinction opened up the space of irony, affording creators the distance that New Critics held in such esteem; they claimed the distinction made possible a detachment that allowed for: condensation, polysemy, control, complexity, ambiguity, nuance; and the attendant virtues—regularity of metre, coherence, formal rhyme, and balance. The closure implied by this control had roots in a severe, even pessimistic, ethos. Olson, Duncan, McClure, Ginsberg, and other advocates of open form poetry found this whole business unlikeably timid and unacceptably repressive. They advocated freedom, spontaneity, and ecstasy. They wanted "no persona and no personality," as Olson said of the *Maximus Poems*, and not because they cherished impersonality, but because they considered personality something that enclosed an person in a false construct. What they did want was a "VOICE," for a voice registers an authentic individual. The Projective Poet spoke for the individual, against the repressive order, and strove to produce poetry that would reveal the glory of a completed individual; and in their practice, the Projective Poet strove to embody—literally to give body to—his or her voice. Grammar was a constraint limiting the full disclosure of the full human being. The Open Form poets' refusal of hypotactical constructions and their preference for parataxis is a form of agrammatism. Brakhage shares these beliefs, for he argues that the codes for lighting, colour temperature, exposure, and camera-handling that characterize the Hollywood cinema are similarly repressive, as they eliminate all evidence of the idiosyncrasies of the particular human being who handles the camera and the particular situation in which he or she works.

Olson's view is that "the structures of the real are flexible, quanta do dissolve into vibrations, all does flow."[669] To this he could have added, since he also recognized the continuation of the past, the Whiteheadian qualification that change occurs to reconcile change with permanence, and that change takes place only to the end of being made permanent, since all events move on to qualify a transcendent creativity—that is, to interpret Whitehead's cosmology as an aesthetic theory (as Olson was certainly prone to doing), every creative act moves on to become an enduring influence, both on immediately following activities, and on much later ones. Earlier in the same essay (in a passage which was quoted in part above) Olson had characterized the achievement of the nineteenth century:

> An idea shook loose, and energy and motion became as important a structure of things as that they are plural, and, by matter, mass. It was even shown that in the infinitely small the older concepts of space ceased to be valid at all. Quantity—the measurable and numerable—was suddenly as shafted in, to any thing, as it was also, as had been obvious, the striking character of the external world, that all things do extend out. [Cf. Whitehead's critique of sixteenth-century science that rendered nature as characterless atoms in motion.] Nothing was now inert fact, all things were there for feeling [a term that here has Whiteheadian overtones], to promote it, and be felt; and man, in the midst of it [just where Whitehead placed him], knowing well how he was folded in, as well as how suddenly and strikingly he could extend himself, spring or, without even moving, go, to far, the farthest—he was suddenly possessed or repossessed of a character of being, a thing among things, which I shall call his physicality. It made a re-entry of or

to the universe. Reality was without interruption, and we are still in the business of finding out how all action, and thought, have to be refounded.[670]

But, Olson opined, the course of change (which, when considered from a sufficiently synoptic vantage point becomes history) never progresses linearly, as the Semitic traditions suggest, nor cyclically, as the ancient Greeks, among others, believed. Its outcome is not foreclosed. Olson's view of history resembles Whitehead's analysis of concrescence, for Olson claimed that all history is co-present, but it must be kept going moment to moment. He insisted, further, that the only agency through which history can go on being regenerated is the agency of "actual willful men," as he describes them in "The Special View of History." The lack of tradition and the demand that the individual regenerate history ensures that American history will be anything but progressive, smooth, and continuous.[671]

Olson realized this, indeed he celebrated it: "when traditions go, the DISCONTINUOUS becomes the greener place."[672] Hence Olson's poetry employs collage, fragments, and discontinuity. He favoured compositional forms that use juxtaposition, correlation, and interaction. These are forms of construction that Stan Brakhage also uses frequently.

To emphasize the discontinuity of his poems, Olson used: sentence fragments; rhetorical repetition that has the effect of isolating, through stress, the repeated element; extreme variation in line length; percussive rhythm with frequent caesurae; multiple digressions and interpolations before the sentence's period (if it comes); and almost constant rhetorical emphasis that, at times, makes almost every phrase seem an ejaculation. There is a passage early in the *Maximus Poems*:

> the underpart is, though stemmed, uncertain
> is, as sex is, as moneys are, facts!
> facts, to be dealt with, as the sea is, the demand
> that they be played by, that they only can be, that they must
> be played by, said he, coldly, the
> ear![673]

Look at how Olson breaks apart the movement from "the underpart is" to its resolution, "facts!" In this description, Olson introduces, first, the qualifier, "though stemmed," then amplifies it with "uncertain," then picks up the line from which he had digressed, qualifies its subject by putting down "is," then presents, initially, one comparison, "as sex is," then a different one—"as moneys are"—and then finally comes to the sentence's period, "facts." He even marks "facts" with an exclamation point, to isolate it and to stress its importance; the line break after "facts" further emphasizes its separateness. The use of rhetorical ejaculation to isolate a term continues in the next line, which opens with an isolating repetition of "facts." Olson then glosses "facts" with another isolated phrase, "to be dealt with." Then the momentum of introduced comparisons takes over from the previous line. What seems most simply there, "to be dealt with," in Gloucester is the sea, and so the comparison is "as the sea is." Too, the comparison echoes "as sex is" and so (considering that the poet is male) suggests that the sea is feminine. So Olson leaves the next fragment, "the demand," hanging. As the fracture hints at the pumping rhythms of sex, we realize at that point, if not before, that the staccato phrases convey the energy of sexual activities; and that the alliteration explains elements of the passage's lexicon: "underpart," "stemmed," and "moneys." He follows this with a statement of the demand, then two reformulations of it. Next we have what seems to be an interruption, the words "said he," a statement that Olson immediately qualifies by a quasi-independent adverb, whose isolation he emphasizes by setting it off by commas. The line ends with a definite article, separated from the adjoining noun by a line break, lest the line conform too strictly to the pattern of a statement attribution breaking into a statement. The line break also sets off the incongruous, completely isolated noun, "ear!" The general aural texture formed by the mixture of stopped, voiced consonants, the high frequency of caesurae, and the rhetorical exclamations ("facts!" and "ear!") produce a general impression of urgency and energy associated with its sexual theme.

Olson believed that the intense experience of the vivified body responding to the open field had restorative and reparative potential. By coming to see and hear for oneself, with one's own eyes and ears, one could escape from Heidegger's "they" (*das Mann*), the crowd which substitutes a generalized inauthenticity for the individual percipient and whose collectivity constitutes what Olson called pejorocracy. Thus, in "Song 1" of "The Songs of Maximus," he writes:

               colored pictures
        of all things to eat: dirty
        postcards
                And words, words, words
        all over everything
                        No eyes or ears left
        to do their own doings (all

        invaded, appropriated, outraged, all senses

        including the mind, that worker on what is
                                And that other sense
        made to give even the most wretched, or any of us, wretched,
        that consolation (greased
                        lulled
        even the street-cars

        song[674]

Olson suggests here that inert words conceal reality; that is, he claims that if the power of the word to uncover being goes unsensed and unrealized, beings are obscured. Language conveys only a generalized, abstracted, and overly schematized representation of the world. Pejorocracy is the social order that develops when humans come to deal with the word rather than the world. Olson even attacks picture-making at the beginning of the poem, probably because pictures describe or represent reality rather than transmitting its energies (and so are an inert form of representation). The only hope Olson offered for a way out of pejorocracy is for us to get in touch with our doings, to get back to what Stan Brakhage called, in the context of a similar argument "a world before the 'beginning was the word.'"[675] Language as discourse (for the ear) and as image (for the eye) has depleted our immediate, sensuous perception of objects. As Olson stated, and Brakhage reiterated at the beginning of *Metaphors on Visions*, our mental images are social and linguistic constructs. Language impedes the body's natural tendency to produce a unique form of vision that is uniquely proper to that particular body. Certainly, the eye is capable of seeing without preconceptions, of being phenomenologically reduced (to use Husserl's terminology), but in the time of pejorocracy, a deliberate and even violently forceful banishing of intruder language is necessary to accomplish this phenomenological reduction. Only in this way can we get, as Husserl's maxim has it, *zu den Sachen selbst* (to the thing itself), or as Olson's American colleague, the poet William Carlos Williams put it, to the state in which we know of "no ideas but in things." The similarity between Williams's and Husserl's slogans should say something about the currency of that conviction in the redemptive power that results from transcending "the verbal icon."

Olson maintained, then, that tradition has interfered with the normal functioning of the human organism by interposing a screen between the body and the world. The circuit of the external world/body/senses/imagination/projection-into-the world essential to creativity has been broken, for language (in the form of both discourse and structured imagery) has intervened and obscured the world. Language has disrupted the body's sensitive reaction to the throbbing energy of reality and has lessened the intensity of sensation. It has weakened the intention to act which is the motor-force of imagination. Art made from mimetic or descriptive language does not "get what you are after—so far as a human being goes," viz., life. A poetry of immediacy, that tries to capture experience while it is still alive and hot at least stands some chance of avoiding the inauthenticity of language as discourse and picture.

Olson did have doubts about how a poet (who is, after all, like all modern human beings, implicated in pejorocracy) could escape from its deleterious effects—doubts he related in "Song 2" of "The Songs of Maximus."

Nonetheless he harboured a faith that it is possible. His principal tactic for reconnecting with the energy and emotional value of experience was basically the same as the method that Brakhage relied on from 1957 to about 1980. The tactic was to begin by focusing attention on what was closest to him—himself, his home, his locale, his family. Attention to the particulars that compose any situation can provide artists with the energies and the means—even with the words and images, if they are conceived as vehicles of particular energies—to keep moving from one encounter to another, from one percept to the next, from one instant to the next. Olson would surely have agreed with Brakhage's idea of perception being an adventure.

> This morning of the small snow
> I count the blessings, the leak in the faucet
> which makes of the sink time, the drop
> of the water on water as sweet
> as the Seth Thomas
> in the old kitchen
> my father stood in his drawers to wind (always
> he forgot the 30th day, as I don't want to remember
> the rent[676]

Here self and other, the internal and external worlds, are so close to one another that energy flows easily from one to the other. Thus Olson's work, like Brakhage's, often employs forms that bring their readers/viewers through many layers of the familiar and ordinary until they come to see the commonplace as energized with some force or as possessing some allure that previously escaped their notice. In conversation with Robert Duncan (at a public lecture/discussion at Berkeley in 1965), Olson was absolutely insistent on the importance of one's own locale, one's place, one's body.

> And I don't believe there is a single person in this room that doesn't have the opportunity—the absolute place and thing that's theirs. I mean places and things that are theirs. . . . I don't believe that everyone of us isn't absolutely *specific*. And *has* his specificity. . . . The *reductive* is what I'm proposing. I don't think you can get your recognitions by going out. I think they come from within.[677]

As Brakhage did in most of the works he made in the period 1957-80, Olson used forms that allow for abrupt changes in direction and thus keep the eye and mind of the viewer/reader continually in motion. Olson suggests the heat of the moment by ellipses and by breaking off lines abruptly, Brakhage by using fragments of actions. In both cases, the maker creates the impression of a flow of discontinuous sensations. The forms both artists create often serve to transmit each discontinuous perception as equally important as the rest—so Olson's poetry or Brakhage's cinema rarely offer a final insight in which the work of art comes to rest.[678] Even when Olson or

Brakhage encounter discoveries that seem especially important, they present those moments as ontologically, aesthetically, and experientially fortuitous and not (as they would if they were composing a modernist poem) as formally necessary. Accordingly, both favour cumulative over teleological forms; and both artists have a tendency towards the list form, which both have resisted (and Brakhage counseled against), though some of Olson's followers, including Allen Ginsberg, have given in to that tendency, and produced very compelling work.[679]

We can see the process by which teleological form is transformed into cumulative form in one of Brakhage's breakthrough films, *Anticipation of the Night* (1958). The *fabula* (see glossary) of the film (the narrative action the film represents), though intense, is simple and even conventional: a man, whom we see only in shadow (and first as soft brown shadow), becomes fascinated with a glass sphere, filled with water, and containing a rose; this incident contains echoes of the famous scene of *Citizen Kane* but, aside from suggesting the empty centre that is at the heart of *Anticipation of the Night* as well, this allusion has less importance than the metaphor it offers—as representing innocence being buffeted about by forces larger than itself. The shadow man goes out a door, passing through a beam of light from the open door as he goes (this transition from open to closed is repeated several times in the film, and each time is marked either by a shot of the door swinging inside the house, then outside again, or a tremoring reflection in the door's glazing) walks across a lawn, sees a baby crawling on the grass as though struggling and pushing into trees; he then walks up to a tree, throws a rope over a branch, forms a noose, and hangs himself. While walking across the lawn, between the door and tree, the shadow man experiences visions precipitated by his imminent death.

This structure is a giant elaboration of a passage in Maya Deren's *Meshes of the Afternoon* (1943). The global shape of the earlier film depicts the female protagonist's regression from what the pioneering English child psychoanalyst Melanie Klein called the depressive state to what she called the paranoid-schizoid state and so, like *Anticipation of the Night*, *Meshes of the Afternoon* produces ominous feelings and a sensation that some great menace threatens the protagonist. In one passage of *Meshes of the Afternoon*, the protagonist splits, and one part of her crosses a room, deliberately, and carrying a knife, to kill another version of herself, asleep in a chair. With each footfall, Deren cuts to a new location, so it appears that the journey she takes to kill herself spans many places—perhaps even all times and all places.

Anticipation of the Night elaborates this single passage from *Meshes of the Afternoon* into a work on a much larger scale and of much greater complexity. There are in fact two journeys represented in *Anticipation of the Night*—an

418   The Films of Stan Brakhage

actual journey and a visionary (imagined) journey. But though the visions in *Anticipation of the Night* present an imaginative journey, the "deformations" of the *syuzhet* (see glossary) so elaborate the film's presentation of incident, so thicken the *fabula*'s incidental texture as to almost, but not quite, deconstruct its narrative. In his visions the shadow man goes out the door (this is a common point from which the two real and the imaginary stories diverge) down a road, through an amusement park (which appears more like a demon-ridden realm where menacing fantasies take palpable form), past a temple, and through a nursery.

There are further similarities between the two films. Like *Meshes of the Afternoon*, *Anticipation of the Night*, encloses the action that is the film's core within a frame. The first framing section presents slowly evolving visual forms of light and shadow on the wall (and so expands upon the device central to the first framing section of *Meshes of the Afternoon*, which also presents, primarily in shadow as well, the protagonist and central events which the protagonist elaborates in her mind) and so seems to offer a first-person view on events; moreover, like *Meshes of the Afternoon*, *Anticipation of the Night* uses shadows to evoke the menace of a domestic situation and to adumbrate (though much more indirectly than its antecedent) that strife in the protagonist's marriage drives the protagonist's actions. And, as in *Meshes of the Afternoon*, the *syuzhet* (the manner that we learn about the *fabula*) renders the *fabula* more ambiguous than I have indicated. For example, just as it is not certain whether the protagonist in *Meshes of the Afternoon* actually dies, nor whether the central part of film is actually a dream, it is not really certain that the shadow man actually sees a baby crawling on the grass. The baby first appears in close-up, crawling, only its arm visible; then the camera pans to its face, first from one direction, then from another; the section with the crawling starts, really, with out-of-focus images of flesh, then parts, and the baby seems to take shape from out of this dynamic-coloured light. The filmmaker seems to create the baby as much as he seems to find it, so it could be that the baby is a vision of himself as an infant, that serves to evoke the innocence that life's woes have distorted.[680]

But more important, the complexity of the *syuzhet* somewhat obscures the film's *fabula*. I will grant that I am not the strongest reader of narrative. Still, I had to watch *Anticipation of the Night* many times before I sorted out the story which provides a key through-line for the work (which I have set out above); and I suspect that, although I am probably much slower to understand such matters than most people, the majority of its viewers have to see the film a few times before they fathom the storyline (the *fabula*). For a key feature of the work, the flow of its visual forms is not organized narratively—at least not primarily—but in another way. What determines that flow is complex, and resists being described. We have already noted that the images in Brakhage's film often have an ambiguous status, as representations that depict the contents of consciousness and as pure material constructs that transmit the energy of Brakhage's conscious states to the viewer—*Anticipation of the Night* was the first of Brakhage's films that developed such ambivalence. The visionary aspect of the work is evident and demands little comment, other than to note that one effect of converting the narrative's point of view to the first person is, as in Joyce's work, to attenuate the narrative's forward impetus. But *Anticipation of the Night* is also a pure rhythmic achievement, a piece whose musical construction anticipates the *Prelude* to *Dog Star Man* (a film that is every bit as Romantic as *Anticipation of the Night*, and which also has the tree of life and death as its central image—a still axis around which the film's vortex spins).

The opening section of the film provides a case study in the film's rhythmic intricacy. That section interweaves images of the protagonist's dark brown shadow, passing through a beam of light coming from an open door and from a window, with images of night lights shot with a moving camera. The alternation structure established at the beginning is augmented as the shadows of the rose floating in a glass bowl join, as though in a dance, with those of the shadow of the protagonist and the moving night lights. This alternating series is then further augmented, with the flares of ends of the film, which bring it to its conclusion. The door closes behind the protagonist, and this closing is repeated several times in the film's first fifteen minutes (another variant of *Meshes of the Afternoon*, which depicts the protagonist opening the door several times). This repetition with augmentation is reminiscent of Gertrude Stein's writing, as P. Adams Sitney noted.[681]

When the shadow man goes out the door, Brakhage intercuts shots of the trees reflected in the door's glazing with shots of trees. The door led into the repetition, so, in accordance with the form of repetition-with-advance that appears often in Gertrude Stein's writings, we expect that the film would proceed to a series of shots of trees. It does—specifically it moves on to blurred shots of overexposed (and therefore whitish) foliage, to a series of repeated panning movements, each of which ends on foliage. These pans move in a circular motion, and this Stein-like series of circular sweeps is augmented with the addition of interposed circular pans of the night world.

This series of repetitions is then made even more complex by cutting so as to match rhyming shapes on either side of the cut, at just the point when the pan reaches maximum velocity, so it seems suddenly to reverse itself. This reversal triggers another, as the elements of the opening scene are presented in reverse order: first we see the door, then the window, then the doorway. Such transpositions are also characteristic of Stein's writing.

The next passage, which returns us outdoors, also has a Steinian construction. It begins with an alternation of the spray of water from a garden hose, producing a rainbow, with night lights and film flares (to articulate a contrast among different types of light). This alternation is augmented by shots of the crawling baby—the baby is discovered, as though accidentally, as the camera sweeps over her arm. He returns time and time again to record the crawling infant's motion, approaching the baby from different directions and intercutting these shots with careening shots over grass and leaves that produce a phantasmagoric effect that we surmise might represent the shadow man's imagining of the baby's vision, since the perspective remains that of the filmmaker.

As Olson's poetics instructed, *Anticipation of the Night* stresses film's kinetic properties. The two journeys the shadow man embarks upon are partly a pretext for emphasizing motion and flux. In keeping with this, the scenes in this film are unified primarily through movement (there are many occasions in the film when one shot, of one object matter, with one quality of movement, is joined with another shot, of different object matter, but with the same quality of movement); so, as P. Adams Sitney notes, the rhetoric of the film is one of becoming.[682] The shadow realm, as well as establishing a dark tenor for the film, conveys the sense that everything is flux, everything is insubstantial, everything undergoes change. The reduction of depth that occurs when one shoots shadows, or when one shoots at night, contributes to the role the camera movement plays as a formal unifier.[683] The film's light play also conveys this Heraclitean metaphysics that is embodied in Olson's poetry: the two journeys are also a pretext for presenting menacingly illuminated trees, appearing and disappearing, highway lights and houses flitting by like active but ephemeral events, and for presenting representations of children (the only humans that appear in the film directly and not through shadow) that are as fleeting as childhood innocence itself. To be sure, there is narrative justification for the instability of the film's visual forms: it explains that under the impact of imagined death, the protagonist's vision regresses to the conditions of an infant's (in much the same way as the mental mechanism of *Meshes of the Afternoon*'s protagonist reverts to the paranoid-schizoid state); the visionary realm, as represented in *Anticipation of the Night*, is a realm of childhood, of amusement parks and the nursery. More important, the threat of death breaks down the conventions of seeing, and the images of *Anticipation of the Night* resemble the unstable visual forms of preverbal consciousness. Furthermore, the key section of the film presents (on one interpretation, for the scene is marvellously polysemic and invites more than one interpretation) a baby dreaming of a heron. The heron raises itself and spreads its wings; thus, it changes from a small to a large and threatening bird. Because the film identifies the shadow man with the baby, we can interpret the scene to suggest that the shadow man dreams the bird, and that this transformation conveys the terror of erection and sexuality; and we can interpret this as indicating that the shadow man's anxiety (and possibly marital strife) have their origin in sexual fears. *Anticipation of the Night* immediately followed Brakhage's psychodramas, and the sexual anxiety Brakhage conveys in *Anticipation of the Night* relates it to the psychodramas *The Way to Shadow Garden* (1954) and *Reflections on Black* (1955), which present a sexually troubled protagonist haunted by thoughts of suicide and blindness.

But to explain the film's characteristics in narrative terms is finally less important than to assess their role in the film's formal construction. Formally the film is, as Olson instructed that poetry should be, a rhythmic reoccurrence of basic themes (which we can consider as packets of energy). The principal motifs are: trees, highway lights, amusement park attractions, a sleeping baby, and the heron just referred to; secondary motifs are the rose, the door (the gates of hell?), the baby, the rainbow (the light of heaven, coming at the end of a violent episode?), deer, and a bear. A key feature of Brakhage's manner of introducing these themes suggests anticipation. For each principal motif dominates one of the "subfields" that form the entire field of the film and instills a characteristic force into the subfield it dominates. The principal motifs also appear outside their particular subfields, however, and when they do, they clash with the motif that dominates the other subfields. But Brakhage usually presents at least a brief glimpse (and sometimes more) of a new motif slightly before the beginning of the subfield that it dominates; once we recognize this formal principle, the appearance of a new motif encourages us to anticipate its dominant role in the following section.

Anticipation of the Night uses intense, often violent camera movement— so violent that their destructive energies seem only just contained by the somewhat tenuous organization that the film's editing imposes on the material. The film uses three sorts of camera movement: horizontal camera movements, like a pan, but (like the sort of movement Brakhage advised using in *Metaphors on Vision*) much more shaky than a pan in a Hollywood or a T.V. movie; movements towards or away from the subject that, because of the perspectival explosion or implosion they create, have a violent effect; and swirling movements—vortices that unloose powerful centrifugal forces. The horizontal movements usually convey movement through space, while the movements towards the objects convey a desire to penetrate the object, and the gyrating movements convey a vertiginous mental state such as might be induced by menace. But all in all, the film's kinetic characteristics accord closely with the ideas that Olson was preaching at the time.

While the film presents a narrative, Brakhage attenuates its impact in a number of ways. An important means of which Brakhage makes extensive use is to join diegetically disjunctive spaces into a continuous sequence by matching movement. Thus shots taken from a moving car are joined together by their common kinetic properties. Or the camera moves in on the baby crawling on the lawn; the same speed and direction of motion is maintained in the following shot that presents lights from a passing car; the similarity between the dynamic qualities of the two shots join the two diegetically non-contiguous spaces into a unbroken flow. In the same vein, in the amusement park sequence, the relative frequency of splices that join matched movements is uncommonly high for Brakhage. To achieve this effect, Brakhage often collapses the image's depth. The shots which depict the children on the amusement park rides, with lights behind them, seem strangely flat. Brakhage also facilitates these transitions by having a limited range of colours dominate each scene: the interior scenes at the beginning tended towards old wine brown; the shots of the night colours tended towards blue; the scenes in the garden were green; the scenes in the amusement park tended to orange, and the temple scenes towards brown and orange; the shots of concluding scenes (daybreak) are in red.

Another means Brakhage uses to join diegetically disjunctive spaces is to employ plastic cutting—to join to shots that have similar visual forms on either side of the cut. At one point in *Anticipation of the Night*, for example, Brakhage cuts together a number of doors and windows, on the basis of the similarity of their shapes. Another device, which Fred Camper analyzed with scrupulous care, is substitution: Brakhage cuts from one object to another— substitutes one article for another—that occupies a similar part of the screen to stress that he is joining together different kinds of light. Thus, for example, Brakhage intercuts similar patterns of sunlight on all walls. In these instances, and others like them, the editing draws our attention to the variations in the intensity of light among similarly shaped patterns. That latter emphasis is signal because, as Fred Camper again has pointed out, *Anticipation of the Night* is about light and presents many different ways in which light is formed: the film's opening presents many shadow forms, on a wall, near a door, modulated by the aperture; and in the opening sections of the film there are many images of walls dappled by sunlight reflected from some surface or refracted through some medium, so that over time the light undergoes continual change; we are patches of light on the lawn; light split by water droplets into a rainbow of colours; we see the mysterious light of dusk and daybreak; and we see streetlights, storelights, automobile lights, amusement park lights.

The combined effect of these two means of creating continuity among diegetically disjunctive spaces transforms the film into a riddling, lyrical work rather than an epic film in a narrative form; the primary means of this transposition is to conjoin shots for dynamic rather than causal reasons or reasons having to do strengthening the film's diegesis. More specifically it transforms the film into a continual flux of light, and this flux imbues the film with an unflagging kinesis. A fine example occurs where Brakhage cuts from pan across night lights to a pan across grass: the cut occurs just as the camera, moving in the same direction and at the same rate as in the previous shot of the night lights, enters a dark patch on the grass that matches the dark of the night. Then the light surges up, as the camera passes out of the dark patch and into the light; the light changes. The intercutting of shots of trees in morning light, of closing doors which gradually darken the screen from right to left within an ominous regularity and sombreness of space, or of different aspects of a rainbow, photographed with a moving camera that several times comes to an abrupt stop, creates a dynamic flux of light and space. One could consider that *Anticipation of the Night* is composed of a number of motions that present themselves over and over, in various new combinations, of: jittery night lights; slowly opening and closing doors; the steady flow of objects—trees, houses, stores, lamp-posts, etc.—taken from a car window; the whirling camera, pointed towards the grass or the floor; circular movements; a bird flapping its wings. Considering *Anticipation of the Night* in this way, one would do well to recall Olson's famous declaration that the poem captures the kinetics of reality. For the film's extremely elaborated *syuzhet* almost obscures its *fabula*, and the relation between *fabula* and kinetic constructs is, to all intents and purposes, an apophantic one. Thus the *fabula* is driven into obscurity, and the film's kinetic constructions come to the fore, providing Brakhage with the opportunity to further elaborate them, which further contributes to their foregrounding. The dynamics of the film overlay, and finally overwhelm, the film's narrative, as the flux of light and space undermines the condition of cinematic narrativity, to wit, the stability of diegetic space.

Michael McClure's Poetics: The Body Is an Organism. The Universe Is an Organism. A Poem Embodies an Aspect of the Universe's Evolving Form.

Michael McClure (1932-) has devoted his efforts, both theoretical and practical, to grounding poetics in the body. Olson's manifesto, "Projective Verse," impressed him enormously. He has summarized the importance it had for him:

> It is our overabstracted nature that does not see the complexity, or feel the complexity, of the body. Charles Olson realized that when he wrote his essay, "Projective Verse." Projective verse—likeactionpainting [sic]—comesfromacomplex body [sic]. Olson saw a breath and energy interaction creating the poetic line. The breath, like the word, is part of the body. One must hold a deep view of our organism in order to search for the real, the meatly, the physiological STANCE. Metaphorically, there is a solid ledge of our own substrate from which we must leap out like a predator (or dart from gracefully like a gatherer) in order to create true poetry.[684]

McClure uses the term "meat" to refer to the flesh, presumably because he believes that the word "flesh" (which at its origin simply meant meat) has become something of a euphemism. He wants people to be aware of the meaty nature of flesh and to think about the corporeal nature of thinking. Brakhage has adopted McClure's use of the term "meat" and sometimes uses it in his writing, lecturing, and even in his shoptalk with other poets and filmmakers.

McClure continued to expound on the influence Olson had on him. "A theory of the development of poetry surely will reflect poetry's origins in the body and in the growing complexity and diversity of the body. Thus the "feeled" grows—the *field* on which poetry grows is the *feeled* . . . the felt."[685]

McClure recognizes the circularity of this description but argues for the appropriateness of that circularity. For, in a manner familiar from Olson's insistence on the identity of form and content, McClure claims that an organic poem is always about itself because, like any creature or any created thing, its patterns (like a tree's annular rings) display the process through which it developed. He believes that Olson's poetry—and I think that he would be willing say the same of his own—reveals the circumstances and process of its creation. A poem's self-reflexive character is not primarily directed to the end of revealing the nature of the language but to bringing the poem's form (the organization of energy) into alignment with its content (the actual, bodily energy the poem contains). McClure offered these comments on Olson to Harald Mesch:

> It's as if Charles becomes alight with an idea, as if he's inspired by the outer universe to an idea which he then internalizes, and that internalization calls upon itself to create some kind of rampaging bull within himself that tramples around in the inner residences of his sensorium to create ideas about that which he desired to have ideas. Then he projects outward and examines the ideas. Then, he re-internalizes the ideas and the wild bull of his consciousness tramples around again in the sensorium of what he's experienced and creates another idea which is projected outward which comes to a field which is then perceived and internalized again.[686]

The conception of the relation between self and world that underpins this passage clearly is not the traditional Cartesian version.

In the same interview he summarized more simply the influence "Projective Verse" had on him.

> Olson's recognition that the mind is a construct of the heart, of the nervous system, and his interest in the energy charge that we derive from the subject, whether in mind or in the world, as the motivating force, was a help. Also his recognition that the syllable is a unit of measurement rather than the foot or the word. That gave me a clue.[687]

Like many recent thinkers, McClure repudiates the bifurcation of nature.

> A way of seeing an organism . . . is the view that the organism is, in itself, a tissue or veil between itself and the environment. And it is not only the tissue between itself and the environment—it is also simultaneously the environment itself. The organism is what Whitehead and Olson would think of as a point of novelty comprehending itself or experiencing itself both proprioceptively and at its tissue's edges and at any of its conceivable surfaces.
>   There is, in fact, a central force in the organism and it IS the environment. The organism is a swirl of environment. . . .
>   The organism is a constellation (like a constellation of stars or molecules) of resonances between itself and the outer environment. The organism is a physical pattern of reflections and counterreflections that we call a body and we see it clearly as a physiology.[688]

We have seen that Charles Olson construed Whitehead's metaphysical and cosmological system as a poetics; in *Modernist Montage*, P. Adams Sitney provided a telling illustration of how he did so, by taking a passage in *Process and Reality* and substituting "poem" where Whitehead had region.[689] McClure follows a similar method, and draws on biological theory, particular on biological theory that attempts to demonstrate that the universe, bodies, and cells have analogous structures and undergo analogous processes. McClure takes the biological concept of an organism, uses that as a metaphor for a poem, and then extends the metaphor, to draw out similarities between the way a poem is organized and the way the universe is organized.

McClure applies the idea of the organism to the poem itself for, he points out, like an organism a poem contains resonances of the outer environment. His writings offer nearly the same image of a circuit that Olson's writings do, to represent the world's energy in flux, which flux creates resonances (images, ideas, energies) in the poet's body; and as Olson suggested about his poems, as they go out into the world, the energies that the works release create echoes and resolutions within the whole field of being.[690]

McClure proposes that an organism is a self-organizing system of energy.

> It seems that Meat is thought. Meat is intellective. Brain cells, nerve cells—like any cells—are meat. They mime the functions of all other meat that expands while there is an energy source—forming a great being that beats and feeds upon itself. As an animal, man unconsciously mimes the process of being.[691]

McClure argues that the biological research of the Yale biophysicist Harold Morowitz confirms Olson's claim that content and form are identical in an organic poem, for Morowitz's *Energy Flow in Biology* offers the general thesis that "THE FLOW OF ENERGY THROUGH A SYSTEM ACTS TO ORGANIZE THAT SYSTEM."[692]

McClure expands his beliefs about the biological and physiological roots of art and poetry into spiritual convictions.

> Olson and I were both looking for the world from which poetry comes. That world is a substrate within us—and not a simple dimensional one—not a flat plane.
>
> We ourselves, at our fundament, are composed of complex proteins whose enfolding and use of space resembles a crumpled helix and its double. We are looking for a point that is both inside of ourselves because we are an organism and outside of ourselves because, as organisms, we are created of the environment in an exquisite complex of motions. Another society might say that we were looking for the *spirit area* from which poetry comes—or from which it arrives—or from which verse is energized.[693]

These remarks provide the basis for a conception of primordial awareness.

On the physical identity of such spiritual activities, McClure even proposes to go Olson one better.

> As I came to understand Olson personally and through his work I began to object to his concept of "anagogic," of poetry *leading out*. I believed that the spring of poetry must be more physical, more genetic, more based in flesh, and have less relationship to culture.[694]

McClure insists that the patterns of individual behaviour (and imagination) recapitulate the deep patterns that evolution and the genetic legacy have embedded in what he refers to as "the meat," i.e., the fleshy body. Through the evolutionary process, the turbulence of the universe creates life forms whose structures possess pattern, and life forms—these creatures—in turn reproduce these patterns in whatever those creatures produce, including works of art. Hence we can discover the same patterns of turbulence in both works of art and our bodies' energetic patterns. This idea grounds McClure's assertion that the physical energy that enlivens us is also the surge that organizes tribal systems and that shapes poetry; accordingly McClure claims this energy as an inheritance.[695] He even opines that the energy which creates a poem derives from and so shares an identity with the "Ur-ancient energy of the very first explosion" which created the universe.[696] Or again: "I MAY EVEN ENVISION THE WHIRLING GYRE OF MILLIONIC STARS THAT VAGUELY RESEMBLES THE HELIX DIRECTING MY CELLS."[697]

In an unpublished journal entry from early 1964, McClure suggests (correctly, I think) that Stan Brakhage's epic *Dog Star Man* draws an analogy between "the new man"—whom I construe to be the familiar American Adam—and the universe: "I just wrote Stan that I believe DSM will be in the shape of a Man like Swedenborg's universe being in the shape of a man.[698] But DSM will be in the shape of a new man—an "Absurdist" man. He continues:

> The essence is that from a viewing of the separate sections over a period of time I believe I can already put together the Woodsman-Christ-Fool-Faust who is either fleeing to or from an atomic holocaust and is either dying or being reborn or experiencing thoughts and acts of birth and death within his body that HAS BECOME NATURE IN THE HEIGHT OF HIS STRESS. He is the dog and the star and the sun and mountains crack about him and the seasons and memories of seasons flash by—as birth flashes by and repeats.

He then goes on to expand on his belief in the Dog Star Man's Adamic nature:

> A new man. A man that has not been seen before. . . . Man is being defined as a universe in the way the body knows that it IS the universe. . . . [But] here it is not [as it is in Poe's *Eureka*, an allusion that connects the Dog Star Man back to the Transcendentalists' American Adam] the diffused atoms of the universe that pull together to the original globe of matter before disappearing in a vacuum of non-existence. . . . It is the elaborate structurings of matter in helixes of protein and water and energy that have created the shape of a living individual who will gradually disappear in death and who will reappear in birth as a continuing man who is not less than a star or a sun and not more than a dog.

It is a perceptive commentary on Brakhage's legendary epic.

McClure rejects all approaches to literature that consider poetry the formal product of a disembodied intelligence. He insists that poetic shape (a term he prefers to form) must be seen as an extension of physiology and that physiology must be considered as a product of phylogeny. Like Olson, he believes that sequence is more important than logic, for sequence can embody the movement of "meat-thought":

> I felt that our lives were lines of synaptic stars—literally—and it seemed *that* simple—and it is—and *that* brutal. It is life, not beauty, that we are after, for if there is beauty (and we do live in beauty) it is our perceptions raining lightning upon our fleshly pads that is glorious[699]

Thus, like Olson, McClure is antagonistic to representational forms; like Olson, he claims to seek not mimicry, but an enactment, after the fashion of Action Painting, of one's personal physiology (which of course, includes one's psychological states). He disavows any wish to duplicate the outside world and proclaims instead the aspiration to enact the desires of the body, of feelings that are as surely embedded in the human physiology as the genes. A poem that works is a field of energy, not a neat ordering of formal variations; in this way, it resembles an abstract expressionist art "in which the

428 The Films of Stan Brakhage

painter created transcriptions of arm and brush that are statements, like pawprints of physical being."[700]

In sum, McClure sees poetry as a performative rather than representational art, and that the purpose of performance is to leave a trace of the behaviours of a truly unique individual. This understanding of his art brought him to a problem similar to the one to which Brakhage's performative conception of film led him, too; both found themselves subjected to accusations of narcissism and solipsism. McClure's answer was similar to that which Brakhage gave: when a poet or filmmaker is genuinely creative, his or her actions derive from one's deepest nature, and the deeper one goes into oneself, the more one taps into something that is universal. In the same interview with Harald Mesch we quoted from above, McClure stated:

> The more one discovers one's *bio-self* as opposed to one's *social self*, the more one is moving out, but one has to move *in* to move *out*. The more you discover your biological person and your biological functions, the more you discover your biological self. And the more you discover your biological self, the more value you can be to yourself. The more value you can be to yourself, the more value you can be to those around you. People fear such acts because they believe that their biological self is a monster. That is certainly not the case. I mean, we're social primates, and we have distinct social patterns. The more we find those deeper patterns and the less we are robotized by the cultural patterns, the better we'll be. If so-called narcissism is an escape from the robotism of the culture, I'm all for it.[701]

McClure has taken his bio-poetics as far as attempting to ground our aesthetic preferences in our biological constitution. He wrote this about contemplating an apple as an aesthetic object:

> Assume that I have a three-dimensional screen within my head (perhaps it is the reticular formation). What I feel, see, think, and know is imaged on the screen. This screen IS the best image that I can make, with limited senses, of the world and universe surrounding me. It is also the neuron-sculptural screenformemory-experienceactivity that continuously dances. There appears to be an order of preference for what takes place on the sculpture screen. The order is apparently biological.[702]

He even avers that aesthetic desire has a cosmic dimension.

> Every life is part of the total surge of Life that feeds upon itself as it expands in size and complexity. The whole surge is powered by the sun. It becomes more complex. It grows. It expands.... The desire for movement is internalized. In my case the desire is to write a poem.[703]

McClure thus suggests that we should consider all life to be a single, unitary surge, a single, giant organism, and that our experience of the surge is the universe's experience of itself. This view reappears in Brakhage's *Dog Star Man*, and McClure seems to recognize the parallels with Brakhage's work, for he has dedicated a poem to him entitled "The Surge"[704] is a fragment from it.

> Is all life a vast chromosome stretched in Time?
> Simply a pattern for another thing?
> But the pattern like the chromosomes *is* the Life,
> and the Surge is its vehicle.
>
> It does not matter!
>
> It is the athletic living thing of energy!
> . . . .
> The Surge can never see itself for the Surge is
> its self-sight. And its sight
> and being are simultaneous.
> There is no urge to see or feel—for it *is* sight
> and feeling.

We participate in the Life of the cosmos. That all life is a single, giant organism is evidenced, McClure asserts, by the repetition of the same animal rituals everywhere throughout nature and, indeed, the cosmos, from a wolf surprising his partner to children playing hide-and-seek games.

As we can infer from the echoes that reverberate in this poem from McClure's journal comments on *Dog Star Man*, McClure's dedicating "The Surge" to Brakhage was not offering some loose tribute to Brakhage's dedication, or his general importance in twentieth-century American culture. In fact the poem contains images and ideas that resonate with specific images in Brakhage's films. What is more, like Brakhage, McClure declares that he aspires for a richer, more comprehensive vision. The poem opens with

> THE SURGE! THE SURGE! THE SURGE!
> IT IS THE SURGE OF LIFE
> I SEEK
> TO VIEW . . .

and later states

> . . . There's a calm inertness
> of joy that living beings drift to and from. (And it is far
> back when the Universe began . . .
> and it is here now too.) . . .
> . . . .
> I mean there is a more total view!
> It shifts and changes and wavers,
> and weakens as our nerves do, to finally make
> a greater field and more total sight.

The image of the calm energy that makes the universe and still maintains it, of a calm energy that reverberates in us, appears as well in *Dog Star Man*.

Dog Star Man deals partly with the urge to unify male and female, while "The Surge" celebrates female vision, a vision that McClure considers to be more inclusive and more somatic than male vision (McClure asks, even, whether the male sight of the paradisiacal universe is not "as dead as Hell"). The "dreary theory" filmmakers of the late 1970s and early 1980s picked Brakhage as the exemplar—and, perhaps, even principal exponent—of patriarchy, more by reason of his formidable reputation, it would seem, than the attitudes and represented content of films (where there is any). Indeed, their represented content has tended to be as domestic as Gertrude Stein's writing and Marie Menken's cinema and, probably, more concerned with the joys and worries of childrearing than any artist's oeuvre heretofore has given us. There are female qualities to the texture and forms of the visual constructs that Brakhage has created—the easiest way to confirm this is to attempt to apply Irigaray's commentary on feminine writing to Brakhage's cinema; the match is surprisingly good.

"The Surge" even contains specific images that seem to hail from *Dog Star Man*:

> The high part is a heart! Within it a man's head & shoulders
> rise from a bat-winged heart with thready tail—
> and a heart upon the thread tip. Nearby is a circle
> (a vacuole? a nucleus?) with a shape inside that might
> be any living thing from a vulture to a child.
>
> High and low outside are stars that are
> living sparks or moths.
> . . . .
> . . . The mountains do pour, moving in millionic
> ripples over thousand aeons. Demanding brute reality we forget
> the greater flow and then the black immediate is larger—and it is
> and isn't. But Life, THE PLASM, does not flow like lead does.
> It SURGES! . . .
> . . . .
> Inert matters pour in and out of the Surge
> . . . .
> The Surge can never see itself for the Surge is
> its self-sight. And its sight
> and being are simultaneous.

McClure contends that humans, when acting out of biological impulses, create biomorphic designs. Only as human civilizations degenerate into mass societies do the more violent proclivities in a culture extend geometric perception upon the world and create geometrically formed art. This is a proposition with which Brakhage concurs: Brakhage has criticized Dziga Vertov's *Man with a Movie Camera* for its extensive use of geometric forms and praised Sergej Ejzenstejn's *Ivan the Terrible* for its use of organic curves. He has also commented (not inaccurately) on my film *Illuminated Texts* as displaying the conflict between natural, biomorphically disposed thinking and abstract, mathematically disposed thinking which evidences itself in geometric forms. Further testimony to the intensity of Brakhage's belief on this matter can be found in Brakhage's famous polemic against Renaissance perspective—Brakhage's hostility towards Renaissance perspective is not motivated simply by his belief that this form of visual representation is not natural to the eye or that it represents visual thinking that has been influenced by society, as it is generally thought to be (and as Brakhage himself proposes in the opening section of "The Camera Eye/My Eye" section of *Metaphors on Vision*). Rather, I believe, his anti-perspectival rhetoric is also fuelled by his belief that images that employ Renaissance perspective depend on rectilinearity and impose a geometric grid imposed upon the world. Indeed, his characterization of Renaissance space as evincing the desire to seize the world, to take possession of it, indicates his belief that this spatial form derives from a corrupted self—a self that, as McClure's statement has it, is violent.

McClure's bio-poetics led him to an analysis of meaning similar to Stein's and Brakhage's—to a perlocutionary (and therefore non-denotational) conception that relates meaning to the actual power inherent in the word itself, apart from all reference—a power invested in the energy of a word's sound. In the same interview we quoted from earlier, Harald Mesch remarked to McClure:

> In *Scratching the Beat Surface* you speak at one point about the invisible observer who closes his ears to the meanings of words and only listens to the vocalization as sounds. And you suggest further on that if the intelligence is open and is able to follow the sounds it will hear something.

McClure clarified:

> I'm talking about the split between what we say we're talking about and what we're speaking of. I think what I spoke of was a man and a woman arguing about laundry tickets. But if you listen to the language, if you listen to the sounds coming out of the body, you realize that what is being spoken of is not really the laundry ticket. It's probably about their sex lives, or about their children that they're conversing, because one does not truly speak of laundry tickets with that emotional passion, or that intensity.
>
> In other words, we use limited vocabularies to describe our true emotional states. And that is what I'm suggesting that one listen for.[705]

The claims this passage makes for McClure's own poems are no less true of Brakhage's films: often in Brakhage's films it is not what a visual representation depicts so much as the features internal to the depiction that matter.

Allen Ginsberg: The Breath, the Voice, and the Poem

The poet Allen Ginsberg (1926-97) has, more tenaciously than any of the poets whom Olson influenced, taken up Olson's view that speech separated from the body leads away from truth and results in what Olson calls "pejocracy." Speaking to an epistemology class at Wisconsin State University in 1971, Ginsberg announced that

> Most public speech is pseudo-event in the sense that it is not the product of a literal human being; it's literally non-human. It's passed through so many hands and so many machines that it no longer represents a human organism inspiring and expiring, inhaling and exhaling, rhythmically. The sentence structure no longer has any relation to any affect that could be traced along the lines of inhalation and exhalation—in other words, sad to say, the voice can finally be separated from the body. If the voice is completely separated from the body, it means that the rhythm will be fucked up, it means the affect will be fucked up, it means it no longer has any human content, actually. It probably means it doesn't mean anything, even, finally—by *mean*, anything that could be connected back to the physical universe or the human universe.[706]

In the same seminar, Ginsberg proposed that "the highest form of epistemological research" would be based upon the "use of rhythmic language to rouse the senses, arouse perceptions, and arouse sense of inner space, to alter all of consciousness itself."[707]

William Carlos Williams lived in Paterson, the town in which Allen Ginsberg grew up. Though few people in Paterson (to say nothing of the United States as a whole) knew of the poet's work—actually Allen Ginsberg's own father, Louis Ginsberg, was better known in town as a poet—Ginsberg turned to him for help several times. In March 1950, Williams offered Ginsberg the crucial advice that he should try to cultivate form without deforming language (by which Williams meant that Ginsberg should try to write using the language Americans ordinarily use when speaking). He encouraged Ginsberg to allow the American language, as it is spoken, to determine the rhythmic construction of a poem. He extolled the value of capturing the force that the spoken word possesses, and not to incorporate the poetical conceits of classical English in his poems. This turned out to be excellent advice, as it encouraged Ginsberg to develop his work in the direction of speech-force, and when he did find the means to embody in his poems the force that Williams had drawn to his attention (something which, famously, happened with the composition of *Howl*), he became a very powerful poet. From Williams, too, Ginsberg adopted an "open form," with syllable count and breath length determining the verse form, and these became crucial features of *Howl*.

A little later, in January 1952, Ginsberg turned to him again, and received equally formative advice. Feeling blocked as a writer, he turned to the notebooks he had been keeping—books of word sketches like those Jack Kerouac kept. He found the most intense passages in them, and framed them on the page in lines somewhat like Williams's, balancing them by syllable count, by breath length, or even visually. He sent the results to Williams, almost apologizing for their quality. He did not expect the poet's response: Williams hailed the poems for capturing direct, immediate perception. The ideas that poems could document (in Olson's and Brakhage's sense of the word) the events immediately at hand, and that recording an actual event's immediate effect on consciousness could have aesthetic value, became central to Ginsberg's poetics.

Williams's advice, like so much advice the good doctor gave, was based on long experience. In 1920, Williams had published *Kora in Hell: Improvisations*. The subtitle testifies to the compositional method Williams used to write the book. He embarked upon *Kora in Hell* with no book in mind; rather, he assigned himself the task of writing something, anything, each night when he arrived home, no matter how late. Even if he felt he had nothing in mind, he wrote something—even something which might seem like nonsense; the fatigue he felt when he got home after an especially long day ensured that many of his nocturnal jottings would approach incomprehensibility.

After a period of accumulating material, he had a collection of highly personal, but sometimes nearly uninterpretable jottings. He pondered about the means he might use to form the jottings into a completed work. While he was groping for some idea, he came across a book that Pound had left in his house, *Varie Poesie dell' Abate Pietro Metastasio*, published in Venice in 1795. The Abbot had divided his book into sections by drawing lines across the page, and Williams realized he could do something similar with *Kora in Hell*. The book presents first a passage of improvised writing, then a line drawn across the page (as in the Abate Pietro Metastasio's book) and then, usually, Williams's interpretation of the improvisation. Or so Williams explains the structure of the book; actually, the supposed interpretations do little in the way of helping us in our hermeneutical endeavours. Rather, to a passage written in the very fragmentary style of the automatic compositions, they append a section in a somewhat more measured and controlled style—but nonetheless inscrutable for that, for even the appended passages are improvisations (making the work a double improvisation, consisting of an improvisation and a meta-improvisation).

Williams told Edith Heal (from whom I have taken most of my description of the method Williams used to write *Kora in Hell*) that "[i]t is the one book

I have enjoyed referring to more than any of the others. It reveals myself to me and perhaps that is why I have kept it to myself."[708] The idea that a work of art, composed on the spur of the moment, without its maker being immediately aware of its meanings, could afford deeper self-revelations than intellectual self-analysis could furnish, had considerable impact on the Action Painters, the Projective Poets, and the Beat Poets (and especially Allen Ginsberg, with his belief in "First thought, best thought"), the Free Jazz musicians, and (though perhaps to a more limited degree) Stan Brakhage. Williams avowed—at least sometimes, though at other times he explicitly repudiated the claim—that the business of poetry is to reveal the unconscious, and in *Kora in Hell*, he used improvisation to trace the operation of the unconsciousness. He derived his understanding of improvisation primarily from Wassily Kandinsky's *On the Spiritual in Art*, which describes improvisation exactly as the unconscious and spontaneous expression of the artist's inner being. The fragmentary, elliptical style of the writing, the discontinuities from sentence to sentence or even phrase to phrase that suggest leaps of the mind, the apparent categorical incompatibilities between modifiers and what they modify that give the impression that what they describe belongs to the realm of imagination, and even, the occasional use of asyntax to embue the prose with raw style were all to have enormous influence on subsequent poets. Even more important was Williams's use of the notebook, for the notebook became, for the Beat Poets, a means of engendering spontaneous compositions—of encouraging them to compose by following the forces immediately under hand.

The title of *Kora in Hell* arose from a conversation with Pound, who, because of his Gnostic leanings, attached special importance to the myth of *nekuia* (see glossary); Kora is another name for Persephone—or, in another persona that appears in appears in Williams's mythology, Springtime—who was captured and taken to Hades. Williams's next collection incorporating prose poetry was, as one might have expected, a Return of Spring piece entitled *Spring and All*. The return of spring heralds the triumph of Imagination; his life had been a Hell until he composed this book, but what kept him in Hell, according to his mythology, was repression from which, apparently, the composition of *Kora in Hell* freed him. But the Hell of *Kora in Hell* is not simply a personal Hell; it is also the Hell of a Winter-time when all goes dead, when nothing is vital with meaning, when merely arbitrary connections between words and things are not sufficient to bring them to life. Improvisation, Williams hoped, would forge a new, vital relation between words and the world; and this new relation would be the result of bring the times of reading and the writing into co-incidence, just as abstract expressionist painting bring the times of viewing and making into co-incidence, and just as musical improvisations brings the times of listening (of performance) and composition into co-incidence (all of which, of course, lend to works produced by these methods a feeling, or present immediacy).

Like other modernists who accorded the lyric form privilege, Williams maintained that poetry has an especially close relation with the imagination, so that the more imaginative a piece is, the more poetic it is. And like other modernists, Williams founded his aesthetic doctrines on the distinction between prose (or ordinary language) and poetry. Sometimes the poet's distinction between imaginative awareness and more ordinary awareness can be identified with the distinction between the creation of a new form and the re-use of an existing form; but more often the distinction rests on a matter of dynamics. Thus, in *Spring and All*, Williams allows that "the imagination is an actual force comparable to electricity or steam; it is not a plaything but a power that has been used from the first."[709]

Ginsberg learned from Williams the value of close observation. Many of the finest moments recorded in Ginsberg's poems are moments when he observes intensely—moments when, in a flash, he recognizes the meaning of a gesture, for example. Some of his finest poems, like "Howl," "Witchita Vortex Sutra," and, paradigmatically, the sequence, "Thru the Vortex West Coast to East 1965-1966" in *The Fall of America* are really lists of such moments of recognition of meaning (Williams's "ideas") inherent in things; Ginsberg manages to sustain the list form by the rapidity with which these details/insights flow.[710] Like Williams, Olson, and Brakhage, Ginsberg believes that the intensity proper to a work of art is a matter of dynamics, and like Williams, Olson, and Brakhage, Ginsberg contends that the dynamic force that impels creativity is a push that originates within the artist's body and is directed outwards, at the world. It is quite possible that Ginsberg drew some of these ideas either directly from Whitehead or from discussions of Whitehead that occurred in Olson's circle: One memorable line, among many, of Ginsberg's "Howl" has the best minds of his generation sitting "through the stale beer afternoons" listening "to the crack of doom on the hydrogen jukebox" in "desolate Fugazzi's"; Whitehead had described the process of creativity (one of his Categories of the Ultimate), inasmuch as it involves the successive construction of novel unities, as entailing the passing away of presently existing entities, and so in the creative advance from creature to creature, creativity sounds repeatedly "the crack of doom."[711]

Like Olson and Brakhage, and like Williams, Ginsberg believed that the rhythm that feelings engender in the body is their primary characteristic. In a most revealing statement about his method of composing poetry, he offered:

The poetry generally is like a rhythmic articulation of feeling. . . . [A]t best what happens, is there's a definite body rhythm that has no definite words, or may have one or two words attached to it. . . . [B]efore I wrote "Moloch whose eyes are a thousand blind windows," I had the word, "Moloch, Moloch, Moloch," and I also had the feeling DA de de DA de de DA de de DA DA. So it was just a question of looking up and seeing a lot of windows. . . . So Moloch whose eyes—then probably the next thing I thought was "thousands." O.K., and then thousands *what?* "Thousands blind." And I had to finish it somehow. So I hadda say "windows." It looked good *afterward*.[712]

Ginsberg expanded upon his thoughts about the physiological effects of rhythm in a later interview that he gave at his farm in Cherry Valley, NY, in 1968.

Now, the Sanskrit thing is even deeper in a funny way, cuz—the grammar is all built on yoga—on a physiological body yoga. . . . [The] deployment—[of certain syllables has effects] physiologically in the body, during their pronouncing. . . . [I]t's touching special jiu-jitsu pressure points on the body, by pronouncing them—so it's doing like a physical exercise or a yoga thing involved with the breathing and also the exhalation of the breathing. . . .

Getting back to the Sanskrit prosody, if you have a prosody built on *that*, it's so complex—you can do anything with it—it's like having the basic . . . patterns of . . . physiological reactions built into the language, into the alphabet—and then making combinations of the alphabet you can play like an organ, to get different effects. . . . That's all I know about the Sanskrit prosody—which is just a hint that there's this giant, extremely sophisticated and physiologically based system, that's as complicated as the nature of the human body, practically, or is fitted to the nature of the human body and touches all the key combinations.[713]

He then went on to summarize his discoveries in this area, by reformulating (albeit somewhat tentatively) the idea of absolute rhythm that Pound claimed to have traced back to Guido Calvacanti: "[N]ow I realize that certain rhythms you can get into, are . . . *mean* certain feelings. Well, everybody knew that anyway all along. But some rhythms mean something."[714] And to the remark by interviewer Mark Robison that such rhythms bring "all your physical universe into the thrust of that prosody," Ginsberg responded, "Yeah. And that's exactly what Olson has been talking about all along as **Projective** verse, involving the complete physiology of the poet."[715]

Ginsberg's proposals for literature here really amount to a single vigorous assertion: that literature must be *kerygma*, and *kerygma* only; unless literature be the proclamation of the revelation, it is nothing. And Ginsberg's verse is kerygmatic: his long line endows his verse with the texture of passages in the First Covenant—with, for example, passages in the Book of Lamentations. What Ginsberg's verse has in common with the First Covenant are qualities that are supposed to ensure its revelatory powers. Ginsberg's use of parataxis, often accolating religious terms ("holy," "blessed") and declamatory rhythms also imbue his writing with qualities of the rhetoric of proclamation.

Ginsberg shares with Olson, and Brakhage too, the idea that artmaking should be reactive, not imitative. Thus when speaking of Cézanne's practice of constructing a visual form by simplification, analysis, and recombination, rather than by imitating reality, Ginsberg noted, "Cézanne is reconstituting by means of triangles, cubes, and colours—I have to reconstitute by means of words, rhythms ... phrasings."[716] Conceiving the problem of poetic composition in this way, led Ginsberg to put emphasis on the activities of words and phrases.

Right after making these remarks on Cézanne, Ginsberg went on to demonstrate that he, like Brakhage and Olson, is aware that several things go on in the mind simultaneously, that the mind works by what Ezra Pound referred to as super-position: "The problem is then to reach the different parts of the mind, which are existing simultaneously, the different associations which are going on simultaneously, choosing elements from both."[717]

Like Olson, Ginsberg considers poetry to be projective. Ginsberg's most forceful statement of this appears in a diatribe he launched against "squares" who found Beat poetry impossible to understand, which he entitled "When the Mode of the Music Changes the Walls of the City Shake" with the following rambling, marvellous, sentence

> Trouble with conventional form (fixed line count & stanza form) is, it's too symmetrical, geometrical, numbered and pre-fixed—unlike to my own mind, which has no beginning and end, nor fixed measure of thought (or speech—or writing) other than its own cornerless mystery—to transcribe the latter in a form most nearly representing its actual "occurrence" is my "method"—which requires the Skill of freedom of composition—and which will lead Poetry to the expression of the highest moments of the mind-body—mystical illumination—and its deepest emotion (through tears—love's all)—in the forms nearest to what it actually looks like (data of mystical imagery) & feels like (rhythm of actual speech & rhythm prompted by direct transcription of visual & other mental data)—plus not to forget the sudden genius-like Imagination or fabulation of unreal & out of this world verbal constructions which express the true gaiety & excess of Freedom—(and also by their nature express the First Cause of the world) by means of spontaneous irrational juxtaposition of sublimely related fact, by the dentist drill singing against the piano music; or pure construction of imaginaries, hydrogen jukeboxes, in perhaps abstract images (made by putting together two things verbally concrete but disparate to begin with)—always bearing in mind, that one must verge on the unknown, write toward the truth hitherto unrecognizable of one's own sincerity, including the avoidable beauty of doom, shame and embarrassment, that very area of personal self-recognition (detailed individual is universal remember) which formal conventions, inter-

nalized, keep us from discovering in ourselves & others—For if we write
with an eye to what the poem should be (has been), and do not get lost in it,
we will never discover any new thing about ourselves in the process of actually writing on the table, and we lose the chance to live in our works, &
make habitable the new world which every man may discover in himself, if
he lives—which is life itself, past present & future.[718]

The rambling, associative form of this sentence is, as Creeley insisted writing must be, at one with the poem's content, which concerns going with the
flow of the writing, allowing oneself to get lost in the writing.

Ginsberg also concurs with the proposition that will-lessness is a virtue, a
proposition that both Olson and Brakhage have put forward, and like them,
Ginsberg uses the idea of virtue of will-lessness to justify allowing the evolution of the poem to go its own way.

Thus the mind must be trained, i.e. let loose, freed—to deal with itself as it
actually is, and not to impose on itself, or its poetic artifacts, an arbitrarily
preconceived pattern (formal or Subject)—and *all* patterns, unless discovered in the moment of composition—all remembered and *applied* patterns
are by their very nature arbitrarily preconceived—no matter how wise &
traditional—no matter what sum of inherited experience they represent—
The only pattern of value or interest in poetry is the solitary, individual
pattern peculiar to the poet's moment & the poem *discovered* in the mind
& in the process of writing it out on the page, as notes, transcriptions—
reproduced in the fittest accurate form, at the time of composition.[719]

Ginsberg's verse is famous for its use of the long line, which follows the
contours of thought. This feature, which is Ginsberg's principal contribution
to Projective Verse, brought much condemnation down on him; and those
few who attempted to understand this mode of construction usually connected it with the populist tradition exemplified by Carl Sandburg and Kenneth Fearing. In "When the Mode of the Music Changes," Ginsberg treats
this conjecture with withering contempt, and provides his own list of significant precursors: Hart Crane's "Atlantis"; Federico Garcia Lorca's *Poet in
New York*; such biblical verse as Psalms and Lamentations; Shelley's verse,
along with that of Apollinaire, Rimbaud, Artaud, Mayakovsky, and Pound;
Williams's verse—for its general integrity, its improvised or open form passages, its direct connection to reality achieved by refusing to dominate reality or to impose unduly upon it, its commitment to close observation, its
quotidian subject matter, but especially for its metrical innovations; Christopher Smart's *Rejoice in the Lamb* (in my view, the greatest English-
language list-form poem), and Melville's *Pierre*. He avers with special force
the importance of Artaud's *To have done with the judgment of god*. Ginsberg
protests that complaints about him had been issued "By intellectual bastards
and snobs and vulgarians and hypocrites who have never read Artaud's *Pour

en finir avec le jugement de Dieu and therefore wouldn't begin to know that this masterpiece, which in thirty years will be as famous as *Anabasis* is the actual model of tone for my earlier writing?"

Ginsberg reference to Artaud here is signal. Artaud was members of the Surrealist circle in Paris, and his interest in Surrealism was based in large measure on the Surrealists' use of automatism. The Surrealist had a great influence on the shaping open form practices. Harold Rosenberg, by described Action Painting as what is produced by one who gesticulates and watches for signs of what the emerging artwork will be (to paraphrase one of his definitions of Action Painting), highlighted the Surrealist provenance of the basic principles. In postulating benefits to accrue through relying on a similar spontaneity, the Open Form poets revealed an equally strong relationship to Surrealism. The influence of Surrealism on Action Painting and Projective Verse is considerable greater that scholars were ready to acknowledge a decade ago. One could work out the historical role of Action Painting and Projective Verse by showing how it attempted to reconcile a spiritual strain in abstract art (abundantly evident in Kandinsky's art and writing, as well as in Mondrian's painting) with a materialist/self-reflexive/constructive strain. But Clement Greenberg took a dim view of the spiritual strain, and frequently ferreted out spiritual and occult ideas and condemned the art they led to as excessively literary. In recent years, close study of the role that occult, or, more generally, spiritual ideas played in shaping American art in the 1920s through the 1960s has revealed they had a much greater influence than previously had been admitted. Ginsberg's work, certainly, has strong connections to Surrealist esoterism.

"When the Mode of the Music Changes" continues with a remark that connects back to one of the sources of Artaud's inspiration: "This is nothing but a raving back at the false Jews from Columbia who have lost memory of the Shekinah."[720] The long line of Ginsberg's does have a relationship to Hebrew verse forms, and especially to its kerygmatic metres—a relation that surely is just as strong as his long line's relationship to the extended line of Artaud's automatic (or, at least "inspired") writing, or to Christopher Smart's. That Ginsberg, Artaud, and Smart all made use of the long line is surely enough to indicate that the long line accommodates particularly well inspired writing—writing that is created in an elevated mental state, whether inspiration or para-psychosis. We must therefore ask: What is the relation between the long line and elevated mental states? And when we consider this question, one should bear in mind that Brakhage, too, creates an elevated mental state that he describes as "trance" (and I would prefer to call "total concentration") and that he too tends to use long rolling passages between caesurae.

A clue is to be found in an influence that Ginsberg has often acknowledged (though not in "When the Mode of the Music Changes"). That influence is Ezra Pound's verse. The features of Pound's verse most influenced Ginsberg were its aural properties. We have already shown how Pound, by breaking the pentameter, began to produce verse whose rhythms are supple and more flexible. This flexibility results partly from the use of rhythms that have no fixed metre (but vary according to where they place the stresses and how many stresses there are in a line) and partly from the use of less heavy accentuation.

The music with which Ginsberg and the Projective Poets were most closely associated, a jazz style known as "bebop" or simply "bop," strived for a similar rhythmic flexibility. The precursor jazz styles, from New Orleans jazz to the "swing" style of the large ensembles of the late 1930 and 1940s, usually played in 2/4 time, with the accent coming on the second beat (which is then called the "back beat"). This metre is extremely inflexible and extremely predictable; consequently in the late 1940s, the jazz musicians who invented bebop began to use 4/4 time, and to accent the metre's down-beats more lightly. The result is a more evenly flowing line that tends to expand over the customary eight-bar phrase length; thus bebop musicians began to use longer lines (and these longer lines were less frequently, and less regularly, internally divided than those or pre-bop jazz). The derogators of bebop, consequently, claimed that they were unable to identify where one phrase ended and other began. The music became a single, long, flowing line.

Several commentators have claimed that Ginsberg derived his long line from Kerouac, who in turn derived his from bebop jazz. I think it is just as likely that the source was what he said it was, the poets he mentioned in "When the Mode of the Music Changes," Christopher Smart and Antonin Artaud, and, despite his declaimer in that text, Walt Whitman (the tone of ironic self-mockery that characterizes so many passages in Ginsberg's writing is simply a dead give away). And of course, Ezra Pound; I believe, really, that it was rhythmic innovations of vers libre, and the historical pressure they created, that led to Ginsberg's long line.

The rhythmic innovations of vers libre and Ezra Pound's poetry had taken the emphasis of line boundaries (off the coincident appearance of rhythmic cadence and the conclusion of a thought phrase after a certain number of feet). Thus, to take them for our example, the line breaks in the *Cantos* seem more tentative—we have the feeling, when reading them, that "a single line" is broken into parts and arranged down the length of a page. Ginsberg develops this into the long line characteristic of his verse.

But the long, continually evolving line, whether Pound's or Ginsberg's, has features that resemble those of the stream of consciousness, especially in the evenness of flow and the unpredictability of where it will come to rest (even if only briefly). Furthermore, the long line can take unexpected turns (just consider how often Pound's verse, or Ginsberg's, will shift suddenly from exuberance to sadness, from outrage to tristesse, within a single line) as can the stream of consciousness. This, then, explains the relation between the verse that attempts to convey consciousness' operations as it performs in extreme states and verse that employs long lines. And thus it is that the sequence of thought forms passing through the mind has been the constant subject of all Ginsberg's verse.

As important as Ginsberg's long line—a line that flows with the movement of thought—is, his use of juxtaposition has even greater importance, for parataxis allows the line to turn with the shifts in his thinking. Moreover, his use of juxtaposition continually refreshes his speech and revitalizes its flow, giving the impression of (to borrow that expression of James again) "the continual coming-on of novelty," that feature which characterizes somatic temporality. Many influences swayed Ginsberg towards this form of construction, but Ginsberg highlights one: While still a student at Columbia University, writing a paper on Cézanne for the distinguished art historian Meyer Schapiro, Ginsberg went to New York's Museum of Modern Art several times to examine the painter's watercolours. He noted that Cézanne often juxtaposed colours so that when the eye passed from one to another, it received a little jolt. Ejzenstejn made an entire aesthetic theory and cinematic practice out of this proto-Cubist device—and so in fact did Ginsberg. He began referring to the jolt as an "eyeball kick." "I got a strange shuddering impression looking at his canvases, partly the effect when someone pulls a Venetian blind, reverses the Venetian—there's a sudden shift, a flashing that you see in Cézanne canvases."[721] Part I of *Howl* contains an homage to Cézanne's method: "who dreamt and made incarnate gaps in Time & Space through images juxtaposed . . . jumping with sensation of Pater Omnipotens Aeterne Deus."[722] Ginsberg attempts to recreate the jolting effect of Cézanne's construction by juxtaposing words that have a gap—usually a conceptual gap, but it can be a break created by an unexpected word—between them "which the mind would fill with the sensation of existence."[723]

In conjunction with the long line, such paratactical constructions also have the effect of giving the poem's represented material an ambiguous status; the poem's content (i.e., its "object matter") allows itself to be interpreted as either subjective or objective. Ginsberg's poetry, like Brakhage's earlier films, evidently grows out of quotidian speech; however, since the words of the poem are projected speech, they seem closer to thought than language ordinarily does, and this gives the strange impression that the material of the poem itself (and what the poem represents) is its maker's actual consciousness. We have already seen that Williams's imagery and Brakhage's visual forms have a similarly ambiguous status, and they, too, seem to be actual outerings (literally projections) of the contents of their maker's consciousness.

Ginsberg also came to Olson's recognition of the importance of living gracefully within one's skin, a recognition whose dawning he records in "The Change," perhaps his most important poem after *Kaddish* and *Howl*. The background of the poem lies in 1948, when Ginsberg, while still a student, experienced a vision of William Blake; Ginsberg then spent the years between 1948 to 1963 trying to recreate the mystical experience he had that day. Attempting to recreate that experience involved him striving to get beyond the body, to break out of the body so as to attain a completed consciousness.[724] Then, in 1963, while on a train between Kyoto and Tokyo, Ginsberg came to the recognition that expanding consciousness through psychedelic means was not important and, more significantly, that enlarging consciousness by whatever means was not the moral key to existence. He realized that he must accept the form he had been given, and must learn to love the forms of earthly beings. He realized he must learn to live in the present, and within limits.

> I am that I am I am the
> man & the Adam of hair in
> my loins   This is my spirit and
> physical shape I inhabit
> this Universe Oh weeping
> against what is my
> own nature for now
>
> Who would deny his own shape's
> loveliness in his
> dream moment of bed
> Who sees his desire to be
> horrible instead of Him[725]

Action Painting as Performance

The ideas the Open Field poets promulgated resonates through all the advanced arts of the time. The best-known exponents were not the poets themselves, but a group of painters who by day worked in studios around Tenth Street in New York and by night congregated at the Cedar Tavern. Commentary on their work adopted similar ideas. Of all their critics, Harold Rosenberg was the most eloquent proponent of Action Painting and, in some ways, the furthest seeing. An eloquent and conceptually dense passage on the Dutch-American painter Willem De Kooning (1904-97) captures the vital tone and expounds the key ideas that many painters used to discuss the work of these painters.

> Painting for de Kooning is . . . a real action, comparable to crossing an ocean or fighting a battle. The art of painting is executed in silence, allowing a minimum of exchange with other minds; at times it even divides the artist's own mind, making what he is doing incomprehensible to him. Like prayer this movement of the spirit and intellect evokes extreme states; a succession of psychic tensions passes over into the self affecting the artist's personality and behavior. He is in a condition of constant heightening, depletion, transformation.
>
> The logic of de Kooning's work lies not in its rational consistency but in the artist's unending struggle with painting and its possibilities. Each confrontation of the drawing board or canvas is a singular situation calling for a new act—and the act and the artist are one. The web of energies he has woven between his painting and his living precludes the formation of any terminal idea.[726]

Note the aesthetics of energy, the notion that thought passes into somatic action directly, sometimes without intermediary activity of the intellect, that spirit is embodied in behaviour, that the artwork arises through following a spontaneous line of inspiration, and that artwork produced through such a process has a rather arbitrary beginning and ending. These are all ideas that the exponents of open field poetics also taught.

Rosenberg made the relationship more definite in a commentary on Hans Hofmann (1880-1966).

> If the ultimate subject matter of all art is the artist's psychic state or tension (and this may be the case even in non-individualistic epochs), that state (e.g., grief) may be represented through an abstract sign. The innovation of Action Painting was to dispense with the representation of the state in favor of enacting it in the physical movement of painting. [Cf. Olson's remarks on the kinetic and projective character of Projective Verse.] The action on the canvas became its own representation. This was possible because action which carries the psychic into the material world is by its nature sign-producing; it leaves the trace of a movement whose origin and character are not ever altogether revealed—for instance, the act of love results in a correlation of bodies which, as Freud pointed out, may be mistaken for murder. Yet, once accomplished, the action also exists in the thing which it has transformed as by a scratch on a cheek.
>
> In turning to action, abstract art abandons its alliance with architecture, as painting had earlier broken with music and with the novel, and offers its hand to pantomime and dance.[727]

Hofmann was a European emigré, and had been in Paris from 1904 to 1914, the years of Les Fauves (his early teaching in New York was based largely on Fauve and Expressionist principles and practices) and Cubism. He opened a school of painting first in Munich, from 1915-32, then in New York. His ideas about painting, which were based primarily on his analysis of the enclosed, "interior" space of Synthetic Cubism, though also on Expressionist and Fauve practices (he is said to have been a brilliant commentator on Matisse's use of colour), were testimony to a fierce rigour and intelligence. Among the most influential of his ideas is that of push-pull relations, an idea that had its provenance in Cubism and Fauvism, for the Synthetic Cubists created relations of exactly that sort among their flat, post-collage painted forms. And like the Synthetic Cubists, Hofmann argued that a painting could be understood as integrating quasi-autonomous elements. Another of Hofmann's key ideas was one that animated many comments in the present book, and that is that the business of painting is animating the picture plane.

Among the Action Painters' important achievements, made partly under Hofmann's tutelage, was to have developed Fauve ideas to the point where they could overcome the spatial legacy of Synthetic Cubist painting (which had been such an important part of the Cubists' legacy to Hofmann), and to have done so by detaching the idea of what constitutes a painterly relation from any notion of spatial composition altogether (which idea had also been an important aspect of the Cubists' influence on Hofmann). The Action Painters accomplished this partly by the use of all-over form (of a uniform pattern of strokes repeated across the canvas, without climax or emphasis). But it was also accomplished by according priority to what, as opposed to spatial composition, we can only consider content. Of course, I do not mean "content" in the sense of "reference to object matter"; rather I mean the energy that the painting makes visible—and, it turns out, makes visible through what is essentially a dialectical process, inasmuch as it is a process that absorbs more and more of true painting's features, including features that initially seemed contrary to its nature.

To understand the process, let us consider the relationship between contour and colour. We ordinarily consider these two as being nearly independent of one another—a painter produces an outline form and then colours it; insofar as it encloses a colour it represents, in a sense, its negation. However the abstract expressionists (among other painters of the 1940s and 1950s) attempted to overturn this conception of the relationship between shape and colour by endeavouring to find the shape appropriate to a certain colour. The idea of there being shape appropriate to a certain colour derives from conceiving a colour patch as a general area that possesses a certain intensity of energy. It is this energy that determines the shape appropriate to given colour: if the energy seems more expansive, the appropriate shape will spread itself out; if the energy seems to turn inwards, the shape will be more compact.

Despite his conviction that painting was composition of quasi-autonomous elements, the idea that colour and form could be unified in this way was one of elements of Hans Hofmann's teaching; he showed the younger New York painters how colour could assume the plastic functions that form had traditionally had, and, by assuming these, could take on their role in placing areas in space. He showed them, in short, how to resolve the tension between Fauve ideas on colour and Cubist ideas on the relation of forms in shallow space. The notion that there are shapes appropriate to particular colours (particular intensities of energy) suggests, finally, the essential identity of colour and shape—that shape cannot exist without colour and colour cannot exist with shape—and the identity of colour and shape was one that the emerging action painters took extremely seriously. Even more importantly, they recognized (at least implicitly) that techniques used to identify colour and shape effect a dialectical advance that sublates the opposition between the terms. Consider, for example, the way in which the painting of Ashile Gorky (1904-48) unify the opposites of drawing (as the activity of delineating an image) and painting (as the activity of colouring the canvas in such a way as to assert its flatness). Generally, as Jackson Pollock's (1912-56) paintings show, in Action Painting, line similarly becomes shape, field becomes figure, form becomes light. Action Painting therefore marks a dialectical advance in recent art history, a further stage along the way of the absolute nature of the medium reconciling an ever-increasing range of opposites, and, like Hegel's *Geist*, absorbing the opposing pairs into itself.

But dialectical advances are driven by the expenditure of energy, and the term that recent art history has made equivalent to Hegel's *Geist*, the term that absorbs all other terms into itself and reconciles their differences, is "energy." In Action Painting we see energy (that is, the motor force that drives action) becoming line becoming colour becoming contour becoming field becoming light. And energy/action is exactly what Action Painting strives to convey to audience (just as Projective Verse does).

The ideas on energy and spontaneity that the Action Painters and the Projective Poets elaborated had many sources, but among the primary ones was Surrealism. Surrealism's legacy to painting was twofold: the idea of forging an aesthetic representation of hallucinatory or oneiric content; and the automatist ideal. For obvious reasons, the first became embroiled in illusionist practices (as Dali's idea that is desirable to imbue a painting with attributes of the photograph testifies). Paintings that were to reproduce psychological contents were required to maintain some vestige of form in depth, and the articulation of form in depth relies to some measure of gestalt perception. But spontaneous practices could rarely sustain such spatial illusion—spontaneous construction favours Hofmann's ideal, surface construction. As the painting became more literally a surface construction, it exposed itself increasingly to automatic methods—to, for example, the drip methods that Hans Hofmann pioneered and Jackson Pollock adopted—for those methods have an evident alliance to more primitive, and all-over perceptual processes, such as those that the psychologist Anton Ehrenzweig discusses as scanning vision. Eventually, the spontaneous construction won out over spatial illusion.

As more automatic methods were introduced, the actual process of making the work became more important. The introduction of the notion of process has obvious affinities to the Projective Poets' ideas on open form. What is more, as the "what" of represented content receded, the "how" of process assumed greater importance, so the actual activity of putting the marks on the canvas assumed expressionistic import of exactly the sort possessed by Brakhage's camera handling.

Further, the Action Painters were the first to decisively dispense with the image—as either representation or as a geometric model. The most important consequence of this was transformation of the norms for art that correspond exactly to the transformation in the norms of poetry that T.E. Hulme analyzed in "A Lecture on Modern Poetry." For the image (whether representation or a geometric model) acted as an ideal, a norm of perfection. Action Painters released painting from the belief that the goal of art was to create a perfected, hypostatized ideal. Painting they understood to be act that conveys energy and effects viewers' bodies and minds.

This change, in its turn, impacted on the conception of the character of the experience that painting was understood to elicit. In *Das Zeit des Weltbildes*, Martin Heidegger delineates the relationship between conceiving of the world as a picture and norms of knowledge. Refusing to represent the world as a picture, but presenting one's response to the world in the form of actions also has epistemological implications—it speaks of a celebration of action and of the belief that our most profound understanding of the world comes not from how the world looks to an "outside spectator," but from our interaction with the world.

This new epistemological position derives from a new understanding of the relation between touch, proprioception, and sight implicit in Action Painting. The development of linear perspective in the quattrocento reflected a severing of sight from touch and proprioception: the space of a Renaissance image is a peculiarly non-fleshy thing, one that has not a great deal to do with tactile and kinaesthetic experience. Action Painters on the other hand relied on gesture to fuse optical, tactile, and proprioceptive experience in a single term. This fusing of the senses in the dynamic, proprioceptive body represents a return to primordial experience, after the eye had detached the faculty of cognition from the body. The body assumes its rightful role in the search for understanding.

Abandoning the image (either representational, or idealized in the form of the geometric image, and instead celebrating gesture, represents the culmination of a phase of modernity. As we noted at the beginning of the book, the transition from the pre-modern to the modern paradigm marked a turn towards subjectivity. The modern paradigm depicts human beings as striving to bring values out of themselves, as they have discovered that no values are given in the objective order of existence. From this developed the view that has been so common in modernity, that, since life is strife and struggle, the good is a life lived at fullest intensity. We have seen, too, that the philosophy of Henri Bergson shows how notions of the body that are entailed by, or at least associated with, the desire to live life at its fullest intensity can be encompassed in effort to get in touch with reality: if reality is thought to be (merely) fluxional, as the modern paradigm implies, then one can adopt the position that the internal dynamics of the proprioceptive body (Bergson would be inclined to say the body's sense of time as *durée*) puts us in touch with the dynamics of reality. This is a view that has been advanced by several of the figures we have examined, and it is also the view that lies behind the declarations of the Action Painters concerning their goals, and behind the practices they invented.

This is a very Romantic conception of artistic activity. Like the Romantic poet, the Action Painter hopes to experience the self as a creative, freely acting agent (this was one of Bergson's principal subjects). By eschewing the visual representation, the Action Painter moves into a completely open space, for nothing external to the process guides his or her actions; and in doing so, the action painter connects with the creativity both Bergson and Whitehead extolled.

There is even more to the abandoning of representation, and what that is requires further perpension on the notion of a poetics of embodiment. Like poets Charles Olson, Michael McClure, and Allen Ginsberg, Stan Brakhage founds his aesthetics in the body—but not on the body viewed objectively, as one object among others in the world, but the body as experienced from within, the proprioceptive body. His films concern the inner sensation of embodiment. While he is not unique in this regard—indeed his filmmaking has been enormously influential—his art has such formidable importance that his works and ideas are paradigms of what filmmaking that evolves from a poetics of embodiment can accomplish.

For Brakhage, a film is ideally a document (that is, a work that possesses energy equivalent to what inspired it) of the filmmaker's experiences of vision.[728] He understands vision to be a somatic activity. Though social conditioning renders one individual's way of seeing less intense and more like that of any other person, at its origin and in its essence, each person's visual experiences are unique precisely because everyone's body is unique and seeing is a bodily act. Brakhage proposes that the film artist should aim at recovering (in some form and in some measure) the experiences of vision proper to his or her own body.

Like Olson, Brakhage believes that wisdom is not the result of possessing knowledge, whether exoteric or esoteric, but of adopting the mode of being proper to one's physical constitution, including everything which that physical constitution entails—its unique capacities for sensing being the most important. Again, like Olson, Brakhage suggests that true knowledge is insight that has become so corporeal that it cannot be "verbally separated" (as Olson puts it); thus, in his view, knowledge constitutes a mode of being that one has invested in one's physical life, and so has become instrinsic to what one is—it has become, "As his skin is. As his life. And to be parted with only as that is."[729]

Brakhage maintains that all changes in one's body affect one's faculty of sight; at times, he even seems to believe that the organ of sight is ultimately the entire body. The most important inference he draws from this is that all emotional experiences register in vision, that emotion and seeing are integral to one another. Brakhage advocates that film artists should become aware of the interplay between emotion and seeing.

Brakhage has even argued that artistic forms derive from our embodied nature—that artworks' characteristics derive from our somatic constitution. His speculations about rhythmic form make clear his reasons for believing that art has a bodily basis; they also makes evident that he intends to to make a place for the personal body in rhythm. For Brakhage insists that rhythm derives from the the the heartbeat. But, as McClure suggested with his image of three-dimensional "mind/brain-screen," Brakhage believes that physiology decides what we see and what forms artists produce. The conception of cinema that he offered from the early 1980s through the early 1990s—that it presents "moving visual thinking"—also depended on his ideas about the body. Brakhage has used the term "moving visual thinking" to refer to thought's *materia prima*, that primordial form of awareness that precedes a thought's taking on definite form. The idea of "moving visual thinking" founds Brakhage's claim that film's great strength is that it, alone among all art media, can present the prime matter of thought—thought before it passes through the filter of language or assumes picture form. Adults are ordinarily unaware of the prime matter of thought, but, he claims, the foetus or the child is. This prime matter derives immediately from and reflects the nature of somatic processes. Brakhage goes as far as to identify thought with neurological processes and so insists that his films actually present the "sparking of the synapses" or "the light in the brain."[730] He avers that his films present, not pictures of visual thinking, but visual thinking itself: by this he seems to mean visual forms impart to the viewer the energy of thinking (the "kinetics" of the process, as Olson would have it), for he seems to believe that thought *is* energy, that it literally *is* a "sparking" or "electrical discharge" of the synapses. One suspects that Olson's anti-mimeticism had some role in bringing Brakhage to these conclusions, for Brakhage accepts, and adapts for film, Olson's belief that in reawakening the energies of an experience in a reader's body, one recreates the experience. A similar belief undergirds Brakhage's claim that his films do not represent the synaptic events he identifies with primordial consciousness, but actually present triggers for those events. This, as I pointed out when commenting on *Scenes from Under Childhood*, is tantamount to a Swedenborgian-style claim for film's correspondence with the body/reality. Sometimes Brakhage works out his correspondence claim for film differently: he sometimes claims that reality is light (or, alternately, he claims that his sensibility, or sometimes human sensibility, is, as a tropism, oriented towards light) and because his films are made of light, their moving visual forms and the events they embody are, to all intents and purposes, identical. Or he works it out yet another way, involving not one but two point-to-point mappings: because films are made of light, identical to (or at least very similar to) the light-events that triggered his own brain-events, which are also light-events ("sparkings"), film can convey the brain-events that correspond to events in reality (as both are light-events). However the correspondence is construed, Brakhage maintains that a film engenders in the viewer's mind virtually the same experience that inspired him to make it (or, according to a somewhat different version, that he experienced in making it).

In the section entitled "Margin Alien" in his compendium of aesthetic propositions, *Metaphors on Vision*, Brakhage twice quotes Olson's statement "ONE PERCEPTION MUST IMMEDIATELY AND DIRECTLY LEAD TO A FURTHER PERCEPTION"; and, as well, he quotes there Olson's "one perception must must MOVE, INSTANTER, ON ANOTHER!" Brakhage's writing gives further evidence of his allegiance to Olson's poetics, for he testifies that it is "that entire section of Charles Olson's STATEMENTS ON POETICS [by which title he is clearly referring to "Projective Verse"] which most perfectly describes for me the working processes which have come increasingly into their own thru each attempt on my part while filming and editing to avoid John's Cage, per chance, these last several years."[731] Brakhage's creative methods do indeed resemble the creative methods Olson advocated: like Olson, he seems to hold that energy is primary and to agree that a work of art has the task of getting energy from where the artist got it over to the viewer/reader.[732]

Brakhage's cinema is renowned for his use of the hand-held, moving camera.[733] So important does he deem his abilities in camera handling that he used to do calisthenics with his camera almost every day in order

> to explore the possibilities of exercise, to awaken my senses, and to pre-
> pare my muscles and joints with the weight of the camera and the neces-
> sary postures of holding it so that I can carry that weight in the balance of
> these postures through my physiological *re*action during picture taking and
> *to* some meaningful *act* of edit.[734]

Brakhage's manner of camera handling relates to two intertwined aspirations for his work: on the one hand, his films present a record of an individual's experiences with vision, so the camera movement imitates (roughly) the movement of the eye, or (somewhat less roughly) the mind's movement; at the same time, in the trace of the movement on the screen, its energy, force, and dynamics are apparent, and this energy affects viewers immediately and proprioceptively, evoking the quality of the movement Brakhage engaged in and so the character of his feelings (however fleeting they might have been) at the very moment he performed that movement. This is analogous to the effects of the traces left by the painter of Action Paintings. Hence, Brakhage's camera movement has both mimetic and expressionistic import. Even this relationship between the mimetic and expressive functions has physiological grounds for, Brakhage would argue, one's emotional state affects the way one's eyes move—for example, they might dart about incessantly when one feels agitated.

Schopenhauer held similar ideas about the interaction of body and spirit/emotion, about the role of external influences both on immediate feelings and on one's intellectual development, and about the illusionary nature of all beliefs in the intellect's autonomy. He stated his views this way in *The World as Will and Representation*.

> [A]s even scholars have, as a rule, become such merely through external
> causes, we should regard them primarily as men who are really destined
> by nature for farming and wood-cutting. In fact, even professors of philos-
> ophy should be estimated according to this standard, and then their
> achievements will be found to come up to all reasonable explanations....
> Physiologically, it is remarkable that the preponderance of the mass of the
> brain over that of the spinal cord and nerves, which according to Sömmer-
> ing's clever discovery affords the true and closest measure of the degree of
> intelligence both in animal species and in individual men, at the same time
> increases the direct mobility, the agility, of the limbs.... Heaviness in the
> movement of the body, therefore, indicates a heaviness in the movement of
> thoughts and ideas; and it is regarded as a sign of dullness and stupidity
> both in individuals and in nations, just as are flabbiness of the facial fea-
> tures and feebleness of the glance. Another sympton of the physiological
> facts of the case referred to is the circumstance that many people have at

once to stand still, as soon as their conversation with anyone accompanying them begins to have some connexion. For as soon as their brain has to
link a few ideas together, it no longer has as much force left over as is
required to keep the legs in motion through the motor nerves; with them
everything is so fine and close-cut.[735]

There is also a somatic basis for Brakhage's use of parataxis. Brakhage's
films often give the impression that he picks up and uses certain images or
clusters of images—which he sometimes repeats, to endow them with additional richness and significance. Often he works with a cluster of forms for a
while and then leaves that set of images behind and takes up another cluster.
His films often seem, in consequence, to be made from a series of discrete
phrases (presented once or several times); they do not build smoothly and
continuously toward a dramatic climax, nor do they conform to the *grande
ligne* of traditional musical composition. Instead, they appear as a series
of fresh, new events (cf. the Steinian and Jamesian sense of the continual
coming-on of novelty) that only the energy of immediate perception can hold
together in a unity, and even the speed of perception can keep them united
only temporarily. A Brakhage film usually acquires its force more through
the accumulating power of the individual image-energies than through its
dramatic development. Furthermore, Brakhage's films rarely rely heavily on
the smooth transitions between visual forms that are common in most films;
and when Brakhage does use a transitional device to get from visual form to
visual form, he usually uses plastic cutting, i.e., cutting between arbitrary
shapes that resemble each other. And plastic cutting itself is not bound by
the codes that govern the construction of an "illusionistic" diegesis and so it
permits greater discontinuities than the mainstream cinema tolerates.

The energy of Brakhage's films, the speed that characterizes no small portion of them, the discontinuities they incorporate, the "out-of-focus" shooting or swish-pans which make the shot's object-matter difficult to identify,
the sense of form-in-evolution they impart (and which elicits the feeling that
they could take unlikely turns or depart in unforeseen directions) all con-
spire to rivet the viewer's attention to the visual flow. One's involvement
with present immediacy—with immediate perception—is so intense that
one has little energy left over for engaging in apperceptive acts. Hence, his
films elicit a strong sense of scoptic identification (since self-reflection
detaches us from—allows us to stand ecstatically apart from—our perceptual
experiences, while identificatory mechanisms turn us over to the flow of our
experiences). This identificatory involvement in the flow of experience operates conjointly with the effects of the paratactical forms of construction to
create a discontinuous sense of the self. This scoptic identification encourages the viewer to enter into his films, to merge with their energy, and

participate in the flow of his shooting. Hence, we feel every abrupt change they undergo—every cut or every change in intensity or direction—as an alteration of one's self. Brakhage's cinema gives the transcendental self no space.[736] The self goes over into its "visionary" experiences.

This evacuated conception of the self is a great irony of the historical process. The self in recent times has assumed a heavy burden: Schopenhauer's philosophy exemplifies the heavy work the body has been required to bear, for Schopenhauer relied on our internal awareness of the body to ground our knowledge of the noumenal realm of Will; poets, painters, dancers, and filmmakers took up Schopenhauer's insight and used it in their efforts to prevent the vanishing of matter into the abyss of nihilism. Moderns generally experience the internally sensed self—the self of throbbing energy and its intense sensations—as the last refuge, as the external world collapses into nothing. What came of this in the end? The self went over into the world of experience and, like the objects of nature, it melted into air.

Glossary

absolute rhythm. As Ezra Pound used the term: a poetic rhythm that corresponds exactly to the shade of emotion the poet endeavours to express. It provides an interpretation of the poet's relation with the world and, accordingly, if achieved, will be genuine, authentic, individual, uncounterfeiting, and uncounterfeitable (as Pound suggests in "A Retrospect," *Selected Literary Essays of Ezra Pound*, p. 9).

accentual verse. Verse whose metre is organized according to stress (i.e., the vocal emphasis on a syllable).

actual entity. As a term from A.N. Whitehead's metaphysics: Whitehead uses the terms "actual entity" and "actual occasion" pretty much interchangeably (though at one point he notes that the word *occasion* implies location, so God, who is a non-temporal actual entity is not an actual occasion). "Actual entities" are the final, real entities of which the world is made up. They have a microcosmic scale; objects that have macrocosmic scale—the entities of everyday experience (automobiles, calculators, evergreen trees, saucepans, humans, etc.) are aggregates of actual entities (see entry for nexus). Whitehead characterizes actual entities as vital, as transient (they are formed through a process he calls "concrescence" [q.v.], endure only for the instant of their becoming, and then immediately go out of existence), and as complex and interdependent drops of experience. Whitehead seems to have modelled the concept of actual entity somewhat after the Leibnizian concept of monad, which had been a topic of concern of his long-time collaborator Bertrand Russell; however, a key difference between Leibniz's monads and Whitehead's actual occasion is that a monad is a "windowless" entity while an actual occasion is "all windows."

actual world. As a term from A.N. Whitehead's metaphysics: the actual world of the actual entity A is the collection of actual entities that form the data for the initial phase of A's concrescence. A's actual world is different from the actual world of any other actual occasion. The concept evidently played a role in Charles Olson's formulation of the idea of a field (q.v.).

all-over form. A form in which a line or shape is repeated across the canvas, without climax or emphasis. The paintings Jackson Pollock (1912-56) did between 1945 and 1950 often exhibit all-over form. All-over forms have the important property of interrelating elements which have (appoximately) equal importance.

alpha element; alpha function. As terms from Wilfred R. Bion's psychoanalytic theory: intermediate data, between beta elements (q.v.) and actual experience, alpha elements are a result of the transformation by alpha functions of beta elements (the rudimentary elements from which experience is assembled) and are capable of being formed (primarily through a concatenative or synthetic process) into data that can be assimilated into the higher mental functions represented by dreams, emotions, memory, and cognition. The formation of alpha elements represents a stage at which the ego is able to accept the sensory and emotional impact of (uncognizable) beta elements.

Alpha functions are processes that transform the beta elements, the raw materials of emotional experience, into alpha elements, i.e., into a form in which they can be accepted by the higher mental process and assimilated into dreams, emotions, cognitions, memories, etc.

My term "primordial experience" is a very loose one, for it is a sort of umbrella concept comprising both what Bion referred to as alpha and beta elements.

anacoluthon (from Greek for "lacking sequence"). A structure that results when a sentence is begun one way and finishes a different way. "Let us go then, you, the tall man, and I am under the stoop."

anacrusis. The rhythmic effect produced by an initial unaccented syllable or unaccented syllables which, since they do not count as part of the metric pattern, delay the beginning of the metrical pattern. The metre of the version of Gertrude Stein's famous single that begins with "A"—"A rose is a rose is a rose"—exhibits anacrusis.

apophansis. A term I use for a process that by revealing one object, feature, or process conceals another—the one being revealed "eclipses" the other. To coin it, I modified a term from rhetoric, *apophasis* (from Greek *apo*, from, and *phanái*, to say), "a figure one uses when one says something while pretending that one is not going say it—statements introduced by "not to mention" are a commonplace example. I chose to create the name for processes that in revealing one object, feature, or process conceal another by modifying the name for the rhetorical figure because both involve similarly coordinated processes of revealing and concealing.

asyntactic (adjective). Applied primarily to literary works, the term refers to passages that seem ungrammatical in sentence structure, loose in overall organization, and ungoverned by conventional principles concerning word order.

autotelic. A term associated primarily with the New Critics, it refers to a quality of an artwork's existence—that it has no other purpose than to be, that it serves no end beyond its own existence.

beta element. As a term from Wilfred R. Bion's psychoanalytic theory: an emotional/somatic element that registers the effect of emotional events and provides the raw material of experience, but belongs to a stage prior to experience. These beta elements must be transformed into alpha elements (q.v.) by alpha functions before they can be acknowledged and assimilated by the higher mental processes represented in dreams, memories, emotions, cognitions, etc.

cathexis. The term that James Strachey used to translate Sigmund Freud's term *Besetzung*, a German term that might be translated, roughly, as "occupation."

caesura. A pause in the reading of a line of poetry that does not affect the metre. The occurrence of a caesura may be determined by grammar, by logic, or by cadence.

causal efficacy. A term from A.N. Whitehead's metaphysics: prehension in the mode of causal efficacy is the more fundamental of the two pure modes of perception—prehension in the mode of presentational immediacy (q.v.) being the other pure mode. Perception in the mode of causal efficacy arises in the first phase of concrescence (q.v.) as conformal feeling (q.v.). It does not involve consciousness and is present in all actual entities, including those which make up inanimate objects. Perception in the mode of causal efficacy transmits feelings from past data—feelings that are vague, massive, and inarticulate, and which are sensed, according to Whitehead, as the efficaciousness of the past. Accordingly, Whitehead characterized perception in the mode of causal efficacy as crude.

conceptual prehension. A term from A.N. Whitehead's metaphysics: a prehension (q.v.) that has as its datum, an eternal object, or, more exactly, has, as an immediate datum, a *definite* eternal object, without there being any participation by a particular realization of the eternal object. Conceptual prehension is the second phase of concrescence. Concrescence begins with a phase of what Whitehead called "conformal," or "physical feelings"; with the onset of the second phase, the emerging actual entity escapes from the tyranny of the given, since conceptual prehensions involve unqualified negation (inasmuch as they extrude any particular realization of the eternal object). The subjective form of a conceptual prehension is valuation—either *adversion* or *aversion*; the effect of this valuation is to enlarge or diminish the importance of the eternal object that is the datum of the prehension in the emerging actual entity. Whitehead considered such valuations to be the most basic form of creative response available to actual entities.

concrescence (from Latin *concrescere*, to grow together, and having the sense of "to unify into one being"). As a term from A.N. Whitehead's metaphysics: the unification (or "growing together") of a variety of elements to create a complex unity. Concrescence is the term Whitehead gives to the process that constitutes, and is, any actual entity (q.v.). The initial phase of this synthetic process involves feeling, disjunctively, all the diverse entities that form data for the emerging actual entity; later phases involve the unification (the "growing together") of these separate feelings into one feeling whose unity Whitehead termed the *satisfaction* of that actual entity. Concrescence, then, can be understood as the process by which many diverse things form a determinate unity though the formation of a superordinate/subordinate relation between each element within this manifold and the novel one. When an actual entity attains satisfaction, it perishes. *See also the entry for* **prehension**.

concrescence, principle of. As a term from A.N. Whitehead's metaphysics: refers to the drive things possess that impels them to actualization, the creative urge towards concrescence, for producing novel advances through the generation of greater interrelatedness. Many thinkers would deem this urge divine, so the principle of concrescence may be considered one of Whitehead's terms for God.

concreteness, fallacy of misplaced. As a term from A.N. Whitehead's metaphysics: refers to what Whitehead considered a fallacy—of taking an abstract quality and treating it as though it had concrete form (as though it were causally efficacious and ontologically prior to the objects that possess that quality).

conformal feeling. As a term from A.N. Whitehead's metaphysics: Whitehead used a number of expressions to refer to the first phase of concrescence: the "conformal phase," the "responsive phase," the "receptive phase," the "initial phase," or the "primary phase." The prehensions that belong to this phase Whitehead called "conformal feelings," or "responsive feelings" or "pure physical feelings." The conformal phase provides the material from which a complex unity of realization is forged. It begins the process of concrescence by linking the past and present—the past is given as objectified *données*, which the response phase absorbs as material for the subjective unity of feeling. Since rejection or extrusion are not involved in conformal feelings (extrusion characterizing only the prehension of eternal objects), Whitehead call the conformal phase of concrescence "the receptive phase." Whitehead characterizes conformal feelings as vectors, since they feel "what is *there* and transform it into what is *here*." In doing so, a conformal feeling transforms objective content in subjective feelings.

consequent nature of God. *See* **primordial nature of God.**

constancy, object. *See* **perceptual object constancy.**

contemporaneous. As a term from A.N. Whitehead's metaphysics: actual events are said to be contemporaneous when they occur without causal dependence on one another. Contemporary regions are known through perception in the mode of presentational immediacy.

counterpoint. As applied to verse (as opposed to music), the term denotes metrical variation. Verse that is written in iambs but contains (if even implicitly) dactyls and trochees, for example, thereby achieves counterpoint.

cross-rhythm. A type of epiploce (q.v.). The rhythmic effect produced when equal units of duration are divided into two parts in two different ways and the resulting metres are heard simultaneously. In this book I often use the term **cross-pulse** to refer to the effect of an implied ternary division of the basic metrical unit that is superimposed in the reader's mind over the rhythm constituted by the primary binary division.

deictic signs. Indexical signs (q.v.) whose referents are affected by the shifts in the speaker's location, e.g., "this," "that," "here," "there."

diegesis. In *The Republic* (392c-395a) Plato used the term "diegesis" to refer to a mode of narration that he labels "pure narration": Socrates notes (in his characteristic manner, by posing questions) that "everything that is said by fabulists or poets [is] a narration of past, present or future things" and goes on to distinguish between two modes of narration—pure or simple narration (*diegesis*) and imitation (*mimesis*).

Plato distinguishes between a mode of narration in which the author (or a stand-in for the author) does not conceal his role in recounting the events that make up the narrative (this is the mode that Plato referred to as "pure" or "simple narration" or "diegesis") and a mode of narration that conceals the role of the author/narrator and creates the impression that the narration actually presents the events that constitute the narrative (this mode Plato referred to as "mimesis.") Plato is quite explicit about the efforts the mimetic artist makes to conceal the mediated status of the narrated events: "When he [Homer, presenting events mimetically] delivers a speech as if he were someone else, shall we not say that he then assimilates thereby his own diction as far as possible to that of the person whom he announces as about to speak?" (393c). "In such a case," he notes, " he and the other poets effect their narration through imitation. . . . But if the poet should conceal [by pretending to be fictive character] himself nowhere, then his entire poetizing and narration would have been accomplished without imitation."

The French aesthetician and semiotician Étienne Souriau, revived the term in 1953, but virtually reversed its meaning: in his writings, it refers to the narrative content (the characters and actions in themselves, considered apart from any discursive mediation). Commentators on film have taken up Souriau's work and proceeded with that; and they often use the term in a more extended sense still—as referring to the illusory world constructed by a narrative. Thus "diegetic space" is illusory space (usually pieced together from a number of parts) in which the narrative action seems to take place. *See also the entries for* ***énoncé***; ***histoire***.

discours (discourse). In Benveniste's literary theories: messages that are marked by the trace of their enunciator are said to be instances of discourse.

In Michel Foucault's sociology: In *Les Mots and les choses* (1966), Foucault used the term to refer to language that had been reduced to representation. In later works, presenting the project of "the pure description of discourse," he uses the term differently. Beginning with *L'Archéologie du savoir* (1969), discourse is the product of the power embodied in institutional languages (Foucault's term for codes relating practices). Foucault describes discursive practices as the set "of anonymous and historical rules, always specific as to time and place, and which, for a given period and within a social, economic, geographic, or linguistic zone, define the framework within which the enunciative practices are exercised" (*The Archeology of Knowledge*, translated by A.M. Sheridan-Smith, pp. 153-54). These discursive practices have a maieutic function, as they bring cultural objects into being by defining them and delimiting their sphere of operation. Thus the discursive practices of psychiatry bring into being mental illness, the mentally-ill person, the mental hospital, and the practitioner who treats mental illness.

emanationism. A doctrine concerning creation, which offers that all reality proceeds apodeictally from a single, perfect, and eternally present being by a series of emanations (overflowings) in which beings spill out from the One who is their source.

emergent property. Regarding properties produced by aggregative processes: qualities that emerge through the synthesis of structures that could not be predicted from characteristics of structure as independent existents. Regarding evolution: the production of emergent properties displays novelty and marks a creative advance.

énoncé. As a term from Emile Benveniste's linguistic theories: Benveniste distinguished the *énoncé*, or what is uttered, from the *énonciation*, or the act of uttering.

en-soi (from French for "in itself" or "in oneself"). As a term from Jean-Paul Sartre's phenomenological ontology: Sartre uses the term *en-soi* to refer—somewhat ambiguously—to: (1) that mode of being possessed by any complete being with a fixed nature; that ontological modality is "closed" in the sense that it expresses either relation (either intrinsically, among features internal to its being, or extrinsically, with some being external to its self), and (2) that sort of being possessed by people who act as though they were inanimate objects, acted upon by external forces and not capable of initiating self-directing action.

epiploce (from Greek for "braiding together"). A term from Classical prosody that refers to a feature of verses that allows them to be scanned in various ways.

épistème. A term coined by the French philosopher Michel Foucault to refer to an ensemble of conditions prevailing at any time that determine the possibility of knowledge.

Eternal Object. As a term from A.N. Whitehead's metaphysics: the forms of definiteness that characterize an experience, and do so by affecting actual occasions. Whitehead patterned his notion of Eternal Objects after the Platonic notion of *eidos*; and Eternal Objects have many of the same roles in Whitehead's metaphysics as has the concept of a universal in metaphysical theories that maintain that the referents of general (universal) terms possess real (usually extra-mental) existence. The most important similarity, perhaps, is that complex Eternal Objects, like Platonic forms, establish the characteristics that define an object. Eternal Objects are of two types (which taxonomy Whitehead seems to have fashioned after John Locke's distinction between primary and secondary properties): first, the "objective species," e.g., geometric objects and relations; and, second, "subjective species": e.g., a colour, emotional intensities, an adversion or an aversion, a pleasure or a pain—whatever can be an element in the subjective form of a feeling.

Eternal Objects are prehended by cognitive modality, which Whitehead calls "conceptual prehension." To be a concrete fact, each actual entity must assume a definite form, which it does by deciding (see entry for concrescence) which Eternal Objects it will allow, and which Eternal Objects it will not, to become ingredient (i.e., to ingress into—see ingression) in its concrescence. Process, which therefore can be identified as concrescence (the growing together) that any actual occasion is, involves the determination of what forms of definiteness will characterize that occasion; this determination takes place by the actual entitities selecting among Eternal Objects according to a scale of valuation. Consequently these actual entities exemplify the ingression of Eternal Objects that represent forms of definiteness that any actual entity can choose among. But the actual entity does not have complete freedom in choosing among these eternal objects; the vector character of the process of concrescence itself, which grades and selects among the forms of definiteness that the past, through the extensive continuum (q.v.), has a significant role in deciding which occasions supersede the present. Eternal Objects belong to the extensive continuum and are part of the primordial nature of God (q.v.).

N.B.: Whitehead does not generally capitalize the term, but I prefer to, to remind readers (and myself) of the similarities between Whitehead's Eternal Objects and Plato's forms.

extensive continuum. As a term from A.N. Whitehead's metaphysics: the first determination of order, representing *real* possibility, that arises out of the general character of the world. The array of Eternal Objects (q.v.) establishes a pure potentiality—that is, a well-defined set of possibilities. The realm of Eternal Objects takes no account of compossibility, i.e., it does not extrude any concerns (regarding the ingression of Eternal Objects into the world) other than those whose nature is purely logical (for example, it extrudes the possibility that the object I am now building will be simultaneously a cube and sphere—the definition of "cube" and "sphere" make it a logical impossibility that it can be both a cube and sphere.) But there are limitations on concrescence other than those of a logical nature—limitations having to do with the past or with compossibility: for example, it is impossible that an aging, flabby man will win the one-hundred-metre dash at the next Olympiad. Real potentiality (as opposed to the pure or logical potentiality) is delimited by restrictions placed upon pure potentiality by the given conditions of the existing world. The extensive continuum, then, is that first determination of co-ordination—the determination of real possibility, resulting from the imposition of limitations that arise from the general character of the world, upon pure possibility. Hence the extensive continuum imposes the first, and the most general, limitation upon pure potentiality—the limitation that each generation of actual entities shall exhibit the general properties of "extensive connection."

fabula. A term from Russian formalist literary criticism that refers to the actions and events recounted in a story, ordered in chronological (and usually causal) sequence, together with the agents that perform those actions and take part in those events and their physical context (the time and location).

feeling. As a term from A.N. Whitehead's philosophy: a positive prehension (q.v.).

field. Suppose we assign the points in space (or space-time) values, and then develop laws (usually by formulating differential equations) that relate those values. The collection of laws relating the values assigned to the points is known as field theory, and the collection of the values assigned to the points is known as a field. John Clark Maxwell's laws of electromagnetism are an example of field theory, with each point in space-time carrying a value for an electric field and a magnetic field. Field theories have the conspicuous advantage, so far as the philosophy of science is concerned, of being able to explain action at distance (actions across spatial distance) without making any assumptions about space-filling substances. Olson's conception of field poetics (which understands a "field" essentially as a collection of environing points, to each of which a vector of energy can be assigned) was clearly influenced by scientific field theory.

Though Whitehead himself was interested in field theory, there are nonetheless difficulties associated with Olson's attempt to combine Whitehead's metaphysics of process and field theory, inasmuch as field theory assumes the existence of space-time points (indeed, the success of field theories in physics is often said to constitute an argument for existence of

space-time points), while Whitehead's *Process and Reality* (1929) is a massive argument for relationalism (i.e., the claim that there are only spatio-
temporal relations, and no independently existing space-time points).

Geist. As a term from the philosophy of G.W.F. Hegel: see Spirit.

Gestalt property. A property which characterizes the whole that some set of elements constitute (in the sense of the pattern or form of their overall configuration), but does not characterize the individual elements by themselves.
Gestalt properties are emergent properties (q.v.); so knowledge of the characteristics of the individual elements does not allow us to predict the gestalt
properties their configuration will possess. See **emergent property.**

histoire. As a term from Benveniste's linguistic theories: messages which are not
marked by a trace of the speaker are said to be instances of *histoire.*

hovering stress or **accent.** Refers to a feature a syllable takes on within a metrical
pattern that allows it to be read as being either heavily or weakly stressed.

hylè (Greek: *hyle*, meaning "matter"). Used to refer to matter (apart from form).

hypotaxis (from Greek for "under arrangement"). Presenting facts or ideas in
superordinate and subordinate clauses, with syntactic joiners.

icon. As a semiotic term: Charles Sanders Peirce coined the term "icon" to designate that sort of sign whose significant powers depend on similarity
between the representamen (q.v.) and the object.

ideograph or **ideogram.** A iconographic grapheme or compound of graphemes of
a pleremic writing system that presents a picture of the object or a representation of the concept for which it stands. Ernest Fenollosa believed that
written characters of Chinese and Japanese are ideographs (though in fact
they are not; Chinese is "logographic," that is, its symbols write out words,
not ideas); and he influenced Ezra Pound, Sergej Ejzenstejn, Charles Olson,
and Stan Brakhage to adopt this belief.

idiolect. The aggregate of all the features of an individual's language use.

illocutionary force. A term from J.L. Austin's linguistic theory: words are often
used to do things. The actions that are performed with an utterance
(promising, sharing an oath, etc.) are referred to as the utterance's illocutionary force.

Imaginary, the (with a capital "I"). A term from Jacques Lacan's psychoanalytic
theory: refers to a stage in the maturational process that is dominated by
perceptual activities; though, to be sure, the mechanisms of the Imaginary
survive that stage, and later behaviours and later ways of making sense of
the world continue to make use of those mechanisms. The stage is preverbal. Its central event is the well-known *stade de mirroir.* The mirror
stage, and the Imaginary stage as a whole, establish the continuing possibility of identification/unification, the formation of binary spatial relations
(inside/outside), and even abstract binary relations (good/evil).

Imagism. A movement in poetry in the early part of the twentieth century; the
poets associated with it believed that a precise, definite clear image is
essential to poetry; that poetry should use common words; should use the
exact word that conveys a given thought or feeling; and should employ as
compact forms as possible. The most aesthetically debilitating verbal constructions, in their view, were clichéd expressions and "dead metaphors";
the most important thinker associated with Imagism, T.E. Hulme, distin-

guished prose and poetry on the basis that the former employs "counter language" that is made up of dead metaphors we shuffle about like so many tokens. The Imagists also strived to create rhythms that were unbridled by conventions, but fit the exact mood they wished to convey.

imagnostic. A term coined by Stan Brakhage, and not intended to be generalized (as I have done in this book). In his note on *Roman Numeral I* (that appears, among other places, in the catalogue of the New York Film-makers' Cooperative), Brakhage tells us that the film begins a new series that would ordinarily be called "abstract," "non-objective" or "non-representational." He expresses his dislike for all such terms, and reports that while making the film and thinking about the problem of what to call such films, the term "imagnostic" repeatedly came to mind. He proposed the term as an alternative to terms like "non-objective," "non-representational," and "abstract." In the note Brakhage also furnishes a para-etymology for the term: *ais* (like) + *gnosis* (knowledge). A very fine article by Phoebe Cohen ("Brakhage's I, II, and III," *Millennium Film Journal* 7/8/9 [Fall/Winter 1980-81]) argues cogently for there being a parallel between Brakhage's idea of imagnostic film and Barnett Newman's idea of the Plasmic Image.

indexical sign. As a term from C.S. Peirce's semiotics: a sign vehicle is an index if its signifier is really affected by its signified. A weather vane is the common example.

ingression. As a term from A.N. Whitehead's metaphysics: the term refers to the unification, though a process of co-ordination that involves prehensions (q.v.) and a process of concrescence (q.v.) of potential occurrences, into complexes.

inscape and **instress.** Coinages of the poet Gerald Manley Hopkins. "Inscape" refers to the distinctive form of a natural object that constitutes its "oneness." "Instress" refers to the ontogenic energy that constitutes the inscape of a natural object, which we apprehend in a moment of illumination that carries us into the inscape.

interpretant. Charles Sanders Peirce uses the term to refer to the meaning of a sign. In "Logic as Semiotic: The Theory of Signs," Peirce defines a sign, or *representamen*, as "something which stands to somebody for something in some respect or capacity." He goes on to explain the nature and role of the interpretant: "[The sign] addresses somebody, that is, creates in the mind of that person an equivalent sign, or perhaps a more developed sign. That sign which it creates I call the *interpretant* of the first sign."

Peirce distinguished a triad of interpretants on the basis of their different effects on the interpreter's mind. The first category is that of the **immediate interpretant**; it is the potentiality that a sign could affect a mind that reflects on it. The second category is the **dynamic interpretant**; it is the direct effect actually produced by the sign on the mind of the interpreter. There are three subcategories of the dynamic interpretant: the emotional, the energetic, and the logical. The third category is that of the **final interpretant**. It relates to habit and law: it is the interpretation that interpreters would in the end agree upon.

This book argues for the primacy in a certain poetic tradition of the energetic interpretant over the emotional and logical interpretants, and for the reduction—even elimination—of the role of the final interpretant.

introjection. A term from psychoanalytic theory: one of the psychological processes by which elements of the external world are taken into an organism, introjection is the process by which objected representations are turned into self-representations; this occurs, for example, when a child takes parents' demands as his or her own.

kerygma. Literally, the Greek term for the gospel (i.e., the good news, the second testament's message of salvation). The term refers more broadly to the voice of God speaking through human agents. Literary theorists, following Northrop Frye's lead, have expanded the term *kerygma* to refer to a mode of rhetoric, the rhetoric of proclamation, and the adjective "kergymatic" to refer to the features of a rhetoric of proclamation, or to the characteristic manner of words that serve as a vehicle for revealing a higher order. Northrop Frye goes so far (in *Words with Power*, p. 101) to describe *kerygma* as "a mode of language on the *other side* of the poetic," for it makes a prophetic utterance genuinely prophetic. *Kerygma* is also the point where the action and the reception of speech fuse, for language becomes truly perlocutionary: "subject and object merge in an immediate verbal world, where a Word not our own, though also our own, responds. . . . Obviously the ordinary critical value-judgments applied to literature have no relevance to the kerygmatic" (Frye, *Words with Power*, pp. 118-19). I believe the quotation makes abundantly clear the relevance of Frye's development of the concept of *kerygma* to the Projective Poets.

One of the purposes of this book has been to demonstrate the primordiality of kerygmatic utterance.

langue. As a term of Ferdinand de Saussure's semiology: the regulatory codes of the system that governs the use of language; these regulatory codes authorize the individual uses of language, the issuing of utterance or the writing of texts, which Saussure refers to as "paroles." *Paroles* are concrete embodiments of the codes that make up the *langue*.

lyrical film. A term used by P. Adams Sitney to refer to one phase in the diachronic morphology of avant-garde cinema in the United States which he put forward in *Visionary Film*. Sitney uses the term to refer to a cinematic form that he considered the successor form to the trance film or the psychodrama. The lyrical film has many of the features of the lyric poem (especially the Romantic lyric); and while Sitney lays emphasis on the subjective point of view, the lyric film typically has many other of the attributes of the lyric poem: it makes use of many rhythmically independent phrases and a shifting rhythm that suggests the rapid shifts of pre-logical thinking.

mechanical unity. A unity produced by a network of external relations. Antonym: organic unity (q.v.).

monism, neutral. The theory that the fundamental reality of the universe is a neutral element that is neither mental nor physical but on which both the mental and the physical depend—to which, in fact, we can ascribe no characteristics (indeed, it is often considered to be unknowable, since it lacks any characteristics we can apprehend). A consequence of Whitehead's neutral monism is that all objective process necessarily presents itself to a subject, without mediation.

mythopoeic film. A term P. Adams Sitney uses in his diachronic morphology of American avant-garde cinema. Mythopoeic filmmakers engage in *mythopoe-*

sis. These efforts generally produce more extended forms. Their films also rely more on a Jungian rather than a Freudian/Eriksonian sense of the self.

negative capability. Keats's term for the capacity of strong souls to abide with uncertainties and doubts, without seeking resolution in facts or reason.

Olson and Brakhage have extolled negative capability, since for them negative capability is a valuable antidote to our culture's tendency towards rationalization.

negative hallucination. What is left after destruction of all mental representations, which usually occurs under highly charged conditions. The absence of any object of awareness opens a gap in consciousness and precipitates the experience of nothingness; the result is often a *timor mortis*.

nekuia. A tale of visiting the Underworld, or the visit itself.

New Criticism. Strictly, the term "New Criticism" applies to the critical writings of John Crowe Ransom, Allen Tate, R.P. Blackmur, Robert Penn Warren, and Cleanth Brooks, and to the critical principles expounded therein. More generally, and much more commonly, however, the term is applied to any critical writing that subscribes to the view that the work of art is an autotelic (q.v.) object; uses the method of close examination to disclose immanent relations in an artwork; and holds that the language of poetry is of a special kind, distinct from ordinary language.

nexus. As a term from A.N. Whitehead's metaphysics: any actual entity (q.v.) has a microcosmic scale; the entities we encounter in everyday experience—automobiles, calculators, evergreen trees, saucepans, humans—are groupings of actual entities. Whitehead refers to these groupings as nexūs (pl.) or societies. Though societies and nexūs are pretty much interchangeable concepts, Whitehead does distinguish between the two, since, strictly, the category of nexus is more inclusive than that of society—there are nexūs that do not constitute societies, but every society constitutes a nexus—since societies are more complex (more intricately compounded) forms than nexūs.

noumenon. As a term from Immanuel Kant's epistemology: the thing-in-itself (*Ding an sich*) as contrasted with its appearance in consciousness, i.e., the phenomenon (q.v.); that reality (whether power or substance is unknowable) which transcends all knowledge whether by sensation or by Understanding.

objet petit 'a.' A term from Lacanian psychoanalytic theory: here the 'a' stands for *autre* or "other." The first lack that the child experiences, *l'object petit 'a,'* induces a gap in consciousness (an awareness of absence—cf. negative hallucination).

objective theory of art. A term used by M. H. Abrams to refer to those theories which maintain that an artwork's primary significance is as an object in itself, independent of the circumstances of its composition, the states of affairs it purports to imitate, any purposes for it that its creator might have declared, or even its effect on the audience. Later modernists such as Olson can be distinguished from early modernists largely because they reject the last claim, in favour of a perlocutionary theory of artistic meaning. *See also the entries for* **illocutionary force; perlocutionary act.**

objective correlative. A term introduced into criticism by T.S. Eliot in a 1919 essay on *Hamlet* and which enjoyed a popularity that astonished Eliot himself. In that essay, Eliot wrote, "The only way of expressing emotion in the form of art is by finding an 'objective correlative'; in other words, a set of objects, a situation, a chain of events which shall be the formula of that *particular* emotion; such that when the external facts, which must terminate in sensory experience, are given, the emotion is immediately evoked" (see "Hamlet," in Eliot, *Selected Essays*, 1932).

objectivism. A short-lived movement in poetry, associated with William Carlos Williams and Louis Zukofsky. The movement extended the ideas of the Imagists by developing a method of presenting the object and keeping the personality out of the work. Olson's **objectism**, a poetic method of avoiding interference by the lyrical ego, reworks ideas of the objectivists; this relationship helps explain why some of Olson's followers, for example, Robert Creeley, took up the cause of making Zukofsky's poetry known to the public.

Open Form. According to the Classical conception of *poesis*, makers—carpenters, cooks, poets—when they make an object of a particular sort, transcribe from the Forms that manifest the ends that objects of its type serve: when they make real cabinets, or real states, for examples, the cabinet maker or statesperson examines the Forms—that is, the transcendent exemplar of the purposes—of cabinets or states and then conforms his or her cabinet or state to the ideal.

Later moderns, by and large, have rejected the applicability of the Classical conception of *poesis* to the arts; they have found egregious the notion that an artist when making an object transcribes from pre-existing models for objects of its kind. The idea of a pre-existing poem that models the poem that a poet is about to write seemed absurd—as absurd as the idea of a pre-existing form for the aimless recreational perambulation I am about to embark on, allowing myself to follow my whims. Some modern art theorists have distinguished art from craft on just these grounds: The objects that craftspeople make have a purpose, and craftspeople model the object they make after reflecting on the functions that objects of its type serve—thus the slogan "form follows function." Artistic making, by contrast, is unconstrained by any considerations of purpose since art objects are non-functional.

The Open Form poet conceives of the poet existing in a field (q.v.) of energies, and the essential task of Open Form poets as opening themselves up as much as possible to that circumambient field—to feeling that field's changing dynamics in his/her body and nerve endings. The open form method of composition allows the compositional process to be constantly effected by changes in the dynamic conditions of the poet's circumambient field. Accordingly, an open form poem is constantly changing, and each change instills new life and fresh energy into the poem. These changes enact sudden turns of feeling and thought, rapid reversals of opinion, instantaneous formations of associations, and unexpected leaps of comparison. Thus, they externalize the mental activities that the poet engages in while composing them.

Open Form poets, and poetic theorists with an allegiance to the notion of open form, proposed that rather than trying to comprehend reality within some grand system, we should concentrate on the moment of experience, on what *this* very instant of experience reveals. The Projective Poet's ideal was complete responsiveness to the entire content of each moment, that would allow him or her to go wherever it seems to be leading. A complete openness to everything that belongs to every moment of experience can reveal much more about reality than any overarching system can. They strove to experience life with what Olson characterized as "point by point vividness." "Every moment of life is an attempt to come to life," Olson taught. We must open ourselves to the throb of life that every moment of experience conveys.

While neither Olson or Duncan spelled "open form" with initial capitals, I have chosen to use capitals when the term acts as the name of the group (or, better, a loose alliance of individual writers), and with small letters when the term is referring to a notion of poetry. Sometimes, of course, the choice between the two is not clear-cut, and in these cases I have tried to follow my instincts about which is the dominant tenor of the term in the particular instance.

See also the entries for periplum; **Projective Verse.**

paideuma. A term that Ezra Pound adopted from the German anthropologist Leo Frobenius. Something like an implicit worldview, the *paideuma* is a complex of ideas, images, feelings—many of them unconscious, but only felt in the bones—that determines how certain cultural groups see the world. It is a mental pattern that members of a culture impose on experience.

paradigmatic relations. The Swiss linguist Ferdinand de Saussure, who developed the concept of paradigmatic relations, actually used the term "associative relations" to refer to the idea and to distinguish them from **syntagmatic relations** (q.v.). Paradigmatically related terms—be they phonemes, words, or even more complex semiotic constructs—meet the commutativity test (i.e., one term can be exchanged for any other paradigmatically related term in a syntagma). Thus, given a syntagma, e.g., "The cat is on the mat," because the term "dog," and the term "turtle," could take the place of "cat," "cat," "dog," and "turtle" are paradigmatically related terms.

parataxis (from Greek "beside arrangement"). Presenting facts or ideas in a series of co-ordinate clauses that are juxtaposed to each other, without conjunctions between them. The opposite of hypotaxis (q.v.).

parole. As one of the terms of Ferdinand de Saussure's semiology: Saussure defines this term through an opposition to the term *langue* (q.v.) or language system; a parole is an event realized within the codes of a language, an instance of language, issued by a concrete individual, the individual's use of the language in an actual speech act, or in texts.

perceptual object constancy. A mode of perception in which the percept is fixed and possesses unchanging features. One can trace a developmental sequence: from synaesthesia (q.v.): through the wobbly image (q.v.); and through stable percepts which, though they are percepts that are understood to represent enduring objects, nonetheless have changeable qualities; to, finally, perceptual object constancy. Brakhage's *Scenes from Under Childhood* traces such an evolutionary sequence.

I must stress that what I mean by "perceptual object constancy" is quite different from what the distinguished psychoanalytic theorist Hans Hartmann means by "object constancy" (a quality of object relation in which the children's relation to their love objects endures and remains stable and permanent independent of the transitory states of the child's needs). There are, nonetheless, areas of overlap: both are achievements that involve the regulation of the drives; both are involved with children separating out from the environment; both involve the children's capacity to have a stable relation to the environment even as their needs, desires, and interests undergo change; and both require a stable mental representation of the object. Whatever the similarities, the differences between the two phenomena are enormous.

periplum (obj. case of *periplus*). From Homer, for "a circumnavigation." The idea that writing is like a voyage that one cannot plot out in advance, and that its course has to alter as one changes direction to cling to the coastline, obviously had a central influence on the Projective Poets.

perlocutionary act. A term from J.L. Austin's linguistic theory: something done to someone by our use of language. For example, we may frighten someone by speaking, or, if we are good orators, we may engender enthusiasm.

perpetually regenerating forms. A term I use to denote forms that produce a sense of "a continual coming-on of novelty" by constantly renewing themselves—by constantly leaving behind their basic features and assuming new features. At their most extreme, perpetually regenerating forms seem constantly on the verge of collapse, and to avoid the threatened collapse only by altering character from moment to moment. It is evident that such forms are congenial with open form (q.v.) practices. Stan Brakhage's films frequently use perpetually regenerating forms.

phenomenon (from Greek *phainomenon*, from *phainesthai*, "to appear," and *phainein*, "to show"). As a term from Immanuel Kant's epistemology: refers to that which is immediately perceived, to the object of experience as it appears in consciousness. Its antonym is "noumenon" (q.v.). What appears in consciousness, according to Kant, is interpreted through the categories. Nature is the sum total of phenomena as they are connected throughout.

pour-soi (from French for "for oneself" or "for itself").

pragmatic meaning. There is often considerable discrepancy between the literal meaning of an utterance and what the utterance is used to say. Suppose you walk into a room with a friend and the friend were to say to you, "It's kind of dark in here." It is rather unlikely that the meaning your friend would have intended you to take involved reporting on the lighting conditions of the room. Rather, your friend probably meant to encourage you to engage in some behaviour (e.g., adjusting the potentiometer on the lighting control, or getting amorous). This meaning is the utterance's pragmatic meaning. Pragmatic meaning, then, concerns what language is actually used to do. Pragmatic meaning comprises illocutionary meaning (q.v.) and perlocutionary meaning (q.v.), and possibly other sorts of meaning. This book concerns the pragmatic and, specifically, the perlocutionary force of poetic statements. *See also the entries for* illocutionary force; perlocutionary act.

prehension. A term from A.N. Whitehead's metaphysics: prehensions are the means by which one actual entity becomes objectified in another or by which eternal entities ingress into actual entities. Prehensions are like vectors in that they "feel what is *there* and transform it into what is *here*." Actual entities are formed by concrescences (q.v.) of prehensions. Prehensions have three factors: (1) the prehending "subject" (the actual entity of which that prehension is a concrete element; (2) the prehended "datum"; and (3) the prehension's "subjective form," i.e., how the subject prehends the datum. There are two sorts of *pure prehensions*: (a) physical prehensions, whose data are actual entities, and (b) conceptual prehensions, whose data are Eternal Objects. Prehensions whose data comprise both actual entities and eternal objects are *impure prehensions*. A hybrid prehension is a prehension by one actual entity (the "subject") of a conceptual prehension or an impure prehension that belongs to mentality of another subject.

presence. As a philosophical term: it is at once richer and more specific than in its everyday use. According to its philosophic use (and this includes its use in aesthetics, as in "presentational modes of art") presence is always something apprehended in an encounter in which the depths of one being meets the depths of another.

presentational immediacy, prehension in the mode of. A term from A.N. Whitehead's metaphysics: one of the two pure modes of perceptions, and the more complex. The other pure mode of perception is prehension in the mode of causal efficacy (q.v.); and the two pure modes combine to form a mixed mode of perception that Whitehead calls symbolic reference. Prehension in the mode of presentational immediacy sets upon the vague, emotional data furnished by prehension in the mode of causal immediacy and forms them into sharp qualities that are projected onto the contemporary region surrounding the prehending actual occasion. The result is something like an immediate awareness of a quality ("red, there").

primordial nature of God. A term from A.N. Whitehead's metaphysics: unlike the entities of the temporal world, which begin with physical prehensions (q.v.), God originates with the conceptual valuation of the real by means of eternal objects (q.v.); this conceptual valuation Whitehead terms the primordial nature of God (since it comes first in the order of occurrences that establishes His nature). While for actual entities, conceptual prehension follow physical prehension, for God this order is reversed, with physical prehension succeeding conceptual prehensions. The **consequent nature of God** is constituted by God's physical prehension of actual entities. But for both God and temporal entities alike, the process of concrescence (q.v.) is completed by phases of comparative feeling in which physical feelings and conceptual feelings are integrated to produce a **superjective nature** in which the actual entity's specific situation qualifies transcendent creativity.

process philosophy. The paradigmatic exponent of process philosophy was A.N. Whitehead, but William James, Charles Sanders Peirce, and Henri Bergson all anticipated its principal themes. Process philosophy lays stress on the continuous progress of nature as a creative adventure that results in novelty. Process philosophers hold that process is the fundamental ground of reality (and not substance as most other philosophers have). Because they wish to avoid any tendency to spatialize time, and because they hold the idea that any real entity undergoes change to be incoherent (inasmuch as change to any real entity would demand that it be both the same and not the same), process philosophers maintain that time is a continuum, but comes in discrete occasions of finite duration.

Projective Verse. The term "projective" comes from the Latin roots *pro* ("forward") and *jacto* ("I throw"). Olson adopted the term to indicate his belief in the possibility of creating verse that consists of sounds projected from the body. ("Speech-force" means "projective" or "projectile," Olson suggested.) By "projective verse" Olson meant verse that propels over to the reader the energy the poet felt, that prompted him or her to write the poem. But it must not have escaped Olson that "projective" also means "propelling forward," for "projective verse" evolves out of the force that propels the poet forward through the composition. Every word that a poet writes down exerts a push. This force is what the poet must attend to while writing, not what he or she wanted to say. Poets write poems by attending to the evolution of the poem that he or she is creating, by opening oneself to the anti-inertial push exerted by all the syllables and all the lines so far put down, and, even more, to the interrelations among these forces (i.e., to the entire field of the poem) and by heeding where the forces generated by those interrelations are leading (for, after all, like all elements of a charged poem, they are all vectors, and they have a direction).

Olson did not write "Projective Poetry" with initial capitals; however, as with the term "Open Form," I have chosen to use capitals when the term acts as the name of group (or better, a loose alliance of individual writers), and with small letters when the term is referring to a notion of poetry. Sometimes, of course, the choice between the two is not clear cut, and in these cases I have tried to follow my instincts about which is the dominant tenor of the term in the particular instance.

proprioception. Strictly, sensations transmitted by receptors located in subcutaneous tissues (muscles, tendons, and joints) that respond to the stimuli arising within the body. Poet Charles Olson expands the term somewhat to refer to all internal sensation (to denote "what happens within"); and I have used the term with Olson's enlarged intention.

push-pull relations (or **push-and-pull relations**). Relations between areas which, usually by reason of their colours, seem to proceed or recede in different degrees.

quality. The measure of stress on a syllable. English metres generally organize patterns of stress and so are known as **"qualitative metres."** Verse that is organized by qualitative metres is known as **qualitative verse.**

quantity. The measure of duration of a syllable's sound. The Classical verse metres organize durational or quantitative patterns (rather than stress patterns, as accentual verse does). Verse that is organized by **quantitative metres** is known as **quantitative verse.**

radical empiricism. A term coined by Leonard B. Meyer, and used in his book *Music, the Arts, and Ideas: Patterns and Predictions in Twentieth-Century Culture*. A notion about mind, expounded by Ralph Waldo Emerson, William Carlos Williams, Gertrude Stein, Charles Olson, John Cage, and Stan Brakhage, that stresses the benefits of attention to the individual, discrete, concrete entities that make up the furniture of the world, or, alternatively (here there is considerable difference among these thinkers, and even among different phases in one thinker's life), that make up the contents of the manifold of consciousness. Any preconceptions, or considerations of relationships, is usually thought to obscure the perception of the particular. As a doctrine in art theory, radical empiricism proposes that it is best to attend to the individual elements that make up a work of art, and to not engage in making predictions about where the work is leading or any other sort of activity that would distract one's attention from the direct perception of the individual element immediately given.

Real, the (spelled with a capital "R"). A term from Lacanian psychoanalytic theory: the Real is plenitude: it is that which is full, that which lacks nothing; thus it is a form of presence (q.v.).

relation, external. If an individual **I** has relation **R** to some other person, thing, or state of affairs, **S**, and if there is no property **I** such that, by reason of having that property, **I**'s relation to **S** is apodeictic, then **R** is an external relation. Less formally: one thing has an external relation to another if the relation is essential to, or affects the natures of, what it relates.

relation, extrinsic. A relation between a property that characterizes a work of art and a property that characterizes something outside the work of art.

relation, internal. If an individual **I** has a property **P** which is such that, by reason of possessing that property, **I** has an apodeictic relation **R** to some other person, thing, or state of affairs, **S**, then **R** is an internal relation of **I**. Less formally: one thing has an internal relation to another if the relation is essential to, or affects the natures of, what it relates. **The doctrine of internal relations** is the thesis that all relations are internal relations. The idea that artworks are characterized by organic unity is application of that doctrine to a restricted domain.

relation, intrinsic. A relation between two properties that are internal to an entity.

representamen. A term from the semiotic theory of Charles Sanders Peirce: in Peirce's theory "representamen" is a synonym for a sign, that is, for something which stands to somebody for something in some respect or capacity. A sign creates in the mind of the person it addresses an equivalent, or perhaps more developed, sign (which Peirce terms the sign's interpretant). The sign stands for something, and that something Peirce calls the **object**; it stands for the object in some respect or capacity, and that respect of capacity Peirce calls the sign's **ground**.

shifter. A deictic sign (q.v.).

simple location, fallacy of. A term from A.N. Whitehead's metaphysics: refers to the belief, which he considered fallacious, that reality is composed of particles of matter, each of which exists, isolated from all others, at a specific location in space and time.

Spirit (*Geist*). As a term from Hegel's philosophy: Hegel uses the term "Spirit," construed in a general sense, to denote the realm of the truly ideal, that is, the human mind and its products (in contrast to Nature) and, construed in a more specific sense, to denote what he calls "the subjective spirit" (i.e., the psychological subject—that is, the cognitive and, most importantly, the moral subject) which is the agent of all psychological life, including thinking and willing (the inclusion of the latter explains why Hegel deems that the subjective spirit is also the moral subject). Spirit, in Hegel's philosophy, is anything that is *für sich* (for itself), and not merely *an sich* (in itself); that is, for something to be Spirit it must possess the capacity of self-reflection.

sprung rhythm. A term coined by Gerald Manley Hopkins, it refers to the rhythm effect created by lines that are measured by the number of stresses, each corresponding to a stress that a syllable would have in ordinary speech.

Symbolic, the (spelled with a capital "S"). A term from Lacanian psychoanalytic theory: refers to the final stage of the maturational process. The Symbolic phase is initiated by the individual's acquisition of language. The structure of language then becomes a model for all structures—including social and sexual relations. Lacan analogizes the structure of this mode of thinking to the structure of language: language's arbitrary relation with the world frees the terms of language so that they can be arranged in new ways (possibly ways that deny the order of the Real; similarly, after the individual has entered into the realm of the Symbolic, he or she is freed from the immediacy of the Real (of the tyranny of presence, for the acquisition of language makes it possible to imagine what is not the case) and the "presencing" implicit in the perceptualism of the Imaginary phase. The acquisition of language makes it possible to conceive abstract and shifting relations. Language brings the conception of such relations with it. Hence language, by its very character, affects our thinking; so, in a sense, we do speak language, but it speaks us. *See also the entries for* **the Imaginary;** *l'objet petit 'a';* **the Real.**

Symbolism. A European art movement of the years between the mid-1890s and the end of World War I. Against the idea that artworks should capture the appearance of concrete things, they proposed that immediate, personal, fleeting, and incommunicable experience is the proper subject of art. The English critic Arthur Symons (in *The Symbolist Movement in Literature*) described Symbolism as the evocation of an unseen world, beyond the world known through ordinary perception; the Symbolists, he explained, saw the world as an "infinitely gentle/ Infinitely suffering thing." There are affinities between the ideas of the Symbolists and Henri Bergson's philosophy.

synaesthesia. The simultaneous response of two or more of the senses to the stimulation of one, so that one hears (as well as sees) sights, tastes (as well as smells) odours, etc.

syntagmatic relations. A term from Ferdinand de Saussure's semiology. Syntagmatic relations concern the relation between successive semiotic units (at whatever level of analysis)—with their "horizontal" as opposed to "vertical" (see **paradigmatic relations**) relations. Thus, while paradigmatic relations involve choosing one semiotic element from a stack that represents the set of all possible semiotic elements that could occupy a given slot in a semiotic structure, syntagmatic relations concern the combining of semiotic units into a sequential structure.

syuzhet. The actions and events recounted in a story, ordered in the sequence in which the story recounts them, along with the agents who perform those actions and take part in those events, and their physical context (the time and location).

thing-in-itself. *See* **noumenon.**

tmesis (from Greek, "a cutting"). The insertion of a word or a phrase within a phrase or a sentence.

topos (from Greek, literally "a place or region"). The term originally referred to a conventionalized expression or passage in a text (a place one returns to).

This sense was extended to include the standard metaphors and standard "topics" (e.g., a wood as Arcadia). They indicate established schemes of thought. A poem that is composed almost entirely of *topoi* is Milton's *Lycidas*, his lament for his friend Edward King. Charles Olson used the term with a different (idiolectic) meaning; on this see his letter to Elaine Feinstein.

transcendental subject. Our inner, unchanging sense of the unity of our consciousness, of the aspect of one's consciousness that perdures through change. Immanuel Kant argued that the transcendental unity of apperception (synonym of transcendental subject) is the unity of the subject that makes possible their ordered or meaningful organization of our perceptions.

Transcendentalism, New England. A literary movement with religio-philosophical undergirdings that flourished in New England from 1835 to 1860. The intellectual leader of the movement was Ralph Waldo Emerson, and the group included Henry David Thoreau, Bronson Alcott, and Theodore Parker. Its roots lay in Romanticism (q.v.). Like the Romantics, the Transcendentalists (who did not give themselves that name, but adopted it from their enemies) believed, ironically, that the Divine is immanent in nature.

transitional object; transitional phenomenon. Terms from D.W. Winnicott's psychoanalytic theory: the first transitional object, and the truest, is the first "not-me" object with which the child identifies and bonds, something inanimate but greatly treasured, usually a blanket, a teddy bear, or some soft toy.

Transitional objects are not recognized as being fully independent objects; and as self-objects, they mediate between "the me" and "the not-me." Yet they have a paradoxical status, for their value as self-objects depends upon their not being imaginary objects or objects that belong exclusively to the child's consciousness or self. Their existence does not depend on the child's actions, and so their existence itself is not subject to the vicissitudes of the child's attention and transitory emotional states. On the other hand, they become transitional objects by acts the child performs. Transitional objects and the thinking characteristic of the transitional area allow the child to create what he/she discovers and to discover in the world what he/she creates.

vates. A poet who possesses prophetic powers. Hence **vatic** is used of anyone who possesses the powers of a prophet or a seer.

vers libre (French for "free verse"). Verse with no regular metre or line length, that depends instead on the rhythms of natural speech and on contrapuntal relations between accented and unaccented syllables.

vitalism. The doctrine states that the activities of any living organism are due to a vital principle (a form of energy regarded as different from mechanical, chemical, electrical, or molecular energy, and usually conceived of as non-physical, invisible, intangible, but exemplified in the activities of living beings).

Vorticism. A movement in the fine arts in the 1910s, led by Wyndham Lewis and Ezra Pound. The term "vortex" itself was contributed by Pound, and intended, in part, the modern spirit in the arts. Like Futurism, Vorticism was committed to assaulting the bourgeois spirit in the arts; it celebrated aggression, dynamism, and innovation. The vortex is "a point of maximum energy," Pound stated. "An image is not an idea," Pound wrote (*Gaudier-Brzeska: A Memoir*, p. 92), "It is a radiant node or cluster; it is what I can, and must perforce, call a VORTEX, from which, and through which, and into which ideas are constantly rushing. In decency one can only call it a VORTEX. And from this necessity came the name 'vorticism.'" As the point of maximum energy, it is a still point around which activity whirls. Brakhage's *Dog Star Man* has many affinities with Vorticism; there the point of stillness is the pivot (to use Pound's related term) of the creative imagination, which spins images out of itself.

wobbly image, the. Before the child acquires language, his or her percepts are in constant flux, and mutate continuously—one distinguished psychoanalyst, J.M. Davie, coined the term "wobbly image" to suggest the nature of such percepts. The mental representation is affected by transitory conditions of the subject. The wobbly image is probably a partially resolved synthesis of assorted bits of the alpha element (q.v.).

Notes

1 George Steiner, *A Reader* (New York: Oxford University Press, 1984), pp. 312-14. Originally published in George Steiner, *On Difficulty* (New York: Oxford University Press, 1978).

2 Wittgenstein's discussion of the topic, which includes his famous commentary on the ambiguous figure that we can see either as a duck or as a rabbit, occurs in the *Philosophical Investigations*, translated by G.E.M. Anscombe (Oxford: Oxford University Press, 1953), Part II, Section XI. The applicability of Wittgenstein's idea of "seeing-as" to visual aesthetics is shown in Roger Scruton's *Art and Imagination: A Study in the Philosophy of Mind* (London: Routledge & Kegan Paul, 1974), pp. 107-33.

3 Charles Olson, *The Special View of History*, edited by Ann Charters (Berkeley: Oyez, 1970), p. 48.

4 Friedrich Nietzsche, *Thus Spoke Zarathustra*, Par. A: First Part, Section 4 ("On the Despisers of the Body"), in *The Portable Nietzsche*, translated and edited by Walter Kaufmann (New York: Viking Portable Library, 1982), p. 146.

5 Michel Foucault, "Nietzsche, Genealogy, History," in D.F. Bouchard, ed., *Michel Foucault: Language, Counter-Memory, Practice: Selected Essays and Interviews* (New York: Cornell University Press, 1977), p. 148.

6 Isadora Duncan, *My Life* (New York: Horace Liveright, 1927), p. 75.

7 Ibid., p. 175.

8 A detail from the portrait, by Ludwig Sigismund Ruhl, in the Universitätsbibliotek, Frankfurt am Main, appears on R.J. Hollingdale's selection and translation of passages from *Parerga and Paralipomena*, issued by Penguin Classics under the title *Essays and Aphorisms* (1970). A detail of the portrait, by J. Schäfer, also at the Universitätsbibliotek, dating from thirty or so years later—and a much more familiar image of the philosopher, looking crabbed, miserable, frustrated, and generally wizened in soul—appears, among other places, on the cover of the Dover edition of E.F.J. Payne's translation of *The World as Will and Representation*. Schopenhauer had spent many of the years between the two portraits inveighing against the standing that Fichte and Hegel's philosophy enjoyed in the academy, and the commonplace acceptance that they (and especially Hegel) were the *summi philosophi*. The difference between the portraits suggests a hardening of the soul, and should be a lesson to those who concern themselves with public fame, or even with academic status.

9 Though Schopenhauer, interestingly, did not deem Kant's *Critique of Judgement* to be as fine an achievement as either of the other Critiques, and did not pursue the parallels, that really are very obvious, between Kant's theory of aesthetic experience and his own.

10 Arthur Schopenhauer, *The World as Will and Representation*, translated from the German by E.F.J. Payne, 2 vols. (New York: Dover Publications, 1966), Vol. 2, Supplements to the Second Book, chap. 22: "Objective View of the Intellect," p. 273.

11 Ibid., Vol. 1, Second Book, "The World as Will," First Aspect, Section 21, pp. 109-10.

12 Ibid., Section 18, pp. 99-100 (emphasis in original).

13 This assertion, to be sure, is not really paradoxical. To overcome the prima facie appearance of contradiction is to recognize that the physiological processes are as ideal as all else. All that the claim really does, in the end, is to assimilate the world to the self, and to propose a version of monism.

14 Schopenhauer, *The World as Will and Representation*, Vol. 2, Supplements to the Second Book, chap. 22, p. 273.

15 Ibid., chap. 20, p. 259.

16 Ibid., Vol. 1, Third Book, Section 31, p. 175 (emphasis in original). Schopenhauer devotes the whole of the thirty-first section to establishing that the Idea is the most adequate objectivity of the Will, and the arguments are convoluted and extremely troubled. Schopenhauer's usual stylistic grace gives way here, and that it does is telling.

17 Ibid., Section 52, p. 260.

18 Ibid., p. 262.

19 Ibid., p. 264.

20 Ibid., Vol. 1, Second Book, Section 18, p. 102.

21 Friedrich Nietzsche, "Rückblick auf meine zwei Leipziger Jahre" (written in the autumn of 1867), quoted in Ronald Hayman, *Nietzsche: A Critical Life* (Harmondsworth, Middlesex: Penguin Books, 1980), p. 172.

22 Friedrich Nietzsche, "On Truth and Lie in an Extra-Moral Sense," in *The Portable Nietzsche*, edited and translated by W. Kaufmann (New York: Viking, 1982), pp. 46-47. I invite readers to consider how similar Nietzsche's views about language and truth are to T.E. Hulme's ideas about counter language (discussed in Chapter 1). Also, I point out the emphasis that Nietzsche lays on the loss of language's capacity to evoke a sensuous response—an emphasis that has been somewhat obscured by use that has been made of this passage in recent years.

23 Friedrich Nietzsche, *The Will to Power*, translated by Walter Kaufmann and R.J. Hollingdale and edited by Walter Kaufmann (New York: Vintage Books, 1967), p. 283.

24 G.W.F. Hegel, *Aesthetics: Lectures on Fine Art*, translated by T.M. Knox (Oxford: Oxford University Press, 1975), Vol. 1, pp. 80-81.

25 Ibid., pp. 518-19.

26 Mikel Dufrenne, "Author's Preface," in *In the Presence of the Sensuous: Essays in Aesthetics*, edited by Mark S. Roberts and Dennis Gallagher (Atlantic Heights, NJ: Humanities Press International, 1987), p. x.

27 Discourse (*discours*) in the sense that Foucault used in *Les Mots et les choses* (Paris: Gallimard, 1966), i.e., simply language reduced to transparent representation; starting with *The Order of Things: An Archaeology of the Human Sciences* (New York: Vintage Books, 1973)—in the project which he characterizes as "the pure description of discursive events"—Foucault uses *discours* in a very different sense, to refer to everything that signs do, over and above representing things.

28 Saussure's semiology is notable for its exclusion of the referential object, a character of the system that seems to support Foucault's thesis.

29 Francis Bacon, *Of the Advancement of Learning* (London: J.M. Dent & Sons, 1930), p. 24.

30 Ezra Pound, "A Retrospect," in *Literary Essays of Ezra Pound*, edited with an Introduction by T.S. Eliot (London: Faber and Faber, 1960), p. 9.

31 Northrop Frye, *Anatomy of Criticism: Four Essays* (Princeton, NJ: Princeton University Press, 1957), p. 251.

32 Gerard Manley Hopkins, from the Preface to the original *Poems: 1876-1889*, in Gerard Manley Hopkins, *The Poems of Gerard Manley Hopkins* (London: Oxford University Press, 1967), p. 46.

33 René Wellek and Austin Warren, *Theory of Literature* (New York: Harcourt, Brace & World, 1956), p. 170.

34 But this should alert us that the convention of favouring fluent writing is more historically than materially based and, therefore, considerably less compelling.

35 William Wordsworth, "Poems of the Imagination," in *Poetical Works*, new ed. revised by Ernest de Selincourt (London: Oxford University Press, 1967), pp. 164-65.

36 Anon., "Edward," in Alexander M. Witherspoon, ed., *The College Survey of English Literature* (New York: Harcourt, Brace, 1951), p. 138.

37 Ibid., p. 139.

38 Thomas Nashe, "Litany in Time of Plague," in Alexander M. Witherspoon, ed., *The College Survey of English Literature* (New York: Harcourt, Brace, 1951), p. 286.

39 William Wordsworth, "Sonnet XXVII," in *Poetical Works*, new ed. revised by Ernest de Selincourt (London: Oxford University Press, 1967), p. 204.

40 William Wordsworth, "Lines Composed a Few Miles Above Tintern Abbey," in ibid., pp. 163-64. I have introduced the emphasis to illustrate my point; it is not present in the original.

41 Emile Benveniste, "Man and Language: Relationships of Person in the Verb," *Problems in General Linguistics* (Coral Gables, FL: University of Miami Press, 1971), p. 199.

42 Ibid., pp. 199-200.

43 Jan Mukařovský, "Standard Language and Poetic Language," in Paul L. Garvin, ed., *A Prague School Reader on Esthetics, Literary Structure, and Style* (Washington, DC: Georgetown University Press, 1964), p. 19

44 Pound, "A Retrospect," p. 9.

45 Ezra Pound, *I Gather the Limbs of Osiris*, in *Selected Prose, 1909-1965*, edited by William Cookson (London: Faber and Faber, 1973), p. 41.

46 Ezra Pound, Canto XIII, in *The Cantos of Ezra Pound* (New York: New Directions, 1972), p. 58.

47 What other motivation could he possibly have had for wishing to resurrect polytheism?

48 The idea that language is basically nominal also subtends the extravagant notion that most sentences have a subject-predicate form.

49 Hence speech's complicity in founding idealism.

50 It is surely not without relevance that nearly all the artists who have propounded the idea of immediate seeing are empiricists. Few any longer believe in the proto-empiricistic assertions about language that I alluded to when discussing Dryden's views on language. But people commonly do believe them, if not in word, then at least in deed, about films (for people do continue to go to movies to be frightened, horrified, or aroused by what the film conveys).

51 Stan Brakhage, *Metaphors on Vision*, edited and with an Introduction by P. Adams Sitney (New York: *Film Culture*, 1963), not paginated. The quotation appears on p. 2 of the main body of text.

52 Ezra Pound, *The Spirit of Romance* (New York: New Directions, 1968), pp. 160-61.

53 *Blast: Review of the Great English Vortex*, Nos. 1-2 (1914-15). Originally published London: John Lane, The Bodley Head, June 1914; reprinted New York: Kraus Reprint Corp., 1967, p. 32.

54 Wyndham Lewis, "The Skeleton in the Cupboard Speaks," in *Wyndham Lewis the Artist: From 'Blast' to Burlington House* (London: Laidlaw and Laidlaw, 1939), p. 78.

55 From *Blast* 1 (June 1914): 39; quoted in Jane Farrington, with contributions by John Rothenstein, Richard Cork, and Omar S. Pound, "What Was Vorticism?" in *Wyndham Lewis* (London: Lund Humphries, 1980), p. 24, whence I have drawn it.

56 Ibid., p. 24.

57 Wyndham Lewis, *Note for the Catalogue of the Vorticist Exhibition, the only exhibition to be held by the Blast group, which opened at the Doré Galleries, New Bond Street, on 10 June 1915*; reprinted in Wyndham Lewis, *Wyndham Lewis on Art: Collected Writings 1913-1956*, with introductions and notes by Walter Michel and C.J. Fox (New York: Funk & Wagnalls, 1969), p. 96.

One basis for the criticism of the cinematographic method is that it is too strictly representational; despite his announced dislike of Bergson's thought, Lewis's claims about the cinematographic method were probably influenced by Henri Bergson's condemnation (in *Creative Evolution*, translated by Arthur Mitchell with a Foreword by Irwin Edman [New York: The Modern Library, Random House, 1944], e.g., pp. 332-43 and especially pp. 332-33) of the mind's proclivity to employ a cinematographic method. (The French edition of *Creative Evolution* was originally published in 1907 and experienced enormous and immediate popularity.)

58 Ezra Pound, "Vorticism," *Blast* 1 (June 1914): 469. "Vorticism" is included in Ezra Pound's *Gaudier-Brzeska: A Memoir* (New York: New Directions, 1970); the quotation appears on p. 92.

59 Ezra Pound, *Literary Essays of Ezra Pound*, edited with an Introduction by T.S. Eliot (London: Faber and Faber, 1960), p. 3.

60 Ibid., p. 4.

61 Brakhage's film *Western History* (1971) is partly a gloss on his reservations about conceiving history as an epic.

62 Wyndham Lewis, "Long Live the Vortex!" *Blast* 1 (June 1914): 7. "Long Live the Vortex!" is reprinted in Wyndham Lewis, *Wyndham Lewis on Art: Collected Writings 1913-1956*, with introductions and notes by Walter Michel and C.J. Fox (New York: Funk & Wagnalls, 1969), p. 25. I have relied on Michel and Fox's text.

63 Pound did not actually use this slogan during his Vorticist period; later he used it in many different ways, sometimes (especially in the *Cantos*) to promote the Confucian ethic of a continual personal and cultural renewal, and sometimes to advocate the revitalization of tradition, by dispensing with what had become outmoded and inventing forms appropriate to the time.

64 This is just one of a number of meanings of Pound's dictum, considering it as offering simply aesthetic advice (while in fact it also provides moral instruction concerning the attitude one should adopt towards daily living).

65 Ezra Pound, "Affirmations ... 1. Arnold Dolmetsch," *New Age*, January 14, 1915, p. 246, and Ezra Pound, "Vortex," *Blast* 2 (July 1915): 154. These are quoted in Michael H. Levenson, *A Genealogy of Modernism: A Study of English Literary Doctrine 1908-1922* (Cambridge: Cambridge University Press, 1984), p. 126.

66 Bergson distinguishes between the vital and geometric orders, and argues for the priority of the former in *Creative Evolution*, pp. 257-58.

67 Pound, *Gaudier-Brzeska: A Memoir*, pp. 89-90.

68 Ezra Pound, "Fratres Minores," poems from *Blast*, in *Collected Shorter Poems by Ezra Pound* (London: Faber and Faber, 1968), p. 168.

69 Huysmans's tribute to Mallarmé (1842-98) in *A rebours*—a work published eight years after Mallarmé's *L'après-midi d'un faune*—first brought attention to the poet's writing.

70 These quotations appear in R.C. Grogin, *The Bergsonian Controversy in France: 1900-1914* (Calgary: The University of Calgary Press, 1988), p. 43. Grogin's topic is broader than his title makes it out to be: the book is really a history of the reception of Bergson's philosophy. It is a very fine piece a work—a model of what intellectual history should be.

71 We shall see that the poet Michael McClure maintains similar beliefs, and that they serve as a basis for his practice. He explains them partly through concepts derived from biology, and partly through concepts derived from the philosopher Alfred North Whitehead.

72 Henri Bergson, "The Image and Reality," in *Matter and Memory*, translated by Nancy Margaret Paul and W. Scott Palmer (London: George Allen & Unwin, 1950), pp. 43-44.

73 Leszek Kolakowski, *Bergson* (Oxford: Oxford University Press, 1985), p. 2.

74 Henri Bergson, *An Introduction to Metaphysics*, translated by T.E. Hulme with an Introduction by T. Goudge, 2nd ed. (Indianapolis, IN: Library of Liberal Arts, Bobbs-Merrill, 1955), pp. 49-56 (emphasis in original).

75 Of course, Hulme's break with Bergson was not clean; Bergson's thought continued to exert some influence on Hulme until 1912.

76 T.E. Hulme, *Further Speculations*, edited by Sam Hynes (Lincoln: University of Nebraska Press, 1962), p. 53.

77 Ibid., p. 30.

78 Ibid., pp. 29-30.

79 The resemblance of this point to one of Kant's is striking. Like Bergson's, Kant's philosophy was a response to the mechanistic materialism which Newtonian science had stimulated. Like Bergson, Kant was willing to concede that the sciences are founded in mechanistic assumptions (every action has a cause; action is the result of force acting on a body; every body preserves its mass wherever it is located in space; et al.) and that this foundation determines its limitations. Kant, however, had greater admiration for science than did Bergson. While Kant wanted to defend the foundations of science from the implications of David Hume's philosophy, Bergson laid such heavy stress on the distortions of reason and the futility of attempts to acquire a comprehensive rational understanding of the world that his philosophy at times reads almost as a celebration of irrationalism. Kant was a devout Lutheran Pietist, and so, like Bergson, was concerned with issues of religion, aesthetics, and morality; the key purpose of Kant's philosophy is to show that Newtonian mechanism, which had been so spectacularly successful at predicating results in the material world, does not constrain (or, more accurately, that the categories which guarantee that Newtonian principles apply to the world we know through the senses do not constrain) moral action or determine aesthetic efficacy.

80 Thus Bergson turned Kant's methods against Kant's conclusions. Kant believed that he had shown that the categories which organize the world as we know it derive from the mind and are essential forms of understanding, for thus he attempted to justify our organizing the experienced world according to the foundational categories of Newtonian science. Kant also assessed the limits of the domain to which the categories applied. He did so by showing that people sometimes use the categories inappropriately, by extending them beyond what is experienced.

Bergson proposed to the contrary that the foundational categories of Newtonian science are inappropriately used exactly when they are applied to experience.

81 Bergson, *Creative Evolution*, p. 210.

82 Bergson explains the relation of the life force to matter by drawing a comparison to a water fountain: the water shooting forth is the life force, the water falling back is matter. This comparison implies that Bergson's distinction between matter and life force is not a strict ontological dualism.

83 Henri Bergson, *The Creative Mind: An Introduction to Metaphysics*, translated by Mabelle L. Andison (New York: Philosophical Library, 1946), pp. 17-18.

84 There is a reason why Bergson's turns of phrase seem so Gnostic: one of the sources of Gnostic ideas was Alexandrian neo-Platonism, and Bergson was an avid reader of Plotinus (and became increasingly more enthusiastic about the mystical philosopher in his later years). Thus Bergson maintained that there are people who have intimate knowledge of *élan vital*, to whom it is translated in its entirety. They make contact with a creative energy that "is of God, if it is not God Himself." Bergson asserted that this contact is achieved not through intellect, but by intuition. Bergson also offered the Gnostic-like idea that the principal obstacle to the spread of mystical experience is that too many people have too great an involvement with matter.

85 Bergson, *Creative Evolution*, p. 27.

86 Bergson, *The Creative Mind*, p. 21.

87 In Chapter 2, we will see that philosopher Alfred North Whitehead refers to the process that generates true novelty as creativity in order to recognize its resemblance between the human and the metaphysical processes.

88 Peirce characterized as tychastic any theory, such as Darwin's, that proposes that evolution proceeds by producing many random (unmotivated) changes, and that those

changes that adapt the organism to its environment are "naturally selected," while those that do not are eliminated.

89 Charles Sanders Peirce, "Evolutionary Love," in *Philosophical Writings of Peirce*, selected and edited with an Introduction by Justus Buchler (New York: Dover Publications, 1955), p. 365.

90 We shall see that the same example has played an important part both in the development of modern poetics and in Stan Brakhage's formulation of his ideas on art and filmmaking.

91 Ezra Pound makes a very similar point when he argues that the logical end of Impressionist art (and Pound certain had not much admiration for "depicting light on haystacks") is the cinematographic method (see Pound, *Gaudier-Brzeska: A Memoir*, p. 89).

92 This claim implies that the world we perceive contains elements of the past; and the proposition that present percepts contain elements from the past entails the denial that reality forms a continuum—the present is not, not even for the pictorial form of perception, a point of infinitessimal magnitude.

93 Charles Sanders Peirce, "Synechism, Fallibilism, and Evolution," in *Philosophical Writings of Peirce*, selected and edited with an Introduction by Justus Buchler (New York: Dover Publications, 1955), p. 356.

94 William James supplied the classic formulation of the principle *"The true is the name of whatever proves itself to be good in the way of belief"* (William James, *Pragmatism* [(Cambridge, MA: Harvard University Press, 1975], p. 42. Italics appear in the source).

95 The resemblance these claims bear to Bergson's theory of creative evolution, and particularly to its notions concerning the preservation of effective functioning, should be noted.

96 Bergson, *The Creative Mind*, p. 79.

97 Bergson, *An Introduction to Metaphysics*, p. 25.

98 Bergson used this as the basis of an argument that mind is likely independent of matter.

99 Ezra Pound, "Treatise on Metre," in *ABC of Reading* (London: Faber and Faber, 1961), p. 199.

100 One should take the word "describes" here in the sense it has in geometry, when we speak, for example, of a moving point describing a line. Such a conception of the significance of the verb "to describe" underlies some of Charles Olson's and Robert Duncan's remarks on Open Form poetics, as well as some of Stan Brakhage's remarks on how an artwork's form evolves.

101 Stan Brakhage, "To Michael McClure," in *Brakhage Scrapbook: Collected Writings 1964-1980*, edited by Robert A. Haller (New Paltz, NY: Documentext, 1982), p. 41.

102 Henri Bergson, "The Multiplicity of Conscious States, The Idea of Duration: Two Aspects of the Self," in *Time and Free Will: An Essay on the Immediate Data of Consciousness*, translated by F.L. Pogson (New York: Harper & Row, 1960), p. 129.

103 Pound found the comment in Lawrence Binyon's *The Flight of the Dragon*, and quoted it approvingly in *Blast* 2 (July 1915); the quotation reappears in "Chronicles from Blast," in Ezra Pound, *Pavannes and Divagations* (New York: New Directions, 1958), p. 149.

104 Brakhage's frequently expressed scepticism about language also has its roots in the belief that reality is flux and in his convictions about direct experience.

105 Aestheticians commonly get themselves off the horns of this dilemma by claiming that the formal intricacy of a strong work derives from a basic human drive, the urge for form. The argument is circular: in fact, its circularity resembles that of Molière's famous attribution (in *Le malade imaginaire*) of a potion's sleep-inducing powers to the "dormative" potential inherent in it.

106 Hollis Frampton, "A Pentagram for Conjuring the Narrative," *Circles of Confusion—Film, Photography, Video: Texts 1968-1980* (Rochester, NY: Visual Studies Workshop Press, 1983), p. 62.

107 Hugh Kenner, "Knot and Vortex," in *The Pound Era* (Berkeley: University of California Press, 1971), pp. 146-47.

108 Ibid., p. 147.

109 William Carlos Williams, "Della Primavera Transportata Al Morale," in *The Collected Poems of William Carlos Williams*, Vol. 1: *1909-1939*, edited by A. Walton Litz and Christopher MacGowan (London: Paladin Grafton Books, 1991), p. 336.

110 Sanford Schwartz, *The Matrix of Modernism: Pound, Eliot, and Early Twentieth-Century Thought* (Princeton: Princeton University Press, 1985).

111 Hulme, *Further Speculations*, p. 71. Hulme's comment on "perfect form" illustrates how Hulme took Bergson's idea that the celebration of perfect, and therefore changeless, form reflects the Platonic devaluation of the world of flux and change and applied this idea to a critique of a prevalent idea about artistic form. It also reflects general beliefs that Hulme held regarding the mischief that religion causes humans by imposing upon them the ideal of perfection; this is a central tenet of his neo-Kantian "Critique of Satisfaction."

112 Henri Bergson, "Form and Becoming," in *Creative Evolution*, translated by Arthur Mitchell with a Foreword by Irwin Edman (New York: The Modern Library, Random House, 1944), p. 328 (emphasis in original).

113 Hulme, *Further Speculations*, pp. 71, 74.

114 Ibid., p. 72.

115 Ibid., pp. 71-72.

116 With what great irony, then, do we of the last years of the century (and millennium) read Hulme's early-twentieth-century attacks on Romanticism? For the keystone of Romantic aesthetics, the concept of organic unity, was a concept framed to explain that there are vital integrities whose unity is not of the sort that can be appraised by objective measure and proportion—a form of unity whose relation to the life force that permeates all of nature, including its manifestation within human being as feeling and imagination, is more important than anything with which the canons that are epitomized by the golden ratio can deal.

117 We should exercise care in the use of words such as "subjective" and "personal," however. These terms are ambiguous: when we say that people's views are personal or subjective, we sometimes mean that they are clouded by self-interest and ambition. Using the term this way, we imply that as people overcome ambition, their viewpoints become more impersonal. When we use the terms "personal" and "subjective" in this way, artistic perception is quite impersonal, for it depends upon sweeping aside our usual way of relating to the world—a form of relatedness based in calculations of utility—and on seeing things freshly.

At other times, however, we use the terms quite differently. Sometimes we ascribe these terms to vision, speaking of "highly personal vision" or "highly subjective awareness." When we use the terms in this way, we use them in a sense somewhat akin to that of "idiosyncratic"—we mean that the person's awareness of the world displays marks of his or her own personality.

Sometimes we even use the terms to ascribe to a person's consciousness a degree of self-awareness—to say that a person is sufficiently authentic to have overcome conventionalized ways of understanding the world and to be able to conceive it in ways that are true to him- or herself. When the terms are used in this manner also, artistic perception can be said to be highly personal.

The words "subjective" and "objective" or "personal" and "impersonal" are used differently in the different cases. Confusions caused by the different meanings they have when they are used differently have caused no end of mischief in discussions of art. Debates about whether art is personal or impersonal usually proceed by alternating between the different meanings of the terms, and so they go absolutely nowhere.

These confusions hamper our efforts to gain understanding of some the most radical innovations in recent art. One of the key concepts of the strain of modernist art theory that we have been examining—and a concept of vital importance to Brakhage—is the concept of direct or immediate perception. The notion was made central to artistic theory and practice by Ford Madox Ford. Ford based his approach to writing, which he confusingly called Impressionism, on the information that is contained in the actual moment of seeing. Ford condemned Tennyson's verse for its use of comparison: commenting on Tennyson's description of bats that "haunt the dusk with ermine capes/ And wooly breasts and beady eyes," Ford protested that no one, exactly at the moment when he or she sees a bat, could note its ermine colour or the woolliness of its breast or the beadiness of its eyes. Tennyson did not confine himself to the impressions of the moment, Ford complained, but went beyond exactly what he saw at the time to reach out for the comparisons that the poem presents. Like William Carlos Williams, Ford thought that such comparisons give evidence of seeing one thing in terms of another, a habit that hampered direct seeing. The method that Ford proposed to combat such deleterious proclivities and to foster immediate perception was the cultivation of instantaneous perception, to catch impressions and ideas exactly as they come to us. This method, Ford proposed, eschews chronology and uses instead the sequence of impressions and ideas.

Ford insisted that his method was objective. He claimed that his Impressionism was a kind of realism—the rendering of the exact facts of life, without comment. Yet he also claimed his Impressionism was a form of egotism, and justified this assertion by pointing out that it offered the exact expression of a personality. Can these apparently contradictory claims be reconciled? The difficulty lies with our limited and confused understanding of the nature of the self. Fleeting impressions are supposed to be highly subjective phenomena. Yet any commitments to investigation of the immediate phenomena of consciousness are destructive to the sense of the self. David Hume noted this when he sought the impressions from which our idea of the self arises and came to the despairing conclusion that the only self he could know through experience was "a bundle or collection of different perceptions, which succeed each other with an inconceivable rapidity, and are in a perpetual flux and movement. . . . The mind is a kind of theatre, where several perceptions successively make their appearance; pass, repass, glide away, and mingle in an infinite variety of postures and situations" (David Hume, *A Treatise of Human Nature*, 2 vols. [London: J.M. Dent & Sons, 1964], Vol. 1, pp. 239-40. First included in Everyman's Library, 1911).

The self dissolves under the pressure of Hume's self-scrutiny, as it is revealed to be subjectivity that lacks a subject. This discovery is a paradigmatic moment in the modern mind's experience, repeated time and again over the next three centuries. Hume was the first philosopher to come to the conclusion that the conception of the self is simply an empty notion. Time and again moderns have confirmed that the coherent self dissolves as the attention is focused on the momentary sensations we ordinarily suppose it contains. Poets have seized on this as an advantage: this dissolving of the self can be felt as loss of the self or, conversely, as the self opening up to the world or, again, as the world rushing against and demolishing the self.

Selfless experience we describe as objective; so, the extreme of inward or subjective attention opens one to a new kind of objective experience. Under intense self-scrutiny, the self breaks down and makes way for the other.

How confused these terms "subjective" and "objective," "inner" and "outer," "self" and "other" are!

118 Many people have been troubled by Brakhage's claim to be a documentary filmmaker. One such person is the insightful critic/historian of the American avant-garde, P. Adams Sitney. Sitney was among the first critics to recognize Brakhage's colossal importance and has written some of the best analyses of Brakhage's films. However, as a student of Harold Bloom, he considers Brakhage to be a member of "the visionary company," and so he analyzes Brakhage's films for the evidence they give of celebrating the triumphs of the imagination; and, again like Bloom, he proposes that the greatest glory of the imagination is its capacity to reconcile consciousness and nature.

Brakhage believes that in stressing the imaginativeness of his work, and in tracing Brakhage's affiliation to a literary tradition that celebrates the image, Sitney underestimates the documental aspect of his work. He makes such a complaint in the following illuminating exchange with Hollis Frampton, a splendid piece of advocacy on behalf of considering his films as documents—"documents of consciousness" (following Gerry O'Grady), I call them:

> *Brakhage:* . . . [T]he minute P. Adams refused to search for his own hypnagogic vision, we had our next quarrel, which sprang up when I said I am the most thorough documentary film maker in the world because I document the act of seeing as well as everything that the light brings me. And he said nonsense, of course, because he had no fix on the extent to which I was *documenting.* He and many others are still trying to view me as an imaginative film maker, as an inventor of fantasies or metaphors.
>
> *Frampton:* You are saying, along with Confucius: "I have added nothing."
>
> *Brakhage:* Yes, I have added nothing. I've just been trying to see and make a place for my seeing in the world at large, that's all. And I've been permitting myself to be used by some forces that are totally mysterious to me, to accomplish something that satisfies me more than what I *thought* I was setting out to do.
>
> Art is the reaching out to this phenomenon or light or moving creatures around us—I don't even know what the hell to call it. I have no name for it. And the extent to which different societies at different times have decided that everyone shares this or that relationship with the world is all some social usage of art, long after the fact of its creating and usually after the fact of the artist's living. (From Hollis Frampton, "Stan and Jane Brakhage [and Hollis Frampton] Talking," *artforum* 11, no. 5 (January 1973), reprinted in Stan Brakhage, *Brakhage Scrapbook: Collected Writings 1964-1980*, edited by Robert A. Haller [New Paltz, NY: Documentext, 1982], pp. 188-89)

I believe that Brakhage is justified in his complaint; for, in my view, Sitney does underestimate the documental character of Brakhage's work. I believe that he has diminished exactly what Brakhage complains that he has—and that is Brakhage's insight into sensation. One of Brakhage's great strengths is his gift of understanding, on his nerve ends, the character of primordial awareness.

119 Stan Brakhage, "Hypnagogically Seeing America," in *Brakhage Scrapbook: Collected Writings 1964-1980*, edited by Robert A. Haller (New Paltz, NY: Documentext, 1982), pp. 104 and 105-106. Ellipses and capitalization follow the original. In the original, however, the title *23rd Psalm Branch* is placed between quotation marks; I have italicized the title and removed the quotation marks.

120 Gail Camhi, "Notes on Brakhage's *23rd Psalm Branch," Film Culture* 67-68-69 (1979): 97. Brakhage's comments on the film, made before and after a screening of the film at the Film-Maker's Cinematheque in New York City on April 22, 1967, appears in the same issue, pp. 109-29. (The comments on war as natural disaster appear on pp. 116ff.) Brakhage's remarks and answers also appear in *Brakhage Scrapbook*, pp. 110-12ff.

121 See ibid., p. 98. Actually, I do not believe that Brakhage's visual forms really represent visionary experience—rather they attempt to provoke equivalent visionary experience by embodying types of energy characteristic of the different modes of vision. (I am also stretching a point when I say that Camhi actually attributes representational status to Brakhage's visual forms, for she does not explicitly do so, though she often writes as though she believes that they possess that status.)

122 In *Sirius Remembered* (1959), Brakhage over and over again returned to the site in the woods where he had left the corpse of the dog, Sirius, and photographed the various stages in its decomposition. Brakhage used camera movement in the film in a desper-

ate attempt to reanimate the dog. Brakhage's use of painting-on-film here resembles his use of camera movement in *Sirius Remembered*.

123 Camhi, "Notes on Brakhage's *23rd Psalm Branch*," p. 98.

124 P. Adams Sitney, *Visionary Film: The American Avant-Garde* (New York: Oxford University Press, 1974), p. 248.

125 Stan Brakhage, "Stan Brakhage Speaks on *23rd Psalm Branch* at Film-Makers' Cinematheque, April 22, 1967," *Film Culture* 67-68-69 (1979): 125ff. On the top of p. 126, in response to a question about *23rd Psalm Branch*'s rhythm, Brakhage testifies that Messiaen was one of the film's primary sources of inspiration. He goes on to extol Messiaen's *Le livre d'orgue* and the synaesthetic interests that undergird Messiaen's theories on *chromoharmonie*. When Ken Jacobs and Jerome Hill, two extremely fine filmmakers who were in the audience that night, revealed that they, too, took a lively interest in Messiaen's music, Brakhage offers the endearing ejaculation (which reveals much about his feelings concerning the plight of creativity that *23rd Psalm Branch* conveys): "We must all get together and send him a cable and write him a letter or something . . . because I'm sure he's very lonely" (pp. 127-28).

126 Sitney, *Visionary Film*, p. 250.

127 Camhi, "Notes on Brakhage's *23rd Psalm Branch*," p. 252.

128 Sitney, *Visionary Film*, p. 251.

129 Ibid., p. 252.

130 The last set of images comes from the earliest representation of warriors in combat that Brakhage could find. He remarks that this representation has the character of an "ur-cartoon," for as one scans along the band of images, a narrative unfolds. That some of the oldest representations of humans show the engaged in combat highlights the persistence of violence.

131 What they are dragging is not clear—I originally described it as "a sac," and conjectured, on the basis of the women's manner, that it contained stolen goods. Actually, it was a Christmas tree (at the time, not allowed in the German Democratic Republic)—and that it was a Christmas tree is a fact that could be easily associated with longing to be home at Christmas, "being away," and also of the lamb.

132 Plato's ideas about artmaking offer legendary difficulties to an interpreter. It is well known that Plato offered a stinging rebuke to artists in *The Republic*. The criticism he offered there rests on the proposition that while all other sorts of *poesis* rely on the artisan's looking towards the form of the thing that he is making and producing an object that imitates that form, artmaking does not. Thus, to make a chair, carpenters look towards the form of the chair (which defines the good for objects that serve the purposes that chairs do) to guide them in their making. Artists, however, do not look towards the form of whatever they want to imitate (or represent—the Greeks would use a term derived from *mimesis* for both concepts), but towards some material object that is a less than perfect embodiment of the form. In producing a representation of a chair, artists do not look towards the form of the chair, but towards actually existing chairs, and model what they make on them. Since the form of the chair represents features that fit some object (or person, or attribute of an object or person) to serve some end, artists do not possess any real understanding of the purposes that chairs serve, or of the way that actual chairs are fitted to serve the purposes that chairs serve. Hence, their making is of a low-grade order.

This is the gist of the criticism of the arts that *The Republic* offers. Other passages in Plato's writings are not so negative towards the arts, and in these Plato sometimes speaks as though artists have actual acquaintance with the forms of the things their works represent. If anyone wishes in light of this to object to the recklessness of my saying that Plato stated that artists model their making on the form of the objects that they make, he or she could simply replace in this account the word "artist" with "maker" and "making" with "*poesis*" and note that (while Plato himself did not think of artmaking as like other kinds of making—he explicitly denied that writing a poem was a typical act of *poesis*—since it is not modeled on an understanding of the form of what the artist imitates/represents), it is a simple enough thing to imagine what Plato might have offered by way of an account of the art that did not involve such a distinction—that he saw artmaking as a form of *poesis* like any other.

Leo Strauss put forward an interpretation of *The Republic* which denies that Plato believed that the form of government *The Republic* offers actually was the ideal: Strauss has claimed that Plato's not believing that the form of government *The Republic* offers is the ideal could possibly account for the differences between *The Republic* and the *Laws*. But I do not accept the Straussian interpretation of *The Republic*.

133 Many modern artists have argued that creativity provides the most cogent demonstration of our freedom. Some have even argued that this freedom is a nearly godlike attribute, and to engage in that free creation is virtually a divine act.

For the sake of greater precision, I point out that the conception that artworks are products of free creation comes in voluntarist and non-voluntarist variants. The voluntarist model represents the artist's will as transcendent and suggests that momentary states of the artist's will determine the outcome of any creative process. Out of this conception there has issued a rhetoric concerning artists' battles with material reality and their triumph, by the grandeur of their talents and the strength of their skills, which are completely available to their will even when they are not aware what they will. This strength allows artists to impose on intractable, sometimes even hostile, matter the forms their wills crave.

The non-voluntarist model, which I discuss at length in the next chapter, holds a more organic conception of the creative process. It maintains that the creative process relies upon the artists complete and utter openness to their environment and upon their highly developed sensibility that responds to every slight change in the whole field of energies, which constitutes the environment in which they create their work. This position has given rise to a rhetoric of self-abnegation concerning the benefits that result from artists surrendering their will—the benefits that result when every bit of an artist's self is identified with the whole field of energies which, really, creates the work (a whole that, to be sure, is identical with the field of being itself) and is sensitive to every minute change in the field of being. On this view, the work of art becomes the whole cosmos and the artist's spirit is just one more part of the cosmos or, to state the same idea more radically, simply a site on which these cosmic energies interact.

134 Hulme, *Further Speculations*, pp. 71-72.

135 Brakhage, *Metaphors on Vision*, not paginated. This extract appears on the first page of the main body of text, in the introduction to the section entitled "The Camera Eye/My Eye."

136 Ibid. These remarks appear on the fifteenth page counting from the first page of the interview. In the source cited, all film titles appear in capital letters; I have used italics when giving titles.

137 Brakhage possesses a deep understanding of Symbolism, his reservations about the movement notwithstanding. He has taken an abiding interest in the composer Claude Debussy, in Olivier Messiaen, in many regards Debussy's principal heir and the composer who has worked out the most interesting extensions of Debussy's musical ideas, in the Symbolist writer Maurice Maeterlinck, as well as in Edmund Wilson's *Axel's Castle*, a great study of the influence of the Symbolist influence on modernist literature (in fact, the first time I engaged in table talk with Brakhage was when he invited Michael Snow, Joyce Wieland, my wife, and me for dessert after screening *The Text of Light*; the conversation concerned, *inter alia*, the Symbolist influences on Ejzenstejn's later films, and the possibility that he knew of Edmund Wilson's commentary on the Symbolist roots of modernist art—in fact, Brakhage reported, Annette Michelson had confirmed that the volume was in Ejzenstejn's library).

138 From this stems the interest in self-reference that dominated literary theory for so long. From this comes, too, the cardinal idea of Jacques Derrida's theories of language, that

everything is textual (*il n'y a pas d'hors texte*)—that words always refer to other words which refer to other words (his idea of deferral, one aspect of his coinage, "différance"), and never connect with the world. In fact, Derrida's philosophical adventure could be interpreted as a giant exfoliation of the implications of Symbolism, as well as a transformation by applying to it one of its own founding principles from which it had conveniently exempted itself. The Symbolists had treated musical language as though it provided insight into the dynamics of a higher realm. Derrida did not allow them this way out—he has held them to the principle that words are without reference to reality, that there is no Transcendental Signifier. What becomes of Symbolism when musical language is emptied of reference is what Derrida's philosophy of language expounds.

139   Elisabeth Kübler-Ross, *On Death and Dying* (New York: Macmillan, 1969). Kübler-Ross describes the luminous experiences reported by people who have been pronounced dead and brought back to life. I believe that these experiences are profoundly regressive—that the near-death experience dissolves the ego and allows early experiences to be reawakened. Further I believe that while the regressiveness of the experience pertains more to the form than the content of the experience, it does have the content of the earliest experiences of infancy, the experiences the infant has when he or she first emerges from the birth canal. There is mounting evidence that, at this moment, the child's eye follows light, but lacks the ability to focus that light. I suspect that what the child sees resembles the contents of *The Text of Light*.

140   Brakhage, *Metaphors on Vision*, not paginated. All the quotations in this section come from the first page of text, after Brakhage's interview with Sitney.

141   Brakhage continued to shoot through refractive media (through prisms and through glass that is not optically perfect) and through media that tint the light in later "imagnostic films" (e.g., the *Roman Numeral Series*, the *Arabic Numeral Series*, the *Egyptian Series*, and the *Babylon Series*).

142   Brakhage attributed the quotation to Duns Scotus Erigena—presumably a sort of portmanteau name, combining that of John Duns Scotus, a Scottish metaphysician (1266-1308) with that of John Scotus Erigena, an Irish-born theologian (ca. 810-77). Pound himself actually attributes the quotation to Erigena, an attribution Brakhage later adopted, though the attribution is questionable.

The phrase appears in part and, later, complete, in Canto LXXIV (in *The Cantos of Ezra Pound*, p. 429): "in the light of light is the *virtù*/ 'sunt lumina' said Erigena Scotus"; and: "'sunt lumina' said the Oirishman to King Carolus,/ 'OMNIA,/ all things that are are lights.'" It also appears in Canto LXXXVII (in *The Cantos of Ezra Pound*, p. 571): "Y Yin, Ocellus, Erigena:/ 'All things are lights.'/ Greek tags in Erigena's verses." (This last line has to do with Erigena's incorporating Greek phrases in his discourse, which Charles the Bald [King Carolus] found made them excellent, lively, and joyous.)

Carroll F. Terrell points out (*A Companion to* The Cantos *of Ezra Pound* [Berkeley and Los Angeles: University of California Press, 1993], p. 367) that the passage derives from Étienne Gilson's citation in *La philosophie du moyen âge*, 2nd ed. (Paris: Payot, 1944), p. 214. But he also offers this interesting remark about the citation in Canto LXXXVII: "Because Pound associates Erigena with light-philosophers, he attributes to him the phrase from Grosseteste, "All things are lights," as a way of suggesting his agreement with Grosseteste.

This attribution is highly plausible, as it represents the essence of Grosseteste's emanationist metaphysics. I note that Pound usually associates the phrase with an acknowledgment that Erigena incorporated citations in writings; and Pound was certainly familiar with the Chinese practice of endorsing a phrase by another by making it one's own. Furthermore, Pound also remarks (in the quotation above) on Erigena's use of "Greek tags" in his verses (Canto LXXXV and Canto LXXXVII); what was primarily remarkable about this was that Erigena was one of the very few in the ninth century who could read and write Greek.

I cannot locate the passage in Erigena; and there is nothing of what I know of Erigena's that says anything like what Pound attributes to him. I conjecture (but, I stress, on the basis of incomplete information) it was the fact that Erigena knew Greek, along with the fact that in *De divisione naturae* Erigena offers an emanationist cosmogony—though not a version that identifies light as The One, that brought Pound to surmise that Erigena belonged to the brotherhood of Eleusis (Canto XC), and, because the mysteries involved revelations about light, to suppose that Erigena shared Grosseteste's views. So he attributes to him a phrase from Grosseteste.

143 Brakhage, *Metaphors on Vision*, not paginated. This quotation appears on the first page of the main body of text, in the section entitled "The Camera Eye/My Eye."

144 Stan Brakhage, quoted in the New York *Film-Makers' Cooperative Catalogue No. 7* (New York: Film-Makers' Cooperative, 1989), p. 57.

145 Stan Brakhage, quoted in ibid., p. 49.

146 In other regards, the note aligns itself with a central tradition in twentieth-century art: Brakhage's comments on the role of memory in thought resemble comments Bergson offered; the idea that memory has a crucial role in thought and perception is one that influences Brakhage's filmmaking as well—we shall examine its role in shaping his film *Scenes from Under Childhood* (1967-70).

147 Pound included the essay "Psychology and Troubadours" in later editions of the *The Spirit of Romance* (New York: New Directions, 1968). The quotation appears in *The Spirit of Romance*, pp. 92-93.

148 The forms of some of Brakhage's later work, on the other hand, are determined by implicit cosmological principles which maintain that the Divine is not immanent in nature, but transcends all creation. *For Marilyn* (1992), for example, testifies to a more orthodox, Christian notion of the Divine, in particular to an idea that has been common in American Christianity since Jonathan Edward's time, that a marriage is a sacred space filled with love and the desire to leave a living legacy to God, and that in the matrimonial space, the marriage partners come into contact with the Divine and work out the pattern of their redemption. The clearest image that Brakhage has given us of a transcendent divine appears in *Visions in Meditation #3: Plato's Cave* (1990). *Plato's Cave* depicts three realms of being, the subterranean, the terrestrial, and the superterrestrial (perhaps, even, the celestial) realms. The first realm is the realm of darkness, of negativity, the last the realm of light, truth, and being. Thus, *Plato's Cave* embodies the central conception of the Great Chain of Being, that of a hierarchy of realms of existence. The tornado in *Plato's Cave* suggests God's transcendence, for the film depicts it as the finger of God who reaches out of the heavens to touch the earth and shake it with His power.

This contrast between Brakhage's earlier and later films establishes a parallel between his evolution of his oeuvre and that of poet Robert Creeley. Creeley's career opens intensely Romantic and intensely brooding with works—*For Love* (1962) and *The Gold Diggers* (1965)—that meditate on a wounded ego, on pain, and on suffering. Brakhage's career opens with works of the same ilk, such as *Anticipation of the Night* (1958) and *The Dead* (1960). In these early works, Brakhage and Creeley defined the lyric for their times. Creeley, abruptly, with *Pieces* (1969), and Brakhage, more gradually, assume a more positive outlook, but perhaps *The Text of Light* (1974) marks the change more emphatically than any other work in his oeuvre, which expresses itself through the use of repetition. Creeley, in *Presences* (1976) and *Hello* (1978), and Brakhage, in the *Visions in Meditation* series, extended their oeuvres to comprise works that, while no less intense than the earlier ones, tend to celebrate the energy of the phenomenal world rather than to lament it. Finally, the later work of Creeley shows an even more intense awareness of language, just as Brakhage's later work reveals an even more intense interest in the material of light.

149 Ann Mellor's *English Romantic Irony* (Cambridge, MA: Harvard University Press, 1980) makes much of this, and already has become the *locus classicus* for the propositions I offer here.

150 *Dog Star Man* makes extraordinary use of self-reflexive constructions. These constructions serve both to bring the process of the film's coming-into-being into evidence and to reveal the fictitiousness of its patternings of human experience.

151 T.E. Hulme, *Speculations: Essays on Humanism and the Philosophy of Art* (London: Routledge & Kegan Paul, 1987; originally published in 1924), p. 132. Hulme, writing shortly after Russell's famous paper, could well be using the term "definite description" in a technical manner. In Russell's use of the term, a definite description is not an elaborate portrait of a thing; rather, it is a term that allows us to pick a unique object (e.g., as the term the "Prime Minister of Canada" enables us to pick out a particular individual, and so serves almost like a name). Some uses of names, because they are indexical (see glossary), seem to hover between being presentational and being representational in just the same way that ostensive definitions do.

We need not, therefore, take "the definite descriptions" which Hulme claims constitute the content of poetry and art to be precise verbal representations—or as representations at all. Hulme associated himself with Bergson's vitalism (see glossary) and Pound's Vorticism, which both affirm that the reality of the mind is the surging and ebbing of energy. If one believes that the mind is an organization of energies, and that artworks, too, are organizations of energy, then it is easy to see how one can argue that an artwork can embody the energy that an object stirs in the mind when the mind apprehends it.

152 Frampton, "Stan and Jane Brakhage (and Hollis Frampton) Talking," pp. 169-70.

153 William Carlos Williams, *In the American Grain: Essays by William Carlos Williams*. Originally published in 1925, this work has been reprinted in paperback with an Introduction by Horace Gregory (New York: New Directions, 1956).

154 Stephen Fredman, *The Grounding of American Poetry: Charles Olson and the Emersonian Tradition* (Cambridge: Cambridge University Press, 1993).

155 Brakhage, *Metaphors on Vision*, not paginated. These excerpts appear on the first page of the main body of the text, in the section entitled "The Camera Eye/My Eye."

156 Henri Bergson, *Time and Free Will: An Essay on the Immediate Data of Consciousness*, translated by F.L. Pogson (New York: Harper & Row, 1960), pp. 131-32.

157 Ibid., p. 231. The expression "we are acted rather than act ourselves" has two importances. First, it describes the type of thinking that occurs when (in Hulme's phrase) the words of language are valued as just so many counters. In such a state, the mathematically and grammatically possible rearrangement of words, and the proximity of certain words within a linguistic space constitutes our thinking. Secondly, it alludes to a question that was at the heart of the Bergsonian philosophy, viz., whether humans are free. Bergson offers one conventional conception of human freedom which claims that when we think in a routine and habituated way, our thinking (behaviour) is determined by factors outside ourselves. (Bergson also believes the converse, that when our thinking is not determined by factors outside ourselves, but by internal factors, then our consciousness is free. He argues that this possibility can be, and often is, actualized.)

158 Proper nouns are an aberrant case, Brakhage seems to believe, for he occasionally suggests that proper nouns moderate the deleterious effects of language. A language that consisted only of proper nouns would not possess such negative features. Brakhage does not make explicit the line of reasoning that led him to conclude that proper nouns have a different status than other nouns do, but his interest in the poetics of Charles Olson (an interest we take up in the next chapter) suggests the following factors that may account for it. A proper noun has meaning only by ostensive definition and an ostensive definition can be understood as proposing a direct connection between words and things that does without the mediating role of sense (*Sinn*). We can imagine that sense, whatever it is, is mental, and so that it belongs to the inventory of items which prevent direct seeing and direct connection with the physical world. It is a form of interference by the "lyrical ego," which Olson referred to, that hampers the reconciliation of mind and nature. But ostensive definition leads out of

the closed realm of language—a realm whose closure is indicated by the way that words of language are defined in terms of other words—and into the world of things. Furthermore, the referent of proper noun is a specific existent, while the referent of an ordinary noun is a concept (or at least something with general characteristics, and not a specific existent).

159 Some psychoanalytic investigations suggest that before children acquire language, their percepts mutate continuously. J.M. Davie coined the term "wobbly perception" to characterize these percepts. Language, Davie insists, has a role in stabilizing perception.

160 Hulme, *Speculations: Essays on Humanism and the Philosophy of Art*, p. 134. Hulme uses the word "intuition" in the sense that Henri Bergson used it: to refer to a non-conceptual faculty of cognition that presents immediate experience (experience uncorrupted by abstraction)—a faculty that does not use the static concepts of reason but fluid concepts that befit the "very movement of the inward life of things."

161 Ibid., p. 151.

162 Actually this tendency of formulating arguments by petitioning to terms' etymologies has a fairly widespread tendency in Central European philosophy in this century—consider the writings of Voegelin, Rahner, and Patočka.

More directly relevant to Brakhage's etymological beliefs are the views of Ralph Waldo Emerson. In the extraordinary essay "The Poet" he writes,

> the poet is the Namer or Language-maker, naming things sometimes after their appearance, sometimes after their essence, and giving to every one its own name and not another's, thereby rejoicing the intellect, which delights in detachment or boundary. The poets made all the words, and therefore language is the archives of history, and, if we must say it, a sort of tomb of the muses. For though the origin of most of our words is forgotten, each word was at first a stroke of genius, and obtained currency because for the moment it symbolized the world to the first speaker and to the hearer. The etymologist finds the deadest word to have been once a brilliant picture. Language is fossil poetry. (Ralph Waldo Emerson, *The Portable Emerson*, edited by Carl Bode in collaboration with Malcolm Cowley [Harmondsworth, Middlesex: Penguin Books, 1981; originally published in 1946], p. 253)

While these are exactly Heidegger's ideas on the subject of etymology, they are also Brakhage's. But their sources are very different: Heidegger's views derive from a sense of crisis that has been so prevalent among Central European thinkers this century, while Brakhage's derive from the desire to discover/create/re-create an Adamic language that the American Adam might speak.

I take up further parallels between Brakhage and Emerson in Chapter 2.

163 T.E. Hulme, "A Lecture on Modern Poetry," in *Further Speculations*, edited by Sam Hynes (Lincoln: University of Nebraska Press, 1962), p. 73.

164 Bergson, *An Introduction to Metaphysics*, pp. 27-28.

165 See the New York *Film-Makers' Cooperative Catalogue No. 7*, p. 49.

166 Pound, *ABC of Reading*, p. 52.

167 Bergson's objections to the image appear, among other places, in his criticism of Marey's chronophotography. While Henri Bergson did not believe that imagery is necessarily fixed and stable, for the eye itself makes saccadic leaps, scans images, glances at things as well as fixing its gaze on them, he argued that the mind (specifically the intellect) has a tendency to freeze the moment; consequently, dynamic images are uncommon. Gilles Deleuze criticizes Bergson for overemphasizing the static, and reconstructs Bergson's philosophy to take into account the "movement-image"; his diagnosis of Bergson's shortcomings explains why Deleuze attaches the importance to the cinema that he does.

168 Henri Bergson, "The Soul and the Body," in *Mind-Energy* (New York: Henry Holt, 1920), pp. 56-57.

169 Henri Bergson, "The Intensity of Psychic States: The Aesthetic Feelings," in *Time and Free Will: An Essay on the Immediate Data of Consciousness*, translated by F.L. Pogson (New York: Harper & Row, 1960), p. 15.

170 T.E. Hulme, "Romanticism and Classicism," in *Speculations: Essays on Humanism and the Philosophy of Art* (London: Routledge & Kegan Paul, 1987; originally published in 1924), p. 134.

171 T.E. Hulme, "Bergson's Theory of Art," in ibid., p. 163.

172 T.E. Hulme, "Notes on Bergson," in *Further Speculations*, edited by Sam Hynes (Lincoln: University of Nebraska Press, 1962), p. 10 (emphasis mine).

173 Brakhage, *Metaphors on Vision*, not paginated. This statement appears on the first page of the main body of the text, in the section entitled "The Camera Eye/My Eye."

174 Hulme, *Further Speculations*, p. 84.

175 Williams gives a precise statement of his annoyance with Pound (which was mixed with great respect) in Part 4 of "From: A Folded Skyscraper," in William Carlos Williams, *The Collected Poems of William Carlos Williams*, Vol. 1: *1909-1939*, edited by A. Walton Litz and Christopher MacGowan (London: Paladin Grafton Books, 1991), pp. 276-77.

176 Emerson, *The Portable Emerson*, p. 51.

177 Ibid., pp. 70-71.

178 Ibid., pp. 160-61.

179 Williams, *In the American Grain*, p. 219 (up to first ellipsis), p. 222 (from first to second ellipses), p. 224 (from second to third ellipses), and pp. 225-26 (from third ellipsis to end).

180 John Cage, *Silence: Lectures and Writings by John Cage* (Hanover, NH: Wesleyan University Press, 1961), pp. 10, 12.

181 Leonard B. Meyer, *Music, the Arts, and Ideas: Patterns and Predictions in Twentieth-Century Culture* (Chicago: University of Chicago Press, 1967). Meyer's book is one of the most interesting works on the theoretical implications of art since the era of high modernism; it dismays me that it is so seldom mentioned by writers on film and literature.
   Meyer presents the essence of his ideas on radical empiricism on pp. 72 and 76.

182 William Carlos Williams, "Prologue" to *Kora in Hell: Improvisations*, in William Carlos Williams, *Imaginations*, edited with an Introduction by Webster Schott (New York: New Directions, 1970), p. 14.

183 Ibid., p. 18.

184 Ibid.

185 William Carlos Williams, "Père Sebastian Rasles," in *In the American Grain: Essays by William Carlos Williams*, with an Introduction by Horace Gregory (New York: New Directions, 1956; originally published in 1925), p. 109.

186 William Carlos Williams, "Edgar Allan Poe," in ibid., p. 216.

187 William Carlos Williams, *Spring and All* (Dijon: Contact Editions, 1923). *Spring and All* is included in the paperback, *Imaginations*, edited with an Introduction by Webster Schott (New York: New Directions, 1970),

188 Williams, *Spring and All*, in Williams, *Imaginations*, pp. 88-89.

189 Ibid., p. 192.

190 William Carlos Williams, "Choral: The Pink Church," in *The Collected Poems of William Carlos Williams*, Vol. 2: *1939-1962*, edited by Christopher MacGowan (London: Paladin Grafton Books, 1991), p. 177. The idea that such integration of process and structure yields aesthetic rewards is a node that unites Ezra Pound, Buckminster Fuller, Hugh Kenner, Hollis Frampton, William Carlos Williams, and, indeed, Stan Brakhage.

191 William Carlos Williams, *Spring and All*, in *The Collected Poems of William Carlos Williams*, Vol. 1: *1909-1939*, edited by A. Walton Litz and Christopher MacGowan (London: Paladin Grafton Books, 1991), p. 182.

192 Williams, "Della Primavera Trasportata Al Morale," p. 332.

193 William Carlos Williams, *"The Wedge*: Author's Introduction," in *The Collected Poems of William Carlos Williams*, Vol. 2: *1939-1962*, edited by Christopher MacGowan (London: Paladin Grafton Books, 1991), p. 54.

194 Williams, *Spring and All*, in *The Collected Poems of William Carlos Williams*, Vol. 1: *1909-1939*, p. 188

195 Ibid., p. 198.

196 Williams, knowingly or not, here repeats ideas that C.S. Peirce had offered on this matter. Peirce claimed that matter acquires habits in just the same way that people do, for all existents have a tendency to "copy" antecedent states ("A Guess at the Riddle," in *Peirce on Signs: Writings on Semiotic by Charles Sanders Peirce*, edited by James Hoopes [Chapel Hill, NC: University of North Carolina Press, 1991], p. 200):

> [I]f the same cell which was once excited, and which by some chance had happened to discharge itself along a certain path or paths, comes to get excited a second time, it is more likely to discharge itself the second time along some or all of those paths along which it had previously discharged itself than it would have been had it not so discharged itself before. This is the central principle of habit; and the striking contrast of its modality to that of any mechanical law is most significant. The laws of physics know nothing of tendencies or probabilities; whatever they require at all they require absolutely and without fail, and they are never disobeyed. Were the tendency to take habits replaced by an absolute requirement that the cell should discharge itself always in the same way, or according to any rigidly fixed condition whatever, all possibility of habit developing into intelligence would be cut off at the outset. . . . It is essential that there should be an element of chance in some sense as to how the cell shall discharge itself; and then that this chance or uncertainty shall not be entirely obliterated by the principle of habit, but only somewhat affected.

Habit makes things persist in their sameness. However, everything also possesses the possibility for acting in several different ways. (This is, in fact, Peirce's pragmatic definition of what it is to be a thing—an entity is simply the sum of its possible behaviours. The proposition that a poem [or, alternatively, its meaning] is simply the sum of its possible effects [behaviours] is the basis for the theory of poetic meaning for Stein, Olson, and Brakhage, according to which the meaning of a poetic term is the sum of its possible effects.) When something acts differently than "on a former like occasion" the "copying" that goes on within the flux of events is inexact. This inexactitude is what makes evolution possible.

197 William James, *Essays in Radical Empiricism* (London: Longmans, Green, 1912), p. 23.

198 T.S. Eliot, *Knowledge and Experience in the Philosophy of F.H. Bradley* (London: Faber and Faber, 1964), p. 20.

199 Pound, "Vorticism," p. 89.

200 Ginsberg offers comments on the first two pages of *Improvised Poetics* that suggest that he believes that the contents of his poems have a similarly ambiguous status. See Allen Ginsberg, *Improvised Poetics*, edited with an Introduction by Mark Robison (San Francisco: Anonym Press, 1972).

201 Robert Duncan, "Often I Am Permitted to Return to a Meadow," in *The Opening of the Field* (New York: New Directions, 1960), p. 7.

202 William Carlos Williams, "The Beginnings of an American Education," in *The Embodiment of Knowledge* (New York: New Directions, 1974), p. 6. One might recall that T.E. Hulme advocated that poetry should be "tentative and half-shy."

203 Ibid., p. 7. Here Williams wrote of the compositional process in a way not dissimilar to that which the Open Form or Projective Poets used to describe their approach to writing.

204 There was another precedent that simply must be mentioned: Gerard Manley Hopkins, a poet so original and innovative that his Victorian contemporaries hardly knew he existed. He proposed a notion of "sprung [i.e., sudden] rhythm" (see glossary).

Sprung rhythm allows any kind of foot to follow any other, and so creates a pressure to use paratactical forms of construction (though Hopkins somewhat attenuated the rhythmical pressure towards the use of paratactical constructions by extending the unit of scansion from the line to the entire stanza). Hopkins's disregard for conventional word order and his tendency to use large word groups provides further motivation for parataxis. Since the rediscovery of Hopkins's poetry, his ideas have exerted considerable influence on the development of poetic theory. His idea of sprung rhythm probably influenced William Carlos Williams's idea of the variable foot. Hopkins's assertion that a poet should take actual speech as his or her model had widespread influence (including, likely, on Williams). Hopkins described poetry, in what has become one of his better-known statements, as "speech framed to be heard for its own sake and interest even over and above its interest of meaning" (Gerard Manley Hopkins, "Poetry and Verse," in *The Journals and Papers of Gerard Manley Hopkins*, edited by Humphry House and completed by Graham Storey [London: Oxford University Press, 1959], p. 289).

Hopkins had fallen under the influence of the Oxford Movement while a student, adopted Roman Catholicism, and eventually entered the priesthood. So it is not surprising that it was to medieval verse that he turned for examples after which to fashion the new poetry that he imagined. Alliterative verse from the medieval era influenced him especially strongly. He restored the medieval poet's practice of using qualitative rather than quantitative metres (i.e., metres that depend on a number of stressed sounds rather than on the actual number of syllables). Hopkins's interest in qualitative measure was shared by the Open Form (see glossary) poets Charles Olson and Robert Duncan. And while, in a strict sense, the stanza, not the line, is the basic unit of scansion in Hopkins's prosody, Hopkins does show a tendency to create lines that use the four-beat stress of earlier English poetry. In all this, he assisted considerably in the initiative against pentameter. Finally, like that of many Open Form poets who were his true successors (a fact which, doubtless, explains why a writer-friend of mine quotes Hopkins's poetry at the drop of a hat), Hopkins's poetry was immediate and sensuous. He wanted his poems to convey his apprehension of a pattern in the natural phenomena that surrounded him—of what he called the phenomenon's "inscape" (see glossary). What the Open Form poets could not accept was his belief that the inscape reflects an unchanging Reality behind the various appearances of things, for the Open Form poets averred that reality fluxes and that the concrete particular has ultimate reality; in this they concurred with the fundamental metaphysical propositions Henri Bergson had offered.

205 Williams, *Kora in Hell: Improvisations*, p. 14.
206 In this affirmation of the transcendentality of the image, Brakhage reverts to the aesthetics of earlier phase of modernism, before the Open Form poets, exemplified by Eliot, Pound, and Joyce. Brakhage's monograph *Gertrude Stein: Meditative Literature and Film* (Boulder: The Graduate School, University of Colorado at Boulder, 1990), written about the same time that he made *A Child's Garden and the Serious Sea*, is also extremely Platonic, and accepts that the artwork is isolated from the real: "For it is in the nature of Image that it is received as a clustering of object-shapes to be individually perceived. . . . The forms within The Film will answer only to each other *and* the form of the paradigm the entirety-of-forms finally is" (pp. 4-5). The quotation comes from his commentary on an image of the oldest church in Maine that appears in *Visions in Meditation #1*. He argues for a version of transformationalism when he asserts that the image assumes relations with other elements in the film (and the whole) and it is utterly changed. I outline the basis of transformationalism in *A Body of Vision: Representations of the Body in Recent Film and Poetry* (Waterloo, ON: Wilfrid Laurier University Press, 1997).

But didn't I suggest that Brakhage has been influenced by Olson, and that one of the main effects of Olson's push was to bring the image down from the Platonic heavens, and use it as a dynamic element, like any other force in reality? I believe the explanation for this shift is simple, and cogent. Earlier in his career, the Emersonian in Brakhage demanded a completely individual religion, and fostered a small degree of hostility towards institutional religion; all this meant that Brakhage's relation with religion was somewhat conflicted. From the time of making *A Child's Garden*, Brakhage has affirmed his faith—recently, when Brakhage was interviewed for a biography a TV station was doing on him (July 1997), he acknowledged that he would call himself a Christian, though this acknowledgment, preposterously, did not make it into the edited film. Hardly surprising, then, that he adopted the Platonism of earlier tradition.

Anyway, one should never accuse Brakhage of not changing his mind, and often.

207 Several of my favourites among Brakhage's films have water as their primary object matter: *Made Manifest, A Child's Garden and the Serious Sea*, and *The Mammals of Victoria*. Too much significance should not be attached to this—after all, water, like trains, is one of film's exemplary subjects, for a body of water is a dynamic thing which modules light as it moves; the tension between surface and the shallow space its movement establishes is most intriguing; and its movement combines repetition with variation in a most satisfying manner. Just consider Ralph Steiner's great film of 1928, H_2O or his later *Look Park* (1974). But I don't believe that one would be guilty of over-interpretation to suggest that Brakhage's success with films whose primary (even exclusive) object matter is water relates to water's movement providing a marvellous image of flux, and its dynamism as conveys the energy that drives that flux.

208 William Carlos Williams, "Young Sycamore," in *The Collected Poems of William Carlos Williams*, Vol. 1: *1909-1939*, edited by A. Walton Litz and Christopher MacGowan (London: Paladin Grafton Books, 1991), pp. 266-67.

209 William Carlos Williams, "Letter to Jim Higgins," undated, cited in Lisa M. Steinman, *Made in America: Science, Technology, and American Modernist Poets* (New Haven: Yale University Press, 1987), p. 96.

210 Brakhage, *Gertrude Stein: Meditative Literature and Film*.

211 William Carlos Williams, *Interviews with William Carlos Williams: "Speaking Straight Ahead,"* edited with an Introduction by Linda Welshimer Wagner (New York: New Directions, 1976), p. 98.

212 Brakhage's note on the film (New York *Film-Makers' Cooperative Catalogue No. 7*, p. 59) consists of a quotation from 1 Corinthians 3:13: "Every man's work shall be made manifest, for the day shall declare it, because it shall be revealed by fire and the fire shall try every man's work of what short it is." The note implies a similar connection between fire and water as does the film *Fire of Waters* (discussed later). I think the coincidence is not entirely by chance, for both I suggest are films about the birth of vision, and both use water as an equivalent for the liquidity of the internal body, the stirrings of the mind, and the flux of matter.

213 Williams, "Père Sebastian Rasles." However, Williams also made it clear in this passage that history inheres in all things, and to understand any thing, one must know its history. He continued by stating that "what has been morally, aesthetically worth while in America has rested upon peculiar and discoverable [sic] ground."

214 *Contact* 1 (January 1921).

215 William Carlos Williams, *The Selected Letters of William Carlos Williams*, edited with an Introduction by John C. Thirlwall (New York: McDowell, Obolensky, 1957), pp. 330, 134.

216 William Carlos Williams, "Writer's Prologue to a Play in Verse," in *The Collected Poems of William Carlos Williams*, Vol. 2: *1939-1962*, edited by Christopher MacGowan (London: Paladin Grafton Books, 1991), p. 59.

217 For Olson's views on the matter, see Charles Olson, "Maximus of Gloucester, Letter 15," in *The Maximus Poems*, edited by George F. Butterick (Berkeley and Los Angeles: University of California Press, 1983), pp. 71-75. Olson suggested that the spirit of poetry might have become central to early American life, but for the Puritan

John Smith's frugality. He adds to this, in "A Later Note on Letter #15" (in ibid., p. 249 [II. 79]), that writing continued in the debased conditions that Puritan frugality left it "until Whitehead, who cleared out the gunk/ by getting the universe in (as against man alone" [Olson did not close the parenthesis] (ibid., p. 249). Gunk? Gummy stuff, that prevents the mind from running smoothly—those aspects of language that have allowed abstract thought to substitute for direct connection with things (a connection that involves the rhythm of the body participating in the rhythm of fluxing circumambient conditions, to recognize the identity of the body's energies with those energies). It was Olson's faith, as it is Brakhage's, that thought can be rich when it is not abstract—that far from enriching thought, abstraction renders thinking less vital, less true, and less complex.

218 William Carlos Williams, "Voyage of the Mayflower," in *In the American Grain: Essays by William Carlos Williams*, with an Introduction by Horace Gregory (New York: New Directions, 1956; originally published in 1925), p. 67.

219 Ibid.

220 Ibid., p. 112.

221 Ibid., p. 113 (emphasis in original).

222 Elsewhere in this book there is commentary, in greater or lesser detail, on all these films.

223 Ibid., p. 157.

224 Ibid., p. 177.

225 William Carlos Williams, "Jacataqua," in *In the American Grain: Essays by William Carlos Williams*, with an Introduction by Horace Gregory (New York: New Directions, 1956; originally published in 1925), pp. 175, 179.

226 William Carlos Williams, "Against the Weather: A Study of the Artist," in *Selected Essays of William Carlos Williams* (New York: Random House, 1954), p. 196.

227 Ibid., pp. 197-98 (emphasis in original).

228 Brakhage, *Gertrude Stein: Meditative Literature and Film*, pp. 4-5.

229 Williams, *Selected Essays of William Carlos Williams*, p. 111.

230 William Carlos Williams, "Introduction to *The Wedge*," in *Selected Essays of William Carlos Williams* (New York: Random House, 1954), p. 257 (emphasis in original).

231 Stan Brakhage, "Film and Music (Letter to Ronna Page)," in *Brakhage Scrapbook: Collected Writings 1964-1980*, edited by Robert A. Haller (New Paltz, NY: Documentext, 1982), p. 50 (emphasis in original). Brakhage actually puts the text I have quoted from between quotation marks in the letters for, he explains, he is quoting himself, drawing from an article that appeared in *WILD DOG*.

232 Stan Brakhage, "S.A. #1," in ibid., p. 43.

233 Ibid., p. 44.

234 Williams, "Edgar Allan Poe," pp. 175, 179.

235 Williams, *Selected Essays of William Carlos Williams*, pp. 118-19.

236 By 1913 or 1914, Hulme rejected many of the polemical propositions he had formulated in 1908-1909. His later aesthetics was rooted in Wilhelm Worringer's once astonishingly popular work, *Abstraktion und Einfühlung*. As the title of the work implies, the conceptual basis of Worringer's work was an absolute polarization of the concepts of abstraction and empathy. There are two types of art, Worringer proposed, and they are utterly different. The former is a detached and autonomous construction wholly indifferent to humans' interests. The latter reflects the interests and feeling of its spectators or audience. The distinction between these two types of works mirrors the difference between two ways of relating to the world: empathy is the result of a "happy pantheistic relationship of confidence between man and the phenomena of the outside world," while abstraction is the product of a more troubled relationship between humans and the outside world. Empathy inclines artworks towards organic forms and naturalism (i.e., the imitation of the forms of nature) while abstraction "finds its beauty in the life-denying inorganic, in the crystalline or, in general terms, in all abstract law and necessity."

Hulme visited Berlin in 1913 and met with Worringer. He returned to England wholly converted to this new set of ideas. Thus, in January 1914, he gave a lecture to the Quest Society on the topic of "Modern Art and Its Philosophy" in which he argued three theses:

> (1) There are two kinds of art, geometrical and vital, absolutely distinct in kind from one another.... (2) Each of these arts springs from and corresponds to a certain general attitude towards the world.... (3) ... this is really the point I am making for—that the re-emergence of geometrical art may be the precursor of the re-emergence of the corresponding attitude towards the world, and so, of the break up of the Renaissance humanistic attitude. (This and the previous two quotations are from T.E. Hulme, "Modern Art," in *Speculations: Essays on Humanism and the Philosophy of Art* [London: Routledge & Kegan Paul, 1987; originally published in 1924], pp. 77-78)

Even in this phase of his work, Hulme's thinking anticipated future developments in aesthetics and art theory; before too long art theorists and art critics could be heard expounding on the "objecthood" of the work of art, insisting upon the fundamental importance of the artwork's autonomous status and its indifference to human emotion, and artists could be found using severely geometric forms in an effort to expel "human" (i.e., empathetic) content from art. And as this movement rose in prominence, Brakhage railed that artists were forsaking the true (human) vocation of art and pointing out that no feature of recent art had given more convincing evidence of this than its geometric forms. In this period he also launched a defence of organic form.

This phase of Hulme's work is hardly known. An excellent summary description of it can be found in chapter 6 ("Hulme: The Progress of Reaction") of Michael H. Levenson's *A Genealogy of Modernism: A Study of English Literary Doctrine 1908-1922* (Cambridge: Cambridge University Press, 1984). Another excellent study of the enthusiasm for Bergsonianism and the reaction against it (which includes a discussion of the right-wing reaction against Bergsonianism which Hulme took up, of Julien Benda and Pierre Lasserre, and commentary on Hulme's relations with the two), is R.C. Grogin's aforementioned study of the reception of Bergsonian philosophy in France just before the outbreak of World War I, *The Bergsonian Controversy in France: 1900-1914*; especially important is chap. 7, "Rationalists, Anti-Rationalists, and Academicians."

237 This, no doubt, explains why *Blast* "blasted" Henri Bergson (i.e., listed him as deserving of opprobrium), and not the sanitary reasons William C. Wees gives in the Appendix of his study of Vorticism (a book which displays a sometimes astonishing lack of concern with Vorticism's intellectual context).

238 Hulme, *Speculations: Essays on Humanism and the Philosophy of Art*, p. 150.

239 Frampton, "Stan and Jane Brakhage (and Hollis Frampton) Talking," pp. 183-86.

240 Algernon Charles Swinburne, *Atalanta in Calydon*, in Alexander M. Witherspoon, ed., *The College Survey of English Literature* (New York: Harcourt, Brace, 1951), p. 1129.

241 Ezra Pound, Canto XLVII, in *The Cantos of Ezra Pound*, pp. 237-38.

242 Ezra Pound, Canto LXXVII, in ibid., p. 474.

243 Ezra Pound, Canto LXXXVI, in ibid., p. 560.

244 Ezra Pound, Canto LXII, in ibid., p. 350.

245 Ezra Pound, Canto LXXIV, in ibid., p. 449.

246 Ezra Pound, Canto CV, in ibid., pp. 747-48.

247 My summary of the principles of Anglo-Saxon prosody draws heavily on Christine Brooke-Rose's very instructive Introduction to Pound's *Cantos* in *A ZBC of Ezra Pound* (Berkeley and Los Angeles: University of California Press, 1971), pp. 88-89.

248 Ezra Pound, Canto LXXXI, in *The Cantos of Ezra Pound*, pp. 519-20.

249 Ibid., p. 520.

250 Ibid.

251 Ibid.

252 Pound, "A Retrospect," p. 9.

253 Ezra Pound, *Translations*, with an Introduction by Hugh Kenner (Norfolk, CT: New Directions, 1963), pp. 23-24.

254 Two proleptic points. First, if you deem that this assertion overestimates the role of geometry, consider that Spinoza's philosophy was *more geometrico demonstrata*, or, more generally, that throughout the period when the modern paradigm held sway, that Euclid's *Elements* was held up as the model of how to establish certain knowledge. Or that we have clear evidence that the modern paradigm is about to lose its hegemonic status when thinkers make desperate efforts (it's the desperation that's the key here) to extend the axiomatic method to a wide range of disciplines, that it is waning when paradoxes are found to arise in the set theoretical foundations of mathematics, when Euclid's fifth axiom is deemed non-intuitive, and alternatives for it are developed, some of which are clearly counter-intuitive, and internally consistent geometries are developed from sets of axioms including those counter-intuitive substitutions; and is, to all intents and purposes, a spent force by the time that Kurt Gödel develops his famous proof that not arithmetic cannot be developed as complete, closed axiomatic system.

Second, if you deem that this assertion overestimates the role that the conception of space-time plays in the modern paradigm, then I suggest that you do what I always do when I consider modernity's founding beliefs, and that is to turn to Kant. Recall the role of space and time in the *Kritik der reinen Vernunft*.

255 In proposing that the Chinese way of writing affected the way that Chinese people conceive reality, Fenollosa was proposing a version of the Sapir-Whorf hypothesis, for which the intellectuals of Fenollosa's day had much enthusiasm.

256 Ernest Fenollosa, "The Chinese Written Character as a Medium for Poetry," in Karl Shapiro, *Prose Keys to Modern Poetry* (New York: Harper & Row, 1962), p. 139.

257 Ibid., p. 142 (emphasis in original).

258 Ibid., pp. 141-42.

259 Ibid., p. 145.

260 Ezra Pound, "A Serious Artist," in *Literary Essays of Ezra Pound*, edited with an Introduction by T.S. Eliot (London: Faber and Faber, 1960), p. 49.

261 A few critics have questioned the extent of the influence, noting that Pound had used paratactical forms before meeting Fenollosa's widow in 1913 and apprising himself of the details of Ernest's work. The tendency to think in images, and by juxtaposing concrete images (cf. parataxis), was likely an inherent disposition of his thought. The latter claim acquires a degree of confirmation from the fact that the later cantos, the *Rock-Drill* and *Thrones* cantos (in which a latent tendency towards what Lev Vygotsky calls "autistic thinking" seems to have taken over), are even more than usually elliptic and paratactical, and in them Pound refuses to identify progressively more of the allusions and references. It was this sort of thinking that led Wyndham Lewis, after receiving a letter written in the same style as the later cantos, to write back, half in concern, half in anger: "Your last letter undecipherable, just cannot imagine what lies beneath the words. Have you anything really to say?"

262 Fenollosa, "The Chinese Written Character as a Medium for Poetry," pp. 140-41 (emphasis in original).

263 Ibid., p. 140.

264 Ibid., p. 148.

265 Brakhage cites Pound's "marvellous mistranslation of a Chinese ideogram" as one of the inspirations that urged him to make his film *Sincerity I*. See the New York *Film-Makers' Cooperative Catalogue No. 7*, p. 50.

266 Fenollosa, "The Chinese Written Character as a Medium for Poetry," p. 142.

267 Ibid., p. 154.

268 Ibid., p. 142.

269 Ibid.

270 Ibid., p. 140.

271 Ibid. (emphasis in original).

272 Ezra Pound, *Lustra*, in *Selected Poems*, edited with an Introduction by T.S. Eliot (London: Faber and Faber, 1948), p. 113.

273 Pound, *Gaudier-Brzeska: A Memoir*, p. 89 (emphasis mine).

274 Ezra Pound, Canto LXXVIII, in *The Cantos of Ezra Pound*, p. 533.

275 T.S. Eliot, "The Love Song of J. Alfred Prufrock," in *Collected Poems 1909-1962* (London: Faber and Faber, 1963), p. 13.

276 T.S. Eliot, "Preludes," in ibid., p. 23.

277 Ezra Pound, Canto XVI, in *The Cantos of Ezra Pound*, p. 68.

278 Ezra Pound, Canto LXXXIII, in ibid., pp. 530-31.

279 Tu Fu, "Snow Storm," in Kenneth Rexroth, *One Hundred Poems from the Chinese* (New York: New Directions, 1965), p. 6. I realize only too well how sloppy I am being when I use Rexroth's version of Tu Fu's poem to illustrate a quality that some Chinese verse possesses—this was the first Chinese verse I translated. The experience gripped me with an exhilaration I shall never forget. My own poor efforts at translation made me realize just how great Rexroth's version really is. He has made the poem entirely his own, and it is more reasonable to refer to it as one of the great American poems of the twentieth century than to cite it as an example of Chinese verse.

280 In R.H. Blyth, "Four Great Haiku Poets," in *Haiku*, Vol. 1: *Eastern Culture* (Tokyo: Hokuseido Press, 1949), p. 334.

281 The building is the juvenile home where Brakhage lived between the ages of nine and nineteen (though there is nothing in the film that definitely identifies it as such). We can speculate that the private association, for Brakhage, is that the building brings back memories of being at risk, just as his little boy is now at risk. That is not an association available to the film's viewers, however. What viewers can take from these images is that the father is examining details of the building's anatomy as the physician scrutinizes the little boy's. The father's activity clearly suggests anxiety—we might extend this by suggesting that the father is all the more anxious because he is reduced to examining the building's anatomy when he would rather be checking out his son (but that no good would come of it), and that he is all more the troubled for being displaced from a position of usefulness by the attending physician.

282 Marjorie Keller, in the first major study of the representation of childhood in avant-garde cinema, *The Untutored Eye: Childhood in the Films of Cocteau, Cornell, and Brakhage* (Cranbury, NJ: Associated University Presses, 1986), pp. 203-13, interpreted the film as telling the story of Brakhage having to come to terms with the restrictions that his primary role as a filmmaker impose on him, keeping him from turning himself over fully to his human obligations and commitments.

>   Since Brakhage finds himself most effective as a seer, his response to the boy's need is predictable. He studies the look of illness and its surroundings. Jane carries the boy, drives the car, and leads him to the doctor. Brakhage films—knowing, showing, all the while that he is inadequate. But the inward difficulty, at the time of editing, is fully directed toward himself and at seeing what aspect of his experience is manifested in his son's own. (p. 212)

>   Keller's commentary is extremely interesting as is her treatment of Brakhage's films generally; however, she underestimated the ambiguity of the film's point of view. In fairness, she did acknowledge that, as is "often the case in Brakhage's films ... there is no fixed point of view. One sees the child and alternately sees as the child might" (p. 204) and even argues that there is an evolution of point of view in the film, as "[w]hat at first is an indecipherable mixture of viewpoints later becomes a distinguishable solo point of view. ... The opening scenes, which begin from an adult's point of view, but quickly shift to include the children's eye view, stand in stark contrast to the individual version at the end of the film" (p. 204).

However, Keller also maintained that one point of view dominates the film (even though others are present). I believe that this claim is doubtful (and that the efforts she had to go through in order to render it plausible provides prima facie evidence of the magnitude of the problems she faced asserting it). What is more, she overburdened the significance of a shot of the boy appealing to the filmmaker, "in need of loving attention" (though even the shot seems to me more direct perception, and so far more ambiguous than Keller makes it out to be).

283 Pound, *Gaudier-Brzeska: A Memoir*, p. 89.

284 Ezra Pound, Canto LII, in *The Cantos of Ezra Pound*, pp. 260-61.

285 Fenollosa, "The Chinese Written Character as a Medium for Poetry," p. 148

286 Ibid., p. 149.

287 Ezra Pound, "Calvacanti," in *Literary Essays of Ezra Pound*, edited with an Introduction by T.S. Eliot (London: Faber and Faber, 1960), p. 154.

288 Ibid.

289 This quotation was taken from Kenner, *The Pound Era*, p. 155.

290 Stan Brakhage, "Poetry and Film," a lecture recorded at the University of North Carolina, Chapel Hill, March 22, 1977; originally published in *Credences*, nos. 5-6, and reprinted in Stan Brakhage, *Brakhage Scrapbook: Collected Writings 1964-1980*, edited by Robert A. Haller (New Paltz, NY: Documentext, 1982), pp. 224-25. I have added quotation marks around the arrow.

291 Stein actually compared her use of repetition to the means by which cinema creates a dynamic impression (thus suggesting that in her writing, repetition is the means for creating the impression of movement. See Gertrude Stein, *Lectures in America* (New York: Random House, 1935), p. 177.

292 Gilles Deleuze understands Bergson taking as his principal mission the demonstration that there is genuine novelty and genuine variety in the world. In his book *Bergsonianism* (translated by Hugh Tomlinson and Barbara Habberjam [New York: Zone Books, 1988]) he claims that what makes Bergson's philosophy great is that, against the entire Western philosophical tradition, Bergson accords ontological priority to difference and change.

293 William James, "On the Notion of Reality as Changing," Appendix to *Essays in Radical Empiricism* and *A Pluralistic Universe* (Gloucester: Peter Smith, 1967), p. 350.

294 William James, "The Stream of Thought," in *The Principles of Psychology*, 2 vols. (New York: Dover Publications, 1950), Vol. 1, p. 231 (emphasis in original).

295 This line appears in variant forms in Stein's oeuvre. Sometimes it is presented: "Rose is a rose is a rose." Sometimes, however, that phrase is preceded by the indefinite article: "A rose is a rose is a rose." To remind readers that this phrase appears in variant forms in Stein's oeuvre, I write: "(A) rose is a rose is a rose," with the article in parentheses. While writing it this way serves as a useful caution, it represses an important ambiguity associated with the variant that lacks the indefinite article—that the first word in that form could be a woman's name.

296 The brilliant Toronto artist Michael Snow has given us a comparable achievement. In the years from 1962 to 1967, Snow created a series, *Walking Woman*, in which he rendered a single form—a stylized figure of a woman, caught in mid-stride and shown in profile—in a huge variety of materials, in many (and sometimes very witty) variations, and placed in a variety of contexts. The series is a major accomplishment of twentieth-century art. Among the features that make it so great is that Snow was the first artist to take a completely systematic approach to demonstrating in operation the modernist principle that when an element assumes new relations it undergoes internal transformation. Snow's precise, highly focused method showed exactly how a single form undergoes change when, placed in a new context, it assumes new relationships. Stein's "(A) rose is a rose is a rose" demonstrates much the same point.

297 Brakhage, *Metaphors on Vision*, not paginated. This comment appears on the sixth page of the interview with Sitney. I have given the film title in italics while the original put it in capital letters.

298 Gertrude Stein, "Composition as Explanation," in *A Stein Reader*, edited and with an Introduction by Ulla E. Dydo (Evanston, IL: Northwestern University Press, 1993), p. 498. I think Stein was being a little coy here, for I believe that James, who knew something about the phenomenology of time consciousness and of the temporality of consciousness, might have known why it was done.

299 From the transcript of a lecture ("Poetry and Film") Stan Brakhage delivered at the University of North Carolina, Chapel Hill, March 22, 1977, and reprinted in *Brakhage Scrapbook*, pp. 225-26. I have inserted the "shows" between brackets for explanatory purposes.

   Brakhage's remark that this famous poem first appeared in a book for children is interesting, for the rhymes and rhythms of children's stories and poems are surely built into the fibre of our bodies.

300 Stein, *Lectures in America*, p. 231.

301 Ibid., pp. 231-32.

302 Ibid., p. 237.

303 Gertrude Stein, "America," in *Everybody's Autobiography* (New York: Cooper Square Publishers, 1971), p. 242.

304 Gertrude Stein, "What Are Master-Pieces and Why Are There So Few of Them," in *What Are Masterpieces* (New York: Pitman, 1970), p. 90.

305 Gertrude Stein, "Oval," in *Bee Time Vine and Other Pieces [1913-1927]*, Vol. 3 of the Yale Edition of the *Unpublished Writings of Gertrude Stein* (New Haven: Yale University Press, 1953; reprinted New York: Books for Libraries Press, 1969); cited in Henry M. Sayre, "The Artist's Model: American Art and the Question of Looking like Gertrude Stein," in Shirley Neuman and Ira B. Nadel, eds., *Gertrude Stein and the Making of Literature* (Boston: Northeastern University Press, 1988), p. 27.

306 Again, the issue of absence that inhabits the signifier, and that of relation between self-reference and the absence of extrinsic reference, are topics that only recently have attained widespread currency.

307 The Surrealist painter Salvador Dalí referred to forms that render this sort of equivalence as "a double image."

   There is a related cinematic construction. The filmmaker joins a shot that highlights an object with another that highlights a similarly shaped object at the same place on the screen. Filmmakers refer to such a cut as a "plastic cut" or a "cut on shape" or even (adopting Juan Gris's term) as a "rhyming cut." It is one of Brakhage's favourite editing devices.

308 Gertrude Stein, "An Elucidation," in *A Stein Reader*, edited and with an Introduction by Ulla E. Dydo (Evanston, IL: Northwestern University Press, 1993), p. 440.

309 Ibid., p. 430.

310 Gertrude Stein, "Tender Buttons: Objects," in *Selected Writings of Gertrude Stein*, edited with an Introduction and Notes by Carl Van Vechten and with an Essay by F.W. Dupee (New York: Vintage Books, 1972), p. 461.

311 The remarks Brakhage made at the earlier date appeared in a letter to Gerard Malanga, published in "On Marie Menken," *Filmwise* 5-6 (1967); reprinted in Stan Brakhage, *Brakhage Scrapbook: Collected Writings 1964-1980*, edited by Robert A. Haller (New Paltz, NY: Documentext, 1982), pp. 91-93.

312 Brakhage, *Gertrude Stein: Meditative Literature and Film*, pp. 3 and 1.

   At the time Brakhage wrote this, he was teaching a course in "Philosophical Film" that included my own films, and dealt with my opposition to narrative (as well as the difference between our two conceptions of film).

313 Ibid., p. 1.

314 Ibid., pp. 2-3.

315 Ralph Waldo Emerson, "Self-Reliance," in *The Portable Emerson*, edited by Carl Bode in collaboration with Malcolm Cowley (Harmondsworth, Middlesex: Penguin Books, 1981; originally published in 1946), p. 151.

316 It should be allowed that Brakhage's enlarged conception of vision expands outward to embrace primordial and, therefore, synaesthetic experience; so Brakhage frequently provides close-ups of highly textured objects; in doing so, he creates visual forms that engender a tactile response.

317 P. Adams Sitney, *Modernist Montage: The Obscurity of Vision in Cinema and Literature* (New York: Columbia University Press, 1990), p. 147.

318 The form of objectivism they espouse, I believe, is entirely consistent with the position of radical empiricism I have suggested is one of the key legacies of the Emersonian tradition; and radical empiricism is more strongly oriented towards the objective than Sitney allows. (He proposes that Stein's writing, like that of all writers belonging to the Emersonian tradition as a whole, is a throughly subjective affair.)

319 Stan Brakhage, "Stan Brakhage at Millennium: November 4, 1977," *Millennium Film Journal* 16/17/18 (Fall/Winter 1986-87): 297-307 (transcription of a talk and question-and-answer session at the Millennium Film Workshop in New York City). Brakhage doesn't explicitly identify iambic (or trochaic) pentameter as the form of construction he intends, but at other times he has made that connection between hoof-beat rhythms and iambic pentameter explicit.

320 Ralph Waldo Emerson, "Self-Examination: Myself, Sunday April 18, 1824," in *Journals of Ralph Waldo Emerson*, edited by Edward Waldo Emerson and Waldo Emerson Forbes (New York: Houghton Mifflin, 1909), p. 361.

321 Ralph Waldo Emerson, "The Poet," in *The Portable Emerson*, edited by Carl Bode in collaboration with Malcolm Cowley (Harmondsworth, Middlesex: Penguin Books, 1981; originally published in 1946), p. 260. The similarity of their thoughts is no doubt one of the reasons both Bergson and James praised Emerson's philosophical abilities.

322 Ralph Waldo Emerson, "Nature," in ibid., p. 22.

323 Harold Bloom, *The American Religion: The Emergence of the Post-Christian Nation* (New York: Simon & Schuster, 1992).

324 This history, in addition to the wariness he, like every artist worth his or her salt understandably shows at being categorized as anything at all, probably accounts for Brakhage's leeriness about being categorized as Emersonian.

325 The New York *Film-Makers' Cooperative Catalogue No. 7*, p. 41.

326 Sitney, *Visionary Film*, p. 193.

327 Brakhage recounts this in *Metaphors on Vision*, not paginated (p. 14).

328 These bursts presage the bas-relief images to come, which is the major device Brakhage uses to interrupt the smooth dynamic flow that characterizes *The Dead*'s montage. These flashes are an example of what Brakhage calls the interruptive flash frame, a single frame that makes reference to something that has come before or something that is still to come, interpolated into a longer shot. (I use the term "interruptive frames" to refer to shots that have essentially the same character and function, but are longer than a single frame, as some of the interruptive shots in *The Dead* are.)

   The success Brakhage has had with the device depends upon the modality of temporal experience that Brakhage's films elicit. As I have noted, Brakhage films seem to transpire the immediate presence, a moment unconditioned by recollection of the past or anticipation of the future. The interruptive frame suggests recollection or anticipation, but, at least as Brakhage uses it, does not elicit anticipation or recollection. A certain tension arises therefore.

   Brakhage claims to have invented the interruptive flash frame, when he made *Cat's Cradle* (1959). (See Stan Brakhage with Ted Perry, "Seminar," *Dialogue on Film* 2, no. 3 [January 1973]: 5.) It was picked up by Gregory Markoupoulos, and used to suggest the mechanics of psychological process in *Twice a Man* and, later, in some of his portraits, more formally. Eventually Hollywood picked it up.

329 Perhaps the most impressive use of superimposition of negative and positive versions of the same shot, but slightly out of register with one another, is Jack Chambers's *Hart of London*. That film is one in which the filmmaker confronts the idea of death, and the

experience opens up a gap in consciousness, which the filmmaker strives to fill with a desperate surfeit of images. On this topic, see my discussion of the film in *Image and Identity: Reflections on Canadian Film and Culture* (Waterloo, ON: Wilfrid Laurier University Press, 1989). I recommended the film to Brakhage when he visited Canada in 1974, and he was extremely taken with it—so impressed that he wrote a program note on the film and made efforts, that met with some success, to get it shown at American film centres.

330 *The Dead* (1960) is not the only film by Brakhage that concludes in the spectral realm of negative: so do *The Way to Shadow Garden* (1954) and *Cat of the Worm's Green Realm* (1997).

331 Emerson, "The Poet," p. 244.

332 Ibid.

333 Ibid., p. 248.

334 Ibid., pp. 249-50.

335 It would be quite profitable to read this assertion through the ideas Donald W. Winnicott has expounded on the transitional area and transitional objects. See D.W. Winnicott, *Playing and Reality* (Harmondsworth, Middlesex: Penguin Education, 1980; originally published by Tavistock in 1971). "Transitional Objects and Transitional Phenomena," "Creativity and Its Origins," and "The Location of the Cultural Experience" are especially important.

336 Gertrude Stein, "Plays," quoted in P. Adams Sitney, "The Sentiment of Doing Nothing: Stein's Autobiographies," in *Modernist Montage: The Obscurity of Vision in Cinema and Literature* (New York: Columbia University Press, 1990), p. 150.

337 Ibid., p. 151.

338 Implicit in the passage too is a problematic concerning the relation between these mental representations and the world. When one looks at a green ball and sees green, does the word "green" have a role in making us see green (do we see sound?), or, perhaps, do words play some other role in making the experience (in our seeing green)? These are very interesting questions (and they have relevance to the opening of *Metaphors on Vision*), but to pursue them would divert us from the real subject of our commentary.

339 Vestigial remnants of that belief remain, as is apparent when, engaged in table chat, we try to apprise ourselves of people's attributes by reflecting on their names.

340 In Sitney, *Modernist Montage: The Obscurity of Vision in Cinema and Literature*, p. 151. He cites as the reference for the Mallarmé: Stéphane Mallarmé, *Oeuvres Complètes*, edited by Henri Mondor (Paris: Gallimard, 1959), p. 368.

341 Northrop Frye, "The Order of Words," in *The Great Code: The Bible and Literature* (Toronto: Academic Press, 1982), p. 6.

342 Charles Olson, *Selected Writings of Charles Olson*, edited with an Introduction by Robert Creeley (New York: New Directions, 1966), p. 58.

343 Frye, *The Great Code: The Bible and Literature*, p. 7. Frye's conception of hieroglyphic language was affected by the writings of the great Canadian thinker Eric Havelock, especially *Preface to Plato* (Cambridge, MA: The Belknap Press of Harvard University, 1963).

344 Gershom Scholem wrote an extraordinary letter to Franz Rosenzweig on December 26, 1926, in which he predicts that language will have vengeance on the Jews for Hebrew, a sacred language, the language they use in Israel to buy groceries and conduct business. The letter is still unpublished, as far as I know. (I received a mimeographed copy of it when I studied with Jacques Derrida.)

345 Frye, *The Great Code: The Bible and Literature*, p. 211.

346 For all these reasons, Pound had a penchant for the list form. Consider:

> And
>
>> I came here in my young youth
>>> and lay there under the crocodile
>> By the column, looking East on the Friday,

> And I said: Tomorrow I will lie on the South side
> And the day after, south west.
> And at night they sang in the gondolas
> And in the barche with lanthorns;
>> (Canto XXVI, in *The Cantos of Ezra Pound*, p. 121)

When one reads this, one tends to break into a singsong after the fourth line (for up to there the metric variations were sufficient to restrain the urge to read the passage in this way).

> And before him had been Pietro Leopoldo
> that wished state debt brought to an end;
> that put the guilds under common tribunal;
> that left names only as vestige of feudal chain;
> that lightened mortmain that princes and church be under tax
> as were others; that ended the gaolings for debt;
> that said thou shalt not sell public offices;
> that suppressed so many *gabelle*;
> that freed the printers of surveillance
>> and wiped out the crime of lèse majesty;
> that abolished death as a penalty and all tortures in prisons
> which he held were for segregation;
> that split common property among tillers;
>> (Canto XLIV, in *The Cantos of Ezra Pound*, pp. 227-28)

And, of course, the best known of all the cantos:

> With usura hath no man a house of good stone
> each block cut smooth and well fitting
> that design might cover their face,
> with usura
> hath no man a painted paradise on his church wall
> *harpes et luz*
> or where virgin receiveth message
> and halo projects from incision,
> with usura
> seeth no man Gonzaga his heirs and his concubines
> no picture is made to endure nor to live with
> but it is made to sell and sell quickly
> with usura, sin against nature,
> is thy bread ever more of stale rags
> is thy bread dry as paper,
> with no mountain wheat, no strong flour
> with usura the line grows thick
> with usura is no clear demarcation
> and no man can find site for his dwelling.
>> (Canto XLV, in *The Cantos of Ezra Pound*, p. 229)

Pound's use of "hath," "thy," "paradise," "virgin," "receiveth," and other such "King James words" confirms that Pound saw the list form as close to a sacred use of language.

347 *A List* appears in Gertrude Stein, *A Stein Reader*, edited and with an Introduction by Ulla E. Dydo (Evanston, IL: Northwestern University Press, 1993), pp. 400-14. In her headnotes to the selection, Dydo comments significantly, "She strings words together like beads or *phrases in prayer*, putting them in varied sequences" (ibid., p. 383 [emphasis mine]).

The contemporary novelist and critic William H. Gass has a penchant for lists, and has commented on the form in interviews. He declares that his interest in lists stems from the fact that a list has a potentially infinite extent.

348 Stein, "Composition as Explanation," p. 500.

349 Gertrude Stein, "If I Told Him: A Completed Portrait of Picasso," in *A Stein Reader*, edited and with an Introduction by Ulla E. Dydo (Evanston, IL: Northwestern University Press, 1993), p. 464.

350 Stein doubtless knew that Shakespeare's view was that there is plenty in a name. *Romeo and Juliet*, after all, is a play whose central conflict arises from names: "Capulet" and "Montague." Therefore Shakespeare raises the many variants on the idea of names in the play. Near the beginning of the play, in Act 1, scene 2, Capulet hands his servant a piece of paper and charges him to "find those persons out/ Whose names are written there." The servant is immediately in a quandry, as for him the names are inert—he cannot read, and so he "can never find what names the writing person hath here writ"; but the fact that, for the servant, these names are inert should alert readers to Shakespeare's idea that words are active (or at least under the right conditions they are). The first thing that Juliet wants to know on seeing Romeo (Act 1, scene 5) is "his name." In Act 2, scene 2, in the same speech to which Stein's little poem alludes, Juliet states that "'Tis but thy name that is my enemy," while Romeo acknowledges that his name "is hateful to myself,/ Because it is an enemy to" Juliet; later in the same scene, Juliet invokes the story of Echo to allude to the power of uttering names; in Act 2, scene 3, Romeo says of "Rosalind" (the Friar has just suggested that Romeo had been with Rosalind) that "that name's woe"; in Act 2, scene 4, Romeo and a bawdy nurse josh about the powers of names, alluding to the dog's growl contained in the first letter of the name "Romeo"; we know that Romeo's love for Juliet will be abiding when in Act 3, scene 1, Romeo identifies his feelings towards the formerly hated name with his own—"And so, good Capulet—which name I tender/ As dearly as mine own"—thereby magically bringing Juliet and himself together in blissful union; in Act 3, scene 2, Juliet responds magically to the charm of Romeo's name: "But Romeo's name speaks heavenly eloquence"; immediately thereafter, she magically identifies harm to Romeo with mangling his name: "what tongue shall smooth thy name/ When I, thy three-hours wife, have mangled it?"; in Romeo's paired scene, Act 3, scene 3, Romeo speaks of the magic, lethal power of names: "As if that name,/ Shot from the deadly level of a gun,/ Did murder her; as that name's cursèd hand/ Murdered her kinsman"; he then asks where a name's physical power lies: "O, tell me, Friar, tell me,/ In what vile part of this anatomy/ Doth my name lodge? Tell me, that I may sack/ The hateful mansion."

There are illocutionary uses of names: in Act 2, scene 1, Mercutio conjures "in his mistress' name"; in Act 3, scene 1, a citizen orders Benvolio: "Up, sir, go with me./ I charge thee in the Prince's name, obey."

The motif of the ornament in the work also relates to the idea of names (the word "ornament" even contains the word "name"); and that relationship raises the issue of whether one's name (or a name) is an essential part of one's being, or simply an ornament.

I think it should be evident to all that Stein's use of allusion here is simply brilliant. And yet the remark seems so very simple!

351 Though overcoming all that a word brings with it is the role of irony, the agent of *poesis*.

352 This indicates another reason why Brakhage has found Stein's writing so interesting, and why Stein has had a major influence on Brakhage's work. In "And Now," a piece published in *Vanity Fair* in September 1934, Stein explained that a crisis over her sense of identity had put her to work on an autobiographical project (the work was to appear under the title *Everybody's Autobiography*): "now everything that is happening is once more happening inside, there is no use in the outside, if you see the outside you see just what you look at and that is no longer interesting, everybody says so or at least everybody acts so and they are right because now there is no use in looking at anything." Brakhage could well agree with the point Stein propounds here. That

Brakhage's visual form related to contents of his mind is well known—and sometimes their subjective quality is so extreme that his mode of vision seems to border on solipsism. For whatever unlikely reason, this is one of his oeuvre's most frequently criticized features. However, attacks on the hyperbolized subjectivity of advanced works of cinematic art are hardly new: Maya Deren offered the first such attack I know of in the written history of avant-garde cinema, in "Cinematography: The Creative Use of Reality" (though she probably directed her attack towards Sidney Peterson and not Brakhage).

> While the [photographic] process permits some intrusion by the artist as a modifier of that image, the limits of its tolerance can be defined as that point at which the original reality becomes unrecognizable or is irrelevant (as when a red reflection in a pond is used for its shape and color only and without contextual concern for the water or the pond).
>
> In such cases the camera itself has been conceived of as the artist, with distorting lenses, multiple superimpositions, etc., used to simulate the creative actions of the eye, the memory, etc. Such well-intentioned efforts to use the medium creatively, by forcibly inserting the creative act into the position it traditionally occupies in the visual arts, accomplish, instead, the destruction of the photographic image as reality. (In P. Adams Sitney, ed., *The Avant-Garde Film: A Reader of Theory and Criticism* [New York: New York University Press, 1978], p. 68)

Whomever the intended target of her attack may be, Deren knew well where her real quarrel with Brakhage's work lay. Brakhage's adherence to the Romantic tradition involves a commitment to the idea that what happens on "the inside" is all of a piece with what occurs on "the outside"; furthermore, Brakhage's transformations of the image have the end of revealing the operations of the imagination. It is the effect that the concrete particular has on consciousness, or, more accurately, the role that consciousness plays in bringing the concrete particular into existence, that is the focus of Brakhage's interests (this is an aspect of what I refer to when I mention the phenomenological cast of his word). Deren believed to the contrary that cinematography, as a photographically based medium, has a strong commitment to unmanipulated reality and that any distortion of reality through "optical" or photographic "tricks" is inconsistent with the nature of the medium; basically, she argues that the still or movie camera has a disposition towards "the outside"—towards, even, presenting "the outside" accurately. Brakhage's Romanticism has led him to conclude that if that disposition of the camera cannot be overcome, the camera is worthless as an artistic instrument. For, as Stein put it, "now everything that is happening is once more happening inside, there is no use in the outside, if you see the outside you see just what you look at and that is no longer interesting." (For her part, Deren argued that even though this disposition of the camera renders cinematography essentially uncreative, nonetheless this proclivity must be respected. If the cinema has any creative potential, it must lie in some aspect other than cinematography. Deren identified this aspect as its temporal character claiming, essentially that film as a creative art is an art of time, not space.)

353 For the past decade and a half, the Stein scholar Ulla E. Dydo has been doing work in Yale University's Stein archive on the two phases in the creation of many (not all) of Stein's works: one took place in what Dydo refers to as *carnets* (because *carnets* are little pocket notepads), the other in what Dydo calls *cahiers* (because *cahiers* are the more formal notebooks, of the sort that students keep their class notes in). The *carnets* include all sorts of incidental materials—grocery lists, addresses, guest lists, and the like—as well as jottings that, we might presume, Stein recorded as they came to her (or as she worked them out in her head); the *carnets*, then, incorporate intimacies of daily living. The *cahiers* contain the texts that Stein was working on. Sometimes Stein composed directly in the *cahiers*, but at other times she copied out material that

had originally appeared in a *carnet*, sometimes revising it in the process. Dydo's painstaking analysis of the relations between the material in the *carnets* and the texts in the *cahiers* illuminates the role of "dailiness" in Stein's work. Her forthcoming book on Stein, *The Language that Rises*, promises to transform Stein scholarship. An inkling of contents can be gleaned from her introduction and headnotes for the splendid Stein anthology she edited, *A Stein Reader*, and from her many articles.

354 Gertrude Stein, "Portrait of Mabel Dodge at the Villa Curonia," in *A Primer for the Gradual Understanding of Gertrude Stein*, edited by Robert Bartlett Haas (Los Angeles: Black Sparrow Press, 1974), pp. 59-60.

355 Gertrude Stein, "Guillaume Apollinaire," in *A Stein Reader*, edited and with an Introduction by Ulla E. Dydo (Evanston, IL: Northwestern University Press, 1993), p. 279.

356 Harriet Scott Chessman, *The Public Is Invited to Dance: Representation, the Body, and Dialogue in Gertrude Stein* (Stanford: Stanford University Press, 1989), p. 162.

357 Gertrude Stein, "Saving the Sentence," in *How to Write*, with a New Preface and Introduction by Patricia Meyerowitz (New York: Dover Publications, 1975), p. 19. *How to Write* contains a motherlode of examples of anacoluthon.

358 Gertrude Stein, *Four in America* (New Haven: Yale University Press, 1947). I have taken the quotation from Ulla E. Dydo, "Gertrude Stein: Composition as Meditation," in Shirley Neuman and Ira B. Nadel, eds., *Gertrude Stein and the Making of Literature* (Boston: Northeastern University Press, 1988), p. 44.

359 Joseph Jacobs, "Lawkamercyme," in *More English Fairy Tales* (New York: Putnam, 1969; originally published in 1894), pp. 65-66; quoted in Chessman, *The Public Is Invited to Dance: Representation, the Body, and Dialogue in Gertrude Stein*, p. 162.

360 Of course, Stein uses repetition in her writings to the exact same end.

361 Quoted in Peter Nicholls, "Difference Spreading: From Gertrude Stein to L=A=N=G=U=A=G=E Poetry," in Anthony Easthope and John O. Thompson, eds., *Contemporary Poetry Meets Modern Theory* (Toronto: University of Toronto Press, 1991), p. 118 (emphasis in original).

362 Stein, *Lectures in America*, pp. 74-75.

363 Ibid., pp. 76-77.

364 The parallels between Snow's ideas and Stein's are telling: in fact, I think that the relation between Pound and Stein is isomorphic to that between Brakhage and Snow.

One fact that presents some troubles for this claim is that Brakhage's conception of meaning is so close to Stein's (this indeed is one of the principal facts I have set out to establish). That trouble can be easily enough accommodated by pointing out, as Demetres P. Tryphonopoulos does in *The Celestial Tradition: A Study of Ezra Pound's* The Cantos (Waterloo: Wilfrid Laurier University Press, 1992), that the *Cantos* do not so much describe an initiation rite as re-enact one for the reader. This idea was put forward too by the poet Robert Duncan (who was raised by parents who believed in the principles of the unorthodox tradition): Michael McClure recounts (in *Lighting the Corners on Nature, Art, and the Visionary: Essays and Interviews* [Albuquerque: University of New Mexico, College of Arts and Sciences, 1993], p. 122) that Duncan believed the *Cantos* "were something like a seance. He believed that Pound was calling up voices from the spirit box." Duncan, we may take it, believed that the *Cantos* were a theurgical effort, and theurgy, of course, depends on a sense of meaning as action— "zaza zaza" means something because it does something, either in the spirit world or to the consciousness of those who utter, or hear, the sound. Its significance resides in its potential for effect. This suggests the intrinsic relation between theurgical conceptions (which, if Leon Surrette's *The Birth of the Modern* is correct, lie at the origin of modernism in the arts) and a perlocutionary theory of meaning—that, indeed, the perlocutionary theory of meaning lay at the heart of the modernists' revision of poesis of artmaking in general.

Another fact that presents some troubles for the claim that the relation between Pound and Stein is isomorphic to that between Brakhage and Snow is that Pound's

Cantos strives towards an all-consuming unity in which everything is joined together in a single, effulgent light. Brakhage is much closer to Stein in his desire to preserve the distinctiveness of each concrete particular.

365 No doubt moved to do so, partly, by his interests in Stein's writing and what Stein's writing derived from the Cubists, partly through his own interest in the Cubists' work, and especially that of Georges Braque; but a major motivation for Brakhage's use of demotic objects has been the great work of Marie Menken.

366 This very Messiaenic handling of rhythm structure is due partly to the influence that Pierre Boulez, a former student of Olivier Messiaen, had on this particular film and, more generally, on Brakhage's ideas about rhythm and structure during the period when he made *Unconscious London Strata* (shot 1979, completed 1981), *Creation* (1979), and *Made Manifest* (1980). Though Brakhage is very devoted to Messiaen's music (he seems, in fact, more interested in Messiaen than in Boulez), the influence of Boulez's masterwork, *Le marteau sans maître*, is especially important in shaping Brakhage's ideas on rhythm during this phase of his career. Boulez's composition is a musical setting of several poems by the popular French Surrealist poet René Char. Boulez fragmented Char's poems and musically reassociated the fragments. The rhythms of *Le marteau sans maître* are as angular as the rhythms of *Unconscious London Strata*—both those works are based on Messiaen's ideas about rhythm, *Le marteau sans maître* directly and *Unconscious London Strata* both directly and, more especially, through *Le marteau sans maître*.

Whether Brakhage dug out a translation of the Char poems that Boulez had set I do not know, but it is (at least) a remarkable coincidence that at the centre of Boulez's composition is a poem, *"bel édifice"* which is just that sort of impression that Brakhage formed of Westminster Abbey, and that he conveys in *Unconscious London Strata*. Furthermore, the whole sense of the Char poem is, as the title suggests, of technological/material civilization gone out of control, oppressing the individual and forcing him or her to march onward towards the doom that will befall us all; Brakhage photographed Westminster Abbey (primarily, but other buildings as well) in a similar manner, to give a sense of a civilization dominated by horrifying forces of doom.

Further, *Le marteau sans maître* recreates the feelings of reading a poem and experiencing its echoes in the mind (exactly as Brakhage's 1994 film *First hymn to the Night Novalis* does), while *Unconscious London Strata* captures the way that the sight of an imposing, terrifying edifice reverberates through consciousness—or the way that memory wells up from beneath consciousness.

Aside from the general affinities between Boulez's *Le marteau sans maître* and *Unconscious London Strata*, and their emotional tone, are more exact resemblances in their use of rhythm and form. *Le marteau sans maître* derives its rhythmic intensity from fusing the use of imitation cells that had provided rhythmic intensity in Boulez's earlier pieces (e.g., *Livre pour quatuor*) and the serial principle which, with this very work, Boulez extended to the construction of a duration row and whose use as the primary determinant of the succession of durations characterized many of Boulez's succeeding compositions. In the *"bel édifice"* section of *Le marteau sans maître*, for example, Boulez uses a more insistently repetitive rhythmic structure, at first using units of 3 and 5, later in 7 and 9, than he does in most other parts of the work (except for the *"bourreaux de solitude"* and the *"l'artisinat furieux"* sections); this insistently repetitive rhythmic form is all the more striking because, for the most part, in *Le marteau sans maître* Boulez does not create a sense of a regular, periodic recurrence, but simply marks the passing of time by a reappearance that is unmarked by any insistence on a metrical pattern). Nonetheless, throughout most of the composition, the duration blocks seem very often on the verge of transmuting into something quite metrical. In this regard, the relation of the metrical character of the *"bel édifice,"* the *"bourreaux de solitude,"* and the *"l'artisinat furieux"* passages to other passages in *Le marteau sans maître* resembles the relation of the more "representational" passages of

Unconscious London Strata to its more "abstract" passages. The isomorphism can be summed up in the following way: Boulez's balancing metrical and non-metrical repetition is analogous to Brakhage's balancing of representation and abstraction. Furthermore, Brakhage insistently avoids metrical editing in *Unconscious London Strata*, and this resembles Boulez's use of non-metrical construction of duration and his use of irregular units of repetition ("irregular" in the sense of "asymmetrical," i.e., related by odd-number relations such as 3, 5, 7, and 9) and his use of rubato in the *"bel édifice"* section.

There are other similarities: at the opening of the "Commentary II on *bourreaux de solitude"* Boulez shatters the musical movements that seem to be developing through the impetus of motivic self-development, by his use of unprepared-for silences which abruptly halt the movement. Brakhage's handling of camera movement in most of *Unconsciousness London Strata* is equally halting and unpredictably staccato. Finally, as the use of an ensemble that includes xylophone, marimba, guitar, and viola (that is played pizzicato as often as it is bowed) gives *Le marteau sans maître* an edgy, percussive texture, so does Brakhage's handling of the camera in *Unconscious London Strata*.

Brakhage shot *Unconscious London Strata* in London in 1979, during the Third Avant-Garde Film Festival. I, too, had been invited to the event, and I happened to see Brakhage shooting—not the footage for *Unconscious London Strata*, but footage of the Thames seen from the patio of the South Bank Arts Centre. He used a Super-8 camera at the time; with the hand that held the camera, he rocked the camera back and forth, somewhat irregularly, and, with the other hand, tapped it, also at irregular intervals. My goal in life is to become a percussionist for a raks sharki ensemble (or a dance company of any sort), and I have squandered more time and effort in the pursuit of that pipe dream than I care to acknowledge. As a would-be percussionist I was very impressed with Brakhage's abilities to constantly vary the polyphonic rhythm. But I was also interested to watch this demonstration that gave such compelling evidence of the importance that, at the time, Brakhage laid on a percussive, but aperiodic, texture. The demonstration also gave me an idea of how Brakhage created a tempo in *Unconscious London Strata* that is as variable and fluctuating as the tempo of *Le marteau sans maître*.

There are also homologies among the "polyphonic" relations in the two works— among the relations between the different layers of visual forms in *Unconscious London Strata* and the relations between voice and instrumental music and *Le marteau sans maître*. Boulez's composition makes use of many different ways of emitting vocal sounds, while Brakhage makes use of a wide range of ways of forming images, from more naturalistic to more abstract. At the opening of *"bel édifice,"* the text is as much spoken as sung, while in the opening section, *"l'artisinat furieux,"* the text is treated very melismatically. There is only sometimes a voice part; and when there is one, it sometimes doubles the instrumental setting and sometimes seems almost independent of the setting. There is a similar range of relations between superimpositions (including those created through dissolves) in *Unconscious London Strata*.

367 Perhaps these impressions are only the result of my constitutional inabilities, for friends for whom I have the greatest admiration, who probably know more about Pound's writing than I do, and certainly know more about Stein's, disagree utterly with me.

368 I have introduced a qualifying phrase here because Pound is not entirely consistent on the matter. Sometimes he longs for light to unify all beings, and sometimes he wishes to accord concrete particulars their rightful place, by acknowledging that they are independent beings whose existence cannot be reduced to any others.

369 The text is from Gertrude Stein, *Tender Buttons*, the full text of which is reprinted in Gertrude Stein, *Look at Me Now and Here I Am: Writings and Lectures*, edited by Patricia Meyerowitz (Harmondsworth: Penguin Books, 1971), and in part in Gertrude Stein, *Selected Writings of Gertrude Stein*, edited with an Introduction and Notes by Carl Van Vechten and with an Essay by F.W. Dupee (New York: Vintage Books, 1972),

p. 461. It also appears, and is discussed, in Peter Nicholls, "Difference Spreading: From Gertrude Stein to L=A=N=G=U=A=G=E Poetry." My discussion of the single is informed by the fine reading of it Nicholls presents there. Nicholls does a nice job of making evident what is at stake in *Tender Buttons*, one of Stein's most difficult (and widely ridiculed) texts.

370 Though during the grand moment when high Analytical Cubism had fully consolidated itself (roughly 1910-12), the tension that gave life to Cubist canvases underwent a basic change: the elaboration of surface complexity; the adjustment of the geometric relations among the aspectual facets to articulate visual rhymes, rhythms, and, generally, patterns; and the reduction of the range of colours to a nearly common hue and value all lessened the representational tug on the work. The tension between form as image and form as object, so fruitful in traditional, representational art, was daringly set aside in favour of the tensions articulated by intrinsic relations. With the shift to Synthetic Cubism in 1912, the earlier sort of tension returned.

371 This does not describe all that is implied by Stein's characterizing the glass as "blind." P. Adams Sitney, in *Modernist Montage: The Obscurity of Vision in Cinema and Literature*, does a fine job of demonstrating that the theme of the "blank" in vision, or a blindness of some sort, is a motif in American modernist poetry and film.

372 Gertrude Stein, "How Writing Is Written," in *How Writing Is Written: Volume II of the Previously Uncollected Writings of Gertrude Stein*, edited by Robert Bartlett Haas (Los Angeles: Black Sparrow Press, 1974), p. 153.

373 T.S. Eliot, "The Epistemologist's Theory of Knowledge," in *Knowledge and Experience in the Philosophy of F.H. Bradley*, p. 134.

374 Stein, "How Writing Is Written," p. 155. The work of Stein's middle period rarely respects chronology—in fact not only do her writings of this time avoid presenting tales diachronically, but Stein uses every possible grammatical, lexical, and syntagmatic means to eliminate any sense of succession.

375 Brakhage's photographed films and those of his painted films that treat "moving visual thinking" have similar qualities.

376 Stein, "How Writing Is Written," pp. 152-53.

377 Ibid., p. 153.

378 Ibid., pp. 155-56.

379 Henri Bergson, "The Divergent Directions of the Evolution of Life—Torpor, Intelligence, Instinct: Life and Consciousness," in *Creative Evolution*, p. 194. Stein described her purpose in writing *Tender Buttons* as capturing "the rhythm of the visible world."

380 Statements of these ideas can be found throughout Bergson's oeuvre; I have based my summary of them on versions that appear in *Creative Evolution*, pp. 182, 34, and 194 (following the order in which my text propounds them).

381 Bergson, "The Organization of Conscious States—Free Will: Real Duration and Causality," in *Time and Free Will*, pp. 199-200.

382 Ralph Waldo Emerson, *The Collected Works of Ralph Waldo Emerson*, edited by Robert E. Spiller et al., 5 vols. (Cambridge, MA: Harvard University Press, 1971-), Vol. 1, p. 9

383 Bergson, "The Organization of Conscious States—Free Will: Psychological Determinism," in *Time and Free Will*, pp. 161-62. This text states some of the ideas that made Bergson so interesting to Marcel Proust and indicates why Bergson's philososphy exercised such a great influence on Proust's writing.

384 Brakhage, *Metaphors on Vision*, not paginated. This quotation appears on the first page of the main section of text.

385 At the outset, we discussed Schopenhauer's enthusiasm for Immanuel Kant's epistemology, and noted that Schopenhauer's enthusiasm had to do with Kant's having been the first in history to recognize the active role that the mind plays in forming what we see. Emerson too stresses the mind's active role (this is just further evidence of the influence Kant had on Romanticism) though, to be sure, Kant used the term "percep-

tion" to refer to the mind's apprehension of objects, while Emerson is deeply distrustful of that term's connotations of passivity. (On that, see Ralph Waldo Emerson, *Natural History of the Intellect*, in *The Complete Works of Ralph Waldo Emerson*, edited by Edward W. Emerson, 14 vols. (Boston: Houghton Mifflin, 1903-1904), Vol. 12, p. 44. The *Natural History of the Intellect* is the principal source for the ideas I set out in this section of the text.

386 This is exactly why, in Section IV of *The Phenomenology of Spirit*, Hegel goes to great lengths to critique the stage of self-certainty, which is a phase of the odyssey of consciousness when self-consciousness is simply immediate being-for-itself, self-identity to the exclusion of every other.

387 Brakhage's celebration of the imagination is sometimes so extreme that he overestimates its role in constructing the objects in the manifold of vision, and underestimates the importance of objective givenness at least of the raw material of sensation (arguing that all synaptic stimulation—which, as we have noted, he idealizes in the fashion of Schopenhauer—is on an equal footing, just as earlier, at the time of writing the opening section of *Metaphors on Vision*, he argued for establishing hallucination and perception on the same footing).

388 Stein, "Portrait of Mabel Dodge at the Villa Curonia," pp. 59-60.

389 Examples of films that risk using a surfeit of diversity are: *Visions in Meditation #1* (1989), *Visions in Meditation #4: D.H. Lawrence* (1990), or, paradigmatically, the *Prelude* of *Dog Star Man* (1961). Examples of films that risk slackening tension through excessive repetition are: *Sirius Remembered* (1959), *Made Manifest* (1980), or *A Child's Garden and the Serious Sea* (1991).

390 Perhaps the best example would be the "My Mountain" section of *Song 27*.

391 One of Brakhage's films challenges this idea of mind as creating the world anew, with every passing moment, in a triumphant act of the imagination. That work is *I . . . Dreaming*. Brakhage made *I . . . Dreaming* in collaboration with composer Joel Haertling, who created an evocative collage of fragments of popular songs, mostly by Stephen Foster. The film purports to give us scenes from a long night, in which the filmmaker, alone and troubled, ponders his situation. Brakhage presents himself in this film, not as the heroic artist that the Romantics (including the New England Transcendentalists) celebrated, but as a man of limited means, alone, contemplating the emptiness of it all. We see the room where Brakhage lives, the landscape out the window, two children touching one another (the children, significantly, seem remarkably aloof from the filmmaker), Brakhage sitting and fretting, Brakhage getting into bed alone, and Brakhage awaking with a start, seemingly in terror. We have a sense of a terrible absence, perhaps conditioned by a loss of love.

During the film, Brakhage scratches words, most of which seem to be associations with the lyrics on the soundtrack, into the film's emulsion. The words are inscribed at various places on the emulsion, and at various angles. Some of these words suggest the filmmaker's longing, and his regret for bygone times. And, at other times, they have a more radical effect: they suggest that what we see on screen is an illustration of a feeling the filmmaker wants to convey. The suggestion is telling, for the film's imagery, though skillfully constructed to evoke a sense of loneliness and alienation, does not so triumphantly reformulate reality as most of Brakhage's other photographed films do—the images in this film do not so forcefully convey that the imagination co-operates with the senses in bringing forth the world the film presents.

A signal moment in the film occurs when Brakhage gives us a landscape, and scratches the word "void" over it. The landscape had figured in several of Brakhage's films (paradigmatically *The Machine of Eden*, which situates the family within a glowing, stunningly beautiful mountain landscape, *Star Garden*, which depicts mostly the interior of Brakhage's mountain home, but also its environment, in radiant detail, and *Creation*, which depicts the seacoast of Alaska and the Canadian Northwest as an awesome sublime) as a redemptive agency: establishing a salutary relation with nature erases the corrupting effects of civilization and history, and brings one into contact with what is immediate and what is local. This moment uses the image of nature differently; Brakhage is isolated from the landscape, it remains something beyond him, outside the window. Nature seems diminished, and so does he. Moreover, while the landscape conveys a sombre mood, it is not reformulated by the imagination—like much of the rest of the film it looks rather more like a product of what Emerson calls "perception" than of what he calls "imagination." Finally, there is shocking dissonance between the sombre landscape and the word scratched over it: "void." There can be no image of the void—in fact no way whatsoever to convey the fear one feels as the void opens up before one. In fact, there can be no way of conveying any deep feelings about the void, for the feeling has no intentional object. The void which opens up before the filmmaker only reflects the emptiness of film, and, perhaps, of all art. There is a terrible feeling of confusion and impotency here, the thoughts and feelings a child might have when trying to understand the vicissitudes of emotional life, and the terrible losses and terrible wounds life brings with it (it is surely significant that words are carved into the film's flesh). The landscape seems so alien, rather as it might to a child. And the dominant feeling of the film is of a confused child waiting for who knows what.

This despondent conclusion hints at Brakhage's doubts (one hopes *momentary* doubts) about the capacity of the imagination to reshape what raw material the senses give into a form that is adequate to human needs.

392 Stein, "Composition as Explanation," pp. 502-503.
393 Robert Duncan, "The Rites of Participation," in *H.D. Book*, Part 1, chap. 6; quoted in Fredman, *The Grounding of American Poetry*, p. 25.
394 Gertrude Stein, "Stanza XV" from *Stanzas in Meditation*, in *The Yale Gertrude Stein*, selections with an Introduction by Richard Kostelanetz (New Haven: Yale University Press, 1980), pp. 366-67. Selections from *Stanzas in Meditation*, including "Stanza XV," also appear in the Dydo anthology, *A Stein Reader*, pp. 569-87. Dydo's version, though incomplete, gives Stein's unredacted version. Dydo traced the troubled history of *Stanzas in Meditation*, and discovered a quarrel between Alice B. Toklas and Stein (over the presence in *Stanzas in Meditation* and other works of references to May—Mabel Haynes, who had been involved in a lesbian triangle between Stein and Toklas). The quarrel led Stein to purge all allusions to "May" from the work. The Kostelanetz edition prints the redacted version, the Dydo the unredacted. (Dydo outlines the history in her headnotes to the text of *A Stein Reader*, p. 568.)
395 I analyzed at some length the paradoxes associated with artistic constructions that evoke a sense of being disembodied phenomena, even while their purpose is to engender somatic effects, in *A Body of Vision*.
396 Gertrude Stein, *A Long Gay Book* (see Dygo anthology, p. 242), quoted in *A Primer for the Gradual Understanding of Gertrude Stein*, edited by Robert Bartlett Haas (Los Angeles: Black Sparrow Press, 1974), p. 149.
397 Donald Sutherland, "Gertrude Stein and the Twentieth Century," in ibid., p. 149.
398 Gertrude Stein and Robert Bartlett Haas, "A Transatlantic Interview" (1946), a portion of Gertrude Stein and Robert Bartlett Haas, "Gertrude Stein Talking—A Transatlantic Interview," *The UCLAN Review* (Summer 1962 and Spring 1963). The interview is reprinted in part in Gertrude Stein, *A Primer for the Gradual Understanding of Gertrude Stein*, edited by Robert Bartlett Haas (Los Angeles: Black Sparrow Press, 1974), p. 15.
399 Ibid., p. 18.
400 Stéphane Mallarmé, *Mallarmé*, edited and translated with an Introduction by Anthony Hartley (Baltimore, MD: Penguin Books, 1965), p. 171.
401 Stein, *Tender Buttons*, in *Selected Writings of Gertrude Stein*, p. 479.
402 In an essay on Melville, "Equal, That Is, to the Real Itself," Olson writes, "As the Master said to me in the dream, of rhythm is image/ of image is knowing/ of knowing there is/ a construct" (in *Selected Writings of Charles Olson*, edited with an Introduction

by Robert Creeley [New York: New Directions, 1966], p. 50). From that point, he goes on to offer several Whiteheadian assertions: "Melville couldn't abuse object as symbol does by depreciating it in favor of subject. Or let image lose its relational force by transferring its occurence as allegory does. It was already aware of the complementarity of each of two pairs of how we know and present the real—image & object, and action & subject—both of which have paid off so decisively since. At this end I am thinking of such recent American painting as Pollock's and Kline's" (ibid., pp. 50-51). "Equal, That Is, to the Real Itself" is Olson's most Whiteheadian composition.

403 Stan Brakhage, "TIME ... on dit," *Musicworks: The Canadian Journal of Sound Exploration* 48 (Autumn 1990): 38 (emphasis in original).

404 Ibid.

405 Stein, *Lectures in America*, p. 236.

406 As regards Stein, I offer this proposition only tentatively. This much is certain, though: Stein gives the woman's body an important place in her writing, as "Susie Asado" and "Lifting Belly" evidence, and the place she accords them relates to the immediate manner in which infants perceive their mothers' bodies. Take, for example, a line in the latter (that reads almost as a concrete): "All belly belly well" ("Lifting Belly," in *The Yale Gertrude Stein*, selections with an Introduction by Richard Kostelanetz [New Haven: Yale University Press, 1980], p. 4). The lilting *l*s in that line give it a flowing movement, and the alternations of *l*s and *b*s make it resemble a fragment of infant babbling. (The very word we use to refer to an infant's vocalizations, through onomatopoeia, contains similar sounds), a quality strenghtened by the repeated short *e*, followed by an *a*.

Yet these qualities of infant vocalizations pertain to the infant's intimacy with a woman's body. This intimacy is embodied in the little "poem" I just quoted, which conjoins one "belly" with another, and surrounds that repetition with the sound "Ah" (from the initial "all" and the terminal "well"), to convey delight. There could be no more immediate, concrete way of conveying the pleasure of juxtaposing bodies/bellies.

407 Brakhage, "TIME ... on dit," p. 38.

408 Ibid.

409 Ibid.

410 Ibid.

411 Brakhage, *Metaphors on Vision*, not paginated. This quotation appears on the first page of the main section of text.

412 Dydo, "Gertrude Stein: Composition as Meditation," p. 43.

413 Stein, *Four in America.* I have taken the quotation from Dydo, "Gertrude Stein: Composition as Meditation," p. 44.

414 Quoted in Charles Caramello, "Gertrude Stein as Exemplary Theorist," in Shirley Neuman and Ira B. Nadel, eds., *Gertrude Stein and the Making of Literature* (Boston: Northeastern University Press, 1988), p. 4.

415 Ibid.

416 Stein, *How to Write*, p. 32. My discussion of the passage is influenced by Dydo's commentary on the work in *A Stein Reader* (pp. 48-49).

417 Perhaps one reason why Stein's work presents its maker in this way is that Stein might have accepted William James's idea that consciousness lacks depth, that it is all surface (what you see/feel/think is what there is). I believe that this Jamesian idea had a momentous role in establishing Stein's approach to writing.

418 Brakhage acknowledged the phenomenological quality of his work when he screened *Visions in Meditation #3* and *#4* at the Art Gallery of Ontario in March 1991.

419 James, *The Principles of Psychology*, Vol. 1, pp. 300-301; quoted in James M. Edie, *William James and Phenomenology* (Bloomington and Indianapolis, IN: Indiana University Press, 1987), pp. 38-39 (emphasis in original).

420 Gertrude Stein's *Stanzas in Meditation* have very much the same character, which may explain what draws Brakhage especially to that formidably difficult work. Ulla E.

Dydo's very fine headnotes to the excerpts from *Stanzas in Meditation* in her anthology, *A Stein Reader* (pp. 568-69), suggests that the work focuses on mental landscapes that do not cohere, and speaks of the tension that the work evokes; she also quotes Stein to suggest that the work is meant to convey "an exactitude of abstract thought." The struggle to make the fragments cohere is indeed the primary impression that *Stanzas in Meditation* makes, and I believe it is from feeling the energies of the relationships amongst the work's motifs, rhythms, and aural patterns that the work's form becomes clear. In other words, Stein's freeing language from nominal meaning makes the proprioceptive body responsible for apprehending meaning.

This is Stein's great lesson to Brakhage, I believe.

421 Dydo, "Gertrude Stein: Composition as Meditation," pp. 54-55.

422 Gertrude Stein, "After the War—1919-1932," in *The Autobiography of Alice B. Toklas* (New York: Vintage Books, 1961), pp. 224-24.

423 Brakhage, *Metaphors on Vision*, not paginated. This quotation appears on the first page of the main body of text.

424 Stein, *How to Write*, p. 73.

425 Gertrude Stein, *Selected Writings of Gertrude Stein*, edited with an Introduction and Notes by Carl Van Vechten and with an Essay by F.W. Dupee (New York: Vintage Books, 1972), p. 481.

426 Both quotations are taken from Edie, *William James and Phenomenology*, p. 70.

427 James, *The Principles of Psychology*, Vol. 1, pp. 341-42.

428 Stein, *Selected Writings of Gertrude Stein*, p. 500.

429 This is the basis for the (subjective) idealism toward which Brakhage's work seems so often to veer (an implication of Sitney's comments on the Emersonian tradition in *Modernist Montage* is that the writers whose works belong to that tradition, and Brakhage, actually adopt [subjective] idealism totally); I believe to the contrary (and one of the principal points I have wished to establish in this book is that what brings it back to its more complex ontology is the radical empiricism that is its real basis).

430 Cassius Longinus (the Pseudo-Longinus), *On the Sublime*, XXXIX, translated by W. Hamilton Fyfe (New York: G.P. Putnam's Sons, 1927), p. 235 (emphasis in original).

431 William Wordsworth, "On the Power of Sound," in *Poetical Works*, new ed. revised by Ernest de Selincourt (London: Oxford University Press, 1967), p. 185, lines 3-13.

432 William Wordsworth, *The Prelude, Book XIV*, in ibid., p. 584, lines 59-62.

433 William Blake, *The Complete Writings of William Blake*, edited by Geoffrey Keynes (London: Oxford University Press, 1966), p. 216.

434 Schopenhauer, *The World as Will and Representation*, Vol. 1, p. 264.

435 W.H. Auden, "The Composer," in *W.H. Auden: Collected Poems*, edited by Edward Mendelson (New York: Random House, 1976), p. 148.

436 But others have too. In "Craft Interview," with the *New York Quarterly*, one of the finest interviews he has given, poet Gary Snyder talks about his use of "open form" method (in which, he acknowledges, he was influenced by Olson): "The first step is the rhythmic measure, the second step is a set of preverbal visual images which move to the rhythmic measure, and the third step is embodying it in words." He then goes on to discuss how he works out the verbal construction. Thus Snyder presents the same sequence as Olson had: rhythm, image, knowing (word), construct (Gary Snyder, "Craft Interview" (1973), in Gary Snyder, *The Real Work: Interviews & Talks 1964-1979*, edited with an Introduction by Wm. Scott McLean [New York: New Directions, 1980], p. 32).

437 I have commented on this Latin phrase, and the vexing questions concerning its provenance, in an earlier footnote. The site on which filmmakers' interests converge with those of the proponents of light metaphysics are more sharply marked out in Robert Grosseteste's writings on optics.

438 This is somewhat loosely stated, for in fact, there is no distinction, either, between primordial sensation and primordial reality; primordial awareness knows no difference

between subject and object—there is simply a "knowing," and all "knowings" have an inherent subject.

439 The Mexican philosopher José Vasconcelos (1882-1959) expounded a metaphysical theory, which he termed aesthetic monism, that develops these views (many of Vasconcelos's ideas anticipate those of Deleuze). The key term of this theory was energy. His theory lays stress on the particular, heterogeneous elements that compose reality and, above all, their fluent conditions. In its promordial condition, energy is unformed, Vasconcelos proposed; but it takes on organic order. Intuition, developed in part through aesthetic experience, is the cognitive means we use to apprehend the forms into which energy organizes itself.

Vasconcelos's work represents a gigantic development of some of the topics central to the present book. The relationships between Vasconcelos's work and that of thinkers whose ideas are central to the present work should be developed; but, surely, I have already taxed the reader's patience sufficiently that it would be foolhardy to take on this topic as well. Perhaps someday I will have the opportunity to expound these relationships; in the meantime, Vasconcelos's work can be consulted: *Pitágoras: Un teoría de ritmo* (1916), *El monismo estético* (1918), and *Estética* (1936) are the key works.

440 Gilles Deleuze, *Expressionism in Philosophy: Spinoza*, translated by Martin Joughin (New York: Zone Books, 1990), p. 95. Originally published as *Spinoza et le problème de l'expression* (Paris: Éditions de Minuit, 1968).

441 Gilles Deleuze, *Spinoza: Practical Philosophy*, translated by Robert Hurley (San Francisco: City Light Books, 1988), p. 97. Originally published in French as *Spinoza: philosophie pratique* (Paris: Presses Universitaires de France, 1970).

442 Thus he stakes the claim that his works have an affinity with Kantian ideas, for they reveal the constitutive role of the subject/imagination.

443 Henry David Thoreau, *Walden and Civil Disobedience*, edited by Owen Thomas (New York: W.W. Norton, 1966), p. 1.

444 I do not wish to imply that Brakhage was directly influenced by Bergson. Whatever influence there was (and it was certainly very small, if it was evident at all), must have been indirect. As *Metaphors on Vision* makes clear, Brakhage was an avid reader of Charles Olson—and, I think, a sufficiently intelligent and perspicacious reader to have worked out for himself the basic features of the metaphysic implicit (actually, in many passages aspects of that metaphysic become explicit) in Olson's writings. Olson was an avid reader of Alfred North Whitehead, and Whitehead in turn took great interest in Bergson's philosophy, and, despite Bergson's anti-science leanings, praised his work quite highly at a time when it had already gone out of fashion.

445 These rhythms do not exactly resemble the energies of vision (or of imaginative life generally), for they belong to a different order of reality. Nonetheless what they resemble cannot be pictured, so this resemblance is as exact as resemblance can be.

446 Brakhage's thinking about art, and artmaking, is similarly conflicted, for sometimes (perhaps under the influence of William Carlos Williams, Ezra Pound, and Gertrude Stein), Brakhage adopts ideas close to those of the early modernists, that extol aesthetic unity over the flux of particulars, that celebrate the transformative powers of *poesis*/the imagination to rework every element that work incorporates, so as to integrate it perfectly into an ideal form; and sometimes (perhaps under the influence of Charles Olson) Brakhage speaks as though conveying the flux of the concretely actual has greatest value. As the ratio in his oeuvre of painted films to photographed films has increased, so, it seems, has Brakhage's acceptance of the earlier view.

447 I must insist, however, that the assertion does not contradict the claim that the irrational response the paratactical method elicits might have affiliations with the reactionary views Pound expounded on politics. Any conscionable thinker must admit that it is impossible to let Pound off the hook by saying: "What he says is dreadful, but how he says it is beautiful"; the method of the *Cantos* and their content are integral. But I think it is also important to see just where exactly the political mischief gets in—and I

would say it gets in exactly where Olson implies it does: in the tendency towards total-izing (a tendency that, I caution, has rationalist as well as irrationalist versions).

448 The criticism that Brakhage's writings on other filmmakers are really writings about himself and his encounters with master artists and that they present simply his fan-tasies about their works is somewhat unfair. For one thing, Brakhage is meticulous about checking his facts. When he chronicles a career or describes a work made by a living artist, he usually checks his report with the filmmaker. (I know this as Brakhage has written about my work and taken pains to check his descriptions with me.) When he writes about the career or works of a filmmaker who is no longer alive, Brakhage scrupulously checks his impressions with source materials. Admittedly, Brakhage does invent fictions of history, but when he does so, he is careful to note that he is engaging in speculation or deliberate (and self-aware) confabulation.

Nonetheless, there is an idiosyncratic quality to his writings on other artists, as one might expect of an artist who insists on the importance of personal encounter and on the unique character of each individual's experience; and this is the quality of his his-torical writings that, likely, these critics intend. As a critic much influenced by Harold Bloom, Sitney tends to see Brakhage's encounters with his colleagues as exemplifying Harold Bloom's theories of misreading. He might have achieved a different and, I believe, more profound insight into the significance of Brakhage's writings on film his-tory by taking into account another aspect of Bloom's writing on American poetry, viz., its Emersonian character. Had he made Bloom's claims about the Emersonian charac-ter more central to the project, he might have considered that marvellous line of William Carlos Williams that is so germane to Brakhage's writings on film history: "That of the dead which exists in our imaginations has as much fact as have we our-selves. The premise that serves to fix us fixes also that part of them which we remem-ber" ("The Virtue of History," in *In the American Grain: Essays by William Carlos Williams*, with an Introduction by Horace Gregory [New York: New Directions, 1956; originally published in 1925], p. 189).

Then again, it would hardly be surprising for one who, like Brakhage, accepts Olson's etymology (Olson cites this etymology, among other places, in *The Maximus Poems*, p. 104) for historian (*historein*) as one who investigates and discovers for one-self to want to write history as one sees—and to write personally.

449 Robert Duncan, "Changing Perspectives in Reading Whitman," in Edwin Haviland Miller, ed., *The Artistic Legacy of Walt Whitman* (New York: New York University Press, 1970), p. 100.

450 D.H. Lawrence, "Introduction to 'New Poems'" (1918), in *Selected Literary Criticism*, edited by Anthony Beal (New York: Viking Press, 1966), p. 87.

451 D.H. Lawrence, *Apocalypse and the Writings on Revelation*, edited by Mara Kalnins (Cambridge: Cambridge University Press, 1980), p. 93.

452 Lawrence, "Introduction to 'New Poems,'" p. 86.

453 D.H. Lawrence, "Poetry of the Present" (Introduction to the American Edition of *New Poems* [1918]), in *The Complete Poems of D.H. Lawrence*, collected and edited with an Introduction and Notes by Vivian de Sola Pinto and Warren Roberts (New York: Viking Press, 1964), p. 183.

454 Lawrence, *Apocalypse and the Writings on Revelation*, p. 95.

455 Ibid. p. 96.

456 This quotation and the previous one are from Kenneth Rexroth, "Introduction," in D.H. Lawrence, *Selected Poems*, selected and with an Introduction by Kenneth Rexroth (New York: Viking Press, 1959), p. 2.

457 Ibid., p. 11.

458 Ibid., p. 17.

459 A significant exception is John W. Longo, *Whitehead's Ontology* (Albany: State Univer-sity of New York Press, 1972). This book is, despite its brevity, the most astute and penetrating commentary on Whitehead's metaphysic with which I am acquainted.

Another exception, and a fine introduction to Whitehead for those who find *Process and Reality* tough slogging, is W. Mays, *The Philosophy of Whitehead* (New York: Collier Books, 1962).

460 Though, as we shall see, Whitehead attempted to reconcile permanence with change (actually, to show that flux needs eternity to complete it, and eternity needs flux to complete it) and to show that, while reality is flux, it nevertheless has an unchanging (though ideal) aspect. Nonetheless, what he called "actual entities" or "actual events" are fleeting, and their transitory character is an essential aspect of their being.

461 The warrant for asserting the equivalence—or, actually, the near co-extensiveness—of the two terms is Alfred North Whitehead, *Process and Reality: An Essay in Cosmology* (New York: Macmillan, 1929), p. 27. There were many errors in the original publication of *Process and Reality*. Some say that Whitehead was remarkably indifferent to the tasks of book publication, though I am of the opinion that the explanation for Whitehead's many slips is simply that it is difficult—far more difficult than people are wont to acknowledge—to think and write at the same time, for thinking abstractly involves a free-floating feeling of the interrelations among diverse elements, while writing demands an extremely focused form of attention (and I know few thinkers who can resist the temptation to rethink a problem as they revise what they have said about it). But for whatever reason, the original publication of *Process and Reality* does contain hundreds of typographical errors, missing phrases, and incorrect references. A corrected edition was produced by David Ray Griffin and Donald W. Sherburne as: Alfred North Whitehead, *Process and Reality: An Essay in Cosmology. Corrected Edition*, edited by David Ray Griffin and Donald W. Sherburne (New York: The Free Press, 1978). Griffin and Sherburne's edition is meticulously produced, and there is little in it one can reasonably quibble with; nevertheless, because they took an interventionist approach, hereafter, in citing from *Process and Reality*, I give the page number both to the version Whitehead produced and to Griffin and Sherburne's edition. In this case, the reference in Griffin and Sherburne's edition is to p. 18.

462 Whitehead, *Process and Reality*, p. 227; Griffin and Sherburne edition, p. 150. The idea of applying that statement to a poem must have appealed to Olson.

463 A principle that, as we shall see, Charles Olson found very intriguing as a proposition about a poem.

464 This was a theme of Bergson's philosophy as well. Bergson wrote, *"There are changes, but there are underneath the change no things which change: change has no need of a support. There are movements, but there is no inert or invariable object which moves: movement does not imply a mobile"* ("The Perception of Change," in *The Creative Mind*, p. 147 [emphasis in original]).

465 Whitehead, *Process and Reality*, p. 28; Griffin and Sherburne edition, p. 18.

466 Ibid., pp. 27-28; Griffin and Sherburne edition, p. 18.

467 Alfred North Whitehead, *Science and the Modern World* (New York: The Free Press, 1967; originally published in 1925), p. 152.

468 Ibid., pp. 50-51. Whitehead also scrupulously pointed out that he did not agree with Bergson that representing reality as simply located instantaneous configurations of matter is the inevitable work of the intellect (probably because he arrived at his organicist metaphysics in a thoroughly intellectual manner, by considering the ontological implications of the theory of relations).

469 Whitehead, *Process and Reality*, p. 269; Griffin and Sherburne edition, p. 177.

470 Ibid., p. 71; Griffin and Sherburne edition, p. 45.

471 Ibid., p. 43; Griffin and Sherburne edition, p. 29.

472 Ibid., p. 134; Griffin and Sherburne edition, p. 87.

473 The idea that whatever occurs immediately moves on to qualify a transcendent creativity would have attracted Olson and the other Open Form poets.

474 Olson did not become acquainted with Merleau-Ponty's work until late in his life but, when he discovered it, he was very excited, as Merleau-Ponty gave philosophical for-

Notes to pages 317-21

mulation to many of the ideas he had been working out. Olson's enthusiastic discovery of Merleau-Ponty is recorded in "Under the Mushroom: The Gratwick Highlands Tape," in *Muthologos: The Collected Lectures & Interviews*, edited by George F. Butterick (Bolinas, CA: Four Seasons Foundation, 1978), Vol. 1, pp. 57-58. Brakhage has worked on Merleau-Ponty's writings, especially *The Phenomenology of Perception*, with the assistance of Forrest Williams, a colleague at the University of Colorado.

475 An irony enfolds Merleau-Ponty's interest in gestalt psychology, for the gestalt psychologists were the intellectual heirs of the neo-Kantian philosophers/psychologists.

476 Maurice Merleau-Ponty, "Eye and Mind," in *The Primacy of Perception and Other Essays on Phenomenological Psychology, the Philosophy of Art, History and Politics*, edited with an Introduction by James M. Edie (Evanston, IL: Northwestern University Press, 1964), pp. 162-63.

477 Mikel Dufrenne, "Eye and Mind," translated by Dennis Gallagher, in *In the Presence of the Sensuous: Essays in Aesthetics*, edited by Mark S. Roberts and Dennis Gallagher (Atlantic Highlands, NJ: Humanities Press International, 1987), p. 71. There would be considerable justification for claiming that Brakhage's films concern "the visible rising from the invisible." One might also consider the relevance of these ideas to Brakhage's famous effort to reanimate forms of vision that antedate the acquisition of language, and to his hostility to the use of geometric forms in art. More generally, I believe that what Dufrenne calls the "the savage" in vision resembles what I have been calling primordial awareness.

478 Maurice Merleau-Ponty, *The Structure of Behavior*, translated by Alden L. Fisher (Boston: Beacon Press, 1963), pp. 162-63.

479 Maurice Merleau-Ponty, "Sense Experience," in *Phenomenology of Perception*, translated by Colin Smith (London: Routledge & Kegan Paul, 1962), p. 235.

480 Sartre conceived of the distinction between the *pour-soi* and the *en-soi* to involve negation—the *en-soi* is everything that the *pour-soi* is not. The *pour-soi*'s relation to the *en-soi* is determined by the capacity of the *pour-soi* to say no to what is and to imagine that different beings could exist and that the beings that do exist could be ordered differently. Many French philosophers who worked in the wake of Sartre's phenomenological ontology realized that Sartre's complete and radical distinction between the *pour-soi* and the *en-soi* (a relation he characterized exclusively in terms of negation) makes it impossible to understand both labour and historical efficacy, since both can be analyzed only in terms of the *pour-soi*'s affecting the *en-soi*. They pointed out that if the *en-soi* is so stubbornly self-identical as Sartre casts it as being, then it is difficult to see how the *pour-soi* can affect the *en-soi*.

481 Maurice Merleau-Ponty, *The Visible and the Invisible: Followed by Working Notes*, edited by Claude Lefort and translated by Alfonso Lingis (Evanston, IL: Northwestern University Press, 1968), p. 266 (emphasis in original).

482 Ibid., p. 199.

483 Sartre's analysis of intersubjectivity and *Mit-Sein* can be found in Jean-Paul Sartre, *Being and Nothingness: An Essay in Phenomenological Ontology*, translated and with an Introduction by Hazel E. Barnes (New York: Washington Square Press, 1966), p. 304.

484 Maurice Merleau-Ponty, "The Experience of the Body and Classical Psychology," in *Phenomenology of Perception*, translated by Colin Smith (London: Routledge & Kegan Paul, 1962), p. 93.

485 Ibid., p. 95.

486 This remains true whether that primary consciousness is the pre-reflexive cogito, as it is in the earlier Merleau-Ponty (of the time of *Phenomenology of Perception*), or whether it is something more primary which we conceive as a cogito only by sifting through the sedimentation of language, as it is in the later Merleau-Ponty (of the time of *The Visible and the Invisible*).

487 Charles Olson, "Against Wisdom as Such," in *Human Universe and Other Essays*, edited by Donald Allen (New York: Grove Press, 1967), p. 68.

488 Merleau-Ponty, *The Visible and the Invisible*, p. 138.
489 Merleau-Ponty, "Eye and Mind," p. 178.
490 Dufrenne, "Eye and Mind," p. 71.
491 Dufrenne, "Author's Preface," p. xi. The term *Urbildliche*, which Dufrenne invokes here, draws upon Klee's famous slogan, *Vom Vorbildlich zur Urbildlich*—"from the presenting image (what is set before us, a representation, a *natura naturata*) to the originary image (a creating image, a *natura naturans*)" (emphasis in original).
492 Williams, *Spring and All*, in *The Collected Poems of William Carlos Williams*, Vol. 1: *1909-1939*, p. 199.
493 Dufrenne, "Eye and Mind," p. 73.
494 Merleau-Ponty, *The Visible and the Invisible*, p. 142. Brakhage would probably argue against Merleau-Ponty's word choices in referring to "a vision in general." Nonetheless, the idea that vision is the product of the flesh of the world acting in us is one he expounds frequently. Moreover, Brakhage has frequently considered the relation between his notions of the absolute individuality of the artist and this universal which acts through us. His deliberations on the topic are rich and complex but, simplifying greatly, they amount to the claim that when we dig down into the deepest layers of the self, we reach something universal. Consider this in terms of field theory: imagine beings that can respond to all the forces in their environing field, and that the response was perspectival, i.e., the intensity of the response to some activity somewhere in this field depended partly on the distance between the subject and that activity. Then no subject could have the same experience as any other subject, yet all subjects would nonetheless register something that others would feel if they were in the same place. Now suppose that the subject's constitution made a difference—how much flesh the subject has, how much energy one has, what one's background is, etc. Taking all these matters into account, we can see that vision and sensation might be highly individual, yet reflect something that could be explained by universal principles.
495 In attaching this value to process, Whitehead joined the company of the French philosopher Henri Bergson and the Americans William James, Charles Sanders Peirce, and, implicitly, Gertrude Stein.
496 Alfred North Whitehead, "Nature and Thought," in *The Concept of Nature* (Cambridge: Cambridge University Press, 1964), p. 3.
497 Whitehead, *Science and the Modern World*, pp. 122-23.
498 Whitehead, *Process and Reality*, p. 224; Griffin and Sherburne edition, p. 148. The first edition has "are constituents" for "is a constituent."
499 Ibid., p. 471; Griffin and Sherburne edition, p. 309. The first edition has a comma after "bodies" (emphasis in original).
500 Ibid., p. 247; Griffin and Sherburne edition, p. 116.
501 Alfred North Whitehead, *Nature and Life* (New York: Greenwood Press, 1968; originally published in 1934), p. 46.
502 Whitehead, *Process and Reality*, p. 386; Griffin and Sherburne edition, p. 253.
503 Olson, "Equal, That Is, to the Real Itself," in *Selected Writings of Charles Olson*, edited with an Introduction by Robert Creeley (New York: New Directions, 1966), p. 51.
504 Whitehead, *Process and Reality*, p 361; Griffin and Sherburne edition, p. 236.
505 Alfred North Whitehead, *Adventures of Ideas* (New York: New American Library, 1955; originally published in 1933), pp. 190-91. One should note the lexical similarities of this passage with Fenollosa's essay on the Chinese written character.
506 There is controversy regarding Whitehead's concept of Eternal Objects (Whitehead was not even wholly consistent in capitalizing the term, and wrote it more often entirely in small letters; however, I prefer to capitalize the term to indicate the similarity of Whitehead's concept to Plato's notion of the Forms or Ideas). The most common view regards them as rather similar to Platonic forms. I go a good distance in agreeing with this, and even rely on this as a mode of explanation in the glossary. However, I believe a more correct way of regarding them is in the fashion W. Mays expounds, in

the fourth chapter of *The Philosophy of Whitehead*, that is, as the result of applying the logical forms of propositions to the structure of experience. Consider, however, that Plato's forms are terms that can be predicates in subject-predicate propositions; notwithstanding the fact that mistaken conclusions based on our proclivity for using subject-predicate forms were Whitehead's philosophical bogeymen, this relationship between Platonic forms, Whiteheadian Eternal Objects, and sentence forms explains why one doesn't go too horribly astray when one considers Eternal Objects to be like Platonic Forms.

507 Olson, "A Later Note on Letter #15," p. 249, [II. 79].
508 The dictum that each actual entity is internally determined and externally free Whitehead classifies as the ninth of his Categorial Obligations. He discusses this principle in *Process and Reality.*, pp. 73ff; Griffin and Sherburne edition, pp. 46ff.
509 Whitehead, *Adventures of Ideas*, p. 254.
510 Whitehead, *Process and Reality*, p. 315; Griffin and Sherburne edition, p. 207.
511 Olson, of course, underplayed this side of Whitehead's philosophy.
512 Ibid., p. 70; Griffin and Sherburne edition, p. 42.
513 Ibid., p. 32; Griffin and Sherburne edition, p. 22.
514 This assertion, which relates worldly creativity and divine Creativity, must also have been attractive to many in the artistic community who were drawn to Whitehead's philosophy.
515 Ibid., p. 527; Griffin and Sherburne edition, p. 347.
516 Ibid., p. 524; Griffin and Sherburne edition, p. 345.
517 Bergson's argument that the mind's tendency to dynamic sensation at a specific location, at a particular point in space, and (what is worse) point in time, is a principal source of philosophical mischief is one of the leitmotifs of *Creative Evolution*. One place the idea is stated is on pp. 326-28.
518 Whitehead's use of the term "symbol" (which I explain in the parenthetical remark) was based on the term's etymology, according to which a symbol is a sign that furnishes the basis for making inferences about objects or states of affairs.
519 Thus the same relation between the many and the one that characterizes the physical universe also characterizes subjective experience. Demonstrating that the same processes characterize both the physical and the subjective realm is Whitehead's basic tactic for overcoming the bifurcation of nature.
520 Whitehead, *Process and Reality*, p. 479; Griffin and Sherburne edition, pp. 314-15.
521 Ibid., p. 480; Griffin and Sherburne edition, p. 315. (The first edition has a colon that Griffin and Sherburne replaced with a semicolon.)
522 Whitehead, *Adventures of Ideas*, p. 187.
523 Whitehead, *Process and Reality*, pp. 31-32; Griffin and Sherburne edition, p. 21.
524 Ibid., p. 249; Griffin and Sherburne edition, p. 164.
525 In this regard they are more like Giordano Bruno's monads.
526 Whitehead, *Process and Reality*, p. 52; Griffin and Sherburne edition, p. 35.
527 Ibid., pp. 50-51; Griffin and Sherburne edition, p. 34.
528 Ibid.
529 Olson, "Equal, That Is, to the Real Itself," in *Selected Writings of Charles Olson*, pp. 60-61. To construe accurately Olson's comment on "symbol" one should recall Whitehead's stress on the concreteness of reality. The remark might well prompt the reader to recall the remarks Brakhage made on (small *s*) symbolism in his interview with P. Adams Sitney (which appears at the beginning of *Metaphors on Vision*), as the two were discussing *Thigh Line Lyre Triangular*. But behind both Olson's comment and Brakhage's remarks one should hear echoes of the Symbolists' ideas of the image, and the lesson that Symbolism taught about detaching the symbol from concrete reference. That historical lesson must have led Olson (and probably Brakhage) to take the term "symbol" as implying abstraction.
530 Charles Olson, *Human Universe and Other Essays*, edited by Donald Allen (New York: Grove Press, 1967), p. 52.

531 Recall here that Ernest Fenollosa extolled the written Chinese language for presenting not things, but the transference of forces between things.
532 Stan Brakhage, *The Brakhage Lectures* (Chicago: The GoodLion, 1972), p. 104 (ellipses in original).
533 Emerson, "The Poet," p. 260.
534 This quotation appears in Robert Duncan's article "The Self in Postmodern Poetry," in *Fictive Certainties* (New York: New Directions, 1985), pp. 219ff. It is cited in Robin Blaser, "The 'Elf' of It," in Christopher Wagstaff, ed., *Robert Duncan: Drawings and Decorated Books*, Catalogue for an Exhibition at the University Art Museum and Pacific Film Archive (Berkeley, CA: Rose Books, 1992), pp. 48-49.
535 Emerson, "Self-Reliance," pp. 149-50.
536 Duncan, "The Self in Postmodern Poetry," pp. 219ff.
537 Walter J. Ong, *Orality and Literacy: The Technologizing of the Word* (London: Methuen, 1982), pp. 31-32.
538 Ibid., pp. 34-35. The reference to Jousse is: M. Jousse, "Le parlant, la parole et le souffle," *L'Anthropologie du geste*, préface par Maurice Hours, École Pratiques des Hautes Études (Paris: Gallimard, 1978).
539 Ibid., p. 37.
540 Ibid., p. 41.
541 Ibid., p. 42.
542 Ibid., pp. 45-46. Ong put the notion thus: "For an oral culture learning or knowing means achieving close, empathetic, communal identification with the known (Havelock), 'getting with it' "—and "getting with it" is certainly something that Olson advocates. Ong continues: "Writing separates the knower from the known and thus sets up conditions for 'objectivity,' in the sense of personal disengagement or distancing.... [T]he individual's reaction is not expressed as simply individual or 'subjective' but rather as encased in communal reaction, the communal 'soul' " (ibid., p. 46).

The Havelock reference is to an important book by a great Canadian classicist, Eric Havelock, *Preface to Plato*, pp. 145-46.
543 Compare Ong's ideas on speech-force, and the speech-force that Olson's poetry actually conveys, with Northrop Frye's conception of the kerygmatic power of poetry.
544 Hans Jonas, "Heidegger and Theology," in *The Phenomenon of Life: Towards a Philosophical Biology* (New York: Dell Publishing, 1968), p. 240.

A fine book by Martin Jay, *Downcast Eyes: The Denigration of Vision in Twentieth-Century French Thought* (Berkeley and Los Angeles: University of California Press, 1993), takes up the theme of disparagement of vision. While Jay concentrates on thinkers rather than creators, there are as clear parallels between the themes his book deals with and the ideas that Ong advances (as there are between Ong's themes and Olson's); so the book makes profitable reading for those interested in the question why artists such as Brakhage should want to replace "the static image" (or what Brakhage disparaging calls "picture") with dynamic forms that are often, as in Brakhage's case, much closer to touch than to sight.

All this lends an irony to Brakhage's celebration of vision. But it must be understood that the form of awareness that Brakhage calls vision (and this is even more true of more recent remarks concerning moving visual thinking) is closer to primordial awareness—that is, to bodily awareness as it exists before the differentiation of the senses—than to conventional eyesight. I believe the principal reasons for his talking about vision (and moving visual thinking) rather than a synaesthetic form of primordial awareness are threefold: first, it is wretchedly difficult to talk—especially at public gatherings such as film screenings—about a form of awareness most people are too terrified to acknowledge (and with good reason, for if one makes a living at a university and is so foolhardy as to risk articulating what one truly experiences, I can assure you, dear reader, that some vice-president will see to it that one enjoys the experience of being suspended without pay pending a satisfactory psychiatric assessment); second, light seems like the electrical nervous energy that provides Brakhage with his basic metaphor for the inward sensation of this primordial form of awareness; third, he needs some principle to allow him to work out why he believes that film can reawaken this primordial form of awareness and he finds it in the idea that because film is a light-borne medium, it is close to the energy that excites the synapses.

All this means that Brakhage, in working out his aesthetic ideas, was bound to confront the deleterious, distancing effects of sight discussed by Walter Ong and French thinkers with whom Martin Jay deals. He did, and he faced the problem squarely: his response to the first of these proposals took the form of statements about the means a film artist might use to avoid these deleterious effects. These proposals were expounded at first as a polemic against Renaissance perspective. Renaissance perspective has the effect of focusing attention towards the vanishing point: all-over forms, to the contrary—the sort of form we find in Jackson Pollock, Barnett Newman, and Mark Rothko's paintings which repeat an element or elements across the entire canvas— spread one's interest across the canvas. This spreading out of attention has a tendency to provoke a scanning rather than focused sort of vision, the dynamic and primordial character of which has best been explained by Anton Ehrenzweig in *The Hidden Order of Art*. More recently, Brakhage has argued that there is another sort of vision (which I think is akin to Ehrenzweig's scanning vision, and it is this similarity that relates the arguments of these two stages in Brakhage's thought, and provides his aesthetic theory with its coherence) that we see struggling for recognition in the history of art, but always suppressed to some degree. The paintings of Hieronymus Bosch and Lawren Harris are two places where he discovers traces of this alternative way of seeing. Brakhage's later work is devoted to releasing this important, primordial awareness that has been suppressed in the history of Western representation. This is true of his photographic works (*Scenes from Under Childhood* is an early work given over almost entirely to this effort, but *Unconscious London Strata* and *Crack Glass Eulogy*, 1992, are paradigmatic examples of the most highly developed stage of the endeavour). But it is also true of his non-photographic works (all the films Brakhage painted between 1985 and 1992 are splendid examples; however, only some of the painted films he made after 1993 have anything to do with consciousness, for *First hymn to the Night Novalis* [1994] and *Last hymn to the Night* [1997] deal with primordial perception, while many of those he painted between 1992 and 1996 do not).

545 Charles Olson, "Projective Verse," in *Human Universe and Other Essays*, edited by Donald Allen (New York: Grove Press, 1967), p. 52.

546 This comment appears in David Perkins, *A History of Modern Poetry: Modernism and After* (Cambridge, MA: The Belknap Press of Harvard University Press, 1987), p. 493.

547 Charles Olson, "The Resistance," in *Selected Writings of Charles Olson*, edited with an Introduction by Robert Creeley (New York: New Directions, 1966), p. 23, and "Equal, That Is, to the Real Itself," in ibid., p. 55.

548 Olson, "Projective Verse," in *Human Universe and Other Essays*, pp. 52-53.

549 There is some tension in Brakhage's thought and work concerning this. On the one hand, Brakhage avows that artworks must not be the products of nostalgia; on the other, he has made films that do engage in retrospection: The *Sincerity Series*, the *Duplicity Series*, and parts of *Scenes from Under Childhood* are examples. However, Brakhage usually treats the issue of how memory has lasting effects (of how the past comes into and shapes the present). Thus Brakhage's desire to understand the continuing presence of the past does not undo his concern for creating a work that transpires entirely in the present; but the effort expended in accelerating the past into the present certainly promotes tension.

550 Fredman, *The Grounding of American Poetry*, p. 77.

551 Ed Dorn's poetry, and especially his great epic, *Gunslinger*, is especially important for highlighting the difference between Brakhage's method and the general method of "composition by the field." For Dorn is a supremely intellectual poet—*Gunslinger*

takes on many of the key themes of Western philosophy. The eponymously named hero poem keeps company with a Stoned Horse (sometimes called Heidegger), and Claude Lévi-Strauss, who sometimes fails to remember his proper place, as a beast of burden, and rides inside the wagon he should be pulling and "I," a person in search of meaning, who dies, is preserved in a vat of LSD, and returns as the secretary of Parmenides (the philosopher of flux) and the Poet who strums his "abso-lute" while singing love songs that allude to cybernetics. See Ed Dorn, *Gunslinger*, with a new Introduction by Marjorie Perloff (Durham, NC: Duke University Press, 1989).

552 Robert Duncan, "Preface: Articulations," in *Bending the Bow* (New York: New Directions, 1968), p. ix.

553 Allen Ginsberg, *Indian Journals: March 1962-May 1963* (San Francisco: Dave Haselwood Books and City Lights Books, 1970), p. 40. The passage is worth quoting:

> No, thought flows freely thru the page space. Begin new ideas at margin and score their development, exfoliation, on the page organically, showing the shape of the thought, one association on depending indented on another [*sic*], with space-jumps to indicate gaps & relationships between Thinks, broken syntax to indicate hesitancies & interruptions,—GRAPHING the movement of mind . . .—the arrangement of lines on the page *spread out* [emphasis in original] to be a rhythmic scoring of the accelerations, pauses & trailings-off of thoughts in their verbal forms as mouth-speech.

He continues (p. 41) by formulating a version of Projective poetics that, uncharacteristic of Ginsberg, verges on the discorporate.

> To the reader who wants to know the what-how of his fellow-man Poet's mind, the content is laid out in its naked practical pattern & is easy to follow.
>   Easier than the arbitrary pattern of a sonnet, we don't *think* in the dialectical rigid pattern of quatrain or synthetic pattern of sonnet: We think in blocks of sensation & images. IF THE POET'S MIND IS SHAPELY HIS ART WILL BE SHAPELY. That is, the page will have an original but rhythmic shape—inevitable thought to inevitable thought, lines dropping inevitably in place on the page, making a subtle infinitely varied rhythmic SHAPE [emphases in original].

554 Olson, *Selected Writings of Charles Olson*, p. 20 (emphasis in original).

555 Ibid., p. 21.

556 Charles Olson, "Letter to Elaine Feinstein," in *Selected Writings of Charles Olson*, edited with an Introduction by Robert Creeley (New York: New Directions, 1966), pp. 28-29.

557 Ibid., p. 27. Capitalization and use of parentheses follows the original.

558 Ibid., pp. 28-29.

559 Whitehead, *Process and Reality*, p. 417; Griffin and Sherburne edition, p. 309.

560 The actuality of these effects contributes to the impression (which, in this case, represents the fact of the matter) that the film (which anyway we ought to identify with what it conditions when it becomes the variable part of the projection apparatus, determining how coloured light changes over time, and what it conditions, of course, is a play of energies through the viewer's body) transpires in the immediacy of the present.

561 Ralph Waldo Emerson, *The Complete Works of Ralph Waldo Emerson*, edited by Edward W. Emerson, 14 vols. (Boston: Houghton Mifflin, 1903-1904), Vol. 6, p. 43.

562 Charles Olson, *Muthologos: The Collected Lectures & Interviews*, edited by George F. Butterick (Bolinas, CA: Four Seasons Foundation, 1978), Vol. 1, p. 64.

563 Charles Olson, "Human Universe," in *Selected Writings of Charles Olson*, edited with an Introduction by Robert Creeley (New York: New Directions, 1966), p. 56 (emphases in original).

564 The reference to Sitney is P. Adams Sitney, *Modernist Montage: The Obscurity of Vision in Cinema and Literature* (New York: Columbia University Press, 1990), pp. 165-66.

565 Fredman, *The Grounding of American Poetry*, p. 62. In fairness to Fredman, whose work I have leaned on heavily while writing this passage, I should point out that I have arrived at a different conclusion than he did concerning the significance of Olson's famous claim regarding meaning.

566 The coincidence is not accidental. Olson certainly would have known that Pound used to call the *Dao*, "the process"; and the *Dao*, as I have pointed out, has important similarities with Whitehead's idea of process. The most important similarity between Whitehead's conception of process and the Daoist conception of "the process" is that, for both, process is an agent of creativity. This similarity would have appealed to Olson, as Olson tended to mine Whitehead's metaphysical theories for ideas about art (after all, a work of art is an object that belongs to reality, and so has features that it shares with the rest of reality; artworks differ from the rest of reality only insofar as they manifest the creative processes that go in the rest of reality).

567 Charles Olson, "Experience and Measurement," quoted in Fredman, *The Grounding of American Poetry*, p. 64.

568 Merleau-Ponty tends to conceive everything in nature as having a meaning and phenomena as the descriptions that we can make about them; this is his way of reconciling nature and consciousness. Whitehead's manner of reconciling the two terms is similar, but not identical, for Whitehead's term 'experience' has a similar role as Merleau-Ponty's 'meaning' and it too mediates between self and world.

   Merleau-Ponty's analysis suggests that it makes sense to speak of a text of experience. The idea that experience is a text and that the difficulty of aligning the descriptions in that text with the realm that we experience (difficulties similar to those which the Symbolists experienced consequent to the withdrawal of language and consciousness into extreme inwardness) became concerns of the post-phenomenological phase of French intellectual life: Derrida, for example, maintains that experience is a text and writes incessantly of the impossibility of an originary, ante-predicative world, a world before the word. What many interpret as Derrida's nihilism is really not so much nihilism of the pure Nietzschean mode as the claim that the discourse of experience is always wide of its source and that there is no way of transcending the text of experience to reach its originary source. The argument is—to characterize it in a brutally summary form—Kantianism without a faith in the noumenal to ground ethical and aesthetic norms, or what is just about the same, Nietzscheanism without the *Übermensch*, the idea of eternal return, or the anthrocentric focus.

569 Maurice Merleau-Ponty, "Physical, Vital, and Human Orders," in *The Structure of Behavior*, translated by Alden L. Fisher (Boston: Beacon Press, 1963), p. 133.

570 A transcription of Olson's interview with National Educational Television appears in Olson, *Muthologos: The Collected Lectures & Interviews*, Vol. 1; the remark I quoted appears on p. 186. (The program, which also included an interview with the Anglo-American poet Denise Levertov was released on film, under the title *Denise Levertov and Charles Olson*; it can be found in the film collections of many university libraries, including York University's [Toronto] Sound and Moving Image library.) Butterick's comment appears in George F. Butterick, A Guide to the Maximus Poems of Charles Olson (Berkeley and Los Angeles: University of California Press, 1978), pp. 358-59. Butterick also reveals that the poet met the philosopher in 1938.

571 Olson, "Projective Verse," in *Human Universe and Other Essays*, pp. 59-60.

572 Ibid., p. 60

573 Charles Olson, "Human Universe," in *Human Universe and Other Essays*, edited by Donald Allen (New York: Grove Press, 1967), pp. 9-10.

574 Charles Olson, "The Metrical," in *The Special View of History*, edited by Ann Charters (Berkeley: Oyez, 1970), p. 27.

575 Compare this to Williams's claims about the importance of eliminating metaphor, and all forms of comparison, from direct perception.

576 Mikel Dufrenne, "Painting, Forever," translated by Dennis Gallager and Mark S. Roberts, in *In the Presence of the Sensuous: Essays in Aesthetics*, edited by Mark S. Roberts and Dennis Gallagher (Atlantic Heights, NJ: Humanities Press International, 1987), p. 144 (emphasis in original).

577 Charles Olson, "The Stance," in *The Special View of History*, edited by Ann Charters (Berkeley: Oyez, 1970), p. 20.

578 Olson, "Human Universe," in *Selected Writings of Charles Olson*, p. 53.

579 Olson, "Projective Verse," in *Human Universe and Other Essays*, p. 60.

580 From a letter from Charles Olson to Robert Creeley, dated February 19, 1952, printed in George F. Butterick, *A Guide to the Maximus Poems of Charles Olson* (Berkeley and Los Angeles: University of California Press, 1978), p. 15.

581 James, *Essays in Radical Empiricism*, p. 19.

582 Olson, "Human Universe," in *Human Universe and Other Essays*, p. 4.

583 Olson, "Against Wisdom as Such," in *Human Universe and Other Essays*, p. 70. The filmmaker Hollis Frampton extended Olson's ruminations on the Hopi language in a piece entitled "A Stipulation of Terms from Maternal Hopi," a most interesting piece of writing, a sort of Borgesian philosophical fantasy, that John Cage and Merce Cunningham drew upon when creating a music/dance piece. The piece can be found in *Circles of Confusion*, a collection of Frampton's writings.

584 Stan Brakhage, "TIME . . . on dit," *Musicworks* 55 (Spring 1993): 55.

585 Ibid. The idea that the transmitting medium imposes its character on the energy (signal) it transmits is one upon which Whitehead put great stress in his analysis of causal efficacy.

I wish to state that the present topic is a matter on which Brakhage and I have a fundamental disagreement. We have debated it, discussed it on the telephone, exchanged correspondence over it, been interviewed on the topic; and, I am pleased to say, he has formulated some of his recent statements on art and artmaking on the basis of our disagreement: the (lamentably) still unpublished *The Domain of Aura* is the outstanding example.

This attempt to root artistic forms in biology strikes me as simply fantastic, a revision, really, of the equally fantastic (to me) Swedenborgian dream of an absolute language. What interests me in the fantasy is that Brakhage ties his visual forms to biological entities/processes which he then treats rather as Swedenborgian hieroglyphs (as the *Egyptian Series* and the *Babylon Series* makes evident), natural forms with what amount to (within the Brakhagian *Weltbild*) cosmic meanings that require a knowing seer to interpret. Two aspects of Brakhage's transformation of the Swedenborgian dream of an absolute language interest me especially. First, that Brakhage transforms the hieroglyphs from entities to traces of process (a transformation that parallels Whitehead's replacing "static stuff" with "fluent energy"); this says much about the privilege Brakhage attaches to film. Second, that hieroglyphs are said to belong to the body's fluent energies, rather than, as in the Swedenborgian view of correspondences (that traces far back, past Meister Eckhart, into some unknown historical provenance and, I should think, back into primordial modes of consciousness) to the created order of nature. Two principal arguments of this book are, first, that as belief in a divinely created, providential order of nature has waned, so concern with the body has intensified, and, second, that a concern for the inner sense has led us to reconceive cosmology (for the body, for certain modes of thought, corresponds to, or is even identified with, the cosmos), and to picture the universe as a fluent organism, a system of exchanges of dynamic energy.

586 Ibid., pp. 55-56.

587 Whitehead, *Process and Reality*, pp. 78-79; Griffin and Sherburne edition, pp. 49-50.

588 Charles Olson, "Review of Eric A. Havelock's *Preface to Plato*," in *Additional Prose: A Bibliography on America Proprioception & Other Notes & Essays*, edited by George F. Butterick (Bolinas, CA: Four Seasons Foundation, 1974), p. 52.

589 Ibid.

590 To be sure, the term "actually" here is massively indeterminate (and for good reason): one could read the statement as saying that attention is devoted to so-called "real world" occurrences; but even that formulation of the idea could be (and has been, by people working with similar claims) interpreted differently.

One way it has been construed is as proposing that the artwork must register the immediate response to an actual, "real world" occurrence, and must do so in a form that rivets attention to resultant response, so that the artwork gives the impression of occurring in the immediate moment. This is the basis we have explored for the rhetoric concerning spontaneity, for some (not all) of Olson's ideas on poetics, and for some (not all) of Brakhage's artistic ideas—for example, Brakhage's assertion that his films register immediate moments of crisis serves to identify a film's content with real-world dynamics.

But another, and probably more fruitful, way of interpreting this proposal is by asserting that the poem/the artwork should itself be converted into an object, into an active thing—into something that does something. This is the motivation for Olson's assertion that artistic meaning is perlocution, just as it is the basis for Brakhage's conception of film as perlocution. For their beliefs of perlocution construe a poem/a film into a sort of generator that produces somatic effects, i.e., into something that is effective in the "real world."

591 Charles Olson, "A Footnote to the Above," in *The Maximus Poems*, edited by George F. Butterick (Berkeley and Los Angeles: University of California Press, 1983), p. 149 [I. 144].

592 Charles Olson, "Mayan Letters," in *Selected Writings of Charles Olson*, edited with an Introduction by Robert Creeley (New York: New Directions, 1966), p. 113. The original lacks closing parentheses.

593 Olson, *The Special View of History*, p. 14. I have substituted "they are" for "he is" in the original.

594 Charles Olson, "On Poets and Poetry," in *Human Universe and Other Essays*, edited by Donald Allen (New York: Grove Press, 1967), p. 64.

595 Olson, "Human Universe," in ibid., p. 7.

596 Ibid., p. 6 (emphasis in original).

597 Olson, "On Poets and Poetry," in *Human Universe and Other Essays*, p. 63.

598 This, again, is the very lesson that Symbolism disclosed: as language and thought withdrew into a terrible inwardness, they lost all contact with the circumambient world. Language became language about language, and the self became enclosed within the circle of subjectivity that does not open upon the world.

Yet, for those who recognized how withdrawn language had become, to restore referentiality to language hardly seemed a worthy goal. After all, to conceive of the word as being of one type, the referent as being an entity of a wholly other type, and of the two types of beings as related through the relation reference is to give the game over to the logic of history—that history began with Descartes and ended with language and thought trapped in the maze of Symbolism from which there is no exit. It retains thought within the logical space of logocentrism.

The alternative? Just what Olson and the perlocutionary theory proposed. Consider a work of art not as an entity that makes reference to the world of objects, or describes the world of objects, but as an object in its own right that, like other objects, does things. What they do is impact physically upon our bodies—they direct their energy towards our senses and affect us. These affects are what is called meaning.

These semiotic propositions showed artists and thinkers the way beyond the word, to the thing.

599 Ibid., p. 65.

600 Note that, on the one hand, Olson accepts the Sapir-Whorf hypothesis that the structure of language creates the word's referent (a thesis that, in the end, implies that it

would impossible for the sign to be detached from a referent, as the sign makes the referent), and, on the other hand, stakes such claims as these.

601 Lobachevski, Cayley, and Klein are nineteenth- and early-twentieth-century mathematicians; Olson cites them, presumably, for their contributions to the development of a new conception of space and time that achieved greatest renown through the impact that Einstein's theories of relativity had on the popular mind. Lobatschewsky (according to Olson's orthography, but more commonly Nicolai Ivanovich *Lobachevski*, 1793-1856) developed one of the first non-Euclidean geometries—a hyperbolic geometry in which a point outside a line has at least two parallels to a given line (in the sense that their instantaneous direction is the same of the given line); such a geometry is said to be hyperbolic because it can be modeled by lines inscribed on a saddle. Arthur Cayley (1821-95) was a brilliant English mathematician who developed ideas in matrix theory and multi-dimensional geometry that became keys to the development of relativity theory and quantum mechanics. Felix Klein (1849-1925) developed geometry by applying group theoretic principles to its study.

602 Charles Olson, "Equal, That Is, to the Real Itself," in *Human Universe and Other Essays*, edited by Donald Allen (New York: Grove Press, 1967), p. 120. My interpretation of these remarks is loose, as this is not Olson's most lucid piece of writing. Frankly, I don't think that his grasp of higher mathematics was very secure.

603 Whitehead devotes chapter 5, Section IV of *Process and Reality* to explaining why "the possibility of coincidence" cannot be the meaning of "congruence." He devotes chapter 6 to showing what congruence would mean in what we now call "non-Euclidean geometries" (and cites Cayley in the process). His demonstration involves rewriting Euclid's fifth axiom (the famous parallel axiom) as a triple (a set of three values), the point **P**, a line l not passing through **P**, and a plane **Pi**, and working out what possible sets could comprise l.

604 Olson, "Equal, That Is, to the Real Itself," in *Human Universe and Other Essays*, pp. 118-19.

605 Olson makes the suggestion that the body can register experience without any subjective effects being present in his essay "Human Universe":

> And it has gone so far, that is, science has, as to wonder if the fingertips, are not very knowing knots in their own rights, little brains (little photo-electric cells, I think they now call the skin) which, immediately, in responding to external stimuli, make decisions! It is a remarkable and usable idea. For it is man's first cause of wonder how rapid he is in his taking in of what he does experience. (*Human Universe and Other Essays*, p. 9)

It should be noted, regarding Olson's reference to photo-electric cells, that this essay was written in the era of Norbert Wiener's cybernetics. Olson is referring to the idea that feedback loops can create intelligent systems that lack consciousness.

Ed Dorn, who has understood Olson better than anyone, dramatizes the repudiation of the ego and subjectivity in his great epic poem, *Gunslinger*. One of the principal characters of that poem is I; so in describing the characters in exploits in the third person, he uses the first-person pronoun: " 'What is this?' I [the name of a character] asked," "I did that" (the device obviously calls into question the lyric voice). Further, I seems to be in search of meaning, and that quest is anachronistic, so I dies in Book II, and is preserved in LSD until he re-emerges as the secretary of Parmenides (the philosopher of flux). But I's (the ego's) disappearance is a key to this poem. Dorn gets rid of "the lyrical ego," searching for a shared mind. The poem first questions, then eliminates, the first-person singular. (This, of course, is quite unlike Brakhage, though Brakhage's photographed films seem to long to establish connection with the common, observable world—consider the *Pittsburg Trilogy*—as a brake on the intense subjectivism of his filmmaking, which reaches an apogee in the imagnostic works.) Dorn recognized astutely that the non-egoic consciousness would render effects more immediately: "I got there ahead of myself/ I got there ahead of my I/ is the fact/ which not a few mortals/ misread as intuition."

606 Olson, "Human Universe," in *Human Universe and Other Essays*, p. 9.

607 Charles Olson, "The Resistance," in *Human Universe and Other Essays*, edited by Donald Allen (New York: Grove Press, 1967), pp. 47-48.

608 Charles Olson, "Human Universe," in *Selected Writings of Charles Olson*, p. 57.

609 Olson, "The Resistance," in ibid., p. 13.

610 Charles Olson, "The Gate and the Center," in *Human Universe and Other Essays*, edited by Donald Allen (New York: Grove Press, 1967), p. 23.

611 Charles Olson, *Letters for Origin: 1950-1956*, edited by Albert Glover (New York: Paragon House, 1969), p. 23.

612 Charles Olson, *Charles Olson & Ezra Pound: An Encounter at St. Elizabeths*, edited by Catherine Seelye (New York: Grossman Publishers, 1975), p. 82.

The proposal for "a record in the perfectest language I can manage of the HEART, BRAIN, LIVER, KIDNEY, the organs, to body them forth, to give a full sense of the instrument of the organism, approached on the simplest of premises" more than a little resembles *The Domain of Aura*, an unpublished book by Brakhage (written partly in response to my film work and to declare the aesthetic divisions that set our oeuvres apart).

The Domain of Aura argues vigorously that pictures (that is, according to Brakhage's idiolect, representations of "nameable things") belie experience, as it occurs at our nerve ends. It was directed against my use of "pictures" in *Lamentations* (though I wish to acknowledge, lest this note be misconstrued, that Brakhage has also written, and spoken, very, very flatteringly about my films). Since I consider that all the works of art that humankind has produced to be a giant repository of life-sustaining energies, that daily refreshes our living and, in times of travail (such as are produced when none-too-bright senior bureaucrats take pleasure in acting recklessly, to prosecute silly, trumped-up charges), sustain our lives; and since all that any decent artist hopes to do is to contribute to this repository of energies, so that another's life may be revitalized, I delight in being of use to Brakhage in this way, or most any other.

613 Olson, "Human Universe," in *Human Universe and Other Essays*, p. 6.

614 This quotation and the previous one are from D.H. Lawrence, *Selected Literary Criticism*, edited by Anthony Beal (New York: Viking Press, 1966), p. 86-87.

615 Olson, "The Gate and the Center," in *Human Universe and Other Essays*, p. 23.

616 P. Adams Sitney has written a fine analysis of Charles Olson's poem "The Librarian," which deals with this feature of its construction (*Modernist Montage: The Obscurity of Vision in Cinema and Literature*, pp. 169-78).

617 Charles Olson, "Projective Verse," in *Selected Writings*, p. 19.

618 Ibid., p. 25.

619 Olson, "Human Universe," in *Human Universe and Other Essays*, p. 10. Note Olson's emphasis on a perlocutionary conception of artistic meaning: "Art does not seek to describe but to enact."

620 For a very interesting illustration of Olson's reading of Whitehead's cosmology as an aesthetic/poetic theory, see Sitney, *Modernist Montage: The Obscurity of Vision in Cinema and Literature*, pp. 264-66.

It should be recalled that Whitehead makes the emotional appreciation of contrasts and rhythms inherent in the concrescence of actual occasions, occurring at the "phase of intensifications," a goal of creativity (a goal which is ensured of realization by God's patient work of harmonization). The phase of intensification is the phase when blue becomes more intense by reason of contrasts (Whitehead's term for unification with other attributes of the occasion that emerges through concrescence) and shape becomes dominant because of loveliness (see *Process and Reality*, pp. 325 and 526; Griffin and Sherburne edition, pp. 213 and 346).

621 Charles Olson, *Call me Ishmael* (San Francisco: City Lights Books, 1947), p. 11.

622 Ibid., p. 12.

623 Olson, "Human Universe," in *Human Universe and Other Essays*, p. 11.

624 Charles Olson, "Introduction to Robert Creeley," in *Human Universe and Other Essays*, edited by Donald Allen (New York: Grove Press, 1967), p. 127.

625 Ibid.

626 Ibid., pp. 127-28.

627 For example, the background of *The Garden of Earthly Delight*, which shifts back and forth between pure black and pure white, thwarts all efforts to map the film's space into the space of the world. Brakhage went to great trouble to create this alternation between white and black grounds, for it is very tricky to create a collage film with a black background, and in which yellow flowers, for example, turn out yellow, rather than yellow's complement, blue. (For you cannot glue the flowers onto black leader—you have to use clear leader, as the medium that is glued onto it must be transparent if you are going to be able to print the film. But you cannot glue the yellow flowers onto a clear ground, and then reverse the colours, for then the yellow will end up blue. Filmmaker and archivist Jonas Mekas worked out the means to achieve the goal; but it demanded great labour on Brakhage's part to achieve it.)

628 In almost all these films, the degree of abstraction changes from moment to moment, though *Commingled Containers* remains a nearly organic (or biomorphic) abstraction across its entire length.

629 Fredman, *The Grounding of American Poetry*, p. 30. This, of course, is just the advice that Northrop Frye gave to students: choose one mind—Olson in fact had a more objective conception of the sustaining relation—live inside it, and learn its ins and outs. This, Frye asserted, is the ideal education, and, he reports, it was the way he learned literature, by occupying William Blake's capacious mental universe, the extent of which gave his mind space to develop, and to sprawl.

630 Olson, "Projective Verse," in *Human Universe and Other Essays*, p. 53; ibid., p. 55 (emphasis in original); ibid., p. 60; ibid., p. 61.

631 Whitehead, *Science and the Modern World*, p. 154.

632 Ibid., pp. 154-55.

633 Olson, "Projective Verse," in *Human Universe and Other Essays*, p. 60. Readers aware of the history of film theory might note that Olson's arguments concerning the poem's status as a natural object—that "the thing [the artist] makes [takes] its place alongside the things of nature"—because they are produced by natural energies coincide closely with those which André Bazin offered on photography at exactly the same time Charles Olson propounded his arguments. This coincidence is due partly to the religious ideas that shaped both men's thinking: in Bazin's system, the unity of nature is a result of the fact that the whole order of nature derives from the Creator and is providential; Olson's system derives the unity of nature from a Whiteheadian conception of the relatedness guaranteed by the Creativity. (The major differences are these: first, Bazin stresses the natural character of the *process* that creates photographs rather than the energies that produce them, but that is due to the less "scientific" provenance of his ideas; and, second, a major one, Bazin emphasizes the order of created nature, that is on fixed structure, while Olson celebrates the evolving order of creation. The later difference highlights the different theological conceptions which subtend the two thinkers' writings: Bazin was a devout Catholic, though of Personalist persuasion, while Olson adopted much of Whitehead's "process theology.")

634 Olson, "Projective Verse," in *Human Universe and Other Essays*, p. 56.

635 Olson, "Equal, That Is, to the Real Itself," in *Selected Writings of Charles Olson*, p. 51.

636 Brakhage offered this assessment at a graduate seminar that Annette Michelson conducted at the Anthology Film Archives, February 15, 1972. A few of the remarks Brakhage made at that seminar are noted by Daniel H. Levoff in "Brakhage's *The Act of Seeing with One's Own Eyes*," *Film Culture* 56-57 (Spring 1973).

637 Leacock's favourite among his films, *Quints*, or *Happy Mother's Day*, is not based on a contest; in fact, there is hardly any conflict in it, and it is vastly more episodic than Leacock's other films. Perhaps this shows that the conflict structure in his other films

results from Robert Drew's influence, while Leacock would have preferred to make more observational films. *Chiefs*, a later film that Leacock did on his own, lends support to this conjecture.

638 Brakhage consistently acknowledges another derivation for the title: seeing with one's own eyes *is* autopsy (autopsy = *auto* + *opsis*, with one's own eyes). I am quite sure, given his interest in word play, that Brakhage would not have missed the pun that the historian (one who sees for oneself) is one who does autopsies, who goes over the corpse of a time past (and not live time). The historian/filmmaker Brakhage is going over the corpse of dead society (or at least death-driven society)—and Pittsburgh evidences its death.

639 However, *The Act of Seeing with One's Own Eyes* is rather close stylistically (and in its use of shocking content) to *Window Water Baby Moving* (1959) and *Loving* (1957), key works in the Brakhage canon. That alone should have given people reason to see that Brakhage had long been interested in document (and in the idea of the filmmaker as a historian). However, Levoff's article on the *The Act of Seeing with One's Own Eyes* reports on how the film was received in New York City: in retreating from the complex formal dynamics of his early films (and in particular *Dog Star Man*, which, unfortunately, has constituted the norm by which many people measure Brakhage's films), Brakhage was giving evidence, it was said, that his talent was in decline. I've heard that same story for twenty-five years now, with each subsequent shift in this very protean filmmaker's work. And, frankly, it is tiresome and annoying; I am simply astounded at how unflagging his inventiveness has been—for when, from time to time, I get caught up on his latest works, I always learn something new and wondrous about film, and about the imagination.

Ironically, many of the people who complain whenever Brakhage's new productions deviate from their norms also condemn his prolificness, saying, "Oh, all his films are the same" (that assessment is a real chestnut of film conferences). I can't think of any other oeuvre of comparable diversity in all the history of film.

640 We will soon see that poet Michael McClure offered Brakhage the interesting observation the *Dog Star Man* has the form of the Swedenborgian man. In fact there are many Swedenborgian dimensions to Brakhage's thought, the most important of which is the belief in correspondence and in the reality of an absolute language (which, for Brakhage, is film). I also point out, when commenting on Brakhage's views on absolute language, that I find it signal that Brakhage alters the Swedenborgian idea of the hieroglyph, the natural forms that found the absolute language and that, if properly interpreted, provide us with clues about the cosmic order, by asserting that hieroglyphs are found not in nature, but in the internal experience of the body.

Brakhage's depiction of the practice of autopsy has to be understood in this context: the pathologists are searching the corpse for clues about life, and, indeed, for clues about being itself. Their quest is doomed, however, for the corpse doesn't contain the energies that dynamize life. What is more, the autoscopic body, the body that pictures itself like an object among other objects, cannot be identified with the body disclosed through inner sense.

641 When he and his family were living near Rollinsville, Colorado, Brakhage would sometimes mount screenings for his children and their friends that included some of his own. Brakhage takes delight in telling that his greatest hit among young ones was *The Act of Seeing with One's Own Eyes*. One can image a living room full of little people shrieking, "Oh gross! Let's see it again!" Good evidence, I think, of beauty's proximity to horror.

642 The identification tag relates to a motif of cataloguing and recording. The motif plays to roles: he articulates an analogy to the filmmaker's actions; and it suggests the loss of individuality right after our loss moments. The people autopsied are measured, observed, submitted to a regimen of scientific observation, but they are not seen as individuals (for science cannot see the individual). Brakhage's response is to imagine

the person as a sexual being. So right after seeing the tag, we see the pathologists handling the corpse's penis and inflamed scrotum with surprising tenderness and respect.

643 Levoff, "Brakhage's *The Act of Seeing with One's Own Eyes*," p. 74. The example is not his.

644 Frye, *Anatomy of Criticism*—on the lyric's associative rhythm, pp. 270ff.; on escape from the plausibility principle, p. 272. I dealt more extensively with Brakhage's use of associative rhythm in *A Body of Vision: Representations of the Body in Recent Film and Poetry* (Waterloo, ON: Wilfrid Laurier University Press, 1997).

645 Frye, *Anatomy of Criticism*, pp. 278, 280.

646 Ibid., p. 280.

647 Ibid.

648 But no donuts, and no bribes, despite this being a film on cops.

649 Fred Camper, *"Western History* and *The Riddle of Lumen,"* *artforum* 11, no. 5 (January 1973): 68.

650 Ibid., p. 67.

651 David C. Hunt, "Elvin Jones: The Rhythmic Energy of Contemporary Drumming," in Pauline Rivelli and Robert Levin, eds., *Giants of Black Music* (New York: Da Capo Press, 1979), p. 51.

652 See ibid., p. 53.

653 Quoted in ibid., p. 50.

654 Quoted in Robert Levin, "Sunny Murray: The Continuous Cracking of Glass," in Pauline Rivelli and Robert Levin, eds., *Giants of Black Music* (New York: Da Capo Press, 1979), p. 56.

655 Olson, "Human Universe," in *Human Universe and Other Essays*, p. 10, and Olson, "Equal, That Is, to the Real Itself," in ibid., p. 119.

656 Charles Olson, "Apollonius of Tyana," in *Human Universe and Other Essays*, edited by Donald Allen (New York: Grove Press, 1967), p. 41.

657 Charles Olson, "Syllabary for a Dancer," *Maps* 10, no. 4.

658 Olson, "The Resistance," in *Selected Writings of Charles Olson*, pp. 13-14.

659 As for Brakhage, these attitudes are evident in *The Dead* (1960).

660 Olson, "On Poets and Poetry," in *Human Universe and Other Essays*, p. 64.

661 Charles Olson, "On the Way to the Fathers," cited in Sherman Paul, *Olson's Push* (Baton Rouge: Louisiana State University Press, 1978), p. 48.

662 Charles Olson, quoted in Robert von Hallberg, *Charles Olson: The Scholar's Art* (Cambridge, MA: Harvard University Press, 1978), pp. 71-72.

663 Cid Corman, "On Poetry as Action," *Maps* 4, p. 67. Corman's comment about the end arriving at every moment echoes remarks that I have offered concerning both Brakhage's perpetually regenerating forms and his use of an ecstatic temporality.

664 Whitehead, *Process and Reality*, p. 95; Griffin and Sherburne edition, p. 61.

665 Whitehead offered remarks of this ilk in *Process and Reality*, p. 262 (Griffin and Sherburne edition, p. 172); pp. 481-83 (Griffin and Sherburne edition, pp. 315-17); and pp. 491-96 (Griffin and Sherburne edition, pp. 322-25).

666 Olson, *Letters for Origin: 1950-1956*, p. 10.

667 See Olson, "Projective Verse," in *Human Universe and Other Essays*, p. 53.

668 Of course, it would be wholly impossible for humans to get rid of all higher forms of awareness, and get back to prehension in the mode of causal immediacy—no complex society can do that. But the idea of a mode of awareness that does not involve consciousness (and the pernicious taint of ideas), but is immediate, direct, physical—simply the exchanges of energy between an entity and the entire history of all the precursors that led to its coming-to-be is a very attractive one to anyone who wants to find a way out of the impasse into which the metaphysical tradition has led us, a trap that the errors of Cartesianism, with its isolated subject, has made abundantly clear.

669 Olson, "Human Universe," in *Human Universe and Other Essays*, p. 122.

670 Ibid., pp. 118-19.

671 Olson's idea of there being a demand that arises anew with every passing moment to regenerate time and history has formal parallels in Stan Brakhage's use of what I call perpetually regenerating forms.

672 Quoted in Paul, *Olson's Push*, p. 52.

673 Olson, *The Maximus Poems*, p. 6 [I. 2].

674 Charles Olson, "The Songs of Maximus: Song 1," in *The Maximus Poems*, edited by George F. Butterick (Berkeley and Los Angeles: University of California Press, 1983), p. 17 [I. 13].

675 Brakhage, *Metaphors on Vision*, not paginated. The passage cited appears on the first page of the main body of the text.

676 Charles Olson, "The Songs of Maximus: Song 3," in *The Maximus Poems*, edited by George F. Butterick (Berkeley and Los Angeles: University of California Press, 1983), p. 18 [I. 14].

677 Charles Olson, "Causal Mythology," in *Muthologos: The Collected Lectures & Interviews*, edited by George F. Butterick (Bolinas, CA: Four Seasons Foundation, 1978), Vol. 1, p. 95 (emphasis in original).

678 Hence the question many viewers have when they first see Brakhage's films: "How does he [Brakhage] know when he has finished making a particular work? What does it mean to say that work has been completed?," when the implication is that to finish a work is to create closure, and closure seals a work off from reality.

679 That the poetics of Charles Olson favours cumulative forms helps explain why Ginsberg & Co., disciples and associates of Olson, helped to bring the work of the very great, but (until recently) seldom-read poet, Christopher Smart.

680 This is one of several instances in Brakhage's oeuvre of passages which implies that life emerges out of that primordiality which has been the subject of this book and which I have often referred to as "primal experience," though here it is important to avoid implying that primordiality has either an objective or a subjective status. One might even be inclined to identify this first image in the passage that concerns the crawling baby as the "First Instance of Primordiality" in Brakhage's filmmaking (the adumbrations of primordiality Brakhage created by such means as scratching on film in *Reflections on Black*, or by using the negative in *The Way to Shadow Garden* being really anticipations of the first fully realized equivalent). Form emerging from light is also a topic of *Dog Star Man* and *Text of Light*; but perhaps the film that is closest to this section of *Anticipation of the Night* in suggesting the creation of life from dynamic light is *Creation* (1979), a film whose form hints that colour and movement give rise to water, which is light's kin: and water and dynamic energy give rise to the first solid form, which is ice, and then to ice's kin, rock and landscape; and then, though the mediation of land, to life.

681 Sitney, *Visionary Film*, p. 182.

682 Ibid.

683 As P. Adams Sitney noted (see ibid., pp. 182-83).

684 Michael McClure, *Scratching the Beat Surface* (San Francisco, CA: North Point Press, 1982), p. 44.

685 Ibid., p. 45.

686 Harald Mesch, "Writing One's Body (An Interview with Michael McClure)," in Michael McClure, *Lighting the Corners on Nature, Art, and the Visionary: Essays and Interviews* (Albuquerque: University of New Mexico, College of Arts and Sciences, 1993), p. 14.

687 Ibid., p. 15.

688 McClure, *Scratching the Beat Surface*, pp. 43-44.

689 Sitney, *Modernist Montage: The Obscurity of Vision in Cinema and Literature*, pp. 165-66. (I've pointed out earlier the use Olson makes of a passage from *Process and Reality* concerning actual entities' vector character.)

690 Poet Gary Snyder (who acknowledges that he reads Michael McClure's works closely)
    makes the analogy between forms that energy creates in the natural world and poetic
    forms explicitly. Speaking with John Jacoby, a professor of English literature, he
    remarks:

> [T]rees, animals, mountains are in some sense individualized turbulence
> patterns, specific turbulence patterns of the energy flow that manifest
> themselves temporarily as discrete items, playing specific roles and then
> flowing back in again. I like to think of poetry as that, and as that, let's see,
> as the knot of the turbulence, whorl or a term that Pound was fond of from
> his friend Wyndham Lewis, "vortex." Or Yeats's term "gyre" too.

Snyder goes on say that we live within the energies of language, but there is little to
distinguish one moment of energy within this field from any other. However:

> [T]he poem or the song manifests itself as a special concentration of the
> capacities of the language and rises up into its own shape. Now the ques-
> tion that people ask inevitably is, does this shape then mean a formal form,
> is that the shape it takes? And the question of course about pre-modern
> traditional English poetic forms as against what has been taking place the
> last few decades of the so-called free verse or open poetry. And the ques-
> tion is, are these formless—to which the answer is of course they're not
> formless.
> Nothing is formless. Everything takes strict pattern including the flow-
> ing water in the stream which follows the physical laws of wave movement,
> or the physical laws by which clouds move, or gases move, or liquids move,
> amongst each other. . . . All these things are form, but there is more or less
> fluidity in the form, and there is also the possibility that the formal pattern-
> ing is to be found in a longer range measuring periodicity than is provided
> by our traditional ways of patterning. [Hear! Hear!] (Gary Snyder, "Knots
> in the Grain" [an interview with John Jacoby, 1973], in Gary Snyder, *The
> Real Work: Interviews & Talks 1964-1979*, edited with an Introduction by
> Wm. Scott McLean [New York: New Directions, 1980], pp. 44-45)

691 McClure, *Scratching the Beat Surface*, p. 145.
692 Cited in ibid., p. 57. Capitalization follows McClure's citation.
693 Ibid., p. 51 (emphasis in original).
694 Ibid., p. 54 (emphasis in original).
695 Ibid., p. 57.
696 Ibid., p. 69.
697 Ibid., p. 148 (capitals as in original).
698 I obtained a copy of McClure's journal comments on *Dog Star Man* from the filmmaker.
699 McClure, *Scratching the Beat Surface*, p. 89 (emphasis in original).
700 Ibid., p. 137.
701 Mesch, "Writing One's Body (An Interview with Michael McClure)," p. 11.
702 McClure, *Scratching the Beat Surface*, p. 119. McClure's statement of this idea has res-
    onances in comments that Stan Brakhage has made about his aesthetic beliefs:
    Brakhage, too, uses the term "dance" to describe the movement of elements in expe-
    rience and, adopting McClure's terms, talks of aesthetic orders that are based in "the
    meat" and of "brain movies."
703 Ibid., pp. 120-21.
704 Michael McClure, "THE SURGE: *for Brakhage*," in *Star* (New York: Grove Press,
    1970), pp. 47-52. Brakhage, incidentally, has mutual respect for McClure—McClure
    appears in Brakhage's *Song 15: 15 Song Traits* (1965).
705 Mesch, "Writing One's Body (An Interview with Michael McClure)," pp. 17-18.
706 Allen Ginsberg, *Allen Verbatim: Lectures on Poetry, Politics, Consciousness*, edited by
    Gordon Ball (New York: McGraw-Hill, 1974), p. 28 (emphasis in original).

707 Ibid., p. 30.

708 William Carlos Williams, *I Wanted to Write a Poem: The Autobiography of the Works of a Poet*, reported and edited by Edith Heal (New York: New Directions, 1978), p. 26.

709 Williams, *Spring and All*, in *The Collected Poems of William Carlos Williams*, Vol. 1: *1909-1939*, p. 207.

710 I have stressed throughout that the image in modernist verse has an ambiguous status, that it is situated indeterminately between the subjective and objective realms. Wanting to call the moments both "insights" and "details" indicates that images in Ginsberg's verse have a similarly indeterminate status. This quality of his imagery reflects the influence of Williams ("no ideas but in things") and Pound ("the precise instant when a thing outward and objective transforms itself, or darts into a thing inward and subjective").

711 For the citation from Ginsberg, see Allen Ginsberg, *Howl and Other Poems* (San Francisco: City Lights Books, 1956), p. 10. For the citation from Whitehead, see Whitehead, *Process and Reality*, p. 348; Griffin and Sherburne edition, p. 228.

712 George Plimpton, ed., "Allen Ginsberg," in *Writers at Work: The* Paris Review *Interviews, Third Series* (New York: Viking Press, 1967), pp. 289-90 (emphasis in original). Compare Ginsberg's comments with Olson's: "Of rhythm is image/ of image is knowing/ of knowing there is construct."

713 Ginsberg, *Improvised Poetics*, pp. 19-22 (emphasis in original). The very idea of improvising poetics (for the title suggests that the theory itself is improvised, as much as that it is a theory of improvised poetry) is significant, inasmuch as poetics, as a relative of aesthetics, is usually deemed to be a subject fitted for long and careful deliberations of a most rigorous and demanding sort. Ginsberg's idea of improvising a poetic theory (or, at least, of improvising the expression of a poetic theory) indicates how thoroughgoing his attachment to the idea of spontaneous creativity is.

714 Ibid., p. 22 (emphasis in original).

715 Ibid., p. 26 (boldface in original).

716 Plimpton, ed., "Allen Ginsberg," p. 296.

717 Ibid.

718 Allen Ginsberg, "When the Mode of the Music Changes the Walls of the City Shake," in Richard Kostelanetz, ed., *Esthetics Contemporary* (Buffalo: Prometheus Books, 1978), pp. 333-34. This denunciation of academic ideas about poetry originally appeared in 1961, at the height of public controversy over the Beat poetry and the Beat lifestyle.

719 Ibid., p. 334.

720 Ibid., p. 335.

721 This quotation, and information concerning the origins of Ginsberg's use of parataxis, is taken from Barry Miles, *Ginsberg: A Biography* (New York: HarperPerennial, 1990), p. 97.

722 Ibid. Barry Miles notes that the Latin quotes a letter that Cézanne wrote to Émile Bernard.

723 Ibid.

724 Ginsberg took up meditative practices to help him; he also frequently enlisted psychotropic agents to assist the effort.

725 Allen Ginsberg, "THE CHANGE: Kyoto-Tokyo Express," in *Planet News: 1961-1967* (San Francisco: City Lights Books, 1968), p. 60.

726 Harold Rosenberg, "De Kooning: On the Borders of the Act," in *The Anxious Object: Art Today and Its Audience* (New York: Collier Books, 1973), p. 124.

727 Harold Rosenberg, "Hans Hofmann: Nature into Action," in ibid., p. 158.

728 Brakhage uses the term "vision" in an expanded sense. For him vision comprises perception, memory, images, fantasy, dream—day or night dream—images, eidetic images, hallucinations, "closed-eye vision," or hypnagogic images (in Andrew Lang's sense of the term, not Freud's, i.e., visual phenomena produced by physically stimulat-

ing the retina (for example, by rubbing the eyes). Brakhage insists in *Metaphors on Vision* that all of these be allowed to enter the realm of perception and that none should be derogated: "Allow so-called hallucination to enter the realm of perception, allowing that mankind always finds derogatory terminology for that which doesn't appear to be readily usable, accept dream visions, day-dreams or night-dreams, as you would so-called real scenes, even allowing that the abstractions which move so dynamically when closed eyelids are pressed are actually perceived" (Brakhage, *Metaphors on Vision*, not paginated—the quoted text appears on the first page of the main body of the text). A careful reading of this passage will reveal that it is a forceful statement of a subjective idealist ontology.

729 Olson, "Against Wisdom as Such," in *Human Universe and Other Essays*, p. 68.

730 In this, Brakhage shares a belief with the dancer/choreographer Deborah Hay (1941-). For Hay insists that dance forms evolve out of the body, that teaching dancing is teaching people to become aware of the body, and that, in dancing, one becomes aware of the body's constitution, right down to the cellular level. "I dance by directing my consciousness to the movement of every cell in my body simultaneously so that I can feel all parts of me from the inside, from the very inside out moving" (Deborah Hay, "Dance Talk," *Dance Scope* 12, no. 1 [Fall-Winter 1977-78]: 21).

731 Stan Brakhage, the "Margin Alien" section of *Metaphors on Vision*, not paginated. The first quotation appears on the third page (counting inclusively) from the section heading; the second quotation appears on the sixth page; and the third quotation appears on the third page.

732 In "Film:Dance" Brakhage associates this with being an American artist, for he states: "Film, as this dance, is particularly American. . . . Its permital abstract is pure energy (as Buckminster Fuller defines 'efficiency,' American-wise, as: 'empheralizing *toward* pure energy')" (Stan Brakhage, "Film:Dance," in *Brakhage Scrapbook: Collected Writings 1964-1980*, edited by Robert A. Haller [New Paltz, NY: Documentext, 1982], p. 121).

733 Cynics have often characterized Brakhage as the chief exponent of "the shaky camera school of filmmaking."

734 Stan Brakhage, "Film:Dance," p. 123 (emphases in original).

735 Schopenhauer, *The World as Will and Representation*, Vol. 2, Supplements to the Second Book, chap. 22, pp. 284-85.

736 To be sure, there is no form that can actually represent the transcendental self, and no space required by it, for it is, as a condition of experience, itself beyond experience. But films such as Brakhage often uses, that encourage a viewer to identify entirely with their percepts, and that are always at the point of breaking down, and often engender a sense of collapse that seems to involve subject and percept mutually, do seem to undo the condition that the transcendental self is supposed to ensure—that the stream of experiences belongs to a self-same subject, that remains identical through all the vagaries of experience.

Selected Bibliography

Auden, W.H. *W.H. Auden: Collected Poems*. Edited by Edward Mendelson. New York: Random House, 1976.

Bacon, Francis. *Of the Advancement of Learning*. London: J.M. Dent & Sons, 1930.

Benveniste, Emile. *Problems in General Linguistics*. Coral Gables, FL: University of Miami Press, 1971.

Bergson, Henri. *Creative Evolution*. In the Authorized Translation by Arthur Mitchell, with a Foreword by Irwin Edman. New York: The Modern Library, Random House, 1944.

_____ . *The Creative Mind: An Introduction to Metaphysics*. Translated by Mabelle L. Andison. New York: Philosophical Library, 1946.

_____ . *Essai sur les données immédiates de la conscience*. In *Oeuvres*. Edited by André Robinet. Paris: Presses Universitaires de France, 1970.

_____ . *An Introduction to Metaphysics*. Translated by T.E. Hulme with an Introduction by T. Goudge. 2nd ed. Indianapolis, IN: Library of Liberal Arts, Bobbs-Merrill, 1955.

_____ . *Matter and Memory*. Translated by Nancy Margaret Paul and W. Scott Palmer. London: George Allen & Unwin, 1950.

_____ . *La pensée et le mouvant*. In *Oeuvres*. Edited by André Robinet. Paris: Presses Universitaires de France, 1970.

_____ . "The Soul and the Body." In *Mind-Energy*. New York: Henry Holt, 1920.

_____ . *Time and Free Will: An Essay on the Immediate Data of Consciousness*. Translated by F.L. Pogson. New York: Harper & Row, 1960.

Blake, William. *The Complete Writings of William Blake*. Edited by Geoffrey Keynes. London: Oxford University Press, 1966.

Blaser, Robin. "The "Elf" of It." In Christopher Wagstaff, ed., *Robert Duncan: Drawings and Illustrated Books* (pp. 21-53). Catalogue for an Exhibition at the University Art Museum and Pacific Film Archive. Berkeley, CA: Rose Books, 1992.

Bloom, Harold. *The American Religion: The Emergence of the Post-Christian Nation*. New York: Simon & Schuster, 1992.

Brakhage, Stan. *The Brakhage Lectures*. Chicago: The GoodLion, 1972.

_____. "Film:Dance." In *Brakhage Scrapbook: Collected Writings 1964-1980*. Edited by Robert A. Haller. New Paltz, NY: Documentext, 1982.

_____. "Film and Music (Letter to Ronna Page)." In *Brakhage Scrapbook: Collected Writings 1964-1980*. Edited by Robert A. Haller. New Paltz, NY: Documentext, 1982. Originally published in *WILD DOG*.

_____. *Gertrude Stein: Meditative Literature and Film*. Boulder: The Graduate School, University of Colorado at Boulder, 1990.

_____. "Hypnagogically Seeing America." In *Brakhage Scrapbook: Collected Writings 1964-1980*. Edited by Robert A. Haller. New Paltz, NY: Documentext, 1982.

_____. *Metaphors on Vision*. Edited and with an Introduction by P. Adams Sitney. New York: Film Culture, 1963.

_____. "On Marie Menken," *Filmwise 5-6* (1967). Originally a letter to Gerald Malanga and reprinted in *Brakhage Scrapbook: Collected Writings 1964-1980*. Edited by Robert A. Haller. New Paltz, NY: Documentext, 1982.

_____. "Poetry and Film." A lecture recorded at the University of North Carolina, Chapel Hill, March 22, 1977. Originally published in *Credences*, nos. 5-6, and reprinted in Stan Brakhage, *Brakhage Scrapbook: Collected Writings 1964-1980*. Edited by Robert A. Haller. New Paltz, NY: Documentext, 1982.

_____. "S.A. #1." In *Brakhage Scrapbook: Collected Writings 1964-1980*. Edited by Robert A. Haller. New Paltz, NY: Documentext, 1982.

_____. "Stan Brakhage at Millennium: November 4, 1977," *Millennium Film Journal* 16/17/18 (Fall/Winter 1986-87): 297-307. Transcription of a talk and question-and-period at the Millennium Film Workshop in New York City.

_____. "Stan Brakhage Speaks on *23rd Psalm Branch* at Film-makers' Cinematheque, April 22, 1967." *Film Culture* 67-68-69 (1979): 125ff.

_____. "TIME . . . on dit." A series of essays by Brakhage that have appeared quarterly since 1989 in *Musicworks: The Canadian Journal of Sound Exploration*. (I have drawn especially from no. 48 [Autumn 1990], on our experiences of the synapses).

_____. "To Michael McClure." In *Brakhage Scrapbook: Collected Writings 1964-1980*. Edited by Robert A. Haller. New Paltz, NY: Documentext, 1982.

_____, with Ted Perry. "Seminar." *Dialogue on Film* 2, no. 3 (January 1973): 2-11.

Brooke-Rose, Christine. *A ZBC of Ezra Pound*. Berkeley and Los Angeles: University of California Press, 1971.

Butterick, George F. *A Guide to the Maximus Poems of Charles Olson*. Berkeley and Los Angeles: University of California Press, 1978.

Camhi, Gail. "Notes on Brakhage's *23rd Psalm Branch*." *Film Culture* 67-68-69 (1979): 97-108.

Camper, Fred. *"Western History* and *The Riddle of Lumen." artforum* 11, no. 5 (January 1973): 66-71.

Caramello, Charles. "Gertrude Stein as Exemplary Theorist." In Shirley Neuman and Ira B. Nadel, eds., *Gertrude Stein and the Making of Literature*. Boston: Northeastern University Press, 1988.

Cohen, Phoebe. "Brakhage's *I, II,* and *III." Millennium Film Journal* 7/8/9 (Fall/Winter 1980-81): 234-37.

_____ . *"Scenes from Under Childhood."* *artforum* 11, no. 5 (January 1973): 51-55.

Cork, Richard. *Wyndham Lewis*. Manchester: City of Manchester Cultural Services, 1980.

Corman, Cid. "On Poetry as Action." *Maps* 4.

Creeley, Robert. *For Love: Poems 1950-1960*. New York: Charles Scribner's Sons, 1962.

Deleuze, Gilles. *Bergsonianism*. Translated by Hugh Tomlinson and Barbara Habberjam. New York: Zone Books, 1988.

_____ . *Expressionism in Philosophy: Spinoza*. Translated by Martin Joughin. New York: Zone Books, 1990. Originally published as *Spinoza et le problème de l'expression*. Paris: Éditions de Minuit, 1968.

_____ . *Spinoza: Practical Philosophy*. Translated by Robert Hurley. San Francisco: City Lights Books, 1988. Originally published in French as *Spinoza: philosophie pratique*. Paris: Presses Universitaires de France, 1970.

Dorn, Ed. *Gunslinger*. With a new Introduction by Marjorie Perloff. Durham, NC: Duke University Press, 1989.

Dufrenne, Mikel. "Eye and Mind." In *In the Presence of the Sensuous: Essays in Aesthetics*, pp. 69-74. Edited by Mark S. Roberts and Dennis Gallagher. Atlantic Highlands, NJ: Humanities Press International, 1987.

_____ . *The Phenomenology of Aesthetic Experience*. Translated by Edward S. Casey. Evanston, IL: Northwestern University Press, 1973.

Duncan, Isadora. *My Life*. New York: Horace Liveright, 1927.

Duncan, Robert. "Changing Perspectives in Reading Whitman." In Edwin Haviland Miller, ed., *The Artistic Legacy of Walt Whitman*. New York: New York University Press, 1970.

_____ . *The Opening of the Field*. New York: New Directions, 1960.

_____ . "The Self in Postmodern Poetry." In *Fictive Certainties*. New York: New Directions, 1985.

Dydo, Ulla E. "Gertrude Stein: Composition as Meditation." In Shirley Neuman and Ira B. Nadel, eds., *Gertrude Stein and the Making of Literature*. Boston: Northeastern University Press, 1988.

Easthope, Anthony, and John O. Thompson, eds. *Contemporary Poetry Meets Modern Theory*. Toronto: University of Toronto Press, 1991.

Edie, James M. *William James and Phenomenology*. Bloomington and Indianapolis: Indiana University Press, 1987.

Elder, R. Bruce. "Eisenstein, My Contemporary," *Canadian Journal of Film Studies/Revue canadienne d'études cinématographiques* 4, no. 2 (Fall/automne 1995): 33-50.

_____ . *Image and Identity: Reflections on Canadian Film and Culture*. Waterloo, ON: Wilfrid Laurier University Press, 1989.

Eliot, T.S. *The Collected Poems of T.S. Eliot (1909-1963)*. London: Faber and Faber, 1963

_____ . *Knowledge and Experience in the Philosophy of F.H. Bradley*. London: Faber and Faber, 1964.

Emerson, Raph Waldo. *The Collected Works of Ralph Waldo Emerson*. Edited by Robert E. Spiller et al. 5 vols. Cambridge, MA: Harvard University Press, 1971-.

_____. *The Journals and Miscellaneous Notebooks of Ralph Waldo Emerson*. Edited by William H. Gilman et al. 16 vols. Cambridge: Harvard University Press, 1960-82.

_____. *Journals of Ralph Waldo Emerson*. Edited by Edward Waldo Emerson and Waldo Emerson Forbes. New York: Houghton Mifflin, 1909.

_____. *The Portable Emerson*. Edited by Carl Bode in collaboration with Malcolm Cowley. Harmondsworth, Middlesex: Penguin Books, 1981; originally published in 1946.

Farrington, Jane, with contributions by John Rothenstein, Richard Cork, and Omar S. Pound. "What Was Vorticism?" In *Wyndham Lewis*. London: Lund Humphries, 1980.

Fenollosa, Ernest. "The Chinese Written Character as a Medium for Poetry." In Karl Shapiro, ed., *Prose Keys to Modern Poetry*. New York: Harper & Row, 1962. Also published as a monograph San Francisco: City Lights Books, 1968.

Foucault, Michel. *Les Mots et les choses*. Paris: Gallimard, 1966.

_____. "Nietzsche, Genealogy, History." In D.F. Bouchard, ed., *Michel Foucault: Language, Counter-Memory, Practice: Selected Essays and Interviews*. New York: Cornell University Press, 1977.

_____. *The Order of Things: An Archaeology of the Human Sciences*. New York: Vintage Books, 1973.

Frampton, Hollis. "A Pentagram for Conjuring the Narrative." In *Circles of Confusion—Film, Photography, Video: Texts 1968-1980*. Rochester, NY: Visual Studies Workshop Press, 1983.

_____. "Stan and Jane Brakhage (and Hollis Frampton) Talking." *artforum* 11, no. 5 (January 1973). Reprinted in Stan Brakhage, *Brakhage Scrapbook: Collected Writings 1964-1980*. Edited by Robert A. Haller. New Paltz, NY: Documentext, 1982.

Fredman, Stephen. *The Grounding of American Poetry: Charles Olson and the Emersonian Tradition*. Cambridge: Cambridge University Press, 1993.

Frye, Northrop. *Anatomy of Criticism: Four Essays*. Princeton, NJ: Princeton University Press, 1957.

_____. *The Great Code: The Bible and Literature*. Toronto: Academic Press, 1982.

Ginsberg, Allen. *Allen Verbatim: Lectures on Poetry, Politics, Consciousness*. Edited by Gordon Ball. New York: McGraw-Hill, 1974.

_____. *Improvised Poetics*. Edited with an Introduction by Mark Robison. San Francisco: Anonym Press, 1972.

_____. *Indian Journals: March 1962-May 1963*. San Francisco: Dave Haselwood Books and City Lights Books, 1970.

_____. *Planet News: 1961-1967*. San Francisco: City Lights Books, 1968. (Planet News includes "THE CHANGE: Kyoto-Tokyo Express.")

_____. "When the Mode of the Music Changes the Walls of the City Shake." In Richard Kostelanzetz, ed., *Esthetics Contemporary*. Buffalo: Prometheus Books, 1978.

Grogin, R.C. *The Bergsonian Controversy in France: 1900-1914*. Calgary: The University of Calgary Press, 1988.

Hallberg, Robert von. *Charles Olson: The Scholar's Art*. Cambridge, MA: Harvard University Press, 1978.

Hanlon, Lindley P. "1663-1966." An essay in *A History of the American Avant-Garde Cinema*. Exhibition catalogue issued by the American Federation of the Arts, 1976.

Havelock, Eric. *Preface to Plato*. Cambridge, MA: The Belknap Press of Harvard University, 1963.

Hay, Deborah. "Dance Talk." *Dance Scope* 12, no. 1 (Fall-Winter 1977-78).

Hayman, Ronald. *Nietzsche: A Critical Life*. Harmondsworth, Middlesex: Penguin Books, 1980.

Hegel, G.W.F. *Vorlesungen über die Aesthetik*. Edited by Friedrich Bassenge. Frankfurt-am-Main: Suhrkamp, 1965. (Revision of H.G. Hotho compilation from Hegel's notes and those of his students.) English translation: G.W.F. Hegel, *Aesthetics: Lectures on Fine Art*. Translated by T.M. Knox. Vol. 1. Oxford: Oxford University Press, 1975.

Hopkins, Gerard Manley. *The Journals and Papers of Gerard Manley Hopkins*. Edited by Humphry House. Completed by Graham Storey. London: Oxford University Press, 1959.

_____ . *The Poems of Gerard Manley Hopkins*. Oxford: Oxford University Press, 1967.

Hulme, T.E. *Further Speculations*. Edited by Sam Hynes. Lincoln: University of Nebraska Press, 1962.

_____ . *Speculations: Essays on Humanism and the Philosophy of Art*. London: Routledge & Kegan Paul, 1987; originally published in 1924.

Hume, David. *A Treatise of Human Nature*. 2 vols. London: J.M. Dent & Sons, 1964. First included in Everyman's Library, 1911.

Hunt, David C. "Elvin Jones: The Rhythmic Energy of Contemporary Drumming." In Rauline Rivelli and Robert Levin, eds., *Giants of Black Music*. New York: Da Capo Press, 1979. This article originally appeared in *Jazz & Pop* (March 1970).

James, William, *Essays in Radical Empiricism*. London: Longmans, Green, 1912.

_____ . *Essays in Radical Empiricism* and *A Pluralistic Universe*. Gloucester: Peter Smith, 1967. (This work includes, as an Appendix, the essay "On the Notion of Reality as Changing.") It should be noted that not all the essays in the original *Essays in Radical Empiricism* are included in this volume.

_____ . *Pragmatism*. Cambridge: Harvard University Press, 1975.

_____ . *The Principles of Psychology*. 2 vols. New York: Dover Publications, 1950.

Jay, Martin. *Downcast Eyes: The Denigration of Vision in Twentieth-Century French Thought*. Berkeley and Los Angeles: University of California Press, 1993.

Jonas, Hans. *The Phenomenon of Life: Towards a Philosophical Biology*. New York: Dell Publishing, 1968.

Keller, Marjorie. *The Untutored Eye: Childhood in the Films of Cocteau, Cornell, and Brakhage*. Cranbury, NJ: Associated University Presses, 1986.

Kenner, Hugh. *The Pound Era*. Berkeley: University of California Press, 1971.

Kolakowski, Leszek. *Bergson*. Oxford: Oxford University Press, 1985.

Kostelanetz, Richard, ed. *Esthetics Contemporary*. Buffalo: Prometheus Books, 1978.

Kübler-Ross, Elisabeth. *On Death and Dying*. New York: Macmillan, 1969.

Lango, John W. *Whitehead's Ontology*. Albany: State University of New York Press, 1972.

Lawrence, D.H. *Apocalypse and the Writings on Revelation*. Edited by Mara Kalnins. Cambridge: Cambridge University Press, 1980.

_____ . *The Complete Poems of D.H. Lawrence*. Collected and edited with an Introduction and Notes by Vivian de Sola Pinto and Warren Roberts. New York: Viking Press, 1964.

_____ . "Poetry of the Present" (Introduction to the American edition of *New Poems* [1918]. In *The Complete Poems of D.H. Lawrence*. Collected and edited with an Introduction and Notes by Vivian de Sola Pinto and Warren Roberts. New York: Viking Press, 1964.

_____ . *Selected Literary Criticism*. Edited by Anthony Beal. New York: Viking Press, 1966.

_____ . *Selected Poems*. Selected and with an Introduction by Kenneth Rexroth. New York: Viking Press, 1959.

Levenson, Michael H. *A Genealogy of Modernism: A Study of English Literary Doctrine 1908-1922*. Cambridge: Cambridge University Press, 1984.

Levin, Robert. "Sunny Murray: The Continuous Cracking of Glass." In Pauline Rivelli and Robert Levin, eds., *Giants of Black Music*. New York: Da Capo Press, 1979.

Levoff, Daniel H. "Brakhage's *The Act of Seeing with One's Own Eyes*." *Film Culture* 56-57 (Spring 1973): 73-81.

Lewis, Wyndham. *Tarr*. London: Methuen, 1951.

_____ . *Wyndham Lewis on Art: Collected Writings 1913-1956*. With introductions and notes by Walter Michel and C.J. Fox. New York: Funk & Wagnalls, 1969.

_____ . *Wyndham Lewis the Artist: From 'Blast' to Burlington House*. London: Laidlaw and Laidlaw, 1939.

Longinus, Cassius (the Pseudo-Longinus). *On the Sublime*. Translated by W. Hamilton Fyfe. New York: G.P. Putnam's Sons, 1927.

Mallarmé, Stéphane. *Mallarmé*. Edited and translated with an Introduction by Anthony Hartley. Baltimore, MD: Penguin Books, 1965.

Mamber, Stephen. *Cinéma-Vérité in America: Studies in Uncontrolled Documentary*. Cambridge, MA: MIT Press, 1974.

Mays, W. *The Philosophy of Whitehead*. New York: Collier Books, 1962.

McClure, Michael. *Lighting the Corners on Nature, Art, and the Visionary: Essays and Interviews*. Albuquerque: University of New Mexico, College of Arts and Sciences, 1993.

_____ . *Scratching the Beat Surface*. San Francisco: North Point Press, 1982.

_____ . *Star*. New York: Grove Press, 1970. (This book contains "THE SURGE: *for Brakhage*.")

Merleau-Ponty, Maurice. *The Phenomenology of Perception*. Translated by Colin Smith. London: Routledge & Kegan Paul, 1962.

_____ . *The Primacy of Perception and Other Essays on Phenomenological Psychology, the Philosophy of Art, History and Politics*. Edited with an Introduction by James M. Edie. Evanston, IL: Northwestern University Press, 1964. (This work includes the important essay "Eye and Mind.")

_____ . *The Prose of the World*. Translated by John O'Neill. Evanston, IL: Northwestern University Press, 1973.

_____. *Sense and Non-Sense*. Translated by Herbert L. Dreyfus and Patricia Allen Dreyfus. Evanston, IL: Northwestern University Press, 1964.

_____. *Signs*. Translated by Richard C. McCleary. Evanston, IL: Northwestern University Press, 1964.

_____. *The Structure of Behavior*. Translated by Alden L. Fisher. Boston: Beacon Press, 1963.

_____. *The Visible and the Invisible: Followed by Working Notes*. Edited by Claude Lefort and translated by Alfonso Lingis. Evanston, IL: Northwestern University Press, 1968.

Mesch, Harald. "Writing One's Body (An Interview with Michael McClure)." In Michael McClure, *Lighting the Corners on Nature, Art, and the Visionary: Essays and Interviews*. Albuquerque: University of New Mexico, College of Arts and Sciences, 1993.

Messiaen, Olivier. *La technique de mon langage musical*. Paris: Alphonse Leduc Editions Musicales, 1955-66. The later edition consists of two volumes and includes an English translation by John Statterfield and a German translation.

Meyer, Leonard B. *Music, the Arts, and Ideas: Patterns and Predictions in Twentieth-Century Culture*. Chicago: University of Chicago Press, 1967.

Miles, Barry. *Ginsberg: A Biography*. New York: HarperPerennial, 1990.

Miller, E.H., ed. *The Artistic Legacy of Walt Whitman*. New York: New York University Press, 1970.

Mukařovský, Jan. "Standard Language and Poetic Language." In Paul L. Garvin, ed., *A Prague School Reader on Esthetics, Literary Structure, and Style*. Washington, DC: Georgetown University Press, 1964.

Nesthus, Marie. "The Influence of Olivier Messiaen on the Visual Art of Stan Brakhage in *Scenes from Under Childhood*, Part One." *Film Culture* 63-64 (1977): 39-56 (Notes pp. 179-81).

Neuman, Shirley, and Ira B. Nadel editors. *Gertrude Stein and the Making of Literature*. Boston: Northeastern University Press, 1988.

Nicholls, Peter. "Difference Spreading: From Gertrude Stein to L=A=N=G=U=A=G=E Poetry." In Anthony Easthope and John O. Thompson, eds., *Contemporary Poetry Meets Modern Theory*. Toronto: University of Toronto Press, 1991.

Nietzsche, Friedrich. *Gesammelte Werke*. München: Musarion-Ausgabe, 1926-1991.

_____. *The Portable Nietzsche*. Translated and edited by Walter Kaufmann. New York: Viking Portable Library, 1982. (This selection includes *Thus Spoke Zarathustra* and "On Truth and Lies in an Extra-Moral Sense.")

_____. "On Truth and Lie in an Extra-Moral Sense." In *The Portable Nietzsche*. Edited and translated by W. Kaufmann. New York: Viking Press, 1982.

_____. *The Will to Power*. Translated by Walter Kaufmann and R.J. Hollingate. Edited by W. Kaufmann. New York: Vintage Books, 1982; this translation originally published in 1967.

Olson, Charles. *Additional Prose: A Bibliography on America Proprioception & Other Notes & Essays*. Edited by George F. Butterick. Bolinas, CA: Four Seasons Foundation, 1974.

_____. *Call me Ishmael*. San Francisco: City Lights Books, 1947.

_____. *Charles Olson & Ezra Pound: An Encounter at Saint Elizabeths*. Edited by Catherine Seelye. New York: Grossman Publishers, 1975.

_____. *Human Universe and Other Essays*. Edited by Donald Allen. New York: Grove Press, 1967. (This work includes "Human Universe," "Equal, That Is, to the Real Itself," "The Resistance," "The Gate and the Center," "Introduction to Robert Creeley," and "On Poets and Poetry.")

_____. *Letters for Origin: 1950-1956*. Edited by Albert Glover. New York: Paragon House, 1969.

_____. *The Maximus Poems*. Edited by George F. Butterick. Berkeley and Los Angeles: University of California Press, 1983.

_____. *Muthologos: The Collected Lectures &Interviews*. Vol. 1. Edited by George F. Butterick. Bolinas, CA: Four Seasons Foundation, 1978. (*Muthologos* contains "Under the Mushroom: The Gratwick Highlands Tape" and "Causal Mythology.")

_____. "Projective Verse." In *Selected Writings of Charles Olson*. Edited with an Introduction by Robert Creeley. New York: New Directions, 1966.

_____. *Selected Writings of Charles Olson*. Edited with an Introduction by Robert Creeley. New York: New Directions, 1966. (*Selected Writings of Charles Olson* includes "Projective Verse," "Against Wisdom as Such," and "Letter to Elaine Feinstein.")

_____. *The Special View of History*. Edited by Ann Charters. Berkeley: Oyez, 1970.

Ong, Walter J. *Orality and Literacy: The Technologizing of the Word*. London: Methuen, 1982.

Paul, Sherman. *Olson's Push*. Baton Rouge: Louisiana University Press, 1978.

Peirce, Charles Sanders. "Evolutionary Love." In *Philosophical Writings of Peirce* (pp. 361-74). Selected and edited with an Introduction by Justus Buchler. New York: Dover Publications, 1955. (The Buchler anthology was originally published as *The Philosophy of Peirce: Selected Writings*. London: Routledge & Kegan Paul, 1940).

_____. "A Guess at the Riddle." In *Peirce on Signs: Writings on Semiotic by Charles Sanders Peirce* (pp. 186-202). Edited by James Hoopes. Chapel Hill, NC: University of North Carolina Press, 1991.

_____. "Logic as Semiotic: The Theory of Signs." In *Philosophical Writings of Peirce* (pp. 98-119). Selected and edited with an Introduction by Justus Buchler. New York: Dover Publications, 1955.

_____. "Synechism, Fallibilism, and Evolution." In *Philosophical Writings of Peirce* (pp. 354-60). Selected and edited with an Introduction by Justus Buchler. New York: Dover Publications, 1955.

Perkins, David. *A History of Modern Poetry: Modernism and After*. Cambridge, MA: The Belknap Press of Harvard University Press, 1987.

Plimpton, George, ed. "Allen Ginsberg." In *Writers at Work: The Paris Review Interviews, Third Series*. New York: Viking Press, 1967.

Pound, Ezra. *ABC of Reading*. London: Faber and Faber, 1961. (This work includes Pound's "Treatise on Metre.")

_____. *The Cantos of Ezra Pound*. New York: New Directions, 1972.

_____ . *Collected Shorter Poems by Ezra Pound*. London: Faber and Faber, 1968.

_____ . *Gaudier-Brzeska: A Memoir*. New York: New Directions, 1970.

_____ . *Literary Essays of Ezra Pound*. Edited with an Introduction by T.S. Eliot. London: Faber and Faber, 1960. (This collection includes Pound's reflections on Imagism, "A Retrospect," his essay on William Carlos Williams, "A Serious Artist," and "Calvacanti.")

_____ . *Pavannes and Divagations*. New York: New Directions, 1964.

_____ . *Selected Poems*. Edited with an Introduction by T.S. Eliot. London: Faber and Faber, 1948.

_____ . *Selected Prose 1909-1965*. Edited by William Cookson. New York: Faber and Faber, 1973.

_____ . *The Spirit of Romance*. New York: New Directions, 1968.

_____ . *Translations*. With an Introduction by Hugh Kenner. Norfolk, CT: New Directions, 1963.

Rexroth, Kenneth. *One Hundred Poems from the Chinese*. New York: New Directions, 1965.

Rivelli, Pauline, and Robert Levin, eds. *Giants of Black Music*. New York: Da Capo Press, 1979.

Rosenberg, Harold. *The Anxious Object: Art Today and Its Audience*. New York: Collier Books, 1973.

Samuel, Claude. *Entretiens avec Olivier Messiaen*. Paris: Éditions Pierre Belfond, 1967.

Sartre, Jean-Paul. *Being and Nothingness: An Essay in Phenomenological Ontology*. Translated and with an Introduction by Hazel E. Barnes. New York: Washington Square Press, 1963.

Schopenhauer, Arthur. *The World as Will and Representation*. Translated from the German by E.F.J. Payne. 2 vols. New York: Dover Publications, 1966.

Schwartz, Sanford. *The Matrix of Modernism: Pound, Eliot, and Early Twentieth-Century Thought*. Princeton: Princeton University Press, 1985.

Scruton, Roger. *Art and Imagination: A Study in the Philosophy of Mind*. London: Routledge & Kegan Paul, 1974.

Sitney, P. Adams. *Modernist Montage: The Obscurity of Vision in Cinema and Literature*. New York: Columbia University Press, 1990.

_____ , ed. *The Avant-Garde Film: A Reader of Theory and Criticism*. New York: New York University Press, 1978.

Snyder, Gary. *The Real Work: Interviews & Talks 1964-1979*. Edited with an Introduction by Wm. Scott McLean. New York: New Directions, 1980.

Stein, Gertrude. *The Autobiography of Alice B. Toklas*. New York: Vintage Books, 1961.

_____ . "Composition as Explanation." In *A Stein Reader*. Edited and with an Introduction by Ulla E. Dydo. Evanston, IL: Northwestern University Press, 1993.

_____ . *Doctor Faustus Lights the Lights*. In Gertrude Stein, *Last Plays and Opera*. Edited with an Introduction by Carl Van Vechten. New York: Vintage Books, 1975. pp 89-118

_____ . "An Elucidation." In *A Stein Reader*. Edited and with an Introduction by Ulla E. Dydo. Evanston, IL: Northwestern University Press, 1993.

_____. *Everybody's Autobiography*. New York: Cooper Square Publications, 1971.

_____. *Four in America*. New Haven: Yale University Press, 1947.

_____. "Guillaume Apollinaire." In *A Stein Reader*. Edited and with an Introduction by Ulla E. Dydo. Evanston, IL: Northwestern University Press, 1993.

_____. "How Writing Is Written." In *How Writing Is Written: Volume II of the Previously Uncollected Writings of Gertrude Stein*. Edited by Robert Bartlett Haas. Los Angeles: Black Sparrow Press, 1974.

_____. "If I Told Him: A Completed Portrait of Picasso." In *A Stein Reader*. Edited and with an Introduction by Ulla E. Dydo. Evanston, IL: Northwestern University Press, 1993.

_____. *Lectures in America*. New York: Random House, 1935.

_____. *A List*. In *A Stein Reader*. Edited and with an Introduction by Ulla E. Dydo. Evanston, IL: Northwestern University Press, 1993.

_____. *Look at Me Now and Here I Am: Writings and Lectures*. Edited by Patricia Meyerowitz. Harmondsworth: Penguin Books, 1971.

_____. "Portrait of Mabel Dodge at the Villa Curonia." In *A Primer for the Gradual Understanding of Gertrude Stein*. Edited by Robert Bartlett Haas. Los Angeles: Black Sparrow Press, 1974.

_____. "Saving the Sentence." In *How to Write*. With a New Preface and Introduction by Patricia Meyerowitz. New York: Dover Publications, 1975.

_____. *Selected Writings of Gertrude Stein*. Edited with an Introduction and Notes by Carl Van Vechten and with an Essay by F.W. Dupee. New York: Vintage Books, 1972.

_____. *Stanzas in Meditation*. In *The Yale Gertrude Stein*. Selections with an Introduction by Richard Kostelanetz. New Haven: Yale University Press, 1980. (*Stanzas in Meditation* also appears in the Dydo anthology.)

_____. *Tender Buttons. Look at Me Now and Here I Am: Writings and Lectures*. Edited by Patricia Meyerowitz. Harmondsworth: Penguin Books, 1971.

_____. *What Are Masterpieces*. New York: Pitman, 1970.

_____, and Robert Bartlett Haas. "Gertrude Stein Talking: A Transatlantic Interview." This interview originally appeared in *The UCLAN Review* (Summer 1962 and Spring 1963) and is reprinted in Gertrude Stein, *A Primer for the Gradual Understanding of Gertrude Stein*. Edited by Robert Bartlett Haas. Los Angeles: Black Sparrow Press, 1974.

Steiner, George. *A Reader*. New York: Oxford University Press, 1984.

Steinman, Lisa M. *Made In America: Science, Technology, and American Modernist Poets*. New Haven: Yale University Press, 1987.

Tenney, James. *META+HODOS: A Phenomenology of 20th-Century Musical Materials and an Approach to the Study of Form* and *META Meta+Hodos*. Oakland, CA: Frog Peak Music, 1988; originally published in 1964.

Terrell, Carroll F. *A Companion to* The Cantos *of Ezra Pound*. Berkeley and Los Angeles: University of California Press, 1993.

Thoreau, Henry David. *Walden and Civil Disobedience*. Edited by Owen Thomas. New York: W.W. Norton, 1966.

Tryphonopoulos, Demetres P. *The Celestial Tradition: A Study of Ezra Pound's* The Cantos. Waterloo, ON: Wilfrid Laurier University Press, 1992.

Wagstaff, Christopher, ed. *Robert Duncan: Drawings and Illustrated Books*. Catalogue for an exhibition at The University Art Museum and Pacific Film Archive. Berkeley: Rose Books, 1992

Wellek, René, and Austin Warren. *Theory of Literature*. New York: Harcourt, Brace & World, 1956.

Whitehead, Alfred North. *Adventures of Ideas*. New York: New American Library, 1955; originally published in 1933.

———. *The Concept of Nature*. Cambridge: Cambridge University Press, 1964.

———. *Nature and Life*. New York: Greenwood Press, 1968; originally published in 1934.

———. *Process and Reality: An Essay in Cosmology*. New York: Macmillan, 1929.

———. *Science and the Modern World*. New York: The Free Press; originally published in 1925.

Williams, William Carlos. *The Collected Poems of William Carlos Williams*. Vol. 1: *1909-1939*. Edited by A. Walton Litz and Christopher MacGowan. London: Paladin Grafton Books, 1991.

———. *The Collected Poems of William Carlos Williams*. Vol. 2: *1939-1962*. Edited by Christopher MacGowan. London: Paladin Grafton Books, 1991.

———. *The Embodiment of Knowledge*. New York: New Directions, 1974.

———. *I Wanted to Write a Poem: The Autobiography of the Works of a Poet*. Reported and edited by Edith Heal. New York: New Directions, 1978.

———. *Imaginations*. Edited with an Introduction by Webster Schott. New York: New Directions, 1970. (This work includes *Spring and All* and *Kora in Hell: Improvisations*).

———. *In the American Grain: Essays by William Carlos Williams*. With an Introduction by Horace Gregory. New York: New Directions, 1956; originally published in 1925.

———. *Interviews with William Carlos Williams: "Speaking Straight Ahead."* Edited with an Introduction by Linda Welshimer Wagner. New York: New Directions, 1976.

———. *Selected Essays of William Carlos Williams*. New York: Random House, 1954. (This book includes Williams's essays "Against the Weather: A Study of the Artist" and "Introduction to *The Wedge*.")

———. *The Selected Letters of William Carlos Williams*. Edited with an Introduction by John C. Thirlwall. New York: McDowell, Obolensky, 1957.

Winnicott, D.W. *Playing and Reality*. Harmondsworth, Middlesex: Penguin Education, 1980; originally published by Tavistock in 1971.

Witherspoon, Alexander M., ed. *The College Survey of English Literature*. New York: Harcourt, Brace, 1951.

Wittgenstein, Ludwig. *Philosophical Investigations*. Translated by G.E.M. Anscombe. Oxford: Oxford University Press, 1953.

Wordsworth, William. *Poetical Works*. New ed. revised by Ernest de Selincourt. Oxford: Oxford University Press, 1967.

Stan Brakhage
Filmography

Films are silent unless otherwise noted.

1952

Interim, b&w, 16mm, 25 mins. Music by James Tenney.

1953

Unglassed Windows Cast a Terrible Reflection, b&w, 16mm, 35 mins.
The Boy and the Sea (lost), b&w, 16mm, 2 mins.

1954

Desistfllm, b&w, 16mm, 7 min., sd.
The Extraordinary Child, b&w, 16mm, 10 mins.
The Way to Shadow Garden, b&w, 16mm, 11 mins., sd.

1955

Untitled film of Geoffrey Holder's wedding, made with Larry Jordan in response to
    an invitation by Maya Deren, col., 16mm.
In Between, col., 16mm, 10 mins. Music by John Cage.
Reflections on Black, b&w, 16mm, 12 mins., sd.
The Wonder Ring, col., 16mm, 6 mins. Suggested by Joseph Cornell, who used the
    footage to make his own *Gnir Rednow*.
Footage for an incomplete film, *Tower House*. Suggested by Joseph Cornell, who
    used the footage to make his own *Centuries of June*.

1956

Zone Moment (lost), col., 16mm, 3 mins.
Flesh of Morning, b&w, 16mm, 22 mins. (Reissued with new sound track in 1986.)
Nightcats, col., 16mm, 9 mins.

1957

Daybreok and Whiteye, b&w, 16mm, 10 mins., sd.
Loving, col., 16mm, 5 mins.

1958

Anticipation of the Night, col., 16mm, 41 mins.

1959

Wedlock House: An Intercourse, col., 16mm, 11 mins.
Window Water Baby Moving, col., 16mm, 13 mins.
Cat's Cradle, col., 16mm, 8 mins.
Sirius Remembered, col., 16mm, 11 mins.

1960

The Dead, col., 16mm, 11 mins.

1961

Thigh Line Lyre Triangular, col., 16mm, 7 mins.
Films by Stan Brakhage: An Avant-Garde Home Movie, col., 16mm, 4 mins.

1961-64

Dog Star Man
1961: *Prelude: Dog Star Man*, col., 16mm, 26 mins.
1962: *Dog Star Man: Part I*, col., 16mm, 31 mins.
1963: *Dog Star Man: Part II*, col., 16mm, 6 mins.
1964: *Dog Star Man: Part III*, col., 16mm, 8 mins.
1964: *Dog Star Man: Part IV*, col., 16mm, 7 mins.

1961-65

The Art of Vision, col., 16mm, 4 hours. Derived from *Dog Star Man*.

1962

Blue Moses, b&w, 16mm, 11 mins., sd.
Silent Sound Sense Stars Subotnik and Sender (lost), b&w, 16mm, 2 mins.

1963

Oh Life—A Woe Story—The Test News, b&w, 16mm, 6 mins.
Footage for the film *Meat Jewel*, which was incorporated into *Dog Star Man: Part II*,
     col., 16mm
Mothlight, col., 16mm, 4 mins.

1964-69

Songs
1964: *Song 1*, col., 8mm, 3 mins.; *Songs 2* and *3*, col., 8mm, 4 mins.; *Song 4*, col.,
     8mm, 3 mins.; *Song 5*, col., 8mm, 4 mins.; *Songs 6* and *7*, col., 8mm, 4 mins.
     (these films were reissued in 1980 as *Songs 1-7*, col., 16mm, 19 mins.);
     Song 8, col., 8mm, 3 mins.
1965: *Songs 9* and *10*, col., 8mm, 7 mins.; *Song 11*, col., 8mm, 3 mins.; *Song 12*,
     b&w, 8mm, 3 mins.; *Song 13*, col., 8mm, 3 mins.; *Song 14*, col., 8mm, 3 mins.
     (these films were reissued in 1980 as *Songs 8-14*, col., 16mm, 22 mins.);

15 Song Traits, col., 8mm, 31 mins. (reissued in 1981 in 16mm); *Song 16*, col., 8mm, 7 mins.; *Songs 17* and *18*, col., 8mm, 5 mins.; *Songs 19* and *20*, col., 8mm, 8 mins.; *Songs 21* and *22*, col., 8mm, 6 mins. (these films were reissued in 1983 as *Songs 16-22*, col., 16mm, 26 mins.).

1966-67: *23rd Psalm Branch*, col., 8mm, 67 mins. (Film comprises Parts I, II, and Coda. Part I, which is dated 1966, was reissued in 1979 in 16mm; Part II and the Coda, which are dated 1967, were reissued in 1980 in 16mm.)

1967: *Songs 24* and *25*, col., 8mm, 6 mins.

1968: *Song 26*, col., 8mm, 6 mins. (these films were reissued in 1984 as *Songs 24-26*, col., 16mm, 12 mins.); *My Mountain Song 27*, col., 8mm, 20 mins. (reissued in 1987 in 16mm).

1969: *Song 27 (Part II) Rivers*, col., 8mm, 27 mins. (reissued in 1988 in 16mm); *Song 28*, col., 8mm, 3 mins., *Song 29*, col., 8mm, 3 mins. (these films were reissued in 1985 as *Songs 28* and *29*, col., 16mm, 6 mins.); *American 30's Song*, col., 8mm, 23 mins. (released in 1996 in 16mm); *Window Suite of Children's Songs*, col., 8mm, 18 mins. (films made by Brakhage's five children; Brakhage arranged them in this form but did not edit them).

1965

Three Films (Blue White, Blood's Tone, and Vein), col., 16mm, 9 mins.
Fire of Waters, b&w, 16mm 7 mins., sd.
Pasht, col., 16mm, 6 mins.
Two: Creeley/McClure, col., 16mm, 4 mins.
Black Vision, b&w, 16mm, 3 mins.

1965-98

Female Mystique and Spare Leaves (for Gordon), col., 16mm, 5 min.

1967

Eye Myth, col., 35mm, 9 seconds. Released in 1972 in 16mm; not shown in 35mm until 1981, at the Telluride Film Festival.

1967-70

Scenes from Under Childhood
1967: *Scenes from Under Childhood: Section No. 1*, col., 16mm, 25 mins. Until the late 1970s a sound version of this section of the film was in distribution; it is now available in both sound and silent versions.
1969: *Scenes from Under Childhood: Section No. 2*, col., 16mm, 41 mins.; *Scenes from Under Childhood: Section No.3*, col., 16mm, 28 mins.
1970: *Scenes from Under Childhood: Section No. 4*, col., 16mm, 46 mins.

1968

The Horseman, the Woman and the Moth, col., 16mm, 19 mins.
Lovemaking, col., 16mm, 36 mins. (Film comprises Parts I-IV.)

1970

The Weir-Falcon Saga, col., 16mm, 30 mins.
The Machine of Eden, col., 16mm, 11 mins.
The Animals of Eden and After, col., 16mm, 36 mins.

1970-72

Sexual Meditations
1970: *Sexual Meditation No. 1: Motel*, col., 8mm, 6 mins. (reissued in 1980 in 16mm).
1971: *Sexual Meditation: Room with View*, col., 16mm, 4 mins.
1972: *Sexual Meditation: Hotel*, col., 16mm, 6 mins.; *Sexual Meditation: Faun's Room Yale*, col., 16mm, 3 mins.; *Sexual Meditation: Office Suite*, col., 16mm, 3 mins.; *Sexual Meditation: Open Field*, col., 16mm, 6 mins.

1971

The Pittsburgh Trilogy
eyes, col., 16mm, 36 mins.; *Deus Ex*, col., 16mm, 33 mins.; *The Act of Seeing with One's Own Eyes*, col., 16mm, 33 mins.
Fox Fire Child Watch, col., 16mm, 4 mins.
Angels', col., 16mm, 3 mins.
Door, col., 16mm, 3 mins.
Western History, col., 16mm, 9 mins.
The Trip to Door, col., 16mm, 14 mins.
The Peaceable Kingdom, col., 16mm, 8 mins.

1972

Eye Myth, col., 16mm, 190 frames, 9 seconds.
Eye Myth Educational, col., 16mm, 2 mins.
The Process, col., 16mm, 8 mins.
The Riddle of Lumen, col., 16mm, 14 mins.
The Shores of Phos: A Fable, col., 16mm, 10 mins.
The Presence, col., 16mm, 3 mins.
The Wold Shadow, col., 16mm, 3 mins.

1973

Gift, col., Super-8mm, 6 mins.
The Women, col., 16mm, 3 mins.

1973-80

Sincerity
1973: *Sincerity*, col., 16mm, 27 mins.
1975: *Sincerity II*, col., 16mm, 38 mins.
1978: *Sincerity III*, col., 16mm, 37 mins.
1980: *Sincerity IV*, col., 16mm, 37 mins.; *Sincerity V*, col., 16mm, 41 mins.

1974

Skein, col., 16mm, 4 mins.
Aquarien, col., 16mm, 3 mins.
Sol, col., 16mm, 5 mins.
Flight, col., 16mm, 5 mins.
Dominion, col., 16mm, 4 mins.
Hymn to Her, col., 16mm, 3 mins.
Clancy, col., 16mm, 5 mins.
Star Garden, col., 16mm, 22 mins.
The Stars Are Beautiful, col., 16mm, 19, mins., sd.
The Text of Light, col., 16mm, 70 mins.
he was born, he suffered, he died, col., 16mm, 8 mins.

1975

Short Films: 1975, col., 16mm, 38 mins. (Film comprises Parts I-X.)

1976

Short Films: 1976, col., 16mm, 21 mins.
Tragoedia, col., 16mm, 39 mins.
Gadflies, col., Super-8mm, 10 mins.
Sketches, col., Super-8mm, 7 mins.
Airs, col., Super-8mm, 18 mins. (reissued in 1978 in 16mm).
Window, col., Super-8mm, 7 mins. (reissued in 1978 in 16mm).
Trio, col., Super-8mm, 7 mins. (reissued in 1978 in 16mm).
Desert, col., Super-8mm, 10 mins. (reissued in 1978 in 16mm).
Rembrandt, Etc and Jane, col., Super-8mm, 14 mins. (reissued in 1978 in 16mm).
Highs, col., Super-8mm, 5 mins. (reissued in 1978 in 16mm).
Absence, col., Super-8mm, 6 mins. (reissued in 1978 in 16mm).
The Dream, NYC, the Return, the Flower, col., Super-8mm, 18 mins. (reissued in 1978 in 16mm).

1977

Soldiers and Other Cosmic Objects, col., 16mm, 20 mins.
The Governor, col., 16mm, 58 mins.
The Domain of the Moment, col., 16mm, 14 mins.

1978

Nightmare Series, col., 16mm, 20 mins.
Purity and After, col., 16mm, 5 mins.
Centre, col., 16mm, 10 mins.
Bird, col., 16mm, 3 mins.
Thot Fal'n, col., 16mm, 10 mins.
Burial Path, col., 16mm, 8 mins.,
Sluice, col., 16mm, 3 mins.

1978-80

Duplicity
1978: *Duplicity*, col. 16mm, 23 mins.; *Duplicity II*, col., 16mm, 15 mins.
1980: *Duplicity III*, col., 16mm, 23 mins.

1979

@, col., 16mm, 6 mins.
Creation, col., 16mm, 17 mins.

1979-81

Roman Numeral Series
1979: *I*, col., 16mm, 6 mins.; *II*, col., 16mm, 8 mins.
1980: *III*, col., 16mm, 2 mins.; *IV*, col., 16mm, 3 mins.; *V*, col., 16mm, 3 mins.; *VI*,
    col., 16mm, 10 mins.; *VII*, col., 16mm, 5 mins.
1981: *VIII*, col., 16mm, 4 mins.; *IX*, col., 16mm, 3 mins.

1980

Salome, col., 16mm, 3 mins.
Other, col., 16mm, 3 mins.
Made Manifest, col., 16mm, 12 mins.
Aftermath, col., 16mm, 8 mins.
Murder Psalm, col., 16mm, 18 mins.

1980-82

Arabics
1980: *1*, col., 16mm, 3 mins.; *2*, col., 16mm, 4 mins.; *3*, col., 16mm, 7 mins.
1981: *4*, col., 16mm, 3 mins.; *5*, col. 16mm, 6 mins.; *6*, col., 16mm, 8 mins.; *7*, col.,
    16mm, 8 mins.; *8*, col., 16mm, 4 mins.; *9*, col., 16mm, 9 mins.; *0+10*, col.,
    16mm, 21 mins.; *11*, col., 16mm, 7 mins.; *12*, col., 16mm, 18 mins.; *13*, col.,
    16mm, 3 mins.
1982: *14*, col., 16mm, 4 mins.; *15*, col., 16mm, 5 mins.; *16*, col., 16mm, 6 mins.; *17*,
    col., 16mm, 7 mins.; *18*, col., 16mm, 7 mins.; *19*, col., 16mm, 8 mins.

1981

Nodes, col., 16mm, 4 mins.
RR, col., 16mm, 8 mins.
The Garden of Earthly Delights, col., issued in both 35mm and 16mm, 3 mins.
Unconscious London Strata, col., 16mm, 23 mins.
Hell Spit Flexion, col., issued in both 35mm and 16mm, 45 seconds (reissued in
    1987 as the second part of *The Dante Quartet*).

1984

The Egyptian Series, col., 16mm, 18 mins.
Tortured Dust, col., 16mm, 94 mins.

1986

Jane, col., 16mm, 13 mins.
Caswallon Trilogy: The Aerodyne, col., 16mm, 4 mins.; *Fireloop*, col., 16mm, 3 mins., sound by Joel Haertling; *Dance Shadows*, col., 16mm, 4 mins.
The Loom, col., 16mm, 43 mins.
Night Music, col., 16mm, 30 seconds.
Confession, col., 16mm, 24 mins.

1987

Loud Visual Noises, col., 16mm, 3 mins. Music compilation by Joel Haertling.
The Dante Quartet, col., issued in both 35mm and 16mm, 8 mins.
Kindering, col. 16mm, 3 mins. Music by Architects Office.

1987-89

Faustfilm
1987: *FaustFilm: An Opera*, col., 16mm, 43 mins. Music by Rick Corrigan.
1988: *Faust's Other: An Idyll*, col., 16mm, 44 mins., sound and music by Joel Haertling; *Faust 3: Candida Albacore*, col., 16mm, 27 mins., music by Doll Parts, sound by Rick Corrigan.
1989: *Faust 4*, col., 16mm, 37 mins. Music by Rick Corrigan.

1988

Matins, col., 16mm, 2 mins.
I . . . Dreaming, col., 16mm, 7 mins. Music by Joel Haertling (and Stephen Foster).
Marilyn's Window, col., 16mm, 8 mins.
Rage Net, col., 16mm, 30 seconds.

1989

City Streaming, col., 16mm, 25 mins.
The Thatch of Night, col., 16mm, 6 mins.

1989-90

Babylon Series
1989: *Babylon Series*, col., 16mm, 5 mins.; *Babylon Series #2*, col., 16mm, 3 mins.
1990: *Babylon Series #3*, col., 16mm, 4 mins.
Visions in Meditation
1989: *Visions in Meditation #1*, col., 16mm, 18 mins.
1990: *Visions in Meditation #2: Mesa Verde*, col., 16mm, 18 mins.; *Visions in Meditation #3: Plato's Cave*, col., 16mm, 18 mins., music by Rick Corrigan; *Visions in Meditation #4: D.H. Lawrence*, col., 16mm, 18 mins.

1990

Glaze of Cathexis, col., 16mm, 4 mins.
Passage Through: A Ritual, col., 16mm, 45 mins. Music by Philip Corner.
Vision of the Fire Tree, col., 16mm, 4 mins.

1991

Delicacies of Molten Horror Synapse, col., 16mm, 10 mins.
Christ Mass Sex Dance, col., 16mm, 5 mins. Music by James Tenney.
Agnus Dei Kinder Synapse, col., 16mm, 4 mins.
A Child's Garden and the Serious Sea, col., 16mm, 80 mins.

1992

Crack Glass Eulogy, col., 16mm, 7 mins. Music by Rick Corrigan.
Interpolations I-V, col., 35mm, 12 mins.
For Marilyn, col., 16mm, 12 mins.
Boulder Blues and Pearls and, col., 16mm, 30 mins.

1993

Blossom Gift Favor, col., 16mm, 1 mins.
Autumnal, col., 16mm, 5 mins.
The Harrowing, col., 16mm, 2 mins.
Tryst Haunt, col., 16mm, 3 mins.
Three Homerics, col., 16mm, 6 mins.
Stellar, col., 16mm, 2 mins.
Study in Color and Black and White, col., 16mm, 2 mins.
Ephemeral Solidity, col., 16mm, 3 mins.

1994

Elementary Phrases (in collaboration with Phil Solomon), col., 16mm, 35 mins.
Black Ice, col., 16mm, 2 mins.
First hymn to the Night Novalis, col., 16mm, 3 mins. at 18 frames per second.
Naughts, col., 16mm, 5 mins.
Chartres Series, col., 16mm, 9 mins.
Paranoia Corridor, col., 16mm, 2 mins.
In Consideration of Pompeii, col., 16mm, 4 mins.
The Mammals of Victoria, col., 16mm, 35 mins.
I Take These Truths, col., 16mm, 35 mins.
We hold These, col., 16mm, 12 mins.

1994-95

Trilogy, col., 16mm, 77 mins. (Comprises *I Take These Truths*, *We Hold These*, both
      1994, and *I . . .* , 1995.)

1995

Cannot Exist, col., 16mm, 2 mins.
Cannot Not Exist, col., 16mm, 4 mins.
Earthen Aerie, col., 16mm, 2 mins.
Spring Cycle, col., 16mm, 10 mins.
I . . . , col., 16mm, 40 mins.
The "b" Series, col., 16mm, 20 mins.

The Lost Films, col., 16mm, 60 mins.
Paranoi Corridor, col., 16mm, 3 mins., sd.

1995-97

Preludes
1995: *Preludes 1-6*, col., 16mm, 20 mins.
1996: *Preludes 7-12*, col., 16mm, 20 mins.; *Preludes 13-18*, col., 16mm, 11 mins.
1997: *Preludes 19-24*, col., 16mm, 9 mins.

1996

Beautiful Funerals, col., 16mm, 5 mins.
Blue Value, col., 16mm, 2 mins.
Concrescence, col., 16mm, 2 mins.
The Fur of Home, col., 16mm, 4 mins.
Polite Madness, col., 16mm, 4 mins.
Sexual Saga, col., 16mm, 2 mins.
Spring Cycle, col., 16mm, 8 mins.
Two Found Objects of Charles Boultenhouse, col., 16mm, 17 mins.
Zone Moment, col., 16mm, 3 mins.
Through Wounded Eyes (Stan Brakhage/Joel Haertling), col., 16mm, 7 mins.

1997

Cat of the Worm's Green Realm, b&w, 16mm, 18 mins., sd.
Commingled Containers, col., 16mm, 5 mins., sd.
Divertimento, col., 16mm, 2 mins.
Last hymn to the Night, col., 16mm, 25 mins.
Self Song/Death Song, col., 16mm, 3 mins.
Shockingly Hot, col., 16mm, 4 mins.
Yggdrasill, Whose Roots Are Stars in the Human Mind, col., 16mm, 17 mins.

1998

"*. . .*" *Reel 1*, col., 16mm, 22 mins.
"*. . .*" *Reel 2*, col., 16mm, 15 mins.
"*. . .*" *Reel 3*, col., 16mm, 15 mins.
"*. . .*" *Reels 4* and *5* will be finished in 1998; *Reel 4* is accompanied by *Flocking*, a
    musical composition by James Tenney.

Other

James Broughton, *Nuptiae*, 1969. Col., 16mm, 14 mins. Photographed by
    Brakhage for Broughton. Music by Lou Harrison.

Index